TO THE STUDENT: A study guide for this textbook is available through your college bookstore under the title STUDY GUIDE AND WORKING PAPERS TO ACCOMPANY COLLEGE ACCOUNTING PROCEDURES: A COMPETENCY BASED APPROACH Chapters 1–15 by Douglas Cloud, Edwin D. Waters, and Don R. Cook. The study guide can help you with course material by serving as a tutorial, review and study aid. If the study guide is not in stock, ask the bookstore manager to order a copy for you.

COLLEGE ACCOUNTING PROCEDURES

CHAPTERS 1–15

The manuscript for this book was developed under the guidance of Hussain Emin, Consulting Editor for The John Wiley Series in Career Accounting. Professor Emin is the Chairman of the Accounting and Business Department at Nassau Community College, Garden City, New York.

COLLEGE ACCOUNTING PROCEDURES

A COMPETENCY BASED APPROACH

CHAPTERS 1–15

DOUGLAS CLOUD D.B.A.
Professor of Accounting

EDWIN D. WATERS Ph.D., C.P.A.
Professor of Accounting

DON R. COOK Ph.D., C.P.A.
Professor of Accounting

TENNESSEE TECHNOLOGICAL UNIVERSITY

JOHN WILEY & SONS
NEW YORK / CHICHESTER / BRISBANE / TORONTO / SINGAPORE

Library of Congress Cataloging in Publication Data:

Cloud, Douglas.
College accounting procedures: a competency based approach: chapters 1–15.

Includes index.
1. Accounting. I. Waters, Edwin R. II. Cook, Don R. III. Title.
HF5635.C645 1984 657'.044 84-13038
ISBN 0-471-08896-X

Printed in the United States of America

10 9 8 7 6 5 4 3 2

preface

Accounting is the language of business. Every firm needs accounting information to make sensible business decisions. Only by using this information can management know if the operation is financially successful. The larger firms must have detailed financial information to divide resources properly and to present financial results to their owners.

College Accounting Procedures is organized to develop student understanding by using a competency based approach to learning tasks. In this book students are introduced to the various tasks that they must understand to accomplish the required accounting procedures. *College Accounting Procedures* is designed for students with no previous accounting background, who have completed high school and have chosen to continue their education by enrolling in a proprietary business school, a community college, or a junior college. The material has been developed with the needs and abilities of these students in mind, and is based on the authors' years of teaching introductory accounting courses. The book is written in a conversational tone and is provided with ample illustrations to make the discussions more meaningful.

The primary objective of the approach used is to build one competency on another until the student has the skill to carry out the day-to-day accounting requirements of a firm.

Organization

Three versions of this book are available to meet the needs of students in various courses. They are:

1. A one-quarter version (Chapters 1–11).
2. A one-semester version (Chapters 1–15).
3. A two-semester or three-quarters version (Chapters 1–26).

This book is divided into three major sections:

1. Accounting for a Service Business (Chapters 1–4).
2. Accounting for a Merchandising Business (Chapters 5–11).
3. Accounting for Assets and Liabilities (Chapters 12–15).

Each chapter begins with a statement of an overall competency in terms of what is expected to be accomplished by the student on completion of the chapter. This overall competency is divided into tasks (career objectives) that the student should be able to perform successfully.

Supplementary Learning Aids for Students

A number of learning aids have been prepared for use with this textbook.

1. Two practice sets.
   a. Sunbrite Laundry Company—A computerized practice set involving a service-type firm that provides laundry and dry cleaning services. November is accounted for manually, whereas December and January are worked by using a computer.
   b. Coggins Auto Supply—A two-month practice set for a merchandising firm. The first month is prepared manually, whereas the second month has the option of being computerized or continued using the manual approach.
2. A study guide with working papers.
3. A microcomputer-aided learning system. This is a tutorial program, designed to be used in conjunction with the text and the study guide, that enables the student to review accounting concepts using a microcomputer.

For Instructors

Instructor's manual (Chapters 1–15).

a. Lesson plans for Chapters 1–15.
b. Solutions to questions, exercises, and problems.
c. Test bank containing objective questions and short problems.
d. Selected accounting forms suitable for photocopying.

Key Terms

Each chapter contains a list of the key terms used in that particular chapter. A glossary defining these terms appears at the end of the textbook with a cross-reference to the chapter where a more detailed discussion is presented.

Questions, Exercises, and Problems

Ample questions, exercises, and problems are provided at the end of each chapter with a statement of the competency tested in each problem. Spaces for problem solutions are provided in the study guide that accompanies this textbook.

Two demonstration problems, with the solutions, are provided. The first one is located at the end of Chapter 10, and the second one is located at the end of Chapter 11. These demonstration problems are designed to illustrate the accounting cycle.

Comprehensive Problems

To review the competencies collectively, two comprehensive problems are included. The first problem is located at the ends of Chapters 2, 3, and 4 and focuses on the business cycle of a service-type business (Magic Carpet Travel). The second comprehensive problem is found after Chapters 6, 9, 10, and 11 and focuses on the accounting cycle of a merchandising business

(Reed Supply Company). Instructors may use these comprehensive problems as "mini" practice sets. Forms for both comprehensive problems can be found in the study guide.

Acknowledgments

Numerous people have contributed to the publication of this textbook. We gratefully acknowledge the helpful comments made by the following reviewers: Rosemary Grant, Lane Community College; Peter A. Mihas, Moraine Park Technical Institute; Joyce G. Cherry, Lenoir Community College; Frances Miller, Albany Junior College; Esther B. Grant, Hillsborough Community College; Robert F. Lilly, Clackamas Community College; Rheba M. Stancliff, Pensacola Junior College; Gerald E. Svendor, West Shore Community College; Pat Rittenbach, Blue Mountain Community College; Walter Doehring, Genesee Community College; Wayne D. Claflin, St. Clair County Community College; Philip L. Tarpley, Madison Area Technical College; Joyce Loudder, Houston Community College; Greg Harpole, Lane Community College; Rocco M. Santoro, Berkeley School; Donald L. Hollin, Union University; Thomas E. Brown, State University of New York; Dot T. Butler, State Area Vo-Tech School; Barbara J. Pennington, Indian Valley Colleges; Augusto C. Breschi, College of the Siskiyous; David Smith, Glen Oaks Community College; Anthony Mercadante, Roberts-Walsh Business School; Charlotte McGregor, McMinnville Area Vo-Tech; Louise Brown, McMinnville Area Vo-Tech; Norina A. Litton, Oneida State Area Vo-Tech; Nancy Allstun, Harriman Area School; Mary E. Armbrecht, Nashville Area School; Darlene Wills, West Covina, California; Rodney Jurist, Rider College; Judy Imperial, Midland Park, New Jersey; Darold Russell, International Business College; Chris Constantynowicz, Robert Morris College; Gerald F. Jedlicka, Terrell College Center; Larry Lamont, Mequon, Wisconsin; Brenda Hartman, Ellsworth Community College; George Wagaman, Pasco Hernando Community College-East Campus; Phyllis Whitney, Frankfort, Kentucky; Phil Tarpley, Rio, Wisconsin; John Chestnutt, Santa Maria, California; Gilbert J. Ribera, Hayward, California.

We also thank Harold Wilson of Middle Tennessee State University and Belford Carver of Southeastern Louisiana University for their help with Chapter 24, and Don Thornberry and W. E. Wiebush of Safeguard Business Systems for their assistance in preparing Chapters 25 and 26. We are deeply indebted to Joy Henshall of Tennessee Technological University for her editing and to the many students who were involved in the numerous proofing of questions, exercises, and problems.

Finally, we sincerely thank Professor Hussain Emin, Chairman of the Accounting and Business Department at Nassau Community College, Garden City, New York, for his valuable contributions as Consulting Editor.

Douglas Cloud
Edwin D. Waters
Don R. Cook

contents

part one

ACCOUNTING FOR A SERVICE BUSINESS

chapter 1
THE BASIC ACCOUNTING EQUATION

overall competency THE ABILITY TO ANALYZE BUSINESS TRANSACTIONS AND PREPARE SIMPLE FINANCIAL STATEMENTS

career objectives Before you can become a competent accountant, you must be able to analyze and record business happenings. When you have gained skill in analyzing and recording, you will be on your way to providing managers and owners with vital information about the financial health of their firms.

This chapter is a simple one, but do not underestimate its importance. The foundation provided in this chapter will make your task of analyzing transactions accurately considerably easier when you do the work required in future chapters. After completing Chapter 1, you should be able to perform the following tasks:

- STATE THE ACCOUNTING EQUATION AND IDENTIFY EACH OF ITS COMPONENTS.
- EXAMINE TRANSACTIONS FOR THE ACCOUNTING PERIOD AND DECIDE WHAT EFFECT EACH TRANSACTION WILL HAVE ON THE ACCOUNTING EQUATION.
- PREPARE A SIMPLE INCOME STATEMENT.
- PREPARE A CAPITAL STATEMENT.
- PREPARE A SIMPLE BALANCE SHEET.

Owners of small firms are concerned about the financial strength of their businesses since achieving success requires a great deal of money and effort. To plan wisely for the future, owners must have accurate financial information. Critical decisions involving expanding or reducing services, or even closing down, are based on this information. Bankers and creditors lend money and extend credit only when accurate information about the health of the firm is available. In addition, governmental agencies require accurate records from small businesses for taxing and regulation purposes.

Accurate records help the owner answer such questions as: Can I expand now? Can I afford to buy a new delivery truck? Can I give the clerk a much deserved raise? Should I sell the business and work for someone else? Some owners and managers try to run a business by "the seat of their pants." Instead of relying on proper accounting techniques, they make business choices by instinct. This approach may be the right course of action in some cases, but over the long run, it is risky.

As the business grows in size and complexity, proper accounting records become even more important to the success of the firm. Many large companies have an entire staff of accountants with access to computers to assist in keeping track of the financial happenings of the business. In this textbook, the primary emphasis will be on learning how to keep the books of a single-owner business, known as a **proprietorship.** This form of ownership contrasts with those of multiowner businesses like partnerships and corporations. These kinds of ownership are discussed in Chapters 16 through 18.

the accounting cycle

It is important for you to see an overview of the next four chapters. In these chapters we will be covering the *accounting cycle,* the step-by-step procedure followed in keeping a firm's books and preparing statements for the owner. We will begin with a business that sells only service; later we will deal with firms that deal in merchandise. The steps in the accounting cycle and the related chapters are shown in Illustration 1-1.

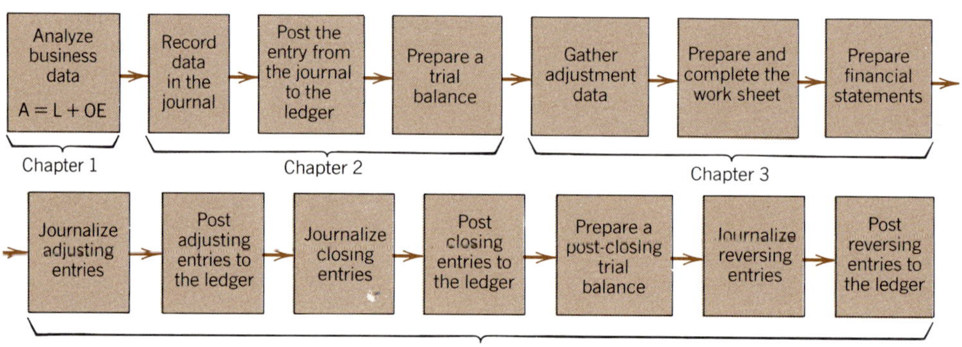

illustration 1-1 the accounting cycle.

early history of accounting

Archeologists tell us that civilized man has always attempted to account for financial happenings. For example, Imhotep, a physician, statesman, and architect, built the first known pyramids for King Zoser about 2650 B.C., relying on mathematical concepts and record-keeping procedures. Also, the biblical account of Joseph's directing that grain be stored for the famine he foresaw tells us that the grain was stored in such abundance that Joseph stopped measuring it. Joseph, therefore, must have used a record-keeping process to account for the grain intake. Later, in the second century B.C., a letter from one Egyptian priest to another warned that an inspector of temple finances had arrived in the area and planned to review the accounts.

The first procedure resembling our modern accounting system was used in Italian trading centers before the thirteenth century A. D. Early in the fifteenth century the invention of movable type made possible the widespread publication of all kinds of material. In 1494, an Italian priest named Luca Pacioli took advantage of this new technique to have his book, *Everything about Arithmetic, Geometry, and Proportions,* published. Primarily a discussion of mathematics, this book is important to accountants because it included a section on double-entry bookkeeping. As mass printing facilities became available, Pacioli's book—and the bookkeeping approach described—spread throughout Europe.

• task STATE AND APPLY SOME OF THE BASIC CONCEPTS OF ACCOUNTING

Entity concept

When a dentist collects money from a patient for filling a tooth or a merchant pays a utility bill, a financial happening takes place. In accounting, this financial event is known as a **transaction.** The question arises as to just when we should record a transaction on the company's books and when we should not record it. To help us answer this question, we use the **entity concept.** To illustrate this concept, let's assume that Jack Paulson owns a dairy. This dairy, like the dental office, is considered an accounting entity. It is a business separate from all other businesses, including Jack's personal affairs. If Jack trades some of his dairy's cows for a delivery truck to be used by the dairy and later makes a cash purchase of a typewriter from Stone's Office Equipment Company for his personal use, should both transactions be recorded on the dairy's books?

To answer this question, refer to Illustration 1-2. The circle represents the dairy, with the business (and its books) inside the circle. Any transaction that pierces the circle should be recorded on the dairy's books. Note that when the cows left the firm and the truck was received, both actions pierced the circle. The entity concept requires that this transaction be recorded on the dairy's books. The second transaction between Jack and the office equipment company had nothing to do with the dairy (it does not pierce the circle), so the entity concept indicates that Jack should ignore this event on his dairy's books.

illustration 1-2
entity concept.

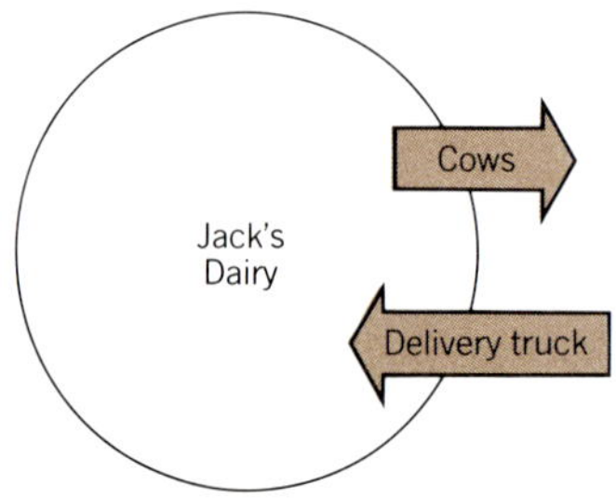

Except for internal transactions, which will be discussed in Chapter 3, Jack will record only those events that cross the entity line. The previous discussion should illustrate that each entity is separate, independent, and self-contained. If Jack owns a bakery in addition to the dairy, then he has two separate entities, and a separate set of books should be kept for each company.

The accountant must keep personal expenditures and business expenditures separated. Since Jack's nonbusiness life is a separate entity, his expenditures for personal items (such as buying the typewriter) should not be recorded on either the dairy's or the bakery's books. An exception to this rule arises when Jack invests personal funds or other assets in the business or withdraws funds or other assets from the business for personal use. The use he makes of a withdrawal is of no importance to the firm, but the fact that an asset is leaving the entity is important.

The same reasoning applies to an investment. How Jack obtained the asset that he is investing in the firm is of no concern to the entity (as long as it was legal); the important point is that the entity is receiving an asset. Few people keep formal double-entry records on a personal entity, so our attention will focus entirely on the business entity. As a business grows, the entity circle gets larger, but the concept remains the same.

Cost concept

When two people bargain about the purchase price of an item of merchandise or the cost of a service, the cost concept eventually enters the picture. For example, Jack decides to buy five more cows for his dairy, and the asking price is \$50 each. The salesman assures Jack that the cows are really worth \$60 each, but he is overstocked at the moment. After some negotiating, Jack buys the cows for \$45 each. Should Jack record the cows at \$60 each? How about \$50 each? The answer to both proposals is no. According to the **cost concept** (also referred to as the **historical cost concept**), the amount paid must be the basis for recording the transaction on the books. In Jack's case, the cows are recorded on the dairy's books at \$45 each.

What is the logic behind the cost principle? The accountant should record the transaction at the most realistic and measurable figure. We have to assume that two individuals looking out for their own interests will arrive at such a figure. Some people have urged the use of appraised value rather than cost so that "more realistic" information will be shown. The problem with this idea is that appraised figures may not be accurate due to personal judgment and interests.

Going-concern concept

For accounting information to be useful, we must assume that the business is a **going concern,** that it will continue indefinitely. This concept allows the accountant to spread the cost of major items, such as buildings and equipment, over their useful lives and to account for their decreasing value or efficiency to the firm over that period. You will learn more about accounting for such items in Chapters 10 and 15.

If we did not follow the going-concern concept, we would have to report the items owned by the business at "liquidation value," the selling price of an item assuming that the business is under pressure to sell everything and close down operations.

review exercises

1. Ralph bought a used car from a friend to be used in the business. He paid $4,000 for the car, knowing that a similar car on the used car lot would have cost him $4,500. What amount should be used to record the purchase of this car on the business books? What concept did you use in making your decision?
2. Harry Williams, promoter for The Wrong Side of the Campus, a singing group, paid $5,000 for posters to publicize an upcoming six-month tour. What accounting concept allows you to record this payment as an item of value when no concert tickets have been sold yet?
3. Rodney Eugene owns both a drugstore and a service station. If the service station repairs the drugstore's delivery truck, should the transaction be recorded on:
   (a) The drugstore's books only?
   (b) The service station's books only?
   (c) Both sets of books?
   (d) Neither set, since the same person owns both businesses?

• **task** EXAMINE TRANSACTIONS FOR THE ACCOUNTING PERIOD AND DETERMINE THE EFFECT EACH TRANSACTION WILL HAVE ON THE ACCOUNTING EQUATION

Basic accounting equation

At the heart of accounting is the following **basic accounting equation:**

Assets	=	Liabilities	+	Owner's Equity
(own)		(owe)		(net worth)

Before showing you how to apply the formula, we must define the items that make up the equation. **Assets** are items *owned* by the business that have future benefit to the firm. Trucks, cash registers, buildings, tools and equipment, and goods held for sale fall into this category. Amounts that the business *owes* are known as its **liabilities.** Debts caused by purchasing items on credit and by borrowing money from a bank are common examples. In accounting language, the **net worth** of a proprietorship is referred to as **net assets, capital,** or **owner's equity.** In this text, we have chosen to use the term **owner's equity.** This term can be better illustrated as net worth by rearranging the equation. If we transfer liabilities to the left side of the equation, the sign changes from plus to minus. The result is

Assets	−	Liabilities	=	Owner's Equity
(own)		(owe)		(net worth)

Now, let's return to the original transaction. The right side of this equation might be looked at another way. If the left side tells us what assets are owned, then the right side tells us who owns them (or has a claim to them):

1. Liabilities are the amounts owed to outsiders (creditors) and therefore represent claims on the assets of the business.
2. Owner's equity is the amount that belongs to the owner.

Analyzing transactions with the basic accounting equation

To illustrate how the basic accounting equation works, consider the Jolly Trolley Company owned by Ed Jolly. Ed has \$5,000 in the bank and owns a rebuilt trolley car that cost him \$100,000. The city maintains the tracks and provides electricity without charge to Jolly as a public service. Ed owes \$90,000 on a five-year mortgage held by the bank on the trolley and \$3,000 to Paul Sutton for supplies bought on account. What is owner's equity for Jolly Trolley? By using the basic accounting equation, we get

Assets	=	Liabilities	+	Owner's Equity
\$105,000	=	\$93,000	+	?

and, using some simple math, we find that owner's equity is \$12,000. The completed equation tells us that creditors have an interest of \$93,000 worth of the business and that Ed's equity is \$12,000. You might note, though, that Ed considers the trolley to be "all his," even though he still owes 90 percent of the cost.

To provide better information, the three major categories are broken down further. Under the asset section, the money held by the bank, as well as any money on hand, is known as *Cash.* The trolley falls into a subcategory known as *Equipment.* Two items are included in the liabilities category—the amount owed to Paul Sutton for supplies and listed under *Accounts Payable* and the long-term mortgage listed under *Mortgage Payable.* Owner's equity in a proprietorship is usually identified by using the owner's name followed by the word "Capital"; thus, *Ed Jolly, Capital* would be used here. Each of the italicized items above is known as an **account.** So, in referring to the amount of money available, the accountant would ask about the *Cash* account.

Using these accounts, the basic accounting equation for Jolly Trolley would now appear as:

Assets			=	Liabilities			+	Owner's Equity
Cash	+	Equipment	=	Accounts Payable	+	Mortgage Payable	+	Ed Jolly, Capital
$5,000		$100,000		$3,000		$90,000		$12,000

$105,000 = $105,000

As a more comprehensive illustration, assume that Joe Jackson opens a car repair business and calls the firm the Kar Klinik. In the following pages, we will examine the first month's transactions and see how they relate to the accounting equation.

(a) On July 1, 19X1, Joe Jackson obtains $5,000 by withdrawing all of his savings and $3,000 by selling stock left to him by a rich uncle. Joe transfers this money to a checking account opened for Kar Klinik. First, recall from the entity discussion that Joe's source of cash (from the savings account and from the selling of stock) is unimportant to the new entity. The only notation made on the books of the company is that cash has been received from Joe, giving the business assets of $8,000. Using the basic accounting equation, we can show the investment of money in the firm as follows:

	Assets	=	Liabilities	+	Owner's Equity
	Cash	=		+	Joe Jackson, Capital
(a)	+$8,000		0		+$8,000 investment

At this point, the firm has no liabilities, so owner's equity is also $8,000. Whenever an item increases or decreases the capital account, the accounting clerk must keep track of what causes this change. This step will be helpful later when financial statements are prepared. We will discuss these statements later in this chapter; for now, just note that we are labeling the reason for the change.

(b) On the same day, Joe signs an agreement with McCracken Realty to rent a garage in which to operate his business. He agrees to pay $300 monthly with the first payment due immediately. Paying this rent in advance causes one asset, *Cash,* to be exchanged for another, *Prepaid Rent.* The asset *Cash* decreases because money has been paid out, and the asset *Prepaid Rent* is increased because Joe Jackson has purchased something with future value (the use of the building).

	Assets			=	Liabilities	+	Owner's Equity
	Cash	+	Prepaid Rent	=		+	Joe Jackson, Capital
	$8,000				0		$8,000
(b)	−300		+$300				
	$7,700		$300				$8,000

$8,000 = $8,000

The total of each side of the equation is shown to remind you that the accounting equation, like any equation, must always balance.

(c) To operate his business properly, Joe buys some pulleys, jacks, and other tools related to repairing cars from Greasy's Auto Supply for a total of $900. He pays $400 at the time of purchase (July 2) and agrees to pay the rest in thirty days. This arrangement to pay in the future is known as purchasing "on account" or "on credit." After this transaction, the basic accounting equation for Kar Klinik is as follows:

	Assets					=
	Cash	+	Prepaid Rent	+	Equipment	=
	$7,700		$300			
(c)	−400				+$900	
	$7,300		$300		$900	

Liabilities	+	Owner's Equity
Accounts Payable	+	Joe Jackson, Capital
		$8,000
+$500		
$500		$8,000

$8,500 = $8,500

The same rule applies here that you saw in the Jolly Trolley example. When items are purchased on account, the liability *Accounts Payable* is increased. Before this transaction, Joe owed nothing; now he owes $500.

(d) On July 6, Joe buys a cash register and some supplies for the office on account from Haskins Supply and Equipment Company. The pencils, stationery, and other office supply items cost $50, and the cash register, which will be labeled *Equipment,* costs $250.

	Assets							=
	Cash	+	Prepaid Rent	+	Supplies	+	Equipment	=
	$7,300		$300				$ 900	
(d)					$50		+250	
	$7,300		$300		$50		$1,150	

Liabilities	+	Owner's Equity
Accounts Payable	+	Joe Jackson, Capital
$500		$8,000
+300		
$800		$8,000

$8,800 = $8,800

In this transaction, two assets increased while the liability *Accounts Payable* increased to show that Joe now owes $800 ($500 to Greasy's and $300 to Haskins).

(e) Since his business requires him to pick up car parts at shops of the various distributors, Joe buys a used 1977 pickup on July 9 from E-Z Deal Motors for $2,800 cash. This transaction creates a new asset, *Truck,* and decreases the amount of cash. Notice that this transaction does not change the owner's equity since only assets are involved.

	Assets									=
	Cash	+	Prepaid Rent	+	Supplies	+	Equipment	+	Truck	=
	$7,300		$300		$50		$1,150			
(e)	−2,800								+$2,800	
	$4,500		$300		$50		$1,150		$2,800	

Liabilities	+	Owner's Equity
Accounts Payable	+	Joe Jackson, Capital
$800		$8,000
$800		$8,000

$8,800 = $8,800

(f) Work is completed on cars belonging to Shirley Seal and Sean O'Hara on July 11, and the two customers pay Joe a total of $630. Since this money is received for performing services, it is **revenue** earned by the firm. Revenue increases owner's equity, as can be seen by examining the transaction below. Note again that the change in capital is labeled so that Joe will know the different items that affect owner's equity during the month.

	Assets									=
	Cash	+	Prepaid Rent	+	Supplies	+	Equipment	+	Truck	=
	$4,500		$300		$50		$1,150		$2,800	
(f)	+630									
	$5,130		$300		$50		$1,150		$2,800	

Liabilities	+	Owner's Equity	
Accounts Payable	+	Joe Jackson, Capital	
$800		$8,000	
		+630	Repairs Revenue
$800		$8,630	

$9,430 = $9,430

(g) On July 14, Nick Turner, the only employee on Joe's payroll, is given his paycheck for $400 for two weeks' work (we are ignoring all deductions that normally reduce paychecks). Meeting the payroll represents an **expense** to the firm. Expenses reduce owner's equity.

	Assets									=
	Cash	+	Prepaid Rent	+	Supplies	+	Equipment	+	Truck	=
	$5,130		$300		$50		$1,150		$2,800	
(g)	−400									
	$4,730		$300		$50		$1,150		$2,800	

Liabilities	+	Owner's Equity	
Accounts Payable	+	Joe Jackson, Capital	
$800		$8,630	
		−400	Salary Expense
$800		$8,230	

$9,030 = $9,030

(h) Back on July 6, Joe bought some equipment and supplies on account for $300 (entry *d*). On July 15, he sends Haskins Supply and Equipment Company a check for this amount in full payment. Note in this transaction that nothing is being purchased, even though the asset *Cash* is being reduced. The purchase has already been recorded as an *Account Payable*. Since the amount owed is being reduced, the liability is decreased also.

Assets =

	Cash	+	Prepaid Rent	+	Supplies	+	Equipment	+	Truck	=
	$4,730		$300		$50		$1,150		$2,800	
(h)	−300									
	$4,430		$300		$50		$1,150		$2,800	

Liabilities	+	Owner's Equity
Accounts Payable	+	Joe Jackson, Capital
$800		$8,230
−300		
$500		$8,230

$8,730 = $8,730

(i) Joe and Nick finish rebuilding the motor and transmission of an antique car for Vince Forte on July 15. Vince is short of money and asks Joe if he can pay $250 later in July and the balance of $300 in August. Joe agrees to this arrangement and opens an account called *Accounts Receivable* to record this promise to pay. Joe correctly decides that this item should increase assets since it represents a legal right to collect something of value in the future. Because the service has been performed, revenue has been earned, even though payment has not yet been received. Owner's equity increases because repairs revenue has been earned.

Assets =

	Cash	+	Prepaid Rent	+	Supplies	+	Accounts Receivable	+	Equipment	+	Truck	=
	$4,430		$300		$50				$1,150		$2,800	
(i)							$550					
	$4,430		$300		$50		$550		$1,150		$2,800	

Liabilities	+	Owner's Equity
Accounts Payable	+	Joe Jackson, Capital
$500		$8,230
		+550 Repairs Revenue
$500		$8,780

$9,280 = $9,280

(j) On July 24, Joe decides to take $300 out of the business to buy himself a watch. Cash taken out of the business for personal use is a withdrawal and not a business expense. Joe has reduced his capital account, the amount that represents his ownership of the business, to pay for his watch.

	Assets						=
	Cash	+ Prepaid Rent	+ Supplies	+ Accounts Receivable	+ Equipment	+ Truck	=
	$4,430	$300	$50	$550	$1,150	$2,800	
(j)	−300						
	$4,130	$300	$50	$550	$1,150	$2,800	

Liabilities	+	Owner's Equity
Accounts Payable	+	Joe Jackson, Capital
$500		$8,780
		−300 Withdrawal
$500		$8,480

$8,980 = $8,980

This reduction in owner's equity is known as a *withdrawal* or a *drawing*. However, money does not have to be involved for a withdrawal to take place. The same concept applies if an owner takes supplies or equipment from the business for personal use. In that case, a decrease in owner's equity matches the decrease in the appropriate asset account.

(k) The first electric bill arrives, showing that Kar Klinik owes the local utility company $50. Joe pays this bill on July 26, thus reducing *Cash* and the capital account. As you found in entry (g), expenses decrease owner's equity.

	Assets						=
	Cash	+ Prepaid Rent	+ Supplies	+ Accounts Receivable	+ Equipment	+ Truck	=
	$4,130	$300	$50	$550	$1,150	$2,800	
(k)	−50						
	$4,080	$300	$50	$550	$1,150	$2,800	

Liabilities	+	Owner's Equity
Accounts Payable	+	Joe Jackson, Capital
$500		$8,480
		−50 Utilities Expense
$500		$8,430

$8,930 = $8,930

(l) On July 28, Joe pays Nick, his only employee, $400 for days worked since the July 14 paycheck. This entry is the same as that we used for (g).

Assets =

	Cash	+	Prepaid Rent	+	Supplies	+	Accounts Receivable	+	Equipment	+	Truck	=
	$4,080		$300		$50		$550		$1,150		$2,800	
(l)	−400											
	$3,680		$300		$50		$550		$1,150		2,800	

Liabilities	+	Owner's Equity
Accounts Payable	+	Joe Jackson, Capital
$500		$8,430
		−400 Salary Expense
$500		$8,030

$8,530 = $8,530

You may wonder why Joe Jackson does not receive a salary. Since Joe is the owner, any "salary" he gives himself would be considered a withdrawal, not an expense to the firm. This is the same reasoning that we used in treating a cash input by Joe as an investment rather than a revenue.

(m) On July 30, Joe pays the *Daily Bugle* $40 for two newspaper ads featuring Kar Klinik that appeared during the month.

Assets =

	Cash		Prepaid Rent	+	Supplies	+	Accounts Receivable	+	Equipment	+	Truck	=
	$3,680		$300		$50		$550		$1,150		$2,800	
(m)	−40											
	$3,640		$300		$50		$550		$1,150		$2,800	

Liabilities	+	Owner's Equity
Accounts Payable	+	Joe Jackson, Capital
$500		$8,030
		−40 Advertising Expense
$500		$7,990

$8,490 = $8,490

(n) On July 30, Joe receives $250 from Vince Forte in partial payment of the $550 he has owed Joe since July 15. This payment causes the asset *Cash* to increase and the asset *Accounts Receivable* to decrease.

Assets =

	Cash +	Prepaid Rent +	Supplies +	Accounts Receivable +	Equipment +	Truck =
	$3,640	$300	$50	$550	$1,150	$2,800
(n)	+250			−250		
	$3,890	$300	$50	$300	$1,150	$2,800

Liabilities	+	Owner's Equity
Accounts Payable	+	Joe Jackson, Capital
$500		$7,990
$500		$7,990

$8,490 = $8,490

Note that capital is not increased by this $250 receipt. Joe recorded the revenue on July 15 when the car was turned over to the owner. If revenue were recorded again when the cash is received, then Joe would be reporting the same revenue twice. Note in the basic accounting equation that the firm has more *Cash* since money was received and less *Accounts Receivable* since a claim Joe had on a customer was paid.

(o) On July 30, Joe and Nick complete a major overhaul on Willard McKinnie's car. Willard picks up his car and gives Joe $825 for services rendered. This entry is similar to that used to record transaction (f).

Assets =

	Cash +	Prepaid Rent +	Supplies +	Equipment +	Truck +	Accounts Receivable
	$3,890	$300	$50	$1,150	$2,800	$300
(o)	+825					
	$4,715	$300	$50	$1,150	$2,800	$300

Liabilities	+	Owner's Equity
Accounts Payable	+	Joe Jackson, Capital
$500		$7,990
		825 Repairs Revenue
$500		$8,815

$9,315 = $9,315

For this simple illustration, let's assume that no other transactions take place during July. In Chapter 3 we will discuss updating a number of assets to show that some of the items have been used, but here we have ignored them for simplicity. The transactions for the month are summarized in Illustration 1-3.

	Assets						Liability	Owner's Equity	
	Cash +	Prepaid Rent +	Supplies +	Accounts Receivable +	Equipment +	Truck =	Accounts Payable +	Joe Jackson, Capital	
(a)	+$8,000							+$8,000	Investment
(b)	− 300	+$300							
	$7,700	$300						$8,000	
(c)	− 400				+$ 900		+$500		
	$7,300	$300			$ 900		$500	$8,000	
(d)			+$50		+ 250		+ 300		
	$7,300	$300	$50		$1,150		$800	$8,000	
(e)	− 2,800					+$2,800			
	$4,500	$300	$50		$1,150	$2,800	$800	$8,000	
(f)	+ 630							+ 630	Repairs Revenue
	$5,130	$300	$50		$1,150	$2,800	$800	$8,630	
(g)	− 400							− 400	Salary Expense
	$4,730	$300	$50		$1,150	$2,800	$800	$8,230	
(h)	− 300						− 300		
	$4,430	$300	$50		$1,150	$2,800	$500	$8,230	
(i)				+$550				+ 550	Repairs Revenue
	$4,430	$300	$50	$550	$1,150	$2,800	$500	$8,780	
(j)	− 300						+	− 300	Withdrawal
	$4,130	$300	$50	$550	$1,150	$2,800	$500	$8,480	
(k)	− 50			+				− 50	Utility Expense
	$4,080	$300	$50	$550	$1,150	$2,800	$500	$8,430	
(l)	− 400							− 400	Salary Expense
	$3,680	$300	$50	$550	$1,150	$2,800	$500	$8,030	
(m)	− 40							− 40	Advertising Expense
	$3,640	$300	$50	$550	$1,150	$2,800	$500	$7,990	
(n)	+ 250			− 250					
	$3,890	$300	$50	$300	$1,150	$2,800	$500	$7,990	
(o)	+ 825							+ 825	Repairs Revenue
	$4,715	$300	$50	$300	$1,150	$2,800	$500	$8,815	

illustration 1-3 schedule of transactions.

sample problem Record the following transactions for Cindy Dickerson, CPA, for the month of July, 19X1:

(a) Invested $1,800 cash and a used typewriter valued at $200 in the business.

(b) Purchased office furniture for $800, paying $200 down and promising to pay the balance in two monthly installments.

(c) Performed services during the first half of the month that brought in $450 cash.

(d) Paid $50 for repair work on typewriter.

(e) Completed work for Fred Griffin on account, $25.

(f) Performed services during the second half of the month that produced $680.

(g) Hired Jessie Walters to clean the office. Payment for this part-time job will be $100 per month.

(h) Paid $300 on office furniture bought in (b) above.

(i) Paid telephone bill for month, $75.

(j) Paid utility bill, $60.

(k) Withdrew $500 for personal use.

(l) Paid rental company $240 for use of office space for July.

sample problem solution

	Cash	+	Accounts Receivable	+	Equipment & Furniture	=	Accounts Payable	+	Cindy Dickerson, Capital	
(a)	+1800				+ 200				+2000	Investment
(b)	− 200				+ 800		+600			
	1600				1000		600		2000	
(c)	+ 450								+ 450	Fees Revenue
	2050				1000		600		2450	
(d)	− 50								− 50	Repairs Expense
	2000				1000		600		2400	
(e)			+25						+ 25	Fees Revenue
	2000		25		1000		600		2425	
(f)	+ 680								+ 680	Fees Revenue
	2680		25		1000		600		3105	
(g)		No Entry								
(h)	− 300						−300			
	2380		25		1000		300		3105	
(i)	− 75								− 75	Telephone Expense
	2305		25		1000		300		3030	
(j)	− 60								− 60	Utility Expense
	2245		25		1000		300		2970	
(k)	− 500								− 500	Withdrawal
	1745		25		1000		300		2470	
(l)	− 240								− 240	Rent Expense
	1505		25		1000		300		2230	

review exercises

4. Indicate the effect each of the following transactions would have on the basic accounting equation:
   (a) Invested cash in the business.
   (b) Purchased supplies on account.
   (c) Paid utility bill at the end of the month.
   (d) Withdrew cash from the business.
   (e) Received payment on account.
   (f) Paid salaries for the week.
   (g) Received cash for services performed.
5. Linda Maxwell's beginning owner's equity amounted to $1,486.14. During August, revenue of $989.75 was earned, and expenses of $619.23 were incurred. During the month, Linda invested an additional $500 in the business. What would Linda's equity be at the end of the month?
6. Harley Parker withdrew $800 from his business during November. In this same month, he had earned $2,374.00 in revenues and incurred $2,567.13 in expenses. If his beginning owner's equity was $16,656.34, what would be his owner's equity at the end of November?

• task GIVEN THE SUMS OF ALL TRANSACTIONS FOR A PERIOD, PREPARE A SIMPLE INCOME STATEMENT, CAPITAL STATEMENT, AND BALANCE SHEET

The income statement

If we continue Illustration 1-3, you can see that by July 31 Joe may be wondering if he should stay in business or sell the equipment, pay off the bills, and forget the whole thing. He started out with $8,000 in cash, and now he has only $4,715. Does this mean that the young firm is operating at a loss? On the other hand, Kar Klinik owns some equipment and supplies, as well as a promise of $300 from Vince Forte—all of which were not owned by Joe at the beginning of the month. Owner's equity at the end of the month shows $815 more than the beginning amount, and Joe withdrew $300 during the month. To get a clearer picture of operations, Joe needs to prepare financial statements.

First, Joe organizes his information about revenues and expenses by preparing an **income statement.** You can see the results of Joe's work in Illustration 1-4. As a result of his calculations, he decides that Kar Klinik made a *net income* for July since **revenues** are greater than **expenses.** Some people use the term *net profit* when talking about *net income.* We will use **net income** because it is the preferred term in today's business world. Kar Klinik would have shown a **net loss** for July if the expenses were greater than the revenues.

illustration 1-4
income statement.

Kar Klinik
Income Statement
For Month Ending July 31, 19X1

Repairs Revenue		2005 –
Operating Expenses:		
Salary Expense	800 –	
Utility Expense	50 –	
Advertising Expense	40 –	
Total Operating Expenses		890 –
Net Income		1115 –

Note that every item that appears on this statement was taken from the Owner's Equity column of Illustration 1-3. While you are looking at Illustration 1-4, examine the heading of this statement. On the first line, Joe has written the name of the firm—not his own name, even though he is the owner. The second line gives the name of the statement, and the third line tells the reader of this statement that the period of time required for Kar Klinik to make the $1,115 net income was one month. This period of time is known as the **fiscal period.** Most firms use an annual, or twelve-month, fiscal period; however, shorter fiscal periods are also common. In this illustration, we used a period of one month for simplicity. Note how the lines are drawn below the numbers. A straight line drawn entirely across the amount column makes the work attractive. A single line indicates that an addition or subtraction is to be made; a double line signifies that the calculation is complete. All statements should be prepared as neatly as possible.

The capital statement

A second statement that Joe prepares is the capital statement. This statement shows the increase and decrease in owner's equity resulting from earnings, investments, and withdrawals. In other words, it tells the reader why the capital account changed from the beginning balance to the ending balance. Some accountants prefer to call this statement a **statement of owner's equity.** Note in Illustration 1-5 that the heading is similar in design to the heading of the income statement. The name of the firm is on the first line, and the title of the statement is on the second line. The third line tells the reader what period of time is accounted for in this report.

illustration 1-5
capital statement.

Kar Klinik
Capital Statement
For Month Ended July 31, 19X1

Joe Jackson, Capital, July 1, 19X1		-0-	
Add: Net Income	1,115 –		
Investment	8,000 –	9115 –	
Less Withdrawals		300 –	
Joe Jackson, Capital, July 31, 19X1			8815 –

Recall in Illustration 1-3 that *Joe Jackson, Capital,* changed from zero to \$8,815. This change was caused by (1) an investment of \$8,000 (item "a" in Illustration 1-3), (2) net income of \$1,115 (determined from the income statement), and (3) withdrawals of \$300 (item "j"). Since the expense and revenue items are part of the calculation of net income, these items don't appear on the capital statement. If Kar Klinik had experienced a net loss of \$413, the capital statement would reflect this change, as can be seen in Illustration 1-6. In summary, investments increase owner's equity and withdrawals decrease it. Likewise, net income increases owner's equity and net loss decreases it. Note that net income and net loss are caused by activities of the business, while investments and withdrawals are direct actions of the owner.

illustration 1-6
capital statement.

Kar Klinik
Capital Statement
For Month Ended July 31, 19X1

Joe Jackson, Capital, July 1, 19X1		-0-	
Add: Investment		8000 –	
Less: Net Loss	\$413		
Withdrawals	300	713 –	
Joe Jackson, Capital, July 31, 19X1			7287 –

After a firm has been in operation for one period, a beginning capital balance usually exists. Assume that Kar Klinik is an established firm with a beginning balance of \$10,000. If the company made a net income of \$360 and the owner withdrew \$300 during July, the completed capital statement would look like the one in Illustration 1-7.

illustration 1-7
capital statement.

Kar Klinik
Capital Statement
For Month Ending July 31, 19X1

Joe Jackson, Capital, July 1, 19X1	10000 –	
Add: Net Income	360 –	
Total	10360	
Less: Withdrawals	300	
Joe Jackson, Capital, July 31, 19X1		10060 –

The balance sheet

Finally, Joe would prepare a **balance sheet** to tell the reader what the business owns (its assets), what the business owes (its liabilities), and the worth of the firm (its owner's equity). A better title would be **statement of financial position.** Unfortunately, this title has not received wide acceptance, so we will use balance sheet. The balance sheet is designed to show that all of the firm's assets equal the sum of the firm's liabilities and owner's equity.

As in the income statement and the capital statement, the heading of the balance sheet requires three lines. The first two lines tell the reader the firm's name and the name of the statement. However, the third line differs significantly in that it gives only the date of the statement. The income statement and the capital statement report income or loss and the change in the capital account over a specific time period. By contrast, the balance sheet says, "Stop! Let's see what amounts are in the firm's accounts on this particular date." Just like the electric meter reader who makes monthly rounds, the proprietor takes a "reading" of the firm's assets, liabilities, and owner's equity at a particular time. On this date the company owns so much, it owes so much, and it is worth so much.

Now go back and take another look at how the account totals given in Illustration 1-3 are transferred to the balance sheet in Illustration 1-8. Each amount shown on the balance sheet is taken from the column total in Illustration 1-3. For example, the *Cash* account column in Illustration 1-3 shows a final amount of $4,715. This amount is entered in the balance sheet because that is how much cash Kar Klinik has on July 31. Once each asset is listed with its total, these amounts are added to produce the *Total Assets* figure. If there were more than one liabilites account, each would be listed under *Liabilities* in a similar fashion. Note that *Liabilities* and *Owner's Equity* are added to produce a total. If this total does not agree with the *Total Assets* figure, there is an error somewhere in the accounts.

illustration 1-8
balance sheet.

Kar Klinik
Balance Sheet
July 31, 19X1

Assets		
Cash	4715 –	
Prepaid rent	300 –	
Supplies	50 –	
Accounts receivable	300 –	
Equipment	1150 –	
Truck	2800 –	
Total Assets		9315 –
Liabilities & Owner's Equity		
Liabilities		
Accounts Payable		500 –
Owner's Equity		
Joe Jackson, Capital, July 31, 19X1		8815 –
Total Liabilities & Owner's Equity		9315 –

As you may have noticed, the amount used for *Joe Jackson, Capital* on the balance sheet can be taken either from the total of *Joe Jackson, Capital* in Illustration 1-3 or from the final figure in the capital statement.

sample problem Ann McCracken owns and operates a lawn care service known as Ann's Lawn Care. After analyzing all of the transactions for May, she has the following account totals:

Cash	$ 448.16
Accounts Receivable	115.00
Lawn Equipment	896.45
Truck	6,600.00
Accounts Payable	316.35
Notes Payable	1,340.00
Ann McCracken, Capital, May 1, 19X1	6,814.14
Expenses during the period:	
Rent	200.00
Telephone	75.00
Utilities	90.34
Gas and Oil	48.19
Repairs	32.12
Lawn Repairs Revenue	634.77
Withdrawals by owner	600.00

Prepare an income statement, a capital statement, and a balance sheet for Ann's Lawn Care, May 31, 19X1.

sample problem solution

Ann's Lawn Care
Income Statement
For Month Ended May 31, 19X1

Lawn Repairs Revenue		$634.77
Operating Expenses:		
Rent Expense	$200.00	
Telephone Expense	75.00	
Utilities Expense	90.34	
Gas and Oil Expense	48.19	
Repairs Expense	32.12	445.65
Net Income		$ 189.12

Ann's Lawn Care
Capital Statement
For Month Ended May 31, 19X1

Ann McCracken, Capital, May 1, 19X1	$6,814.14
Add: Net Income	189.12
	$7,003.26
Less: Withdrawal	600.00
Ann McCracken, Capital, May 31, 19X1	$6,403.26

Ann's Lawn Care
Balance Sheet
May 31, 19X1

Assets		
Cash	$ 448.16	
Accounts Receivable	115.00	
Lawn Equipment	896.45	
Truck	6,600.00	
Total Assets		$8,059.61
Liabilities and Owner's Equity		
Liabilities		
Accounts Payable	$ 316.35	
Notes Payable	1,340.00	
Total Liabilities		$1,656.35
Owner's Equity		
Ann McCracken, Capital, May 31, 19X1		6,403.26
Total Liabilities and Owner's Equity		$8,059.61

review exercises

7. Prepare a capital statement for Bob's Auto Body Shop for the month of August, assuming:

Bob Harper, Capital, August 1, 19X1	$7653.00
Investment during month	1200.00
Expenses for August	2416.21
Revenues for August	3176.54

8. Prepare a capital statement for Warren's Answering Service based on the following facts:

Betty Warren, Capital, Feb. 1, 19X1	$8232.87
Withdrawals during February	1650.00
February Expenses	642.56
February Revenues	591.43

9. Using (I) for income statement, (B) for balance sheet, and (C) for capital statement, indicate which statement would show each of the following items: (a) *Rent Expense*; (b) *Bill Carver, Drawing;* (c) *Rental Revenue;* (d) *Accounts Payable*; (e) *Equipment*; (f) *Net Loss;* (g) *Accounts Receivable.*

10. Edgar Phillipi prepared a schedule similar to the one shown in Illustration 1-3 for his business, Ed's Fixit Shop. The Owner's Equity column showed the following events for the month of November:

Edgar Phillipi, Capital	
$3,500	
+150	Service Revenue
$3,650	
−100	Supplies Expense
$3,550	
−400	Salary Expense
$3,150	
+240	Service Revenue
$3,390	
+2,000	Investment
$5,390	
−170	Rent Expense
$5,220	
+200	Service Revenue
$5,420	
−120	Utility Expense
$5,300	

Prepare an income statement for Edgar for the month of November, 19X1.

chapter highlights

Having studied this chapter, you should now be able to:

- State the basic accounting equation in terms of a company's accounts.
- Analyze a transaction to identify which accounts are affected and whether they are increased or decreased.
- Prepare a simple income statement.
- Prepare a simple capital statement.
- Prepare a simple balance sheet.

The procedure we have used in this chapter is suitable only for an extremely small business. In the following chapters, we will expand this system to show an approach more convenient for handling complex business transactions. To receive the maximum benefit from this text, it is important to keep the competency task in mind as you do each exercise or problem the instructor assigns.

check figures to review exercises

1. $4,000, cost concept

2. Going-concern concept

3. (c)

4. (a) +A, + OE
(b) +A, + L
(c) −A, −OE
(d) −A, −OE
(e) +A, −A (no effect)
(f) −A, −OE
(g) +A, +OE

5. $2,356.66
6. $15,663.21
7. Ending capital, $9,613.33
8. Ending capital, $6,531.74
9. (a) I, (b) C, (c) I, (d) B, (e) B, (f) C and I, (g) B
10. Net loss, $200

key terms

The following important terms are discussed in Chapter 1 and are defined in the Glossary at the end of the book:

account
asset
balance sheet
basic accounting equation
capital statement
cost concept
entity concept
expense
fiscal period
going concern
income statement
liability
net income
net loss
owner's equity
proprietorship
revenue
transaction

questions

1. Which accounting concept assumes that the business will last indefinitely?
2. Which accounting concept assumes that the amount spent should be the amount recorded on the company's books?
3. State the basic accounting equation and define each term.
4. What type of items decrease owner's equity?
5. What exactly is meant by "Accounts Receivable"?
6. What is included in the heading of an income statement? How does this differ from the heading of a balance sheet?
7. *Arthur Kramer, Capital,* at the beginning of the period was $10,000, and Kramer invested $2,500 during the period. If the ending capital balance is $12,000, how much net income or net loss did the company have?
8. Give another acceptable title for the capital statement.
9. Give another acceptable title for the balance sheet.
10. What is meant by "fiscal" period?

exercises

1. Barbara Wallace owns a beauty shop with the following items: *Cash,* $2,000; *Equipment,* $10,000; *Accounts Payable,* $3,000; *Mortgage Payable,* $8,000. What is the net worth of the beauty shop?

2. Classify these as an asset, a liability, an expense, or a revenue:
   (a) Salary Expense
   (b) Equipment
   (c) Accounts Payable
   (d) Accounts Receivable
   (e) Rent Income
   (f) Supplies Expense
   (g) Cash

3. Indicate the effect on the basic accounting equation of each of the following transactions:
   (a) Purchased supplies for cash.
   (b) Bought truck by issuing note payable.
   (c) Received cash for services rendered during the period.
   (d) Paid employee for one week's work.
   (e) Provided services for the month with expected receipt of money next month.
   (f) Collected the money in (e) above.
   (g) Paid utilities for the month.

4. Dr. Ross had *Dental Fees Revenue* of $2,500 during July and the following expenses: rent, $300; utilities, $120; technician's salary, $800; supplies, $250. Using + and − under the equation A = L + OE, indicate how each of the following transactions would affect the basic accounting equation:
   (a) Purchased equipment for $600 using cash.
   (b) Invested $5,000 cash in the business.
   (c) Provided services to customers on account, $200.
   (d) Bought supplies on account, $20.
   (e) Withdrew $500 from the business.
   (f) Paid for the supplies purchased in (d).
   (g) Paid the utility bill for the month, $180.
   (h) Collected cash for (c) above.

5. Calculate the missing information in each of the following situations:
   (a) Beginning capital, $6,000; investments, $1,000; withdrawals, $2,500; net loss, $453.16. What is the ending capital balance?
   (b) Beginning capital, $3,250; net income, $3,128.73; ending capital, $4,600. How much was withdrawn for personal use?
   (c) Beginning capital, $16,432.12; investments, $2,000; net loss, $2,400.45. What is the ending capital balance?

6. Given the following information, prepare a balance sheet for January for Harry's Dog Grooming Service: *Cash,* $400; *Accounts Receivable,* $700; *Supplies,* $350; *Delivery Truck,* $7,000; *Accounts Payable,* $600; *Notes Payable,* $6,500; *Harry Walker, Capital* (you calculate).

problems

1. COMPETENCY TESTED The ability to analyze transactions for a new business and to determine their effect on the basic accounting equation.

   Magic Carpet Travel Agency had the following transactions during the first month of operations, September, 19X1.

   (a) Edna May invested $5,000 in the business.
   (b) Paid rent for the month, $350.
   (c) Purchased office supplies from Sherri Supply Company, $75, paying cash.
   (d) Bought a typewriter from Brown Equipment Company, $600, on account.
   (e) Paid $600 for desks and chairs.
   (f) Paid employee's salary for first half of September, $400.
   (g) Received commissions for first half of month, $1,020.
   (h) Withdrew $100 for personal use.
   (i) Paid $150 on account to Brown Equipment Company.
   (j) Received commissions of $960 for the second half of the month.
   (k) Paid the telephone bill, $183.
   (l) Paid the employee salary for the second half of September, $400.
   (m) Paid the utility bill, $75.
   (n) Paid $40 to the local newspaper for an ad.
   (o) Bought supplies, $80, on account.

   Instructions Using the following account headings, prepare a schedule similar to the one found in Illustration 1-3: *Cash, Supplies, Equipment, Accounts Payable,* and *Edna May, Capital.*

2. COMPETENCY TESTED The ability to analyze transactions for a new business and to determine their effect on the basic accounting equation.

   Bonnie's Beauty Parlor began operations in August of the current year. Bonnie Herald rented space in a shopping mall and hired one assistant hairdresser. The following transactions took place during August:

   (a) Invested $2,000 in the beauty parlor.
   (b) Paid rent for one month, $450 (treat as an expense).
   (c) Purchased equipment, paying $500 cash and signing a note payable for $4,500.

(d) Purchased supplies on account, $150.

(e) Brought a typewriter from home to be used in the business; it has a current market value of $300 (Bonnie is investing the typewriter in the business).

(f) Performed services for the month and earned $2400.

(g) Paid the employee's salary of $600.

(h) Paid the telephone bill, $55.

(i) Paid the utility bill, $140.

(j) Paid $50 toward supplies bought in (d).

(k) Gave a $50 permanent to Doris Smith, who promises to pay the first of next month.

(l) Purchased a new washing machine for her home by taking money out of her personal savings account, $350.

(m) Paid $10 for a radio ad.

Instructions Using the following account headings, prepare a schedule similar to the one found in Illustration 1-3: *Cash; Accounts Receivable; Supplies; Equipment; Accounts Payable; Notes Payable; Bonnie Herald, Capital.*

3. COMPETENCY TESTED The ability to analyze transactions for an established firm and to determine their effect on the basic accounting equation.

Sam's Income Tax Service has the following account balances on March 1: *Cash,* $600; *Accounts Receivable,* $200; *Supplies,* $220; *Equipment,* $2,040; *Accounts Payable,* $540; *Notes Payable,* $1,400; *Sam Brown, Capital,* $1,120. The following transactions took place during March:

(a) Received $50 from a customer on account.

(b) Paid rent for month, $250 (treat as an expense).

(c) Sam invested an additional $500 in the business.

(d) Sold an old typewriter for its cost, $200.

(e) Collected $1,500 for preparing tax returns.

(f) Paid assistant a salary of $600.

(g) Withdrew $200 for personal use.

(h) Paid $1,000 on note payable.

(i) Bought $50 of supplies on account.

(j) Collected $150 on account.

(k) Paid utility bill, $93.

(l) Paid telephone bill, $67.

(m) Prepared tax returns and charged $1,640. Collected all but $40, which is expected to be received in April.

(n) Paid assistant a salary of $600 for second half of month.

Instructions Prepare a schedule similar to the one in Illustration 1-3 for the month of March for Sam's Income Tax Service.

4. COMPETENCY TESTED Given the account balances, the ability to construct financial statements.

On December 31, 19X1, Wilson Tire Repair completed its fiscal year. Hal Wilson ended the year with the following account totals:

Cash	$ 690
Accounts Receivable	450
Supplies	214
Equipment	4,000
Building	100,000
Accounts Payable	550
Mortgage Payable	80,000
Hal Wilson, Capital	?

During the year he had the following changes in the capital account:

Supplies Expense	$ 1,000
Repairs Expense	650
Utilities Expense	1,400
Salaries Expense	8,500
Telephone Expense	640
Insurance Expense	440
Service Revenue	10,300
Investments	1,200
Withdrawals	1,800

Hal Wilson had a beginning capital balance on January 1 of $27,734.

Instructions Prepare an income statement, a capital statement, and a balance sheet for the year ending December 31, 19X1.

5. COMPETENCY TESTED The ability to prepare financial statements.

Kristie's Child Care Center had the following account totals as of February 28, 19X1.

Cash	$350
Accounts Receivable	130
Supplies	219
Equipment	900
Accounts Payable	295
Notes Payable	400
Kristie Cheese, Capital, Feb. 28	904
Kristie Cheese, Capital, Feb. 1	850

During February, Kristie paid the following expenses:

Salaries	$375
Utilities	80
Telephone	48
Rent	150

In addition, Kristie took out $312 for personal use and had revenue from child care amounting to $1,019.

Instructions Prepare an income statement, a capital statement, and a balance sheet for the month of February, 19X1.

6. COMPETENCY TESTED The ability to analyze transactions and prepare financial statements.

Willie's Trailer Park began the month of June with the following balances: *Cash,* $1,500; *Accounts Receivable,* $440; *Notes Receivable,* $500; *Supplies,* $97; *Equipment,* $4,000; *Accounts Payable,* $128; *Notes Payable,* $2,700; *Willie Faulkner, Capital,* $3,709. During June, the following transactions took place:

(a) Paid rent for the month, $1,000. (Treat as an expense.)

(b) Collected $100 owed on account.

(c) Bought new swing set on account, $480.

(d) Received cash for rental of trailer spaces, $2,200.

(e) Paid $200 toward note payable.

(f) Paid employee's salary, $400.

(g) Withdrew $500 for personal use.

(h) Took money received in (g) and purchased a new television set for personal use.

(i) Paid telephone bill, $44.

(j) Paid utilities, $390.

(k) Received cash for rental on trailer spaces, $2,400.

(l) Made an arrangement to accept $25 in July from Sam Short, a renter unable to pay on time.

(m) Paid employee's salary, $400.

Instructions Using a form similar to the one in Illustration 1-3, prepare (a) a schedule of transactions for June and (b) an income statement, a capital statement, and a balance sheet for June.

7. COMPETENCY TESTED The ability to prepare a capital statement.

Clark's Summer Camp operated for three months during the current year—June, July, and August. After the summer was over, Sarah Clark looked back over her first summer of operation and calculated these ending amounts: *Cash,* \$300; *Accounts Receivable,* \$1,819; *Supplies,* \$85; *Equipment,* \$2,115; *Accounts Payable,* \$219; *Notes Payable,* \$1,900. Expenses for the three months amounted to \$3,000, while revenue amounted to \$3,500. During this time, Sarah invested \$2,000 and withdrew \$300.

Instructions Prepare a capital statement for the three-month period ending August 31. Keep in mind that this is the first year of operations. Prove the ending capital balance using the basic accounting equation.

chapter 2
THE RECORDING PROCESS

overall competency THE ABILITY TO RECORD TRANSACTIONS IN THE GENERAL JOURNAL, POST THEM TO THE LEDGER, AND PREPARE A TRIAL BALANCE

career objectives Although Chapter 1 gave you some solid basics to build upon, they are adequate only for a very small business. In this chapter, you will learn how to use three accounting tools essential to preparing financial statements—the journal, the ledger, and the trial balance.

Upon completing this chapter, you should be able to

- RECORD DAILY TRANSACTIONS IN THE GENERAL JOURNAL.
- POST TO THE LEDGER THE INFORMATION FOUND IN THE JOURNAL.
- PREPARE A TRIAL BALANCE FROM THE COMPLETED LEDGER.
- QUICKLY LOCATE MISTAKES MADE IN JOURNALIZING, POSTING, AND PREPARING THE TRIAL BALANCE.

The starting point for the accounting process is information taken from some type of business document—a sales ticket or an invoice, for example. This information is recorded first in a **journal** and then transferred to various accounts in a **ledger.** By using the journal and the ledger, you will find that a large number of transactions can be processed. As you work with these new concepts, you should be able to relate the new material to what you learned in Chapter 1.

• task ANALYZE TRANSACTIONS AND DETERMINE WHICH ACCOUNTS ARE AFFECTED AND WHETHER THE ENTRY INCREASES OR DECREASES THE ACCOUNT

Ledger accounts and the ledger

The *account* approach to analyzing transactions allows you to group information about each account in a very useful way. In its simplest form, the ledger account is designed in the shape of a T that displays three parts: the heading, the left side, and the right side.

Account Title	
Left side	Right side

The left side of the account is known as the **debit;** and the right side is the **credit.** Thus, when we talk about entering a transaction on the *debit* side, we simply mean that the number is entered on the left side. In accounting language, we are *debiting* the account. When entries are made to the right side of an account, we are *crediting* the account. The terms debit and credit are used so often that they are abbreviated. The letters "Dr." mean *debit,* and the letters "Cr." mean *credit.*

The classification of the account controls the effect of an entry, that is, whether the account is increased or decreased. Illustration 2-1 shows how an entry affects each major category in the basic accounting equation.

illustration 2-1
chapter comparisons.

Item	Chapter 1 Procedure	Chapter 2 Equivalent
1. To show increase/ decrease in account	Use of plus (+) or minus (−)	Use of debit or credit
2. Nature of increase/ decrease	Assets + to increase − to decrease Liabilities + to increase − to decrease Owner's Equity Investment + to increase Revenues + to increase Expenses − to decrease Drawing − to decrease	Assets Debit to increase Credit to decrease Liabilities Credit to increase Debit to decrease Owner's Equity Investment Credit to increase Debit to decrease Revenues Credit to increase Debit to decrease Expenses Debit to increase Credit to decrease Drawing Debit to increase Credit to decrease

Now, by showing these changes in T-account format, we can see that the basic accounting equation is kept in balance.

Assets		=	Liabilities		+	Owner's Equity	
Dr.	Cr.		Dr.	Cr.		Dr.	Cr.
+	−		−	+		−	+

Since the income statement uses only revenue and expense accounts, these two categories are separated from owner's equity and given their own identity.

illustration 2-2
owner's equity category.

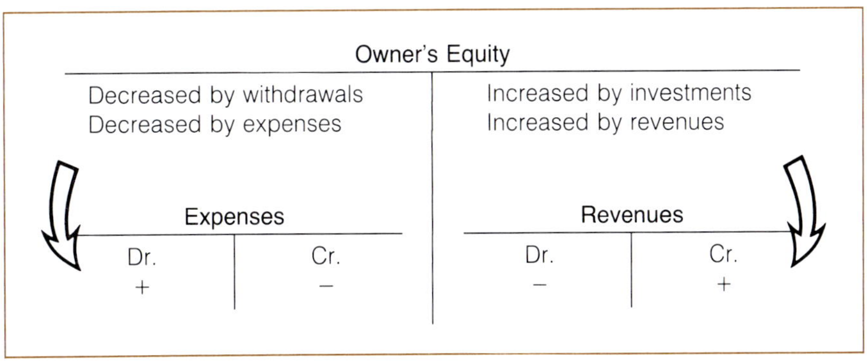

You may need to think about why expenses decrease owner's equity but increase the category itself. As before, expenses decrease owner's equity with debit entries. When we create a separate category for *expenses,* any account in the category becomes larger as it is debited. Firms receive better information about the amount and type of expenditures being made by having numerous expense accounts.

Revenue items increase through credits, just like owner's equity. Since revenue increases owner's equity, it follows that both should increase on the *credit* side. With expenses and revenues entered in their own account categories, the only daily transactions that affect owner's equity will show investments and withdrawals by the owners. Putting all of this together, we now have the following expanded basic accounting equation:

Assets		=	Liabilities		+	Owner's Equity		−	Expenses		+	Revenues	
+	−		−	+		−	+		+	−		−	+
Dr.	Cr.		Dr.	Cr.		Dr.	Cr.		Dr.	Cr.		Dr.	Cr.

illustration 2-3 expanded basic accounting equation.

Recall in Chapter 1 that you had to keep the basic accounting equation in balance as each transaction was made. To assist you in doing this when debits and credits are used, always keep in mind that debits must equal credits in each transaction. By keeping this basic rule in mind, you will avoid recording problems later.

Applying the debit and credit procedure

To see how the debit–credit approach works, let's try a few transactions. Assume that on March 15, a check is written for $75 to pay the newspaper for past advertising. Let's analyze this transaction using the T accounts in Illustration 2-3. First, the firm now has more expenses, so we need to plus, or debit, the expense account (since expenses are increased by debits). Next, since *Cash* is an asset that is decreasing, we must credit the asset. In terms of Illustration 2-3, we have done the following:

Asset (Cash)		Expense (Advertising Expense)	
	75 (to decrease, credit)	75 (to increase, debit)	

As you can see, debits equal credits in this transaction. As another example, assume that the firm collects $125 for services rendered that day. The asset *Cash* must be increased, and assets are increased on the debit side. At the same time, the revenue account *Service Revenue* must be increased through a credit. In T-account form, we now have the following transaction:

Asset (Cash)	
125 (to increase, debit)	

Revenue (Service Revenue)	
	125 (to increase, credit)

In the first transaction, the firm experienced an increase and a decrease, but in the second, both accounts increased. These illustrations emphasize the fact that the pattern using debits and credits is not based on the concept of plus and minus, but on the equality of debits and credits.

Classification of ledger accounts

Earlier we mentioned that each account has a separate page in the ledger. In Chapter 1 you should have developed a *feel* for the type of accounts in each category. Using this approach, you should think of a transaction in terms of its effect on the individual account, as well as on the category. To illustrate, assume that the employees are paid $1,250 for work performed during the month. Your analysis of the situation should go something like this: The firm has $1,250 more expenses now than it did before, so the expense category should be increased by a debit, which actually decreases owner's equity. Since a business usually has a number of expense accounts, you must decide on the type of expense. In this case, a salary expense is involved. Therefore, you should debit *Salary Expense* for $1,250. The cash account is an asset account and should be decreased. Therefore, your conclusion should be to credit *Cash* for $1,250.

A brief discussion of the different types of accounts within each major group will give you a better grasp of the concept.

assets

Cash

The *Cash* account of the business includes coin, currency, checks, and money in checking accounts.

Accounts receivable

Services are often performed and products sold with an agreement that cash will be received later. These transactions are recorded in the asset account *Accounts Receivable.*

Office supplies

Blank business documents, stationery, paper, pencils, and paper clips are examples of office supplies. Purchases of these items are recorded as increases in the asset account. At the end of an accounting period, the value of supplies used during the period is shown by debiting an expense account and by crediting *Office Supplies.*

Prepaid insurance

Insurance premiums are usually paid in advance and shown as an increase in the asset *Prepaid Insurance.* Later the part "used up" as time passes is shown as an expense. Procedures for transferring the expired portion from the asset account will be described in a later chapter. Several other prepaid items, such as *Prepaid Rent* and *Prepaid Taxes,* are handled in a manner similar to that used for *Prepaid Insurance.*

Land, buildings, and equipment

Values for land, buildings, and equipment should be shown in separate accounts. Purchases of any of these items are shown as an increase in the respective asset account, and selling, trading, or discarding them requires a decrease in the respective asset accounts.

liabilities

Accounts payable

Equipment, supplies, and services are often purchased on account, to be paid for later. The obligations to pay cash in the future are recorded as increases to the liability account called *Accounts Payable.*

Notes payable

Sometimes a firm signs a written document known as a *note* in exchange for merchandise or equipment. This legal document is a liability that calls for payment of interest in addition to the principal, or face amount, of the note by a certain date or within a stated period of time. *Notes Payable* is also used when money is borrowed from a bank and a note is signed and given to the bank as written evidence that the firm agrees to this liability. Notes will be discussed in detail in Chapter 13.

Mortgage payable

A **mortgage** is a written promise to repay a debt, usually over a relatively long period of time and usually in connection with expensive purchases such as purchases of land, buildings, or major equipment. Under a mortgage agreement, the item for which the mortgage is issued can be claimed in payment for the debt if the business cannot make its mortgage payments.

Other liabilities

Salaries Payable, Taxes Payable, and *Interest Payable* are examples of other obligations recorded and presented in the financial statements.

owner's equity

Capital

The capital account balance shows the owner's claim on the assets after outsiders' claims are deducted. As was shown in Chapter 1, capital is increased by investments in the business and by net income, and it is decreased by withdrawals and net losses.

Drawing

Withdrawals of cash and other assets are routinely made by the owner of the firm. Such withdrawals are looked upon by the owner as *payment* for work performed or risks taken. When an owner removes an asset from the business entity for personal use, the owner's drawing account is debited. Later, this account balance is transferred to the capital account. The drawing account has a debit balance, so the final effect of these withdrawals is to reduce the capital of the owner.

Revenues

Performance of services and sales of products increase revenue accounts. *Fees Earned* and *Commissions Earned* are examples of revenue accounts. Keep in mind that revenue accounts are really owner's equity accounts that have been temporarily separated to permit easier preparation of the income statement.

expenses Expenses are costs incurred for doing business during the current accounting period. Cash payments have been made or are expected to be made in the future for these expenses. When an asset, such as supplies, is used up during an accounting period, the amount used becomes an expense or is said to be an "expired cost." Examples are *Salaries Expense, Rent Expense, Supplies Expense,* and *Utilities Expense.*

Normal balances

Because most accounts have more increases than decreases, a balance on the *increase* side of the account is said to be **normal.** For asset and expense accounts, a normal balance will be on the debit (left-hand) side. Liabilities, revenues, and owner's equity usually have credit (right-hand) balances. If the business is operating routinely and profitably, accounts are expected to have normal balances in the ledger after transactions have been entered properly and each account has been summarized.

Abnormal balances

A firm might occasionally have an account with an *abnormal* balance. For example, a firm's checking account might be overdrawn as a result of a miscalculation. The owner, thinking that the account has a larger balance, might pay a bill or purchase supplies for cash. After this transaction is recorded, the *Cash* account will have a credit balance.

Typically, an account does not have a zero balance. However, if a small firm with a few liabilities should choose to pay them off, the transaction would produce a zero balance. It is also possible to use up advertising purchased in advance (*Prepaid Advertising*). The important point is that if an account has a balance, it normally is on the increase side.

Applying the debit and credit rule to entries

To see how a series of entries affects the ledger accounts, examine the following transactions and analyze the effect that each has on the different accounts:

(a) Diana Lee began a business by investing cash of $2,000 and equipment valued at $12,000.

Cash	
(a) 2,000	

Diana Lee, Capital	
	(a) 14,000

Equipment	
(a) 12,000	

(b) Diana paid $700 for two months' rent of store space.

Cash	
(a) 2,000	(b) 700

Diana Lee, Capital	
	(a) 14,000

Prepaid Rent	
(b) 700	

Equipment	
(a) 12,000	

Note that the credit to *Cash* is placed on the first available line on the credit side.

(c) Office supplies costing $80 were purchased from Village Supply on account.

Cash	
(a) 2,000	(b) 700

Accounts Payable	
	(c) 80

Prepaid Rent	
(b) 700	

Diana Lee, Capital	
	(a) 14,000

Office Supplies	
(c) 80	

Equipment	
(a) 12,000	

(d) Diana performed counseling services and received $1,200 in cash.

Cash

(a)	2,000	(b)	700
(d)	1,200		

Accounts Payable

		(c)	80

Prepaid Rent

(b)	700		

Diana Lee, Capital

		(a)	14,000

Office Supplies

(c)	80		

Consulting Revenue

		(d)	1,200

Equipment

(a)	12,000		

(e) The monthly telephone bill was paid, $78.

Cash

(a)	2,000	(b)	700
(d)	1,200	(e)	78

Accounts Payable

		(c)	80

Prepaid Rent

(b)	700		

Diana Lee, Capital

		(a)	14,000

Office Supplies

(c)	80		

Consulting Revenue

		(d)	1,200

Equipment

(a)	12,000		

Telephone Expense

(e)	78		

These transactions should give you a "feel" for making entries. Remember these key points:

1. Make certain that each transaction has matching debits and credits. As you saw in entry (a), it is possible to have more than one debit. It is also possible to have more than one credit.
2. Enter the transaction in the next available space.
3. Most or all accounts should have normal balances.

Selecting an account title may give you some concern. The best rule to follow is to use an account title that describes the category as clearly as possible.

sample problem Make the following entries for Beverly's Answering Service:

(a) Beverly Williams invested $500 in the business.
(b) Paid rent for month, $250.
(c) Purchased a desk from Colson Office Equipment for $375 on account.
(d) Purchased office supplies from Hedgecoth Supplies, paying $25.
(e) Billed customers for month, $1,250.
(f) Received $1,117 from customers from monthly billing in (e).
(g) Withdrew $625 for personal use.
(h) Paid telephone bill, $174.
(i) Paid utilities, $62.

sample problem solution

Cash

(a)	500	(b)	250
(f)	1,117	(d)	25
		(g)	625
		(h)	174
		(i)	62

Accounts Receivable

(e)	1,250	(f)	1,117

Prepaid Rent

(b)	250		

Office Supplies

(d)	25		

Equipment

(c)	375		

Accounts Payable

		(c)	375

B. Williams, Drawing

(g)	625		

B. Williams, Capital

		(a)	500

Billed Revenue

		(e)	1,250

Telephone Expense

(h)	174		

Utilities Expense

(i)	62		

review exercises

1. Indicate whether each of the following items would be an asset, liability, or owner's equity item:
   (a) stationery
   (b) building
   (c) Joe Washington, Drawing
   (d) deposit in bank
   (e) amount owed to creditor

(f) amount owed by customer
(g) pencils and paper clips
(h) mortgage payable in 10 years

2. Fill in the basic accounting equation. Then indicate the side that increases with a plus (+), and the side that decreases with a minus (−).

__________ = __________ + __________ − __________ + __________

3. Analyze the following *Cash* account and indicate which entries must be in error:

Cash

Investment by owner	10,000	Payment of utilities	80
Payment from customers	493	Payment of salaries	800
Purchase of equipment	550	Payment for ad	70
Collection from services		Payment for rent	250
performed	869	Withdrawal by owner	100
		Net Income	792

• task ANALYZE TRANSACTIONS, RECORD THEM IN THE JOURNAL, AND POST THEM TO THE LEDGER

The journal

In Chapter 1, we recorded transactions in a table using the basic accounting equation as our guide. Earlier in this chapter we introduced you to using debits and credits to record transactions in the ledger. The ledger approach would be fine if all we wanted was a listing of transactions in chronological order within each account. In other words, we have no "diary" of all the company's financial events. To produce such a record, we use a bound book called a **journal.** Each transaction is recorded *first* in this book, then transferred later to the ledger. In this way, we have not only a grouping of all information about each account (that is, all cash receipts and payments are in the *Cash* account) but also a record of the transaction in chronological order. The process of recording a transaction in the journal is called *journalizing.* The journal enables us to keep accurate daily records, as well as to write a short explanation to remind ourselves about the specifics of the actual transaction.

Since the journal is the first place a transaction is recorded in the company's books, it is called the **book of original entry.** The name **journal** reflects the French word *jour,* meaning day, since this record is designed to show day-to-day transactions. Each business transaction must be analyzed thoroughly before the journal entry can be made. The purpose of this analysis is to determine which accounts to debit and credit so that the proper accounts are increased or decreased. If you are a beginner, you should use a step-by-step procedure to analyze the transactions. Later you may be able to think through numerous steps at the same time or, as we might say in accounting, think in terms of debits and credits.

Steps in analyzing a transaction for recording

1. Determine the broad types of classifications affected, such as assets, liabilities, revenues, expenses, or owner's equity. In some cases, two accounts in the same classification may be affected, such as two asset accounts.
2. Determine the effects in terms of increases or decreases. If two account types are involved, there may be two increases, two decreases, or an increase and a decrease.
3. Determine the specific ledger accounts affected and identify their broad classifications.
4. Record first the debit and then the credit in equal amounts.

If more than two ledger accounts are involved in a single transaction, we use a **compound entry.** Any combination of debits and credits is proper if the total debits equal the total credits.

To illustrate the steps, let's trace a transaction. Assume a delivery truck is purchased for $5,000 with $2,000 in cash and a note for the balance. Your analysis should go something like this:

Steps 1 and 2. One asset account is increased, one asset account is decreased, and one liability account is increased.

3. *Delivery Truck,* an asset account, *Cash,* an asset account, and *Notes Payable,* a liability account, are affected.

4. *Delivery Truck* is debited $5,000 (to increase the asset), *Cash* is credited $2,000 (to decrease the asset), and *Notes Payable* is credited $3,000 (to increase the liability). The single debit of $5,000 equals the two credits of $2,000 and $3,000.

In this procedure, did you note the emphasis on analyzing the situation? In the words of one accounting educator: "There are three important things we must learn to do in accounting—the first is to analyze; the second is to analyze; the third is to analyze." To assist your analysis, be on the alert for the words *received* and *paid.* When *received* is used, more than likely the item received was cash, so the asset *Cash* should be increased by a debit. Since most entries have only a single debit and a single credit, your major concern will be to decide what account to credit. When *paid* is found in the wording, you can feel fairly certain that money has been spent, so *Cash* must be decreased, or credited. Now all you have to do is determine the account to be debited.

A very important point that we have stressed in this section needs repeating. In Chapter 1, we used an accounting equation table (A = L + OE) as the first place to record a transaction. Earlier in this chapter, we introduced the ledger and recorded transactions directly to the T accounts. These approaches were used strictly for teaching. *With few exceptions, the journal should be the first place a transaction is recorded.* Then, as we will discuss later in this chapter, the transaction information is transferred to the ledger.

Steps in making a journal entry. To familiarize you with how the journal works, let's make a few entries using the Kar Klinik illustration from Chapter 1. On July 1, Joe Jackson invested $8,000 in the business. On the same day, he rented shop space by paying the owner one month's rent in advance. The steps listed below were used to record the entries from the Kar Klinik illustration. Examine Illustration 2-4 as you go through these steps:

1. Write the year at the top of the page in the month column. Unless the year changes, this will be the only time the year will appear on this page.
2. Record the month and day of the transaction. Unless the month changes, it will not be repeated.
3. Next, enter the debit account. Since cash increased, the *Cash* account is debited.
4. Since *Cash* is increased by $8,000, enter this amount in the debit amount column. We sometimes use a dash in the cents column if no cents are involved. Some people prefer to use zeros. Either approach is acceptable. Also, some instructors like to use dollar signs. When actual accounting paper is used, it is understood that dollars are being listed. Again, this usage is a matter of preference, so follow your instructor's procedure.
5. Indent the account title to indicate the credit portion. While we have no set standard as to how far to indent, the credit entry should be indented enough to indicate the nature of the entry.
6. Complete the entry by entering the amount in the credit column.
7. Provide a brief explanation of the transaction. If more than one line is needed, indent each additional line to match the start of the first explanation line.
8. Skip one line before the next transaction.

illustration 2-4 steps in journalizing.

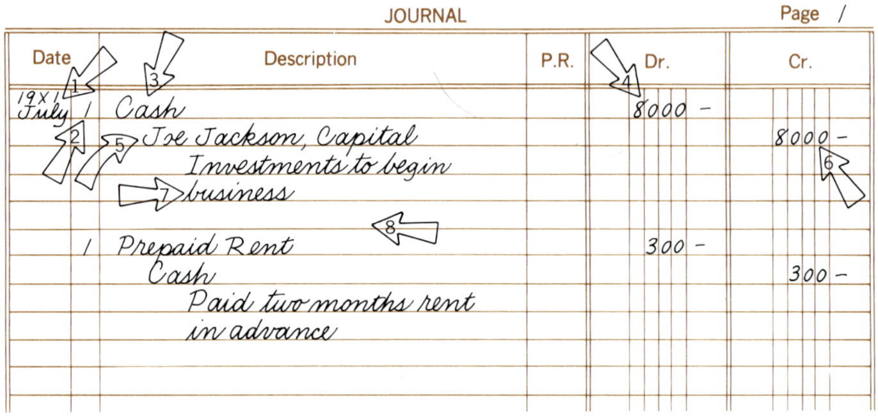

In this text, when we do not use actual accounting forms, we will use dollar signs so that you will not have any doubt as to the purpose of the column. Finally, never divide an entry between two pages. If an entry will not fit, just leave the space blank and go to the next page where you will have enough room. Dividing an entry could cause you to miss an error.

Posting to the ledger

Now we need to transfer the information from the journal to the **ledger.** You may wonder why we need to put the information in both the journal and the ledger. As we mentioned earlier, the journal is a diary of financial events for a business. However, it does not group all the transactions involving a specific account, like buying supplies or paying salaries. To do this, we need to get the information into the ledger accounts. This process, which is known as **posting,** may be done daily or every few days. The ledger must contain a ledger sheet for each account title written in the journal. The ledger is in loose-leaf form, like a notebook, so that accounts may be added or removed.

Before we illustrate the posting process, let's take a moment to see how to number accounts in the ledger. Numbers are used to enable the accountant to find each account quickly. The first digit indicates the type of account (asset, for example), and the second (and third or fourth if there are a large number of accounts) identifies a particular account within the group (*Cash,* for example). In this text, we use a widely accepted numbering system:

First Digit	Type of Account
1	Assets
2	Liabilities
3	Owner's equity
4	Revenue
5	Cost
6	Expense

We will not use cost accounts until Chapter 5, so this chapter will not have any accounts with 5 as the first digit. In our two-digit system, Account 13 is the third account in the asset section. If we used a three-digit system, an account numbered 614 would be the fourteenth account in the expense section. To assist the accounting clerk in selecting accounts to use in journal entries, a **chart of accounts** is usually prepared. We will show such a chart in the Kar Klinik illustration presented in the next section. In contrast to the ledger numbering system, the journal, which is bound, uses a simple page numbering system (that is, 1, 2, 3, and so forth).

Now we are ready to illustrate the posting process. The first transaction from Illustration 2-4 showed a cash investment of $8,000 by Joe Jackson to begin a business. Illustration 2-5 shows how the two ledger accounts, *Cash* and *Joe Jackson, Capital,* should be posted.

illustration 2-5 posting to the ledger.

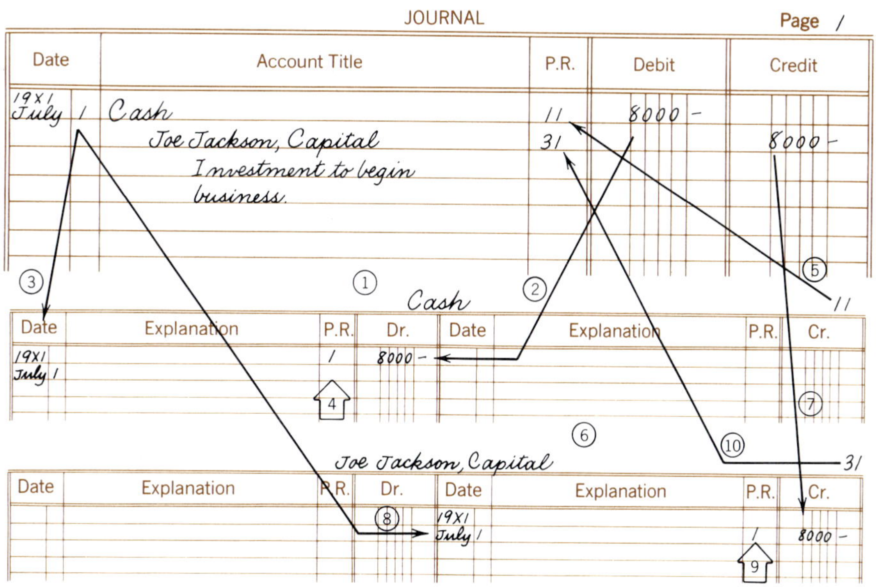

The following steps were used in Illustration 2-5 and should be used as a pattern in all of your posting:

1. Find the account to be debited in the ledger.
2. Transfer the debit amount from the journal to the debit side of the ledger.
3. Transfer the date to the debit side of the ledger.
4. Record the number of the journal page in the ledger's posting reference column.
5. Record the ledger page number in the journal's posting reference column.

6. Locate the account to be credited in the ledger.
7. Transfer the credit amount to the ledger.
8. Transfer the date to the credit side of the account.
9. Record the journal page number in the ledger's posting reference column.
10. Record the ledger page number in the journal's posting reference column.

Transactions recorded and posted

To help you understand how to journalize transactions, we are using the Kar Klinik illustration from Chapter 1. The transactions given below are repeated for your convenience.

July 1	Joe Jackson invested $8,000 to start the Kar Klinik. He withdrew $5,000 from his personal savings and sold stock left to him by an uncle for $3,000.
1	Paid two months' rent in advance, $300.
2	Purchased equipment from Greasy's Auto Supply for a total of $900, paying $400 cash and agreeing to pay the balance in 30 days.
6	Purchased equipment, $250, and supplies, $50, on credit from Haskins Supply and Equipment Company.
9	Purchased a 1977 pickup for $2,800 cash.
11	Collected $630 for fixing cars belonging to Shirley Seal and Sean O'Hara.
14	Paid salary for two weeks to employee, $400.
15	Paid $300 to Haskins Supply and Equipment Company for items bought on July 6.
15	Completed car repairs for Vince Forte totaling $550. Vince agrees to pay part of this later in July and the rest in August.
24	Joe Jackson withdrew $300 for personal living expenses.
26	Paid utilities, $50.
28	Paid employee for second two-week period, $400.
30	Paid the *Daily Bugle* for two newspaper ads that appeared during July, $40.
30	Received from Vince Forte $250 of the $550 for repair service previously performed and recorded on July 15.
30	Received $825 for completing major car overhaul.

The following *chart of accounts* was prepared to allow the accounting clerk to see what accounts were available and also to assist in locating an account quickly in the ledger:

illustration 2-6
chart of accounts.

Assets		Revenue	
11	Cash	41	Repairs Revenue
12	Accounts Receivable		**Expenses**
13	Supplies	61	Salary Expense
14	Prepaid Rent	62	Utilities Expense
16	Equipment	63	Advertising Expense
18	Truck		
	Liability		
21	Accounts Payable		
	Owner's Equity		
31	Joe Jackson, Capital		
32	Joe Jackson, Drawing		

A copy of this chart could be taped to the inside cover of the ledger binder for easy reference. This chart should be kept current by updating its contents as accounts are added or removed.

The transactions for Kar Klinik are journalized in Illustration 2-7. Observe in particular how the dates are handled, how the rule of debits and credits is followed, and how the explanations are displayed. Next, note how the information in the journal is posted to the various ledger accounts in Illustration 2-8. We have used the T-account form to simplify the illustration. A posting reference number is shown in both the ledger (referring to the journal page) and the journal (referring to the ledger page). You should post the journal transactions in order so that no entry is overlooked. *Do not fill in* the posting reference column as an afterthought. This column serves two purposes: (1) to show that the posting has been completed, and (2) to indicate the page in the ledger to which the information was transferred.

Let's compare what we just covered with what you learned in Chapter 1. In Chapter 1 you learned how to summarize an account by totaling each column. This procedure would work well in a very small operation, but it would prove cumbersome if many transactions were involved. In this chapter, we transferred the transactions from a journal to the ledger accounts to summarize each account without having to go through the plus and minus approach. Compare Illustration 1-3 with the ledger accounts in Illustration 2-8, and you will see that the column totals are now shown as account balances. A notable improvement is gained by showing greater detail in the revenue and expense items. You may have noticed also that the total of the capital account in Illustration 1-3 does not match the account balance in Illustration 2-8. We will be dealing with another step later that will take care of this situation.

illustration 2-7
Kar Klinik's journal.

JOURNAL Page

Date		Description	P.R.	Dr.	Cr.
19X1 July	1	Cash	11	8000 –	
		Joe Jackson, Capital	31		8000 –
		Investment to begin business.			
	1	Prepaid Rent	14	300 –	
		Cash	11		300 –
		Paid Smith Realty for two months rent in advance.			
	2	Equipment	16	900 –	
		Cash	11		400 –
		Accounts Payable	21		500 –
		Purchased repair equipment from Greasy's Auto Supply.			
	6	Equipment	16	250 –	
		Supplies	13	50 –	
		Accounts Payable	21		300 –
		Purchased supplies and cash register on credit from Haskin Supply & Equipment Co.			
	9	Truck	18	2800 –	
		Cash	11		2800 –
		Purchased a used delivery truck for cash.			
	11	Cash	11	630 –	
		Repairs Revenue	41		630 –
		Completed performance of repairs on O'Hara's cars.			
	14	Salary Expense	61	400 –	
		Cash	11		400 –
		Paid Nick Turner for two weeks salary.			

JOURNAL

Page 2

Date		Description	P.R.	Dr.	Cr.
19X1 July	15	Accounts Payable	21	300 —	
		Cash	11		300 —
		Paid Haskins Supply & Equipment Co. full amount owed.			
	15	Accounts Receivable	12	550 —	
		Repairs Revenue	41		550 —
		Completed repairs for Vince Forte on credit.			
	24	Joe Jackson, Drawing	32	300 —	
		Cash	11		300 —
		Owner withdrew cash for personal use.			
	26	Utilities Expense	62	50 —	
		Cash	11		50 —
		Paid utilities with cash.			
	28	Salary Expense	61	400 —	
		Cash	11		400 —
		Paid Nick Turner for two weeks salary.			
	30	Advertising Expense	63	40 —	
		Cash	11		40 —
		Paid Daily Bugle for ads.			
	30	Cash	11	250 —	
		Accounts Receivable	12		250 —
		Received cash from Vince Forte on account.			
	30	Cash	11	825 —	
		Repairs Revenue	41		825 —
		Received cash for work performed for Willard McKinnie.			

Cash 11

Date	Ref.	Debit	Date	Ref.	Credit
July 1	1	8,000	July 1	1	300
11	1	630	2	1	400
30	2	250	9	1	2,800
30	2	825	14	1	400
		9,705	15	2	300
			24	2	300
Bal. 4,715			26	2	50
			28	2	400
			30	2	40
					4,990

Accounts Receivable 12

Date	Ref.	Debit	Date	Ref.	Credit
July 15	2	550	July 30	2	250
Bal. 300					

Supplies 13

Date	Ref.	Debit	Date	Ref.	Credit
July 6	1	50			

Prepaid Rent 14

Date	Ref.	Debit	Date	Ref.	Credit
July 2	1	300			

Equipment 16

Date	Ref.	Debit	Date	Ref.	Credit
July 2	1	900			
6	1	250			
		1,150			

Truck 18

Date	Ref.	Debit	Date	Ref.	Credit
July 9	1	2,800			

Accounts Payable 21

Date	Ref.	Debit	Date	Ref.	Credit
July 15	2	300	July 2	1	500
			6	1	300
					800
			Bal. 500		

Joe Jackson, Capital 31

Date	Ref.	Debit	Date	Ref.	Credit
			July 1	1	8,000

Joe Jackson, Drawing 32

Date	Ref.	Debit	Date	Ref.	Credit
July 24	2	300			

Repairs Revenue 41

Date	Ref.	Debit	Date	Ref.	Credit
			July 11	1	630
			15	2	550
			30	2	825
					2,005

Salary Expense 61

Date	Ref.	Debit	Date	Ref.	Credit
July 14	1	400			
28	2	400			
		800			

Utilities Expense 62

Date	Ref.	Debit	Date	Ref.	Credit
July 26	2	50			

Advertising Expense 62

Date	Ref.	Debit	Date	Ref.	Credit
July 30	2	40			

illustration 2-8 **Kar Klinik's ledger.**

sample problem Phyllis Davidson started a sign painting service during the current year. She decided to rent a small building and hired one helper. Journalize and post the following selected April transactions:

Apr.	3	Phyllis invested $1,000 in a business she called Quality Signs.
	4	Hired Molly Walters, an assistant, who agreed to work for $675 a month.
	4	Rented space to operate for $250 a month, payable in advance.
	5	Bought a used panel truck for $3,500, paying $500 down and signing a note for the balance.
	8	Finished a sign for Big Pop Grocery. Big Pop promised to pay Phyllis by the end of the month, $85.
	29	Received check from Big Pop as promised.
	30	Performed services and collected $1,134 for other painting assignments.
	30	Paid $64 for gas and oil.
	30	Paid salary to Molly, $675.
	30	Paid telephone bill, $42.

sample problem solution

Apr.	3	Cash	$1,000	
		Phyllis Davidson, Capital		$1,000
	4	No entry		
	4	Prepaid Rent	250	
		Cash		250
	5	Equipment	3,500	
		Cash		500
		Notes Payable		3,000
	8	Accounts Receivable	85	
		Sign Revenue		85
	29	Cash	85	
		Accounts Receivable		85
	30	Cash	1,134	
		Sign Revenue		1,134
	30	Gas and Oil Expense	64	
		Cash		64
	30	Salary Expense	675	
		Cash		675
	30	Telephone Expense	42	
		Cash		42

Cash	
1,000	250
85	500
1,134	64
	675
	42

Accounts Receivable	
85	85

Prepaid Rent	
250	

Equipment	
3,500	

Notes Payable	
	3,000

Phyllis Davidson, Capital	
	1,000

Sign Revenue	
	85
	1,134

Gas and Oil Expense	
64	

Salary Expense	
675	

Telephone Expense	
42	

review exercises

4. Journalize the following transactions:

May 15	Ellen Brooks invested $4,000 cash, $500 in office supplies, and equipment valued at $2,500 in a new business.
18	Paid $900 for three months' rental of office space.
21	Performed bookkeeping services totaling $95 for Ted Phillips. Ted promised to pay on May 25.
25	Received payment from Ted Phillips for service performed on May 21.

5. Harvey Winkle decided that he would speed up the posting process by posting all the entries involving *Cash* first. Harvey reasoned that then he could go back and pick up the other accounts. He felt that this approach would save him time because he would not have to look up the same account over and over again. Typically, Harvey posts to *Cash* from five or six journal pages before going back and posting less frequent items. Comment on Harvey's method.

6. Indicate the first digit in the ledger account number that would be used for each of the following accounts: (a) *Salaries Expense;* (b) *Rental Revenue;* (c) *Interest Payable;* (d) *Accounts Receivable;* (e) *Andrea Albright, Capital;* (f) *Utilities Expense;* (g) *Office Equipment.*

• task GIVEN THE LEDGER ACCOUNT BALANCES, CONSTRUCT A TRIAL BALANCE

The trial balance

The **trial balance** is a statement that shows whether the total debits are equal to the total credits for an accounting period. As you can see in Illustration 2-9, it lists all accounts in the order in which they appear on the ledger, with the balance for each account.

illustration 2-9
trial balance.

Kar Klinik
Trial Balance
July 31, 19X1

Account	Debit	Credit
Cash	4715 –	
Accounts Receivable	300 –	
Supplies	50 –	
Prepaid Rent	300 –	
Equipment	1150 –	
Truck	2800 –	
Accounts Payable		500 –
Joe Jackson, Capital		8000 –
Joe Jackson, Drawing	300 –	
Repairs Revenue		2005 –
Salary Expense	800 –	
Utilities Expense	50 –	
Advertising Expense	40 –	
	10505 –	10505 –

If the account has a debit balance in the ledger, it is shown as a debit on the trial balance. Likewise, a credit balance in the ledger is shown as a credit on the trial balance. Debit and credit amounts are then totaled to test for equality. If the total debits equal the total credits, indicate this equality by drawing a double line below the money columns. If they do not match, you must find the error that was made in the accounts or in transferring amounts to the trial balance.

Trial balance analysis

The agreement of debit and credit totals does not guarantee the accuracy of each step from journalizing to preparing a trial balance. It proves only that total debits equal total credits; however, if the totals are not equal, it definitely proves that you have a mistake.

Errors may have been made that do not affect the equality of debits and credits in recording transactions (posting from journal to ledger accounts, summarizing the ledger accounts, listing accounts and amounts in the trial balance, or in adding the debit and credit columns in the trial balance). For example, a credit to *Accounts Receivable* could have been posted to *Accounts Payable* rather than to *Accounts Receivable.* Even though *Accounts Payable* is increased with a credit and *Accounts Receivable* is shown at an amount larger than it should be, the totals of the trial balance would be unaffected.

If the trial balance does not agree, repeating the steps of the process in reverse is generally recommended. In other words, go through the following steps until you find the error:

1. Add both columns in the trial balance.
2. Trace each figure in the trial balance to the ledger accounts balances.
3. Recalculate the balance in each account.

4. Retrace the postings from the journal to the ledger.
5. Examine each journal entry to make certain that the proper accounts were debited and credited.

During the search for the error, you should be alert for any amount that is the same amount as the difference from equality in the trial balance. For example, if the debit total is $23,695.13 and the credit total is $22,695.13, you may have omitted $1,000 in recording account totals on the trial balance, or $1,000 may be listed twice. Also, be alert for half the difference of equality in the trial balance. In the previous example, assume that *Accounts Payable* of $500 was incorrectly listed on the debit side. Since the credit side is $500 less than it should be and the debit side is $500 more than it should be, the difference is $1,000 when the mistake is only $500.

Sometimes an error may be located rather quickly by testing the amount to see if a slide or a transposition has been made. A **slide** takes place when a number is moved over one place, and a **transposition** is an exchange of two or more digits. For example, writing $900 rather than $9,000 and $2,000 for $200 would be slides. Writing $659.23 for $695.23 or $79.47 for $97.47 would be a transposition. When a slide or transposition is made, the difference is exactly divisible by 9. For example, the difference between $9,000 and $900 is $8,100, a number that may be divided by 9 without producing a remainder. Likewise, the difference between $695.23 and $659.23 ($36) is exactly divisible by 9, so a handy tool to locate a mistake is to see whether the difference between trial balance totals is divisible by 9. If it is, check for a slide or a transposition error.

Possible errors in the various steps from journalizing to preparing the trial balance are too numerous to detail. An important step to follow in error situations is to reason through each action that has been completed and try to isolate the error or errors. This process of analysis will become easier as you gain experience in accounting.

sample problem Given the following account balances, prepare a trial balance for Hargrove Service Center for November 30, 19X1.

Cash	$15,000
Accounts Receivable	8,000
Prepaid Rent	800
Equipment	18,000
Accounts Payable	4,000
Notes Payable	5,000
Ted Hargrove, Capital	14,400
Ted Hargrove, Drawing	2,500
Supplies Expense	1,500
Utilities Expense	150
Salaries Expense	2,400

Service Revenue	25,600
Miscellaneous Expense	650

Assume that all of the accounts have normal balances.

sample problem solution

Hargrove Service Center
Trial Balance
November 30, 19X1

Cash	$15,000	
Accounts Receivable	8,000	
Prepaid Rent	800	
Equipment	18,000	
Accounts Payable		$ 4,000
Notes Payable		5,000
Ted Hargrove, Capital		14,400
Ted Hargrove, Drawing	2,500	
Supplies Expense	1,500	
Utilities Expense	150	
Salaries Expense	2,400	
Service Revenue		25,600
Miscellaneous Expense	650	
	$49,000	$49,000

review exercises

7. On December 31, 19X1, the ledger for Drab's Cleaners has the following balances:

Cash	$ 4,351
Accounts Receivable	8,640
Notes Receivable	3,000
Supplies	590
Equipment	3,922
Building	88,000
Accounts Payable	9,460
Mortgage Payable	59,600
Dan Drab, Capital	50,804
Dan Drab, Drawing	12,400
Cleaning Revenue	26,654
Salaries Expense	14,990
Supplies Expense	3,587
Advertising Expense	1,012
Utilities Expense	4,670
Telephone Expense	1,356

Prepare a trial balance for Drab's Cleaners.

8. What is wrong with the following simple trial balance?

King's Service
Trial Balance
August 31, 19X1

	Dr.	Cr.
Cash	$180	
Accounts Receivable	260	
Accounts Payable	24	
Phil King, Capital		$296
Phil King, Drawing	50	
Service Revenue		250
Telephone Expense		80
	$514	$626

9. Identify the type of error or errors involved in each situation given below:

(a) *Equipment* was listed on the trial balance as a debit of $14,326.14 instead of the correct amount, $13,426.14.

(b) *Robert Cunningham, Drawing* was listed as a debit of $5,000, rather than $500.

chapter highlights

You can see that the use of a journal and a ledger makes gathering information about each account a much easier task than that afforded by the method presented in Chapter 1. At the same time, you should have found that the method of analyzing each transaction for increases and decreases is the same as the one you used before, except that now you have the debit and credit tools instead of the simple plus and minus concept.

Having studied Chapter 2, you should now be able to:

- Identify account classifications by account number.
- Journalize transactions.
- Post to the ledger.
- Prepare a trial balance.
- Locate and correct errors quickly.

At this point, let us encourage you to use accounting "common sense." In handling all transactions based on the basic accounting equation, you should be able to check yourself to see whether a transaction makes sense. For example, ending with a credit balance in *Rent Expense* should be a strong clue that something is wrong. Try to work the exercises and problems using this "accounting sense" rather than memorizing procedures and entries.

check figures for review exercises

1. (a) asset
   (b) asset
   (c) owner's equity
   (d) asset
   (e) liability
   (f) asset
   (g) asset
   (h) liability

2.

A		=	L		+	OE		−	E		+	R	
+	−		−	+		−	+		+	−		−	+

3. Purchase of equipment in on the wrong side, and net income is not a cash item, so it should not be in the *Cash* account.

4.

Date	Account	Debit	Credit
May 15	Cash	$4,000	
	Office Supplies	500	
	Equipment	2,500	
	Ellen Brooks, Capital		$7,000
18	Prepaid Rent	900	
	Cash		900
21	Accounts Receivable	95	
	Bookkeeping Revenue		95
25	Cash	95	
	Accounts Receivable		95

5. Harvey's posting procedure of skipping accounts and returning later to pick them up promotes error. Making sure that each entry is posted would probably take more time than that required to use proper procedure.
6. (a) 6, (b) 4, (c) 2, (d) 1, (e) 3, (f) 6, (g) 1
7. Column totals, $146,518
8. *Accounts Payable* should be a credit, and *Telephone Expense* should be a debit.
9. (a) transposition, (b) slide

key terms

The following important terms are discussed in Chapter 2 and are defined in the Glossary at the end of the book:

book of original entry | **debit** | **posting**
chart of accounts | **journal** | **slide**
compound entry | **ledger** | **transposition**
credit | **normal balance** | **trial balance**

questions

1. What is a ledger?
2. What is included under the heading Owner's Equity?

3. How does a note payable differ from a mortgage payable?

4. Define net assets.

5. How would you explain the term *debit* to a friend who has no understanding of accounting?

6. Why is the journal referred to as the *book of original entry?*

7. What kind of journal entry has three debits and one credit?

8. What is the purpose of posting?

9. Are the trial balance and the balance sheet the same? If not, how do they differ?

10. Does equality of debits and credits on the trial balance prove correct journalizing and posting?

11. Writing $975.83 for $957.83 is what type of error?

12. When $10 is incorrectly recorded as $100, what type of error is involved?

13. What is a quick test to determine whether you have errors like those mentioned in Questions 11 and 12?

exercises

1. By analyzing the information in the *Cash* account below, determine the other half of each entry for Dr. Joel Rose, D.D.S.

Cash

(a) Received from customer for past services	1,463	(e) Paid utilities	208
(b) Owner invested	5,000	(f) Purchased truck	6,000
(c) Received for current services	579	(g) Owner's withdrawal	500
(d) Sold typewriter	300	(h) Paid salaries	1,200
		(i) Paid rent	490

2. Using + and −, fill in the accounting equation shown below:

Assets	=	Liabilities	+	Owner's Equity	+	Revenues	−	Expenses

3. Determine the major classification of each of the following items by indicating whether it is an asset; a liability; owner's equity; an expense; or revenue. Then indicate whether the normal balance would be a debit or credit for that account.

(a) *Notes Payable*

(b) *Service Revenue*

(c) *Cash*

(d) *Howard Lamberson, Capital*

(e) *Accounts Receivable*

(f) *Rent Revenue*

(g) *Mortgage Payable*

(h) *Building*

(i) *Salary Expense*

(j) *Howard Lamberson, Drawing*

(k) *Equipment*

(l) *Prepaid Insurance*

4. Journalize the following transactions using these accounts: *Accounts Receivable; Prepaid Rent; Equipment; Accounts Payable; Notes Payable; Cash; Joe Wilson, Capital; Joe Wilson, Drawing; Service Revenue; Utilities Expense;* and *Salary Expense.*

(a) Paid rent for August, $235.

(b) Sold services on account, $550.

(c) Paid employees for month, $2,450.

(d) The owner, Joe Wilson, withdrew $135 for personal use.

(e) Bought a new adding machine, giving $95 cash and a note for $200.

(f) Paid utility bill for August, $63.

(g) Collected for services performed in (b).

(h) Invested equipment worth $500 and cash of $1,000 in the firm.

5. Arrange the following procedures in the proper order for posting:

(a) Journal page number is recorded in the PR column.

(b) Debit account is found in the ledger.

(c) Ledger account number is recorded in the PR column of the journal.

(d) Debit amount is transferred from the journal to the ledger.

(e) Credit account is located in the ledger.

(f) Date is recorded on the debit side of the ledger.

(g) Credit amount is transferred from the journal to the ledger.

(h) Date is recorded on the credit side of the ledger.

Note: SOME OF THE STEPS ABOVE MAY BE USED MORE THAN ONCE.

6. Given the following accounts, prepare a simple trial balance for Stark Company for December 21, 19X1.

Cash	$2,869
Accounts Receivable	87

Office Supplies	$ 686
Prepaid Rent	400
Office Equipment	400
Delivery Truck	4,800
Accounts Payable	1,512
Willie Stark, Capital	7,511
Willie Stark, Drawing	620
Service Revenues	2,563
Salary Expense	1,500
Utilities Expense	87
Advertising Expense	137

problems

1. COMPETENCY TESTED The ability to classify accounts and state the normal balance.

Analyze the following accounts.

(a) Equipment
(b) Salary Expense
(c) Office Supplies
(d) Dan Bunyon, Drawing
(e) Notes Payable
(f) Miscellaneous Expense
(g) Service Revenue
(h) Hair Dressing Fees
(i) Cash
(j) Advertising Expense
(k) Prepaid Insurance
(l) Accounts Payable
(m) Dan Bunyon, Capital
(n) Supplies Expense
(o) Accounts Receivable

Instructions (a) Using the code A = Asset, L = Liability, OE = Owner's Equity, R = Revenue, and E = Expenses, classify the accounts above. (b) Indicate the normal balance of each account.

2. COMPETENCY TESTED The ability to understand the basic accounting equation.

	A	L	OE	R	E
(a) Sold equipment for cash					
(b) Invested cash in the firm					
(c) Performed services on account					
(d) Paid monthly telephone bill					
(e) Received cash from customer on cash sale					
(f) Owner withdrew cash from the business					
(g) Paid semi-monthly salaries					
(h) Paid on account					
(i) Bought a typewriter by issuing cash and a note payable					
(j) Paid cash on note payable					

Instructions Indicate the effect of each of the transactions above on the expanded basic accounting equation by placing a plus or a minus under the affected classification. In some cases, it is possible to have both a plus and a minus under the same classification.

3. COMPETENCY TESTED Expertise in recording transactions in general journal form.

Little Music Service was opened as a proprietorship by Joseph Little on April 1, 19X1. Little gives guitar and accordion lessons. The following transactions took place during the first month of operations:

April	1	Little invested $1,000 in the business, $400 in cash and $600 in musical instruments.
	1	Rented studio space for $275 payable in advance.
	3	Paid for April 2 advertising on radio, $35.
	4	Purchased office supplies, $60.
	4	Bought a typewriter by giving $50 down and a note of $250 for the balance.
	5	Received $80 for services rendered.
	6	Purchased a desk on credit from Cecil Office Equipment, $297.
	8	Collected $130 for services rendered.
	9	One client, Harold Twitty, was provided lessons on account, $25.
	11	Little withdrew $225 for personal use.
	15	Paid $100 toward the desk purchased from Cecil Office Equipment on April 6.
	16	Hired an assistant instructor for $700 per month.
	17	Collected $90 for services rendered.

22 Collected the $25 from Harold Twitty owed since April 9.
28 Collected for services rendered, $265.
29 Paid utilities for month, $62.
30 Paid telephone bill, $38.
30 Paid salary for one-half month, $350.

Instructions Record the entries above using the following accounts: *Cash; Accounts Receivable; Office Supplies; Prepaid Rent; Office Equipment; Accounts Payable; Notes Payable; Joseph Little, Capital; Joseph Little, Drawing; Lesson Revenue; Advertising Expense; Salary Expense; Utilities Expense; Telephone Expense.*

4. COMPETENCY TESTED Skill in journalizing and posting transactions and preparing a trial balance.

Polly McCracken owned and operated Polly's Travel Agency, a long-established proprietorship. Account balances on January 1, 19X1 were: *Polly McCracken, Capital,* $1,000, and *Cash,* $1,000. Open the following T accounts: *Cash; Prepaid Rent; Supplies; Office Equipment; Accounts Payable; Notes Payable; Polly McCracken, Capital; Commission Revenue; Salaries Expense; Utilities Expense; Advertising Expense; Repairs Expense; Telephone Expense;* and *Miscellaneous Expense.* During January, 19X1, the following transactions occurred:

Jan. 2 Paid January rent, $425.
4 Collected a deposit of $100 that the agency must send to Halibut Cruise Lines.
5 Received commission checks totaling $147.
6 Cash sales for airline tickets totaled $1,649. The travel agency keeps $153 and must send the balance to the Air Traffic Conference. (*Note*: Make a compound entry.)
9 Purchased supplies on account from Heady Office Supply, $43.
10 Paid $173 to KNOB for radio ads broadcast from January 3 through January 6.
11 Bought a typewriter from Wilson Equipment Company, paying $100 down and signing a note for $800.
12 Received commission checks totaling $92.
13 Cash sales for airline tickets amounted to $1,346. Commissions earned, $117.
14 Sent check for amount due to the Air Traffic Conference, $2,725.
15 Received $5,200 final payment on African safari. The entire amount is deposited in the agency's account with plans to send a check for this amount to African Safari Company on January 16.
15 Paid employees' salaries, $1,200.
16 Sent check for $5,200 to African Safari Company.
18 Paid $43 to Heady Office Supply for purchase of January 9.
19 Paid Wilson Equipment $69 for repair to equipment.

20 Received commission checks, $293.

20 Cash sales of airline tickets for week, $2,196. Commissions earned, $105.

22 Paid client $15 to cover expenses paid as a result of error in itinerary (charge to *Miscellaneous Expense*).

24 Paid utility bill, $88.

26 Paid telephone bill, $460.

27 Received commission check from African Safari Company, $400.

27 Cash sales of airline tickets for week, $1,865. Commissions earned, $89.

29 Received deposit of $200 from client for trip to Hawaii. Agency deposited $200 and plans to send the full amount to Hawaiian Tours.

30 Paid $200 to Hawaiian Tours on account.

31 Paid $400 on note of January 11.

Instructions

(a) Journalize the January transactions.

(b) Post the transactions to the ledger.

(c) Prepare a trial balance.

5. COMPETENCY TESTED Expertise in journalizing and posting transactions and preparing a trial balance.

Paul's Portraits is a successful proprietorship owned by Paul Ethridge. The firm's books are kept on an annual basis. At the beginning of February, 19X1, Paul's accounts show the following balances: *Cash,* $7,893.12; *Accounts Receivable,* $425; *Supplies,* $3,862.52; *Equipment,* $3,580; *Building,* $85,000; *Accounts Payable,* $1,484.15; *Mortgage Payable,* $65,000; *Paul Ethridge, Capital,* $25,379.17; *Paul Ethridge, Drawing,* $6,000; *Portrait Revenue,* $34,916; *Advertising Expense,* $238; *Salaries Expense,* $18,920; *Telephone Expense,* $413.69; *Utilities Expense,* $314.77; *Miscellaneous Expense,* $132.22.

The firm uses a standard two-digit ledger numbering system.

Assets

11 Cash
12 Accounts Receivable
13 Supplies
14 Equipment
15 Building

Liabilities

21 Accounts Payable
22 Mortgage Payable

Owner's Equity

31 Paul Ethridge, Capital
32 Paul Ethridge, Drawing

Revenue

41 Portrait Revenue

Expenses

61 Advertising Expense
62 Salaries Expense
63 Telephone Expense
64 Utilities Expense
65 Miscellaneous Expense

February transactions were as follows:

Feb. 2 Finished three portraits for Adabelle Harper at $150 each; client will pay later.
4 Paid $380 on mortgage (ignore interest).
7 Paid $261.14 on account for debts from last month.
9 Received $450 from Adabelle Harper on account.
11 Purchased supplies on account from Oster Supplies, $149.50.
14 Collected $690 for work finished on the 14th.
15 Paid salaries, $1,800.
16 Paid utility bill, $76.39.
17 Withdrew $800 for personal use.
18 Received $2,130 for services rendered.
20 Paid $75 for radio advertising run during the previous week.
22 Paid $10 for miscellaneous items.
24 Paid $493.88 on account.
25 Received $4,940 for services rendered.
28 Paid telephone bill, $67.14.
28 Paid salaries for second half of month, $1,760.
28 Bought a display case, $789.

Instructions

(a) Journalize the February transactions.

(b) Post to the ledger.

(c) Prepare a trial balance.

6. COMPETENCY TESTED Skill in journalizing and posting transactions and preparing a trial balance.

Crane's Janitorial Service, a proprietorship, provides cleaning services for the local public schools. On September 1, the ledger showed the following balances (ledger account numbers are shown in parentheses): *Cash* (11) $420; *Accounts Receivable* (12) $231; *Cleaning Supplies* (13) $55; *Prepaid Rent* (14) $0; *Cleaning Equipment* (15) $2,600; *Service Truck* (16) $0; *Notes Payable* (21) $500; *Accounts Payable* (22) $240; *John Crane, Capital* (31) $5,192; *John Crane, Drawing* (32) $4,000; *Cleaning Services Revenue* (41) $8,615; *Advertising Expense* (61) $90; *Salary Expense* (62) $6,000; *Utilities Expense* (63) $246; *Telephone Expense* (64) $536; *Gas and Oil Expense* (65) $369. During September, 19X1, the following transactions took place:

Sept. 2 John Crane invested $1,000 cash and a new buffer valued at $285.
4 Billed Lincoln Elementary for past services, $312.88.

5 Purchased cleaning supplies on account, $114.62.
6 Received payment on account from Jefferson High School, $231.
7 Bought a used van as a service truck for the business, $3,040, paying $500 down and signing a note for the difference.
8 Billed Washington Elementary for services performed, $319.23.
9 John Crane withdrew $450 for personal use.
10 Paid gas and oil bill, $35.
12 Received payment from Lincoln Elementary, $312.88.
14 Paid helper, Jack Smith, $375.
15 Invested $2,000 in the business.
16 Paid telephone bill, $67.23.
17 Paid rent for month, $400.
19 Billed Roosevelt Junior High for past services, $234.67.
21 Received amount due from Washington Elementary.
22 Paid for cleaning supplies purchased on Sept. 5.
24 Bought a new scrubbing machine, $723.95, paying $100 down and agreeing to pay the balance to Matthew's Equipment Company next month.
25 Paid for radio ad, $15.
26 Billed Lincoln Elementary for services performed, $298.16.
27 Paid utility bill, $29.33.
29 Purchased cleaning supplies on account, $193.16.
30 Paid gas and oil bill, $49.43.
30 Paid helper, Jack Smith, $375.

Instructions

(a) Journalize the September transactions.
(b) Post to the ledger.
(c) Prepare a trial balance.

7. COMPETENCY TESTED The ability to locate errors and correct a trial balance.

Cash

Bal. 1,640	420
315	200
1,400	50
125	75
	25
	25
	300

Accounts Receivable

275	125

Supplies

25	

Accounts Payable

150	250 Bal.

Notes Payable

425	2,730 Bal.

Prepaid Rent	
420	

Equipment	
Bal. 4,815	

George Harris, Capital	
	3,475 Bal.
	315

George Harris, Drawing	
50	
75	

Clinic Revenue	
	275
	1,400

Salary Expense	
300	

Utilities Expense	
200	

Advertising Expense	
25	

From the ledger, Harris prepared a trial balance.

George Harris
Trial Balance
For the month ended August 31

Cash	$1,810	
Accounts Receivable		$150
Supplies	25	
Prepaid Rent	420	
Equipment	4,851	
Accounts Payable		250
Notes Payable		2,205
George Harris, Capital		3,790
George Harris, Drawing		125
Clinic Revenue		1,675
Salary Expense	300	
Utilities Expense	200	
Advertising Expense	25	
	$7,631	$8,195

Instructions George has called you in, asking for your help in finding the mistake. Prepare a corrected trial balance for George.

comprehensive problem

MAGIC CARPET TRAVEL (PART 1)

Magic Carpet Travel opens in November of the current year to sell airline tickets on domestic carriers, rail tickets, and to act as an agent for hotels, car rental firms, and cruise lines.

Instructions Daily transactions for the month of November are listed below. Record each transaction in journal form using the accounts listed. When journalizing is completed, post to the ledgers. Finally, to test the accuracy of your work, prepare a trial balance.

Assets

11 Cash
12 Accounts Receivable
13 Office Supplies
14 Prepaid Rent
15 Prepaid Insurance
16 Equipment

Liabilities

21 Accounts Payable
22 Mortgage Payable

Owner's Equity

31 Sarah Harper, Capital
32 Sarah Harper, Drawing

Revenue

41 Commissions Earned

Expenses

61 Advertising Expense
62 Salaries Expense
63 Utilities Expense
64 Telephone Expense

Nov.	1	Sarah Harper invested $10,000 cash and $2,000 in equipment in the new proprietorship.
	1	Paid Booker Realty $800 to rent a building for two months.
	1	Sold airline tickets for $709.91, earning a commission of $55.09. (*Hint:* Show the amount due the airlines as *Accounts Payable.* In this case, it would be $654.82.)
	1	Paid Wadson Printer $28 for advertising brochures.
	1	Received $850 from a client as a deposit on an around-the-world cruise. No commission is recorded at this time since the entire deposit must be sent to the cruise line.
	2	Issued check for $850 to Seabrook Cruise Lines in payment of client's deposit of Nov. 1.
	2	Sold airline tickets for $1,679 cash; commissions earned, $143.22.
	3	Sold airline tickets totaling $945 cash; commissions earned, $73.06.
	3	Sold railroad tickets totaling $250 to Markell on account; commissions earned, $25.
	3	Sold airline tickets totaling $840 to Burgess on account; commissions earned, $84.
	4	Sold airline tickets totaling $1,021.54 for cash; commissions earned, $94.80.
	7	Sold airline tickets totaling $2,549 for cash; commissions earned, $199.87.
	8	Received a commission check from Delford Inn for $8.46.
	8	Sold a cruise, collecting the entire amount due of $935; commissions earned, $91.10.
	9	Sold a tour to a client, receiving a deposit of $200. The entire amount must be sent to Luckett Tours Company.
	9	Sold $1,224.55 in airline tickets for cash; commissions earned, $109.18.
	10	Issued check to Happy Cruise Line for the cruise sold on Nov. 8.

10 Received $840 from Burgess, Inc. for sale of Nov. 3.

10 Paid $7,094.41 to Air Traffic Conference for all debts due to the airlines for tickets sold between Nov. 1 and 7.

10 Issued check to the railroad in payment of the sale made on Nov. 3.

11 Sold airline tickets for $2,375. Of these, tickets amounting to $375 were sold to the Butone Company on account, while the rest were for cash. Commissions earned on the total sales were $175.35.

14 Received a commission check from Donover Hotel, $15.

14 Received $100 as a deposit from a client for Dive Inn. No commission is recorded at this time.

15 Shirley Silversmith was hired at the beginning of November. She was issued a salary check for $350 for the first half of the month.

15 Issued check for $100 deposit to Dive Inn.

16 Sold airline tickets totaling $692 in cash sales; commissions earned, $46.17.

17 Received payment from Butone Company for $375 in payment of tickets they bought on November 11.

17 Paid $3,315.02 to the Air Traffic Conference for all airline tickets sold between Nov. 8 and 14.

18 Paid Feller Insurance Agency for fire insurance, $180.

18 Bought office supplies on account from Hall Office Supply, $75.

21 Sold airline tickets totaling $724; commissions earned, $54.76.

21 Paid utility bill of $63.15.

21 Sold railroad tickets totaling $140, receiving cash; commissions earned, $14.00.

22 Sold airline tickets to Wilson Supply Company on account, $318; commissions earned, $20.61.

23 Issued check in payment of debt to Hall Office Supply created on Nov. 18.

24 Received $2,500 in full payment for a tour using Zing Away Tour Company; commissions earned, $250.

24 Issued check for the amount due Zing Away Tour Company.

25 Sold airline tickets totaling $1,048 for cash; commissions earned, $77.22.

25 Paid *Daily News* $75 for ad.

25 Paid $1,315.07 to the Air Traffic Conference for all airline ticket sales from Nov. 15 through Nov. 21.

28 Received commission check from Holiday House, $8.15.

28 Received $318 from Wilson Supply Company for sale of Nov. 22.

29 Sold airline tickets for cash totaling $1,131; commissions earned, $128.39.

29 Received a deposit of $100 from a client for Hawaiian Tours.

30 Issued check for $100 to Hawaiian Tours.

30 Sold airline tickets totaling $1,731; commissions earned, $76.95.

30 Received a commission check from Friendly Car Rentals, $64.08.
30 Paid the employee for the second half of November, $350.
30 Paid telephone bill, $260.
30 Sarah Harper withdrew $1,000 for personal use.

This comprehensive problem will be continued at the end of Chapter 3 and concluded at the end of Chapter 4.

chapter 3
COMPLETING THE ACCOUNTING CYCLE (PART I)

overall competency THE ABILITY TO PREPARE ADJUSTING ENTRIES AND FINANCIAL STATEMENTS FOR A SERVICE-TYPE BUSINESS

career objectives The firm's manager or owner needs financial statements that provide current information. To provide this information, the accounting clerk must identify the account balances that are not current and update them. A work sheet is used to organize this information in a logical order for easy analysis. From this work sheet, the accounting clerk can journalize the **adjusting entries** and prepare the financial statements.

When you complete this chapter, you should be able to perform these tasks correctly:

- PLAN THE ADJUSTING ENTRIES BY USING THE WORK SHEET AS A PLANNING TOOL.
- COMPLETE THE WORK SHEET FOR A SERVICE-TYPE BUSINESS.
- PREPARE THE FINANCIAL STATEMENTS FROM A COMPLETED WORK SHEET.

After all the everyday business transactions of a firm have been recorded in the journal and posted to the ledger, some account balances will need adjustments to report items not previously recorded. Examples of these adjustments are salaries owed but not paid, or supplies that have been used but are still shown as an asset on the books.

If the owner or manager is to obtain useful information, the financial statements must present a fair picture of the business. The income statement must include all revenue earned and all expenses paid. Reporting expenses on the same statement with related revenues is known as the **matching concept.** Likewise, the balance sheet must include only those assets that are still usable on the statement date. Thus, equipment that has been sold or supplies that have been used should not be included. The balance sheet should include all liabilities that represent debts to be paid after the statement date. If adjusting entries are made after the everyday entries have been posted, the information in the financial statements will be current.

This chapter contains some very important concepts that you must make a special effort to understand. The accounting tools presented in this chapter will help you understand other chapters in this textbook. The key to success in understanding how to make adjusting entries and how to construct financial statements from a work sheet is to analyze carefully each step you are planning to take to see whether it will give you the desired result.

• task PLAN THE ADJUSTING ENTRIES NEEDED AT THE END OF THE ACCOUNTING PERIOD TO BRING THE LEDGER ACCOUNT BALANCES UP TO DATE

Adjusting entries

Preparing **adjusting entries** takes thoughtful planning. Later in this chapter, we will show you how the work sheet can help you do this planning. However, before you can fully understand how to plan on the work sheet, you must see the effects that adjusting entries have on the ledger. It is important to understand that *adjusting entries are not correcting entries.* Correcting entries are made to correct errors; adjusting entries are made to show current information in the accounts. A number of situations require adjusting entries; these four involve deferrals and accruals:

1. When payments are made this period for benefits covering future accounting periods.
2. When cash is received this period for services to be performed in future accounting periods.

3. When accrued expenses have not been recorded.
4. When accrued revenues have not been recorded.

The first two items are **deferrals,** and the last two are **accruals.** In the next section, we will discuss each of these in detail.

Deferral. In the simplest terms, a **deferral** is a delay in recognizing either an expense or a revenue. To examine a situation in which payments are made in the current period for benefits covering future accounting periods, assume that $900 of rent is paid on April 1 for three months. When the cash is paid, *Prepaid Rent* is debited. On April 30, one-third of the asset is used up. The following adjusting entry is needed to show the current ledger account balances:

Date		Description	P.R.	Dr.	Cr.
19X1 Apr.	30	Rent Expense		300 –	
		Prepaid Rent			300 –
		To record rent that expired.			

After this entry is posted, *Rent Expense* is increased by $300, and *Prepaid Rent* will show a balance of $600, the amount still prepaid for May and June.

Prepaid Rent		Rent Expense	
Apr. 1 900	Apr. 30 300	Apr. 30 300	

On February 1, Franklin's Video Games purchased supplies costing $75. At that time, the asset *Supplies* was debited. Assume that on February 28, a count of supplies on hand showed that $45 in supplies had been used. To transfer the used portion from an asset account to an expense account, the following adjusting entry is needed:

JOURNAL Page 1

Date		Description	P.R.	Dr.	Cr.
19X1 Feb.	28	Supplies Expense		45 –	
		Supplies			45 –
		To record supplies used.			

As you saw in the rent illustration, the part of the asset that has been used up becomes an expense. *Supplies* has an ending balance of $30, and *Supplies Expense* now shows that $45 of supplies were used.

Supplies	
Feb. 1 75	Feb. 28 45

Supplies Expense	
Feb. 28 45	

When a number of deferrals resulting from prepayments are combined into one item on the balance sheet, they are referred to as *prepaid expenses.*

Deferrals also result from receiving cash for services to be performed partly during this period and partly in future periods. To illustrate, assume that Colonial Mall owns a building with empty store space. Jess Phillips rents the space for $4,800 for a period covering one year from August 1, 19X1. Since Colonial Mall *owes* one year's use of the store space, a liability is credited on its books.

JOURNAL Page 1

Date		Description	P.R.	Dr.	Cr.
19X1 Aug.	1	Cash		4800 —	
		Unearned Rent Revenue			4800 —
		Received twelve months			
		rent in advance from			
		Jess Phillips.			

Unearned Rent Revenue is a term that is widely used to represent this liability even though it does not end with the word *payable.* On August 31, one month's rent is earned. To bring the accounts up to date, the following adjusting entry is made:

JOURNAL Page 1

Date		Description	P.R.	Dr.	Cr.
19X1 Aug.	31	Unearned Rent Revenue		400 —	
		Rent Revenue			400 —
		Rent earned for one			
		month.			

In T-account form, the accounts involved look like this:

Unearned Rent Revenue	
Aug. 31 400	Aug. 1 4,800

Rent Revenue	
	Aug. 31 400

Each month that passes, Colonial Mall earns $400 ($4,800 ÷ 12). By allowing Jess to use the space, Colonial Mall no longer owes that portion of the service. The adjusting entry forces the two accounts to show the revenue (*Rent Revenue* increases from zero to $400) and the reduction of the liability (*Unearned Rent Revenue* decreases by $400).

Accrual. At the end of the accounting period, some expenses and revenues have usually built up without being recorded. The continual building up of an expense or a revenue until it is paid is known as an **accrual.** You might think of an accrual as somewhat like a conveyor belt that adds coal to a pile. The pile gets larger and larger until a front-end loader scoops it up and carries it away. In the same way, accruals become larger and larger until payment is made or received. Let's use this example: Nick Turner is paid $400 on July 28 in the Kar Klinik illustration. If Nick is paid on Friday, July 28, for the two-week period ending on that date, and he works again on Monday, July 31, he will not receive payment during July for working that one day. Since Nick earns $40 a day, Kar Klinik must record this liability and its related expense in July, even though it will not be paid until August 11. Examine Illustration 3-1 to understand the timing of the payment.

illustration 3-1
accrued salary.

	Monday July 24	Tuesday July 25	Wednesday July 26	Thursday July 27	Friday July 28
Salary per Day . . .	$40	$40	$40	$40	$40
					payday

	Monday July 31
Salary per Day . . .	$40

The following adjusting entry records this debt:

JOURNAL Page 1

Date		Description	P.R.	Dr.	Cr.
19X1 July	31	Salary Expense		40 –	
		Salary Payable			40 –
		To record accrued salary expense.			

When Nick is paid in August for ten days' work, the accrued salary will be paid as part of the regular salary in August.

Revenues accrue in a similar manner. If a service is provided without any record of earned revenue when the accounting period ends, an adjusting entry is needed. To illustrate, assume that on Thursday, July 27, Joe Jackson accepts a car needing major repair. By closing time on July 31, $280 has been earned. Joe expects the job to be completed on August 2. To show revenue earned on this car repair, the following adjusting entry is made:

JOURNAL Page 1

Date		Description	P.R.	Dr.	Cr.
19X1 July	31	Accounts Receivable		280 –	
		Repairs Revenue			280 –
		Accrued revenue from car			
		repair.			

The same approach is used for revenue earned but not recorded for items like interest and rent. To describe the transaction more clearly, we make the debit to *Interest Receivable* or *Rent Receivable* and show the type of revenue in the account title of the credit, such as *Interest Revenue*. Note that only revenue items that are earned but not reported at the end of the fiscal period are handled this way.

Mixed accounts

When you compare deferrals with accruals, you will notice a unique characteristic of deferrals in that they are **mixed** before the adjusting entry separates the accounts. These accounts are considered mixed because they are either part asset and part expense or part liability and part revenue. For example, a payment for rent is totally an asset when the rent is first paid. As time passes, a portion becomes an expense even though the entire amount remains in the asset account. An adjusting entry is needed to remove the expense portion from *Prepaid Rent* and to transfer it to an expense account, *Rent Expense*.

Depreciation

In addition to deferrals and accruals, other accounts need adjusting. One group in particular includes long-lived operational assets like buildings and equipment used in the business. As time passes, these assets become less efficient unless expensive repairs and alterations are made. This loss of efficiency may be due simply to wearing out, or it may be due to the appearance on the market of better models or those less expensive to operate. A technique known as **depreciation** is used to record this loss of efficiency. Even though we will discuss depreciation in more detail in later chapters, you will need some understanding of it now.

To illustrate the concept, assume that on July 6, when Kar Klinik bought the cash register for $250, it was expected to have a useful life of 50 months. Using one of the simplest approaches to calculating depreciation, the accounting clerk divides the cost by 50 months and finds that the cash register is depreciating at the rate of $5 each month. Therefore, the following adjusting entry is recorded on July 31:

JOURNAL — Page 1

Date		Description	P.R.	Dr.	Cr.
19X1 July	31	Depreciation Expense, Store Equipment		5 –	
		Accumulated Depr., Store Equipment			5 –
		To record depreciation for one month.			

In the entry above, we introduced a new account called *Accumulated Depreciation, Store Equipment.* This account is classified as a *contra* (or negative) *asset* and is subtracted from the *Store Equipment* account on the balance sheet. The difference between the cost of an asset and the total accumulated depreciation is its **book value.** It is very important that you understand that *book value does not mean market value.* Depreciation is the accounting method of transferring the asset balance to the expense account over the life of the asset. It does not show the asset's current value.

You might wonder why the *Store Equipment* account was not credited. Think back to what is happening when an asset is credited. The asset is either being used up physically, as when supplies are used, or the asset is leaving the entity, as when cash is paid. Since neither situation fits the use of the cash register in our illustration, a helper account is created to show that a loss of efficiency is taking place. This helper account is called *Accumulated Depreciation* followed by the type of item being described, such as *Building, Equipment,* or *Machinery.*

In the adjusting entry for depreciation, as in all adjusting entries, note that there is one balance sheet account and one income statement account. If a compound entry is used, the rule requires at least one account from each statement. If you can remember this simple rule, it may keep you from making an error when planning your adjusting entries.

sample problem Hillary's Suntan Shoppe shows the following unadjusted ledger balances on its books on March 31, 19X1:

Supplies	$175.00
Prepaid Insurance	214.00
Prepaid Rent	350.00

On this date, the firm actually had $87 of supplies on hand, $144 in prepaid insurance, and $180 of prepaid rent. In addition, Hillary owes her employees $132 in wages. Make the necessary adjusting entries:

sample problem solution

Supplies Expense	$ 88	
Supplies		$ 88
Insurance Expense	70	
Prepaid Insurance		70
Rent Expense	170	
Prepaid Rent		170
Wages Expense	132	
Wages Payable		132

review exercises

1. The *Supplies* account on January 1, 19X1, has a balance of $215. During the month, supplies amounting to $106 were purchased. At the end of January, a count showed $55 in supplies on hand. Make the required adjusting entry.
2. On May 1, *Prepaid Insurance* shows a $240 debit balance representing two years' insurance coverage beginning on May 1. Make the adjusting entry on May 31 to show that one month's insurance has expired.
3. On April 1, 19X1, $1,200 was received representing rent for April through June. Make the necessary adjusting entry on April 30.
4. Employees of Jarvis Supply Company work a five-day week for a total of $600 per day. The month ends on Thursday, June 30. Make the required adjusting entry assuming the employees are paid each Friday.

• **task** GIVEN AN UNADJUSTED TRIAL BALANCE, ALONG WITH INFORMATION ABOUT ACCOUNTS THAT SHOULD BE BROUGHT UP TO DATE, PREPARE A WORK SHEET FOR A SERVICE-TYPE BUSINESS

Unadjusted trial balance

In the previous section, we discussed a number of accounts that need adjusting. Without these adjustments, the financial statements would be misleading since expenses and revenues would be incorrect.

illustration 3-2 unadjusted trial balance.

Kar Klinik
Trial Balance
July 31, 19X1

Cash	4715 –	
Accounts Receivable	300 –	
Supplies	50 –	
Prepaid Rent	300 –	
Equipment	1150 –	
Truck	2800 –	
Accounts Payable		500 –
Joe Jackson, Capital		8000 –
Joe Jackson, Drawing	300 –	
Repairs Revenue		2005 –
Salary Expense	800 –	
Utilities Expense	50 –	
Advertising Expense	40 –	
	10505 –	10505 –

As we mentioned in the introduction, these adjustments can be determined best by planning them on a **work sheet.** The starting point in preparing a work sheet is to take a trial balance similar to the one we prepared in Chapter 2 and transfer this same information to the first two columns of a work sheet. For reference, we have repeated the unadjusted trial balance in Illustration 3-2. Note that we are referring to this trial balance as **unadjusted.** To change an unadjusted trial balance to an adjusted trial balance, adjusting entries must be *journalized and posted.* Journalized entries, such as the ones we made in the previous section, should first be *planned.* Once we have shown you how to plan adjusting entries in this chapter, we will show you how to journalize and post them in Chapter 4.

The work sheet

Procedures at the end of the accounting period can be time consuming unless an orderly procedure is established. One tool that can help make this period-ending process orderly is a work sheet. The **work sheet** is a **planning sheet** that permits the accounting clerk to (1) test equality of the debits and credits shown on the unadjusted trial balance, (2) plan the adjusting entries and test their equality, (3) prepare an adjusted trial balance to test the equality of debits and credits, and (4) divide the accounts on the adjusted trial balance between the balance sheet and the income statement. To begin, we will introduce you to the ten-column format (so called because there are ten amount columns). Later, when you develop confidence in using the work sheet, we will change to an eight-column format.

Now let's take a look at how a work sheet is prepared for Kar Klinik for July. As we mentioned earlier, the first step is to enter the information from the trial balance in Illustration 3-2 in the first two columns of the work sheet in Illustration 3-3. Since the work sheet is a planning sheet, and not for management's use, you should use a pencil so you can erase your mistakes (you might make one or two). Unless the firm's management wants a formal trial balance, preparing a trial balance like the one in Illustration 3-2 can be skipped.

illustration 3-3
first two columns of a work sheet.

Account Titles	Trial Balance Dr.	Trial Balance Cr.
Cash	4715 –	
Accounts Receivable	300 –	
Supplies	50 –	
Prepaid Rent	300 –	
Equipment	1150 –	
Trucks	2800 –	
Accounts Payable		500 –
Joe Jackson, Capital		8000 –
Joe Jackson, Drawing	300 –	
Repairs Revenue		2005 –
Salary Expense	800 –	
Utilities Expense	50 –	
Advertising Expense	40 –	
	10505 –	10505 –

After the equality of the unadjusted trial balance is verified, the adjustments are planned. A review of the accounts of Kar Klinik shows that the following accounts should be adjusted:

(a) *Supplies* A count is taken of supplies on hand, and the value of supplies not used is $20. Since supplies costing $30 have been used, they should be shown as an expense of doing business. The asset *Supplies* is reduced by $30.

(b) *Prepaid Rent* One-half of the rent service has been provided from an advance payment of $300 for two months on July 1 (1/2 x $300 = $150.) The *Prepaid Rent* account is reduced by $150 and a new account, *Rent Expense,* is set up with a debit of $150.

(c) *Equipment* Equipment is composed of a cash register purchased for $250 (50-month life) and $900 of repair equipment (90-month life). Total depreciation of equipment for July is calculated like this:

Cash register ($250 ÷ 50) =	$ 5
Repair equipment ($900 ÷ 90) =	10
Total equipment depreciation	$15

Depreciation Expense and *Accumulated Depreciation, Equipment,* should be increased by $15.

(d) *Truck* The truck is to be depreciated over 40 months ($2,800/40), or $70 per month. Using the same type of adjusting entry that we used for the depreciation of equipment, *Depreciation Expense, Truck* and *Accumulated Depreciation, Truck* are increased by $70.

(e) *Salary Expense* Kar Klinik owes Nick Turner $40 for working on Monday, July 31. *Salary Expense* and *Salary Payable* are increased by $40 to show this unrecorded accrual.

Compare these entries with the adjustments columns in Illustration 3-4 to be certain that you fully understand each one. Also note two items of special interest in Illustration 3-4. First, it was necessary to add some accounts below those already listed for the unadjusted trial balance. This step is necessary only if an account in the adjusting entry does not appear in the unadjusted trial balance. *Supplies, Prepaid Rent,* and *Salary Expense* are not repeated in the listing of accounts. Some accountants prefer to list all the accounts in the unadjusted trial balance—even those that do not have a balance. This approach is acceptable, and your instructor may direct you to use it. We feel that the approach shown in Illustration 3-4 requires less effort because some accounts may not be used during the fiscal period and therefore do not need to be listed.

illustration 3-4
work sheet with adjustments.

Account Titles	Trial Balance Dr.	Trial Balance Cr.	Adjustments Dr.	Adjustments Cr.
Cash	4715 –			
Accounts Receivable	300 –			
Supplies	50 –			(a) 30 –
Prepaid Rent	300 –			(b) 150 –
Equipment	1150 –			
Trucks	2800 –			
Accounts Payable		500 –		
Joe Jackson, Capital		8000 –		
Joe Jackson, Drawing	300 –			
Repairs Revenue		2005 –		
Salary Expense	800 –		(e) 40 –	
Utilities Expense	50 –			
Advertising Expense	40 –			
	10505 –	10505 –		
Supplies Expense			(a) 30 –	
Rent Expense			(b) 150 –	
Depr. Expense, Equipment			(c) 15 –	
Accum. Depr., Equipment				(c) 15 –
Depr. Expense, Trucks			(d) 70 –	
Accum. Depr., Trucks				(d) 70 –
Salary Payable				(e) 40 –
			305 –	305 –

Second, a small letter is placed in parentheses next to each entry to identify the debit and its related credit. Although you may think that this step could be skipped, we encourage you to include these letters because they are helpful in locating errors.

Because the trial balance has equality of debits and credits and because the adjusting entries also show an equality of debits and credits, it stands to reason that all accounts should remain in balance after the adjusting entries are made. Keeping this equality throughout the work sheet is very important. Always make certain that debits and credits are equal by adding the columns before moving to the next step.

Adjusted trial balance

After the account balances in the unadjusted trial balance are combined with the adjustments, the adjusted trial balance columns of the work sheet are completed. A close examination of Illustration 3-5 shows that the adjusted balances are calculated by

1. adding debits to debits, or
2. adding credits to credits, or
3. subtracting debits from credits, or
4. subtracting credits from debits.

illustration 3-5 partially completed work sheet.

Account Titles	Trial Balance Dr.	Trial Balance Cr.	Adjustments Dr.	Adjustments Cr.	Adjusted Trial Balance Dr.	Adjusted Trial Balance Cr.
Cash	4715 -				4715 -	
Accounts Receivable	300 -				300 -	
Supplies	50 -			(a) 30 -	20 -	
Prepaid Rent	300 -			(b) 150 -	150 -	
Equipment	1150 -				1150 -	
Trucks	2800 -				2800 -	
Accounts Payable		500 -				500 -
Joe Jackson, Capital		8000 -				8000 -
Joe Jackson, Drawing	300 -				300 -	
Repairs Revenue		2005 -				2005 -
Salary Expense	800 -		(e) 40 -		840 -	
Utilities Expense	50 -				50 -	
Advertising Expense	40 -				40 -	
	10505 -	10505 -				
Supplies Expense			(a) 30 -		30 -	
Rent Expense			(b) 150 -		150 -	
Depr. Expense, Equipment			(c) 15 -		15 -	
Accum. Depr., Equipment				(c) 15 -		15 -
Depr. Expense Trucks			(d) 70 -		70 -	
Accum. Depr., Trucks				(d) 70 -		70 -
Salary Payable				(e) 40 -		40 -
			305 -	305 -	10630 -	10630 -

To describe the procedure another way, this step requires that you add or subtract *horizontally*. The columns are totaled to test again for equality of debits and credits.

Now that we have brought all of the accounts up to date, we must divide the account balances between the income statement and the balance sheet. Since the capital statement is actually a breakdown of the capital account, the drawing account is considered a part of the balance sheet. Once you have gained skill in preparing the work sheet, you may decide not to use the adjusted trial balance column by taking the adjusted balances directly to the income statement and balance sheet columns.

Transferring balances to the statement columns

Once the adjusted trial balance is complete, your skill in identifying and classifying accounts becomes very important. You must be able to determine by the account title whether it belongs on the income statement or on the balance sheet. Using the work sheet in Illustration 3-5, the accounting clerk decides that cash of $4,715 is an asset and belongs on the balance sheet. The next step is deciding whether the item is a debit or a credit. This decision is very easy because debits in the adjusted trial balance remain as debits in the financial statement columns, and credits remain credits.

Once the decision is made that *Cash* is a balance sheet item, it *must* be a balance sheet debit. The accounting clerk continues to transfer all the account balances from the adjusted trial balance to the financial statement until every item is transferred. Examine Illustration 3-6 to make certain that you fully understand this step. We strongly urge you not to memorize patterns on the work sheet.

illustration 3-6
work sheet.

Kar Klinik
Work Sheet
For Month Ended July 31, 19X1

Account Titles	Trial Balance		Adjustments		Adjusted Trial Balance		Income Statement		Balance Sheet	
	Dr.	Cr.	Dr.	Cr.	Dr.	Cr.	Dr.	Cr.	Dr.	Cr.
Cash	4715 -				4715 -				4715 -	
Accounts Receivable	300 -				300 -				300 -	
Supplies	50 -			(a) 30 -	20 -				20 -	
Prepaid Rent	300 -			(b) 150 -	150 -				150 -	
Equipment	1150 -				1150 -				1150 -	
Trucks	2800 -				2800 -				2800 -	
Accounts Payable		500 -				500 -				500 -
Joe Jackson, Capital		8000 -				8000 -				8000 -
Joe Jackson, Drawing	300 -				300 -				300 -	
Repairs Revenue		2005 -				2005 -		2005 -		
Salary Expense	800 -		(e) 40 -		840 -		840 -			
Utilities Expense	50 -				50 -		50 -			
Advertising Expense	40 -				40 -		40 -			
	10505 -	10505 -								
Supplies Expense			(a) 30 -		30 -		30 -			
Rent Expense			(b) 150 -		150 -		150 -			
Depr. Expense, Equipment			(c) 15 -		15 -		15 -			
Accum. Depr., Equipment				(c) 15 -		15 -				15 -
Depr. Expense, Trucks			(d) 70 -		70 -		70 -			
Accum. Depr., Trucks				(d) 70 -		70 -				70 -
Salary Payable				(e) 40 -		40 -				40 -
			305 -	305 -	10630 -	10630 -	1195 -	2005 -	9435 -	8625 -

Some students fall into the practice of looking for assets first, then liabilities, then owner's equity, and so on. This works only to a point; it can lead to poor procedures and errors when the work sheet becomes very complicated. Try to learn to place accounts in the proper columns by using good accounting basics—not by memorizing patterns.

Completing the work sheet

The final step in preparing a work sheet is to determine whether the firm made a net income or a net loss. To do this, all four statement columns must be added. Unless the situation is unusual, none of the four totals should be the same. As can be seen in Illustration 3-6, all four column totals differ. The key is the *difference* between the columns for each statement. To help you see this better, look at Illustration 3-7. The income statement difference is $810 ($2,005 − $1,195), a figure that matches the balance sheet difference ($9,435 − $8,625).

illustration 3-7 bottom of work sheet.

Account Titles	Income Statement Dr.	Income Statement Cr.	Balance Sheet Dr.	Balance Sheet Cr.
	1195 –	2005 –	9435 –	8625 –
Net Income	810 –			810 –
	2005 –	2005 –	9435 –	9435 –

To determine whether this $810 is net income or net loss, we must know the types of accounts that the balances in each column represent. First, examine the income statement columns in Illustration 3-6. The debit column contains only expenses, while the credit column contains a single revenue item. Since the revenue column is greater than the expense column, Kar Klinik made a net income. Using the same approach on the balance sheet columns is not as easy. The debit column contains mostly assets, while the credit column contains mostly liabilities and the capital account at the beginning of the period. Since the debit column is $810 larger than the credit column, the firm made a net income. If the difference between the two income statement columns exactly matches the difference between the two balance sheet columns, you are ready to complete the work sheet.

The net income or net loss is inserted in the columns on the *smaller amount side* of each statement. In Kar Klinik's case, the firm's net income of $810 is placed on the debit side of the income statement and on the credit side of the balance sheet. All four columns are added to verify that debits now equal credits for each statement. Once this is done, a double line is drawn below the totals to indicate that the work sheet is complete. To give you a total picture, the completed work sheet for Kar Klinik is shown in Illustration 3-8.

Before you leave your preparation of a work sheet, make certain that the words *Net Income* or *Net Loss* are written under the account title heading on the same line on which you have written the difference between the financial statement columns.

Kar Klinik
Work Sheet
For Month Ended July 31, 19X1

Account Titles	Trial Balance Dr.	Trial Balance Cr.	Adjustments Dr.	Adjustments Cr.	Adjusted Trial Balance Dr.	Adjusted Trial Balance Cr.	Income Statement Dr.	Income Statement Cr.	Balance Sheet Dr.	Balance Sheet Cr.
Cash	4715 -				4715 -				4715 -	
Accounts Receivable	300 -				300 -				300 -	
Supplies	50 -			(a) 30 -	20 -				20 -	
Prepaid Rent	300 -			(b) 150 -	150 -				150 -	
Equipment	1150 -				1150 -				1150 -	
Trucks	2800 -				2800 -				2800 -	
Accounts Payable		500 -				500 -				500 -
Joe Jackson, Capital		8000 -				8000 -				8000 -
Joe Jackson, Drawing	300 -				300 -				300 -	
Repairs Revenue		2005 -				2005 -		2005 -		
Salary Expense	800 -		(e) 40 -		840 -		840 -			
Utilities Expense	50 -				50 -		50 -			
Advertising Expense	40 -				40 -		40 -			
	10505 -	10505 -								
Supplies Expense			(a) 30 -		30 -		30 -			
Rent Expense			(b) 150 -		150 -		150 -			
Depr. Expense, Equipment			(c) 15 -		15 -		15 -			
Accum. Depr., Equipment				(c) 15 -		15 -				15 -
Depr. Expense, Trucks			(d) 70 -		70 -		70 -			
Accum. Depr., Trucks				(d) 70 -		70 -				70 -
Salary Payable				(e) 40 -		40 -				40 -
			305 -	305 -	10630 -	10630 -	1195 -	2005 -	9435 -	8625 -
Net Income							810 -			810 -
							2005 -	2005 -	9435 -	9435 -

illustration 3-8 completed work sheet.

sample problem Complete the work sheet for Taylor's Book Repairs for July. This exercise tests your understanding of how to transfer items from the adjusted trial balance to the financial statements:

	Adjusted Trial Balance Dr.	Adjusted Trial Balance Cr.
Cash	$6,650	
Accounts Receivable	450	
Prepaid rent	60	
Supplies	75	
Equipment	1,400	
Accounts Payable		$ 990
Joe Taylor, Capital		6,970
Joe Taylor, Drawing	60	
Rent Expense	240	
Salaries Expense	550	
Utilities Expense	60	

	Adjusted Trial Balance	
	Dr.	Cr.
Advertising Expense	$ 35	
Repairs Revenue		$1,700
Supplies Expense	110	
Depreciation Expense, Equipment	35	
Accumulated Depreciation, Equipment		35
Salaries Payable		30
	$9,725	$9,725

sample problem solution

	Income Statement		Balance Sheet	
	Dr.	Cr.	Dr.	Cr.
Cash			6,650	
Accounts Receivable			450	
Prepaid Rent			60	
Supplies			75	
Equipment			1,400	
Accounts Payable				990
Joe Taylor, Capital				6,970
Joe Taylor, Drawing			60	
Rent Expense	240			
Salaries Expense	550			
Utilities Expense	60			
Advertising Expense	35			
Repairs Revenue		1,700		
Supplies Expense	110			
Depr. Expense, Equipment	35			
Accum. Depr., Equipment				35
Salaries Payable				30
	1,030	1,700	8,695	8,025
Net Income	670			670
	1,700	1,700	8,695	8,695

review exercises

5. From the following list of trial balance accounts, indicate the ones that most likely will need adjusting: (a) *Cash;* (b) *Unearned Rent Revenue;* (c) *Notes Receivable;* (d) *Supplies;* (e) *Equipment;* (f) *Accounts Payable;* (g) *Hugh Sliger, Capital;* (h) *Hugh Sliger, Drawing;* (i) *Prepaid Rent;* (j) *Salaries Expense;* (k) *Building;* (l) *Depreciation Expense, Building;* (m) *Accumulated Depreciation, Building.*

6. What would be the difference in the totals of a trial balance and which side would be larger if each of the following separate mistakes was made:

   What if an accounting clerk showed:
   (a) *David Henner, Drawing* as a $250 credit?
   (b) *Salaries Payable* as a $530 debit?
   (c) No entry for *Supplies Expense,* $28?
   (d) *Telephone Expense,* $78, twice on the debit side?
   (e) *Equipment* costing $1,980 as a debit of $1,890?

7. Equipment is composed of three items: A truck that depreciated $1,500 this year, a desk and chair that depreciated $40, and an adding machine that depreciated $25. Prepare a single adjusting entry to bring the accounts up to date.

• task FROM A COMPLETED WORK SHEET, PREPARE A FIRM'S FINANCIAL STATEMENTS

The financial statements represent brief summaries of operations. For larger companies many transactions have to be made, classified, analyzed, and adjusted by considering a mass of underlying data. A work sheet brings together the many accounts and provides the information for the principal financial statements—the balance sheet, the income statement, and the capital statement. Preparing these three statements from a completed work sheet will be discussed and illustrated now.

The income statement

The income statement provides useful information for the owner or manager of a business. The information needed to prepare the income statement is taken from the income statement section of the work sheet. This statement reports total revenues and total related expenses for a definite period of time. An income statement provides information about the different kinds of expense and the amounts that have been expended and accrued. It is also possible to classify the expenses according to the *nature* or *function* of the cost. Two broad classifications of income statement expenses are **selling expenses** and **administrative expenses.** Selling expenses are those incurred in connection with sales and marketing activities. Administrative expenses are those that relate to the general management and office routines of the firm. These account titles describe specific expenses for each of these two categories:

Selling	Administrative
Sales Salaries Expense	Office Salaries Expense
Depreciation Expense, Display Fixtures	Administrative Salaries Expense
Advertising Expense	Depreciation Expense, Building
Delivery Expense	Bad Debt Expense
Entertainment Expense	Depreciation Expense, Office Machines and Equipment
Sales Commissions Expense	Insurance Expense
	Property Taxes Expense
	Office Supplies Expense

This list makes no attempt to be complete, and some of the expenses may be common expenditures for both broad categories. For example, accounts like *Depreciation Expense, Buildings; Insurance Expense;* and *Property Taxes Expense* might be divided between sales and administrative functions in some fair manner. Managers are responsible for the expenditures and accountable for expenses incurred in the areas they control. For instance, the sales manager is responsible for planning and controlling travel, customer contracts, advertising, and similar marketing functions that sell products and services to customers. A proper classification of the sales expenses will inform top management as to how well these functions are performed by the sales manager. Similar reasoning is used to classify the administrative expenses.

Firms often have revenues and expenses that do not arise from *normal business operations.* These revenue and expense accounts should be classified as *Other Revenues* and *Other Expenses* and displayed in the bottom section of the income statement. This approach emphasizes to the reader of the income statement that these accounts came from events not related to normal operations. Assume that a firm had income from normal operations of $3,561 and revenues from both rent and dividends and expenses for payment of interest on borrowed money. A portion of an income statement included as Illustration 3-9 shows how *Other Revenues* and *Other Expenses* should be displayed.

illustration 3-9 partial income statement.

Income From Operations		3561 –
Other Revenues:		
Dividend Revenue	225 –	
Rent Revenue	800 –	
Total Other Revenue	1025 –	
Other Expenses:		
Interest Expense	85 –	940 –
Net Income		4501 –

If *Other Expenses* amount to more than *Other Revenues,* the net figure is subtracted from *Income from Operations.* Other accounts that often appear in the "other" category are *Interest Revenue, Gain on Sale of Equipment,* and *Loss on Sale of Building.*

To provide continuity with the work sheet, a simplified income statement that shows representative expenses is prepared in Illustration 3-10. Data for the income statement are contained in the debit and credit columns of the income statement section of the work sheet shown in Illustration 3-8.

illustration 3-10
preparing the income statement.

Account Titles	Income Statement Dr.	Income Statement Cr.
Accounts Payable		
Joe Jackson, Capital		
Joe Jackson, Drawing		
Repairs Revenue		2005 –
Salary Expense	840 –	
Utilities Expense	50 –	
Advertising Expense	40 –	
Supplies Expense	30 –	
Rent Expense	150 –	
Depr. Expense, Equipment	15 –	
Accum. Depr., Equipment		
Depr. Expense, Trucks	70 –	
Accum. Depr., Trucks		
Salary Payable		
	1195 –	2005 –
Net Income	810 –	
	2005 –	2005 –

Kar Klinik
Income Statement
For Month Ended July 31, 19X1

Revenue:		
Repairs Revenue		2005 –
Operating Expenses:		
Salary Expense	840 –	
Utilities Expense	50 –	
Advertising Expense	40 –	
Supplies Expense	30 –	
Rent Expense	150 –	
Depreciation Expense, Equipment	15 –	
Depreciation Expense, Trucks	70 –	
Total Operating Expenses		1195 –
Net Income		810 –

Must be the same amount as shown on work sheet

Because Kar Klinik's operations are very simple, we have little need to classify its expense items. In a small service company like this one, most expenditures are made to provide a service, and administrative expense is usually a small percentage of the total. However, separating *Other Revenues* and *Other Expenses* might be useful even in the smallest company.

The capital statement

After completing the income statement, the accounting clerk has the information needed to show why the capital account balance changed from the beginning of the period to the end of the period. For Kar Klinik, the beginning balance was zero. During the period, Joe invested $8,000, the firm made a net income of $810, and Joe withdrew $300. Put in T-account form, owner's equity would look like this:

Owner's Equity

Withdrawal	300	Investment	8,000
		Net Income	810

The capital statement should provide the reader with this same information. You can see that this is the case in Illustration 3-11.

illustration 3-11
capital statement.

Kar Klinik
Capital Statement
For Month Ended July 31, 19X1

Joe Jackson, Capital, July 1, 19X1		-0-
Add: Net Income	810 —	
Investment	8000 —	8810 —
		8810 —
Less: Withdrawals		300 —
Joe Jackson, Capital, July 31, 19X1		8510 —

From work sheet

Information to prepare the capital statement is taken mostly from the work sheet. We say "mostly" since the capital account cannot be used directly unless there are no investments during the fiscal period. In Illustration 3-11, both the amount of net income and the amount of withdrawals are found in the balance sheet columns—net income at the bottom and withdrawals in the *Joe Jackson, Drawing* account. Since Joe invested $8,000 during the period, the beginning balance must be taken from the general ledger. Here we find that the beginning balance was zero. If the capital account had begun the month with an $8,000 balance, and Joe had not made any investments, the amount shown for *Joe Jackson, Capital* on the balance sheet credit column would have been usable.

The balance sheet

Earlier we discussed the balance sheet and pointed out that it shows the financial condition of the business on a specific date. All but the capital amount is taken from the work sheet when a formal balance sheet is prepared. Examine Illustration 3-12 to see how the information is transferred from the balance sheet columns to the statement. *Joe Jackson, Capital* must be taken from the capital statement so that this amount shows the end of the period balance.

Account Titles	Balance Sheet Dr.	Balance Sheet Cr.
Cash	4715 –	
Accounts Receivable	300 –	
Supplies	20 –	
Prepaid Rent	150 –	
Equipment	1150 –	
Trucks	2800 –	
Accounts Payable		500 –
Joe Jackson, Capital		8000 –
Joe Jackson, Drawing	300 –	
Depr. Expenses, Equipment		
Accum. Depr., Equipment		15 –
Depr. Expenses, Trucks		
Accum. Depr., Trucks		70 –
Salary Payable		40 –

To statement of owner's equity

From statement of owner's equity

Kar Klinik
Balance Sheet
July 31, 19X1

Assets			
Current Assets:			
Cash		4715 –	
Accounts Receivable		300 –	
Supplies		20 –	
Prepaid Rent		150 –	
Total Current Assets			5185 –
Plant and Equipment:			
Equipment	1150 –		
Less: Accum. Depr., Equipment	15 –	1135 –	
Trucks	2800 –		
Less: Accum. Depr. Trucks	70 –	2730 –	
Total Plant and Equipment			3865 –
Total Assets			9050 –
Liabilities and Owner's Equity			
Current Liabilities:			
Accounts Payable		500 –	
Salary Payable		40 –	
Total Liabilities			540 –
Owner's Equity			
Joe Jackson, Capital			8510 –
Total Liabilities and Owner's Equity			9050 –

illustration 3-12 preparing the balance sheet.

In Chapter 1, you were told that all items are recorded on the basis of their cost; therefore, the balance sheet values for assets used to operate a business do not attempt to reflect fair market values. The equipment owned by Kar Klinik may have a market value above or below the $1,135 book value ($1,150 less accumulated depreciation of $15) on the balance sheet date. From the point of view of a going concern, the company expects to remain in business and to depreciate most of the cost of the equipment. Therefore, market value is unimportant when historical accounting procedures are used.

To give you an idea of how a balance sheet appears if the assets and liabilities are classified into subcategories, we have prepared Kar Klinik's balance sheet using the **classified balance sheet** style. Assets are classified mainly as *Current Assets, Plant and Equipment Assets,* and *Other Assets* on the balance sheet. *Current Assets* are cash or those assets that will be converted into cash, usually within one year. Equipment and truck are operational assets and represent long-term investments. Assets like the equipment and the truck used at Kar Klinik to provide sales and repair service are classified as *Plant and Equipment.* Because current liabilities are usually settled more quickly than long-term debt, these two types of liabilities are usually separated. *Current Liabilities* are usually those we expect to pay within one year. *Long-Term Liabilities* are usually obligations that extend beyond one year.

sample problem From the partial work sheet of Quality Printing Service, prepare an income statement, a capital statement, and a balance sheet for January, 19X1.

Account	Income Statement Dr.	Income Statement Cr.	Balance Sheet Dr.	Balance Sheet Cr.
Cash			$ 4,210	
Accounts Receivable			650	
Supplies			220	
Equipment			3,000	
Delivery Truck			4,800	
Accounts Payable				$ 2,340
Notes Payable				600
Bill Lamberson, Capital				9,140
Bill Lamberson, Drawing			600	
Printing Income		$3,080		
Rent Expense	$ 400			
Utilities Expense	80			
Wages Expense	780			
Advertising Expense	50			

Account	Income Statement Dr.	Income Statement Cr.	Balance Sheet Dr.	Balance Sheet Cr.
Truck Expense	$ 70			
Supplies Expense	380			
Depreciation Expense, Truck	100			
Accumulated Depreciation, Truck				100
Depreciation Expense, Equipment	50			
Accumulated Depreciation, Equipment				50
Wages Payable				80
	1,910	3,080	13,480	12,310
Net income	1,170			1,170
	$3,080	$3,080	$13,480	$13,480

sample problem solution

Quality Printing
Income Statement
For Month Ended January 31, 19X1

Revenue:		
Printing Income		$3,080
Operating Expenses:		
Rent Expense	$400	
Utilities Expense	80	
Wages Expense	780	
Advertising Expense	50	
Truck Expense	70	
Supplies Expense	380	
Depreciation Expense, Truck	100	
Depreciation Expense, Equipment	50	
Total Operating Expense		1,910
Net Income		$1,170

Quality Printing
Capital Statement
For Month Ended January 31, 19X1

Bill Lamberson, Capital, January 1		$9,140
Add: Net Income	$1,170	
Less: Withdrawals	600	
Increase in Owner's Equity		570
Bill Lamberson, Capital, January 31		$9,710

Quality Printing
Balance Sheet
January 31, 19X1

Assets

Current Assets:			
Cash		$4,210	
Accounts Receivable		650	
Supplies		220	
Total Current Assets			$5,080
Plant and Equipment:			
Equipment	$3,000		
Less: Accumulated Depreciation, Truck	100	2,900	
Delivery Truck	4,800		
Less: Accumulated Depreciation, Equipment	50	4,750	
Total Plant and Equipment			7,650
Total Assets			$12,730

Liabilities and Owner's Equity

Current Liabilities:		
Accounts Payable	$2,340	
Notes Payable	600	
Wages Payable	80	
Total Liabilities		$ 3,020
Owner's Equity:		
Bill Lamberson, Capital, Jan. 31		9,710
Total Liabilities and Owner's Equity		$12,730

review exercises

8. Which of the following items are selling expenses and which are administrative expenses? (a) *Sales Salaries Expense;* (b) *Property Taxes Expense;* (c) *Office Supplies Expense;* (d) *Office Salaries Expense;* (e) *Depreciation Expense, Delivery Truck;* (f) *Advertising Expense.*

9. On a classified balance sheet, specifically where would each of the following accounts appear? (a) *Prepaid Rent;* (b) *Salaries Payable;* (c) *Delivery Truck;* (d) *Julie Wright, Capital;* (e) *Accounts Receivable;* (f) *Mortgage Payable;* (g) *Accounts Payable;* (h) *Cash.*

10. At the beginning of the fiscal period, March 1, 19X1, Linda's Linens accounts showed a capital balance for Linda Valeni of $14,916.13. During March, Linda withdrew $1,200 for personal use, and the firm made a net income of $896.76. Prepare a capital statement.

11. Bill McClain of McClain Builders wants you to prepare a capital statement. The ledger shows that his capital account on February 1 was $9,554.08. During February, Bill invested $2,000 in the business and suffered a $534.21 net loss.

chapter highlights

You have now learned to identify accounts that must be adjusted and planned when updated on a work sheet. The work sheet helps in preparing adjustments for certain accounts on the unadjusted trial balance and in adding new accounts as needed. After the accounts have been adjusted, they are separated into income statement and balance sheet columns to determine net income and to segregate the balance sheet accounts. From the completed work sheet, you prepared an income statement, a capital statement, and a balance sheet.

Having studied Chapter 3, you should be able to:

- Plan necessary adjusting entries at the end of the accounting period.
- Prepare a work sheet for a service-type business.
- Prepare the financial statements from the completed work sheet.

check figures for review exercises

1. *Supplies* should be credited for $266.
2. *Insurance Expense* should be debited for $10.
3. Debit *Unearned Rent Revenue,* credit *Rent Revenue,* $400.
4. Debit *Salaries Expense,* credit *Salaries Payable,* $2,400.
5. (b), (d), (i), (j), (l), and (m).
6. (a) $500, Cr.
   (b) $1,060, Dr.
   (c) $28, Cr.
   (d) $78, Dr.
   (e) $90, Cr.
7. Dr. *Depreciation Expense, Equipment* and credit *Accumulated Depreciation, Equipment,* $1,565.
8. Selling Expenses: (a), (e), and (f).
9. (a) Current Assets
   (b) Current Liabilities
   (c) Plant and Equipment
   (d) Owner's Equity
   (e) Current Assets
   (f) Long-Term Liabilities
   (g) Current Liabilities
   (h) Current Assets
10. Ending capital, $14,612.89.
11. Ending capital, $11,019.87.

key terms

The following important terms are discussed in Chapter 3 and are defined in the Glossary at the end of the book.

- **accrual**
- **adjusted trial balance**
- **adjusting entries**
- **administrative expenses**
- **capital statement**
- **classified balance sheet**
- **deferral**
- **matching concept**
- **mixed account**
- **selling expenses**
- **unadjusted trial balance**
- **work sheet**

questions

1. What is the purpose of an adjusting entry?
2. What is a mixed account? Give an example. What is a contra account? What type of balance does *Accumulated Depreciation, Equipment* have?
3. If salaries are paid for work from Monday through Friday and accounting period ends on Tuesday, why bother making an adjust. entry?
4. What is the purpose of a trial balance?
5. Contrast the purpose of the adjusted trial balance with that of the trial balance.
6. After the adjusting entry, will *Prepaid Rent* have a debit or a credit balance? Assuming that no mistakes were made, is it possible to have a different balance in the adjusted trial balance for this account than that found in the trial balance?
7. What is the purpose of a work sheet?
8. On the work sheet, if the debit column total on the income statement column is larger than that for the credit column, would the firm have a net income or a net loss?
9. If the total of the debits in the balance sheet column of the work sheet is smaller than the total of the credit column, would a firm have a net income or a net loss?
10. What is the purpose of an income statement?
11. What type of accounts appear on an income statement?
12. Indicate which of the following expenses are selling expenses and which are administrative expenses: (a) *Sales Salaries Expense;* (b) *Depreciation Expense, Store Equipment;* (c) *Insurance Expense, Office Equipment;* (d) *Delivery Expense;* (e) *Office Supplies Expense.*
13. How does the balance sheet differ from the trial balance?
14. What is the difference between a current liability and a long-term liability?

exercises

1. One year's rent of $3,600 was paid in advance on August 1, 19X1. Assuming a rental rate of $300 a month, make the necessary adjusting entry on August 31, 19X1, to bring the accounts up to date.
2. Supplies on hand at the beginning of 19X1 amounted to $100. During the year, $550 of supplies were purchased. By the end of 19X1, the inventory count showed that $400 of the supplies had been used. Make the required adjusting entry.
3. Assume the same facts as in Exercise 2, except this time assume that the count of supplies showed $150 of supplies still on hand on December 31. Make the adjusting entry.
4. Ten employees who earn $50 each per day when they work a five-day week, worked only Monday, December 30, and Tuesday, December 31, before the accounting period ended. What adjusting entry would be used to record these accrued salaries assuming the employees are paid on Friday?
5. Depreciation on a typewriter, adding machine, and other office equipment was estimated at $500 for the current year. Prepare the necessary adjusting entry.
6. Black and Blue Cab Company had the following trial balance at the end of 19X1 (small numbers have been used to help you concentrate on the concepts involved):

Black and Blue Cab Company
Trial Balance
December 31, 19X1

	Dr.	Cr.
Cash	$ 4	
Accounts Receivable	8	
Prepaid Rent	5	
Prepaid Insurance	3	
Supplies	4	
Equipment	13	
Accounts Payable		$ 6
Accumulated Depreciation, Equipment		7
Bill Barter, Capital		13
Bill Barter, Drawing	2	
Cab Revenue		22
Salaries Expense	4	
Utilities Expense	2	
Advertising Expense	3	
	$48	$48

Draw a rough work sheet form on plain paper; then prepare a work sheet for Black and Blue Cab Company for the year ending December 31, 19X1 using the following data:

(a) Rent of $3 on the cab company's office space is still prepaid at the end of the year.
(b) A count of supplies on hand shows $1 in supplies still available for use.
(c) Insurance of $1 has expired by December 31.
(d) Depreciation on the cab and other equipment amounts to $3 for the year.
(e) A salary of $2 has accrued for the cab driver by year end.

7. Using the completed work sheet in Exercise 6, prepare (a) an income statement, (b) a capital statement, and (c) a balance sheet.

problems

1. COMPETENCY TESTED The ability to journalize adjusting entries.

Purple Company has been operating a medium-size retail store for several years. In addition to daily transactions posted to the ledger accounts, certain adjusting transactions must be made at the end of the year. Ledger accounts have 19X1 balances as shown before adjusting entries.

Prepaid Rent	
3,000	

Salary Expense	
11,800	

Store Supplies	
600	

Delivery Equipment	
9,000	

Accumulated Depreciation, Delivery Equipment	
	3,200

(a) Journalize adjusting entries based upon the following information:
  (1) Rent was paid in advance for three years on January 1, 19X1.
  (2) Accrued *Salary Expense* for the last week in 19X1 was $500.
  (3) A count of store supplies showed $200 of store supplies on hand.
  (4) Delivery equipment had an estimated scrap value of $1,000 and was being depreciated over an estimated 5 years at $1,600 per year.

(b) (1) From the information in the T accounts, determine the amount of expenses to be listed on the income statement prior to adjusting entries.
  (2) What were the total expenses after adjustments?
  (3) What were the decreases in assets after adjustments?
  (4) What were the increases in liabilities after adjustments?

2. **COMPETENCY TESTED** Skill in preparing a work sheet and the financial statements.

Brown Company had the following incomplete work sheet for the year ended December 31, 19X1:

Brown Company
Work Sheet
For Year Ended December 31, 19X1

Account	Trial Balance		Adjustments		Adjusted Trial Balance		Income Statement		Balance Sheet	
	Dr.	Cr.	Dr.	Cr.	Dr.	Cr.	Dr.	Cr.	Dr.	Cr.
Cash	5				5				5	
Accounts Receivable	7				7				(j)	
Store Supplies	3			(a)	(d)				1	
Equipment	10				10				10	
Accumulated Depreciation, Equipment		3		(b)		6				(k)
Accounts Payable		4				4				4
Charles Brown, Capital		12				12				(m)
Charles Brown, Drawing	1				(e)				(l)	
Sales		11				11		(h)		
Salaries Expense	4		(c)		(f)		5			
	30	30								
Store Supplies Expense			(a)		(g)		2			
Depreciation Expense			(b)		3		(i)			
Salaries Payable				(c)		1				(n)
			6	6	34	34	10	11	24	23
Net Income							1			(o)
							11	11	24	(p)

Instructions

(a) Complete the work sheet above by filling in the correct amount by the letter given.

(b) Prepare an income statement from the work sheet.

(c) Prepare a capital statement.

(d) Prepare a balance sheet.

3. **COMPETENCY TESTED** The ability to prepare a work sheet.

Legal Beaver Law Firm keeps its books on an annual fiscal year ending each March. At the end of March the following unadjusted trial balance was prepared:

Account	Dr.	Cr.
Cash	$ 6,992	
Accounts Receivable	8,638	
Office Supplies	967	
Equipment	14,032	
Accumulated Depreciation, Equipment		3,911
Building	180,000	
Accumulated Depreciation, Building		52,000
Accounts Payable		2,915
Mortgage Payable		88,677
Earl Beaver, Capital		52,303
Earl Beaver, Drawing	29,600	
Legal Fees		69,424
Salaries Expense	26,800	
Utilities Expense	915	
Advertising Expense	200	
Travel Expense	655	
Repairs Expense	187	
Interest Expense	244	
	$269,230	$269,230

Data for adjustments:

Office supplies used	$ 668
Depreciation on equipment	1,640
Depreciation on building	4,850
Accrued salaries	980
Accrued interest expense	45

Instructions Prepare a work sheet for Legal Beaver Law Firm for the year ending March 31, 19X1.

4. COMPETENCY TESTED Expertise in preparing financial statements.

Jay's Tennis Pro School operates on a calendar fiscal year ending December 31. Below is a partial work sheet for the current year.

Jay's Tennis Pro School
Work Sheet
For the Year Ended December 31, 19X1

Account	Income Statement Dr.	Income Statement Cr.	Balance Sheet Dr.	Balance Sheet Cr.
Cash			$ 3,462	
Accounts Receivable			915	
Shop Supplies			437	
Prepaid Insurance			148	
Prepaid Rent			400	
Equipment			2,450	
Accumulated Depreciation, Equipment				$ 940

Account	Income Statement Dr.	Income Statement Cr.	Balance Sheet Dr.	Balance Sheet Cr.
Accounts Payable				$ 869
Notes Payable (short-term)				500
Jay Christie, Capital				7,594
Jay Christie, Drawing			$ 4,200	
Lesson Revenue		$14,600		
Salary Expense	$ 8,600			
Rent Expense	800			
Utilities Expense	643			
Telephone Expense	890			
Shop Supplies Expense	914			
Insurance Expense	434			
Depreciation Expense, Equipment	350			
Salaries Payable				140
	12,631	14,600	12,012	10,043
Net Income	1,969			1,969
	$14,600	$14,600	$12,012	$12,012

Instructions From the work sheet above, prepare (a) an income statement, (b) a capital statement, and (c) a balance sheet.

5. COMPETENCY TESTED Skill in using the completed work sheet properly.

The last six columns of Hal's Fix-It Shop's eight-column work sheet for the year ending on December 31, 19X1 are shown below:

	Adjustments Dr.	Adjustments Cr.	Income Statement Dr.	Income Statement Cr.	Balance Sheet Dr.	Balance Sheet Cr.
Cash					3,100	
Accounts Receivable					4,000	
Prepaid Insurance		(a) 200			1,000	
Supplies		(b) 400			800	
Equipment					15,000	
Accum. Depreciation		(c) 800				8,200
Accounts Payable						1,800
Hal Lunn, Capital						9,900
Hal Lunn, Drawing					2,000	
Service Revenue				17,000		
Salaries Expense	(d) 700		7,300			
Depreciation Expense	(c) 800		800			
Salaries Payable		(d) 700				700

	Adjustments		Income Statement		Balance Sheet	
	Dr.	Cr.	Dr.	Cr.	Dr.	Cr.
Rent Expense			3,000			
Insurance Expense	(a) 200		200			
Supplies Expense	(b) 400		400			
	2,100	2,100	11,700	17,000	25,900	20,600
Net Income			5,300			5,300
			$17,000	$17,000	$25,900	$25,900

Instructions

(a) Prepare an income statement.

(b) Prepare a capital statement.

(c) Prepare a balance sheet.

comprehensive problem

MAGIC CARPET TRAVEL (PART 2)

Use the information completed in Part 1 to complete this comprehensive problem, which was started in Chapter 2.

Instructions

(a) Transfer the trial balance prepared in Part 1 to the first two columns of the work sheet. Be sure to put the proper heading on the work sheet.

(b) Using the following information, make the necessary adjustments in the adjusting entry columns of the work sheet:

(1) Rent still prepaid on November 30, $350.

(2) Office supplies on hand, November 30, $15.

(3) Unused insurance as of November 30, $165.

(4) Depreciation for the month on equipment, $50.

(c) Complete the work sheet.

(d) Prepare the income statement for November.

(e) Prepare the capital statement for November.

(f) Prepare the balance sheet for November.

chapter 4
COMPLETING THE ACCOUNTING CYCLE (PART II)

overall competency THE ABILITY TO MAKE ADJUSTING, CLOSING, AND REVERSING ENTRIES

career objectives The accounting clerk must be able to use the completed work sheet as part of a planning stage that updates accounts by making adjusting entries. After this step, ledger account balances will match the information shown on the financial statements. Next, the accounting clerk must close all of the temporary accounts back into the capital account. The post-closing trial balance tests the accuracy of this closing process. Finally, reversing certain adjusting entries to prepare the accounts for the next fiscal period completes the process.

When you complete Chapter 4, you should be able to accomplish the following tasks:

- JOURNALIZE AND POST THE ADJUSTING ENTRIES.
- JOURNALIZE AND POST THE CLOSING ENTRIES.
- PREPARE A POST-CLOSING TRIAL BALANCE.
- JOURNALIZE AND POST THE REVERSING ENTRIES.

In Chapter 3 you were introduced to the work sheet on which adjusting entries were planned, but no changes were made in the ledger accounts. To update the accounts, we must journalize and post the adjusting entries. After this work has been done, the expense and revenue items must be made ready for the next fiscal period. These two steps are needed to accomplish the desired results:

1. Journalize the adjusting entries and post to the ledger. For the adjusting entries, use information from the adjustment columns of the work sheet.
2. Journalize the closing entries and post to the ledger. Information for these closing entries is taken from the income statement columns of the work sheet.

• task JOURNALIZE AND POST THE PLANNED ADJUSTING ENTRIES FROM A COMPLETED WORK SHEET

Journalizing the adjusting entries

When you prepared the work sheet, we encouraged you to place letters next to the amounts in the adjustment columns. Now, by using these letters, you will be able to make the adjusting entries without much effort. You analyzed and planned the adjusting entries when you prepared the work sheet in Chapter 3.

The work sheet for Kar Klinik that was prepared in Chapter 3 is shown again as Illustration 4-1. The journal entries shown in Illustration 4-2 are made by using the following steps:

1. Turn to the last entry in the general journal and skip one line.
2. Write the words "Adjusting Entries" in the items column.
3. Record the date of the work sheet in the general journal date column. The month is used only if this is the first entry on the journal page.
4. Find Item (a) in the work sheet's adjustment debit column. In this case, it is a debit of $30 to *Supplies Expense.*
5. Debit *Supplies Expense* for $30 in the general journal.
6. Find the credit for Item (a) in the work sheet's adjustment column. It is a credit of $30 to *Supplies.*
7. Credit *Supplies* for $30 in the general journal. Do not write an explanation.
8. Find Entry (b) in the work sheet's adjustment debit column and continue the process until all items are journalized.

Since the words "Adjusting Entries" are written in the center of the items column, an explanation after each entry is unnecessary.

Kar Klinik
Work Sheet
For Month Ended July 31, 19X1

Account Titles	Trial Balance Dr.	Trial Balance Cr.	Adjustments Dr.	Adjustments Cr.	Adjusted Trial Balance Dr.	Adjusted Trial Balance Cr.	Income Statement Dr.	Income Statement Cr.	Balance Sheet Dr.	Balance Sheet Cr.
Cash	4715 -				4715 -				4715 -	
Accounts Receivable	300 -				300 -				300 -	
Supplies	50 -			(a) 30 -	20 -				20 -	
Prepaid Rent	300 -			(b) 150 -	150 -				150 -	
Equipment	1150 -				1150 -				1150 -	
Trucks	2800 -				2800 -				2800 -	
Accounts Payable		500 -				500 -				500 -
Joe Jackson, Capital		8000 -				8000 -				8000 -
Joe Jackson, Drawing	300 -				300 -				300 -	
Repairs Revenue		2005 -				2005 -		2005 -		
Salary Expense	800 -		(e) 40 -		840 -		840 -			
Utilities Expense	50 -				50 -		50 -			
Advertising Expense	40 -				40 -		40 -			
	10505 -	10505 -								
Supplies Expense			(a) 30 -		30 -		30 -			
Rent Expense			(b) 150 -		150 -		150 -			
Depr. Expense, Equipment			(c) 15 -		15 -		15 -			
Accum. Depr., Equipment				(c) 15 -		15 -				15 -
Depr. Expense, Trucks			(d) 70 -		70 -		70 -			
Accum. Depr., Trucks				(d) 70 -		70 -				70 -
Salary Payable				(e) 40 -		40 -				40 -
			305 -	305 -	10630 -	10630 -	1195 -	2005 -	9435 -	8625 -
Net Income							810 -			810 -
							2005 -	2005 -	9435 -	9435 -

illustration 4-1 **Kar Klinik's work sheet.**

illustration 4-2 **Kar Klinik's adjusting entries.**

JOURNAL Page

Date		Description	P.R.	Dr.	Cr.
19X1 July	30	Cash	11	825 -	
		Repairs Revenue	41		825 -
		Collection from Willard McKinnie for repairing car.			
		Adjusting Entries			
	31	Expense		30 -	
		Prepaid Supplies			30 -
	31	Rent Expense		150 -	
		Prepaid Rent			150 -
	31	Depreciation Expense, Equipment		15 -	
		Accumulated Depreciation, Equipment			15 -
	31	Depreciation Expense, Truck		70 -	
		Accumulated Depreciation, Truck			70 -
	31	Salary Expense		30 -	
		Salary Payable			30 -

Posting the adjusting entries

In previous discussions, we have used the T-account form for the general ledger accounts. This form is a good teaching tool, but most firms use either a three- or a four-column account. We will be using the four-column style in this textbook. Note in Illustration 4-3 that the four columns allow debit and credit entries as well as debit and credit balances. If the account has a debit balance, this amount is placed in the left-hand balance column. If a credit balance exists, the balance is placed in the right-hand balance column. This approach is in keeping with the T-account structure, except that the four-column format allows for a running balance.

illustration 4-3
four-column ledger form.

ACCOUNT TITLE ACCOUNT NO.

Date	Item	P.R.	Dr.	Cr.	Balance	
					Dr.	Cr.

Now let's return to posting the adjusting entries for Kar Klinik. This procedure is a good one to follow:

1. Transfer the debit amount to the ledger account debit column.
2. Transfer the date. Notice the single date column in this format.
3. Indicate the general journal page number in the posting reference column of the ledger page.
4. Write the words "Adjusting Entry" in the items columns.
5. Indicate the ledger page number in the posting reference column of the journal.
6. Transfer the credit amount to the credit column of the ledger account.
7. Transfer the date.
8. Indicate the journal page number in the posting reference column of the ledger account.
9. Indicate the ledger page number in the posting reference column of the journal.

This procedure is shown more clearly by Illustration 4-4, in which each step mentioned above is labeled so that you can follow the procedures easily.

illustration 4-4 posting to a four-column ledger.

JOURNAL Page 2

Date		Description	P.R.	Dr.	Cr.
	31	Supplies Expense	64	30 –	
		Supplies	13		30 –

Supplies Account No. 13

Date		Item	P.R.	Dr.	Cr.	Balance Dr.	Balance Cr.
19X1 July	6		1	50 –		50 –	
	31	Adjusting Entry	2		30 –	20 –	

Supplies Expense Account No. 64

Date		Item	P.R.	Dr.	Cr.	Balance Dr.	Balance Cr.
19X1 July	31	Adjusting Entry	2	30 –		30 –	

After you have posted the adjusting entries, all accounts except the capital account should have the same balance as that shown on the financial statements. We will discuss how to make the capital account match the balance sheet figure in our discussion of closing entries. In Illustration 4-5, you can see the ledger for Kar Klinik *after* the adjusting entries have been posted.

illustration 4-5 adjusted general ledger.

Cash Account No. 11

Date		Item	P.R.	Dr.	Cr.	Balance Dr.	Balance Cr.
19X1 July	1		1	8000 –		8000 –	
	1		1		300 –	7700 –	
	2		1		400 –	7300 –	
	9		1		2800 –	4500 –	
	11		1	630 –		5130 –	
	14		1		400 –	4730 –	
	15		1		300 –	4430 –	
	24		1		300 –	4130 –	
	26		1		50 –	4080 –	
	28		1		400 –	3680 –	
	30		1		40 –	3640 –	
	30		2	250 –		3890 –	
	30		2	825 –		4715 –	

illustration 4-5 (continued)

Accounts Receivable — Account No. 12

Date		Item	P.R.	Dr.	Cr.	Balance Dr.	Balance Cr.
19x1 July	15		1	550 –		550 –	
	30		2		250 –	300 –	

Supplies — Account No. 13

Date		Item	P.R.	Dr.	Cr.	Balance Dr.	Balance Cr.
19x1 July	6		1	50 –		50 –	
	31	Adjusting Entry	2		30 –	20 –	

Prepaid Rent — Account No. 14

Date		Item	P.R.	Dr.	Cr.	Balance Dr.	Balance Cr.
19x1 July	1		1	300 –		300 –	
	31	Adjusted Entry	2		150 –	150 –	

Equipment — Account No. 16

Date		Item	P.R.	Dr.	Cr.	Balance Dr.	Balance Cr.
19x1 July	2		1	900 –		900 –	
	6		1	250 –		1150 –	

Accumulated Depreciation, Equipment — Account No. 17

Date		Item	P.R.	Dr.	Cr.	Balance Dr.	Balance Cr.
19x1 July	31	Adjusting Entry	2		15 –		15 –

Trucks — Account No. 18

Date		Item	P.R.	Dr.	Cr.	Balance Dr.	Balance Cr.
19x1 July	9		1	2800 –		2800 –	

Accumulated Depreciation, Trucks — Account No. 19

Date		Item	P.R.	Dr.	Cr.	Balance Dr.	Balance Cr.
19X1 July	31	Adjusting Entry	2		70 –		70 –

Accounts Payable — Account No. 21

Date		Item	P.R.	Dr.	Cr.	Balance Dr.	Balance Cr.
19X1 July	2		1		500 –		500 –
	6		1		300 –		800 –
	15		1	300 –			500 –

Salary Payable — Account No. 22

Date		Item	P.R.	Dr.	Cr.	Balance Dr.	Balance Cr.
19X1 July	31	Adjusting Entry	2		40 –		40 –

Joe Jackson, Capital — Account No. 31

Date		Item	P.R.	Dr.	Cr.	Balance Dr.	Balance Cr.
19X1 July	1		1		8000 –		8000 –

Joe Jackson, Drawing — Account No. 32

Date		Item	P.R.	Dr.	Cr.	Balance Dr.	Balance Cr.
19X1 July	24		1	300 –		300 –	

Repairs Revenue — Account No. 41

Date		Item	P.R.	Dr.	Cr.	Balance Dr.	Balance Cr.
19X1 July	11		1		630 –		630 –
	15		1		550 –		1180 –
	30		2		825 –		2005 –

illustration 4-5
(continued)

Salary Expense Account No. 61

Date		Item	P.R.	Dr.	Cr.	Balance Dr.	Balance Cr.
19X1 July	14		1	400 –		400 –	
	28		1	400 –		800 –	
	31	Adjusting Entry	2	40 –		840 –	

Utilities Expense Account No. 62

Date		Item	P.R.	Dr.	Cr.	Balance Dr.	Balance Cr.
19X1 July	26		2	50 –		50 –	

Advertising Expense Account No. 63

Date		Item	P.R.	Dr.	Cr.	Balance Dr.	Balance Cr.
19X1 July	30		2	40 –		40 –	

Supplies Expense Account No. 64

Date		Item	P.R.	Dr.	Cr.	Balance Dr.	Balance Cr.
19X1 July	31	Adjusting Entry	2	30 –		30 –	

Rent Expense Account No. 65

Date		Item	P.R.	Dr.	Cr.	Balance Dr.	Balance Cr.
19X1 July	31	Adjusting Entry	2	150 –		150 –	

Depreciation Expense, Equipment Account No. 66

Date		Item	P.R.	Dr.	Cr.	Balance Dr.	Balance Cr.
19X1 July	31	Adjusting Entry	2	15 –		15 –	

Depreciation Expense, Trucks Account No. 67

Date		Item	P.R.	Dr.	Cr.	Balance Dr.	Balance Cr.
19X1 July	31	Adjusting Entry	2	70 –		70 –	

sample problem From the partial work sheet of Sincere Cleaners, prepare the necessary adjusting entries for the year ending on December 31, 19X1.

Account	Adjustments Dr.		Adjustments Cr.	
Cash				
Accounts Receivable				
Notes Receivable				
Supplies			(a)	$ 850
Equipment				
Accumulated Depreciation, Equipment			(d)	800
Building				
Accumulated Depreciation, Building			(e)	2,400
Accounts Payable				
Notes Payable				
Phil Noe, Capital				
Phil Noe, Drawing				
Cleaning Revenue				
Advertising Expense				
Wages Expense	(b)	$ 640		
Supplies Expense	(a)	850		
Interest Expense	(c)	50		
Interest Payable			(c)	50
Wages Payable			(b)	640
Depreciation Expense, Equipment	(d)	800		
Depreciation Expense, Building	(e)	2,400		
		$4,740		$4,740

sample problem solution

Adjusting Entries

19X i			
Dec. 31	Supplies Expense	$ 850	
	Supplies		$ 850
31	Wages Expense	640	
	Wages Payable		640
31	Interest Expense	50	
	Interest Payable		50
31	Depreciation Expense, Equipment	800	
	Accumulated Depreciation, Equipment		800
31	Depreciation Expense, Building	2,400	
	Accumulated Depreciation, Building		2,400

review exercises

1. Which of the following accounts would normally need adjusting? (a) *Lee Kardatzke, Capital;* (b) *Prepaid Advertising;* (c) *Rent Expense;* (d) *Lee Kardatzke, Drawing;* (e) *Supplies;* (f) *Machinery;* (g) *Interest Payable.*
2. Phillip Company pays weekly salaries of $10,000 on Friday for a five-day week ending on that day. Journalize the adjusting entry necessary at the end of October, 19X1, assuming that the fiscal period ends on (a) Wednesday, (b) Thursday.
3. The *Supplies* account has a balance of $842 on December 31, 19X1, the end of the fiscal period. A physical count reveals that $640 has been used. Make the necessary adjusting entry.
4. Marvin Adkins' Campgrounds show unrecorded depreciation on its buildings of $850 and unrecorded depreciation on its equipment of $690. Make the necessary adjusting entries.

• task FROM A COMPLETED WORK SHEET, JOURNALIZE AND POST THE CLOSING ENTRIES

Journalizing the closing entries

After the adjusting entries have been journalized and posted, the expenses and revenues should be current, and all the items on the balance sheet, with the exception of capital, should be in good order. Typically, most accounts that appear on the balance sheet have balances, so they are referred to as **real** or **permanent** accounts. For example, it would be unusual (but possible) for *Cash, Accounts Receivable,* or *Supplies* to have a zero balance.

In contrast to real accounts, expense and revenue accounts should be closed at the end of each accounting period, much like a stopwatch is returned to zero after each race in a 100-meter dash. This procedure allows a reading to be made of each expense and revenue account for a specific period of time. These accounts, known as **nominal** or **temporary** accounts, are typically found on the income statement. Unless this approach is followed, preparing an income statement for a specific period, such as the one we did for Kar Klinik's July transactions, would be difficult.

This process of transferring the balances out of the nominal accounts is done with **closing entries.** A temporary account called *Income Summary* will be used to assist in the closing process. First, we will transfer all the revenue and expense accounts to this *Income Summary* account, then we will close the *Income Summary* account to the capital account. Finally, we will close out the drawing account to the capital account. The end result is basically the same as that which we started with in Chapter 1: All changes in owner's equity (revenues, expenses, withdrawals) are combined into the owner's capital account. These steps are used in the closing procedure:

1. Close out all accounts in the *Income Statement* credit column of the work sheet.
2. Close out all accounts in the *Income Statement* debit column of the work sheet.
3. Close the balance of *Income Summary* to the capital account.
4. Close the balance in the drawing account to the capital account.

You can find the information for Steps 1 and 2 from three possible sources:

1. The work sheet columns for the income statement items.
2. The income statement.
3. The ledger.

We will use the work sheet since it is a very handy source of information.

Step 1 Close out all accounts in the income statement credit column of the work sheet. We have taken the income statement columns and the account titles from Kar Klinik's completed work sheet and displayed them again in Illustration 4-6. You will note that only one account appears in the income statement credit column—*Repairs Revenue.* Since this balance is a credit, it must be closed by a debit.

illustration 4-6
partial work sheet.

Account Titles	Income Statement		Balance Sheet	
	Dr.	Cr.	Dr.	Cr.
Joe Jackson, Drawing			300 -	
Repairs Revenue		2005 -		
Salary Expense	840 -			
Utilities Expense	50 -			
Advertising Expense	40 -			
Supplies Expense	30 -			
Rent Expense	150 -			
Depr. Expense, Equipment	15 -			
Accum. Depr., Equipment				15 -
Depr. Expense, Trucks	70 -			
Accum. Depr., Trucks				70 -
Salary Payable				40 -
	1195 -	2005 -	9435 -	8625 -
Net Income	810 -			810 -
	2005 -	2005 -	9433 -	9435 -

Before the first closing entry is journalized, the words "Closing Entries" should be written in the middle of the items column two spaces below the last adjusting entry. The following closing entry would be journalized to complete Step 1:

JOURNAL — Page 2

Date		Description	P.R.	Dr.	Cr.
19X1 July	31	Repairs Revenue		2005 –	
		Income Summary			2005 –

No explanation is required since the heading preceding the entry tells the reader the purpose of this series of entries.

Step 2 Close out all accounts in the income statement debit column of the work sheet. Illustration 4-6 lists seven accounts in the debit column. To force these accounts to zero balances, each must be *credited.* A line is skipped between the first entry and the one shown below.

JOURNAL — Page 2

Date		Description	P.R.	Dr.	Cr.
19X1 July	31	Income Summary		1195 –	
		Salary Expense			840 –
		Utilities Expense			50 –
		Advertising Expense			40 –
		Rent Expense			150 –
		Supplies Expense			30 –
		Depreciation Expense, Equipment			15 –
		Depreciation Expense, Truck			70 –

Step 3 Close the balance of *Income Summary* to the capital account. After the first two entries are posted, *Income Summary* will have a balance exactly equal to the firm's net income or net loss for the period. In Kar Klinik's case, *Income Summary* has a credit balance of $810. Since this amount is a net income, the effect of Step 3 should be to increase the capital account.

JOURNAL — Page 2

Date		Description	P.R.	Dr.	Cr.
19X1 July	31	Income Summary		810 –	
		Joe Jackson, Capital			810 –

Step 4 Close the balance in the drawing account to the capital account. In Chapter 1, we illustrated that withdrawals reduce capital. Since *Joe Jackson, Drawing* has a debit balance, it must be closed by a credit. The resulting closing entry would be:

JOURNAL Page 2

Date		Description	P.R.	Dr.	Cr.
19X1 July	31	Joe Jackson, Capital		300 –	
		Joe Jackson, Drawing			300 –

Information for this transaction is taken from the debit balance sheet column on Kar Klinik's work sheet. The drawing account is the only nominal account found on the balance sheet of a service-type firm.

Now, we will combine these separate steps into one continuous illustration. Look at Illustration 4-7 to see how this set of entries might look in an actual journal.

illustration 4-7 journalized closing entries.

JOURNAL Page 2

Date		Description	P.R.	Dr.	Cr.
19X1 July	31	Salary Expense	61	30 –	
		Salary Payable	22		30 –
		Closing Entries			
	31	Repairs Revenue		2005 –	
		Income Summary			2005 –
	31	Income Summary		1195 –	
		Salary Expense			840 –
		Utilities Expense			50 –
		Advertising Expense			40 –
		Rent Expense			150 –
		Supplies Expense			30 –
		Depreciation Expense, Equipment			15 –
		Depreciation Expense, Trucks			70 –
	31	Income Summary		810 –	
		Joe Jackson, Capital			810 –
	31	Joe Jackson, Capital		300 –	
		Joe Jackson, Drawing			300 –

Posting the closing entries

Once the closing entries have been journalized, the next step is to post these entries to the general ledger. The procedure is identical to the one you would use for posting adjusting entries except that the words "closing entry" are written in the items column. The completed ledger *after* posting the closing entries for Kar Klinik is shown in Illustration 4-8.

illustration 4-8
general ledger after adjusting and closing entries.

Cash Account No. 11

Date		Item	P.R.	Dr.	Cr.	Balance Dr.	Balance Cr.
19X1 July	1		1	8000 –		8000 –	
	1		1		300 –	7700 –	
	2		1		400 –	7300 –	
	9		1		2800 –	4500 –	
	11		1	630 –		5130 –	
	14		1		400 –	4730 –	
	15		1		300 –	4430 –	
	24		1		300 –	4130 –	
	26		1		50 –	4080 –	
	28		1		400 –	3680 –	
	30		1		40 –	3640 –	
	30		2	250 –		3890 –	
	30		2	825 –		4715 –	

Accounts Receivable Account No. 12

Date		Item	P.R.	Dr.	Cr.	Balance Dr.	Balance Cr.
19X1 July	15		1	550 –		550 –	
	30		2		250 –	300 –	

Supplies Account No. 13

Date		Item	P.R.	Dr.	Cr.	Balance Dr.	Balance Cr.
19X1 July	6		1	50 –		50 –	
	31	Adjusting Entry	2		30 –	20 –	

Prepaid Rent Account No. 14

Date		Item	P.R.	Dr.	Cr.	Balance Dr.	Balance Cr.
19X1 July	1		1	300 –		300 –	
	31	Adjusting Entry	2		150 –	150 –	

Equipment Account No. 16

Date		Item	P.R.	Dr.	Cr.	Balance Dr.	Balance Cr.
19X1 July	2		1	900 –		900 –	
	6		1	250 –		1150 –	

Accumulated Depreciation, Equipment — Account No. 17

Date		Item	P.R.	Dr.	Cr.	Balance Dr.	Balance Cr.
19X1 July	31	Adjusting Entry	2		15 –		15 –

Trucks — Account No. 18

Date		Item	P.R.	Dr.	Cr.	Balance Dr.	Balance Cr.
19X1 July	9		1	2800 –		2800 –	

Accumulated Depreciation, Trucks — Account No. 19

Date		Item	P.R.	Dr.	Cr.	Balance Dr.	Balance Cr.
19X1 July	31	Adjusting Entry	2		70 –		70 –

Accounts Payable — Account No. 21

Date		Item	P.R.	Dr.	Cr.	Balance Dr.	Balance Cr.
19X1 July	2		1		500 –		500 –
	6		1		300 –		800 –
	15		1	300 –			500 –

Salary Payable — Account No. 22

Date		Item	P.R.	Dr.	Cr.	Balance Dr.	Balance Cr.
19X1 July	31		2		40 –		40 –

Joe Jackson, Capital — Account No. 31

Date		Item	P.R.	Dr.	Cr.	Balance Dr.	Balance Cr.
19X1 July	1		1		8000 –		8000 –
	31	Closing Entry	2		810 –		8810 –
	31	Closing Entry	2	300 –			8510 –

illustration 4-8 (continued)

Joe Jackson, Drawing — Account No. 32

Date	Item	P.R.	Dr.	Cr.	Balance Dr.	Balance Cr.
19X1 July 1		1	300 –		300 –	
31	Closing Entry	2		300 –	–0–	

Income Summary — Account No. 33

Date	Item	P.R.	Dr.	Cr.	Balance Dr.	Balance Cr.
19X1 July 31	Closing Entry	2		2005 –		2005 –
31	Closing Entry	2	1195 –			810 –
31	Closing Entry	2	810			–0–

Repairs Revenue — Account No. 41

Date	Item	P.R.	Dr.	Cr.	Balance Dr.	Balance Cr.
19X1 July 11		1		630 –		630 –
15		1		550 –		1180 –
30		2		825 –		2005 –
31	Closing Entry	2	2005 –			–0–

Salary Expense — Account No. 61

Date	Item	P.R.	Dr.	Cr.	Balance Dr.	Balance Cr.
19X1 July 14		1	400 –		400 –	
28		2	400 –		800 –	
31	Adjusting Entry	2	40 –		840 –	
31	Adjusting Entry	2		840 –	–0–	

Utilities Expense — Account No. 62

Date	Item	P.R.	Dr.	Cr.	Balance Dr.	Balance Cr.
19X1 July 26		2	50 –		50 –	
31	Closing Entry	2		50 –	–0–	

Advertising Expense — Account No. 63

Date	Item	P.R.	Dr.	Cr.	Balance Dr.	Balance Cr.
19X1 July 30		2	40 –		40 –	
31	Closing Entry	2		40 –	–0–	

Supplies Expense — Account No. 64

Date		Item	P.R.	Dr.	Cr.	Balance Dr.	Balance Cr.
19X1 July	31	Adjusting Entry	2	30 –		30 –	
	31	Closing Entry	2		30 –	-0-	

Rent Expense — Account No. 65

Date		Item	P.R.	Dr.	Cr.	Balance Dr.	Balance Cr.
19X1 July	31	Adjusting Entry	2	150 –		150 –	
	31	Closing Entry	2		150 –	-0-	

Depreciation Expense, Equipment — Account No. 66

Date		Item	P.R.	Dr.	Cr.	Balance Dr.	Balance Cr.
19X1 July	31	Adjusting Entry	2	15 –		15 –	
	31	Closing Entry	2		15 –	-0-	

Depreciation Expense, Trucks — Account No. 67

Date		Item	P.R.	Dr.	Cr.	Balance Dr.	Balance Cr.
19X1 July	31	Adjusting Entry	2	70 –		70 –	
	31	Closing Entry	2		70 –	-0-	

Pay special attention to the *Income Summary* account. All of the transactions take place on July 31. This account is truly temporary in that it is opened and closed on the same date. The final balance in *Joe Jackson, Capital* is $8,510 ($8,000 investment + $810 net income − $300 withdrawal) as of July 31. This amount now matches the figure shown on the balance sheet, as well as the ending capital balance on the capital statement. If you examine Illustration 4-8, you should note that only real accounts have balances after the adjusting and closing entries have been posted. All of the *nominal* accounts have been condensed into the capital account; therefore, all of these accounts now have zero balances.

sample problem From the partial work sheet of Quality Printing Services, prepare the necessary closing entries for one month ending on January 31, 19X1.

Account	Income Statement Dr.	Income Statement Cr.	Balance Sheet Dr.	Balance Sheet Cr.
Cash			$ 4,210	
Accounts Receivable			650	
Supplies			220	
Equipment			3,000	
Delivery Truck			4,800	
Accounts Payable				$ 2,340
Notes Payable				600
Bill Lamberson, Capital				9,140
Bill Lamberson, Drawing			600	
Printing Income		$3,080		
Rent Expense	$ 400			
Utilities Expense	80			
Wages Expense	780			
Advertising Expense	50			
Truck Expense	70			
Supplies Expense	380			
Depreciation Expense, Truck	100			
Accumulated Depreciation, Truck				100
Depreciation Expense, Equipment	50			
Accumulated Depreciation, Equipment				50
Wages Payable				80
	$1,910	$3,080	$13,480	$12,310
Net Income	1,170			1,170
	$3,080	$3,080	$13,480	$13,480

sample problem solution

	Dr.	Cr.
Printing Income	$3,080	
Income Summary		$3,080
Income Summary	1,910	
Rent Expense		400
Utilities Expense		80
Wages Expense		780
Advertising Expense		50
Truck Expense		70
Supplies Expense		380
Depreciation Expense, Truck		100
Depreciation Expense, Equipment		50

Income Summary	$1,170	
Bill Lamberson, Capital		$1,170
Bill Lamberson, Capital	600	
Bill Lamberson, Drawing		600

review exercises

5. Determine which of the following accounts should be closed: (a) *Wally Lufkins, Drawing;* (b) *Accounts Receivable;* (c) *Supplies Expense;* (d) *Accumulated Depreciation, Equipment;* (e) *Wally Lufkins, Capital;* (f) *Income Summary.*
6. The work sheet's income statement debit columns for Spurlock's Plumbing shows a total of $14,631.14 and a credit total of $18,983.15. If the capital and drawing accounts have balance sheet column amounts of $28,401.34 and $1,400, respectively, what is the ending capital balance after the closing entries?
7. The work sheet showed the following:

Phyliss Davidson, Capital	$13,490.26
Phyliss Davidson, Drawing	850.00
Income statement debit column total	23,916.44
Income statement credit column total	21,642.98

Phyliss invested $1,000 in the business during the month. What would be the ending capital balance after making the closing entries?

• **task** GIVEN THE COMPANY'S LEDGER AFTER THE BOOKS HAVE BEEN CLOSED, PREPARE A POST-CLOSING TRIAL BALANCE AND MAKE THE REQUIRED REVERSING ENTRY

Post-closing trial balance

A **post-closing trial balance** is a listing of the real accounts after the nominal accounts have been closed, that is, an after-closing trial balance. The purpose of this statement is to prove that debits equal credits in the ledger *after* posting the adjusting and closing entries. The July 31, 19X1 post-closing trial balance for Kar Klinik is given in Illustration 4-9. All the ending balances are taken from the firm's general ledger (Illustration 4-8).

illustration 4-9 post-closing trial balance.

Kar Klinik
Post-Closing Trial Balance
July 31, 19X1

Cash	4715 –	
Accounts Receivable	300 –	
Supplies	20 –	
Prepaid Rent	150 –	
Equipment	1150 –	
Accumulated Depreciation, Equipment		15 –
Trucks	2800 –	
Accumulated Depreciation, Trucks		70 –
Accounts Payable		500 –
Salary Payable		40 –
Joe Jackson, Capital		8510 –
	9135 –	9135 –

As you examine Illustration 4-9, notice that all of the accounts with zero balances have been omitted. Also note that the capital account is listed at the after-closing balance. Since the revenue, expense, and drawing account balances have been closed into capital, debits *should equal* credits.

Reversing entries

The accounting process for a fiscal period is completed with the preparation of **reversing entries.** The purpose of reversing entries is to prepare the accounts for normal and routine journal transactions for the next accounting period. To illustrate, an adjusting entry was made to record $40 for the one day worked by Nick Turner on July 31. After the adjusting entry, *Salary Expense* and *Salary Payable* appear as follows:

Salary Payable — Account No. 22

Date		Item	P.R.	Dr.	Cr.	Balance Dr.	Balance Cr.
19X1 July	31	Adjusting Entry	2		40 –		40 –

Salary Expense — Account No. 61

Date		Item	P.R.	Dr.	Cr.	Balance Dr.	Balance Cr.
19X1 July	14		1	400 –		400	
	28		2	400 –		800	
	31	Adjusting Entry	2	40 –		840	
	31	Closing Entry	2		840 –	–0–	

Reversing entries are made as of the first working day of the next accounting period. To accomplish the desired results, the adjusting entry above is merely reversed.

JOURNAL — Page 2

Date		Description	P.R.	Dr.	Cr.
19x1 Aug.	1	Salary Payable		40 –	
		Salary Expense			40 –

Once the reversing entry has been posted, these two accounts would appear as follows:

Salary Payable — Account No. 22

Date		Item	P.R.	Dr.	Cr.	Balance Dr.	Balance Cr.
19x1 July	31	Adjusting Entry	2		40 –		40 –
Aug.	1	Reversing Entry	2	40 –			–0–

Salary Expense — Account No. 61

Date		Item	P.R.	Dr.	Cr.	Balance Dr.	Balance Cr.
19x1 July	14		1	400 –		400 –	
	28		2	400 –		800 –	
	31	Adjusting Entry	2	40 –		840 –	
	31	Closing Entry	2		840 –	–0–	
Aug.	1	Reversing Entry	2		40 –		40 –

Later, on August 11, when the firm pays Nick for two weeks' work, the following entry would be made:

JOURNAL — Page 3

Date		Description	P.R.	Dr.	Cr.
19x1 Aug	11	Salary Expense		400 –	
		Cash			400 –

After posting the August 1 entry, the *Salary Expense* account shows a $360 expense for nine days ($40 × 9).

Salary Expense — Account No. 61

Date		Item	P.R.	Dr.	Cr.	Balance Dr.	Balance Cr.
19X1 July	14		1	400 —		400 —	
	28		2	400 —		800 —	
	31	Adjusting Entry	2	40 —		840 —	
	31	Closing Entry	2		840 —	-0-	
Aug.	1	Reversing Entry	2		40 —		40 —
	11		3	400 —		360 —	

The entry on the credit side of *Salary Expense* prevents the double counting of $40. The difference between the routine payment for two weeks of $400 and the $40 accrued as of July 31 represents the correct salary expense after the first two weeks in August of $360.

Not all adjusting entries are reversed. For the time being, we will just tell you to reverse those adjusting entries involving accruals. In Chapter 10 we will discuss reversing entries in more detail.

sample problem After the closing entries have been posted for Quality Printing Services on January 31, 19X1, the following account balances are found in the ledger.

Cash	$4,210
Accounts Receivable	650
Supplies	220
Equipment	3,000
Accumulated Depreciation, Equipment	50
Delivery Truck	4,800
Accumulated Depreciation, Truck	100
Accounts Payable	2,340
Notes Payable	600
Wages Payable	80
Bill Lamberson, Capital	9,710

Prepare a post-closing trial balance for Quality Printing Services.

sample problem solution

Quality Printing Services
Post-Closing Trial Balance
January 31, 19X1

Cash	$ 4,210
Accounts Receivable	650

Supplies	$ 220	
Equipment	3,000	
Accumulated Depreciation, Equipment		$ 50
Delivery Truck	4,800	
Accumulated Depreciation, Delivery Truck		100
Accounts Payable		2,340
Notes Payable		600
Wages Payable		80
Bill Lamberson, Capital		9,710
	$12,880	$12,880

review exercises

8. Accrued salaries for the last week of the fiscal year amounted to $320. Make the required reversing entry. (Hint: You will have to make the adjusting entry first.)
9. Indicate which of the following accounts will appear on a post-closing trial balance: (a) *Accounts Receivable;* (b) *Salaries Expense;* (c) *Jan Harper, Drawing;* (d) *Service Fees;* (e) *Notes Payable;* (f) *Jan Harper, Capital.*
10. The post-closing trial balance has proven to be unequal because of the following independent situations. What would be the difference in the two totals and which side would be larger?
    (a) *Jay Smith, Drawing,* $400, was included in the statement.
    (b) *Accounts Payable,* $148.63, was shown on the debit side.
    (c) *Store Supplies,* $57.63, was shown twice.
    (d) *Equipment* was listed at $2,614.32 instead of the correct $2,641.32.
    (e) *Jay Smith, Capital,* $14,987.07, was shown at the preclosing figure of $13,006.24.
    (f) *Prepaid Insurance,* $80, was listed on the credit side.

• task REVIEW THE ACCOUNTING CYCLE

We began Chapter 1 by giving you an overall picture of the accounting cycle. Now that you have covered the cycle, we want you to see a list of the steps again.

1. Analyze data to decide recording status.
2. Journalize transactions.
3. Post to ledger accounts.

4. Prepare a trial balance from ledger accounts.
5. Complete the work sheet with necessary adjustments and classifications.
6. Prepare an income statement, capital statement, and balance sheet. Use income statement columns and balance sheet columns, respectively.
7. Record the work sheet adjusting entries in the journal, then post them to the ledger. Use the adjustment columns of the work sheet to obtain this information.
8. Prepare closing entries and post to the ledger.
9. Prepare a post-closing trial balance.
10. Make reversing entries at the beginning of the new fiscal period and post to the ledger.

Once the reversing entries have been posted, the company's accounting records are ready to begin a new fiscal period. The entire cycle begins again with analyzing, journalizing, and posting transactions on a daily basis. The cycle effect gives rise to the term **accounting cycle.**

sample problem Without referring to the previous material, arrange the following events in the accounting cycle in proper sequence:

(a) Journalize closing entries.
(b) Journalize reversing entries.
(c) Analyze data.
(d) Prepare a work sheet.
(e) Post adjusting entries.
(f) Prepare the financial statements.
(g) Journalize daily transactions.
(h) Post reversing entries.
(i) Journalize adjusting entries.
(j) Prepare a post-closing trial balance.
(k) Post daily transactions.
(l) Post closing entries.

sample problem solution The items above should be arranged in the following sequence: (c), (g), (k), (d), (f), (i), (e), (a), (l), (j), (b), (h).

chapter highlights

You have now been through all the basic steps of keeping a set of books for a service-type operation. In Chapter 4 we emphasized the following tasks:

- Journalizing and posting adjusting entries.
- Journalizing and posting closing entries.
- Preparing a post-closing trial balance.
- Journalizing and posting reversing entries.

We also reviewed the accounting cycle to show you how all the various parts we have been discussing fit into a pattern.

check figures for review exercises

1. (b), (c), (e), and (g)

2. (a) Debit *Salaries Expense* and credit *Salaries Payable* for \$6,000. (b) Debit *Salaries Expense* and credit *Salaries Payable* for \$8,000.

3. Debit *Supplies Expense* and credit *Supplies* for \$640.

4.

Depreciation Expense, Building	\$850	
Depreciation Expense, Equipment	690	
Accumulated Depreciation, Building		\$850
Accumulated Depreciation, Equipment		690

5. (a), (c), and (f)

6. \$28,401.34 + \$4,352.01 − \$1,400 = \$31,353.35

7. \$13,490.26 − \$2,273.46 − \$850 = \$10,366.80 (*Note*: The \$1,000 investment would already be included in the work sheet balance of the capital account.)

8. Debit *Salaries Payable* and credit *Salaries Expense* for \$320.

9. (a), (e), and (f)

10. (a) \$400, dr. (d) \$27, cr.
(b) \$297.26, dr. (e) \$1,980.83, dr.
(c) \$57.63, dr. (f) \$160, cr.

key terms

The following terms are discussed in Chapter 4 and are defined in the Glossary at the end of the book.

accounting cycle
closing entries
nominal account
permanent account
post-closing trial balance
real account
reversing entry
temporary account

questions

1. What do we mean when we say that the work sheet allows for planning the adjusting entries?
2. What is the primary advantage of using a four-column style over the T style of ledger account?
3. List the proper steps in posting an adjusting entry.
4. Distinguish between real accounts and nominal accounts.
5. How do closing entries differ from adjusting entries?
6. How many closing entries are needed to close the books?
7. In what way does a post-closing trial balance differ from a trial balance? Specifically, what is the purpose of a post-closing trial balance?
8. Identify the accounts in the following list that should be closed to *Income Summary*: (a) *Equipment;* (b) *Juan Fernandez, Drawing;* (c) *Accounts Receivable;* (d) *Depreciation Expense, Building;* (e) *Salaries Payable;* (f) *Cash;* (g) *Juan Fernandez, Capital;* (h) *Supplies;* (i) *Supplies Expense;* (j) *Rent Revenue.*
9. What are the sources of information for making closing entries?
10. What type of accounts appear on a post-closing trial balance?
11. When a reversing entry is made, exactly what type of previously recorded entry is being reversed?
12. What is the purpose of making a reversing entry when an accrual is involved?

exercises

1. Indicate which of the following transactions is a daily transaction (D); an adjusting entry (A); a closing entry (C); or a reversing entry (R).

	Account	Debit	Credit
(a)	Accounts Receivable	45	
	Service Revenue		45
(b)	Depreciation Expense, Equipment	80	
	Accumulated Depreciation, Equipment		80
(c)	Cash	150	
	Accounts Receivable		150
(d)	Salaries Payable	45	
	Salaries Expense		45
(e)	Insurance Expense	70	
	Prepaid Insurance		70
(f)	Service Revenue	1,950	
	Income Summary		1,950
(g)	Fred Bower, Capital	600	
	Fred Bower, Drawing		600
(h)	Equipment	450	
	Notes Payable		450
(i)	Interest Expense	10	
	Interest Payable		10

2. Identify the following accounts as real (R) or nominal (N).
(a) Salaries Payable
(b) Rent Expense
(c) Income Summary
(d) Land
(e) Notes Payable
(f) Rent Revenue
(g) Dudley Chancey, Drawing
(h) Prepaid Rent
(i) Unearned Concerts Revenue
(j) Dudley Chancey, Capital

3. After all of the revenue and expense accounts have been closed, the *Income Summary* account has a debit balance of \$1,614.41. The capital account for Martha Rothchild shows a balance of \$28,690.93 on the work sheet, and the drawing account has a balance of \$6,800. Make the entries to close (a) *Income Summary* into the capital account, and (b) the drawing account into the capital account.

4. The December 31, 19X1 work sheet for Winter's Enterprises shows the following information:

Income Statement debit total	\$ 8,905
Income Statement credit total	10,080
Martin Winter, Capital	48,770
Martin Winter, Drawing	12,000

Make the necessary closing entries by assuming all expenses are represented by a single account labeled *Expenses* and the only revenue account is *Service Revenue.*

5. Harold Folley closes his books each month. The following transactions involving salaries were made between September 1 and October 2:

Sept.	1	Reversed the August 31 adjusting entry, \$1,000.
	4	Paid the weekly salaries for five days, \$5,000.
	11	Paid the weekly salaries for five days, \$5,000.
	18	Paid the weekly salaries for five days, \$5,000.
	25	Paid the weekly salaries for five days, \$5,000.
	30	Adjusted for accrued salaries, \$3,000.
Oct.	1	Reversed the September 30 entry.
	2	Paid the weekly salaries for five days, \$5,000.

(a) How much *Salaries Expense* should be shown on the income statement for September?
(b) How much expense for salaries will be shown in October for the week ending on October 2?

problems 1. COMPETENCY TESTED The ability to journalize and post adjusting entries.

Rod's Exercise House operates on a monthly fiscal period. As of July 31, 19X1, the following ledger accounts need adjusting:

Prepaid Advertising, $100
Prepaid Rent, $450
Store Supplies, $550
Accumulated Depreciation, Equipment, $450
Salaries Expense, $8,860

Additional Data:

(a) Advertising not used on July 31, $37.

(b) The rent payment was made on July 1 for three months.

(c) A count of store supplies shows that $199 of the supplies are on hand as of July 31.

(d) Salaries of $240 are accrued and unpaid as of July 31.

(e) Depreciation expense is $50 per month.

Instructions Make the necessary adjusting entries and post to the ledger accounts.

2. COMPETENCY TESTED The ability to prepare closing entries.

The adjusted trial balance of Rhodes Company's work sheet for December 31, 19X1 had the following balances:

	Dr.	Cr.
Cash	$ 900	
Accounts Receivable	1,200	
Prepaid Rent	600	
Office Supplies	500	
Office Equipment	2,000	
Accumulated Depreciation		$ 700
Accounts Payable		800
Salaries Payable		300
John Rhodes, Capital		1,500
John Rhodes, Drawing	400	
Service Revenue		6,900
Salaries Expense	1,800	
Rent Expense	2,400	
Depreciation Expense	300	
Heat and Lighting Expense	100	
Office Supplies Expense	200	
Interest Revenue		200
	$10,400	$10,400

Instructions

(a) Complete the work sheet.

(b) Prepare closing entries.

(c) What is the dollar amount increase in the capital account?

3. COMPETENCY TESTED Skill in journalizing adjusting and closing entries.

Clover Stables is owned and operated by Mary O'Mara. She closes her books and prepares financial statements monthly. Mary prepares the following work sheet for February, 19X1. The amounts are purposefully small so that you can concentrate on making the journal entries.

Clover Stables
Work Sheet
For the Month Ended February 28, 19X1

Account	Trial Balance Dr.	Trial Balance Cr.	Adjustments Dr.	Adjustments Cr.	Adjusted Trial Balance Dr.	Adjusted Trial Balance Cr.	Income Statement Dr.	Income Statement Cr.	Balance Sheet Dr.	Balance Sheet Cr.
Cash	$ 7				$ 7				$ 7	
Accounts Receivable	18				18				18	
Prepaid Rent	4			(a) $ 3	1				1	
Prepaid Insurance	3			(d) 2	1				1	
Supplies	9			(e) 3	6				6	
Equipment	14				14				14	
Accumulated Depreciation, Equipment		$ 6		(b) 1		$ 7				$ 7
Accounts Payable		14				14				14
Notes Payable		3				3				3
Mary O'Mara, Capital		32				32				32
Mary O'Mara, Drawing	7				7				7	
Horse Care Revenue		23				23		$23		
Wages Expense	12		(f) $ 2		14		$14			
Utilities Expense	4				4		4			
	$78	$78								
Rent Expense			(a) 3		3		3			
Depreciation Expense, Equipment			(b) 1		1		1			
Interest Expense			(c) 1		1		1			
Interest Payable			(c)	1		1				1
Insurance Expense			(d) 2		2		2			
Supplies Expense			(e) 3		3		3			
Wages Payable				(f) 2		2				2
			$12	$12	$82	$82	$28	$23	$54	$59
Net Loss								5	5	
							$28	$28	$59	$59

Instructions

(a) Journalize and post the adjusting entries.

(b) Journalize and post the closing entries.

4. COMPETENCY TESTED The ability to handle the posting at the end of a fiscal period.

The following journal entries are found on the books of Mang's Oriental Rug Cleaners on December 31, 19X1:

Adjusting Entries

Date	Account	Debit	Credit
19X1			
Dec. 31	Supplies Expense	$ 3,890.16	
	Supplies		$ 3,890.16
31	Unearned Rent Revenue	50.00	
	Rent Revenue		50.00
31	Insurance Expense	380.00	
	Prepaid Insurance		380.00
31	Depreciation Expense, Equipment	1,423.11	
	Accumulated Depreciation, Equipment		1,423.11
31	Depreciation Expense, Building	2,080.34	
	Accumulated Depreciation, Building		2,080.34
31	Wages Expense	154.00	
	Wages Payable		154.00

Closing Entries

Date	Account	Debit	Credit
31	Cleaning Revenue	45,688.70	
	Rent Revenue	2,400.00	
	Income Summary		48,088.70
31	Income Summary	42,400.52	
	Supplies Expense		3,890.16
	Insurance Expense		380.00
	Depreciation Expense, Equipment		1,423.11
	Depreciation Expense, Building		2,080.34
	Wages Expense		30,113.10
	Utilities Expense		2,890.56
	Telephone Expense		1,623.25
31	Income Summary	5,688.18	
	Y. G. Mang, Capital		5,688.18
31	Y. G. Mang, Capital	12,500.00	
	Y. G. Mang, Drawing		12,500.00

Instructions (a) Without listing the ledger account numbers in the posting reference column above (but do it mentally if you don't want to write in the book), post the adjusting and closing entries. (b) Make a reversing entry on January 2, 19X2 for the accrued wages adjusting entry and post to the ledger.

5. COMPETENCY TESTED Skill in preparing a post-closing trial balance.

After posting the closing entries, the accounts of the Thrasher Flight School are as follows:

Cash	$ 8,341.34
Accounts Receivable	1,998.50
Supplies	2,678.26
Equipment	40,577.00
Accumulated Depreciation, Equipment	18,098.45
Accounts Payable	6,445.20
Mortgage Payable	20,600.00
Salaries Payable	160.00
Unearned Lessons Revenue	850.00
Lowell Thrasher, Capital	7,441.45

Instructions Prepare a post-closing trial balance for August 31, 19X1.

6. COMPETENCY TESTED The ability to handle any part of the accounting cycle for a service-type firm.

The books for Seal's Motel are kept on a monthly fiscal period. Transactions for the month of February, 19X1 are as follows:

Feb.	2	Opened the business by depositing $5,000 in the firm's checking account.
	2	Paid Warren Realty $1,600 for two months' rent of the motel.
	3	Paid $480 to Thrasher Insurance for one year's insurance coverage.
	3	Hired Katy McCoin as custodian, $550 per month, payable twice a month.
	4	Paid Balton Sign Company $300 for sign (consider this equipment).
	5	Purchased a cash register from Randolph's Equipment Company for $350.
	7	Revenue from first week's operation totaled $860.
	8	Purchased a used typewriter from Hedgecoth for $100 cash and a $250 note.
	10	Purchased cleaning supplies on account from Bennett Wholesale Supply, $108.
	12	Paid Snow White Cleaners for week's laundry, $78.

Feb. 13 Sent a bill to Wade Construction Company for rooms rented out to their workers during the past week, $240.

14 Revenue from cash operations for the week amounted to $1,040.

15 Paid Katy $300 for two weeks' salary.

17 Withdrew $150 for personal use.

19 Paid $108 to Bennett Wholesale Supply on account.

21 Revenue from motel operations amounted to $890 during the week.

23 Received a check from Wade Construction Company for $240.

24 Paid *Herald-Star* $10 for ad run in last week's paper.

26 Purchased sheets from Institutional Supply on account, $140.

27 Paid telephone bill, $67.

27 Sent a bill to Wade Construction Company for rooms, $316.

28 Paid Katy $300 for two weeks' salary.

28 Paid utility bill, $363.

28 Revenue from motel operations for past week totaled $764.

28 Withdrew $400 for personal use.

28 Paid $117 to Snow White Cleaners for laundry service.

Instructions

(a) Journalize the entries above for the month of February using the following accounts: *Cash; Accounts Receivable; Supplies; Prepaid Rent; Prepaid Insurance; Equipment; Accumulated Depreciation, Equipment; Accounts Payable; Notes Payable; Ed Seal, Capital; Ed Seal, Drawing; Motel Revenue; Telephone Expense; Utilities Expense; Salaries Expense; Laundry Expense;* and *Advertising Expense.*

(b) Post the month's transactions to the ledger.

(c) Prepare a work sheet using the following data:

Rent was paid for two months on February 2.
Supplies on hand on February 28, $25.
Depreciation of sign, cash register, and typewriter, $40.
Unused insurance, $440.
Accrued salary, $30.

(d) Prepare the financial statements for February.

(e) Journalize and post the adjusting and closing entries.

(f) Prepare a post-closing trial balance.

(g) Reverse the adjusting entry you make for the accrued salary, dating it March 1 and then post this entry.

compre-hensive problem

MAGIC CARPET TRAVEL (PART 3)

Using the information completed in Parts 1 and 2, perform the following steps:

(a) Journalize and post the adjusting entries.

(b) Journalize and post the closing entries.

(c) Prepare a post-closing trial balance.

(d) Journalize the reversing entry.

part two

ACCOUNTING FOR A MERCHANDISING BUSINESS

chapter 5
PURCHASING AND ACCOUNTS PAYABLE

overall competency THE ABILITY TO ANALYZE AND RECORD PURCHASES, RETURNS AND ALLOWANCES, AND DISCOUNTS

career objectives The accounting clerk in charge of purchasing and accounts payable is responsible for handling documents like purchase orders, sales invoices received from sellers, and debit and credit memoranda. Also, the accounting clerk must record journal entries related to these documents and post these entries to the general ledger and subsidiary ledgers.

When you complete this chapter, you should be able to complete the following tasks:

- PREPARE A PURCHASE ORDER FOR MERCHANDISE OR SUPPLIES.
- KNOW THE MEANING OF VARIOUS SHIPPING TERMS.
- FROM THE SOURCE DOCUMENT, RECORD THE ACCOUNTING ENTRIES FOR BUYING MERCHANDISE ON ACCOUNT.
- POST THE JOURNAL ENTRIES TO THE GENERAL AND SUBSIDIARY LEDGERS.
- RECORD ACCOUNTING ENTRIES FOR RETURNS AND ALLOWANCES ON MERCHANDISE.

In the first four chapters, you were introduced to accounting for a service-type business. Now we want to show you how to keep the accounting records for a firm that sells merchandise. Many entries are the same for both types of businesses. The most notable difference is in accounting for the buying, handling, and selling of merchandise. In this chapter we will begin with the purchasing function—a very important part of any merchandising business.

• task PREPARE A PURCHASE ORDER FOR MERCHANDISE OR SUPPLIES

Merchandise defined

Items stocked in a store for resale are classified as **merchandise.** Merchandise should be distinguished from items used in the business, such as office supplies, office equipment, desks, copying machines, and buildings. In most cases you will have little trouble deciding the correct classification. However, some owners use merchandise (such as an adding machine in an office equipment company) for business purposes; and then return it to the shelf for sale to the public. If the merchandise is used as office equipment for extended periods of time, serious consideration should be given to showing this item as office equipment rather than as merchandise in the accounting records.

The cost of buying merchandise is recorded in an account called *Purchases.* By introducing this account, we are introducing the last of our major accounting categories. This category appears on the income statement between the revenue section and the expense section and is known as the **cost of goods sold.** An account that falls into this category is known simply as a *cost* account. To tell the difference between a cost account and the other categories, simply use the rule that any purchase of merchandise is debited to a cost account.

The first digit of a cost account number should be 5. The chart of accounts is now complete.

First Digit	Classification
1	Asset
2	Liability
3	Owner's equity
4	Revenue
5	Cost
6	Expense

Like asset and expense accounts, cost accounts normally have debit balances. An easy way to remember the classifications that have normal debit balances is to use the word *ace* (asset, cost, and expense).

Requisition data

A request to order merchandise or other items is sent to the purchasing department. In a small business, the request may be informal; in a large business, the process is likely to be more formal. A requisition form may be required by the purchasing department. This form has lines for (1) the name of the department requesting items, (2) the number of items, (3) a description of items, (4) the date needed, and (5) approval of the department head or supervisor. This form might be similar to the one in Illustration 5-1.

illustration 5-1
sample purchase requisition.

Purchase Requisition

No. 573

No. of items: 20

Description: Classic Terry Robes (Various sizes and colors) @ $18.60 ea.

Date needed 9/14
Requested by JM
Approved by TK

The **purchase requisition** is an internal business document on which it is not necessary to show the name of the business. Notice that the form has a control number in the upper right corner. These forms are consecutively numbered, and all numbers are accounted for by the person responsible. At least two copies should be made—one for the purchasing department and one for the requesting department's files.

Credit terms

Most businesses buy and sell items on credit. Each business has a policy as to the type of **credit terms** allowed each customer. Credit may be with or without **cash discounts.** The credit term *n/30* means that payment of the invoice price is expected within 30 days from the date of the invoice. If a cash discount is allowed by the seller, the terms might be *2/10, n/30*. These terms mean that a 2 percent discount is deducted if the payment is made within ten days from the date of the invoice, and the full amount is to be paid within 30 days. Although the *n* supposedly means *net,* it actually means the invoice amount.

Most businesses have a policy of taking advantage of cash discounts on purchases even if they must borrow at a relatively high interest rate to do so. For example, if the Ultimate Discount Company buys merchandise with an invoice price of $6,000 and credit terms of 2/10, n/30, it should borrow, if necessary, to take the discount of \$120 (\$6,000 × .02). The cost of borrowing, assuming a 12 percent interest rate, would be \$39.20 (\$5,880 × .12 × 20/360). Notice that only \$5,880 would be borrowed (\$6,000 minus \$120), and the amount kept for 20 days since the invoice price is expected within 30 days if the discount is not taken. The simple explanation for a company's borrowing at 12 percent to take a 2 percent discount is that the 12 percent is an annual rate whereas the 2 percent is a flat rate. The word *flat* means that it is not adjusted to an annual rate.

Usually, a strict application of the number of days, such as the ten days used in the earlier illustration, is not made in actual business practice. If the flow of business documents is slow, the payment may be made after the discount period. The seller often allows the discount if the buyer is an important customer.

Purchase order

The **purchase requisition** is analyzed by the purchasing agent or someone working in the purchasing department. If the purchase requisition is for frequently ordered items, the same supplier will probably be used. Factors considered in selecting suppliers are price, timely delivery, quality, and credit terms.

After the supplier has been selected, a **purchase order** is prepared and mailed to the company. An example of a completed purchase order is shown in Illustration 5-2.

illustration 5-2
purchase order. (courtesy of Wilson Jones Company)

JENNISON COMPANY
P.O. Box 789, Highway 32
Happy Hollow, TN 38579

No. 2095
Date Jan. 8, 19X1

Sold To Strips Galore
P.O. Box 101
Boma, TN 38556

Shipped to Same

Salesman: No later than 1/25
Shipped VIA: Overnight Delivery Service
F.O.B.: Shipping Point
Terms: 2/10, n/30

Quantity Ordered	Quantity Shipped	Stock Number Description	Price	Per	Amount
60		X-3 High Strips	10 –	ea	600 –

Wilson Jones
GRAYLINE FORM 44-401 3-PART
© 1974 PRINTED IN U.S.A.

Purchase Order

We have discussed all items on the purchase order in Illustration 5-2 except the term *FOB shipping point.* This term will be explained under the next task.

Distribution of purchase order copies

In addition to the original, three copies of the purchase order should be prepared for distribution.

1. The original is sent to the supplier as an order for the merchandise or other items.
2. One copy is kept in the purchasing department.
3. One copy is sent to the receiving department. The number of items ordered should be blocked out so that receiving will be encouraged to make an independent count of the items received.
4. One copy is sent to the accounting department to be matched with a copy of the receiving report. This copy is also used by the accounting department for recording the purchase and, once authorized, making the payment.

You can see the flow of the purchase order distribution in Illustration 5-3.

illustration 5-3
distribution of the purchase order.

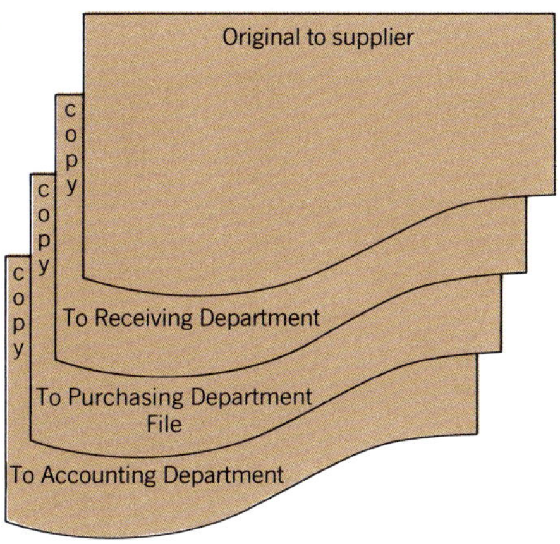

A log should be kept of consecutive purchase order numbers. This record allows control by accounting for all numbers. It can also be used as a quick reference to determine which orders have been filled.

sample problem A purchase requisition received by the purchasing department shows this information:

Items needed, 40 whitewall steel belted radial tires, size P205/70R14. Needed within 30 days. Signed by E. G. Hanson, clerk in inventory for replacement parts and approved by H. A. Agnew, supervisor of replacement parts.

List the steps that should be taken within the purchasing department.

sample problem solution

1. Determine that the two signatures (person signing and person approving) are by authorized persons and are authentic.
2. Determine whether this item has been ordered before. If so, who was the supervisor? Since no brand name was specified, the person requesting the order should be contacted to find out whether any brand is acceptable. Also, compare credit terms offered by different companies. Use this analysis to determine which supplier is best.
3. Fill out the usual form for the purchase order.
4. Mail original to supplier and distribute copies to the receiving and accounting departments.
5. File one copy in the purchasing department.
6. Fill in the control number of the purchase order used in a log to account for consecutive numbering.

review exercises

1. Explain the meaning of each of these credit terms: (a) 2/10, n/30; (b) 1/15, n/45; (c) n/60.

2. A purchase of merchandise for $5,000 is made with credit terms of 2/10, n/30. The company does not have the cash available to take the discount but can borrow cash from the bank at 15 percent interest. Show computations to determine the cost of borrowing and savings from taking the cash discount. Should the loan be taken to earn the discount?

3. List the different elements of information that a purchase order should show.

• task UNDERSTAND SHIPPING TERMS OF THE SUPPLIER.

Timing the recognition of *Purchases* and related *Accounts Payable* is very important, especially near the beginning and ending of the accounting period. In the same way, timing the recognition of *Sales* and *Accounts Receivable* is equally important to the seller. These supplier problems will be dealt with in Chapter 6. Also, whether to include or exclude items from merchandise is a timing problem for both buyer and seller. These inventory items and the related cost of goods sold will be discussed in Chapter 14.

Freight costs

Shipping terms may be stated as **FOB** (free on board) **shipping point** or **FOB destination.** These terms appear on the invoice and indicate the party immediately responsible for paying the common carrier (railroad, trucking firm, barge company, or airline) transporting the goods between the seller and the buyer. An easy way to remember how shipping terms work is to think about what *free on board* really means. Shipping terms indicate who does not have to pay the freight. To illustrate, *FOB shipping point* means that the freight is free to the shipper. Therefore, the buyer must be responsible for the freight cost. In contrast, *FOB destination* means that the buyer is not responsible for the merchandise until it is transferred from the common carrier to the firm's property (loading dock or truck).

To emphasize these terms, Illustration 5-4 shows how FOB shipping point works.

illustration 5-4
FOB shipping point.

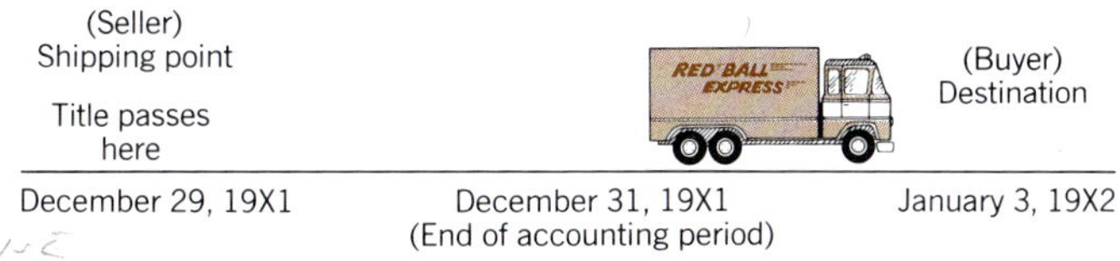

Since the freight costs are "free" to the shipper, the buyer assumes ownership (and freight costs) on December 29 when the goods are transferred to the common carrier. On the other hand, if goods are shipped FOB destination, then ownership (along with the freight costs) passes on January 3, 19X2, when the merchandise arrives at the destination. This situation is shown in Illustration 5-5.

illustration 5-5
FOB destination.

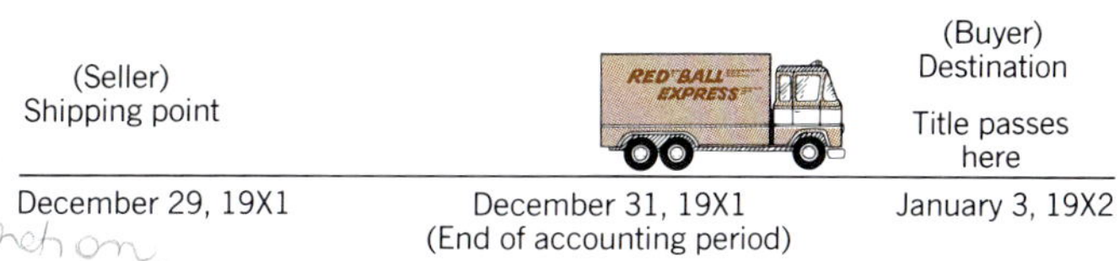

For convenience, the seller may pay the freight charges for the buyer on shipping terms of FOB shipping point and add the freight cost to the invoice when the bill is sent. As an illustration, assume that St. Paul Wholesale (shipping point) ships merchandise FOB shipping point to Denver, Inc. (destination). Since it is "free on board" at the shipping point, the destination should pay the freight charges. St. Paul Wholesale pays Freighter Truckline $125 to handle the $2,000 of merchandise. When St. Paul Wholesale bills Denver, Inc., the invoice will total $2,125.

sample problem The Big 4 Company orders 20 cartons of No. 2 paper cups from the Hefty Supply Company. Hefty pays the trucking company for the shipping cost, but the shipment is made FOB shipping point. Answer the following questions: (1) When does the title pass to Big 4? (2) Who owns the paper cups during shipment? (3) How are the freight charges handled?

sample problem solution

1. Title passes when items are placed on the truck.
2. Big 4 owns the goods during shipment.
3. Hefty pays the trucking company, and this amount is included as a part of the total of accounts receivable from Big 4. Big 4 would include the freight costs as a part of the total accounts payable to Hefty. The freight charges would be shown on Hefty's sales invoice broken out separately or as a part of product cost.

review exercises

4. Supply Limited ships 10 pairs of brake linings to Import Repairs using FOB destination. The shipment is made on December 30 and arrives at the Import Repairs warehouse on January 4. Supply Limited's accounting period ends on December 31. Answer these questions: (1) When does title pass? (2) Which party owns the items at the end of the accounting period? (3) On what date would the purchase be recorded by Import Repairs?

5. Happy Hollow Company orders 16 pairs of blue auto floor mats from Vinyl Manufacturing Company on June 21. The items are shipped FOB shipping point and arrive on July 1. The accounting period ends on December 31 for both companies. Since the shipment is completed in the middle of the accounting period, what importance should be placed on the FOB shipping point notation?

• task GIVEN THE SOURCE DOCUMENT, RECORD ACCOUNTING ENTRIES FOR BUYING MERCHANDISE ON ACCOUNT

Recording transactions

Usually, the purchase of merchandise is recorded upon receipt of the **sales invoice** from the seller. On most occasions, the sales invoice is mailed separately from the shipment of merchandise. An example of the sales invoice is shown in Illustration 5-6.

illustration 5-6 sales invoice. (courtesy of Wilson Jones Company)

STRIPS GALORE COMPANY
P.O. Box 101, Highway 32
Boma, Tennessee 38577

Invoice

No. 6501
Date January 18, 19X1
Shipped to Same

Sold To Jennison Company
P.O. Box 789, Highway 32
Happy Hollow, TN 38579

Your Order No.	Our Order No.	Salesman	
123862	899021	F. J.	
Date Shipped	**Shipped VIA**	**F.O.B.**	**Terms**
1/24/X1	Overnight Delivery Service	Shipping Point	2/10, n/30

Quantity Ordered	Quantity Shipped	Stock Number Description	Price	Per	Amount
60	60	X-3 Wide High Strips	$10 –	ea	600 –
		Freight			50 –
					650 –

Wilson Jones
GRAYLINE FORM 44-401 3-PART
© 1974 PRINTED IN U.S.A.

Original / Invoice

The sales invoice gives the information needed to record the purchases:

JOURNAL — Page 1

Date		Description	P.R.	Dr.	Cr.
19X1 Jan.	21	Purchases		600 –	
		Freight-In		50 –	
		Accounts Payable			650 –
		To record purchases of			
		merchandise; 2/10, n/30			
		FOB shipping point			

Notice that we have introduced a new account—*Freight-In*. *Freight-In* is often recorded separately, as shown above, if the amount is listed as an additional amount on the sales invoice. *Freight-In* is shown on the income statement as an addition to *Purchases*. This separate recording and presentation gives more detailed data and may be used by managers to compare and analyze costs. If the freight charge is included as a part of the total, it is recorded as *Purchases*. The income statement presentation of these items will be shown in a later chapter. Since freight is part of the cost of buying merchandise, *Freight-In* is a *cost* account.

When the merchandise is received, the shipment is inspected to verify the number and condition of items ordered. Also, the receiving clerk compares the order to determine whether the items received are the items ordered. A **receiving report** is filled out as shown in Illustration 5-7.

Date	P.O. No. or Returned Goods	VIA	Freight Bill No.	Prepaid	Collect
Jan. 21, 19X1			25201A		

Received From: Strips Galore Company

Address: P.O. Box 101, Highway 32, Crossville, TN 38555

Quantity	Item No.	Description	Remarks, Condition, etc.
60	X-3	Wide High Strips	As Ordered—ok

No. Packages	Weight	Received By	Checked By	Delivered To
2	62	JAW	HEN	

illustration 5-7 receiving report.

illustration 5-8 flow of receiving report.

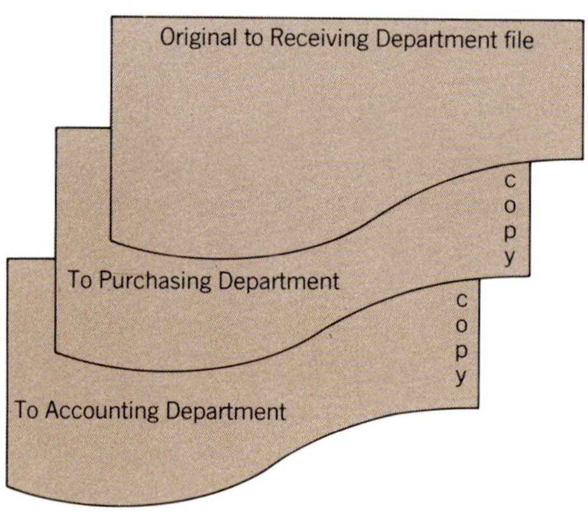

The original receiving report is filed in the receiving department, and copies are sent to purchasing and accounting. In the accounting department, the copy of the receiving report is matched and attached to the purchase order copy and the sales invoice received from the supplier. See Illustration 5-8 for the flow of a receiving report. The terms of purchase and the date of the invoice are examined to find out the date of payment necessary to take the cash discount as discussed earlier in this chapter. On the determined payment date, documents are processed for payment. On the basis of a copy of the check and the supporting documentation, the journal entry is made. A third cost account, *Purchases Discount,* is introduced in this entry. Since *Purchases Discounts* reduces the cost of the merchandise, it is classified as a *contra (minus) cost* account. Here is the complete entry:

JOURNAL Page 1

Date		Description	P.R.	Dr.	Cr.
19X1					
Jan.	30	Accounts Payable		650 -	
		Purchases Discounts			12 -
		Cash			638 -
		To record payment of sales			
		invoice number 6501			
		less 2 percent discount			
		plus freight charge of $50-			

Note that no discount is taken on the $50 freight charge since this $50 is paid in full by the seller to the freight carrier. The documents supporting this payment and attached to the check copy should be marked or perforated to prevent duplicate payment in the future.

Subsidiary ledger and controlling account

When purchasing merchandise and other items on account, you must know how much is owed each creditor. Placing each purchase on account as a credit to *Accounts Payable* gives us only the grand total owed to all creditors. Managers need to know how much is due each creditor. To provide this additional information, a separate ledger is needed. To identify the main ledger that we have been dealing with, we shall refer to it as the **general ledger.** The new supporting ledger is known as a **subsidiary ledger.** This ledger account has three columns with space provided for the name and address. Since creditors are added or deleted periodically, it is not practical to assign each account a number. Instead, the accounts are kept in alphabetical order. In this way, *Carry-Out Wholesale* can be added between *Carlson's TV* and *Carter Electric* without any difficulty.

To maintain control of the various creditor accounts, we must have an account in the general ledger that summarizes this separate subsidiary ledger. This account, which you are already familiar with, is *Accounts Payable.* After all posting has been completed, the balance of the *Accounts Payable* account must be the same as the total when all the creditors' balances are added together. To illustrate this relationship between the controlling account and the subsidiary ledger, assume for simplicity that Markum Company has only three creditors with balances at the end of the fiscal period.

Accounts Payable Ledger		General Ledger
Company W	$ 600	Accounts Payable $1,000
Company Y	200	
Company Z	200	
Total	$1,000	

If posting has been done properly, *Accounts Payable* should have a matching balance of $1,000. In this way, *Accounts Payable* controls the subsidiary ledger. Hence, the general ledger account is known as a **control** or **controlling** account.

To see how the subsidiary account is added to the journal entry, let's use the entry made in the preceding section. Since the merchandise was bought from Strips Galore Company, this information will be added to the entry.

JOURNAL Page 1

Date		Description	P.R.	Dr.	Cr.
19X1 Jan.	21	Purchases		600 –	
		Freight-In		50 –	
		Accounts Payable/Strips Galore Co.			650 –
		Bought merchandise from			
		Strips Galore Company.			

On January 30 a payment of $638 made within the discount period is reflected in the following entry:

JOURNAL Page 1

Date		Description	P.R.	Dr.	Cr.
19X1 Jan.	30	Accounts Payable/Strips Galore Company		650 –	
		Purchases Discounts			12 –
		Cash			638 –
		Paid for merchandise			
		within discount period.			

sample problem The Pretex Company purchases 10 cartons of dry roasted peanuts from Wholesale Foods. The sales invoice from Wholesale is dated May 10 and shows terms of 2/10, n/30, $20 a carton, and a freight charge of $24, FOB shipping point. Pretex follows a policy of taking all possible cash discounts. Prepare journal entries to record the purchase and the payment on May 19.

sample problem solution

May 12	Purchases	200	
	Freight-In	24	
	Accounts Payable/ Wholesale Foods		224
19	Accounts Payable/ Wholesale Foods	224	
	Purchases Discounts		4
	Cash		220

review exercises

6. Gray Company ships 20 television games to Grand Amusement Company for $4,000 plus $63 freight, FOB destination. Explain the meaning of FOB destination and calculate the total amount Grand Amusement should send Gray Company.
7. Major Discount Company's purchasing department receives a purchase requisition from the automotive section to order various sizes of oil filters from Filten, Inc. Briefly describe the process of ordering and receiving these items including the different documents involved.
8. Record the purchase and payment within the discount period for items described in Exercise 7 above if the items cost $430 with freight of $63 on FOB destination and 2/10, n/30 terms.

• task POST JOURNAL ENTRIES TO THE GENERAL AND SUBSIDIARY LEDGERS

The posting process

Posting to the general ledger accounts would be done the same way as you did it earlier, with one major difference—posting to the subsidiary ledger. To emphasize this difference, let's continue with the Strips Galore Company illustration. In Illustration 5-9, you can see that the credit of $650 must be posted twice—first to the *Accounts Payable* account and then to Strips Galore Company.

illustration 5-9
posting involving a subsidiary ledger.

JOURNAL — Page 17

Date		Description	P.R.	Dr.	Cr.
19X1 Jan.	21	Purchases	41	600 –	
		Freight-In	42	50 –	
		Accounts Payable/Strips Galore Company	21/✓		650 –

Date		Description	P.R.	Dr.	Cr.
	30	Accounts Payable/Strips Galore Company	21/✓	650 –	
		Purchases Discounts	44		12 –
		Cash	11		638 –

P.24

The posting reference column has space only for posting to one place, so the accounting clerk must draw in a diagonal line that provides two posting reference spaces for the credit. Since the accounts payable subsidiary ledger account does not have a page number, the posting process is indicated by a check mark (√) in the journal. The same procedure would be followed in posting the January 30 entry. Note, in Illustration 5-10, the posting of the two journal entries to Strips Galore Company's subsidiary ledger account.

Schedule of accounts payable

The total of all the accounts in the accounts payable subsidiary ledger should be compared with the balance of the controlling account at the end of the accounting period and at other regular intervals such as at the end of each month. To illustrate how this information is gathered, assume that on January 31, 19X1, the following accounts appear in the subsidiary ledger:

illustration 5-10
accounts payable subsidiary ledger.

Anson Limited
113 Broad Street
City

Date		Explanation	P.R.	Dr.	Cr.	Balance
19X1 Jan.	1		3		800 –	800 –
	9		6	400 –		400 –
	18		16		225 –	625 –
	26		21	300 –		325 –

Canton Company
1413 Park Avenue
City

Date		Explanation	P.R.	Dr.	Cr.	Balance
19X1 Jan.	8		5		500 –	500 –

Effie Business Systems
412 Main Street
Livingston, TN 38570

Date		Explanation	P.R.	Dr.	Cr.	Balance
19X1 Jan.	7		5		350 –	350 –
	13		10	350 –		–0–
	22		18		810 –	810 –

Mason Company
Box 914
City

Date		Explanation	P.R.	Dr.	Cr.	Balance
19X1 Jan.	15		14		770 –	770 –
	24		20	770 –		–0–

Strips Galore Company
PO Box 101
Crossville, TN 38555

Date		Explanation	P.R.	Dr.	Cr.	Balance
19X1 Jan.	21		17		650 –	650 –
	30		24	650 –		–0–

Using the accounts above, the accounting clerk for Jennison Company would prepare the schedule of accounts payable shown in Illustration 5-11. A creditor who has a zero balance should not be listed on the schedule.

illustration 5-11
schedule of accounts payable.

Jennison Company
Schedule of Accounts Payable
January 31, 19X1

Anson Limited	325 –	
Canton Company	500 –	
Effie Business Systems	810 –	
Total Accounts Payable		1635 –

Accounts Payable — Account No. 21

Date	Item	P.R.	Dr.	Cr.	Balance Dr.	Balance Cr.
19X1 Jan. 1		3		800 –		800 –
7		5		350 –		1150 –
8		5		500 –		1650 –
9		6	400 –			1250 –
13		10	350 –			900 –
15		14		770 –		1670 –
18		16		225 –		1895 –
21		17		650 –		2545 –
22		18		810 –		3355 –
24		20	770 –			2585 –
26		21	300 –			2385 –
30		24	650 –			1635 –

Once the schedule has been prepared, a comparison should be made between the balance of the controlling account, *Accounts Payable,* and the total of all the subsidiary accounts to see whether they agree. If the two numbers do not agree, postings and journal entries must be examined until the error is located. *It is not necessary to prepare a formal statement to make this comparison.* All that is needed is to run an adding machine tape of the subsidiary ledger balances after all postings have been completed. The formal statement is primarily to assist managers in a review of debts to various creditors.

sample problem On August 7, 19X1, the Babco Company purchases merchandise from Yates Corporation on credit with terms of 1/15, n/30. The purchase is for $3,600, including the freight charge. Payment is made on August 20, 19X1. Journalize the purchase and the payment. Post to the *Accounts Payable* account and to the accounts payable subsidiary ledger.

sample problem solution

Date	Account	Dr.	Cr.
Aug. 7	Purchases	3,600	
	Accounts Payable/Yates Corporation		3,600
20	Accounts Payable/Yates Corporation	3,600	
	Purchases Discounts		36
	Cash		3,564

GENERAL LEDGER

Accounts Payable

19X1						
Aug	7			3,600		3,600
	20		3,600			0

ACCOUNTS PAYABLE LEDGER

Yates Corporation

19X1					
Aug.	7			3,600	3,600
	20		3,600		0

review exercises

9. The relationship between the *Accounts Payable* general ledger controlling account and the accounts payable subsidiary ledger is important to every business. Describe this relationship and state why it is important.

10. The Abble Company purchases merchandise in the amount of $4,000 from Cainn Limited on credit with terms stated as 2/10, n/30. Journalize and post the purchase and the payment within the discount period.

• task RECORD PURCHASES IN A PURCHASES JOURNAL

Special journals

We have used a single journal to record all of the firm's transactions. In the business world, very few businesses record all of their transactions in one journal. Journals are specially designed to handle cash receipts, cash payments, purchases, and sales. These journals are known as **special journals.** The two-column journal that you are familiar with will still be used to record transactions that do not fit one of the special journals. We will refer to this journal as the *general journal* to distinguish it from special journals.

Special journals have two advantages: they save labor and make it possible to divide accounting duties. Labor is saved primarily in the posting process, which will be described in the illustrations and discussion for this task. In medium and large businesses, one or two persons may work full time on purchases and accounts payable. If a general journal is used, it would be difficult for several accounting clerks to work with the one journal. Using special journals makes it possible to assign accounting duties to more than one clerk.

Single-column purchases journal

A single-column **purchases journal** is limited to handling only purchases of merchandise on credit. Cash purchases of merchandise or purchases of other items on credit or for cash would be entered in other journals. A single-column purchases journal is shown in Illustration 5-12.

illustration 5-12 posting from the purchases journal.

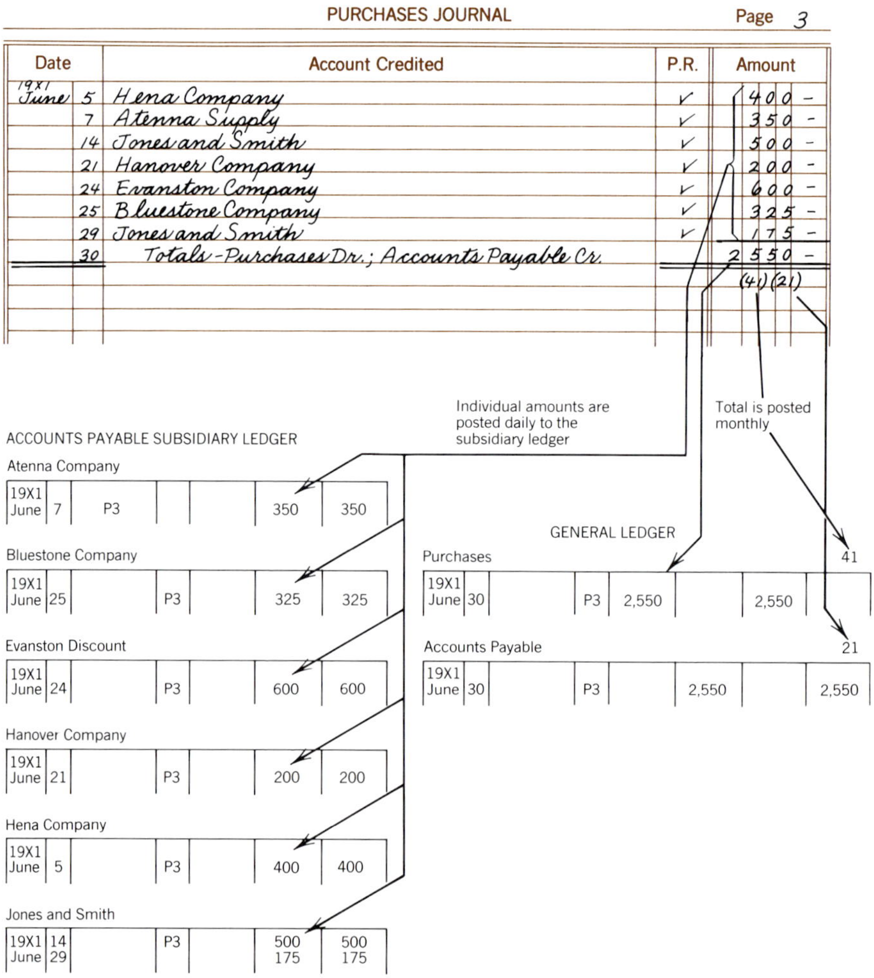

Actually, every transaction recorded in the single-column purchases journal is a debit to *Purchases* and a credit to *Accounts Payable* (and the creditor). Since the debit and credit to these two accounts are always the same, having two amount columns is unnecessary. Also, a great deal of posting can be saved by posting only once to the general ledger. This can be done by posting the total of the amount column once to the debit side of *Purchases* and once to the credit side of *Accounts Payable*. If a firm has 80 entries in the purchases journal, this approach saves 79 postings. The accounting clerk will have to provide the parentheses to indicate the posting of totals as part of the posting process.

Now let's see how the creditors' accounts are handled in Illustration 5-12. Even though the credits are posted as a total to *Accounts Payable,* we must post each entry individually. From now on, we will be using more than one journal, so we will have to use a posting reference more complete than a page number. In this illustration, you can see that this is the third page of the purchases journal. To identify this page in the ledger, we will use "P3" in the posting reference columns of (1) the creditors' accounts in the subsidiary ledger and (2) the two accounts affected in the general ledger. As we mentioned earlier, since the subsidiary ledger accounts do not have numbers, a check mark must be used in the journal to show that the posting has been done.

Multicolumn purchases journal

Some businesses prefer to use a special journal to handle not only purchases of merchandise on account but other purchases as well. The design of the multicolumn purchases journal dictates how much can be included. The purchases journal shown in Illustration 5-13 would be used for the purchase of merchandise, store supplies, or office supplies on account. By adding a miscellaneous (or sundry) column, then the purchase of anything on credit can be recorded in the purchases journal. There are drawbacks to having too many columns, so we will use the design in Illustration 5-13 whenever a multicolumn purchases journal is needed. The *Sundry Accounts Dr.* column is used as a miscellaneous column for recording debits to accounts that do not have special columns.

PURCHASES JOURNAL — Page 9

Date		Account Credited	P.R.	Accounts Payable Cr.	Purchases Dr.	Store Supplies Dr.	Office Supplies Dr.	Sundry Accounts Dr.		
								Account	P.R.	Amount
19X1 July	10	Marshall Company	✓	185 25				Office Equipment	16	185 25
	12	Henderson Discount	✓	214 75	214 75					
	14	Jackson Limited	✓	38 42		38 42				
	16	Hillboro Company	✓	82 11			82 11			
	19	Brown Company	✓	12 88		12 88				
	29	Marshall Company	✓	640 50	640 50					
	31			1,173 91	855 25	51 30	82 11			185 25
				(21)	(41)	(13)	(14)			(✓)

illustration 5-13 multiple-column purchase journal.

Each special column for *Accounts Payable, Purchases, Store Supplies,* and *Office Supplies* must be posted separately each month. The numbers shown below the total for each special column are the numbers of the accounts in the general ledger. In multicolumn journals, as in single-column journals, individual amounts for each business should be posted daily to the accounts payable subsidiary ledger.

sample problem A list of items bought on credit by the Penn South Company are shown below.

Aug. 5 Bought merchandise for $600 on credit, terms 2/10, n/30, from Henson Discount.

10 Bought store supplies for $82 on credit, terms 1/10, n/30, from Jordan Supply.

14 Bought office supplies for $58 on credit, terms n/30, from Erwin Wholesale Company.

19 Bought merchandise for $750 on credit, terms 1/15, n/30, from Conway Company.

22 Bought office supplies for $63 on credit, terms n/30, from Erwin Wholesale Company.

28 Bought merchandise for $350 on credit, terms 2/10, n/30, from Henson Discount.

Instructions Record the transactions above on page 12 of a multicolumn purchases journal.

sample problem solution

PURCHASES JOURNAL — Page 12

Date		Account Credited	P.R.	Accounts Payable Cr.	Purchases Dr.	Store Supplies Dr.	Office Supplies Dr.	Sundry Accounts Dr. Account	P.R.	Amount
19X1 Aug.	5	Henson Discount	✓	600 –	600 –					
	10	Jordan Supply	✓	82 –		82 –				
	14	Erwin Wholesale Company	✓	58 –			58 –			
	19	Conway Company	✓	750 –	750 –					
	22	Erwin Wholesale Company	✓	63 –			63 –			
	28	Henson Discount	✓	350 –	350 –					
	31			1903 –	1700 –	82 –	121 –			–0–
				(21)	(41)	(13)	(14)			

review exercises **11.** The Jamestown Company has the following transactions for the week of April 10 through 16:

April 10 Purchased merchandise on credit, $600.

11 Purchased merchandise for cash, $725.

12 Purchased office supplies on credit, $56.

13 Purchased store supplies on credit, $25.
14 Paid for the April 10 purchase.
15 Sold merchandise on credit, $84.
16 Paid salaries to employees, $680.

Instructions List by month and day the transactions that are entered in a single-column purchases journal.

• task PREPARE ENTRIES FOR THE RETURN OF MERCHANDISE AND ALLOWANCES FOR DAMAGED ITEMS

Debit and credit memoranda

Adjustments to *Purchases* and *Accounts Payable* are often made for returns of merchandise or allowances for merchandise. **Returns** may be made on the basis of agreements between the buyer and seller. **Allowances** may be granted because goods are damaged or do not meet specifications. The business document used to notify the other party of the return or allowance is called a memorandum. If the buyer fills out the document, it is called a **debit memorandum.** The word *debit* on the memorandum shows that *Accounts Payable* will be reduced. If the seller completes the memorandum, it is called a **credit memorandum** since a credit reduces *Accounts Receivable.* The buyer usually initiates the document; therefore, we will emphasize the debit memorandum. A debit memorandum is shown in Illustration 5-14.

illustration 5-14
debit memorandum.

DEBIT MEMORANDUM

No. 29

JENNISON COMPANY
P.O. Box 789, Highway 32
Happyhollow, TN 38

TO: STRIPS GALORE COMPANY
P.O. Box 101, Highway 32
Bomhi, TN 38577

DATE: Jan. 24, 19X1

WE DEBIT YOUR ACCOUNT AS FOLLOWS:

10 units X-3 Wide High Strips at $10 each. Merchandise is defective as verified by your representative M. Gordon— $100.

Recording returns and allowances

The debit memorandum is mailed from the buyer to the seller. A copy of the memorandum is sent to the shipping department, and a copy is kept by the accounting department. If the memorandum shows a return of merchandise, the shipping department accepts this document as authorization to return the goods. The accounting department records the debit memorandum and reduces the subsidiary ledger account. See Illustration 5-15 for the flow of debit memorandum documents. The journal entry made by the buyer for the debit memorandum follows:

GENERAL JOURNAL — Page 1

Date		Description	P.R.	Dr.	Cr.
19X1					
Jan.	24	Accounts Payable/Strips Galore Company		100 –	
		Purchases Returns & Allowances			100 –
		To record debit memorandum			
		No. 29 for defective merchandise			

This entry is recorded in the general journal but *not* in the purchases journal. Some accountants simply credit *Purchases* for the memorandum; but using *Purchases Returns and Allowances* gives the owner more information. This contra cost account is deducted from *Purchases* on the income statement. Let's pause for a moment here to see where we stand with cost accounts. We now have two positive cost accounts—*Purchases* and *Freight-In,* and two negative cost accounts—*Purchases Discounts* and *Purchases Returns and Allowances.* In a later chapter we will show you how these accounts are reported on an income statement.

Now let's continue with the Strips Galore illustration. With the return of part of the original purchase on January 24, Jennison Company owes

illustration 5-15
distribution of the debit memorandum.

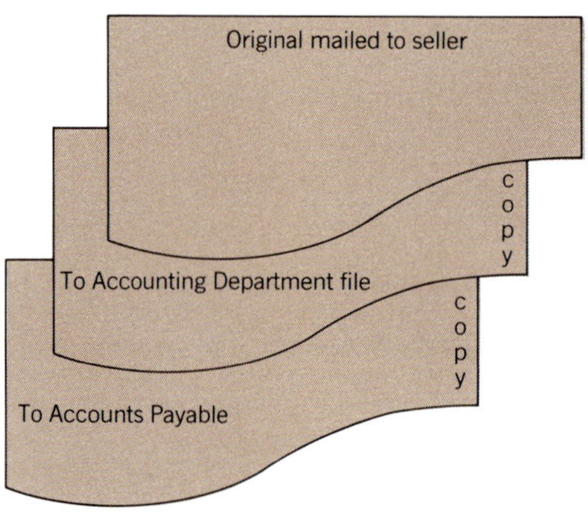

only $550 ($600 − $100 + freight of $50). By paying within the discount period, the purchaser is allowed to reduce payment by $10 ($500 × 2%). It is very important that you understand two points here: (1) the discount is allowed only on the merchandise purchased and kept and (2) the discount is not allowed on the freight charge. When the payment is made on January 28, the following entry would be needed:

GENERAL JOURNAL — Page 1

Date		Description	P.R.	Dr.	Cr.
19X1 Jan	28	Accounts Payable/Strips Galore Company		550 -	
		Purchases Discounts			10
		Cash			540
		Payment on account			

sample problem The Sneva Company has the following balance in *Accounts Payable* accounts at June 1, 19X3:

Accounts Payable, general ledger	$900
Accounts Payable, subsidiary accounts:	
Ferguson Company	$200
Genny Company	300
Lonny Company	400
Total	$900

All purchases are bought with terms of 2/10, n/30, FOB shipping point. Transactions for the month of June, 19X3 follow:

June 5 Paid the Ferguson account less 2% discount.

7 Bought merchandise from Lonny Company for $900 plus freight of $100.

9 Paid Lonny the $400 balance within the discount period.

10 Paid Genny Company the $300 balance within the discount period. A freight charge of $40 is included in the $300.

12 Issued a debit memorandum for $200 to Lonny Company for return of merchandise on the June 7 transaction.

16 Paid the Lonny Company after deducting for the debit memo and discount.

25 Bought merchandise from the Ferguson Company for $1,200 plus freight of $80.

28 Bought merchandise from the Genny Company for $800. No separate freight charge is specified on the invoice.

Instructions

(a) Record all transactions in the general journal.

(b) Prepare a schedule to compare the total of the subsidiary accounts with the general ledger balance at June 30, 19X1.

sample problem solution

(a)

			Debit	Credit
June	5	Accounts Payable/Ferguson Company	$ 200	
		Purchases Discounts		$ 4
		Cash		196
	7	Purchases	900	
		Freight-In	100	
		Accounts Payable/Lonny Company		1,000
	9	Accounts Payable/Lonny Company	400	
		Purchases Discounts		8
		Cash		392
	10	Accounts Payable/Genny Company	300	
		Purchases Discounts		5.20
		Cash		294.80
	12	Accounts Payable/Lonny Company	200	
		Purchases Returns and Allowances		200
	16	Accounts Payable/Lonny Company	800	
		Purchases Discounts		14
		Cash		786
	25	Purchases	1,200	
		Freight-In	80	
		Accounts Payable/Ferguson Company		1,280
	28	Purchases	800	
		Accounts Payable/Genny Company		800

(b) Comparison of general ledger and subsidiary:

Accounts Payable, general ledger		$2,080
Accounts Payable, subsidiary:		
Ferguson Company	$1,280	
Genny Company	800	
Total		$2,080

review exercises

12. A return or allowance for merchandise may be a debit or credit memorandum. What does the debit or credit part of the heading mean for the accounting records?

13. Buyer Corporation receives merchandise from Seller Company with an invoice price of $2,200 with credit terms of 1/15, n/45. Buyer Corporation, at a later date, issues a debit memorandum for $200. The payment is made within the discount period. Prepare the general journal entries for the purchase, debit memorandum, and payment.

Flow chart

The following flow chart shows the steps in purchasing merchandise discussed in this chapter.

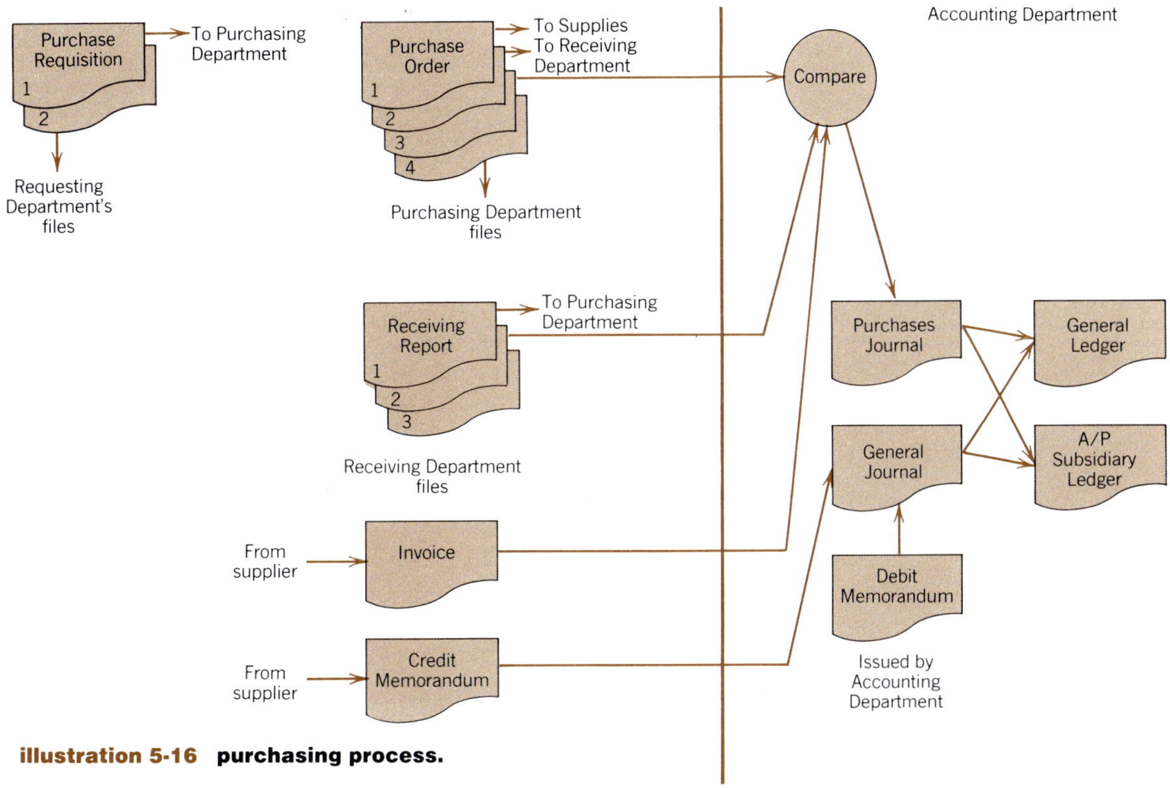

illustration 5-16 purchasing process.

chapter highlights

In this chapter we have covered these areas of study:

- Handling a purchase requisition.
- Handling a purchase order.
- Using various shipping terms.
- Recording the journal entries for buying merchandise.
- Posting journal entries to the general ledger and subsidiary ledgers.
- Handling debit and credit memoranda.

check figures for review exercises

1. Terms of 2/10, n/30 mean that a 2% discount is allowed if an invoice is paid within 10 days from its date, but payment is expected within 30 days with no discount. Terms of 1/15, n/45 mean that a 1% discount is allowed if the invoice is paid within 15 days from its date or payment within 45 days with no discount. Terms of n/60 mean that no discount is allowed, but payment is expected within 60 days from date of the invoice.
2. Savings, $100; cost, $40.83; yes, the loan should be taken.
3. (a) Company order items
   (b) Number of purchase order
   (c) Date of order
   (d) Method of shipment
   (e) Terms of shipment
   (f) Terms of credit sale
   (g) Delivery date
   (h) Quantity ordered
   (i) Description of items ordered
   (j) Unit price
   (k) Total amount
4. (1) When goods are delivered
   (2) Supply Limited, the seller
   (3) As of January 4
5. The shipping terms *FOB shipping point* indicate that the buyer is obligated to absorb the freight charges since the buyer owns the goods during shipment.
6. *FOB destination* indicates that the seller should absorb the freight cost. Grand Amusement should pay only $4,000.
7. The purchasing department completes the purchase order and distributes various copies if the requisition is in order. When goods are received, the receiving department makes an independent count, fills out a receiving report, and distributes various copies to departments. When necessary documents are compared, the payment is made. These business documents—sales invoice, purchase order, and receiving report—serve to justify the payment.
8.

Purchases	$430.00	
Accounts Payable/Filter's, Inc.		$430.00
(The seller absorbs freight costs.)		
Accounts Payable/Filter's, Inc.	430.00	
Purchases Discounts		8.60
Cash		421.40

9. The general ledger control account shows totals for all accounts payable. The subsidiary ledger shows details for each individual supplier. The total of the accounts in the subsidiary should agree with the bal-

ance in the control account. The subsidiary is necessary for accurate and detailed records for each creditor.

10.

Purchases	$4,000	
Accounts Payable/Cainn Limited		$4,000
Accounts Payable/Cainn Limited	4,000	
Purchases Discounts		80
Cash		3,920

11. April 10 transaction

12. A debit memo is issued by the buyer, and it means a reduction in *Accounts Payable.* A credit memorandum is issued by the seller, and it means a reduction in *Accounts Receivable.*

13.

Purchases	$2,200	
Accounts Payable/Seller Company		$2,200
Accounts Payable/Seller Company	200	
Purchases Returns and Allowances		200
Accounts Payable/Seller Company	2,000	
Purchases Discount		20
Cash		1,980

key terms

The following important terms are discussed in Chapter 5 and are defined in the Glossary at the end of the book.

allowances
cash discount
controlling accounts
credit memorandum
credit terms
debit memorandum
FOB destination
FOB shipping point
general ledger
merchandise
purchases journal
purchase order
purchase requisition
receiving report
returns
sales invoice
special journals
subsidiary ledger

questions

1. What is a purchase requisition, and what information is shown on it?
2. What is meant by credit terms? Give two examples of credit terms.
3. What is a purchase order, and what information is included on this document?
4. How many copies of the purchase order should be made, and to whom are these copies sent?
5. Explain the meaning and importance of these shipping terms: *FOB shipping point* and *FOB destination.*

6. If the seller pays the freight charges to the common carrier and the buyer absorbs the freight costs, how is this transfer handled on the seller's records?
7. What does the term *merchandise* mean?
8. Under what conditions is the freight charge debited to *Freight-In* by the buyer?
9. What item(s) is (are) subject to the cash discount?
10. What is the importance of the receiving report to the business?
11. What is meant by accounts payable subsidiary ledger?
12. What is the control account for the creditors' subsidiary ledger?
13. What type of account is *Purchases Returns and Allowances?*
14. Why is the *Purchases Returns and Allowances* account used?
15. What is a debit memorandum? Credit memorandum?
16. What are the advantages of special journals, and why do we use them?
17. What type of transaction can be entered in a single-column purchases journal?

exercises

1. What information is shown on a purchase requisition? Compare and contrast the data on a purchase order and a purchase requisition.
2. With credit terms of 2/10, n/30, at what interest rate could a purchasing business borrow money to take advantage of savings from paying within 10 days?
3. A credit purchase of $6,000 has terms of 1/10, n/45. The debtor must pay 12% interest on a loan to take the 1% discount. Compute the saving and cost of borrowing and paying during the discount period. Should the purchaser borrow and take the discount?
4. Diamond Manufacturing Company sends a purchase order for $12,000 to Star Supply for merchandise. Star Supply ships the items on December 30, FOB shipping point, adds $300 freight charges to invoice, and states the credit terms as 2/10, n/30. The shipment arrives at Diamond's warehouse unloading platform on January 4. The accounting period ends on December 31 for both businesses. Explain the situation described above for passing of title, freight charges, credit terms, and date to record the purchase.
5. Using the data in Exercise 4 above, prepare the journal entries for Diamond Manufacturing Company to record the purchase and payment of the proper amount after the discount period has passed.
6. Using the information in Exercise 4 above, assume a purchase return for $1,000 on January 6 and payment on January 8. Prepare entries for the purchase, return, and payment within the discount period. (Use both control and subsidiary accounts for the payable.)

7. Using the journal entries you made in Exercise 6 above, draw "T" accounts and post all debits and credits including both control and subsidiary accounts for the payable. Ignore posting reference notations.

8. Identify each classification below as to the type of account (asset, liability, etc.).
   (a) Freight-In
   (b) Purchases
   (c) Star Supply Company
   (d) Accounts Payable
   (e) Purchases Returns and Allowances
   (f) Purchases Discounts

9. List the different types of transactions that can be entered in a multi-column purchases journal.

problems

1. COMPETENCY TESTED The ability to prepare a purchase order.

Date—April 8, 19X1
Purchase order No. 2437

Name and address of supplier:

Peachtree Supply Company
8922 Peachtree Street, N.E.
Atlanta, GA 30309

Name and address of buyer:

Warrior Appliance Center
1213 University Drive
Tuscaloosa, AL 35401

Method of shipment—Tri-State Trucking
Term of shipment—FOB destination
Credit terms—2/10, n/30
Delivery date—no later than May 3, 19X1
Description of items—12 white, 15 cubic feet no-frost refrigerators, Model 25J1410
Unit Price—$462 per unit
Freight charge—$325

Instructions Prepare a purchase order.

2. COMPETENCY TESTED The ability to prepare a purchase order.

Date of invoice—August 10, 19X1
Purchase order No. 8227

Name and address of supplier:

Automotive Supply Corporation
9909 Buckeye Street
Cincinnati, OH 45240

Name and addresss of buyer:

All Makes Parts, Inc.
2102 Michigan Avenue
Chicago, IL 60600

Method of shipment—Jiffy Trucking Company
Terms of shipment—FOB shipping point
Credit terms—1/15, n/30
Delivery date—no later than August 30
Description of items—10 rebuilt alternators, 45 amp, part No. H 2298722
Unit price—$41 per unit
Freight charge—$93

Instructions Prepare a purchase order.

3. COMPETENCY TESTED Skill in analyzing credit terms.

For the same products, a company has the two choices below:

Choice A: Total product cost $4,600, freight cost $70, FOB shipping point, credit terms of 2/10, n/30.

Choice B: Total product cost $4,500, freight cost $70, FOB destination, credit terms of 1/15, n/45.

Assuming the purchasing company can borrow from the bank on a short-term basis (up to 90 days) at 12%, analyze the two cases by determining the lower total cost of each supplier. Considering other factors, state which choice you think is the better overall deal.

4. COMPETENCY TESTED Skill in analyzing credit terms.

For the purchase of the same items of merchandise, a company has two choices:

White Company: Total product cost $5,000, FOB destination, credit terms 2/10, n/30.

Red Company: Total product cost $5,050, FOB shipping point, credit terms 1/15, n/45.

The purchasing company has a continuing line of credit with the bank for short-term loans at 12%. Red Ball Express will deliver the goods for $110, billing the responsible party according to FOB terms. Analyze the two suppliers' total packages by determining the lower total cost and considering other factors. Which is the better deal?

5. COMPETENCY TESTED Expertise in journalizing and posting purchase transactions.

The Yellow Company had the following transactions during May, 19X1:

May 2 Purchased merchandise from Blue Company at a cost of $2,900, freight cost $100, FOB shipping point, credit terms 2/10, n/30.

5 Purchased merchandise from White Corporation at a cost of $4,100, freight cost $120, FOB destination, credit terms 1/15, n/30.

11 Paid the Blue Company for the May 2 purchase less discount.

30 Paid White Corporation for the May 5 purchase at the full price.

Instructions

(a) Journalize the transactions.

(b) Post journal entries to the general ledger and subsidiary ledger accounts.

(c) What do you think about Yellow Company paying the full amount to White Corporation on May 30?

6. COMPETENCY TESTED Expertise in journalizing and posting purchase transactions.

The Cranston Company had the following transactions for October, 19X1:

Oct. 1 Purchased merchandise from Church Corporation at a cost of $3,400, freight cost $80, FOB shipping point, credit terms 2/10, n/30.

4 Purchased merchandise from Synder Company at a cost of $5,300, freight cost $110, FOB destination, credit terms 1/15, n/45.

29 Paid Church Corporation for the October 1 purchase at full price.

Instructions

(a) Journalize the transactions.

(b) Post journal entries to general ledger and subsidiary ledger accounts.

(c) Comment on the October 29 payment to Church Corporation after the discount date.

7. COMPETENCY TESTED Skill in journalizing and posting purchasing transactions.

The Inman Company completed the following transactions during June, 19X1:

June 1 Received a sales invoice from the Bass Company with the following data shown: total price of merchandise $1,600, freight cost of $80, FOB destination, credit terms, 2/10, n/30.

3 Bought office equipment from Equipment Unlimited at a total cost of $1,800. Credit terms of 1/10, n/30 were granted.

6 Purchased merchandise from the Kyle Company at total price of $3,100 with credit terms of 2/10, n/45.

June 10 Paid the Bass Company for the June 1 transaction less discount.

11 Paid Equipment Unlimited for the June 3 transaction less the discount. (*Hint:* The discount is a reduction in the cost of the equipment.)

12 Returned goods costing $200 to the Kyle Company and issued a debit memorandum to Kyle.

15 Paid the Kyle Company for the June 6 purchase less the debit memorandum and cash discount.

21 Returned goods costing $100 to the Bass Company along with a debit memorandum. Continued business is expected with this supplier, and this amount should be debited to *Accounts Payable* even though it causes an abnormal debit balance in the account.

Instructions

(a) Prepare general journal entries for the transactions.

(b) Post these entries to general ledger and subsidiary ledger accounts.

8. COMPETENCY TESTED The ability to journalize and post purchase transactions.

The Lee Company completed the following transactions during the month of November.

Nov. 2 Received a sales invoice from the Ellis Company with the following data: total price of merchandise $2,900, freight cost $120, FOB destination, credit terms 2/10, n/30.

4 Bought a delivery truck at a total price of $9,300 and paid cash at purchase date.

5 Purchased merchandise from the Burns Company at a total price of $3,300 with credit terms of 2/10, n/45.

11 Paid the Ellis Company for the November 2 purchase less discount.

12 Issued a debit memorandum to the Burns Company for $150 for damaged goods.

14 Paid the Burns Company for the November 5 purchase less debit memorandum and cash discount.

29 Returned goods to the Ellis Company, along with a debit memorandum for $80.

Instructions

(a) Journalize all transactions.

(b) Post journal entries to the general ledger and subsidiary ledger accounts.

(c) How would you classify the debit balance in *Accounts Payable* in the balance sheet?

9. COMPETENCY TESTED Skill in entering transactions in a single-column purchases journal and a general journal.

Assume that the Davis Company uses a single-column purchases journal and a general journal. The following transactions are for October, 19X1:

Oct.	4	Purchased merchandise from Hardy Supply for $800 with credit terms of 2/10, n/30.
	6	Purchased office supplies from Pannell Limited for $95 with credit terms of n/30.
	10	Purchased merchandise from Hardy Supply for $485 with credit terms of 2/10, n/30.
	15	Paid salaries to employees for the first half of October, $1,600.
	17	Sold merchandise for cash of $995.
	18	Purchased merchandise from the Randall Company for $325 with credit terms of n/30.
	19	Paid Hardy Supply for the October 4 purchase at the full amount and for the October 10 purchase less the discount.
	23	Purchased merchandise from Hardy Supply for cash of $200.
	25	Sold merchandise on credit to Norcom, Inc. for $1,130, terms 2/10, n/30.
	26	Purchased merchandise from the Sames Company for $810 with credit terms of n/30.
	28	Purchased office supplies from Pannell Limited for $118 with credit terms of n/30.
	31	Paid salaries to employees for the second half of October, $1,600.

Instructions

(a) Record the transactions above in either a single-column purchases journal or in a general journal, whichever is more appropriate.

(b) Post the accounts payable transactions to the general ledger account and the subsidiary ledger accounts.

(c) Compare the October 31 total of the accounts in the subsidiary ledger with the balance in the general ledger *Accounts Payable.*

10. COMPETENCY TESTED Skill in entering transactions in a multicolumn purchases journal and a general journal.

The Graves Company uses a multicolumn purchases journal and a general journal. Transactions for February follow:

Feb.	3	Purchased merchandise from Crump Supply for $650 with credit terms of 2/10, n/30.
	4	Purchased store supplies from Simmons Supply for $138 with credit terms of n/30.

Feb. 6 Purchased office supplies from the Cerami Company for $163 with credit terms of 1/15, n/45.

7 Sold merchandise for cash of $900.

9 Purchased merchandise for cash of $775.

11 Purchased merchandise from Crump Supply for $895 with credit terms of 2/10, n/30.

12 Paid Crump Supply for the February 3 purchase less discount.

14 Purchased merchandise from Robinson Supply for $1,250 with credit terms of n/30.

15 Paid salaries to employees, $1,300.

20 Paid the Cerami Company for the February 6 purchase less discount.

21 Paid Crump Supply for the February 11 purchase less discount.

23 Purchased merchandise from the Thaxton Company for $490 with credit terms of 2/10, n/30.

26 Purchased office supplies from the Cerami Company for $205 with credit terms of 1/15, n/45.

27 Sold merchandise to Hall, Inc. for $1,380 with credit terms of 2/10, n/30.

28 Paid salaries to employees, $1,300.

Instructions

(a) Record the transactions above either in the multicolumn purchases journal or the general journal, whichever is more appropriate.

(b) Post the *Accounts Payable* transactions to the general ledger account and the subsidiary ledger accounts.

(c) Compare the February 28 total of the accounts in the subsidiary ledger to general ledger *Accounts Payable* account.

chapter 6
SALES AND ACCOUNTS RECEIVABLE

overall competency THE ABILITY TO ANALYZE AND RECORD SALES, RETURNS, ALLOWANCES, AND DISCOUNTS

career objectives The accounts receivable clerk should be able to keep daily sales records, prepare bills of sale and invoices, and know how to record transactions in the sales journal. Skill in handling these tasks is important to management in determining which items are preferred by customers. The accounting clerk needs competency in handling individual customer accounts so that sales and cash receipts are properly recorded. Proper accounting is needed also to deal with returns, allowances, and discounts.

When statements are mailed to customers, the clerk should be confident that the information shown on each statement is accurate. Such confidence comes from following proper accounting techniques throughout the process of recording, posting, and preparing statements. Customers who receive statements containing errors are likely to believe that the seller's operation is inefficient or dishonest.

Upon completing this chapter, you should be able to:

- PREPARE A BILL OF SALE ACCURATELY WITH INFORMATION AS TO CUSTOMER IDENTIFICATION, ITEMS SOLD, AND THE AMOUNT DUE.
- ENTER DATA FROM A SALES SLIP INTO THE SALES JOURNAL AND POST THE DATA FROM THERE TO THE GENERAL AND THE ACCOUNTS RECEIVABLE LEDGERS.
- PREPARE A CREDIT MEMORANDUM.
- JOURNALIZE AND POST THE CREDIT MEMORANDUM INFORMATION TO THE PROPER CONTROLLING AND SUBSIDIARY ACCOUNTS.

- CALCULATE SALES DISCOUNTS.
- PREPARE A SCHEDULE OF ACCOUNTS RECEIVABLE.
- PREPARE AN AGING SCHEDULE OF ACCOUNTS RECEIVABLE.
- PREPARE A STATEMENT OF ACCOUNT FOR EACH CUSTOMER WITH AN OUTSTANDING BALANCE.

Selling merchandise and services is one of the most important functions of a company. From sales dollars, companies pay current expenses such as salaries, rent, and utilities, and provide dollars to replace inventory that has been sold. After all expenses and costs have been subtracted from revenues, the amount remaining (if positive) is net income or (if negative) net loss.

If the owner is to have an accurate net income or net loss figure, careful records must be kept for both cash and credit sales. Credit sales require more record keeping effort than do cash sales since sales on account must be identified for individual customers. Later, when these customers pay, the individual's account balance must be brought up to date correctly. This analysis requires the accountant to know the discount policy of the company. This chapter will explore the competencies and tasks needed for sales and accounts receivable accounting.

• task PREPARE A SALES INVOICE

Whenever a transaction for a sale takes place, the buyer and seller must agree on the price of the merchandise, the terms of payment, and who will pay the freight charges. A sales invoice provides evidence of definite terms of the transaction, so you need to know how to prepare an invoice properly.

Billing and invoicing procedures

Cash sales records are first recorded automatically on **cash register tapes** as each sale is made. With a modern register, it is possible to identify the type of merchandise sold from inventory numbers attached to the merchandise. You may have seen such a system while checking out at a modern department store or lumber yard where the cashier seemed to be putting into the cash register quite a bit of information about each item. An example of this type of cash register tape is shown in Illustration 6-1. In contrast, sales made on credit require additional detailed record keeping, since information must be kept about the buyer, the items purchased, and

illustration 6-1
cash register tape with inventory control. (courtesy the Kroger Company)

	15	1.39
	KRO 20 MILK	1.89
	GROUND BEEF	2.92
	BSH CHIL BNS	.69
	GROUND BEEF	2.91
	B B MARG	.50
	B B MARG	.50
	NON FOOD	2.00
	PRODUCE	.69
VC	GROCERY	.40-
VC	GROCERY	.25-
	TAX DUE	3.66
	TOTAL	57.20
	CK TEND	57.20
	CHG DUE	.00

11/12/82 16:09 0893/ 6

the amount of the total sale. To keep the necessary information on credit sales, a source document must be prepared in the form of a **bill of sale** or **sales invoice.** Illustration 6-2 shows an example of a simplified bill of sale by Jayson's to S. K. Able of goods sold on account. The main parts of

illustration 6-2
bill of sale. (courtesy of Jayson's)

JAYSON'S
Tops in Fashions
West Side Shopping Center
Cookevill, Tenn.
Phone: 526-5244

CUSTOMER'S ORDER NO. 102 — DATE January 3, 19X1 ← Date sold (1)
NAME Mrs. S. K. Able ← Customer's name and address (2)
ADDRESS 740 North Street City
SOLD BY 5 — CASH — C.O.D. — CHARGE — ON ACCT 2/10 n/30 — MDSE RET'D. — PAID OUT ← Terms of sale (3)

QUAN.	DESCRIPTION	PRICE	AMOUNT
3	Pair of Hose	$2.00	$6.00
1	Hagan Dress	$64.00	$64.00
2	Blouses	$15.00	$30.00
		TAX	6.00
		TOTAL	$106.00

← Items sold (4)
← Sales tax calculation (5)
← Total bill including sales tax (6)

ALL claims and returned goods MUST be accompanied by this bill

202 — Rec'd by ____ — Printed in U.S.A.

the bill are: (1) date sold, (2) customer's name and address, (3) terms of the sale, (4) identification of the merchandise sold, (5) sales tax calculation, and (6) amount of the sale after tax.

To illustrate the procedure, assume that Mrs. Able purchased three pairs of hose at $2 per pair, one dress at $64, and two blouses at $15 each. In compliance with state law, a sales tax of 6 percent is applied to each sale of merchandise to retail customers. Refer again to Illustration 6-2 to see how the sales clerk would report all of this information. Keep this particular sale in mind throughout this chapter so that you can follow it through the recording process.

Sales invoice

A **sales invoice,** a billing showing items sold on credit, provides the same essential information as that shown on a bill of sale. Sales invoices are prepared when orders are received and sent to customers. Their purpose is to bill the customer for payment due.

Let's assume that Jayson's also sells merchandise to other companies. Since sales taxes are charged only to final consumers, they do not apply when merchandise is sold to retail stores. During January, an order is received from the Marx Company for 12 dresses at $50 each, 5 blouses at $10 each, and 10 pairs of socks at $1 per pair. This information would be recorded on a sales invoice similar to the one shown in Illustration 6-3. Note the information provided in this illustration: (1) who sold the mer-

illustration 6-3 sales invoice.

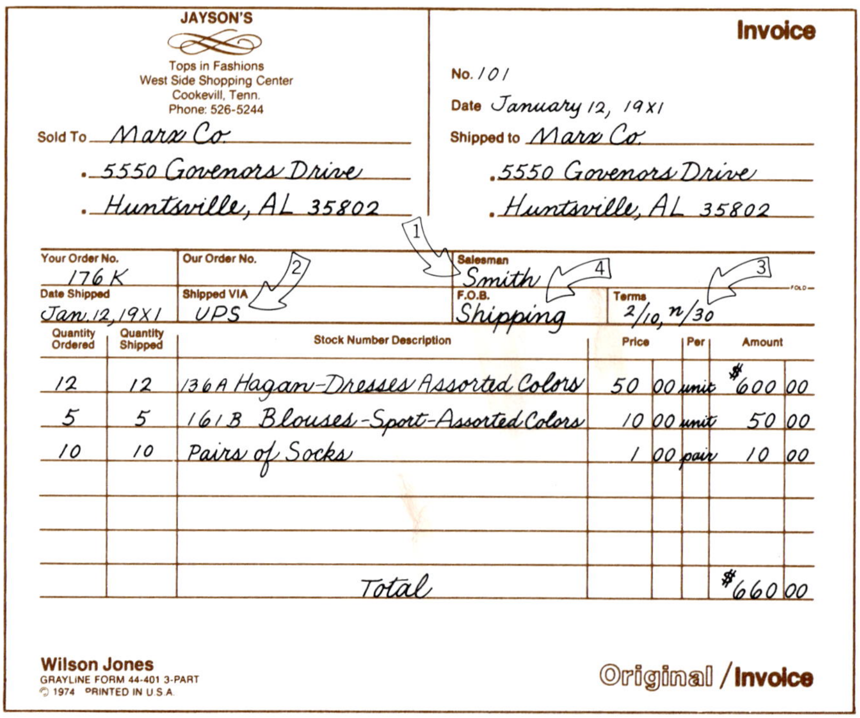
JAYSON'S
Tops in Fashions
West Side Shopping Center
Cookevill, Tenn.
Phone: 526-5244

Invoice

No. 101
Date January 12, 19X1

Sold To Marx Co.
5550 Govenors Drive
Huntsville, AL 35802

Shipped to Marx Co.
5550 Govenors Drive
Huntsville, AL 35802

Your Order No.	Our Order No.	Salesman	
176 K		Smith	
Date Shipped	**Shipped VIA**	**F.O.B.**	**Terms**
Jan. 12, 19X1	UPS	Shipping	2/10, n/30

Quantity Ordered	Quantity Shipped	Stock Number Description	Price	Per	Amount
12	12	136A Hagan–Dresses Assorted Colors	50 00	unit	$600 00
5	5	161B Blouses-Sport-Assorted Colors	10 00	unit	50 00
10	10	Pairs of Socks	1 00	pair	10 00
		Total			$660 00

Wilson Jones
GRAYLINE FORM 44-401 3-PART
© 1974 PRINTED IN U.S.A.

Original / Invoice

chandise, (2) how it was shipped, (3) the credit terms extended, and (4) the shipping terms extended.

More than one copy of many source documents is prepared. For example, Illustration 6-4 shows a possible distribution of the sales invoice to the various parties who need information to control a particular operation.

illustration 6-4
distribution of the sales invoice.

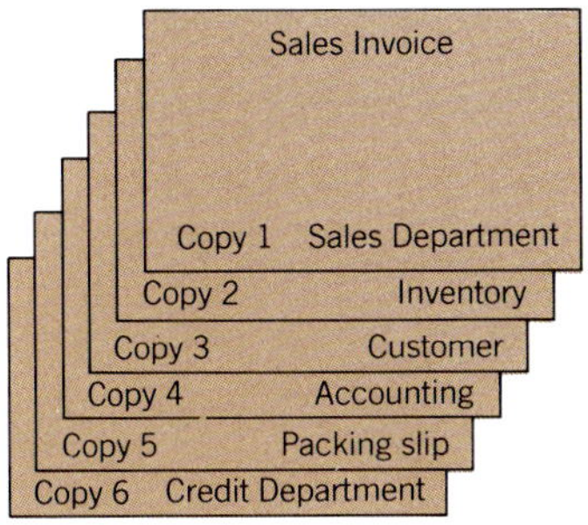

sample problem Draw a rough form of a bill of sale, then complete it for Mrs. N. M. Bass, who purchased the following items on account on January 18: one pair of shoes at $50, one pocketbook at $80, three pairs of socks at $4 each, and a belt for $8. Assume a sales tax rate of 6 percent.

sample problem solution

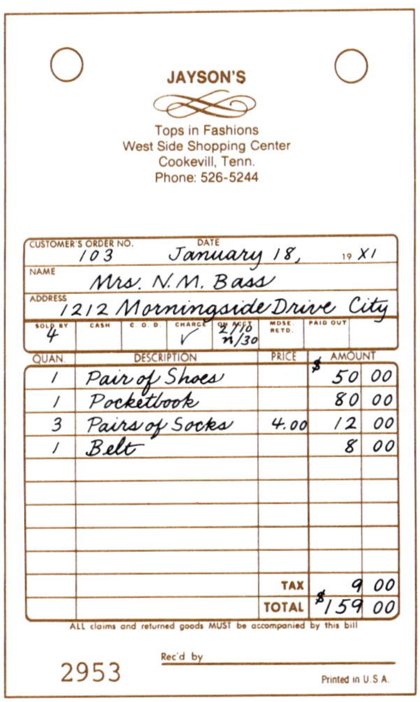

JAYSON'S

Tops in Fashions
West Side Shopping Center
Cookevill, Tenn.
Phone: 526-5244

CUSTOMER'S ORDER NO. 103 DATE January 18, 19 X1
NAME Mrs. N. M. Bass
ADDRESS 1212 Morningside Drive City

SOLD BY	CASH	C.O.D.	CHARGE	ON ACCT.	MDSE. RETD.	PAID OUT
4			✓	2/10 n/30		

QUAN.	DESCRIPTION	PRICE	AMOUNT
1	Pair of Shoes		$ 50 00
1	Pocketbook		80 00
3	Pairs of Socks	4.00	12 00
1	Belt		8 00
		TAX	9 00
		TOTAL	$159 00

ALL claims and returned goods MUST be accompanied by this bill

2953 Rec'd by

Printed in U.S.A.

review exercises

1. For a sale to Judy Wallack of four pairs of hose at $3.50, a dress at $30, and a blouse at $12.80, determine the amount of the billing. How much is the sales tax if the rate is 6 percent?
2. For a bill of sale, list the main parts that show the information needed for cash or credit sales.

3. Determine the total billing for the Dome Company from the following:

10 short leather coats at $85.70 each.
5 belts (leather) assorted colors at $6.10 each.
4 pair of slacks—brown—at $32.20 each.

• **task** USING COMPLETED SALES INVOICES AND BILLS OF SALE, PREPARE ENTRIES FOR BOTH THE GENERAL LEDGER ACCOUNTS AND THE INDIVIDUAL CUSTOMER ACCOUNTS

Accounting transactions

Sales made on account that are recorded on **bills of sales** and **sales invoices** must be entered into the accounting system. The sales information on Mrs. Able and Marx Company is transferred to the accounts receivable clerk for proper recording in the journal. Using a procedure similar to that found in Chapter 5 in dealing with creditors, the clerk posts the journal entries both to the individual customer accounts and to the controlling account. Just as *Accounts Payable* serves as the **controlling account** for the accounts payable ledger, *Accounts Receivable* is the controlling account for the accounts receivable ledger. This posting procedure allows you to keep the balance in the individual accounts of Mrs. Able and Marx Company up to date. It will also give you complete credit information about the individual or company. In addition, you will be able to determine whether the accounts are being paid on a timely basis.

The two transactions for Mrs. Able and Marx Company would be recorded in general journal form as follows:

GENERAL JOURNAL — Page 1

Date		Description	P.R.	Dr.	Cr.
19X1 Jan.	3	Accounts Receivable/S. K. Able		106 —	
		Sales Tax Payable			6 —
		Sales			100 —
		Terms 2/10, n/30			
	15	Accounts Receivable/Marx Company		660 —	
		Sales			660 —
		Terms 2/10, n/30			

Most states have a sales tax on retail sales that is collected from the customer and later paid to the proper taxing authority. Earlier we mentioned that Mrs. Able was being charged a $6 sales tax because this was a retail sale. Since Marx Company is not a retail customer, the sales tax is not applied.

In terms of the accounting equation, these two transactions have increased the asset account, *Accounts Receivable*, by $766. Jayson's will pay the sales taxes at a later date, so a liability, *Sales Taxes Payable*, will increase by $6. *Sales* increases by $760 and, being a revenue account, will be closed to *Income Summary* at the end of the period. The effect of the charge sales to Mrs. Able and Marx Company on the accounting equation would be:

Asset	=	Liability	+	Owner's Equity
Accounts Receivable $766.00		Sales Taxes Payable $6.00		R. Jayson's, Capital $760.00 (Sales)

All sales on account will be recorded in the manner above if the general journal is used. Every time a charge sale is made to a wholesale customer, *Accounts Receivable* and the individual customer's name must be debited and *Sales* must be credited. If a retail customer is involved, *Sales Taxes Payable* also must be credited.

If a number of sales on account are made during the accounting period, recording them in the general journal would not be efficient. The account names would have to be written each time, and you would have to post each general ledger account individually. This procedure would be both repetitious and time consuming.

Sales journal

In Chapter 5 you were introduced to the purchases journal. This special journal saved you time in both journalizing and posting. In this chapter we want to discuss another special journal—the **sales journal.** Like the purchases journal, the sales journal is designed to make the recording of repetitious transactions more efficient. If a transaction is to be recorded in the sales journal, it must meet three requirements. Each transaction must (1) be a sale, (2) involve merchandise, (3) be made on account. If any of these three items is missing, the transaction must be recorded in one of the other journals.

A typical single-column sales journal is shown in Illustration 6-5. To assist you in understanding the single-column format, we are assuming briefly that the firm is located in a state that does not impose a sales tax. The single-column sales journal could have two amount columns—one for debits to *Accounts Receivable* and a second for credits to *Sales*. Using the same logic we used for the single-column purchases journal, only one amount column is provided. Each entry then must represent both the debit and the credit. Postings are similar to those for the purchases journal. The total of $1,250 is posted to the two general ledger accounts, and each sale must be posted individually to the debit side of the customer's account.

illustration 6-5
single-column sales journal.

SALES JOURNAL — Page 1

Date		Account Debited	Inv. No.	P.R.	Amount
19X1 Jan.	3	S.K. Able	101	✓	100 –
	12	Marx Company	102	✓	660 –
	15	N.M. Bass	103	✓	150 –
	25	Loma Company	104	✓	340 –
		Total			1250 –
					(13)(41)

Because most states have a sales tax on retail sales, we will assume again that Jayson's is located in a state that levies this tax on all retail sales. To make accounting easier, a sales journal similar to the one in Illustration 6-6 can be designed to assist in journalizing and posting.

To keep this illustration simple, we have assumed that Jayson's had only four charge sales in January. Let's look at a typical entry to see how the

illustration 6-6
multicolumn sales journal.

SALES JOURNAL — Page 1

Date		Account Debited	Inv. No.	P.R.	Accts. Rec. Dr.	Sales Taxes Payable Cr.	Sales Cr.
19X1 Jan.	3	S.K. Able	101	✓	106 –	6 –	100 –
	12	Marx Company	102	✓	660 –		660 –
	15	N.M. Bass	103	✓	159 –	9 –	150 –
	25	Loma Company	104	✓	340 –		340 –
	31				1265 –	15 –	1250 –
					(14)	(25)	(41)

GENERAL LEDGER

Account Receivable — 14

Date		Item	P.R.	Debit	Credit	Balance Debit	Balance Credit
19X1 Jan	31		S1	1265		1265	

Sales Taxes Payable — 25

Date		Item	P.R.	Debit	Credit	Balance Debit	Balance Credit
19X1 Jan	31		S1		15		15

Sales — 41

Date		Item	P.R.	Debit	Credit	Balance Debit	Balance Credit
19X1 Jan	31		S1		1250		1250

ACCOUNTS RECEIVABLE LEDGER

Able, S.K.
740 North Street
City

Date		Item	P.R.	Debit	Credit	Balance
19X1 Jan	3		S1	106		106

Bass, N. M.
1212 Movingsite Dr.
City

Date		Item	P.R.	Debit	Credit	Balance
19X1 Jan	15		S1	159		159

Loma Company
P.O. Box 884
City

Date		Item	P.R.	Debit	Credit	Balance
19X1 Jan	25		S1	340		340

Marx Company
5550 Governors Dr.
Huntsville AL 35802

Date		Item	P.R.	Debit	Credit	Balance
19X1 Jan	12		S1	660		660

multicolumn sales journal works. On January 3, $100 of merchandise was sold to S. K. Able using Invoice No. 101. Because the firm is required by state law to collect a sales tax, Able must be billed for an additional $6. Since the sale was for $100 and not $106, it is important *not* to include the sales tax in the revenue account. The $106 total is posted to the debit side of S. K. Able's account in the subsidiary ledger. Since the subsidiary ledger is arranged in alphabetical order and not by number, a check mark is placed in the posting reference column of the sales journal. This procedure is the same as the one you used for the purchases journal in Chapter 5.

At the end of the accounting period (January, in this case), the three totals are posted to their respective accounts in the general ledger. Before posting these totals, it would be wise to crossfoot all multicolumn journals to see if the debit totals equal the credit totals. In this case, $1,250 plus $15 equals $1,265. Note two important points in posting the totals: First, the symbol "S1" is used to designate page 1 of the sales journal; second, the *Sales* account number begins with a "4" to indicate a revenue account.

sample problem Calculate and journalize the following three sales on account. Using a single-column sales journal, post to the controlling account and to the customers' individual accounts with the proper reference numbers and check marks.

Smith Company—Invoice 102 (Feb. 8)
8460 13th Ave. Bloomington, MN. 55420
2 dresses @ $40 each
Perfume, $15
1 pr. slacks @ $25

Noble Company—Invoice 103 (Feb.10)
3002 Casco Circle, Wayzata, MN. 55391
4 blouses @ $20 each
6 pocketbooks @ $30
5 jackets @ $45 each

Jones Company—Invoice 104 (Feb. 20)
3750 St. Clair Ave. St. Paul MN. 55105
3 pr. hose @ $6 each
2 pant suits @ $50
2 belts @ $5 each

sample problem solution

SALES JOURNAL Page 2

Date		Account Debited	Inv. No.	P.R.	Amount
19X1 Feb.	8	Smith Company	102	✓	120 –
	10	Noble Company	103	✓	485 –
	20	Jones Company	104	✓	128 –
	28				733 –
					(13/41)

GENERAL LEDGER

Accounts Receivable Account No. 13

Date		Item	P.R.	Dr.	Cr.	Balance Dr.	Balance Cr.
19X1 Feb.	28		S2	733 –		733 –	

Sales Account No. 41

Date		Item	P.R.	Dr.	Cr.	Balance Dr.	Balance Cr.
19X1 Feb.	28		S2		733 –		733 –

ACCOUNTS RECEIVABLE SUBSIDIARY LEDGER

Jones Company
3150 St. Clair Avenue
St. Paul, MN. 55105

Date		Explanation	P.R.	Dr.	Cr.	Balance
19X1 Feb.	20		S2	128 –		128 –

Noble Company
3002 Casco Circle
Wayzata, MN. 55391

Date		Explanation	P.R.	Dr.	Cr.	Balance
19X1 Feb.	10		S2	485 –		485 –

Smith Company
8460 13th Avenue
Bloomington, MN. 55420

Date		Explanation	P.R.	Dr.	Cr.	Balance
19X1 Feb.	8		S2	120 –		120 –

review exercises

4. The following sales were made on account in March:

Green Company	$140.25
Brown Company	110.30
Boone Company	85.50

What is the total amount to be posted to the controlling account? If Boone Company had a previous balance of $78.80 in the subsidiary account on March 1, what is the total amount that Boone Company owes to the firm? If *Accounts Receivable* had a total balance of $240.60 on March 1, what is the balance on March 31?

5. What are the advantages of using a special journal for the information listed in Exercise 4?

• task THE SKILL TO PREPARE A CREDIT MEMORANDUM AND TO JOURNALIZE AND POST THE INFORMATION ACCURATELY

Sales returns and allowances

Merchandise sold to customers on credit is sometimes returned. As we discussed in Chapter 5, the reason for the *return* is usually dissatisfaction caused by having received wrong items or goods damaged during shipment. Sometimes the customer finds that the merchandise ordered is not needed and seeks to return it. An *allowance,* in contrast, is granted when the customer agrees to keep the incorrect or damaged merchandise at a reduced cost rather than to return it to the vendor. This agreement is usually more attractive to the seller than paying return freight and possibly facing the problem of loss on the resale of damaged merchandise. In either case, the customer should contact the vendor to receive permission to return the merchandise or to reduce the amount due.

In accounting for a return or an allowance, the **credit memorandum** (also called a **credit memo**) becomes the source document for recording transactions to the *Accounts Receivable* control account and the customer's account in the subsidiary ledger. The completed credit memorandum must contain the following information:

1. Name and address of person or business returning the merchandise.
2. Description of merchandise returned.
3. Reason for the return or allowance.
4. Amount of the credit memorandum.
5. Signature of the person giving approval.

The credit memorandum should be prepared in four copies and distributed to the different persons or departments shown in Illustration 6-7.

illustration 6-7 credit memorandum distribution.

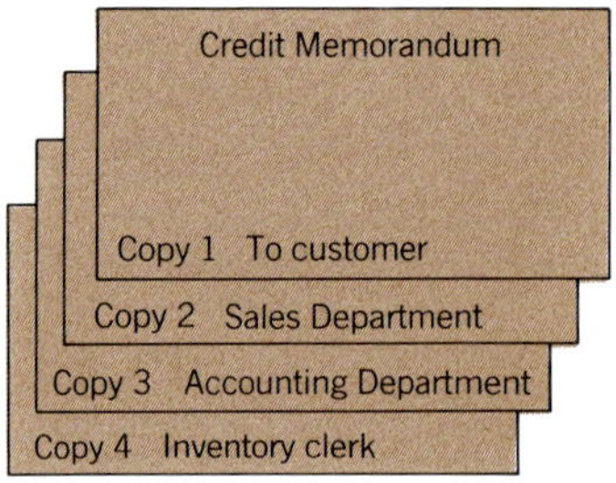

Assume that on January 7, Mrs. Able returned one blouse originally billed at $15 and one pair of hose billed at $2 from the sale made on January 3. In addition to giving credit for the returned merchandise, the tax liability must be reduced by $1.02 ($17 × .06). The completed credit memorandum appears in Illustration 6-8.

illustration 6-8 credit memorandum.

Credit Memorandum

S. K. Able
740 North Street
City

Date: January 7, 19X1

We credited your account for $18.02 for the following returned merchandise:

1 blouse @ $15.00
1 pr. hose @ $2.00
Sales taxes: $1.02

Reason: Blouse was wrong color and hose were damaged

Approval: Sally Johnson

On the basis of the copy of the approved credit memorandum, a general journal entry is prepared to show the reduction in *Sales* and *Accounts Receivable.* As you would expect, the customer's individual account will also be reduced to keep it in agreement with the controlling account. Since sales taxes were charged to a retail customer, that total must be reduced in *Sales Taxes Payable* and in *Accounts Receivable* for S. K. Able. *Sales* could be debited to reduce that account, but *Sales Returns and Allowances* is used instead to provide information on the frequency and amount of sales returned. The general journal entry appears below:

GENERAL JOURNAL Page

Date		Description	P.R.	Dr.	Cr.
19X1 Jan.	7	Sales Returns and Allowances		17 –	
		Sales Taxes Payable		1 02	
		Accounts Receivable/S.K. Able			18 02
		Merchandise returned			
		from January 3 sale			

Posting

The entry above will be posted to the accounts as indicated in the general journal entry. The general ledger accounts and subsidiary account for S. K. Able are shown below in Illustration 6-9.

illustration 6-9
partial ledgers.

GENERAL LEDGER

Accounts Receivable — Account No. 14

Date		Item	P.R.	Dr.	Cr.	Balance Dr.	Balance Cr.
19X1 Jan.	1	Balance	✓			3100	
	7		G1		18 02	3081 98	

Sales Taxes Payable — Account No. 23

Date		Item	P.R.	Dr.	Cr.	Balance Dr.	Balance Cr.
19X1 Jan.	1	Balance	✓				186 –
	7		G1	1 02			184 98

Sales Returns and Allowances — Account No. 42

Date		Item	P.R.	Dr.	Cr.	Balance Dr.	Balance Cr.
19X1 Jan.	7		G1	17 –		17 –	

ACCOUNTS RECEIVABLE SUBSIDIARY LEDGER

S.K. Able
740 North Street
City

Date		Explanation	P.R.	Dr.	Cr.	Balance
19X1 Jan.	3		S1	106		106 –
	7		G1		18 02	87 98

Posting references in the general ledger accounts and the accounts receivable subsidiary ledger identify the journals from which the transactions were posted. Refer to the general journal, and you will notice that a check mark has been placed in the posting reference column by *Accounts Receivable/S. K. Able* to indicate that the subsidiary account has also been posted. A common error among beginning accounting students is to omit this posting.

sample problem From the data you prepared for the month of February, assume that on February 25, Jones Company returned one pants suit and two belts because the merchandise was damaged. Jones Company is located at 1100 East Street, Duncan, Kansas 64272. From the completed credit memorandum, prepare the necessary journal entries and post to the proper accounts in the general and subsidiary ledgers.

sample problem solution

Credit Memorandum

Jones Company
1100 East Street
Duncan, Kansas 64272

Date: February 25, 19X1

We credited your account for $60.00 for the following returned merchandise:

1 Pants suit @ $50.00
2 Belts @ $5.00

Reason: Pants suit is wrong color. Belts were torn.

Approval: Billy King

GENERAL JOURNAL

Page 20

Date		Description	P.R.	Dr.	Cr.
19X1 Feb.	25	Sales Returns and Allowances	42	60 –	
		Accounts Receivable/Jones Company	13/✓		60 –
		To record credit memo.			

GENERAL LEDGER

Accounts Receivable — Account No. 13

Date		Item	P.R.	Dr.	Cr.	Balance Dr.	Balance Cr.
19X1 Feb.	25		G20		60 –		60 –

Sales Returns and Allowances — Account No. 42

Date		Item	P.R.	Dr.	Cr.	Balance Dr.	Balance Cr.
19X1 Feb.	25		G20	60 –		60 –	

Accounts Receivable Subsidiary Ledger

Jones Company
1100 East Street
Duncan, Kansas 64272

Date		Explanation	P.R.	Dr.	Cr.	Balance
19X1 Feb.	20		S 2	128 –		128 –
	25		G 20		60 –	68 –

review exercises

6. Marke Company sold $800 in merchandise to the Swak Company on January 5, 19X1. On January 10, Swak Company returned $120 in merchandise to Marke Company because of damage. Prepare the general journal entry and post to the proper ledgers.
7. Indicate the normal balances of the following accounts: (a) *Sales;* (b) *Sales Returns and Allowances;* (c) *Accounts Receivable;* (d) individual customer accounts in the accounts receivable subsidiary ledger.

• task CALCULATE DISCOUNTS ALLOWED FOR PROMPT PAYMENTS

Sales discount

Selling on credit is a common business practice. To encourage prompt payment, merchants often allow **sales discounts.** Since the approach used for sales discounts resembles the approach used for purchases discounts, the procedure should be familiar to you.

Refer again to Illustration 6-3 and note that the terms of the sale are 2/10, n/30. These credit terms mean that the customer can take a 2 percent discount if the invoice is paid within ten days of the invoice date. After the ten days have passed, the customer has up to 30 days from the invoice date to pay the full amount. In Illustration 6-3, if Marx Company paid the amount due within the discount period, $646.80 would be received ($660 less 2% of $660).

Total Bill	$660.00	
Less 2% discount	13.20	(0.02 × $660)
	$646.80	

Terms of 2/10, n/30 are the most common, but each firm is free to set its own terms—and some rather creative credit terms can result. For example, *2/10, 1/15, n/30* means that a 2 percent discount is allowed if the invoice is paid within ten days, 1 percent if paid between the 11th and 15th days, and the gross amount is due if the invoice is paid between the 16th and 30th days from the invoice date. Terms such as *3/10, EOM* mean that a discount of 3 percent is allowed if payment is made within ten days after the end of the month.

Shipping terms are often included as part of the sales transaction. As we discussed in Chapter 5, terms of *FOB shipping point* require the buyer to pay for shipping charges, while terms of *FOB destination* require the seller to pay the shipping charges. When the terms are FOB shipping point and the shipper pays the freight charges, the customer must reimburse the seller for this amount. If the customer pays within the discount period, the discount **does not** apply to the freight charge. To illustrate, assume that Walters Company sold merchandise for $300 to Edwards Company. Terms of the invoice are 1/10, n/30, and FOB shipping point. The freight company requires the $40 payment to be made before the merchandise is shipped, so Walters Company pays this bill. The invoice shows a total cost of $340 ($300 for the merchandise and $40 for the freight charges). If Edwards Company pays within the discount period, a check for $337 must be sent. The amount due would be calculated as follows:

Cost of the merchandise	$300
Less 1% discount	3
	$297
Add the freight charge	40
Amount of the check	$337

When merchandise that has been sold on account is returned, no discount should be taken on this merchandise. To illustrate, assume that Marker and Sons sold $800 of merchandise to Baker and Daughter with terms of 2/10, n/30, and FOB destination. Due to an error in filling the order, Baker was allowed to return $60 of the merchandise. The freight cost was $50. Marker and Sons should receive a check for $725.20 if the invoice is paid within the discount period.

Original invoice price	$800.00
Freight cost to be paid by customer	0.00
	$800.00
Less returned merchandise	60.00
Amount subject to the discount	$740.00
Less discount at 2%	14.80
Amount due within discount period	$725.20

sample problem Determine the amount to be collected from the following sale to Farr Company if the customer pays within the discount period. Terms of the sale are 2/10, n/30 and FOB shipping point.

Sold: 3 coats @ $30 each
5 pairs of shoes @ $20 per pair
6 pocketbooks @ $25 each

Hamilton Truck Lines charged the seller $35 to ship this merchandise. The customer was given a $10 allowance due to the pocketbooks being the wrong color.

sample problem solution

Original Invoice	$340.00
Less allowance	10.00
Amount subject to a discount	$330.00
Less discount ($330 × .02)	6.60
	$323.40
Plus freight charges	35.00
Total amount due if paid within discount period	$358.40

review exercises

8. Larder Company sold $1,200 of merchandise to Bull Company on March 17. Terms of the sale were 4/10, n/30 and FOB shipping point. Bull Company was billed $32 by the trucking firm for the freight charges. On March 20, Bull Company returned $200 of the merchandise. If Bull Company sent a check on March 25 to settle this invoice, what amount should be paid?
9. Assume in Review Exercise 8 that the freight company billed Larder Company for the freight charges rather than Bull Company. How much would Bull Company have to pay in settlement on March 25?

• task PREPARE A SCHEDULE OF ACCOUNTS RECEIVABLE AND PROVE THE BALANCE WITH THE CONTROL ACCOUNT

Schedule of accounts receivable

After all postings from the sales journal and the general journal have been made, a **schedule of accounts receivable** is prepared. This schedule gives the balances owed by each customer. Let's assume that on January 27, Marx Company, a customer, paid $500, only a part of their bill. The receipt of this cash is shown on the next page.

GENERAL JOURNAL — Page 1

Date		Description	P.R.	Dr.	Cr.
19X1 Jan.	27	Cash	11	500 –	
		Accounts Receivable/Marx Company	14/✓		500 –
		To record receipt on account			

The *Accounts Receivable* control account has the following balances after all January transactions are posted. *Accounts Receivable* would have a credit

Accounts Receivable — Account No. 14

Date		Item	P.R.	Dr.	Cr.	Balance Dr.	Balance Cr.
19X1 Jan.	7		G 1		18 02		18 02
	27		G 1		500 –		518 02
	31		S 1	1265 –		746 98	

balance on January 27 since the total of charge sales from the sales journal will not be posted until the end of January. After all postings from the sales journal in January have been completed, the accounts receivable subsidiary ledger accounts will have the following balances:

illustration 6-10
accounts receivable subsidiary ledger.

S.K. Able
740 North Street
City

Date		Explanation	P.R.	Dr.	Cr.	Balance
19X1 Jan.	3		S 1	106 –		106 –
	7		G 1		18 02	87 98

N.M. Bass
1212 Morningside Drive
City

Date		Explanation	P.R.	Dr.	Cr.	Balance
19X1 Jan.	25		S 1	159 –		159 –

Loma Company
P.O. Box 884
City

Date		Explanation	P.R.	Dr.	Cr.	Balance
19X1 Jan.	25		S 1	340 –		340 –

Marx Company
5550 Governors Drive
Huntsville, AL 35802

Date		Explanation	P.R.	Dr.	Cr.	Balance
19X1 Jan.	12		S 1	660 –		660 –
	27		G 1		500 –	160 –

The schedule of accounts receivable shown below in Illustration 6-11 lists customers' names and amounts due to Jayson's.

illustration 6-11 schedule of accounts receivable.

Jayson's
Schedule of Accounts Receivable
January 31, 19X1

Able, S.K.	87 98	
Bass, N.M.	159 –	
Loma Company	340 –	
Marx Company	160 –	
Total Accounts Receivable		746 98

The total of the individual accounts in Illustration 6-11, $746.98, is equal to the balance in *Accounts Receivable*. If these two amounts did not match, we would have to locate the error and make the correction. Errors could be caused by misadding, improper posting, or omissions. In Chapter 2, we mentioned that an easy test for a slide or a transposition is to see whether the difference between the two numbers is divisible by 9. To refresh your memory, if $275 is posted as $257, the difference of $18 ($275 − $257) is divisible by 9 (18 ÷ 9 = 2). This tells us we are looking for a transposition, which should speed up the search.

sample problem From the following balances in ledger accounts, prepare a schedule of accounts receivable and compare the balance of this schedule with the controlling account for Boxx Company as of December 31, 19X1.

GENERAL LEDGER

Accounts Receivable 13

12/31	Bal.	6,000		6,000	

Sales 41

12/31	Bal.		20,000	20,000

ACCOUNTS RECEIVABLE SUBSIDIARY LEDGER

Wint Bower
1160 Castle Place,
San Jose, CA 95123

12/31	Bal.	1,200		1,200

Jack Cone
1418 West 14th St.,
Sunnyvale, CA 94088

12/31	Bal.	2,500		2,500

Ken Stone
3814 Homestead Road
Daly City, CA 94015

12/31	Bal.	1,500		1,500

Bill Webster
P.O. Box 263
St. Jose, CA 95123

12/31	Bal.	800		800

sample problem solution

Boxx Company
Schedule of Accounts Receivable
December 31, 19X1

Bower, Wint	$1,200	
Cone, Jack	2,500	
Stone, Ken	1,500	
Webster, Bill	800	
Total Accounts Receivable		$6,000

review exercises

10. From the following account balances in the accounts subsidiary ledger, prepare a schedule of accounts receivable for the Kyle Company as of December 31, 19X1.

ACCOUNTS RECEIVABLE SUBSIDIARY LEDGER

Bob Clark

12/31	Bal.	825		825

Spence Dunn

12/31	Bal.	350		350

Dole Mang

12/31	Bal.	780		780

11. The *Accounts Receivable* control account had a balance of $1,900 on December 31, 19X1. What is the difference in the total from your schedule in Exercise 10 and the balance in the *Accounts Receivable* control accounts? How would you go about locating the error?

• task PREPARE AN AGING SCHEDULE OF ACCOUNTS RECEIVABLE TO ASSIST THE COMPANY IN THE DEVELOPMENT OF CREDIT POLICIES

Bad debts/aging of accounts receivable

The length of time that a debt has been outstanding has a bearing on the possibility of its future collection. An account 60 days past due is more likely to be collected than an account five months past due. Accountants age the *Accounts Receivable* to determine the length of time that a customer's account is past due. **Aging of Accounts Receivable** can be accomplished by a schedule similar to the one in Illustration 6-12.

illustration 6-12 aging of accounts receivable.

Jayson's
Aging of Accounts Receivable
December 31, 19X1

Name	Balance	Not Due	Days Past Due				
			1-30	31-60	61-90	91-120	over 120
Adams Electric	195.23	195.23					
T.J. Barr	86.14			86.14			
Carson Co.	618.69		286.52	332.17			
L.P. Case	300.00	300.00					
Cumber Co.	249.49	249.49					
Dalton Shoe	190.00					190.00	
...							
	26,908.10	23,090.12	914.60	625.50	776.80	530.30	970.78

sample problem From the limited number of accounts presented below, prepare an aging of accounts receivable schedule as of December 31, 19X1. Terms of all sales are 2/10, n/30 for the Foxx Company.

sample problem solution

L.V. Cody
834 Spring Street
Hartford, CT 06106

19X1 Sept. 28		S19	$100		$100

J.C. Dunn
19 Broad Street
Windsor, CT 06095

19X1					
Sept. 4		S19	$225		$225
10		G21		$225	0
Oct. 20		S24	130		130

Friend Company
828 Cervens Road
Tolland, CT 06084

19X1					
Apr. 10		S16	$300		$300
25		G30		$150	150
Nov. 1		S22	40		190

Home Company
436 Warehouse Street
Hartford, CT 06106

19X1					
Nov. 15		S21	$140		$140

sample problem solution

Aging of Accounts Receivable
Foxx Company
December 31, 19X1

Name	Balance	31-60	61-90	91-120	Over 120
L. V. Cody	$100			$100	
J. C. Dunn	130		$130		
Friend Co.	190	$ 40			$150
Home Co.	140	140			
Totals	$560	$180	$130	$100	$150

review exercises

12. From the two accounts of Fred Cone and Joe Gordon, prepare an aging of accounts receivable schedule as of December 31, 19X1 for the Gore Company. (Use the categories found in the sample problem solution.) Terms are 2/10, n/30.

Fred Cone
1116 Charles Avenue
Tallahassee, FL 32303

19X1					
Nov. 2		S17	$50		$ 50
Dec. 6		S18	45		105

Joe Gordon
2410 Holly Street
Tallahassee, FL 32303

19X1					
Sept. 5		S11	$180		$180
15		CR40	160	$20	
Oct. 20		S15	90		110

• task PREPARE A STATEMENT OF ACCOUNT FOR EACH CUSTOMER WITH AN OUTSTANDING BALANCE

Customer statement

Periodically, the selling firm's accounting clerk prepares a **statement of account** from a customer's accounts receivable account. This statement informs the customer of the amount owed and identifies the items purchased. Customers compare these statements with their appropriate accounts payable subsidiary ledger accounts. Errors on the part of either the seller or the buyer can be located by using this statement.

To illustrate how to prepare a statement of account, assume that Moss Company had the following charge sales, sales returns, and payments during January. From this customer's subsidiary ledger, a statement can be prepared and mailed. Sales invoices will provide information as to the item sold and its price. Moss Company's accounts receivable subsidiary account for January is given in Illustration 6-13.

illustration 6-13 customer's accounts receivable ledger account.

Moss Company
362 Kendall Street
City

Date		Explanation	P.R.	Dr.	Cr.	Balance
19X1 Jan.	2		S4	200 –		200 –
	6		G2		200 –	-0-
	8		S5	150 –		150 –
	9		G4		50 –	100 –
	20		S7	300 –		400 –
	25		S8	180 –		580 –

You can see that the amount on the statement in Illustration 6-14 is equal to the subsidiary account balance.

illustration 6-14 statement of account. (courtesy of Jayson's)

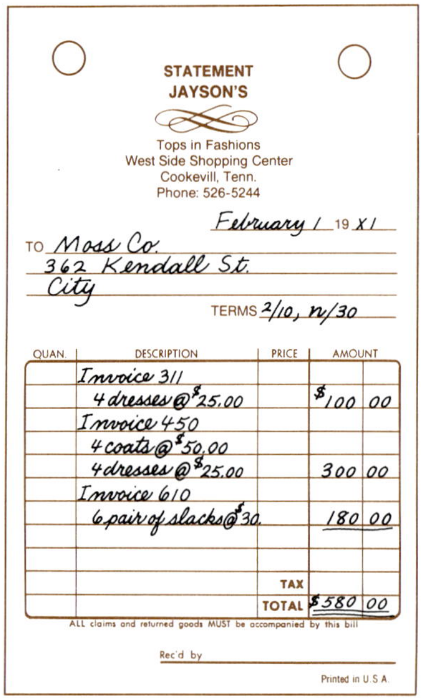
STATEMENT
JAYSON'S

Tops in Fashions
West Side Shopping Center
Cookevill, Tenn.
Phone: 526-5244

February 1 19X1

TO Moss Co.
362 Kendall St.
City

TERMS 2/10, n/30

QUAN.	DESCRIPTION	PRICE	AMOUNT
	Invoice 311		
	4 dresses @ $25.00		$100 00
	Invoice 450		
	4 coats @ $50.00		
	4 dresses @ $25.00		300 00
	Invoice 610		
	6 pair of slacks @ $30.		180 00
		TAX	
		TOTAL	$580 00

ALL claims and returned goods MUST be accompanied by this bill

Rec'd by

Printed in U.S.A.

sample problem Using the information given below, prepare a statement of account for Moore Company to be mailed on February 1, 19X1 to Central Company, 232 First Street, Oldham, Kentucky 42163, terms 2/10, n/30.

Inv. No. 201: Sold 4 sweaters @ \$25 each and 2 blouses @ \$35 each (January 5). Both blouses were the wrong size and were returned on January 10.

Inv. No. 325: Sold 4 coats @ \$50 each (January 15).

Inv. No. 402: Sold 2 dresses @ \$25 each (January 20).

Central Company
232 First Street
Oldham, KY 42163

Date		Explanation	P.R.	Dr.	Cr.	Balance
19X1 Jan.	5			170 –		170 –
	10				70 –	100 –
	15			200 –		300 –
	20			50 –		350 –

sample problem solution

STATEMENT

MOORE COMPANY
1735 Edgewood Drive
Bowling Green, KY 42101

February 1, 19X1

TO Central Co.
232 First Street
Oldham, Kentucky 42163

TERMS 2/10, n/30

QUAN.	DESCRIPTION	PRICE	AMOUNT
	Invoice 201:		
	4 Sweaters @ $25.00		$100 00
	Invoice 325:		
	4 Coats @ $50.00		200 00
	Invoice 402:		
	2 Dresses @ $25.00		50 00
		TAX	
		TOTAL	350 00

ALL claims and returned goods MUST be accompanied by this bill

Rec'd by

Printed in U.S.A.

review exercises

13. Sales to Lark Company for the month of February are shown below:

Feb.	2	Invoice No. 107— 6 shirts @ $20
	14	Invoice No. 112— 2 coats @ $40
	25	Invoice No. 130— 10 belts @ $5

Lark Company's account shows a balance of $150 as of March 1. Prepare a statement to be mailed on that date.

Lark Company
1230 Turner Street
Rome, TN 32706

Date	Item	Post Ref.	Dr.	Cr.	Balance
19X1					
Feb. 2		S10	120		120
14		S11	80		200
15		CR7		100	100
25		S12	50		150

Flow chart of sales on account

Accounting routines that maintain records for sales on account can be illustrated by flow charting. Illustration 6-15 is an example that traces a sale from the original transaction to its final accounting.

illustration 6-15
systems flow chart.

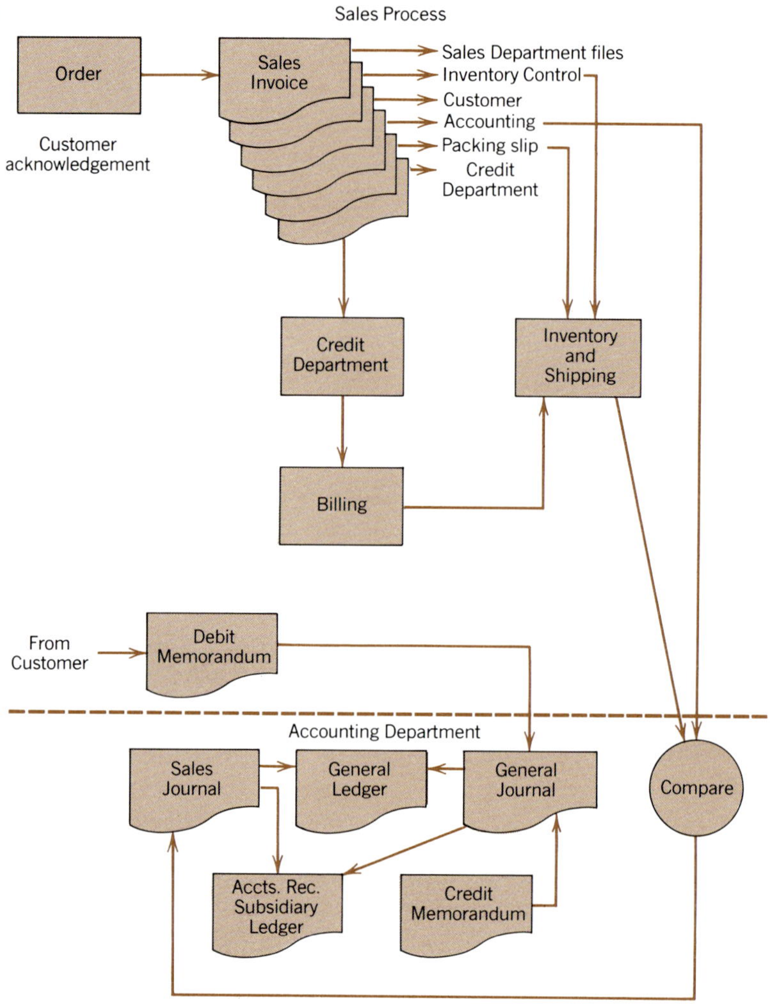

chapter highlights

After studying this chapter, you should be able to:

- Prepare a bill of sale.
- Enter transactions in a sales journal and post to the general and subsidiary ledgers.
- Prepare a credit memorandum.
- Journalize and post the credit memorandum information to the control and subsidiary accounts.
- Prepare a schedule of accounts receivable.
- Prepare an aging schedule of accounts receivable.
- Prepare a statement of account for each customer with an outstanding balance.

check figures for review exercises

1. Total billing $56.80 + sales tax, $3.41 = $60.21.
2. Information pertaining to customer name, terms of sales, and other financial information.
3. Total billing, $1,016.30.
4. $336.05 posted to controlling account for March—Boone owes $164.30. *Accounts Receivable* balance—$576.65.
5. Efficiency, accuracy, and posting advantages.
6. Debit *Sales Returns and Allowances* for $120.
7. Only *Sales* would have a credit balance.

Account	Normal Balance
Sales	Cr.
Sales Returns and Allowances	Dr.
Accounts Receivable	Dr.
Individual Accounts Receivable	Dr.

8. Amount paid, $960.
9. Full settlement, $992.
10. Total of schedule of accounts receivable, $1,955.
11. Difference of $55—locate error by checking the postings and the additions. Check general journal entries for returns not posted to individual customer accounts in the subsidiary ledger.
12. Joe Gordon—($20, 61-90 days), ($90, 31-60 days).
13. Statement to Lark Company—Total $150.

key terms

The following important terms were discussed in this chapter and are also defined in the Glossary at the end of the book:

aging of accounts receivable

bill of sale

cash register tape

controlling account

sales discount

sales invoice

sales journal

schedule of accounts receivable

slide

statement of account

transposition

questions

1. Why do businesses sell on credit?
2. List the source documents used as a basis for all charge sales transactions.

3. What is a sales discount?
4. Why is the account *Sales Returns and Allowances* debited when the accountant journalizes a credit memorandum?
5. Why is it necessary to post individual accounts on a daily basis?
6. What is meant by the term "controlling account"?
7. How is a special sales journal more efficient than a general journal in recording sales on credit and less likely to produce posting errors?
8. What information is contained in an accounts receivable subsidiary ledger?
9. What is the difference between a sales return and a sales allowance?
10. What is the purpose of the schedule of accounts receivable?
11. What are some common accounting errors in accounting for charge sales?
12. Why is the aging of accounts receivable procedure beneficial to management?
13. How do you think a computer could be used to the firm's advantage in accounting for sales on account?
14. Define the following terms in reference to sales on credit: invoice extensions; credit memorandum; subsidiary ledger; general ledger; 2/10, n/30.

exercises

1. Prepare a sales slip to the Kapa Company, 220 East Street, Dyersburg, TN 38024, for a sale made on January 5, 19X1. Items sold were 2 dozen baseball gloves at $20 each and 10 baseball caps at $3 each. Terms were 2/10, n/30. Prepare a general journal entry to record the sale.
2. Noel Company sold merchandise on account during the week to the following customers:

T.J. Lancaster	$430
Johnny Simpson	140
Myrtle Smith	350
Tom Martin	800

   Assume a 6 percent sales tax. Calculate the total amount to be debited to *Accounts Receivable*.
3. From the single-column sales journal shown below, make all postings to the control account and the needed subsidiary accounts (use T accounts).

SALES JOURNAL Page 2

Date	Inv. No.	Customer	P.R.	Amount
19X1				
June 3	1023	S.A. Lion		400
9	1024	Boaz Company		250
15	1025	Kuna Company		630
22	1026	Ziebot, Inc.		180

4. List the general ledger accounts involved with (a) sales for cash and (b) sales made on credit. Indicate the source of the information posted to these accounts. What subsidiary ledger is used to provide information on sales to customers?

5. Prepare a credit memorandum from the following information: Locke Company sold $800 of merchandise on account to Swimmers, Inc. (732 Monroe St., Jonesville, TN 36213), on July 15. On July 25, Swimmers, Inc., returned $200 of merchandise damaged during shipment. From the credit memorandum, prepare a general journal entry.

6. Terms of another sale to Kapa (Exercise 1) were 2/10, n/30. The sale was made on February 10 for $100. (a) What will be the amount of the check to be received if the payment is made within the discount period? (b) Calculate the discount if Kapa had returned $20 of merchandise.

7. The Zuma Company believes that offering sales discounts will prompt most customers to pay their bills within the discount period. Such procedures will increase the amount of cash available to Zuma and help to avoid bad debts. Sales discount terms given by Zuma in September follow:

Blair Company, $400, terms 2/10, n/30
C. B. Diller, $500, terms 1/10, n/30
Silk Company, $250, terms 2/10, n/60
Hasters, Inc., $300, terms 2/10, n/30
A. D. Last, $380, terms 1/10, n/30

All customers paid their charge sales within the discount period except Silk Company. Calculate the total sales discounts and the amount of cash received by Zuma Company.

8. Jones Equipment Company shipped 20 typewriters by the Red Ball Express Freight Lines to Anderson Office Equipment. The invoice showed shipping terms of FOB shipping point and credit terms of 2/10, n/30. If the typewriters sell for $300 each and the shipping charges amount to $50 each, how much will Jones Equipment Company collect if Anderson pays within the discount period and Jones Equipment paid the freight charges?

problems

1. COMPETENCY TESTED The ability to prepare and post general journal entries.

The Blue Company made the following credit sales to customers during January, 19X1:

			Invoice Number
Jan. 2	L. K. Thompson	$500	231
15	J. C. Jones	200	232
20	Moss Company	100	233
25	M. N. Spinner	300	234

Instructions Record the charge sales transactions for Blue Company for January in general journal form. There is no sales tax in the state where Blue Company is located. Post to *Accounts Receivable* and the customers' individual subsidiary accounts.

2. COMPETENCY TESTED The ability to understand returns and credits.

Central Company sold $1,000 of merchandise to L. P. Smith Company on January 5, 19X1. On January 10, 19X1, L. P. Smith returned 4 units at $50 each to Central Company because of flaws in manufacture.

Instructions

(a) Prepare a credit memorandum.

(b) Use the credit memorandum as a source document to prepare the required general journal entry.

(c) Post to the proper general ledger accounts and the customer's subsidiary account.

3. COMPETENCY TESTED Skill in recording and comparing entries in a special sales journal.

From the information provided in Problem 1, record the information in a single-column sales journal. Post to the *Accounts Receivable* and *Sales* accounts and to the customers' individual subsidiary accounts.

Which of the two systems—general journal transactions or special sales journal—did you find to be the least time consuming?

4. COMPETENCY TESTED The ability to use the three-column sales journal.

The Holmes Company uses a three-column sales journal and uses a general journal for all other transactions. Assume a sales tax rate of 5%.

Transactions for August 19X3 follow:

Aug. 3 Sold $620 of merchandise to Laws Company, 2/10, n/30. Invoice No. 436. (No sales tax)

4 Received $500 for cash sale. (No sales tax.)

6 Sold $300 of merchandise to Mason Company, 2/10, n/30. Invoice No. 437. (No sales Tax)

8 Sold $100 of merchandise to D. O. Davis, 2/10, n/30. Invoice No. 438. (Sales tax, 5%)

9 Issued a credit memorandum to Mason Company for $50 as an allowance for keeping damaged merchandise.

14 Received payment in full from Mason Company.

17 Sold $400 of merchandise to B. D. Jones, 2/10, n/30. Invoice No. 439. (Sales tax 5%)

25 Received $120 from Laws Company.

27 Issued a credit memorandum to Laws Company for $80 for returned merchandise.

Instructions

(a) Journalize the August transactions in the sales journal and the general journal.

(b) Post the individual customers' accounts to the subsidiary ledger.

(c) Post the sales journal and the general journal.

(d) Prepare a schedule of accounts receivable.

(e) Does the *Accounts Receivable* control account equal the sum of the individual subsidiary accounts?

5. COMPETENCY TESTED The ability to record general journal entries for sales on account.

Sept. 2 Sold $400 of merchandise to John Jones, 2/10, n/30, FOB shipping point.

6 Sold $800 of merchandise to Henry Johnson, 1/10, n/30, FOB shipping point.

8 Issued a credit memorandum to John Jones for $75 of returned merchandise.

12 Received the amount due from John Jones for the September 2 sale.

15 Cash sales for September 1-15 were $1,200.

17 Received the amount due from Henry Johnson for the September 6 sale. The check was dated September 15 and the envelope was postmarked September 16. (*Hint*: Company will accept the check and give the discount.)

20 Sold $500 of merchandise to David Henry. Cash of $200 was collected at date of sale with $300 on credit with terms of n/30. Freight was paid by the buyer.

Sept. 29 Received the balance due from David Henry for the sale of September 20.

Instruction Prepare the transactions in general journal form.

6. COMPETENCY TESTED The ability to prepare a three-column sales journal.

The Miff Company uses a three-column sales journal. For sales to individuals, assume a sales tax rate of 5%. Sales made by the Miff Company during September were as follows:

Sept. 3	Arnold Company, $300, 2/10, n/30, Invoice No. 106
10	C. M. Cruze, $400, 2/10, n/30, Invoice No. 107
15	Spark Company, $250, 2/10, n/30, Invoice No. 108
22	M. C. Cloan, $180, 2/10, n/30, Invoice No. 109
25	Zedi Company, $220, 2/10, n/30, Invoice No. 110
28	L. D. Sloan, $320, 2/10, n/30, Invoice No. 111

Instructions

(a) Prepare the transactions in the special sales journal.

(b) Total the special journal.

(c) Post to the individual customer's accounts.

(d) Post totals to the three general ledger accounts.

(e) Prepare a schedule of accounts receivable.

7. COMPETENCY TESTED Skill in handling credit transactions, posting, and control account comparisons with subsidiary accounts.

Using a single-column special journal for sales of Winston Company, record the following transactions. Also, post to *Accounts Receivable, Sales,* and to the accounts receivable subsidiary ledger accounts. As a final step, prepare a schedule of accounts receivable and compare the total to the control account total.

Transactions for sales:

Nov. 2	Henson Company, $250, 2/10, n/30. Invoice No. 232.
5	Langford Company, $600, 1/10, n/30. Invoice No. 233.
10	White Company, $425, 1/10, n/30. Invoice No. 234.
16	Bray Company, $300, 2/10, n/30. Invoice No. 235.
24	Berry Company, $350, n/30. Invoice No. 236.
29	White Company, $500, 2/10, n/30. Invoice No. 237.

8. COMPETENCY TESTED The ability to handle a problem involving recording, posting, and preparing a schedule of accounts receivable.

Using a single-column sales journal and a general journal, prepare transactions for the month of July, 19X1, for Dalen Company. The firm is located in a state with no sales tax.

July 3 Sold $500 of merchandise to Miller Company, 2/10, n/30, FOB shipping point. Invoice No. 316.

5 Sold $300 of merchandise to J. B. Carson, 1/10, n/30, FOB shipping point. Invoice No. 317.

7 Sent a credit memorandum to Miller Company for $100 for returned merchandise.

8 Sold $200 of merchandise to L. C. Jones, 2/10, n/30. Invoice No. 318.

9 Received the amount due from Miller Company on the sale of July 3. Invoice No. 316.

12 Sold $700 of merchandise to Miller Company, 2/10, n/30, FOB shipping point. Invoice No. 319.

15 Sold $350 of merchandise to Green Company, 2/10, n/30, FOB shipping point. Invoice No. 320.

16 Cash sales for the two weeks were $1,000.

20 Received the amount due from Green Company.

25 Jones paid $100 on his account.

28 Sold $150 of merchandise to Green Company, 2/10, n/30, FOB shipping point. Invoice No. 321.

29 Issued a credit memorandum to J. B. Carson for $30 for returned merchandise.

Instructions

(a) Record the transactions above.

(b) Post to customers' subsidiary accounts.

(c) Total and rule the sales journal.

(d) Post the sales journal total to the general ledger accounts.

(e) Post the general journal transactions to the general ledger accounts and to the accounts receivable subsidiary ledger.

(f) Prepare a schedule of accounts receivable.

comprehensive problem

REED SUPPLY COMPANY

The Reed Supply Company is a small wholesale supply store that sells merchandise to retail stores. The business operates as a single proprietorship and has two employees. Wages are paid every two weeks after social security taxes and employees' income taxes have been withheld. Reed Supply Company maintains a one-column sales journal, a multicolumn purchases journal, and a general journal. Terms for all sales and purchases are 2/10, n/30. Transportation charges are FOB shipping point for sales of merchandise. Transportation charges are paid by Reed Supply Company when merchandise is purchased. The purchases and sales transactions for the company are for the month of January. The trial balance as of January 1, 19X2, follows:

Reed Supply Company
Trial Balance
January 1, 19X2

Cash	$ 800	
Accounts Receivable	1,850	
Merchandise Inventory	2,000	
Delivery Equipment	8,000	
Accumulated Depreciation, Delivery Equipment		$ 2,400
Accounts Payable		1,200
John Reed, Capital		9,050
	$12,650	$12,650

19X2

Jan. 2 Sold merchandise on account to Stevens Products for $1,250. Invoice No. 595.

2 Sold merchandise on account to Ellis and Foster for $2,580. Invoice No. 596.

3 Purchased merchandise on account from Swan Company for $1,340.

4 Purchased office supplies on account from Dodson Supply Company, $170.

5 Sold merchandise on account to Ellis and Foster for $1,520. Invoice No. 597.

8 Purchased merchandise on account from Rush and Sons, $1,180.

9 Sold merchandise on account to Bolt and Sons for $465. Invoice No. 598.

10 Purchased office supplies for $150 and store supplies for $120 from Dodson Supply Company on account.

10 Returned merchandise to Rush and Sons for $180 from the purchase of January 8.

11 Purchased merchandise on account from Walters Company for $920.

13 Purchased merchandise from Swan Company on account for $1,340.

15 Sold merchandise on account to Nolan Supply Company for $980. Invoice No. 599.

19 Sold merchandise on account to Stevens Products for $750. Invoice No. 600.

23 Sold merchandise on account to Bolt and Sons for $1,300. Invoice No. 601.

Jan. 25 Purchased merchandise from Walters Company for $500 on account.
28 Purchased merchandise from Rush and Sons for $350 on account.
29 Sold merchandise for $900 to Nolan Supply Company. Invoice No. 602.
30 Sold merchandise for $1,600 to Bolt and Sons. Invoice No. 603.

Instructions

1. Record the transactions above in the journals.

NOTE: This comprehensive problem material will be used again in Chapter 9. All the journals needed for this problem are provided in your workbook with the Chapter 6 material.

chapter 7
CASH RECEIPTS AND DISBURSEMENTS

overall competency THE ABILITY TO KEEP RECORDS FOR CASH RECEIVED AND TO HANDLE CASH PAYMENTS

career objectives An accounting clerk must be able to prepare accurate business forms that account for the receipt, disbursement, and control of cash, that is, where a firm's money came from and where it has gone. When cash is received, it must be verified, deposited, and recorded in the accounts. When cash is paid, checks must be written and the payment journalized and posted. The accounting clerk uses special journals to record cash receipts and cash disbursements. This chapter gives you examples of business forms and the accounting records necessary to verify the receipt, disbursement, and control of cash.

When you complete this chapter, you should be able to:

- PREPARE ACCURATE FORMS FOR BUSINESS RECORDS WHEN CASH IS RECEIVED.
- JOURNALIZE CASH RECEIPTS IN A CASH RECEIPTS JOURNAL.
- POST TO THE GENERAL LEDGER AND TO THE SUBSIDIARY ACCOUNTS.
- RECORD CREDIT CARD SALES.
- FILL OUT CHECK STUBS AND WRITE CHECKS TO PAY INVOICES.
- USING THE CHECK STUBS AND OTHER REQUEST FORMS FOR CASH PAYMENTS, ANALYZE THE INFORMATION AND JOURNALIZE THE TRANSACTIONS IN THE CASH DISBURSEMENTS JOURNAL.
- FOOT, PROVE, AND RULE THE CASH DISBURSEMENTS JOURNAL AND THEN POST TO THE SUBSIDIARY LEDGER AND GENERAL LEDGER ACCOUNTS.

Because money has no identifying characteristics that link it to an owner and it is easily carried and widely accepted in exchange for goods and services, it can be stolen or misused quite easily. Reports in the news about fraud and theft should indicate that management must be careful in setting up a system of recording, handling, and protecting cash receipts and cash payments. Failure to provide these safeguards could result in significant losses to the firm.

Cash is collected mainly from daily cash sales and from collections on account. Cash is also received when the firm borrows money, the owner invests in the business, or the firm sells a piece of used equipment. Whatever the source, all cash receipts must be verified and properly recorded. Likewise, cash payments must be carefully controlled to be certain that payments are made only for authorized expenditures. We will examine the special journals available to the accounting clerk to make recording cash much easier.

• task PREPARE ACCURATE FORMS FOR BUSINESS RECORDS WHEN CASH IS RECEIVED

Cash sales

Daily cash sales reports are based upon the amounts shown on **cash register tapes.** Numbers on the left side of the cash register tape in Illustration 7-1 are used for inventory control, while amounts on the right provide the dollars and cents display.

illustration 7-1
cash register tape.

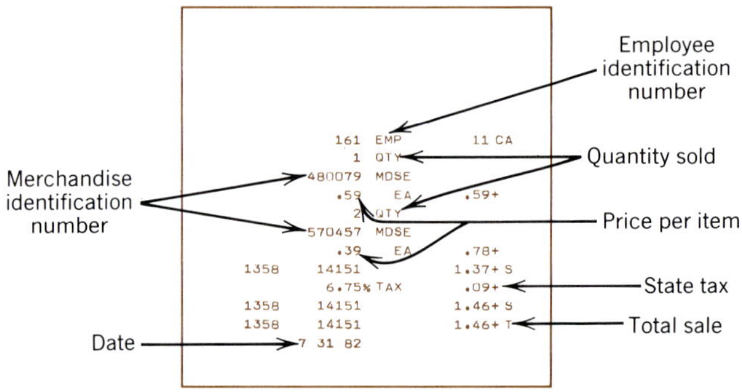

At the end of the business day, the actual amount of cash on hand is verified by a physical count. Any differences are reported as **cash short** or **cash over.** When verifying the actual amount of cash that should be on hand, you must consider the **cash change fund**—the amount of cash placed in the cash registers to make change. An example of the determination of cash short or over follows:

Cash Receipts June 2, 19X1

Total Cash in Register	$335.00
Less Change Fund	50.00
Cash Received	285.00
Cash Register Tape	288.00
Cash Short	$ 3.00

The general journal entry to record this daily cash sales report follows:

GENERAL JOURNAL — Page 1

Date		Description	P.R.	Dr.	Cr.
19X1 June	2	Cash		285 —	
		Cash Short and Over		3 —	
		Sales			288 —
		To record cash sales.			

Cash Short and Over is debited because of the mistake in making change. *Cash Short and Over* usually has a small debit balance since shortages are more common than overages. The best control over cash sales is the cash register that produces the tapes from which cash sales are recorded.

Sales taxes are collected as a part of cash sales and must be recorded. If a 6 percent sales tax were applied to the $288 sales above, an additional $17.28 would be collected. The journal entry to include the sales tax follows:

GENERAL JOURNAL — Page 1

Date		Description	P.R.	Dr.	Cr.
19X1 June	2	Cash		302 28	
		Cash Short and Over		3 —	
		Sales Taxes Payable			17 28
		Sales			288 —
		To record cash sales.			

Collections of accounts receivable

Sales made to customers on credit are collected at a later date according to the credit terms. As indicated in Chapter 6, *2/10, n/30* means that a 2 percent sales discount will be permitted if payment is received within ten days of the billing date. If not, the total amount is due within 30 days. Retail stores, utility companies, manufacturing companies, and other business organizations receive thousands of payments through the mail each week. You must make certain that the proper account is credited and that the correct amount was received.

To provide cash controls, the various procedures necessary to receive, deposit, and record cash should be performed by different persons. Clerks handling cash *should not* be responsible for recording cash transactions in the journal. In addition, a supervisor should approve the work of the others at the end of the day. The clerk who opens the mail should prepare a list of cash receipts each day to identify the customers making payment. The clerk opening the mail could be responsible for counting the cash from the cash register and preparing the change fund. A second clerk could receive the cash and prepare a deposit slip. A third clerk could receive a copy of customer payments and a copy of the deposit slip. After verifying the amounts on both forms, the third clerk could prepare the journal entries. A third copy of the cash receipts can be placed in the hands of a person responsible for reviewing the cash deposits and the journal transactions to make sure that no errors have been made and that all cash receipts are verified by the bank deposit. The flow diagram in Illustration 7-2 can help you identify the different responsibilities of the three clerks.

illustration 7-2
control of cash receipts.

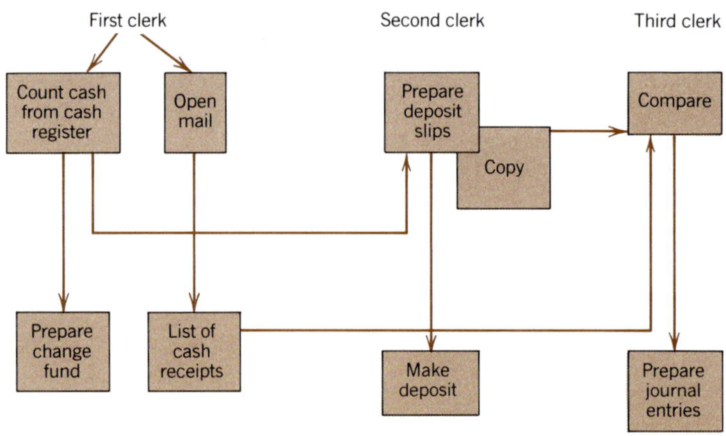

Business forms

A prenumbered **customer's receipt form** can be designed to conform to business needs. The typical receipt form should provide information as to the customer's name, accounts to be debited or credited, date received, explanation, and initials of the person receiving the cash. To save the cost of many different kinds of forms, the same form can be used to record cash receipts that was used to record sales on account. Assume Jayson's collected $86.32 on January 12 from Mrs. Able in full settlement of her account. (You may want to refer to her account in Illustration 6-9 before proceeding.)

Illustration 7-3 presents the details for this transaction on a customer receipt form.

illustration 7-3
customer receipt form. (courtesy of Jayson's)

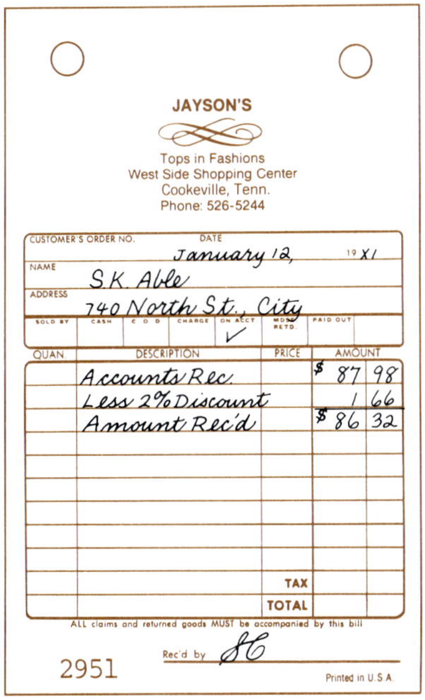
JAYSON'S

Tops in Fashions
West Side Shopping Center
Cookeville, Tenn.
Phone: 526-5244

CUSTOMER'S ORDER NO. — DATE January 12, 19X1
NAME S.K. Able
ADDRESS 740 North St., City
SOLD BY | CASH | C.O.D. | CHARGE | ON ACCT ✓ | MDSE RETD. | PAID OUT

QUAN	DESCRIPTION	PRICE	AMOUNT
	Accounts Rec.		$ 87 98
	Less 2% Discount		1 66
	Amount Rec'd		$ 86 32
		TAX	
		TOTAL	

ALL claims and returned goods MUST be accompanied by this bill

2951 Rec'd by SC Printed in U.S.A.

The general journal entry to illustrate the receipt of cash from Mrs. Able is given below:

GENERAL JOURNAL Page 12

Date		Description	P.R.	Dr.	Cr.
19X1 Jan.	12	Cash		87 98	
		Sales Discounts		1 66	
		Accounts Receivable/S.K. Able			86 32

Another form for the receipt of cash may use the design shown in Illustration 7-4.

illustration 7-4
cash receipt form. (courtesy of Ampad)

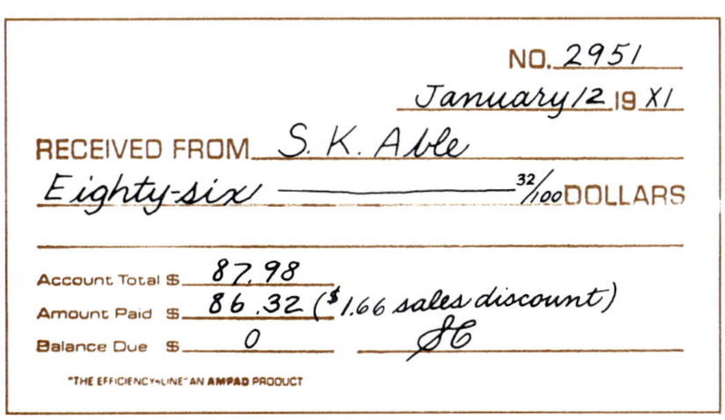
NO. 2951
January 12 19X1
RECEIVED FROM S. K. Able
Eighty-six ——— 32/100 DOLLARS

Account Total $ 87.98
Amount Paid $ 86.32 ($1.66 sales discount)
Balance Due $ 0 SC

"THE EFFICIENCY-LINE" AN AMPAD PRODUCT

The forms used are important in listing cash receipts. Cash can be recorded in the *cash receipts journal* from either of the foregoing two forms or from the cash register tapes. All cash receipts are listed on a **daily cash receipts report.** Because separate cash receipts are prepared for each customer when checks are received, an individual customer name is unnecessary on this receipts report. A daily cash receipts report and proof of cash can use the design shown in Illustration 7-5.

illustration 7-5
cash receipt report.

DAILY CASH RECEIPTS REPORT

Cash Receipt Report		Date January 15, 19X1
Cash Count		$1,022.30
Less Change Fund		100.00
Cash in Register		$ 922.30
Cash Sales	$320.10	
Cash Collected on Accounts Receivable	402.20	
Other Cash Receipts	200.00	
Total Cash Collected		922.30
Cash Short/Over		0

Other cash receipts

While the two main sources of cash receipts are cash sales and collections of accounts receivable, most businesses have other sources of cash receipts. For example, cash is received for the business entity when Mr. Victor Jones, the owner, decides to invest additional cash in the business, as shown below:

GENERAL JOURNAL Page 1

Date		Description	P.R.	Dr.	Cr.
19X1 Feb.	8	Cash		500 —	
		Victor Jones, Capital			500 —
		To invest additional capital			

Another example of cash receipts is cash borrowed by issuing a note payable. If interest is to be paid on the 60-day, 6 percent note payable on the maturity date, the following general journal entry would be recorded:

GENERAL JOURNAL — Page 1

Date		Description	P.R.	Dr.	Cr.
19X1 Feb.	10	Cash		300 —	
		Notes Payable			300 —
		To record issue of a 60 day,			
		6 percent note			

In some circumstances, a creditor may send a check for returned merchandise. The entry to record such a receipt would be:

GENERAL JOURNAL — Page 1

Date		Description	P.R.	Dr.	Cr.
19X1 Feb.	12	Cash		50 —	
		Purchases Returns and Allowances			50 —
		To record returned			
		merchandise			

sample problem The clerk (Sam Carter) responsible for incoming checks received by mail prepares a receipt for each payment received from the customer. The clerk is also responsible for collecting the cash sales receipts from the cash register. A second clerk (Jill West) is responsible for preparing the daily bank deposit. A third accounting clerk (Fred Harper) prepares the journal entries for the cash receipts for the day. The following checks were received in the mail on February 16:

	Owed		Cash Received
L. P. Green Company	\$300	2/10,n/30	\$294
Gene Cone Company	400	2/10,n/30	392
Brown & Brown	250	n/30	250
Lockwood, Inc.	280	n/30	280
Cash sales for the day			\$320

Instructions

(a) Prepare cash receipt form No. 301 for L. P. Green Company.

(b) Prepare the journal entry to record the receipt of cash.

sample problem solution

(a)

NO. 301
February 16 19X1
RECEIVED FROM L. P. Green Co.
Two Hundred Ninety-Four — 00/100 DOLLARS

Account Total $ 300.00
Amount Paid $ 294.00 ($6.00 sales discount)
Balance Due $ 0   SC

"THE EFFICIENCY-LINE" AN AMPAD PRODUCT

(b)

19X1			
Feb. 16	Cash	1,536	
	Sales Discounts	14	
	Sales		320
	Accounts Receivable/L. P. Green Company		300
	Accounts Receivable/Gene Cone Company		400
	Accounts Receivable/Brown & Brown		250
	Accounts Receivable/Lockwood, Inc.		280
	To record daily cash receipts		

review exercises

1. Assume that on February 16, Jones Company receives $154 for cash sales and $1,536 in collections from customers. Total cash deposits for the day are $1,685 of cash counted from the cash register ($1,715, less a change fund of $30). Determine the cash short or cash over.
2. Name two sources of cash collections other than cash sales and collections of accounts receivable.

• task JOURNALIZE CASH RECEIPTS IN A CASH RECEIPTS JOURNAL

Purpose of special journals

Cash receipts as verified by business forms represent one of the most frequent transactions of a business. The accounting clerk must take great care in recording these transactions or errors will be entered into the accounting system. Once errors have been made, they may be difficult to locate because so many transactions have been recorded. Accounting systems are designed to provide an efficient flow of accounting data. *Special journals* are designed to group similar and frequent transactions. These special journals provide a means of recording transactions efficiently and help prevent errors. The **cash receipts journal** is an example of a special journal that can be used for the frequent recording of cash receipts. Sources of cash can be examined easily when all cash receipts are recorded in a special journal.

The cash receipts journal has a special column for each type of frequent transaction that involves a general ledger account. Amounts are collected in these columns and totaled. Since most cash receipts are from cash sales and collections from customers, you should set up special columns for *Cash, Accounts Receivable,* and *Sales.* Other general ledger accounts that may be needed in a cash receipts journal are *Sales Discounts* and *Sales Taxes Payable.* A *Sundry Cr.* column is provided for all credit entries that do not have special columns. A typical cash receipts journal is presented in Illustration 7-6. You can understand the efficiency of this format when considering

illustration 7-6 cash receipts journal.

CASH RECEIPTS JOURNAL Page 7

Date		Account Credited	P.R.	Sundry Cr.	Accounts Receivable Cr.	Sales Cr.	Sales Discounts Dr.	Cash Dr.
19X1 Mar.	3	Milton Company			450 –		9 –	441 –
	4	Office Supplies		10 –				10 –
	5	Sales				1163 –		1163 –
	5	Zwolwinski & Shannon			150 –		3 –	147 –
	6	Jasper, Inc.			500 –		10 –	490 –

the general journal approach for recording cash sales and collections on accounts receivable. For example, if $500 is collected for cash sales and $200 is collected on account, the following entries would be recorded in general journal form.

GENERAL JOURNAL Page 1

Date		Description	P.R.	Dr.	Cr.
19X1 Jan.	2	Cash		500 –	
		Sales			500 –
		Sold merchandise for cash.			
	2	Cash			
		Accounts Receivable/Fred Burton		200 –	
		Collected on account for sale of Dec. 23.			200 –

Cash has been debited two times and should be posted twice. In addition, *Accounts Receivable* must be written every time collections are made on account if general journal procedures are followed. With many thousands of cash transactions to record and post, the accounting clerk finds these methods time consuming. Special columns established for *Cash, Accounts Receivable,* and *Sales* greatly increase efficiency by reducing the detailed repetition otherwise required to handle frequent transactions. Illustration 7-7 shows that these same two transactions require only two lines in the cash receipts journals.

illustration 7-7 cash receipts journal.

CASH RECEIPTS JOURNAL — Page 17

Date		Account Credited	P.R.	Sundry Cr.	Accounts Receivable Cr.	Sales Cr.	Sales Discounts Dr.	Cash Dr.
19X1 Jan.	2	Sales				500 –		500 –
	2	Fred Burton			200 –			200 –

Amount columns for specific ledger accounts enable the accounting clerk to journalize identical types of transactions easily without repeatedly writing the same general ledger account titles required for individual general journal transactions. The format for the cash receipts journal is designed to record the information from business documents that verifies the receipt of cash. The journal provides an easy way of posting this information to the general ledger accounts and the accounts receivable subsidiary ledger.

The *Sundry Cr.* column of a cash receipts journal provides for all other accounts of the general ledger that are credited when *Cash* is debited. For example, the capital account is credited when cash is invested by the owner. Since this type of transaction does not happen often, a separate column for the owner's capital account in the cash receipts journal is unnecessary.

Cash receipts journal entries

The purpose and efficiency of the cash receipts journal can be illustrated best by showing some typical transactions. When recording transactions in the cash receipts journal, remember to

1. Place amounts received on account in the *Accounts Receivable Cr.* column.
2. Place all cash sales in the *Sales Cr.* column.
3. Place all other cash receipts in the *Sundry Cr.* column.

The typical transactions described below represent these three groups. Illustration 7-8 shows how to record them in the cash receipts journal.

(a) Cash collections on account.

Date				Cash Received
19X1				
1/12	S. K. Able	$ 87.98	2/10, n/30	$ 86.32
1/16	Marx Company	660.00	2/10, n/30	646.80
1/24	Loma Company	340.00	2/10, n/30	340.00

(b) Cash sales recorded each day.

(Only three days will be illustrated)

1/7	$100.20
1/20	320.10
1/28	200.40

(c) Other accounts.

1/18	Additional investment by Victor Jones, the owner	$500.00
1/27	Borrowed cash from the Second National Bank by issuing a note payable	300.00

illustration 7-8 cash receipts journal.

CASH RECEIPTS JOURNAL — Page 14

Date		Account Credited	P.R.	Sundry Cr.	Accounts Receivable Cr.	Sales Cr.	Sales Discounts Dr.	Cash Dr.
19X1 Jan.	7	Sales				100 20		100 20
	12	S.K. Able			87 98		1 66	86 32
	16	Marx Company			660 –		13 20	646 80
	18	Victor Jones, Capital		500 –				500 –
	20	Sales				320 10		320 10
	24	Loma Company			340 –			340 –
	27	Notes Payable		300 –				300 –
	28	Sales				200 40		200 40

On January 12, cash of $86.32 collected from S. K. Able is placed in the *Cash Dr.* column. Full credit for the payment is made by crediting *Accounts Receivable* for the $87.98. A debit of $1.66 to *Sales Discounts* is the difference between the cash received of $86.32 and the $87.98 owed by the customer. All collections on account are recorded by this procedure. The *Account Credited* column requires only the name of the creditor. A proof that debits equal credits for each transaction of this type can be illustrated as follows:

Debits		Credits	
Cash	$86.32	Accounts Receivable	$87.98
Sales Discounts	1.66		
	$87.98	⟷	$87.98

The accuracy of each type of transaction in the cash receipts journal can be shown this way.

With a special column for *Sales Cr.*, all cash sales can be recorded quickly with a minimum of writing time for ledger account titles. However, the third type of cash transaction for the sundry or other general ledger accounts requires additional instructions. The accounting clerk must write the name of the general ledger account to be credited in the *Account Credited* column. For example, in Illustration 7-8, the two cash receipts are credits to *Victor Jones, Capital* and to *Notes Payable*. The January 18 transaction journalizes an additional investment by the owner, and the January 27 transaction records the cash received when the company borrowed from the bank.

sample problem Prepare the following four transactions for the Grover Company for February, 19X1, in a cash receipts journal.

Feb. 2 Received from a customer, James Oaks, $500 less 2 percent sales discount.

10 Cash sales, $650.

12 Borrowed $400 from Community Bank by issuing a note payable.

15 Received $300 less 2 percent from a customer, Don Frey.

sample problem solution

CASH RECEIPTS JOURNAL Page 7

Date		Account Credited	P.R.	Sundry Cr.	Accounts Receivable Cr.	Sales Cr.	Sales Disc. Dr.	Cash Dr.
19X1								
Feb.	2	James Oaks			500		10	490
	10	Cash Sales				650		650
	12	Notes Payable		400				400
	15	Don Frey			300		6	294

review exercises

3. Using the sample problem solution given above, determine the total credit to be given to customers for February.
4. Use the solution to Review Exercise 3 to present the journal entry for Don Frey in general journal form. What additional writing did you need to prepare the journal entry in this form?

• task POST TO THE GENERAL LEDGER AND TO THE SUBSIDIARY ACCOUNTS

Posting the cash receipts journal

The greatest efficiency of a special journal is gained in the posting process. When a general journal is used, each general ledger account must be posted individually and there is no opportunity to group identical transactions. Dates, posting reference numbers, and amounts must be posted for each item, a time-consuming and inefficient process.

When a cash receipts journal is used, special amount columns are totaled and posted at the end of the month or fiscal period. Day-by-day posting of general ledger accounts is not needed. End-of-the-month posting of totals is sufficient to prepare the trial balance and the financial statement. Posting individual customer accounts on a current basis, however, is important to maintain up-to-date balances for customers and to avoid credit losses. A quick review of a customer's individual account will show how promptly accounts are being collected. Recall from our discussion of posting to the subsidiary ledger that a check mark is placed in the posting reference column to indicate that individual customer accounts have been posted.

When posting to the general ledger from the cash receipts journal, you must post the general ledger accounts in the *Sundry Cr.* column, as well as totals from the specific account columns. In ruling the cash receipts journal, place double lines across all amount columns. Proving the accuracy of the cash receipts journal is complete when the totals of the debit column equal the totals of the credit column. Equality of debits and credits in the cash receipts journal in Illustration 7-8 is proved by the following totals:

Debit Totals		Credit Totals	
Sales Discounts	$ 14.86	Sundry	$ 800.00
Cash	2,493.82	Accounts Receivable	1,087.98
		Sales	620.70
	$2,508.68	⟵⟶	$2,508.68

Transferring cash receipts data requires three types of posting from the cash receipts journal:

1. Posting to the individual customer accounts (daily).
2. Posting the general ledger accounts from the sundry credit column (daily).
3. Posting the totals from the specific account columns (end-of-month).

Illustration 7-9 shows how the cash receipts journal is posted and ruled.

Ledger account numbers are placed in the posting reference column to indicate postings to *Victor Jones, Capital* and *Notes Payable*. Collections on account are posted to the individual customers' accounts, and a check mark is placed in the posting reference column. The posted accounts receivable

illustration 7-9
posting from a cash receipts journal.

CASH RECEIPTS JOURNAL — Page 14

Date		Account Credited	P.R.	Sundry Cr.	Accounts Receivable Cr.	Sales Cr.	Sales Discounts Dr.	Cash Dr.
19X1 Jan.	7	Sales	✓			100.20		100.20
	12	S.K. Able	✓		87.98		1.66	86.32
	16	Marx Company	✓		660 —		13.20	646.80
	18	Victor Jones, Capital	31	500 —				500 —
	20	Sales	✓			320.10		320.10
	24	Loma Company	✓		340 —			340 —
	27	Notes Payable	23	300 —				300 —
	28	Sales	✓			200.40		200.40
	31			800 —	1,087.98	620.70	14.86	2,493.82
				(✓)	(12)	(41)	(42)	(11)

ACCOUNTS RECEIVABLE SUBSIDIARY LEDGER

S. K. Able
740 North Street
City

19X1 Jan.	12		CR14		87.98	xxx

Marx Company
5550 Governors Drive
Huntsville, AL 35802

19X1 Jan.	16		CR14		660	xxx

Loma Company
P.O. Box 884
City

19X1 Jan.	24		CR14		340	xxx

GENERAL LEDGER

Cash — 11

19X1 Jan.	31		CR14	2,493.82		xxx	

Accounts Receivable — 12

19X1 Jan.	31		CR14		1,087.98		xxx

Notes Payable 23

19X1 Jan.	27		CR14		300.00		XXX

Victor Jones, Capital 31

19X1 Jan.	18		CR14		500.00		XXX

Sales 41

19X1 Jan.	31		CR14		620.70		XXX

Sales Discounts 42

19X1 Jan.	31		CR14	14.86		XXX	

subsidiary ledger can be seen in Illustration 7-10. Because each item in the *Sundry Cr.* column is posted individually, the column total is not posted. A check mark placed in parentheses below the double lines indicates this treatment. All other amount columns are posted in total to the general ledger account shown at the top of the column. This posting is indicated by placing the general ledger account number in parentheses below the double lines.

In this illustration, full payment for three of the four customers entitles them to full credit, even when a discount is taken. S. K. Able paid $86.32

illustration 7-10 posted accounts receivable subsidiary ledger.

S. K. Able
740 North Street
City

Date		Explanation	P.R.	Dr.	Cr.	Balance
19X1 Jan.	3		S1	106 –		106 –
	7		G1		18 02	87 98
	12		CR14		87 98	-0-

N. M. Bass
1212 Morningside Drive
City

Date		Explanation	P.R.	Dr.	Cr.	Balance
19X1 Jan.	15		S1	150 –		150 –

Loma Company
P.O. Box 884
City

Date		Explanation	P.R.	Dr.	Cr.	Balance
19X1 Jan.	5		S1	340 –		340 –
	24		CR14		340 –	–0–

Marx Company
5550 Governors Drive
Huntsville, AL 35802

Date		Explanation	P.R.	Dr.	Cr.	Balance
19X1 Jan.	12		S1	660 –		660 –
	16		CR14		660 –	–0–

on January 12 and was given credit in his subsidiary account for $87.98. The page number of the cash receipts journal is recorded in the posting reference column of the customer's account for quick reference to the journal entry. This page number is preceded by CR to tell the accounting clerk that the information was posted from the cash receipts journal.

sample problem For the previous sample problem with four entries for a cash receipts journal, rule the journal and complete all postings.

sample problem solution

CASH RECEIPTS JOURNAL Page 7

Date		Account Credited	P.R.	Sundry Cr.	Accounts Receivable Cr.	Sales Cr.	Sales Discounts Dr.	Cash Dr.
19X1 Feb.	2	James Oaks	✓		500 –		10 –	490 –
	10	Sales	✓			650 –		650 –
	12	Notes Payable	21	400 –				400 –
	15	Don Frey	✓		300 –		6 –	294 –
				400 –	800 –	650 –	16 –	1834 –
				(✓)	(12)	(41)	(42)	(11)

ACCOUNTS RECEIVABLE SUBSIDIARY LEDGER

Don Frey

19X1 Feb.	15		CR7		300	XXX

James Oaks

19X1 Feb.	2		CR7		500	XXX

GENERAL LEDGER

Cash 11

19X1 Feb.	28		CR7	1,834		XXXX	

Accounts Receivable 12

19X1 Feb.	28		CR7		800	XXX	

Notes Payable 21

19X1 Feb.	12		CR7		400		400

Sales 41

19X1 Feb.	28		CR7		650		XXXX

Sales Discounts 42

19X1 Feb.	28		CR7	16		XXX	

review exercises

5. In the sample problem, why did you credit *Notes Payable* to the *Sundry Cr.* column? Will *Notes Payable* be posted as a part of the total of the *Sundry Dr.* column or individually? Why place check marks in the posting reference column for customer collections?

6. In reference to the sample problem solution, why is posting to the individual customer accounts and also to *Accounts Receivable* necessary?

• task RECORD CREDIT CARD SALES

With the coming of "plastic money," American shopping habits changed dramatically. Instead of presenting money or filling out credit applications each time a purchase is made, the customer may use a **credit card** to buy merchandise or service. Each credit card contains an emblem for the issuing bank or company, an account number, the customer's name, and an expiration date. In addition, the card owner is asked to sign the card before using it. This signature helps the vendor identify unauthorized use.

Bank credit cards

You are probably familiar with credit cards issued by banks. The most popular ones in circulation use the MasterCard® and VISA service marks. To illustrate how to account for a bank credit card sale, assume that Howard Franklin uses his VISA card to buy a blouse and pants. The salesperson takes Howard's card and a **sales draft** (also known as a *sales slip* or *sales voucher*) and makes an impression of the card's raised information and the store's identification plate on the sales draft. You have probably watched this process when using your own card to make a purchase.

Since some abuse the credit card privilege, caution is required by the salesperson in accepting credit cards. A listing of all the numbers of credit cards that should no longer be honored is circulated frequently by banks. A quick check through this numerically arranged list should be made before completing the transactions. The salesperson also has a toll-free number provided by the banks for sales approvals. The bank employee, who verifies available credit sufficient to make the purchase, supplies an authorization code. This number is placed in the proper box on the sales draft. The completed sales draft for the Howard Franklin transaction is shown in Illustration 7-11.

illustration 7-11 credit card sales draft.

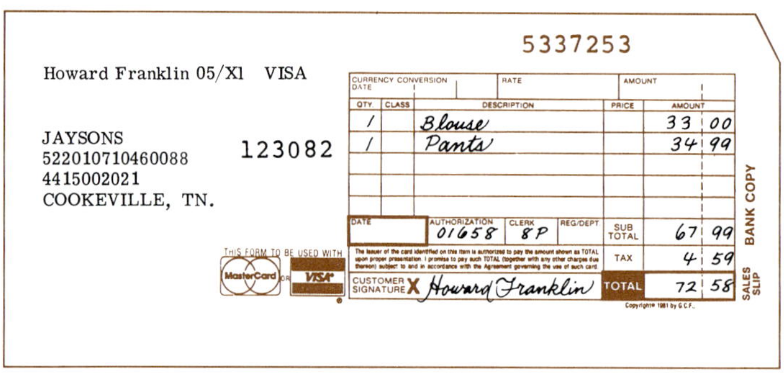

5337253

Howard Franklin 05/X1 VISA

JAYSONS
522010710460088
4415002021
COOKEVILLE, TN.

123082

QTY.	CLASS	DESCRIPTION	PRICE	AMOUNT
1		Blouse		33 00
1		Pants		34 99

AUTHORIZATION 01658 — CLERK 8P

SUB TOTAL 67 99
TAX 4 59
TOTAL 72 58

CUSTOMER SIGNATURE X Howard Franklin

THIS FORM TO BE USED WITH MasterCard OR VISA

BANK COPY — SALES SLIP

"MasterCard" is a registered trademark of MasterCard International, Inc.

The sales draft is completed in three copies: one for the customer, one for the bank, and one for the merchant's records. The burden of collection is on the bank, not the vendor, so the merchant treats the transaction very much like a cash sale. To illustrate, assume that on March 13 Fashionable Suit's accounting clerk totals the merchant's copies of the credit card sales drafts. Clothing sales before taxes total $1,065.96, while sales taxes amount to $63.96. The entry would be recorded as follows:

CASH RECEIPTS JOURNAL Page 75

Date		Account Credited	P.R.	Sundry Cr.	Accounts Receivable Cr.	Sales Taxes Payable Cr.	Sales Cr.	Sales Discounts Dr.	Cash Dr.
19X1 Mar.	13	Sales (Credit Card)				63 96	1 065 96		1 129 92

We have added a *Sales Taxes Payable* Cr. column to Fashionable Suit's cash receipts journal since this vendor enters transactions to this account daily. Later, when the bank statement arrives, *Credit Card Discount Expense* is debited and *Cash* is credited. This approach introduces a new account, but you should treat it as you would a service charge expense.

Nonbank credit cards

Numerous firms encourage sales by providing a credit card usable only for purchases from that particular firm. Sears, Shell Oil, and American Airlines all have such a program. If the credit card operation is local, for example, a building supply firm that has a card for approved contractors, then each sale is a sale on account. This means that you treat the transaction as a credit sale by debiting *Accounts Receivable* (and the customer's account) and crediting *Sales.*

Large operations that have thousands of retail outlets allow these stores to pay the home office for merchandise or services rendered by using the sales draft like cash—but only to the home office. Since so many variations of these plans are used, we will not go into further detail about this arrangement.

Companies may also be set up specifically to deal in credit cards—American Express, Diners Club, and Carte Blanche, for example. Credit card transactions involving this type of card require the accountant to set up an *Accounts Receivable* from the credit card company. To illustrate, assume that Hotel DuVont accepts American Express credit cards. The firm is located in a state that levies an 8 percent hotel tax. When the receipts are counted, 45 sales drafts total $2,916 (including $216 for the hotel tax). The following entry would be made in the sales journal:

SALES JOURNAL — Page 154

Date		Account Debited	P.R.	Accts. Rec. Dr.	Hotel Taxes Payable Cr.	Hotel Revenue Cr.
19X1 July	17	American Express		2916 –	216 –	2700 –

Credit card companies charge a fee known as a *discount* for their service. Assume in this case that the discount rate is 6 percent. When cash is received from American Express, the following entry is journalized:

CASH RECEIPTS JOURNAL — Page 79

Date		Account Credited	P.R.	Sundry Cr.	Accounts Receivable Cr.	Sales Taxes Payable Dr.	Sales Cr.	Sales Discounts Dr.	Cash Dr.
19X1 Aug.	15	American Express			2916				274104
		Credit Card Discount Expense		(17496)					

Note that the debit to *Credit Card Discount Expense* presents an awkward situation. If the entry is placed in the *Sundry Accounts Dr.* column, brackets or red ink must be used to show that it is a debit. A better approach is to use a special column for this account, but having such a column depends primarily on how often entries are made for transactions with firms like American Express and Diners Club.

Credit slips

Occasionally, a customer who used a credit card to purchase merchandise returns the item. The proper accounting treatment depends on the type of credit card. If it is a bank credit card, the entry is a debit to *Sales Returns and Allowances*, a debit to *Sales Taxes Payable* (if appropriate), and a credit to *Cash*. If a nonbank credit card is involved (such as J. C. Penney or American Express), the entry above would show a credit to *Accounts Receivable/American Express*. It is possible to net the sales drafts and credit slips, but such a treatment would not give information about the amount of merchandise being returned.

sample problem On August 6, 19X1, Valley Drugs receives 25 credit card sales drafts from customers. Eight of these totaling $275.15 are on MasterCard credit cards, six totaling $186.34 are on VISA cards, one for $29.50 is on an American Express card, and ten amounting to $76.50 are on Valley Drugs' own charge system. Make a compound journal entry in general journal form to record the 25 sales drafts. Assume that American Express charges a 6 percent discount rate and that the state does not have a sales tax. For the purpose of this sample problem, indicate the subsidiary ledger for Valley Drugs' system with an X.

sample problem solution

Cash	$461.49	
Accounts Receivable/American Express	29.50	
Accounts Receivable/X	76.50	
Sales		$567.49

review exercises

7. Using the information in the sample problem, make the entry (in general journal form) to record receipt of payment from American Express (6 percent charge).

8. Village Shoes accepts VISA and MasterCard credit cards. On January 3, 40 sales drafts and two credit slips are in the receipts. The sales drafts total $935.96, and the two credit slips amount to $41.69. Make the needed entry in general journal form to record this information.

• task FILL OUT CHECK STUBS AND WRITE CHECKS TO PAY INVOICES

Receiving the invoice

When you receive a *purchase invoice,* examine it for accuracy. Match the invoice price with the amounts shown on the purchase order and verify the extensions to see if they have been multiplied properly and that all subtotals and totals have been added correctly. The invoice shown in Illustration 7-12 has been checked for:

1. agreement with the purchase order
2. accuracy of extensions
3. addition of subtotals and totals

In some companies, separate receiving departments prepare a **receiving report** that can be compared with the seller's invoice. A typical receiving report shown in Illustration 7-13 indicates that the merchandise bill to Jayson's in Illustration 7-12 was received in good condition and in the quantity ordered.

HOOPER COMPANY
365 Roosevelt Drive
New York, NY 10158

INVOICE
№ 1308

SOLD TO Jayson's
36 West Broad
West Side Shopping Center
Cookeville, Tenn. 38501

SHIP TO Jayson's

DATE 3/2/X1
SOLD BY Cookeville, Tenn.
TERMS 2% Net FOB NY

STYLE	QUANTITY	DESCRIPTION	PRICE		EXTENSION	
60-5205X	2	White jacket	70	00	140	00
		6968606/15994				
		Color #001				
60-5205X	3	Navy jacket	70	00	210	00
		6968605/15994				
		Color #005				
			SUB TOTAL		350	00
			FREIGHT		3	89
			TOTAL		353	89

illustration 7-12 invoice.

Paying the invoice

One of your jobs as an accounting clerk might be to make certain that all the company's trade debts are paid on time to take advantage of purchase

illustration 7-13
receiving report. (courtesy of Rediform)

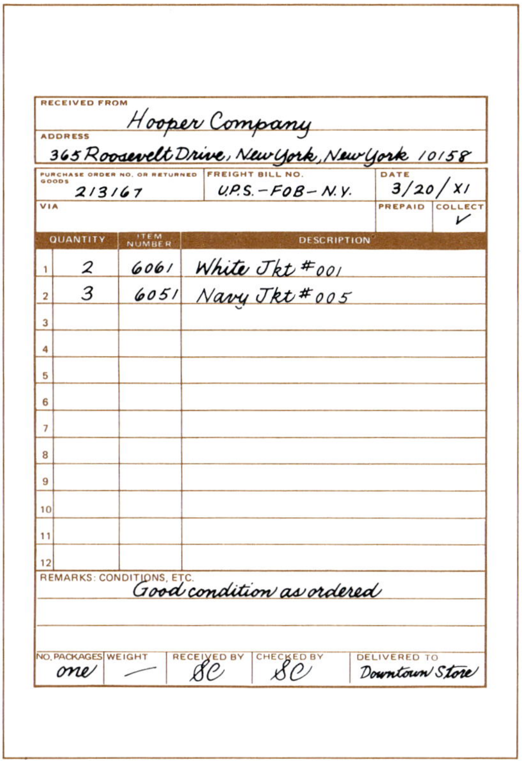

RECEIVED FROM Hooper Company
ADDRESS 365 Roosevelt Drive, New York, New York 10158

PURCHASE ORDER NO. OR RETURNED GOODS	FREIGHT BILL NO.	DATE
213167	U.P.S.-FOB-N.Y.	3/20/X1

VIA | PREPAID | COLLECT ✓

	QUANTITY	ITEM NUMBER	DESCRIPTION
1	2	6061	White Jkt #001
2	3	6051	Navy Jkt #005
3			
4			
5			
6			
7			
8			
9			
10			
11			
12			

REMARKS: CONDITIONS, ETC. Good condition as ordered

NO. PACKAGES	WEIGHT	RECEIVED BY	CHECKED BY	DELIVERED TO
one	—	SC	SC	Downtown Store

discounts and also to maintain a good credit rating. One convenient method of knowing when to pay a bill is to file the invoice in an accordion file (a heavy-duty paper file that opens and closes much like an accordion) by the date on which you wish to pay. Every day the authorized person pulls out the invoices to be paid on that particular day and writes the checks.

Note that because a 2 percent discount on the invoice is permitted if it is paid within ten days of the billing date, a check would be prepared for $346.89 payable to Hooper Company. This check is written by the owner or someone whom the owner has authorized to write checks. Often this person is very busy, and occasionally may fail to complete the check stub properly or, even worse, may leave it blank. The accounting clerk may have to remind the check writer of the additional time, and therefore cost, involved in supplying this information later.

Now that we have the owner or other check writer trained, let's take a closer look at the stub. Most forms have space for the date, the name of the person or firm to whom the check is being written, the purpose, and the amount. Space is limited, so discretion must be used in adding information like the invoice number paid and account number affected. The check stub for the check written to Hooper Company is shown in Illustration 7-14.

illustration 7-14
check stub. (courtesy of John N. Harland Company)

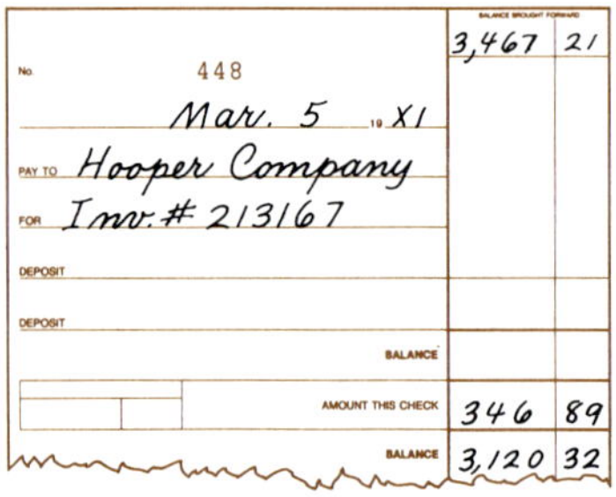

BALANCE BROUGHT FORWARD 3,467 21
No. 448
Mar. 5 19 X1
PAY TO Hooper Company
FOR Inv. # 213167
DEPOSIT
DEPOSIT
BALANCE
AMOUNT THIS CHECK 346 89
BALANCE 3,120 32

Once the check stub has been completed, the authorized person fills in the check. The completed handwritten check is shown in Illustration 7-15. An alternative approach to preparing checks properly is to have the accounting clerk complete both the stub and the check and then present it to the authorized person for signature only.

illustration 7-15
handwritten check. (courtesy of Jayson's)

THIS CHECK IS DELIVERED IN CONNECTION WITH THE FOLLOWING ACCOUNT(S)

DATE		AMOUNT
3/2 X1	213167	350 –
	Freight	3 89
	TOTAL OF INVOICES	353 89
	LESS 2 % DISCOUNT	7 –
	LESS	
	TOTAL DEDUCTIONS	
	AMOUNT OF CHECK	346 89

JAYSON'S
WEST SIDE SHOPPING CENTER
COOKEVILLE, TN 38501
448
87-564
641
Mar. 2 19 X1
PAY TO THE ORDER OF Hooper Company $ 346.89
Three Hundred forty six and 89/100 — DOLLARS
CITIZENSBANK
P.O. Box 70
Cookeville, Tennessee 38501
JAYSON'S
Michael Jayson
⑈046508⑈ ⑆064105640⑆ 07 700 3⑈

Since some people alter information on checks before cashing them, some firms use control devices to reduce this possibility. Illustration 7-16 shows the simplest approach, a check-writing machine to record the amount. Some firms use a machine to enter all the information, including the signature.

illustration 7-16
check with machine-written amount. (courtesy of Cody Office Equipment and Supplies)

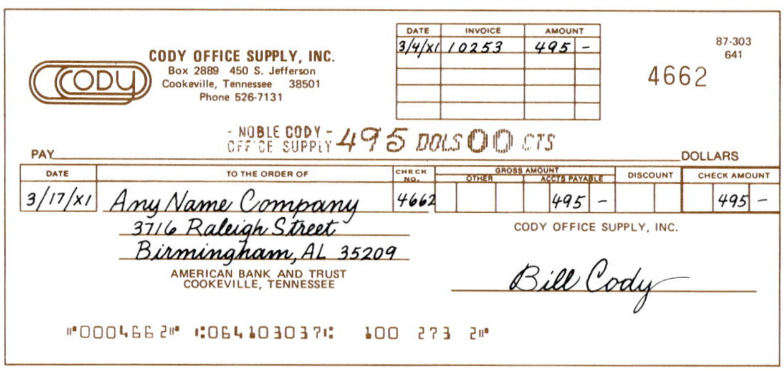

CODY
CODY OFFICE SUPPLY, INC.
Box 2889 450 S. Jefferson
Cookeville, Tennessee 38501
Phone 526-7131

DATE	INVOICE	AMOUNT
3/4/x1	10253	495 –

87-303
641
4662
PAY - NOBLE CODY - OFFICE SUPPLY 495 DOLS 00 CTS DOLLARS

DATE	TO THE ORDER OF	CHECK NO.	GROSS AMOUNT OTHER	GROSS AMOUNT ACCTS PAYABLE	DISCOUNT	CHECK AMOUNT
3/17/x1	Any Name Company	4662		495 –		495 –

3716 Raleigh Street
Birmingham, AL 35209
AMERICAN BANK AND TRUST
COOKEVILLE, TENNESSEE
CODY OFFICE SUPPLY, INC.
Bill Cody
⑈0004662⑈ ⑆064103037⑆ 100 273 2⑈

Check request form

Companies also need to control expenditures for which no regular invoices are received. A **check request form** can be prepared to authorize these expenditures. Again the amount, the name of the person or company to be paid, and the account to be charged are shown. A responsible person within the business is required to approve the payment. A check request form is shown in Illustration 7-17.

illustration 7-17
check request form.

Payable To *Monroe Company*
Address *Davis Street*
City *Hometown* State *TN.* Zip Code *38501*
Amount $ *392 00* Charge to Account No. *619*
Or Charge To
For *Rent Expense – March and April*

Requested by	Approved by *DRH*	Check issued by *BC* Check No. *470*

sample problem As the accounting clerk, you are permitted to fill in the check stub and prepare the check for signature. Use the following facts to draw a rough copy of a check and stub and to prepare it for the owner's signature.

Date: July 17, 19X1
Purpose: Pay Levy Brothers for Inv. 3371 ($852.40 less a 2 percent discount)
Balance in checking account before Check 5514—$2,650.33
Check 5514 is to be used

sample problem solution

Stub:
No. 5514
July 17, 19 *X1*
Pay to *Levy Brothers*
For *A/P – Inv. # 3371*
Balance brought forward *2,650 33*
Deposit
Deposit
Balance
Amount this check *835 35*
Balance *1,814 98*

Check:
JAY SMITH WORLD TRAVEL SERVICE, INC.
400 DUBOIS RD COOKEVILLE MALL
615 528-6491
COOKEVILLE, TN 38501
5514
87-190/641
July 17, 19 *X1*
PAY TO THE ORDER OF *Levy Brothers* $ *835.35*
Eight Hundred thirty five and 35/100 DOLLARS
FIRST TENNESSEE BANK 1ST
N.A. COOKEVILLE COOKEVILLE, TENNESSEE
FOR
⑈005514⑈ ⑆064101903⑆ ⑈0135976⑈

review exercises

9. An invoice is received from Bennett Wholesalers for $596.95. A 2 percent discount is permitted for early payment. Included in the invoice price is freight of $20. In preparing to write the check, determine the amount, assuming the invoice is paid within the discount period.

• task USING THE CHECK STUBS AND OTHER REQUEST FORMS FOR CASH PAYMENTS, ANALYZE THE INFORMATION AND JOURNALIZE THE TRANSACTIONS IN THE CASH DISBURSEMENTS JOURNAL

Cash disbursements journal

Once again we have a repetitive accounting procedure. For day-to-day business transactions, many checks are written to pay the company's debts. Many of the cash payment transactions pay accounts payable. Therefore, a special journal is designed with special columns for debits to *Accounts Payable* and credits to *Cash.* The design of a special journal permits a division of labor for handling all the required accounting routines. Having several different persons involved in an accounting routine also helps to control cash, as explained in our discussion of cash receipts. By providing a **cash disbursements journal** for these frequent transactions, we can both control cash and record the transactions efficiently by reducing recording time. Many of the transactions, such as payment of invoices, are routine, and recorded explanations are unnecessary. By using special column headings, we can group the accounts involved in repeated transactions.

Because all cash payments should be recorded in the cash disbursements journal, we must record payments for such items as salaries, operating expenses, equipment purchases, and other expenditures. If we must also make frequent payments for certain operating expenses, we can use special columns with the account title to provide for them. The cash disbursement journal is flexible enough to provide columns for all accounts that require repeated and frequent recordings.

For purposes of our analysis of the cash disbursements journal, we will assume that other than for payments on account, cash payments are not frequent enough to require a special column. Therefore, as we did in the cash receipts journal, a *Sundry Accounts Dr.* column is provided to account for the other types of payments that a business normally makes. Jayson's cash disbursements journal, shown as Illustration 7-18, includes typical transactions.

Payment of invoices

Follow the payment to Hooper Company by the Jayson Company with Check No. 448. The full amount of $353.89 owed to the company is recorded in the *Accounts Payable Dr.* column to show that Hooper Company has been

CASH DISBURSEMENTS JOURNAL — Page 1

Date		Ch. No.	Payee	Account Debited	P.R.	Sundry Accounts Dr.	Accounts Payable Dr.	Purchases Discounts Cr.	Cash Cr.
19X1 Mar.	5	448	Hooper Company	Hooper Company			353 89	7 –	346 89
	6	449	Sally Doaks	Office Salaries Expense		125 –			125 –
	8	450	Russel Dover Company	Advertising Expense		100 –			100 –
	10	451	Leo Green Company	Leo Green Comany			400 –	8 –	392 –
	12	452	Sall's Discount Store	Sall's Discount Store			250 60		250 60
	13	453	Julia Green	Sales Returns and Allowances		54 –			54 –
	15	454	Borak Distributors	Borak Distributors			580 –	11 60	568 40
	20	455	Carson Office Supply	Office Supplies		200 –			200 –
	22	456	King Wholesale Company	King Wholesale Company			330 50	6 61	323 89
	25	457	Michael Jayson	Jayson, Drawing		300 –			300 –
	26	458	Jones Equipment Company	Office Equipment		420 –			420 –
	30	459	Payroll	Sales Salaries Expense		2000 –			2000 –
	31	460	Smith Company	Smith Company			150 –	3 –	147 –

illustration 7-18 **cash disbursements journal.**

paid in full. Since Hooper Company permitted a 2 percent discount, the purchase discount of $7 ($350 × .02) will be shown in the *Purchases Discount* column. The freight cost of $3.89 shown on the invoice and the check stub is debited to *Freight-In* when *Accounts Payable/Hooper Company* is credited for the full amount owed. The amount of cash actually paid, as shown on the check stub, is $346.89; it should be recorded in the *Cash Cr.* column.

Because purchase returns reduce the amount owed to a creditor, they must be considered before payment is made. For example, assume that a purchase of $200 (2/10, n/30) was made from Smith Company. A return of merchandise of $50 was made on March 25, as shown in the following general journal entry, with final payment on March 31 of $147 [$200 − $50 − ($150 × .02)]. Purchase discounts are never taken on merchandise returned.

GENERAL JOURNAL — Page 1

Date		Description	P.R.	Dr.	Cr.
19X1 Mar.	25	Accounts Payable/Smith Company		50 –	
		Purchases Returns and Allowances			50 –
		To return merchandise.			

Other payments

Follow the payment to Sally Doaks for monthly bookkeeping services that was supported by a request for a check form approved by Michael Jayson. The checks would be payable to Sally Doaks, and the account charged would be *Office Salaries Expense.* Since there is no special column for *Office*

Salaries Expense, the debit would be recorded in the *Sundry Accounts Dr.* column for $125 with a credit to the *Cash Cr.* column.

These additional payments for March are representative of the types of payments required by most companies:

Paid for advertising	$ 100
Cash payment for a returned sales item	54
Bought office supplies	200
Personal withdrawal by owner	300
Bought office equipment	420
Paid sales salaries	2,000

For each of these transactions, the account would be recorded in the *Sundry Accounts Dr.* column because the transactions are infrequent and do not fit into any special columns. Before leaving this section, be certain that you have examined Illustration 7-18 carefully and fully understand what is being done with each transaction. The company maintains a separate payroll checking account to pay its sales employees. Therefore, a check is made payable to payroll.

sample problem The Cashion Company maintains a cash disbursements journal. Record these transactions made during the first week of March:

March 1 Paid Wilson Company for Invoice No. 1120 with Check No. 102 for the amount owed of $400, less discount of 2 percent.

2 Paid Invoice No. 1121 with Check No. 103 to Farmer, Inc. for the amount owed of $850, less 2 percent discount.

3 Purchased office equipment for $320.50 from Jones Company using Check No. 104.

4 Paid sales salaries of $600. Make Check No. 105 payable to payroll.

6 Paid Invoice No. 1122 with Check No. 106 to Morrow Company for amount owed of $576.40. The amount was not paid during the discount period.

sample problem solution

CASH DISBURSEMENTS JOURNAL Page 19

Date		Ch. No.	Payee	Account Debited	P.R.	Sundry Accounts Dr.	Accounts Payable Dr.	Purchases Discounts Cr.	Cash Cr.
19X1 Mar.	1	102	Wilson Company	Wilson Company			400 –	8 –	392 –
	2	103	Farmer Inc.	Farmer Inc.			850 –	17 –	833 –
	3	104	Jones Company	Office Equipment		320 50			320 50
	4	105	Payroll	Sales Salaries Expense		600 –			600 –
	6	106	Morrow Company	Morrow Company			576 40		576 40

review exercises

10. Purchases of merchandise were made from the Glock Company for $560.50 on March 1, on terms of 2/10, n/30. On March 4 merchandise valued at $60.50 was returned to Glock Company. The final payment was made on March 8 for the amount due. Prepare entries in general journal form for the purchase, the return of purchases, and the final payment. Also, indicate any special journals that could be used to record any of the three general journal entries.

11. Record the following four types of transactions in the cash disbursements journal:

March	1	Paid Invoice No. 1093 to Loha Company of $1,050.80 less 2 percent, Check No. 203.
	2	Paid Invoice No. 1060 to Moore Company of $829.50, no discount, Check No. 204.
	3	Purchased office equipment, $540.70, Check No. 205.
	4	Paid sales salaries of $800, Check No. 206.

• task FOOT, PROVE, AND RULE THE CASH DISBURSEMENTS JOURNAL AND THEN POST TO THE SUBSIDIARY LEDGER AND GENERAL LEDGER ACCOUNTS

Footing, proving, and ruling

At the end of the month, the cash disbursements journal is totaled, proved, and ruled. After the columns have been totaled, the accounting clerk determines the accuracy of the recordings in the special journal by checking the equality of debits and credits. When the columns in Illustration 7-18 are totaled, the following amounts are determined:

Sundry Accounts	$3,199.00	Purchases Discounts	$ 36.21
Accounts Payable	2,064.99	Cash	5,227.78
	$5,263.99	⟵⟶	$5,263.99

When total debits equal total credits, as in Illustration 7-18, the journal is ruled. Double lines are drawn across all columns except the *Payee* and *Account Debited* columns, as shown in Illustration 7-19.

Posting

At frequent intervals, the amounts recorded in the *Accounts Payable Dr.* column are posted to individual accounts in the accounts payable subsidiary ledger. A business should keep current balances in the creditors' accounts. A review of the accounts payable subsidiary accounts will show

CASH DISBURSEMENTS JOURNAL — Page 1

Date	Ch. No.	Payee	Account Debited	P.R.	Sundry Accounts Dr.	Accounts Payable Dr.	Purchases Discounts Cr.	Cash Cr.
19x1 Mar. 5	448	Hooper Company	Hooper Company	✓		353 89	7 –	346 89
6	449	Sally Doaks	Office Salaries Expense	65	125 –			125 –
8	450	Russel Dover Company	Advertising Expense	69	100 –			100 –
10	451	Leo Green Company	Leo Green Company	✓		400 –	8 –	392 –
12	452	Sall's Discount Store	Sall's Discount Store	✓		250 60		250 60
13	453	Julia Green	Sales Returns and Allowances	42	54 –			54 –
15	454	Borak Distributors	Borak Distributors	✓		580 –	11 60	568 40
20	455	Carson Office Supply	Office Supplies	14	200 –			200 –
22	456	King Wholesale Company	King Wholesale Company	✓		330 50	6 61	323 89
25	457	Michael Jayson	Jayson, Drawing	32	300 –			300 –
26	458	Jones Equipment Company	Office Equipment	18	420 –			420 –
30	459	Payroll	Sales Salaries Expense	64	2000 –			2000 –
31	460	Smith Company	Smith Company	✓		150 –	3 –	147 –
31					3199 –	2064 99	36 21	5227 78
					(✓)	(21)	(52)	(11)

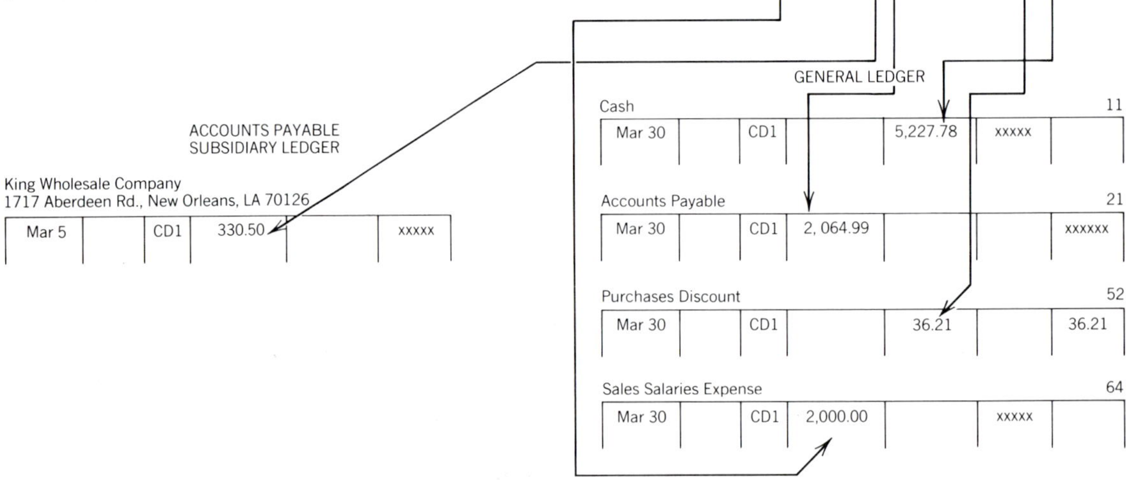

illustration 7-19 posting the cash disbursements journal.

whether creditors have been paid on a timely basis and whether all purchases discounts have been taken. A check mark is placed in the posting reference column of the journal to indicate that postings have been completed to the accounts payable subsidiary ledger. For example, look at the check mark for King Wholesale Company in Illustration 7-19. All subsidiary ledger account postings are indicated in the same manner.

All special column totals provided in the cash disbursements journal are posted as totals at the end of the month. The general ledger posting reference numbers for *Cash, Accounts Payable,* and *Purchases Discounts* are written below the ruling after posting. The *Sundry Accounts Dr.* column total is not posted because the items were posted individually.

All accounts in the *Sundry Accounts Dr.* column must be posted separately to the general ledger. Posting reference numbers for the general ledger accounts are placed in the posting reference column to indicate the completion of this process. For example, in Illustration 7-19 the *Sundry Accounts Dr.* column entry for *Sales Salaries Expense* is posted to Account 64 of the general ledger. Other general ledger accounts have similar posting procedures. Individual postings to the subsidiary ledger and the general ledger are shown in Illustration 7-19. The procedure for posting the cash disbursements journal is very similar to that used in posting the cash receipts journal.

sample problem Total, rule, and post the Cashion Company's cash disbursements journal from the previous sample problem solution.

sample problem solution

CASH DISBURSEMENTS JOURNAL — Page 19

Date		Ch. No.	Payee	Account Debited	P.R.	Sundry Accounts Dr.	Accounts Payable Dr.	Purchases Discounts Cr.	Cash Cr.
19X1 Mar.	1	102	Wilson Company	Wilson Company	✓		400 –	8 –	392 –
	2	103	Farmer Inc.	Farmer Inc.	✓		850 –	17 –	833 –
	3	104	Jones Company	Office Equipment	17	320 50			320 50
	4	105	Payroll	Sales Salaries Expense	62	600 –			600 –
	6	106	Morrow Company	Morrow Company	✓		576 40		576 40
						920 50	1826 40	25 –	2721 90
						(✓)	(21)	(52)	(11)

SUBSIDIARY LEDGER

Farmer, Inc.
12 Manor Avenue
Cocoa, FL 32922

19X1 Mar.	2		CD19	850.00		XXX

Morrow Company
6745 Lakewood Drive
Melbourne, FL 32935

19X1 Mar.	6		CD19	576.40		XXX

Wilson Company
779 Woodsmere Parkway
Rockledge, FL 32955

19X1 Mar.	1		CD19	400.00		XXX

GENERAL LEDGER

Cash 11

19X1 Mar.	31		CD19		2,721.90	XXX	

Office Equipment 17

19X1 Mar.	3		CD19	320.50		XXX	

Accounts Payable 21

19X1 Mar.	31		CD19		1,826.40		XXX

Purchases Discounts 52

19X1 Mar.	31		CD19		25.00		XXX

Sales Salaries Expense 62

19X1 Mar.	4		CD19	600.00		XXX	

review exercises

12. During this month, the following amounts were posted to the accounts payable subsidiary ledger from the cash disbursements journal:

Kane Company	$500.20	Budd Company	$265.30
Ladd Company	300.25	Ware Company	95.40
Dale Company	400.00		

A total of $320.35 was posted to the general ledger accounts from the *Sundry Accounts Dr.* column. Purchases discounts amounted to $31.22. How much cash was paid during the month?

13. The cash disbursements journal for Tudor Company displays these totals:

Sundry Accounts Dr.	Accounts Payable Dr.	Purchases Discounts Cr.	Cash Cr.
400.00	2,000.00	38.00	2,362.00

General ledger accounts in the *Sundry Accounts Dr.* column are *Sales Salaries Expense,* $210; *Office Equipment,* $140; and *Miscellaneous Expense,* $50. These three payments were made to creditors: Johnson Company, $900; Dolan Company, $600; and Pierce Company, $500. Post the subsidiary ledger and the general ledger accounts.

Flow chart

The cash receipts procedure is diagrammed in the flow chart in Illustration 7-20.

illustration 7-20 the cash receipts procedure.

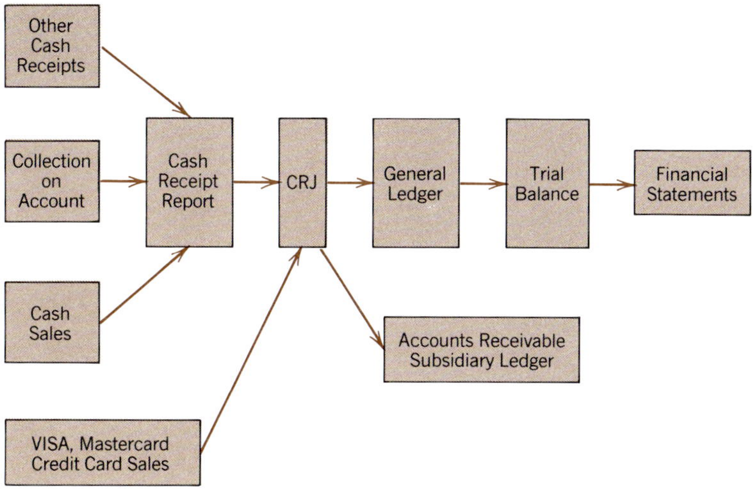

chapter highlights

You have seen that cash control is most important for a business. In this chapter we have looked at how to do these tasks:

- Journalizing cash receipts in the cash receipts journal.
- Posting from the cash receipts journal to the general ledger and to the accounts receivable subsidiary ledger.
- Handling credit card transactions.
- Filling out check stubs and writing checks.
- Journalizing cash payments in the cash disbursements journal.
- Posting from the cash disbursements journal to the general ledger and the accounts payable subsidiary ledger.

key terms

The following important terms are used in Chapter 7 and defined in the Glossary at the end of the book:

cash change fund
cash disbursements journal
cash receipts journal
cash register tape
cash short and over
check register
check request form
credit card
customer receipt form
daily cash receipts report
receiving report
sales draft
voucher register
voucher system

check figures for review exercises

1. Cash short of $5.
2. Investment by owner, sale of equipment, borrow, cash refund.
3. $800 Cr.; both Oaks and Frey receive full credit.
4. Needed to write account titles for *Accounts Receivable, Cash,* and *Sales Discounts.*
5. *Sundry Cr.* column provides for miscellaneous general ledger accounts; *Notes Payable* posted separately. Check marks in the posting reference columns indicate that customer accounts have been posted to the subsidiary ledger accounts.
6. *Accounts Receivable* control account must equal the balances in the customer subsidiary accounts.
7. Dr. *Cash,* $27.72; Dr. *Credit Card Discount Expense,* $1.77; Cr. *Accounts Receivable/American Express,* $29.50
8. Dr. *Cash,* $935.96; Cr. *Sales,* $935.96; Dr. *Sales Returns and Allowances,* $41.69; Cr. *Cash,* $41.69.
9. $585.41 ($596.95 – 2% of $576.95).
10. March 4 Cr. *Purchases Returns and Allowances,* $60.50. March 8 Cr. *Cash* $490.
11. March 1 entry is a credit to *Cash* of $1,029.78.
12. $1,850.28.
13. Debit Dolan Company $600 in the accounts payable subsidiary ledger.

questions

1. List the main sources of cash receipts for a firm.
2. What business forms can be used to assist in verifying cash receipts?
3. What is the best procedure to control cash received by a company?
4. How does cash short or cash over develop in a company? Give an example of the general journal entry required to record a cash shortage.
5. What is the purpose of a special journal?
6. How do you prove the equality of entries made in the cash receipts journal?
7. When posting the cash receipts journal, how do you show that postings have been made to individual customer accounts in the accounts receivable subsidiary ledger?
8. What procedures can a company follow in developing control of cash payments?
9. Why should you post frequently to the accounts payable subsidiary ledger?
10. List the business documents used to determine valid liabilities.
11. How do you prove that transactions have been recorded correctly in the cash disbursements journal?

exercises

1. Stanley Sims owes $500 to the Burns Company on sales made to him on account on May 2, 19X1. Terms of the sale are 2/10, n/30. Full collection of the account sale was made on May 8, 19X1. Prepare entries in general journal form for the sale and collection.
2. Briefly list the steps for controlling incoming cash from the time it is received in the mail until it is recorded in the accounting journals.
3. Assume that cash registers for a particular business contain $500 of change placed in them at the beginning of each working day. Cash register tapes indicate that $6,050 of sales have been made during the day. An actual count of cash gives $6,545. Prepare the general journal entry for cash sales for the day.
4. Indicate how you would post from the partial cash receipts journal given below:

Date		Account Credited	Sundry Cr.	Accounts Receivable Cr.	Sales Cr.	Sales Dis. Dr.	Cash Dr.
	5	Walter Smith		400		8	392
	28	Notes Payable	800				800
			1,000	1,315	100	90	2,325

5. Prepare in general journal form the following cash payments transactions for the Porter Company for June:
   (a) Paid Invoice No. 103 to Lestor Company for $580, less 2 percent discount.
   (b) Paid advertising expenses of $200 for the month.
   (c) Paid Invoice No. 104 to Bolton Company for $420.35. No discount was allowed.
6. Coleman Company purchased merchandise on account from Ryan Company for $1,000, terms 2/10, n/30. Five days later, Coleman Company returned $100 of merchandise. Prepare general journal entries to record (a) the purchase, (b) the return, and (c) the final payment within the discount period.

problems

1. COMPETENCY TESTED The ability to prove cash receipts and make the required journal entries.

   The Monroe Company collected accounts receivable as indicated on the two cash receipt forms listed on the next page:

NO. 7051
Feb 2 19 X1
RECEIVED FROM James Monty Co.
Ninety Eight —— 00/100 DOLLARS
For Collection of Accounts Receivable
Account Total $
Amount Paid $
Balance Due $
SC
"THE EFFICIENCY LINE" AN AMPAD PRODUCT

NO. 7052
Feb 2 19 X1
RECEIVED FROM Joe Lowell, Inc.
One Hundred Ninety Six —— 00/100 DOLLARS
Partial Payment, Acct. Rec.
Account Total $
Amount Paid $
Balance Due $ 100.00
SC
"THE EFFICIENCY LINE" AN AMPAD PRODUCT

In addition, cash sales recorded on cash register tapes were $820.35. The change fund was $50. The cash count was $1,160.20.

Instructions (a) Prepare a proof of cash report with any cash short or over identified. (b) Prepare all entries in general journal form.

2. COMPETENCY TESTED The ability to compare cash receipts recorded in general journal form with those recorded in cash receipts journal.

The following selected cash receipts transactions occurred during February (all sales were 2/10, n/30):

Feb. 2 Cash sales, $325.30.
10 Collected $392 from Fred Smith on account. Total amount owed on sale on account was $400.
15 Collected $196 from Bill Walker. Total amount owed on sale on account was $200.
20 Collected $147 from Jack Green. Total amount owed on sale on account was $150.
25 Borrowed $500 from the local bank.

Instructions

(a) Record the transactions in general journal form.

(b) Record the same transactions in a cash receipts journal.

(c) List the procedures that save time when you use a cash receipts journal.

3. COMPETENCY TESTED The ability to record transactions in a sales journal and a cash receipts journal.

The Monroe Company had the following sales and cash receipts for April. The terms of all sales were 2/10, n/30.

April	2	Issued Invoice No. 101 for sales on account to Loew Company, $520.
	4	Issued Invoice No. 102 for sales on account to Ming Company, $340.
	7	Issued Invoice No. 103 for sales on account to Nome Company, $680.
	9	Received a check for $509.60 from the Loew Company on Invoice No. 101.
	10	Cash sales, $187.00
	12	Issued Invoice No. 104 for sales on account to the King Company for $1,050.
	13	Received a check for the amount due from the Ming Company, less discount.
	15	Monroe Company borrowed $2,000 from the First Putnam Bank. (*Hint*: credit *Notes Payable*).
	16	Dalton Monroe, the owner of the Monroe Company, invested an additional $5,000 in the company.
	20	Received a check from the Nome Company for $680 on Invoice No. 103.
	21	Received a check for the amount due from the King Company, less discount.
	25	Cash sales, $225
	28	Issued Invoice No. 105 to Alex Company, $400.

Instructions

(a) Prepare the transactions in the sales journal and the cash receipts journal.

(b) Total the special journals.

4. COMPETENCY TESTED The ability to post the cash receipts journal to the subsidiary and general ledger accounts.

The Cone Company had entered the following transactions for May in the cash receipts journal:

CASH RECEIPTS JOURNAL 7

Date		Account Credited	P.R.	Sundry Cr.	Accounts Receivable Cr.	Sales Cr.	Sales Disc. Dr.	Cash Dr.
19X1								
May	1	Larkin Company			220.00		4.40	215.60
	4	H.S. Johnson			500.00		10.00	490.00
	6	Notes Payable		300.00				300.00
	7	Cash Sales				435.10		435.10
	12	Don Green			315.60			315.60
	22	Tom Cone, Capital		1,200.00				1,200.00
	24	Cash Sales				120.50		120.50
	29	J.D. Larkin			425.60		8.51	417.09

Instructions

(a) Total and rule the cash receipts journal given in the workbook.

(b) Prove that total debits are equal to total credits.

(c) Post the cash receipts journal to the accounts receivable subsidiary accounts and to all general ledger accounts.

5. COMPETENCY TESTED Skill in determining which transactions should be entered in the cash receipts journal.

Fresh and Easy Company's general ledger accounts pertaining to cash receipts transactions showed the following balances on January 1, 19X1:

Cash	$1,050	
Accounts Receivable	2,080	
Notes Receivable	300	
Store Supplies	100	
Mason, Capital		$3,530
Sales		
Sales Discounts		
Sales Returns and Allowances		
Interest Revenue		

The *Amount* column of the sales journal (page 1) has an ending total of $6,000. Credit terms for all sales were 2/10, n/30.

These checks were received from customers for the amounts due:

Date		Customer	Sales Discounts	Cash
Jan.	2	Bill Jenkins	$10.00	$490.00
	5	Jones Company		327.90
	9	Lowe, Inc.	8.40	311.60
	16	Stanley Company	5.00	245.00

20	Monroe Company	$ 6.72	$329.08
28	James Dorr		85.25

Additional checks received were:

	Accounts	Amounts	Cash
Jan. 6	Notes Receivable	$ 200	
	Interest Income	20	$ 220
15	Mason, Capital	1,000	1,000
21	Store Supplies (Sold)	50	50

The following transaction is related to merchandise returned.

Jan. 14 Credit memo issued to Monroe Company, $105.

Instructions

(a) Prepare transactions for the cash receipts journal and the general journal based on the foregoing transactions.

(b) Post the cash receipts journal, the total of the sales journal, and the general journal to the general ledger and the subsidiary ledger.

(c) The basic accounting equation was in balance before making the January transactions. Prove that it is still in balance.

6. COMPETENCY TESTED The ability to record transactions in a cash disbursements journal.

Record these transactions for Moore Company for 19X1:

May 1	Purchased equipment from Smith Company for $1,500, issuing Check No. 101.
2	Issued Check No. 102 to Martin Realty for monthly rent, $200.
3	Issued Check No. 103 to Lee Company for Invoice No. 420 of $1,200. Purchases discount was 2 percent.
5	Issued Check No. 104 to Brown, Inc. for Invoice No. 450 of $1,800.
12	Issued Check 105 to Union Bank for a note payable of $800 plus interest expense of $8.
13	Issued Check No. 106 for $588 to Walton Supply Company for Invoice No. 461, less $12 discount.
15	Issued Check No. 107 to payroll checking account to pay for sales salaries of $4,000 and office salaries of $2,000.
20	Issued Check No. 108 to Martin Moore, the owner, for $500.

Instructions Prepare the cash payment entries in the cash disbursements journal.

7. COMPETENCY TESTED The ability to prepare entries in a purchases journal, cash disbursements journal, and a general journal.

Stone Company maintains a one-column purchases journal, cash disbursements journal, and a general journal. Terms for all purchases of merchandise are 2/10, n/30 for the year 19X1. Start check numbers with 211.

June	1	Purchased store supplies, $100 from Wilder Supply Company.
	2	Paid June rent, $500, to Lomas Realty.
	3	Purchased equipment for $1,200 from Porter Company.
	4	Purchased merchandise on account from Dillard Company, $1,500.
	8	Purchased merchandise on account from Litton Company, $1,800.
	12	Paid sales salaries of $480.
	13	Paid Dillard Company for amount owed.
	17	Paid Litton Company for amount owed.
	20	Purchased merchandise on account from Cantrell Company for $1,600.
	23	Returned $200 of merchandise to Cantrell.
	25	Paid Cantrell for the merchandise purchased on June 20, less the return on June 23, less 2 percent discount.
	26	Paid Wilson Transport for freight on purchased merchandise, $180.
	28	Paid sales salaries of $480.
	30	Don Stone, the owner of the company, withdrew $160 for personal use.

Instructions Prepare the entries in the appropriate journals.

8. COMPETENCY TESTED The ability to prepare entries for purchases, purchase returns, and cash payments.

Logan Company maintains a cash disbursements journal for all cash payments for June, 19X1.

June	2	Paid the month's rent to Equity Realty, $400.
	4	Purchased merchandise from Jones Company, $500, 2/10, n/30.
	6	Paid sales salaries , $1,200.
	8	Paid for store supplies from Wilbur Distributors, $120.
	10	Purchased merchandise from Doak Company, $345, 2/10, n/30.
	12	Paid Jones Company the amount due on purchase of June 4.
	15	Purchased merchandise from Burson Company, $340, 2/10, n/30.
	19	Paid Doak Company for the amount due on purchase of June 10.
	20	Paid Union Bank for a note payable of $500 principal and $5 interest expense.
	21	Returned merchandise of $60 to Burson Company.
	28	Paid Burson Company the amount due on the purchase of June 15 less return of June 21.
	30	Paid sales salaries, $1,200.

Instructions Journalize the transactions above in the cash disbursements journal, purchases journal, and general journal. Start cash payments with Check No. 151.

appendix A to chapter 7

VOUCHER SYSTEM

To add a degree of control for paying checks, a voucher check disbursement method can be added. When a business is small, the owner can supervise purchase orders closely, inspect merchandise received, and prepare and sign the checks for payment. In larger business organizations, the owner cannot possibly provide for these routines personally. A system must be established to make sure that payments are made to the right persons or companies for the correct amount owed. This control procedure for cash disbursements requires that all except very minor cash payments have voucher approval. The authorization or approval process that permits checks to be written is called a **voucher system.** *The voucher itself is the written form signed by responsible persons to approve payment.*

• task RECORD CASH PAYMENTS WHEN THE VOUCHER SYSTEM IS EMPLOYED FOR CONTROL

Preparing the voucher

Before a voucher is prepared, a liability for making a payment must be established. For merchandise transactions, the description and price on a purchase order must be compared with those on the invoice and receiving report. For payrolls, the payroll supervisor must make sure that all persons for whom checks are to be prepared are still employed. Care should be taken to assure that payments are made only to those to whom the business owes money. Through separation and rotation of duties among personnel, a high degree of control can be established with the voucher system.

When the liability for payment is correctly determined, a voucher form is prepared for approval. Information for the voucher is taken from the invoice accounts to be debited or credited and the amount of the payment. The numbered voucher provides a space for the check number once payment has been made. Thus, a cross reference is established between the approval voucher and the check. A typical design for a two-page voucher is given in Illustration 7A-1.

illustration 7A-1 voucher.

	Voucher Jayson's	Page 1
Date	June 2, 19X1	Voucher No. 402
Payee	Lomax Distributors, Inc. 1191 Pine St. Pittsburgh, TN 31602	
For	June 1, Invoice No. 5421A 2/10, n/30 F.O.B. Pittsburgh	$640.00

		Page 2
	Account:	
	Debits:	
	Purchases	$640.00
	Credits	
	Accounts Payable	$640.00
	Accounts Approved SP	
	Voucher Payment	
Date	June 8, 19X1 Due June 25	Voucher No. 402
Payee	Lomax Distributors, Inc.	
Summary		
	Amount	$640.00
	Discounts	12.80
	Net Payment	$627.20
Payment	Date June 24	Check No. 214
Approved for Payment MJ		
Recorded SP		

The related purchase order, invoice, or receiving report is attached to the two-page voucher. Once payment has been made, these supporting documents should be marked or perforated so that they will not be used again to support a second payment for the same items or services.

Voucher register

The **voucher register** is designed much like the special journals that you have already studied. Every approved voucher must be recorded in the *Voucher Payable Cr.* column along with its voucher number. Other columns established for frequent expenditures and a sundry or miscellaneous column provide for all other accounts debited. To provide for cross reference between the voucher and the check written for payment, the voucher register has special columns for voucher numbers, check numbers, and the date of payment. Using this feature of the voucher register, you can identify all vouchers that have not been paid. When a voucher is paid, you will write the check number and date of payment in the voucher register, which *replaces* the purchases journal.

These are steps to be followed in using a voucher register:

1. Record the voucher in the voucher register. Be sure to place the identifying voucher number in the column provided.
2. In an unpaid voucher file arrange the items according to the due date to avoid loss of purchase discounts.
3. When a voucher is due, have the treasurer or authorized person write the check for payment.
4. Place the voucher in a paid voucher file after payment. Mark all supporting documents attached to the voucher as being paid to avoid possible reuse.
5. Record the date of payment and the check number in the voucher register for the voucher paid.

A voucher register is shown in Illustration 7A-2. Seven vouchers representing valid liabilities have been entered.

Date	Vchr. No.	Payee	When and How Paid		Vouchers Payable Cr.	Purchases Dr.	Freight In Dr.	Sales Salaries Expense Dr.	Advertising Expense Dr.	Office Salaries Expense Dr.	Sundry Accounts Debited		
			Date	Ch. No.							Account Title	P.R.	Amount
19X1 June 1	401	North Realty			400 –						Rent Expense		400 –
2	402	Lomax Distributing Company			640 –	640 –							
5	403	Wholesale Supply			100 –						Office Supplies		100 –
7	404	John Carver			350 –			350 –					
9	405	Brown Supply			420 –						Office Equipment		420 –
10	406	Green Wholesale			170 –						Office Supplies		170 –
12	407	Dunn and Dunn			220 –				220 –				

illustration 7A-2 voucher register.

Check register

When the vouchers are paid, an entry is made in a **check register**, a three-column disbursements journal. Amounts entered in this cash column in the check register are posted to *Vouchers Payable* debit, *Purchases Discounts* credit, and *Cash* credit. The check register replaces the cash disbursements journal when the voucher system is used. All debits for expenses, purchases, and other accounts were recorded in the voucher register when the *Voucher Payable* was established. When a voucher is paid, the voucher number and the check number are recorded in the check register. Then the date and check number are recorded in the voucher register to show that the voucher has been paid. All unpaid vouchers in the voucher register can be identified easily. The payments of Vouchers 401, 402, 403, 404, and 406 are shown in Illustration 7A-3. The payment on June 3 is for an invoice with terms of 2/10, n/30.

illustration 7A-3 check register.

CHECK REGISTER — Page 5

Date	Payee	Vchr. No.	Ch. No.	Vouchers Payable Dr.	Purchases Discount Cr.	Cash Cr.
19X1 June 2	North Realty	401	100	400 —		400 —
3	Lomax Distributing Company	402	101	640 —	12 80	627 20
6	Wholesale Supply	403	102	100 —		100 —
8	John Carver	404	103	350 —		350 —
12	Green Wholesale	406	104	170 —		170 —

After the transactions have been completed in the check register, the date paid and the check number are written in the voucher register. Illustration 7A-4 shows that all vouchers have been paid except Vouchers 405 and 407. Therefore, the total of vouchers to be paid in the unpaid vouchers file is $640 ($420 + $220). These two unpaid vouchers as shown in the voucher register give you the information found on a schedule of accounts payable. With the voucher system, therefore, the separate accounts payable subsidiary ledger may not be needed. Posting procedures for the voucher register and the check register are the same as those required for special journals.

VOUCHER REGISTER — Page 1

Date	Vchr. No.	Payee	When and How Paid: Date	Ch. No.	Vouchers Payable Cr.	Purchases Dr.	Freight In Dr.	Sales Salaries Expense Dr.	Advertising Expense Dr.	Office Salaries Expense Dr.	Sundry Accounts Debited: Account Title	P.R.	Amount
19X1 June 1	401	North Realty	6 2	100	400 —						Rent Expense		400 —
2	402	Lomax Distributing Company	6 3	101	640 —	640 —							
5	403	Wholesale Supply	6 6	102	100 —						Office Supplies		100 —
7	404	John Carver	6 8	103	350 —			350 —					
9	405	Brown Supply			420 —						Office Equipment		420 —
10	406	Green Wholesale	6 12	104	170 —						Office Supplies		170 —
12	407	Dunn and Dunn			220 —				220 —				

illustration 7A-4 voucher register showing payments.

sample problem Doltan Company maintains a voucher system with both voucher and check registers. Five vouchers were approved, and three were paid during the first week of July. Purchase terms are 2/10, n/30.

Date		Voucher No.	Payee	Account	Amount
19X1					
July	1	506	Porter Realty	Prepaid Rent	$500
	3	507	Duset, Inc.	Purchases	350
	4	508	Lusk Advertising	Prepaid Advertising	120
	5	509	Spence Company	Office Equipment	480
	6	510	Brooks Smith	Sales Salary Expense	370

Vouchers 506, 507, and 509 were paid during the week on July 1, 4, and 5, respectively.

Instructions Prepare entries for the vouchers paid in the check register.

sample problem solution

CHECK REGISTER

Date		Payee	Vchr. No.	Ch. No.	Vouchers Payable Dr.	Purchases Discounts Cr.	Cash Cr.
19X1							
July	1	Porter Realty	506	215	$500		$500
	3	Duset Inc.	507	216	350	7	343
	6	Spence Co.	509	217	480		480

review exercises

1. From a review of the sample problem above and its solution, what is the total of the unpaid vouchers payable?
2. Prepare entries in the voucher register for the Lassiter Corporation for the first part of September.

Sept. 1 Recorded Voucher 148 for $600 payable to Mountain Realty, for rent for the month.

3 Recorded Voucher 149 for $2,500, payable to Voltair, Inc., for merchandise. Terms 2/10, n/30.

5 Recorded Voucher 150 for $565, payable to Logan Equipment Company, for office equipment.

6 Recorded Voucher 151 for $180, payable to Foster Company, for office supplies.

check figures for review exercises

1. $490.
2. On Sept. 5—Dr. office equipment, Cr. Vouchers Payable, $565.

problems 1. COMPETENCY TESTED The ability to prepare transactions for a voucher register and a check register.

Boma Company maintains a voucher register and a check register to control cash payments. The following vouchers were approved for May:

Date	Vchr. No.	Payee	Account	Amount
19X1				
May 2	205	Homer Company	Purchases	$1,000
4	206	Dixon Company	Purchases	580
7	207	Doyle Jones	Sales Salaries	250
10	208	Jackson Manufacturing	Office Equipment	320
12	209	Loma Company	Purchases	800
14	210	Doyle Jones	Sales Salaries	250
18	211	Carter Company	Purchases	960
20	212	Billow Agency	Advertising	310
21	213	Doyle Jones	Sales Salaries	250
24	214	Dorr and Sons	Office Supplies	95
25	215	People's Bank	Notes Payable	1,400
			Interest Expense	140
28	216	Doyle Jones	Sales Salaries	250

Payments from the check register follow:

Date	Voucher No.	Check No.	Payee	Amount
19X1				
May 8	207	302	Doyle Jones	$ 250
11	205	303	Homer Company	980
12	206	304	Dixon Company	568.40
15	210	305	Doyle Jones	250
20	209	306	Loma Company	784
22	212	307	Billow Agency	310
22	213	308	Doyle Jones	250
26	215	309	People's Bank	1,540
29	216	310	Doyle Jones	250

Instructions Prepare the entries in the voucher register and in the check register,

2. COMPETENCY TESTED The ability to prepare voucher register and check register entries.

There were four vouchers not paid on October 1, 19X1 (all were for purchases of merchandise) for the Thomas Company.

	Amount	Voucher Number	Date
Kinard Company	$620	102	9/19
Lusky Supply	560	109	9/21
Dover Products	120	115	9/22
Morgan Inc.	460	118	9/25

Additional vouchers for October were:

Date		Voucher No.	Payee	Account	Amount	Terms
19X1						
Oct.	1	120	Jones Supply	Purchases	$ 180	2/10, n/30
	2	121	Dixon Company	Purchases	300	1/10, n/30
	3	122	Farmer Company	Office Equipment	455	
	14	123	Payroll	Sales Salaries	1,000	
	15	124	Doyle Realty	Prepaid Rent	500	
	16	125	Baron Company	Purchases	620	2/10, n/30
	18	126	Dally, Inc.	Purchases	540	2/10, n/30
	20	127	Booker Company	Delivery Equipment	8,000	
	25	128	Nobles Bank	Notes Payable	200	
				Interest Expense	32	
	28	129	Payroll	Sales Salaries	1,000	

Check register entries for October were:

Date	Check No.	Voucher No.	Payee	Amount
Oct. 1	341	102	Kinard Co.	$ 620
2	342	118	Morgan Inc.	450.80
3	343	109	Lusky Supply	560
5	344	122	Farmer Co.	455
10	345	120	Jones Supply	176.40
11	346	121	Dixon Co.	297
15	347	123	Payroll	1,000
17	348	124	Doyle Realty	500
24	349	126	Dally Inc.	529.20
26	350	128	Nobles Bank	232
29	351	129	Payroll	1,000

Instructions (a) Prepare entries in the voucher register and the check register for October. (b) Prepare a schedule of vouchers payable.

chapter 8
PAYROLL ACTIVITIES: RECORDING THE PAYROLL

overall competency THE ABILITY TO RECORD THE PAYROLL AND PAYROLL TAX EXPENSES FOR A SMALL AND MEDIUM-SIZE BUSINESS

career objectives An important part of the accounting clerk's duties is to prepare the payroll—weekly, biweekly (every two weeks), semimonthly (twice a month), or monthly. The skill needed to carry out this duty depends on the complexity of the payroll. Regardless of the size of the firm, certain procedures must be done either by hand or with the aid of a computer. Upon completing this chapter, you should be able to:

- PREPARE PAY CHECKS.
- PREPARE AN INDIVIDUAL EMPLOYEE'S EARNING RECORD.
- PREPARE THE PAYROLL REGISTER.
- JOURNALIZE THE EMPLOYEES' PAYROLL TAXES.
- JOURNALIZE THE EMPLOYER'S PAYROLL TAXES.

Most of you have received payroll checks, so you will understand something about this chapter before you read it. As we mentioned in the career objectives, firms pay their employees at various times. Payment schedules range anywhere from daily for migrant farm workers working on a units-picked basis to annually for those in professional sports. It all depends on the company's policy or the arrangement agreed upon by the employer and employee.

Some workers are paid a salary, and others are paid a wage. A **salary** is designed for workers whose hours are not fixed. For example, if you are a teacher, you receive a set monthly amount whether you work 30 or 80 hours a week (unless you have some special provision for overtime pay). The same is true of a major league baseball pitcher, who may work 3 innings or 18 innings a week. In contrast, the employee might be paid on the basis of the number of units produced or number of hours worked. In this case, the employee is being paid a **wage.**

As you well know either from personal experience or from comments from friends and relatives, what you earn is not what you take home on payday. Deductions are made for everything from Federal income taxes to charitable donations. In this chapter, your task will be to examine each employee's record to make certain that proper deductions are taken.

• task GIVEN THE EMPLOYEES' TIME CARDS, PREPARE THE INDIVIDUAL EMPLOYEE EARNINGS RECORD FOR EACH EMPLOYEE

Calculating the gross pay

For all employees who work for wages, the *Fair Labor Standards Act* (also known as the *Wages and Hours Law*) requires that the employee be paid time and a half for all hours worked over 40 hours. Many people think that those working on Sundays and holidays are entitled to double time (twice the employee's regular pay per hour), but double time is usually paid only to those who have gained such rates through union contracts. In other words, the law requires only time and a half, not double time. To illustrate how an employer complies with the *Fair Labor Standards Act*, assume that Becky Ross works for Edgewood Motel at $5 per hour. Her **time card,** shown in Illustration 8-1, indicates that she worked 44 hours during the past week. Since she is paid on a weekly basis, her **gross pay** is calculated by multiplying the $5 per hour rate by 40 and the additional four overtime hours by 1 1/2 times the $5 (or $7.50 per hour) rate. This calculation results in a gross pay of $230.

Regular pay (40 hours × $5)	$200.00
Overtime pay (4 hours × $7.50)	30.00
Gross Pay	$230.00

illustration 8-1
employee time card. (courtesy of Lathem Time Recorder Company)

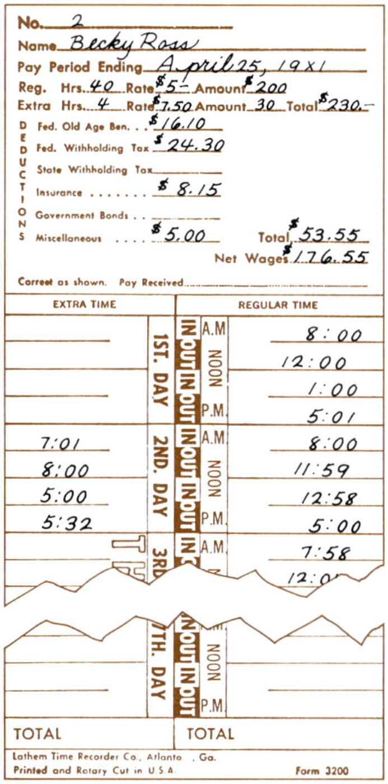
No. 2
Name Becky Ross
Pay Period Ending April 25, 19X1
Reg. Hrs. 40 Rate $5.– Amount $200
Extra Hrs. 4 Rate $7.50 Amount 30 Total $230.–

DEDUCTIONS
Fed. Old Age Ben. . . $16.10
Fed. Withholding Tax $24.30
State Withholding Tax
Insurance $8.15
Government Bonds . .
Miscellaneous . . . . $5.00 Total $53.55
Net Wages $176.55

Correct as shown. Pay Received

EXTRA TIME		REGULAR TIME
	1ST. DAY IN A.M.	8:00
	OUT NOON	12:00
	IN NOON	1:00
	OUT P.M.	5:01
7:01	2ND. DAY IN A.M.	8:00
8:00	OUT NOON	11:59
5:00	IN NOON	12:58
5:32	OUT P.M.	5:00
	3RD. DAY IN A.M.	7:58
	OUT NOON	12:0–
	7TH. DAY IN / OUT / IN / OUT	
TOTAL		TOTAL

Lathem Time Recorder Co., Atlanta, Ga.
Printed and Rotary Cut in U.S.A. Form 3200

Another way to calculate Becky's pay would be to multiply the total number of hours worked by $5, and then add on the extra pay.

Regular pay (44 hours × $5)	$220.00
Overtime pay (4 hours × $2.50)	10.00
Gross Pay	$230.00

Either method gives the same answer, so it is a matter of preference on the part of the accounting clerk.

Usually, employees working on a Sunday or a holiday, such as those in a large discount department store, are not receiving any special pay considerations. However, let's assume that Becky's employer wants her to work on Thanksgiving Day, so she offers Becky double time for that day. Use the same data as before, only assume that the month is November. This would mean that Becky's 44 hours would receive more pay because the time she worked on Thanksgiving day would be doubled. The resulting pay would be $290.

Regular pay (40 hours × $5)	$200.00
Overtime pay (4 hours × $7.50)	30.00
Thanksgiving Day bonus (8 hours × $7.50)	60.00
	$290.00

Overtime pay also can be given to those who work on a salary, but this would be a little unusual since the idea of a salary is to allow a somewhat unstructured schedule. However, if the employees are allowed overtime pay, there are two ways to calculate it. One is to take the annual salary and divide it by 12 to obtain a monthly salary. Next, this monthly salary is divided by 22 (assuming a five-day work week) to get a daily amount. Finally, the daily amount is divided by a typical workday for the salaried person. A fairer method would be to find the annual rate and convert it to an hourly rate. To illustrate, assume Marcia Ledbetter receives a salary of $12,000 per year. To determine the hourly rate, follow the procedure shown below:

Annual salary, $12,000 ÷ 52 weeks = $230.77 per week
$230.77 ÷ 40 hours = $5.77 per hour

Thus, the $5.77 would be used in the same way we used the $4 for Becky in the earlier illustration.

Payroll deductions

To operate the government's many programs, as well as to provide financing for union and charitable organizations, payroll deductions are withheld each time the payroll is made. You will need to be aware of these deductions and how to deal with them. As you perform the payroll duties, keep in mind that the company is simply the collecting agent of the funds once the payroll has been paid. The firm will send the money to the various agencies for which the deductions were withheld. We will discuss this activity in Chapter 9. The most common deductions can be divided into two groups—**involuntary** and **voluntary.** Although some of the voluntary might be considered involuntary, based on the circumstances, the following list offers a general guide:

A. Involuntary
   1. Federal income taxes
   2. State income taxes
   3. Local income taxes
   4. Social Security (FICA) taxes
B. Voluntary
   1. Purchase of U.S. savings bonds
   2. Tax-sheltered annuities
   3. Union dues
   4. Health and life insurance premiums
   5. Contributions to charitable organizations
   6. Deductions for merchandise purchased from the firm
   7. Credit union savings plan

Federal income taxes The amount deducted by the employer for each employee depends on a number of factors. One of these factors is how many **dependents** (**or exemptions**) the employee claims. The employee is allowed one personal exemption, and one each for persons making less than a specific minimum amount and depending upon the employee for over half their support. An additional allowance is granted if the employee or the spouse is over 65 or blind. So, if Wallace Phillips is still working at 67 and his wife is 66 and blind, he could have a total of five exemptions (two for himself and three for his wife since she is allowed one for being blind, one for being over 65, and one regular deduction). The number of exemptions claimed is declared by the employee who completes Form W-4 upon being hired. Illustration 8-2 is an example. If an employee chooses to claim no dependents, more is taken out of each paycheck during the year; but on April 15, the tax due is reduced or the tax refund claim increased.

illustration 8-2
W-4 form.

Form **W-4** (Rev. January 1982)

Department of the Treasury—Internal Revenue Service
Employee's Withholding Allowance Certificate

OMB No. 1545-0010
Expires 4-30-83

1 Type or print your full name: Becky Lee Ross
2 Your social security number: 141 28 1007

Home address (number and street or rural route): 821 Bluebonnet Road,
City or town, State, and ZIP code: Cookeville, TN 38501

3 Marital Status: ☐ Single ☒ Married ☐ Married, but withhold at higher Single rate
Note: If married, but legally separated, or spouse is a nonresident alien, check the Single box.

4 Total number of allowances you are claiming (from line F of the worksheet on page 2) 1
5 Additional amount, if any, you want deducted from each pay . . . . $
6 I claim exemption from withholding because (see instructions and check boxes below that apply):
a ☐ Last year I did not owe any Federal income tax and had a right to a full refund of ALL income tax withheld, AND
b ☐ This year I do not expect to owe any Federal income tax and expect to have a right to a full refund of ALL income tax withheld. If both a and b apply, enter "EXEMPT" here . . . . ▶
c If you entered "EXEMPT" on line 6b, are you a full-time student? . . . . ☐ Yes ☐ No

Under the penalties of perjury, I certify that I am entitled to the number of withholding allowances claimed on this certificate, or if claiming exemption from withholding, that I am entitled to claim the exempt status.

Employee's signature ▶ Becky Lee Ross   Date ▶ July 8, 19 X1

7 Employer's name and address (including ZIP code) (FOR EMPLOYER'S USE ONLY) | 8 Office code | 9 Employer identification number

A second item that affects the amount of Federal income taxes withheld is the employee's marital status. A single person usually pays a higher tax rate than does a married person, and the Federal tax tables reflect this difference. A third consideration is the amount the person makes per period. As mentioned earlier, wages and salaries can be paid daily, weekly, biweekly, and so on. To assist you in calculating the Federal income tax, the **Employer's Tax Guide** is available at any Internal Revenue Service free of charge. A page from this *Guide* is shown in Illustration 8-3. This table is the one to be used for a married person who is paid a wage or salary between zero and $300 per week. There are similar tables for other combinations, such as a married person paid semimonthly and a single person paid monthly. To illustrate using the table for a married person paid weekly, assume that Harvey Walker made $228 during the past week. His W-4 form shows that he claims himself, his wife, and their two children as dependents. By matching the vertical column for 4 dependents with the horizontal column for income of at least $220, but less than $230, we find that we must withhold $13.50 for Federal income taxes. Take a moment to examine Illustration 8-3 to make certain that you know how we arrived at this amount.

illustration 8-3
federal income tax table.

MARRIED Persons—**WEEKLY** Payroll Period
(For Wages Paid After June 1982 and Before July 1983)

And the wages are—		And the number of withholding allowances claimed is—										
At least	But less than	0	1	2	3	4	5	6	7	8	9	10 or more
		The amount of income tax to be withheld shall be—										
$0	$47	$0	$0	$0	$0	$0	$0	$0	$0	$0	$0	$0
47	48	.20	0	0	0	0	0	0	0	0	0	0
48	49	.30	0	0	0	0	0	0	0	0	0	0
49	50	.40	0	0	0	0	0	0	0	0	0	0
50	51	.50	0	0	0	0	0	0	0	0	0	0
51	52	.60	0	0	0	0	0	0	0	0	0	0
52	53	.80	0	0	0	0	0	0	0	0	0	0
53	54	.90	0	0	0	0	0	0	0	0	0	0
54	55	1.00	0	0	0	0	0	0	0	0	0	0
55	56	1.10	0	0	0	0	0	0	0	0	0	0
56	57	1.20	0	0	0	0	0	0	0	0	0	0
57	58	1.40	0	0	0	0	0	0	0	0	0	0
58	59	1.50	0	0	0	0	0	0	0	0	0	0
59	60	1.60	0	0	0	0	0	0	0	0	0	0
60	62	1.80	0	0	0	0	0	0	0	0	0	0
62	64	2.00	0	0	0	0	0	0	0	0	0	0
64	66	2.30	0	0	0	0	0	0	0	0	0	0
66	68	2.50	.20	0	0	0	0	0	0	0	0	0
68	70	2.70	.40	0	0	0	0	0	0	0	0	0
70	72	3.00	.70	0	0	0	0	0	0	0	0	0
72	74	3.20	.90	0	0	0	0	0	0	0	0	0
74	76	3.50	1.20	0	0	0	0	0	0	0	0	0
76	78	3.70	1.40	0	0	0	0	0	0	0	0	0
78	80	3.90	1.60	0	0	0	0	0	0	0	0	0
80	82	4.20	1.90	0	0	0	0	0	0	0	0	0
82	84	4.40	2.10	0	0	0	0	0	0	0	0	0
84	86	4.70	2.40	0	0	0	0	0	0	0	0	0
86	88	4.90	2.60	.30	0	0	0	0	0	0	0	0
88	90	5.10	2.80	.50	0	0	0	0	0	0	0	0
90	92	5.40	3.10	.80	0	0	0	0	0	0	0	0
92	94	5.60	3.30	1.00	0	0	0	0	0	0	0	0
94	96	5.90	3.60	1.20	0	0	0	0	0	0	0	0
96	98	6.10	3.80	1.50	0	0	0	0	0	0	0	0
98	100	6.30	4.00	1.70	0	0	0	0	0	0	0	0
100	105	6.80	4.50	2.10	0	0	0	0	0	0	0	0
105	110	7.40	5.10	2.70	.40	0	0	0	0	0	0	0
110	115	8.00	5.70	3.30	1.00	0	0	0	0	0	0	0
115	120	8.60	6.30	3.90	1.60	0	0	0	0	0	0	0
120	125	9.40	6.90	4.50	2.20	0	0	0	0	0	0	0
125	130	10.20	7.50	5.10	2.80	.50	0	0	0	0	0	0
130	135	11.00	8.10	5.70	3.40	1.10	0	0	0	0	0	0
135	140	11.80	8.70	6.30	4.00	1.70	0	0	0	0	0	0
140	145	12.60	9.50	6.90	4.60	2.30	0	0	0	0	0	0
145	150	13.40	10.30	7.50	5.20	2.90	.60	0	0	0	0	0
150	160	14.60	11.50	8.40	6.10	3.80	1.50	0	0	0	0	0
160	170	16.20	13.10	10.00	7.30	5.00	2.70	.40	0	0	0	0
170	180	17.80	14.70	11.60	8.60	6.20	3.90	1.60	0	0	0	0
180	190	19.40	16.30	13.20	10.20	7.40	5.10	2.80	.50	0	0	0
190	200	21.00	17.90	14.80	11.80	8.70	6.30	4.00	1.70	0	0	0
200	210	22.60	19.50	16.40	13.40	10.30	7.50	5.20	2.90	.60	0	0
210	220	24.20	21.10	18.00	15.00	11.90	8.80	6.40	4.10	1.80	0	0
220	230	25.80	22.70	19.60	16.60	13.50	10.40	7.60	5.30	3.00	.70	0
230	240	27.50	24.30	21.20	18.20	15.10	12.00	8.90	6.50	4.20	1.90	0
240	250	29.40	25.90	22.80	19.80	16.70	13.60	10.50	7.70	5.40	3.10	.80
250	260	31.30	27.70	24.40	21.40	18.30	15.20	12.10	9.10	6.60	4.30	2.00
260	270	33.20	29.60	26.00	23.00	19.90	16.80	13.70	10.70	7.80	5.50	3.20
270	280	35.10	31.50	27.80	24.60	21.50	18.40	15.30	12.30	9.20	6.70	4.40
280	290	37.00	33.40	29.70	26.20	23.10	20.00	16.90	13.90	10.80	7.90	5.60
290	300	38.90	35.30	31.60	28.00	24.70	21.60	18.50	15.50	12.40	9.30	6.80
300	310	40.80	37.20	33.50	29.90	26.30	23.20	20.10	17.10	14.00	10.90	8.00

(Continued on next page)

Page 10

State and local income taxes Most states impose additional taxes on their residents. If the state has an income tax, withholding procedures are similar to those for Federal income taxes. Various states usually provide booklets that shows the deduction, given the number of dependents, the frequency of payment, and the range of salary or wage during that time. Some counties and cities also levy a local payroll tax. The usual procedure is to tax a flat rate percentage, such as 1½ percent of the gross pay, without regard to the number of dependents. A check with the local taxing authority will provide all the information you need to prepare the payroll if you happen to be located in a community with these taxes.

Social Security deductions In 1935, Congress passed the Federal Insurance Contributions Act (FICA) whereby a worker receives a monthly pension upon reaching the age of 62 and continues to receive these benefits until death. More recently, the Act has been amended to provide medical payments known as **Medicare** after the employee reaches 65. In addition, if the employee dies before being covered by the Act, the family receives some benefits. It also provides for a worker who becomes disabled before retirement. In each case, the benefits are determined by the employee's average earnings and the years the person worked under the pension plan.

Since the rate and maximum amount levied are *constantly changing*, we will use amounts only to illustrate the procedure. Check with your instructor as to current requirements. For all illustrations, exercises, and problems, *we will assume* that the first $30,000 earned by the employee during a single year is taxed at 7% (.07).* To illustrate how this tax works, assume that Claudine Whitaker has been working for Selter Enterprises since the beginning of the year at an annual salary of $37,000. By September 30, she has earned $27,750. On October 31, her monthly salary of $3,083.33 would be subject to only $2,250 × 7% of FICA taxes.

Maximum amount to be taxed	$30,000
Amount taxed to September 30	27,750
Amount of the October check subject to FICA taxes	$ 2,250

By multiplying the $2,250 by 7%, we find that this paycheck will have a deduction of $157.50 for FICA taxes. How much of her November check will have these deductions? To answer, ask yourself how much of her gross pay is subject to this tax. The answer: None, because Claudine has earned more than $30,000; therefore, no deduction is made in November or December.

According to the 1935 Act, the employer's responsibilities are to:

1. Pay an amount matching that paid by the employee for FICA taxes.
2. Send payments to the Internal Revenue Service or deposit the funds in an authorized bank for Federal employees' taxes withheld and employer's payroll taxes.
3. File Form 941, an *Employer's Quarterly Federal Tax Return,* at the appropriate times.
4. Provide a W-2 form to each employee.
5. Send a copy of each employee's W-2 and a *Transmittal of Income and Tax Statements* (Form W-3) to the Internal Revenue Service.
6. Keep a current *Employee's Withholding Allowance Certificate* (Form W-4) on file for each employee.

*In 1985, the rate was set tentatively at 7 percent for employees and 7.05 percent for employers based on the first $38,100 earned by each employee. For illustration purposes, we have assumed a matching 7 percent and ceiling of $30,000 for both parties.

Other deductions If employees want to save part of their wages for the future, the employer may withhold the specified amount and purchase U.S. savings bonds or transfer these funds to a credit union. A *credit union* is usually an agency located on the company's property that operates like a savings and loan company for employees. Such deductions would be considered voluntary (in contrast with taxes). Another voluntary deduction is a *tax-sheltered annuity,* an investment-type arrangement for nonprofit organizations. The major difference between this program and others is that wages contributed are not subject to withholding taxes. No taxes have to be paid on them until the funds are withdrawn. Most employees leave these investments in the program until they retire. This arrangement usually reduces taxes because a retired employee is normally in a lower tax bracket than one who is employed currently.

Other voluntary programs available to an employee could include life insurance, contributions to charitable organizations, and union dues. If the employee works for a firm that requires all employees to belong to a union, the latter item is not voluntary. Many employees buy products from their employer and have the purchase price deducted later from their paychecks. This program is made available for the employee's convenience and gives the employer another market. Other deductions, voluntary and involuntary, depend on the location of the firm and the types of programs offered.

Employee's individual earnings record

Once the employee's time card has been collected for the payroll period, the next step is to transfer this information to a cumulative (continuous)

illustration 8-4
employee's earnings record. (courtesy of Boorum & Pease)

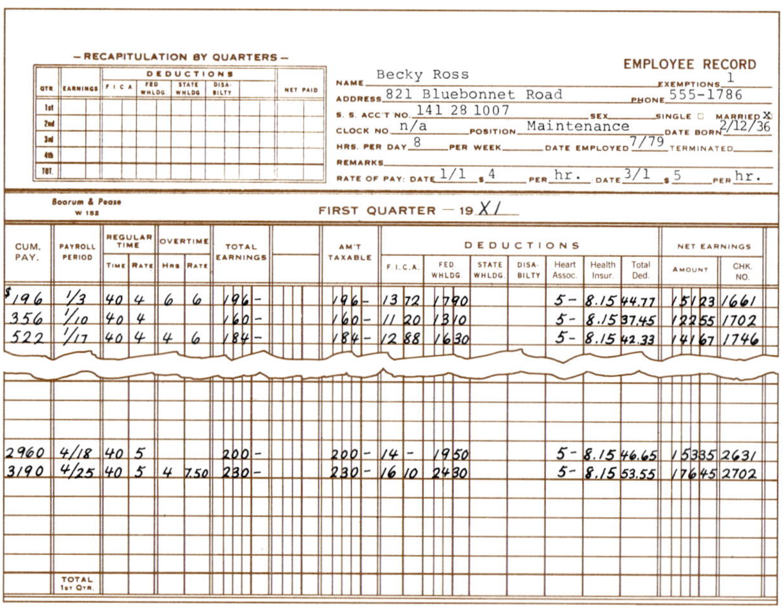

EMPLOYEE RECORD

NAME Becky Ross EXEMPTIONS 1
ADDRESS 821 Bluebonnet Road PHONE 555-1786
S. S. ACC'T NO. 141 28 1007 SEX SINGLE ☐ MARRIED X
CLOCK NO. n/a POSITION Maintenance DATE BORN 2/12/36
HRS. PER DAY 8 PER WEEK DATE EMPLOYED 7/79 TERMINATED
REMARKS
RATE OF PAY: DATE 1/1 $ 4 PER hr. DATE 3/1 $ 5 PER hr.

– RECAPITULATION BY QUARTERS –

QTR	EARNINGS	F I C A	FED WHLDG	STATE WHLDG	DISA-BILTY		NET PAID
1st							
2nd							
3rd							
4th							
TOT.							

Boorum & Pease W 152

FIRST QUARTER — 19 X1

CUM. PAY.	PAYROLL PERIOD	REGULAR TIME Time	REGULAR TIME Rate	OVERTIME Hrs.	OVERTIME Rate	TOTAL EARNINGS		AM'T TAXABLE	F.I.C.A.	FED WHLDG	STATE WHLDG	DISA-BILTY	Heart Assoc.	Health Insur.	Total Ded.	NET EARNINGS Amount	CHK. NO.
$196	1/3	40	4	6	6	196 –		196 –	13 72	17 90			5 –	8.15	44.77	151 23	1661
356	1/10	40	4			160 –		160 –	11 20	13 10			5 –	8.15	37.45	122 55	1702
522	1/17	40	4	4	6	184 –		184 –	12 88	16 30			5 –	8.15	42.33	141 67	1746
2960	4/18	40	5			200 –		200 –	14 –	19 50			5 –	8.15	46.65	153 35	2631
3190	4/25	40	5	4	7.50	230 –		230 –	16 10	24 30			5 –	8.15	53.55	176 45	2702
	TOTAL 1st QTR.																

record known as an **employee earnings record.** An example of this form can be seen in Illustration 8-4 for Becky Ross, an employee of Edgewood Motel. Note in the cumulative pay column that she has made $2,960 after being paid for the week ending April 18. During the week ending April 25, she earned $200 for regular time and $30 for overtime. (The manager gave her a raise to $5 on March 1.) To calculate her pay, you would fill in the total earnings portion of the record sheet from the time card. Next, you would calculate her deductions by first figuring out how much of this gross amount is subject to FICA taxes. By referring either to the FICA tax table in the *Employer's Tax Guide* or multiplying the gross pay of $230 by 7%, you find that this tax deduction is $16.10. Since the cumulative pay is below $30,000, her entire gross pay is subject to this tax.

The next item to consider is Federal withholding. By either checking her W-4 form or, easier yet, looking at the top of the employee record, we can determine her marital status and number of exemptions. We find that she claims one dependent and that she is married. By using the *Guide* (Illustration 8-3), we find that the deduction for Federal tax should be $24.30.

Becky also belongs to the company's group health insurance plan, which requires a deduction of $8.15 per week. In addition, she donates $5 per week to the Heart Association through payroll deductions. These deductions total $53.55, which, when subtracted from the gross pay, gives her a **net pay** of $176.45. After this row on the employee record has been completed, the last step is to add the gross pay for that week to the previous balance, giving Becky a cumulative pay of $3,190 through April 25.

sample problem

Violet's Photography Service has two employees other than the owner (who, you recall, does not get a salary in a proprietorship). Robert Alden receives $6 an hour, while Phyllis Needles receives $7 an hour. Robert worked 45 hours this week, and Phyllis worked the regular 40. Robert is single and claims two dependents. In addition to the involuntary deductions, Robert has $20 taken out for the credit union and $5 for the United Fund. Phyllis has a health insurance plan requiring a $9 deduction, and she also has a $5 weekly payroll deduction for the United Fund.

Instructions Assume that Robert's cumulative pay is $8,600 and Phyllis's is $9,800 going into this week. Robert's Federal income taxes are $49.40. Phyllis's Federal income tax can be determined by using Illustration 8-3. What would gross and net pay be for each person?

sample problem solution

Robert Alden:		
40 hours @ $6	$240.00	
5 hours @ $9	45.00	
Gross Pay		$285.00

Deductions:		
Federal income taxes	$ 49.40	
FICA taxes	19.95	
U. S. Savings bond	25.00	
United Fund	5.00	
Total deductions		99.35
Net Pay		$185.65
Connie Wright:		
Gross Pay (40 hours @ $7)		$280.00
Deductions:		
Federal income tax	$ 34.80	
FICA taxes	19.60	
Credit Union	20.00	
United Fund	5.00	
Total deductions		79.40
Net Pay		$200.60

review exercises

1. Martha West is paid $6.50 per hour. During the current pay period, she works 48 hours. Forty of those are regular hours and six are for overtime on regular work days. During a busy week, Martha agrees to work two hours on Sunday afternoon to get the store presentable for Monday morning. Martha's employment agreement calls for her to receive double time on Sundays and holidays. Calculate Martha's gross pay.
2. The time card of Morgan Walanski for the week ending August 9 shows the following:

	In	Out	In	Out
Aug. 3	8:31	12:00	12:59	5:32
4	8:28	12:01	1:00	6:02
5	8:00	11:58	1:01	6:00
6	8:31	12:00	12:58	5:58
7	8:29	11:59	1:00	5:31

Assuming an hourly rate of $6.50, what is Morgan's gross pay (round all times to nearest 15 minutes)?

3. Fred Fontana is a salaried employee who is paid a set $792 per month; however, he is paid overtime through an agreement with his employer for all hours over 176 in any month. During November, Fred worked a total of 180 hours. What is his gross pay?
4. Wayne Smith earned gross pay of $296 during the past week. He claims five dependents and has voluntary deductions of $9.28 for health insurance, $4 for the Boy Scouts, and $5 for U. S. savings bonds. Assuming that he has made $11,200 to date, calculate his net pay using Illustration 8-3.

• **task** GIVEN THE COMPLETED INDIVIDUAL EMPLOYEE RECORDS, MAKE THE NECESSARY ENTRIES IN THE PAYROLL REGISTER. FROM THE PAYROLL REGISTER, PREPARE THE JOURNAL ENTRY TO RECORD THE PAYROLL

The payroll register

Now let's see if we can take all of the employee records that have been prepared for each worker of Edgewood Motel and record them in the payroll register. Since we did only the one for Becky Ross, assume that the same approach was used for the other employees. First, you can see a typical sheet from a payroll register in Illustration 8-5. To illustrate its use, assume that Edgewood Motel has five employees working on a wage basis. Also, assume that the employees have involuntary deductions for Federal income taxes and FICA taxes and voluntary deductions for health insurance, the Heart Association (HA), and for U.S. savings bonds (SB). Examine Illustration 8-5 closely to see how the information from the individual employee's record for Becky Ross (Illustration 8-4) was transferred to the payroll register. While you are examining this document, note that the gross pay minus the deductions must equal the net pay. Also note that the company check used to pay each worker is listed for better payroll control. Finally, gross pay to the individual employee is classified according to the

Payroll Register
For the Week Ending April 25, 19X1

Name	Regular Time Earnings	Overtime Earnings	Total Earnings	Deductions from Employee's Earnings					Net Pay	Maint. Wages Exp.	Office Wages Exp.	Chk. No.
				FICA Taxes	Federal Income Taxes	Hosp. Insur.	Other Deduct.	Total Deduct.				
Abrams, Betty	250–		250–	17.50	24.80	8.15	SB 25–	75.45	174.55		250–	2700
Baker, Dot	175–	6–	181–	12.67	9.30			21.97	159.03	181–		2701
Ross, Becky	200–	30–	230–	16.10	24.30	8.15	HA- 5–	53.55	176.45	230–		2702
Wright, Connie	275–	10–	285–	19.95	42.80	8.15		70.90	214.10		285–	2703
Ziegler, Faye	180–		180–	12.60	15.60	8.15	HA- 2–	38.35	141.65	180–		2704
	1,080–	46–	1,126–	78.82	116.80	32.60	32–	260.22	865.78	591–	535–	

$1,126.00 – $260.22 = $865.78 $1,126.00

illustration 8-5 payroll register.

department or work section assigned to the employee. This procedure aids in making the required journal entry. In this case, Edgewood Motel has two employees working in the office, so their wages are shown as *Office Wages Expense,* while wages for three employees working in upkeep are shown as *Maintenance Wages Expense.*

When all the employees' individual payroll records for the period are entered, the next step is to add all of the columns. A mathematical check should be made to see that totals for the deduction columns plus the net pay total matches the sum of *Maintenance Wages Expense* and *Office Wages Expense.* Once these figures agree, you are ready to make the journal entry.

Journalizing the payroll

First, by using the payroll register in Illustration 8-5 as our basis, we see that we need to debit *Maintenance Wages Expense* and *Office Wages Expense.* Since the totals are shown on the payroll register as $591 and $535, our work is simplified. The credit part is not quite as easy. As the credits are recorded, we must keep in mind that the funds held back from the employees must eventually be paid to another agency; therefore, we will have to show these amounts as liabilities of the firm. The first deduction is for FICA taxes. The total of $78.82 is credited to *FICA Taxes Payable.* We treat the $116.80 under the Federal income tax column in a similar manner. We must add the word "Employees'." However, to separate this account from the firm's income tax, we will credit *Employees' Federal Income Taxes Payable.*

Next, the voluntary deductions are credited. Since they also must be paid eventually, they are liabilities. These account titles are not set, but should be descriptive. For this example, the deduction of $32.60 for hospitalization is credited to *Employees' Insurance Premiums Payable.* The $25 held out of Betty Abrams' salary is credited to *Employees' Savings Bond Plan Payable,* while the $7 to the Heart Association is credited to *Employees' Heart Association Contribution Payable.* The amount remaining, the take home pay, is credited to *Wages Payable.* Now, putting all of this together, the resulting entry looks like this:

GENERAL JOURNAL Page

Date		Description	P.R.	Dr.	Cr.
19X1 Apr.	25	Maintenance Wages Expense		591 –	
		Office Wages Expense		535 –	
		FICA Taxes Payable			78 82
		Employees' Federal Income Taxes Payable			116 80
		Employees' Insurance Premiums Payable			32 60
		Employees' Savings Bond Plan Payable			25 –
		Employees' Heart Association			
		Contribution Payable			7 –
		Wages Payable			865 78

Accrued payroll

When we made the adjusting entry for wages or salaries in Chapter 3, we simply debited the expense account and credited the liability for the gross amount. From a practical point of view, this same approach can be used when deductions are involved (which is usually the case). Accountants argue that liabilities for charities, unions, Federal taxes, and the like do not accrue in the same way that interest accrues. Federal and state tax withholdings are based on salaries and wages paid rather than salaries and wages accrued. The expense is still the same for the company, regardless of the number or size of the deductions. Because some estimating must be done that later proves to be inaccurate, many firms do not accrue deductions.

The other possibility is to estimate the best that you can so that some idea of the liabilities can be shown. To illustrate, let's continue with the Edgewood Motel example. The last pay period ended on April 25. By Wednesday, April 30, maintenance wages of $349.30 and office wages of $321.00 have accrued for the three-day period. The FICA tax can be determined by multiplying 7% by $670.30 ($349.30 + $321.00). Estimating Federal withholding tax requires projecting what each worker will make and the tax that will have to be paid for that employee. Then this amount would be multiplied by 3/5 to estimate salary for three days. A similar procedure can be used to arrive at the other deductions. Since the first approach is simpler, and since there is support for this position, we will use it in this textbook.

sample problem The individual earnings records of Brian's Ice Cream Barn provide the following facts:

Esther Frazier:	Gross pay, regular	$316.00
	Gross pay, overtime	18.00
	FICA Taxes	23.38
	Federal income taxes	37.00
	United Fund	5.00
	Health insurance	7.53
	Purchased merchandise	10.00
Charles Martin:	Gross pay, regular	$275.00
	FICA taxes	19.25
	Federal income taxes	21.50
	Health insurance	7.53
Alma Warrent:	Gross pay, regular	$360.00
	Gross pay, overtime	20.00
	FICA taxes	26.60
	Federal income taxes	57.30

Instructions Assuming that the firm's accounting clerk does not divide the payroll into various expenses, make the necessary journal entry in general journal form. (*Hint*: On scrap paper you may want to rough out a payroll register.)

sample problem solution

Wages Expense	989.00	
FICA Taxes Payable		69.23
Employees' Federal Income Taxes Payable		115.80
Employees' Health Insurance Premiums Payable		15.06
Employees' Contributions to United Fund Payable		5.00
Accounts Receivable/E. Frazier		10.00
Wages Payable		773.91

review exercises

5. Jack Tuttle, CPA, has two employees—Fred Stanfield and Wanda Cranford. Fred, who was hired in September, has made $5,900 in cumulative pay through November 20, while Wanda has made $29,960. For the week ending November 27, Fred made $805 and Wanda made $750. How much of each employee's salary is subject to FICA taxes?
6. Assume that Fred in Review Exercise 5 has withholdings for Federal income taxes of $197.20, allows $6.80 to be deducted for life insurance, $5 for the United Fund, and $50 for a tax-sheltered annuity plan. Wanda has Federal income tax withholdings of $185.90 but has not authorized any voluntary deductions. Make the required entry in the general journal to record the payroll for the week ending on November 27.

• task FROM THE INFORMATION ON THE LAST COMPLETE LINE OF THE INDIVIDUAL EMPLOYEE'S EARNINGS RECORD, CALCULATE AND JOURNALIZE THE EMPLOYER'S PAYROLL TAXES

Unemployment insurance

Ideally, everyone who wants a job would have one, but this ideal situation doesn't exist, even in a period of economic prosperity. In fact, even in times of booming business, more than 2 percent of the working population are looking for work. Add to this the problems of seasonal unemployment in agriculture, fishing, and the building industries, and unemployment becomes a national problem. In periods of a sluggish economy or, worse yet, in a depression, the unemployment rolls grow.

To assist the unemployed, the government passed the *Federal Unemployment Tax Act,* which requires employers with four or more workers to pay 3.1% on the first $3,000 earned by each employee. The rate has since been changed to 3.5% on the first $7,000, (with another increase planned for 1985),* but the principle involved is still the same. The Act allows for a possible reduction to .8% (.008) in the Federal rate if the state has an unemployment plan that meets Federal standards. The rate that an employer pays for the state unemployment tax varies from close to zero to almost 5% depending on the state and the condition of the Unemployment Compensation Trust Fund. The varying rate is allowed by the states as an **experience rating** (also known as a merit rating). This system rewards the employer for not laying off workers in slack periods. A zero rating would allow an employer to save $162 per employee per year. This employment tax saving would amount to $3,240 per year for a firm with 20 employees. In all states except Alabama, Alaska, and New Jersey, only the employer pays the unemployment tax. In these three states, the employee also contributes.

Journalizing the payroll taxes

From our earlier discussion, recall that the employee and the employer pay a matching amount of FICA taxes. So if Edgewood Motel's employees pay $78.82, the employer must pay this same amount. We will assume that none of the employees has cumulative pay of more than $7,000, so the entire payroll is subject to both state and Federal unemployment taxes. The five employees made a total of $1,126. If the firm pays 2.7% on state and .8% on Federal, the state unemployment tax is $30.40, ($1,126 × .027) while the Federal unemployment tax is $9.01 ($1,126 × .008). The journal entry to record Edgewood Motel's share of payroll taxes for the week is:

GENERAL JOURNAL — Page 1

Date		Description	P.R.	Dr.	Cr.
19X1 Apr.	25	Payroll Taxes Expenses		118 23	
		FICA Taxes Payable			78 82
		State Unemployment Taxes Payable			30 40
		FUTA Taxes Payable			9 01
		To record employees payroll			
		taxes for week ending April 25.			

*In 1985, the state unemployment rate is set to increase from 2.7 percent to 5.4 percent. For illustration purposes, we are using the rate that was in effect in 1984.

Later in the year, assume that the individual employee earning records show that before the payroll for the week ending November 14, the following cumulative payroll amounts are found (note that Faye Ziegler left the firm and was replaced by Rosaline Smith):

Abrams, Betty	$7,250
Baker, Dot	6,930
Ross, Becky	7,025
Smith, Rosaline	1,250
Wright, Connie	5,600

During the week ending November 14, the accounting clerk made the following analysis:

Employee	Gross Pay	Subject to FICA	Subject to Unemployment
Abrams, Betty	$260	$ 260	none
Baker, Dot	180	180	$ 70
Ross, Becky	225	225	none
Smith, Rosaline	165	165	165
Wright, Connie	275	275	275
		$1,105	$510
		(7.0%)	state (2.7%)
			Federal (.8%)

The resulting entry from the foregoing calculations would be:

GENERAL JOURNAL Page 1

Date		Description	P.R.	Dr.	Cr.
19X1 Nov.	14	Payroll Taxes Expense		95 20	
		FICA Taxes Payable			77 35
		State Unemployment Taxes Payable			13 77
		FUTA Taxes Payable			4 08
		To record payroll taxes for			
		the week ending Nov. 14.			

To assist in making the payroll, the register can be expanded to provide the accounting clerk with important information needed to make the employer's tax entry. Such a payroll register can be seen in Illustration 8-6, which is the same as the one shown in Illustration 8-5, except for the additional columns.

Payroll Register
For the Week Ending April 25, 19X1

Name	Regular Time Earnings	Over-Time Earnings	Total Earnings	Cumulative Earnings	Subject to F.I.C.A.	Subject to Unemploy.	Deductions from Employee's Earnings				Net Pay	Maint. Wages Exp.	Office Wages Exp	Chk. No.
							FICA Taxes	Federal Income Taxes	Hosp. Insur.	Other Deductions				
Abrams, Betty	250-		250-	4,340	250-	250-	17.50	24.80	8.15	SB 25-	174.55		250-	2700
Baker, Dot	175-	6-	181-	2,680	181-	181-	12.67	9.30			159.03	181-		2701
Ross, Becky	200-	30-	230-	3,190	230-	230-	16.10	24.30	8.15	HA 5-	176.45	230-		2702
Wright, Connie	275-	10-	285-	4,675	285-	285-	19.95	42.80	8.15		214.10		285-	2703
Ziegler, Faye	180-		180-	2,410	180-	180-	12.60	15.60	8.15	HA 2.-	141.65	180-		2704

illustration 8-6 **payroll register.**

Accrued payroll taxes

When the fiscal period ends, payroll taxes probably will have accrued and should be recorded. To illustrate, let's continue with the Edgewood Motel case. On Wednesday, April 30, three days of FICA taxes, Federal unemployment taxes, and state unemployment taxes have built up. The total pay due at this date is \$670.30. To determine the amounts, we multiply the gross pay by the appropriate rate. Assuming that no employee has made over \$7,000 after this accrued amount is added to the previous cumulative balances, the FICA amount is \$46.92 (\$670.30 × 7%), the state unemployment amount is \$18.10 (\$670.30 × 2.7%), and the Federal unemployment amount is \$5.36 (\$670.30 × .8%). The resulting adjusting entry is:

GENERAL JOURNAL — Page 1

Date		Description	P.R.	Dr.	Cr.
19X1 Apr.	30	Payroll Taxes Expense		70 38	
		FICA Taxes Payable			46 92
		State Unemployment Taxes Payable			18 10
		FUTA Taxes Payable			5 36
		To record employer's payroll taxes			

sample problem The law firm of Hector and Martin has four employees who are paid salaries. A portion of the payroll register for the week ending November 21, 19X1, is shown below. Calculate the missing information, and then prepare the necessary journal entry to record the employer's payroll taxes. Assume that the firm has earned a merit state unemployment rate of 2.2%.

Name	Total Earnings	Cumulative Earnings	Subject to FICA	Subject to Unemployment
Allen, Roy	$ 800	$35,600		
Carlten, Rex	750	16,200		
Manley, Fred	650	4,200		
Padovich, Frank	750	30,600		
	$2,950	$86,600		

Cumulative earnings include this week's gross pay.

sample problem solution

Name	Subject to FICA	Subject to Unemployment Tax
Allen, Roy	$ 0	$ 0
Carlten, Rex	750	0
Manley, Fred	650	650
Padovich, Frank	150	0
	$1,550	$650

Nov. 11	Payroll Taxes Expense	$128.00	
	FICA Taxes Payable		$108.50
	State Unemployment Taxes Payable		14.30
	FUTA Taxes Payable		5.20
	To record employer payroll taxes for the week ending November 11.		

review exercises

7. Joe Throng, CPA, has four employees. The cumulative pay *prior* to this week and this week's salaries can be seen below:

	Cumulative	This Week
Fred Bosinki	$18,900	$650
Wilma Foster	30,200	900
Mildred Hendrix	2,400	550
James Morgenstein	29,600	850

The firm has a merit rating on state unemployment of 1.8%. Prepare the journal entry as of October 17 to record Joe Throng's employer payroll taxes.

8. Weldon's Photo Center employs five workers. The firm's state unemployment rate is 2.2 percent. The cumulative pay *prior* to this week and this week's gross salaries are shown on the next page:

	Cumulative	This Week
Keith Gabeheart	$14,600	$340
Phil Hampston	29,800	650
Mark Iverie	30,200	700
Mary Jackson	2,400	600
Arnold Weiss	6,900	500

Record the employer's payroll taxes.

chapter highlights

After studying Chapter 8, you should be able to handle the payroll for a small firm as far as performing the following tasks:

- Prepare the paychecks or divide the cash properly to pay the firm's employees.
- Prepare the individual employees' earnings records.
- Prepare the payroll register each payday.
- Journalize the payroll, properly recording the voluntary and involuntary withholdings.
- Journalize the employer's payroll taxes.

We will continue with the topic of handling the payroll in Chapter 9. In Chapter 8, we have looked at how to record the expenses and related liabilities caused by the payroll. In Chapter 9, we will look at paying these liabilities and sending the proper forms with the different payments.

check figures for review exercises

1. $344.50
2. $279.50 ($260 + $19.50)
3. $819.00 (4 hours @ $6.75 + $792.00)
4. $296 − ($9.28 + $4 + $5 + $21.60 + $20.72) = $235.40
5. Fred—$805; Wanda—$40 ($30,000 − $29,960)
6.

Nov. 27	Salaries Expense	$1,555.00	
	FICA Taxes Payable		$ 59.15
	Employees' Federal Income Taxes Payable		383.10
	Employees' Life Insurance Premium Payable		6.80
	Employees' Contribution to United Fund Payable		5.00
	Employees' Tax-Sheltered Annuity Plan Payable		50.00
	Salaries Payable		1,050.95

7. Payroll Taxes Expense	$126.30	
FICA Taxes Payable		$112.00
State Unemployment Taxes Payable		9.90
FUTA Taxes Payable		4.40
8. Payroll Taxes Expense	$135.80	
FICA Taxes Payable		$114.80
State Unemployment Taxes Payable		15.40
FUTA Taxes Payable		5.60

key terms

The following important terms are discussed in Chapter 8 and defined in the Glossary at the end of the book.

dependent

employee's earnings record

employer's tax guide

exemption

experience rating

gross pay

involuntary deductions

net pay

salary

time card

voluntary deductions

wage

questions

1. What are the circumstances that usually allow an employee to receive double-time pay?
2. What is the difference between a wage and a salary?
3. What is meant by voluntary deductions? Involuntary deductions?
4. Belford Carver is 68, his 64-year old wife is blind. How many dependents can Belford legally claim on a joint return?
5. What is the purpose of the FICA tax? Who pays this tax?
6. In most states, who pays the state unemployment tax? What is the maximum amount of gross pay that must be paid on for each employee?
7. Using the guidelines given in this chapter, determine how much of Joe Foster's salary of $36,800 would be subject to FICA taxes. How about Federal unemployment taxes?
8. If the employees pay $612.50 in FICA taxes, how much does the employer have to pay?

exercises

1. Lester Adcock is an employee of a firm that has a union contract requiring double-time pay on holidays. During the week ending July 6, Lester's time card showed the following:

	In	Out
July 2	7:30 AM	11:30 AM
2	12:02 PM	5:00 PM
3	7:28 AM	11:30 AM
3	12:00 Noon	4:09 PM
4	7:31 AM	11:30 AM
4	11:59 AM	4:00 PM
5	7:27 AM	11:32 AM
5	12:00 Noon	4:02 PM
6	7:29 AM	11:30 AM
6	12:02 PM	3:59 PM

Calculate Lester's gross pay if he receives $7 per hour and each time is rounded to the nearest 15-minute period.

2. Betty Walker is a travel agent who receives an annual salary of $11,648. She receives time and a half for all hours over 40 per week. During the current week, she worked 45 hours. Calculate her gross pay.

3. Ginny May is a widowed employee with two minor children and her 68 year-old father as dependents. During the week she earned $208. She chooses voluntary deductions of $5 to United Way and $16 for a hospital plan. Calculate her take home pay, assuming that her Federal income tax is $12.30 and that she has earned $15,100 to date.

4. Marty Moss has earned a total of $16,950 from January 1 to August 15. For the week ending August 22, he earns $500. He chooses the following voluntary deductions:

Tax-Sheltered Annuity	$50.00
Health Insurance	8.50
Life Insurance	30.00
Heart Association	2.00

In addition to FICA taxes, he also has $88.70 deducted for Federal income taxes. Calculate his take home pay.

5. For the week ending March 19, Winningham Auto Sales calculated wages for its office personnel of $440 and for its sales personnel, $1,060. Federal income taxes withheld totaled $180.60, deductions for savings bond amounted to $50, and the employees elected to belong to a health insurance program that requires a weekly deduction of $82. Make the necessary entry to record the payroll (assuming the entire payroll is subject to FICA taxes).

6. Using the information in Exercise 5, make the entry to record the employer's payroll taxes, assuming a state unemployment rate of 2.2% and that the entire payroll is subject to unemployment taxes.

7. Sweet Tooth Candy Store has four employees. The cumulative pay prior to the current week and this week's wages are shown on the next page.

	Cumulative Pay	This Week
Allen Cartright	$5,812	$350
Myrtle O'Brien	7,486	380
Hollis Pranzer	2,060	240
Harvey Stein	6,980	370

Due to a poor retention record, the firm currently has a 2.7% unemployment rate. Prepare the necessary entry to record the firm's payroll taxes expense. (*Note:* Make only the employer's tax entry, not the entry to record wages expense.)

problems

1. COMPETENCY TESTED Skill in entering information in the employee's individual earnings record.

In preparing an April 25 payroll, you receive an application sheet on Susie Wehoefer. She lists her home address as 6704 Broad St. and her Social Security number as 987-00-0865. She has been assigned clock-card number 17, and she began work on April 20 as a sales clerk. Her pay will be $4 per hour. By examining her time card, you see that she worked 43 hours during her first week. Her W-4 form indicates that she is married and claims only herself as a dependent. You also find authorization to deduct $2 a week for the Community Chest, $6.25 for a hospitalization plan, and $2.50 for disability insurance.

Instructions Using Illustration 8-3, prepare Susie's individual earnings record (including the heading material).

2. COMPETENCY TESTED The ability to calculate gross pay from time card data.

The Rod & Reel Shop has two employees who work for wages. A breakdown of the time cards for the two show the following work times:

	Date	In	Out
John Averitt:	8/14	10:00 AM	12:30 PM
	8/14	1:00 PM	6:33 PM
	8/15	9:30 AM	12:29 PM
	8/15	1:00 PM	6:30 PM
	8/16	9:00 AM	12:30 PM
	8/16	1:00 PM	6:31 PM
	8/17	10:00 AM	6:30 PM
	8/18	9:32 AM	12:28 PM
	8/18	1:00 PM	6:55 PM
Phil LaRue:	8/14	9:58 AM	12:00 Noon
	8/14	12:30 PM	6:01 PM
	8/15	10:00 AM	11:59 AM

8/15	12:30 PM	7:15 PM
8/16	9:00 AM	12:00 Noon
8/16	12:27 PM	6:32 PM
8/17	9:59 AM	12:01 PM
8/17	12:30 PM	6:59 PM
8/18	8:57 AM	11:29 AM
8/18	12:02 PM	6:31 PM

John is paid $5.50 per hour, while Phil is paid $6.00 for each hour he works. The company's time card policy is to round uneven time to the nearest 15 minutes.

Instructions From the information above, calculate the gross pay for each employee.

3. COMPETENCY TESTED The ability to calculate gross pay and record the payroll.

Max's Catering Service has three employees.

(1) Phillip Cantana receives $6 per hour. This week he worked 46 hours. In addition to social security deductions, he also had the following withheld from his pay: Federal income tax, $25.20; state income tax, $6.80; deduction for U.S. savings bond, $25; contribution to the Kidney Foundation, $5.

(2) Margaret Perry earns $6.80 per hour. This week she worked 42 hours. She authorized you to withhold $10 weekly for the Credit Union and $8 for the Kidney Foundation. Federal income tax amounted to $34, while state income tax withholdings were calculated to be $8.40.

(3) Huffy Zeff, a new employee, makes $3.80 an hour and worked 40 hours this week. He does not want any deductions (including the involuntary ones) taken from his paycheck. Despite this, $20.70 in Federal income taxes, $3.90 in state taxes, and FICA taxes were deducted.

Instructions

(a) Prepare a payroll register for Max's Catering Service. Assume that the highest cumulative pay is Perry's $3,042.

(b) Make the entry to record the current week's payroll.

(c) Make the entry to record the employer's payroll taxes assuming a 2.4% state rate.

4. COMPETENCY TESTED The ability to prepare the payroll register.

Feldhause Drug Store has four employees on the payroll for the week ending July 15. All but Betty work as salespersons. Following is a breakdown on each employee:

Charlotte Baker:	\$4.20 per hour; worked 41 hours during the week; Federal income tax, \$22.80; hospital insurance, \$7.10; U.S. savings bond, \$10.
Marilyn Francis:	\$3.90 per hour; worked 46 hours during the week; Federal income tax, \$18.80; hospital insurance, \$7.10.
Billy Gardner:	\$4.00 per hour; worked 38 hours during the week; Federal income tax, \$22.60; heart fund, \$5.
Betty Zeller:	\$5.90 per hour; worked in the office 42 1/2 hours during the week; Federal income tax, \$30.40; hospital insurance, \$7.10; heart fund, \$10.

Instructions

(a) Prepare the payroll register for the week ending July 15, assuming Checks 4915-18 were used to pay the payroll. Each employee had cumulative wages of less than \$15,000.

(b) Make the required journal entry to record the payroll.

5. COMPETENCY TESTED The ability to calculate various taxes and journalize the payroll entries.

Evelyn's Bakery employs five employees. The individual employee's earnings record for each employee provides the following information (cumulative pay does not include the current week):

PAYROLL REGISTER

Week Ending May 3, 19X1

			Deductions					
Employee	Cumulative Pay	Gross Earnings	FICA	Fed. With.	United Fund	Health Insur.	Net Pay	Subject to Unemploy.
Brown, A.	\$5,615	\$218			\$ 2	\$5.00		
Cravens, M.	7,060	294			5	7.50		
Lolly, J.	6,875	205				5.00		
Nabi, Y.	1,225	230			4	5.00		
Rami, B.	6,990	290			10	7.50		

Brown and Cravens claim a total of three dependents, Lolly and Nabi claim five, and Rami claims six. All of the employees are married; the dependents' claim includes both workers and their spouses.

Instructions

(a) From the data above and by using Illustration 8-3, complete the payroll register for the week ending on May 3.

(b) Prepare, in general journal form, the necessary entry to record the week's payroll.

(c) If the firm has a 1.8% state unemployment merit rating, make the required entry, in general journal form, to record the payroll taxes.

6. COMPETENCY TESTED The ability to calculate and journalize the employer's payroll taxes.

Smooth Sailing Travel Agency employs six travel consultants. The list below shows their cumulative pay before the current week's pay and this week's gross pay:

	Cumulative Pay	Gross Pay
Carlstad, Ron	$4,860	$260
Marquis, Linda	7,220	225
O'Mara, Mike	2,187	240
Paulson, Patty	6,980	210
Riker, Jo	1,550	240
Soo, Ling	6,914	265

Instructions

(a) Calculate the FICA and unemployment taxes assuming that the firm has a 2.2% state unemployment rate.

(b) Make the journal entry to record the employer's payroll taxes. (*Note:* Do not journalize the payroll entry.)

7. COMPETENCY TESTED The ability to prepare accrued payroll entries at the end of a fiscal year for a firm with both salaries and wages.

Patents Limited has three engineers and two engineering assistants on its payroll. All of the workers have been with the firm for the entire fiscal year and each received a paycheck on December 26 for work performed for the week ending on that day. All five employees worked Monday, Tuesday, and Wednesday, December 29, 30, 31, and have received no pay for this effort.

As of the last payday, the three engineers—Dodd, Ethridge, and Unkenhotz—had earned cumulative amounts of $32,500, $33,800, and $28,600, respectively. All three belong to a group insurance plan that requires a daily premium of $2.50 per employee. No other voluntary deductions were authorized. Each of the three engineers is paid a flat daily salary as follows:

Dodd	$125
Ethridge	130
Unkenhotz	110

Accrued Federal income taxes for December 29 through 31 for Dodd, Ethridge, and Unkenhotz amounted to $82.80, $85.02, and $64.10, respectively. Important payroll information for the three accrued days for the two engineering assistants is given below:

	Cumulative Pay	Gross Pay	FICA Taxes	Federal Income Taxes
Hillinsly	$5,430	$188	$13.16	$34.86
Randolph	8,690	150	10.50	21.96

Randolph belongs to the group insurance program and also pays a $2.50 per day premium. The firm has earned a state unemployment merit rating of 2.0%.

Instructions Prepare the necessary entries, in general journal form, to record (a) the accrued payroll and (b) the accrued payroll taxes. (*Note:* You might want to set up a rough payroll register to assist you in working this problem.)

8. COMPETENCY TESTED Skill in completing a complex payroll register.

Jolly Time Toy Company employs a staff of eight who work on a wage basis. Below is a list showing the cumulative pay prior to the current week, the number of hours worked this week, the regular hourly pay, and the Federal income tax withheld:

Employee	Cumulative Pay	Hours Worked	Hourly Pay	Federal Income Tax
Acuff, Babs	$ 7,488	41½	$4.50	$17.40
Clements, Roy	9,650	44¼	6.00	23.10
Everitt, May	6,004	46	3.90	20.90
Fagan, Jewell	1,080	38	5.50	26.20
Hampton, Bob	8,635	40	6.00	16.10
Nantini, Sal	8,040	42	5.75	26.40
O'Kelly, Sean	5,930	50	4.50	30.40
Stephens, Rob	11,284	43½	7.50	43.20

All of the employees except Clements and Fagan belong to a group insurance plan that deducts $9 a week from their take-home pay. Nantini and Stephens have $25 per week deducted for the credit union. Fagan, Hampton, and O'Kelly give $5 each week to the United Fund. Acuff and Fagan work in the office, and the rest are salespersons. The employees were paid by check. Acuff received Check No. 9603.

Instructions Prepare a payroll register for the week ending December 15. Use Illustration 8-5 as an example.

chapter 9
PAYROLL ACTIVITIES: PAYMENTS AND REPORTS

overall competency THE ABILITY TO HANDLE THE PAYROLL FOR A SMALL AND MEDIUM-SIZE BUSINESS

career objectives The accounting clerk must know when and where to send payments for various debts created by the payroll procedure. Some of these payments go to governmental agencies, such as the State Department of Revenue. Other payments are made to private organizations, such as credit unions, the United Fund, and labor unions. Failure to pay the correct amount at the appropriate time may embarrass the firm and make it subject to fines. Managers of small businesses depend on the accounting clerk to fill out the proper forms and to provide the information necessary for prompt and accurate payments.

Upon completing this chapter, you should be able to perform the following tasks:

- PREPARE CASH AND CHECKS FOR THE EMPLOYEES' PAYROLL.
- RECORD PAYMENTS TO THE EMPLOYEES IN THE CASH DISBURSEMENTS JOURNAL.
- MAKE PAYMENTS TO THE FEDERAL GOVERNMENT, USING THE CORRECT AMOUNTS AND FORMS.
- JOURNALIZE PAYMENT OF FEDERAL TAXES.
- PREPARE STATE AND FEDERAL UNEMPLOYMENT TAX RETURNS.
- RECORD UNEMPLOYMENT PAYMENTS IN THE CASH DISBURSEMENTS JOURNAL.

We looked at recording payroll expenses and liabilities in Chapter 8. In this chapter we will look at procedures for paying employees and certain agencies. In journalizing the payroll, two separate events took place: First, we recorded an expense for the workers' salaries or wages. A portion was withheld from each employee for voluntary and involuntary deductions. Voluntary deductions were withheld according to the wishes of the employee, and the involuntary were withheld to comply with the laws of governmental agencies. As a *third party,* the employer must show a liability for these amounts, since the firm is withholding the funds from employee earnings and must pay them to the various agencies. Second, we recorded an expense for the employer for payroll taxes. This entry created three liabilities to various governmental agencies.

Paying taxes and voluntary deductions requires knowledge of how to fill out the required forms properly and how to meet deadlines. We will also look at some nonfinancial forms connected with the payroll activity.

• task PREPARING THE EMPLOYEES' PAYROLL AND JOURNALIZING THE PAYMENT

We will discuss preparing the employees' take home pay and journalizing the payment as if the same person would perform both steps. In actual practice, it is not wise to let the same person who records the information in the company's records also prepare the checks. Unless this person is the owner, this procedure might prove too tempting for the one given these responsibilities. We are showing these steps as a continuous process so that you can have a total picture of the payroll process.

Paying in cash

Some firms prefer to pay their employees in cash to save them from having to go to the bank or being left without cash when payment is made after banking hours. One check is written for the entire **net pay** to provide cash for the individual employees. The money must be received in the proper denominations so that each employee receives exactly the number of dollars and cents specified. Currency is placed in a pay envelope along with a slip explaining the deductions taken. Illustration 9-1 is a typical form used for this purpose.

When the single check is written, an entry is recorded in the cash disbursements journal debiting *Salaries Payable* or *Wages Payable* and crediting *Cash* for the net pay. Because banks have made 24-hour automatic tellers available, the need for payment in cash has become less critical. Paying by cash is a burdensome process and can be justified only when very few employees are involved.

illustration 9-1 payroll deduction statement.

PAYROLL STATEMENT

SALARY OR WAGES $ 230.00

Total Earnings $ 230.00

DEDUCTIONS		
F.I.C.A. $	16	10
Fed. Income Tax	24	30
State Income Tax		
Bonds		
Heart	5	00
Hosp.	8	15

Total Deductions $ 53.55

NET AMOUNT $ 176.45

Employee Becky Ross

Social Security No. 141 28 1007

Employer Edgewood Motel

Employer's Ident. No. 36-1488420

Period From 4/19 To 4/25

Date Paid 4/25

CASCADE® L1-C2419 PRINTED IN U.S.A

Paying by check

Typically, most firms pay their employees with checks. Two approaches are available when checks are used. One is to use the same checkbook that the firm uses to pay all the bills to write the employees' checks. Another approach is to write one check that transfers funds for the full net payroll from the regular checking account to a special payroll checking account.

Standard checking account approach If the firm has only a few employees, management might feel that a separate checking account for the payroll is not needed. One possibility for recording the wages earned by the employees of Edgewood Motel (Illustration 8-5) is to record each check on a separate line. This approach is shown in Illustration 9-2.

CASH DISBURSEMENTS JOURNAL Page 29

Date		Ch. No.	Payee	Account Debited	P.R.	Sundry Accounts Dr.	Accounts Payable Dr.	Purchases Discounts Cr.	Cash Cr.
19X1 Apr.	26	2700	Betty Abrams	Wages Payable		174 55			174 55
	26	2701	Dot Baker	Wages Payable		159 03			159 03
	26	2702	Becky Ross	Wages Payable		176 45			176 45
	26	2703	Connie Wright	Wages Payable		214 10			214 10
	26	2704	Faye Ziegler	Wages Payable		141 65			141 65

illustration 9-2 paying the payroll.

A number of problems arise when a special payroll account is not used:

1. A standard check used for paying bills does not have designated spaces to explain deductions to the employee.
2. Unless the checkbook is kept in a secure place, unauthorized employees might look through the check stubs to see what other employees are making.
3. If the firm has a large number of employees, a sizable amount of time and effort is required to journalize the payroll.

To emphasize the last point, look at Illustration 9-2 again and imagine having 20 or 25 employees. If regular checks are used, 20 to 25 lines would be needed. To show deductions, it might be necessary to provide each employee with a payroll deduction statement similar to the one shown in Illustration 9-1. As we noted in our discussion of the payroll register in Chapter 8, the check number of each payroll check should be shown on the payroll register in the "Check No." column.

Special payroll checking account To provide checks with detachable information stubs, each employee must be given a specially designed check. To do this, one regular check is written for the net pay of all the employees. This step is exactly the same as that used when the payroll is paid in cash, *Wages Payable* or *Salaries Payable* is debited and *Cash* is credited. The payroll is prepared immediately so the special **payroll bank account** has no balance after the payroll checks are written. Anyone looking at the balance sheet would not be aware that funds were transferred to this special bank account. A typical payroll check designed to give the employees information about gross pay, deductions, and net pay is shown in Illustration 9-3.

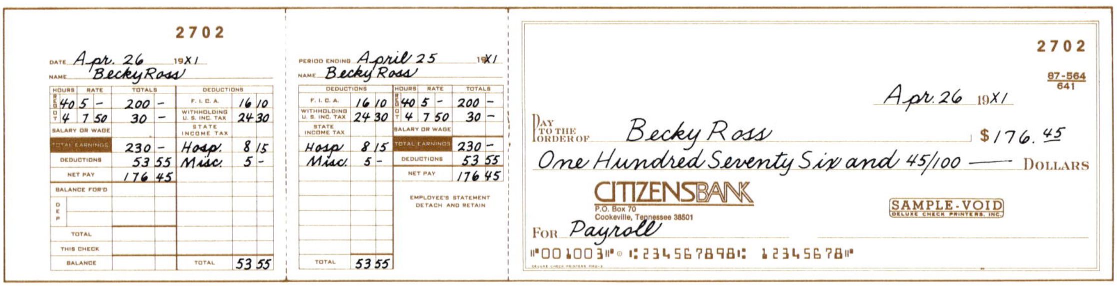
2702
DATE Apr. 26 19X1
NAME Becky Ross
HOURS 40 RATE 5 – TOTALS 200 –
OT 4 7 50 30 –
DEDUCTIONS: F.I.C.A. 16 10; WITHHOLDING U.S. INC. TAX 24 30; STATE INCOME TAX; Hosp. 8 15; Misc. 5 –
TOTAL EARNINGS 230 –
DEDUCTIONS 53 55
NET PAY 176 45
TOTAL 53 55

PERIOD ENDING April 25 19X1
NAME Becky Ross
EMPLOYEE'S STATEMENT DETACH AND RETAIN

2702
87-564/641
Apr. 26 19X1
PAY TO THE ORDER OF Becky Ross $176.45
One Hundred Seventy Six and 45/100 DOLLARS
CITIZENS BANK
P.O. Box 70
Cookeville, Tennessee 38501
SAMPLE-VOID
FOR Payroll
⑈001003⑈ ⑆234567898⑆ 12345678⑈

illustration 9-3 payroll account check.

sample problem The Soup Shoppe employs nine workers on a wage plan for its restaurant operation. Gross and net pay for the week ending August 17, 19X1 are shown below:

Employee	Gross Pay	Net Pay
Beaucamp, Hugh	$142	$119.26
Farris, Robert	160	128.44
Faulkner, Alice	180	141.90
LaSoto, Pierre	148	122.36
Marcelli, Jeannie	120	102.77
Nye, Louis	135	113.30
O'Brien, Pat	160	136.10
Patternson, Marcia	170	128.50
Zwalowski, Jim	142	120.67

Prepare in general journal form the entry or entries to record paying the payroll if the firm uses a special payroll account.

sample problem solution

Aug. 17	Wages Payable	1,113.30	
	Cash		1,113.30

review exercises

1. Weber Farms pays its employees in cash. The net pay for each employee is shown below:

Baldwin	$189.74
Baker	160.30
Khan	218.46
O'Leary	116.88
Ziegler	140.10

You must decide in advance how the currency and coins should be received from the teller so that the exact amount is available for each employee. Assume that a $20 bill is the largest used and that the fewest possible currency items (bills and coins) are used to pay each employee.

2. Nancy is trying to decide whether to use the regular checking account or a special payroll account at the bank to handle the payroll. She chooses to use the special payroll account because it takes fewer checks. Is Nancy correct in her thinking?

• task SEND THE AMOUNTS WITHHELD FROM THE EMPLOYEES' AND THE EMPLOYER'S PAYROLL TAXES, ALONG WITH THE CORRECT DOCUMENTS, TO THE FEDERAL GOVERNMENT

Paying the employees' income taxes and FICA taxes

The employer must pay these four payroll taxes to the United States Treasury Department: (1) employees' income taxes withheld from their paychecks, (2) FICA deductions from the employees' paychecks, (3) a matching amount of FICA taxes, and (4) Federal unemployment taxes payable by the employer (and the employee in a few states). Let's first concentrate on how the employer pays the income taxes and the FICA taxes; then we will look at Federal unemployment taxes.

The Federal government requires that the employer deposit the amount withheld from the employees and the matching employer's share of FICA taxes with an authorized financial institution or a Federal Reserve Bank. When doing this, the employer must submit *Form 501* (Illustration 9-4) and *Form 941* (discussed later). Form 501, which is a *Federal Tax Deposit Form,* has a detachable stub that the bank gives to the employer as proof of the firm's deposit. Notice that this form has a preassigned **employer identification number** that must appear on all documents sent to the Federal government.

illustration 9-4
Federal tax deposit form.

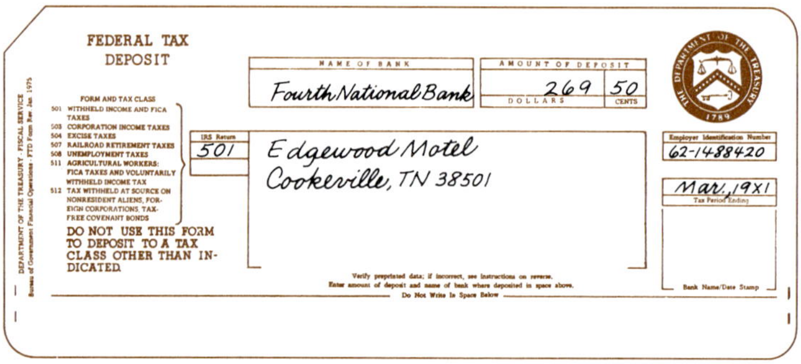
FEDERAL TAX DEPOSIT

DEPARTMENT OF THE TREASURY - FISCAL SERVICE
Bureau of Government Financial Operations - FTD Form Rev. Jan. 1975

FORM AND TAX CLASS
501 WITHHELD INCOME AND FICA TAXES
503 CORPORATION INCOME TAXES
504 EXCISE TAXES
507 RAILROAD RETIREMENT TAXES
508 UNEMPLOYMENT TAXES
511 AGRICULTURAL WORKERS: FICA TAXES AND VOLUNTARILY WITHHELD INCOME TAX
512 TAX WITHHELD AT SOURCE ON NONRESIDENT ALIENS, FOREIGN CORPORATIONS, TAX-FREE COVENANT BONDS

DO NOT USE THIS FORM TO DEPOSIT TO A TAX CLASS OTHER THAN INDICATED

NAME OF BANK: Fourth National Bank

AMOUNT OF DEPOSIT: DOLLARS 269 CENTS 50

IRS Return: 501

Edgewood Motel
Cookeville, TN 38501

Employer Identification Number: 62-1488420

Tax Period Ending: Mar., 19X1

Verify preprinted data; if incorrect, see instructions on reverse.
Enter amount of deposit and name of bank where deposited in space above.

Bank Name/Date Stamp

Do Not Write In Space Below

How often the employer makes a deposit depends on the amount of unpaid Federal taxes (not counting Federal unemployment taxes) that have built up but not been paid. The rule for payment states that if the undeposited taxes for the quarter are less than $500, the employer has the choice of paying the taxes directly to the Internal Revenue Service or depositing them by the end of the next month to a local bank that qualifies. If the three taxes together have an undeposited total of more than $500, but less than $3,000 at the end of the first or second month of that particular quarter, this amount must be deposited within 15 days after the end of the month. If you are thoroughly confused, possibly we can help you with an illustration. Assume that Edgewood Motel has the following Federal payroll items during April:

	Employee's FICA	Employer's FICA	Employee's Federal Income Tax	Cumulative Total
Apr. 4	$69.23	$69.23	$112.40	$ 250.86
11	76.15	76.15	124.60	527.76
18	72.67	72.67	118.10	791.20
25	78.82	78.82	116.80	1,065.64

Since more than $500 of undeposited taxes has accumulated by the end of April, a deposit is due by May 15. The necessary entry is shown in Illustration 9-5. Making this deposit to the authorized financial institution or Federal Reserve Bank on time is required by law. Proof of mailing at least two days before due date must be provided if the deposit is late. If the check is hand delivered, it must arrive before the financial institution or Federal Reserve Bank closes its business day.

CASH DISBURSEMENTS JOURNAL — Page 75

Date		Ch. No.	Payee	Account Debited	P.R.	Sundry Accounts Dr.	Accounts Payable Dr.	Purchases Discounts Cr.	Cash Cr.
19X1 May	15	2721	First Federal Bank	F.I.C.A. Taxes Payable		593 74			
				Employ. Income Taxes Payable		471 90			1 065 64

illustration 9-5 paying Federal taxes.

For firms with large payrolls, the required payments are more frequent. This tax law states that if the undeposited taxes (the employer's and employees' FICA taxes plus the Federal income taxes withheld from the employee) at the end of any **eighth-month** are $3,000 or more, a deposit must be made within three banking days after the end of that eighth-month. To understand what the rule requires, we must understand the term *eighth-month.* An average 30-day month was roughly divided into eight parts. Examine the left-hand column on *Form 941* (Illustration 9-6), and you will see that the 3rd, 7th, 11th, 15th, 19th, 22nd, 25th, and last day of the month mark the end of a period equal to about one-eighth of a month. To illustrate how the $3,000 rule works, let's use a larger firm than Edgewood Motel—Barger Manufacturing Company, a firm that employs 13 workers.

You can see the tax liability, dates of deposit, and total amount deposited by Barger Manufacturing Company in Illustration 9-6. This quarterly return is for the months of July, August, and September. At the end of

Form **941** (Rev. October 1982) Department of the Treasury Internal Revenue Service

Employer's Quarterly Federal Tax Return

▶ For Paperwork Reduction Act Notice, see page 2.

OMB No. 1545–0029 Expires 2–28–83

T | FF | FD | FP | I | T

Your name, address, employer identification number, and calendar quarter of return. (If not correct, please change.) ▶

Name (as distinguished from trade name): James Barger

Date quarter ended: Sept. 30, 19X1

Trade name, if any: Barger Manufacturing Co.

Employer identification number: 36 48778641

Address and ZIP code: 1139 Industrial Drive, Toms River, NJ 08753

If address is different from prior return, check here ▶ ☐

Record of Federal Tax Liability and Deposits (Complete if line 13 is $500 or more)

If you made eighth-monthly deposits using the 95% rule, check here . ▶ ☐

If you are a first-time 3-banking-day depositor, check here . . . . . . ▶ ☐

See the instructions under Rule (4) on page 4 for details.

	a. Date wages paid (Day)	b. Tax liability	c. Date of deposit (Optional)	d. Amount deposited (Optional)
		Overpayment from previous quarter . . ▶		-0-
First month of quarter	1st–3rd A	1,060.84		
	4th–7th B			
	8th–11th C	1,020.06		
	12th–15th D			
	16th–19th E	1,124.40	7/23	3,205.30
	20th–22nd F			
	23rd–25th G	1,216.18		
	26th–last H	1,173.49		
I	Total . . ▶	5,594.97		3,205.30
Second month of quarter	1st–3rd I			
	4th–7th J	1,180.46	8/11	3,570.13
	8th–11th K			
	12th–15th L	1,090.20		
	16th–19th M			
	20th–22nd N	1,040.73		
	23rd–25th O			
	26th–last P	961.81	8/31	3,092.74
II	Total . . ▶	4,273.20		6,662.87
Third month of quarter	1st–3rd Q	1,186.86		
	4th–7th R			
	8th–11th S	1,059.32		
	12th–15th T			
	16th–19th U	1,007.20	9/22	3,253.38
	20th–22nd V			
	23rd–25th W	1,105.38		
	26th–last X			
III	Total . . ▶	4,358.76		3,253.38
IV	Total for quarter (add lines I, II, and III) . .	14,226.93	Column b total must equal line 13	13,121.55
V	Final deposit made for quarter. (Enter 0 if included in line IV.)			-0-

	If you are not liable for returns in the future, write "FINAL" . . . . . . ▶	
	Date final wages paid . . ▶	
1	Number of employees (except household) employed in the pay period that includes March 12th (complete first quarter only) . . . . ▶	13
2	Total wages and tips subject to withholding, plus other compensation . . . . ▶	37,896 40
3	Total income tax withheld from wages, tips, annuities, sick pay, gambling, etc . ▶	
4	Adjustment of withheld income tax for preceding quarters of calendar year . . ▶	
5	Adjusted total of income tax withheld	8,921 43
6	Taxable FICA wages paid: $ 37,896 40 times 14% equals tax .	5,305 50
7 a	Taxable tips reported: $ ______ times 7% equals tax .	
b	Tips deemed to be wages (see instructions): $ ______ times 7% equals tax .	
8	Total FICA taxes (add lines 6, 7a, and 7b)	5,305 50
9	Adjustment of FICA taxes (see instructions) . . . ▶	
10	Adjusted total of FICA taxes .	5,305 50
11	Total taxes (add lines 5 and 10) . . . . ▶	14,226 93
12	Advance earned income credit (EIC) payments, if any . ▶	
13	Net taxes (subtract line 12 from line 11)	14,226 93
14	Total deposits for quarter from your records or from column d . . . . ▶	13,121 55
15	Undeposited taxes due (subtract line 14 from line 13). Enter here and pay to Internal Revenue Service . ▶	1,105 38
16	If line 14 is more than line 13, enter overpayment here ▶ $ ______ and check if to be: ☐ Applied to next return, or ☐ Refunded.	

Under penalties of perjury, I declare that I have examined this return, including accompanying schedules and statements, and to the best of my knowledge and belief it is true, correct, and complete.

Signature ▶ James Barger Title ▶ Manager Date ▶ Oct. 27, 19X1

Please file this form with your Internal Revenue Service Center (see instructions on "Where to File").

Form 941 (Rev. 10–82)

illustration 9-6 employer's quarterly federal tax return.

August, the company had no tax liability, since the deposit made on August 31 covered the outstanding tax debt to that point. Illustration 9-7 shows the Federal liabilities that were created by withholding FICA taxes and Federal income taxes from the employees in September and assuming matching FICA taxes for the employer:

illustration 9-7
Federal taxes in September.

Payday	Employees' FICA	Employer's FICA	Employees' Federal Income Tax	Total	Cumulative Total
Sept. 3	$328.03	$328.03	$530.80	$1,186.86	$1,186.86
10	284.71	284.71	489.90	1,059.32	2,246.18
17	266.35	266.35	474.50	1,007.20	3,253.38
24	298.99	298.99	507.40	1,105.38	4,358.76

The employees are paid on Friday of each week. Refer to Illustration 9-8 and you´will see that September has four paydays, with the first payday on September 3. Since September is the third month of the quarter, and payday is on the third, the total debt of $1,186.86 shown on that week is entered on line Q of Form 941. September 10, the second payday, is entered on line S. The cumulative total of these two amounts is less than $3,000, so no deposit is required. The third payday liability is entered on line U. Since the cumulative total does exceed $3,000, a deposit must be made within three banking days of the eighth-month ending on September 19 (line U range Days 16-19). According to the calendar in Illustration 9-8, the deposit of $3,253.38 must be made by Wednesday, September 22, unless the bank is closed on the 20th through 22nd. For each day the bank or Federal depository is closed, the deposit date is advanced one day.

illustration 9-8
September paydays.

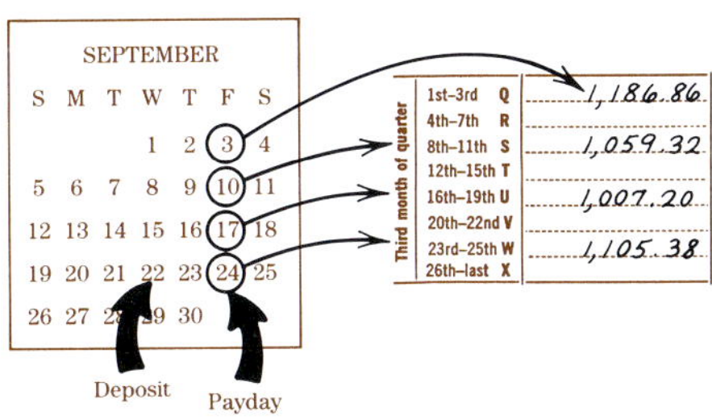

The September 24 payday of $1,105.38 does not require a payment since $3,000 in tax liability has not been accumulated. Refer again to Form 941 in Illustration 9-6. Note that line 6 is multiplied by 14%. This amount is the sum of employees' and employer's FICA taxes (7% × 2 using the FICA rate we chose in Chapter 8). Also, note that the term quarterly is based on the firm's fiscal year. Therefore, the quarters end on March 31, June 30, September 30, and December 31.

Paying the Federal unemployment tax

In Chapter 8 we pointed out that in most states the Federal unemployment tax is paid only by the employer. We will use a rate of 3.5% (.035) on the first $7,000 of wages or salaries paid to each employee during the year. Every employer who pays wages of $1,500 or more in any calendar quarter or who has one or more employees for some part of a day in any 20 weeks during the year must pay this tax. Another set of rules applies to agricultural and household employers, but we will concentrate on the typical business employer.

Earlier, we discussed how the Federal unemployment tax is reduced by the state unemployment tax. The rule also permits employers in Puerto Rico and the U.S. Virgin Islands to take this allowance. This rule allows the employer to deduct 2.7% (.027) of taxable wages and salaries from the Federal tax. In many cases, this allowance simply means that the firm pays .8% to the Federal government and 2.7% to the state government for unemployment. In this section, we want to look at the forms required to pay this unemployment tax.

The *Employer's Annual Federal Unemployment Tax Return* (Form 940) is shown in Illustration 9-9. Firms that owe less than $100 for the Federal unemployment tax must submit this return no later than January 31. For example, the 19X1 return is due by January 31, 19X2. This payment should amount to .8% (.008) of the first $7,000 paid to each employee. As we discussed earlier, the actual rate is 3.5%, but up to 2.7% credit is allowed for payments to state unemployment tax programs.

If an employer owes more than $100 in Federal unemployment taxes after any quarter, a deposit must be made by the last day of the following month to the Internal Revenue Service or to a qualified bank. Look at Part IV of Illustration 9-9 and you will see that Edgewood Motel owed $133.79 by June 30. A deposit was required by July 31, so the firm sent this deposit on July 28. An entry is made in the cash disbursements journal debiting *FUTA Taxes Payable* and crediting *Cash.* If a local bank is used, the check is made to the bank and not to the Internal Revenue Service.

Wage and tax statements

Each employee is to be given a *Wage and Tax Statement (Form W-2)* by January 31 of the following year. If the employee leaves the firm, the employer has until January 31 to provide the W-2 form unless the departing employee asks for one. When such a request is made, the employer has the later of (a) 30 days after the request or (b) the date of the final wage payment.

Information to fill out Form W-2 for each employee is found on the employee's individual earnings record. To illustrate completing a Form W-2, assume that by December 31, Becky Ross's records showed the following information:

Total wages	$7,600.00
FICA taxes withheld	532.00
Federal income taxes withheld	744.60

Form **940** Department of the Treasury Internal Revenue Service

Employer's Annual Federal Unemployment Tax Return

▶ For Paperwork Reduction Act Notice, see page 2.

OMB No. 1545–0028

19X1

T	
FF	
FD	
FP	
I	
T	

If incorrect, make any necessary change. ▶

Mary L. Farmer
Edgewood Motel
Highway 35 and 20th St.
Cookeville, TN 38501

Calendar Year 19X1

Employer identification number 62-1488420

A Did you pay all required contributions to your State unemployment fund by the due date of Form 940? ☒ Yes ☐ No

If you check the "Yes" box, enter amount of contributions timely paid to your State unemployment fund ▶ $

B Are you required to pay contributions to only one State? ☒ Yes ☐ No

If you checked the "Yes" box, (1) Enter the name of the State where you are required to pay contributions ▶ Tennessee

(2) Enter your State reporting number(s) as shown on State unemployment tax return ▶ 207 702

Part I Computation of Taxable Wages and Credit Reduction (To Be Completed by All Taxpayers)

	Amount paid	
1 Total payments (including exempt payments) during the calendar year for services of employees		38,420 00
2 Exempt payments. (Explain each exemption shown, attaching additional sheets if necessary) ▶		
3 Payments for services in excess of $6,000. Enter only the excess over the first $6,000 paid to individual employees exclusive of exempt amounts entered on line 2. Do not use State wage limitation	8,420 00	
4 Total exempt payments (add lines 2 and 3)		8,420 00
5 **Total taxable wages** (subtract line 4 from line 1). (If any portion is exempt from State contributions, see instructions) ▶		30,000 00

6 Credit reduction because of unrepaid advances to the States listed. Enter in lines (a)–(k) the wages included on line 5 above for each State and multiply by the rate shown.

(a) CT ____ × .007 ____	(e) ME ____ × .006 ____	(i) RI ____ × .006 ____
(b) DE ____ × .006 ____	(f) NJ ____ × .006 ____	(j) VT ____ × .006 ____
(c) DC ____ × .006 ____	(g) PA ____ × .006 ____	(k) VI ____ × .006 ____
(d) IL ____ × .006 ____	(h) PR ____ × .006 ____	

7 Total credit reduction (add lines 6(a) through 6(k) and enter on line 2, Part II or line 4, Part III) ▶

Part II Tax Due or Refund (Complete if You Checked the "Yes" boxes in Both Items A and B Above)

1 FUTA tax. Multiply the wages on line 5, Part I, by .007 and enter here	210 00
2 Enter amount from line 7, Part I	
3 **Total FUTA tax** (add lines 1 and 2)	210 00
4 Less: Total FUTA tax deposited from column d, line 5, Part IV	133 79
5 **Balance due** (subtract line 4 from line 3—if over $100, see Part IV instructions). Pay to IRS ▶	76 21
6 **Overpayment** (subtract line 3 from line 4) ▶	

Part III Tax Due or Refund (Complete if You Checked the "No" Box in Either Item A or Item B Above)

1 Gross FUTA tax. Multiply the wages on line 5, Part I, by .034	
2 Maximum credit. Multiply the wages on line 5, Part I, by .027	
3 Enter the smaller of the amount on line 11, Part V, or line 2, Part III	
4 Enter amount from line 7, Part I	
5 Credit allowable (subtract line 4 from line 3)	
6 Total FUTA tax (subtract line 5 from line 1)	
7 Less: Total FUTA tax deposited from column d, line 5, Part IV	
8 **Balance due** (subtract line 7 from line 6—if over $100, see Part IV instructions). Pay to IRS ▶	
9 **Overpayment** (subtract line 6 from line 7) ▶	

Part IV Record of Federal Tax Deposits for Unemployment Tax (Form 508) (Do not include contributions paid to State)

	a. Quarter	b. Liability for quarter	c. Date of deposit	d. Amount of deposit
1	First	66.50		
2	Second	67.27	7/28	133 79
3	Third	67.69		
4	Fourth	8.54		
5	Total for year			133 79

If you will not have to file returns in the future, write "Final" here (see general instruction "Who Must File") ▶

Under penalties of perjury, I declare that I have examined this return, including accompanying schedules and statements, and to the best of my knowledge and belief, it is true, correct, and complete, and that no part of any payment made to a State unemployment fund claimed as a credit was or is to be deducted from the payments to employees.

Date ▶ 1/29/X2 Signature ▶ Mary L. Farmer Title (Owner, etc.) ▶ Owner

illustration 9-9 **employer's annual Federal unemployment tax return.**

This information and other data from her earnings record were used to prepare the Form W-2 shown in Illustration 9-10.

1 Control Number | 22222

2 Employer's name, address, and ZIP code
Edgewood Motel
Highway 35 and 20th St.
Cookeville, TN 38501

3 Employer's identification number	4 Employer's State number
62-1488420	

5 Stat Emp ☐ Deceased ☐ Pension Plan ☐ Legal Rep ☐ 942 Emp ☐ Subtotal ☐ Correction ☐ Void ☐

6	7 Advance EIC payment
	.00

8 Employee's social security number	9 Federal income tax withheld	10 Wages, tips, other compensation	11 FICA tax withheld
141-28-1007	$744.60	$7,600.00	$532.00

13 FICA wages	14 FICA tips
$7,600.00	.00

12 Employee's name, address, and ZIP code
Becky Lee Ross
821 Bluebonnet Road
Cookeville, TN 38501

16 Employer's use

17 State income tax	18 State wages, tips, etc.	19 Name of State
20 Local income tax	21 Local wages, tips, etc.	22 Name of locality

Form **W-2 Wage and Tax Statement 1980**
36-2515832 I R S APP 6/9/80
COPY A For Social Security Administration. *See Instructions for Forms W-2 and W-2P

illustration 9-10 the W-2 and tax statement.

The *Wage and Tax Statement* form comes in a convenient packet designed to make multiple copies. When the employee's name and address are typed on the top copy, an envelope ready for mailing is also prepared. In the case of Becky Ross, four copies are made for: (1) Edgewood Motel to mail to the Social Security Administration; (2) Becky to mail with her Federal tax return; (3) Becky's personal records; (4) Edgewood Motel's files.

If the firm were located in a state with a state income tax, two additional copies would be needed—one for the employer to send to the state taxing authority and one for the employee to file with the state tax return. Two more copies would be needed for a local income tax.

By February 28 following the end of the taxing year, the employer must submit a *Transmittal of Income and Tax Statements (Form W-3).* This form is sent to the Social Security Administration with Copy A of Form W-2 for each employee. The Social Security Administration records FICA information from Form W-3 and then sends the data on to the Internal Revenue Service. A completed Form W-3 for Edgewood Motel is shown in Illustration 9-11.

Schedule of Federal taxes

To give you an overall picture, Illustration 9-12 shows you the most used tax forms and a brief description of when to use these forms.

1 Control number	33333				
☐ Kind of Tax Statements Transmitted ▶	2 941/941E ☐ CT-1 ☐	Military ☐ 942 ☐	943 ☐ Section 218 ☐	3 W-2 ☒ W-2P ☐	4 Original ☒ Corrected ☐	5 With TIN ☒ Without TIN ☐
6 State SSA number 69–	7 Advance EIC payments			8 Number of statements attached 5		
9 Federal income tax $3,513.20	10 Wages, tips, and other compensation $37,350.00			11 FICA tax withheld $2,614.50		
12 Employer's State number	13 FICA wages $37,350.00			14 FICA tips		
15 Employer's identification number 62-1488420				16 Establishment number		
17 Employer's name Edgewood Motel				18 Gross annuity, pension, retired pay, or IRA payment		
Highway 35 and 20th St. Cookeville, TN 38501 19 Employer's address and ZIP code (If available, place label over boxes 15, 17, and 19.)				20 Taxable amount		

Under penalties of perjury, I declare that I have examined this return, including accompanying documents, and to the best of my knowledge and belief, it is true, correct, and complete. In the case of documents without recipients' identifying numbers, I have complied with the requirements of the law by requesting such numbers from the recipients, but did not receive them.

Signature ▶ *Mary L. Farmer* Title ▶ *Owner* Date ▶ *2/25/X2*

illustration 9-11 **transmittal of income and tax statement.**

sample problem Complete the partial Form 941 for Thrasher Corporation by filling in the amount deposited in Column d. Since the date of deposit depends on the arrangement of the two months involved, ignore Column c for this problem.

Record of Federal Tax Liability and Deposits (Complete if line 13 is $500 or more)

If you made eighth-monthly deposits using the 95% rule, check here . ▶ ☐

If you are a first-time 3-banking-day depositor, check here . . . . . . ▶ ☐

See the instructions under Rule (4) on page 4 for details .

	a. Date wages paid		b. Tax liability	c. Date of deposit (Optional)	d. Amount deposited (Optional)
	Day		Overpayment from previous quarter . . ▶		
First month of quarter	1st–3rd	A			
	4th–7th	B	2,196.10		
	8th–11th	C			
	12th–15th	D	3,004.80		
	16th–19th	E			
	20th–22nd	F	2,231.70		
	23rd–25th	G			
	26th–last	H	2,016.10		
I	Total . . ▶		9,448.70		
Second month of quarter	1st–3rd	I	1,886.50		
	4th–7th	J			
	8th–11th	K	2,013.20		
	12th–15th	L			
	16th–19th	M	3,076.90		
	20th–22nd	N			
	23rd–25th	O	2,516.70		
	26th–last	P			
II	Total . . ▶		8,893.30		
	1st–3rd				

illustration 9-12
schedule of Federal tax forms.

Tax	Form	Amount	Deposit Due
Employees' Federal income tax and FICA taxes	501	Less than $500 at end of a quarter	Last day of the month following the end of the quarter
	501	$500 or more, but less than $3,000 by the end of any month	Within 15 days after end of the month
	501	$3,000 or more at the end of any eighth-month period	Within 3 banking days after the end of the eighth-month period that the undeposited taxes reach $3,000
Federal unemployment tax (FUTA)	940	3.5% (less experience rating) on first $7,000 paid each employee. Less than $100 due.	By January 31 of the following year
	940	$100 or more due	Quarter Ending / Due Date Mar. 31 — Apr. 30 June 30 — July 31 Sept. 30 — Oct. 31 Dec. 31 — Jan. 31
Employees' Federal income tax and FICA taxes	941	Does Not Apply	Quarter Ending / Due Date Mar. 31 — Apr. 30 June 30 — June 30 Sept. 30 — Oct. 31 Dec. 31 — Jan. 31
Wage and Tax Statement	W-2	No Limit	Provide copy to employees by Jan. 31 or 30 days after termination of employment. Provide copy to Social Security Administration by Feb. 28 (with Form W-3)
Annual Transmittal of Income and Tax Statements	W-3	No Limit	By February 28 (with Form W-2)
Employee's Withholding Allowance Certificate	W-4	Does Not Apply	Employer must keep on file. Make effective with first wage or salary payment.

sample problem solution

	Amount Deposited
1st-3rd	
4th-7th	
8th-11th	
12th-15th	$5,200.90
16th-19th	
20th-22nd	
23rd-25th	
26th-last	4,247.80
1st-3rd	
4th-7th	
8th-11th	3,899.70
12th-15th	
16th-19th	3,076.90
20th-22nd	
23rd-25th	
26th-last	

review exercises

3. For five employees, the Wash Tub had the following payroll deductions and employer FICA taxes:

	Employees' FICA	Employer's FICA	Employees' Federal Income Tax
July 5	$66.50	$66.50	$ 99.70
12	62.12	62.12	95.10
21	73.15	73.15	118.10
28	76.47	76.47	127.60

Prepare a general journal entry to record the payment that would be made to the Federal government.

4. Delta Corporation has a rather large payroll. For the month of November, the following payroll deductions and employer FICA taxes were shown in the payroll register.

	Employees' FICA	Employer's FICA	Employees' Federal Income Tax
Nov. 4	$2,660.00	$2,660.00	$3,988
11	2,484.00	2,484.00	3,804
18	2,926.00	2,926.00	4,724
27	3,058.80	3,058.80	5,104

When would the first payment have to be made? Make the necessary entry to record this payment.

• task SEND THE STATE AND OTHER AGENCIES THE AMOUNT DUE FOR BOTH VOLUNTARY AND INVOLUNTARY DEDUCTIONS

State unemployment tax

In addition to acting as a trustee of the funds for the Federal government, the employer also retains part of the employees' gross pay for such voluntary deductions as charities, credit unions, insurance premiums, and involuntary deductions, such as state and local income taxes. The employer also owes taxes for state unemployment contributions. We will look at some of these deductions, as well as some miscellaneous forms that might be of interest to the employer.

The employer must pay taxes to the state on the first $7,000 earned by each covered employee in a calendar year. This *taxable* payroll is the same amount that is covered by the Federal unemployment tax law. The rate paid varies from state to state and is based on (1) the firm's employment experience and (2) the amount in the state's trust fund. As we mentioned in Chapter 8, the rate ranges from 0.3% to approximately 5.0%. Due to its widespread use, we will assume a rate of 2.7%.

Since **experience ratings** are important, we should tell you more about how that system works. To put it simply, the more workers a firm lays off, the higher the unemployment rate; the fewer workers laid off, the lower the unemployment rate. The plan is designed to keep a balance in the state's trust fund adequate to ensure payments to qualified unemployed persons.

Most states require the employer to pay into the fund for a set number of years, such as three, before qualifying for experience ratings deductions. Once each year after that, the employer's record is examined to see how much was paid into the fund and how much was paid out in benefits to that firm's former employees. If the state experiences high unemployment and the trust fund drops below a set amount, the rate will not be reduced as much by a good record. In fact, the firm might find itself having to pay a higher rate. The reverse is true in a period of low unemployment. A firm with a good record might find itself receiving a substantial cut in its state tax rate.

To illustrate how the experience rating system works, assume that Wilcox Company is assigned a rate of 2.2% after four years of paying 2.7%. This means that the firm will pay a total of 3.0% for unemployment—2.2% to the state and .8% to the Federal government. In other words, the Federal authorities allow Wilcox a full 2.7% credit (3.5% less 2.7% = .8%) even though Wilcox is paying the state only 2.2%. A firm can assist in keeping the lowest possible rate by:

1. Keeping accurate records.
2. Answering requests for separation information promptly and in detail.
3. Appealing any determination of benefits that appears to be incorrect.
4. Verifying all tax notices received.
5. Filing all reports and paying all taxes when they are due.

State unemployment tax payments are due quarterly within the month following the end of each calendar quarter, the same schedule for submitting Form 941. A *State Wage and Contribution Report* is shown in Illustration 9-13.

An employer must be careful to pay the state unemployment taxes on time. If the state tax is not paid by January 31, the employer owes the full 3.5% Federal tax. By paying this amount to the Federal government, however, the employer *is not* relieved of paying the state debt. Carelessness about paying taxes on time, therefore, may result in delinquent taxes that will cost the employer 3.5% plus the firm's current state unemployment rate. Payment should be made to the state's revenue or employment security department. *State Unemployment Taxes Payable* is debited and *Cash* is credited.

Employees' state and local income taxes

Most states require employers to withhold a portion of each employee's gross pay in the same way that the Federal government collects employees' withholding taxes. Generally, the amount withheld depends on the gross pay and the number of exemptions of the employee. Tax tables similar to the Federal tax table shown in Chapter 8 are provided to the employer by the state.

Timing of deposits and form numbers varies so much from state to state that we can only suggest that you consult with your instructor or obtain a copy of the state taxing requirements for local rules. If you move to a different state, becoming acquainted with the new state laws is very important. Your employer in one state may not have been required to withhold for state income taxes, while a new employer in a different state may be required to do so.

DES 220.5
ES 0317 (R.5/82)

Tennessee Department of Employment Security
WAGE AND CONTRIBUTION REPORT

AREA	FEDERAL ID NUMBER	RATE	QTR/YEAR	STATE ACCOUNT NUMBER
11	62-1488420	2.70	1st	207-702

QTR END DATE	DUE DATE	DATE PAID	DATE RECEIVED	10
3/31/x1	4/30/x1			

Total Number of Workers as of the 12th of Each Month of the Quarter	1st Month	2nd Month	3rd Month
	5	5	5

Item 9 ◆ Social Security Number (1)	NAME First	Middle Initial	Last (2)	TOTAL WAGES PAID THIS QUARTER (3)
141-36-2655	Betty	I.	Abrams	3,354 00
863-44-9625	Dot	J.	Baker	2,089 00
141-28-1007	Becky	L.	Ross	2,457 00
555-11-9912	Connie	L.	Wright	3,650 00
228-60-4422	Faye	A.	Ziegler	1,935 00
PAGE 1 OF 1 PAGES			TOTAL WAGES THIS PAGE	13,485 00

1. TOTAL WAGES	13,485 00	AUDITOR
2. LESS NON-TAXABLE WAGES		MEMO NO.
3. NET TAXABLE WAGES (Item 1 minus Item 2)	13,485 00	CONT. D/C
4. CONTRIBUTION DUE x Item 3)	364 09	CONT. DUE
5. INTEREST DUE		INTEREST DUE
6. PENALTY DUE		PENALTY DUE
7. OUTSTANDING DEBIT OR CREDIT		INTEREST D
8. TOTAL DUE Make check payable to Tennessee Dept of Employment Security	364 09	PENALTY D

SAMPLE

SEE INSTRUCTIONS ON REVERSE SIDE OF LAST SHEET
RETURN BOTH WHITE AND YELLOW COPIES OF THIS REPORT, ANY CONTINUATION SHEETS, AND YOUR CHECK. DO NOT WRITE IN THE SHADED AREA.

Tennessee Department of Employment Security
Contributions Section, Cordell Hull Bldg.
Nashville, Tennessee 37219

"I CERTIFY THAT THE INFORMATION ON THIS REPORT IS TRUE AND CORRECT"

Signature: Mary L. Farmer
Title: Owner
Phone No: 528-1111 Date: 4/19/X1

NAME AND ADDRESS OF PREPARER IF OTHER THAN TAXPAYER:

Signature: ______
Address: ______
Phone No: ______

EMPLOYERS' NAME AND ADDRESS

Edgewood Motel
Highway 135 and 20th St.
Cookeville, Tn. 38501

Illustration 9-13 **state wage and contribution report.**

Some counties and cities have the equivalent of an income tax although it may be called something else, such as an occupational tax. This tax is usually applied as a flat percentage of gross pay. To illustrate, assume that Jon Wood is employed in a city that applies a 1.5% occupational tax. If Jon made $300 during the week, the accountant calculates his pay by deducting $4.50 ($300 × 1.5%) for this tax. When a deposit is made to the local taxing authority, *Employee Occupational Taxes Payable* is debited and *Cash* is credited. A brief schedule of state tax reports is given in Illustration 9-14.

illustration 9-14 schedule of state tax reports.

Tax	Remarks
State quarterly contribution report	Pay within month following end of each calendar quarter. Payment of the state unemployment rate on first $7,000 earned by each employee.
Employer's quarterly wage report	In some states, this form is combined with Quarterly Contribution Report. File at the same time.
Separation notice	Must be furnished to each worker within 24 hours of the separation if separation is expected to last 7 or more days.

Miscellaneous deduction payments

Insurance premiums withheld Voluntary deductions for life and health insurance premiums are usually mailed each payday to the insurance firms involved. Assume that a firm withheld $148.60 for life insurance premiums and $296.30 for health insurance premiums. The entry to record this payment is shown in Illustration 9-15.

CASH DISBURSEMENTS JOURNAL — Page 36

Date		Ch. No.	Payee	Account Debited	P.R.	Sundry Accounts Dr.	Accounts Payable Dr.	Purchases Discounts Cr.	Cash Cr.
19X1 Aug.	19	1475	Continental Life	Life Insurance Premium Payable		148 60			148 60
	19	1476	United Insurance	Health Insurance Prem. Payable		296 30			296 30

illustration 9-15 paying insurance premiums.

Savings accounts Voluntary deductions for credit unions, savings bonds, and other forms of savings are sent to the bank or credit union each payday. The payment entry would be similar to that used for insurance premiums. A descriptive account is debited and *Cash* is credited. For the credit union, the accountant could use *Credit Union Deductions Payable, Employee Credit Union Deductions Payable,* or something more specific like *Southern Colorado Credit Union Deductions Payable.*

Retirement funds and other deductions Some retirement funds are less voluntary than others. Some employees wish to supplement their Social Security benefits with additional retirement plans. The employer may have a group retirement system. If enough employees are interested, a tax-shelter annuity program can be set up. In all of these cases, withholding funds from the employee creates a liability. The accounting clerk must know when and how much to send to each of these funds. When a check is written, an entry is recorded in the cash disbursements journal to debit the appropriate liability and credit *Cash.*

Payments made to charities and unions are handled the same way. An appropriate liability account is debited and *Cash* is credited. The frequency of payment and the form required, if any, depend upon the organization involved.

review exercises

5. Gino's Italian Foods has earned an unemployment rating from the state of 1.6%. If the total payroll for the first quarter of the year is $48,600, calculate these amounts: (a) the employer's portion of FICA taxes, (b) state unemployment taxes, and (c) Federal unemployment taxes. Assume that all employees have earned less than $7,000 each.
6. In Review Exercise 5, if Gino's failed to pay its unemployment taxes on time, what amount would be due to (a) the state and (b) the Federal government?

Payroll flow chart

Illustration 9-16 shows a typical payroll procedure. Note that no change may be made to the payroll without proper personnel files. All payroll deductions must be properly authorized so that the correct amount and types of deductions are taken. In a large operation, the time cards are reconciled with the job time tickets to make certain that all hours worked are charged to the appropriate department.

Note also that updating the employees' individual earnings records each time a payroll is prepared maintains an up-to-date record on each employee. In Illustration 9-16, a special payroll bank account is used. Only a slight modification is required in the drawing if the regular checking account is used for payroll checks.

Maintaining adequate payroll procedures is important to all firms. In this area the law imposes a prison sentence, as well as a fine, for negligence in keeping adequate records.

illustration 9-16
payroll flow chart.

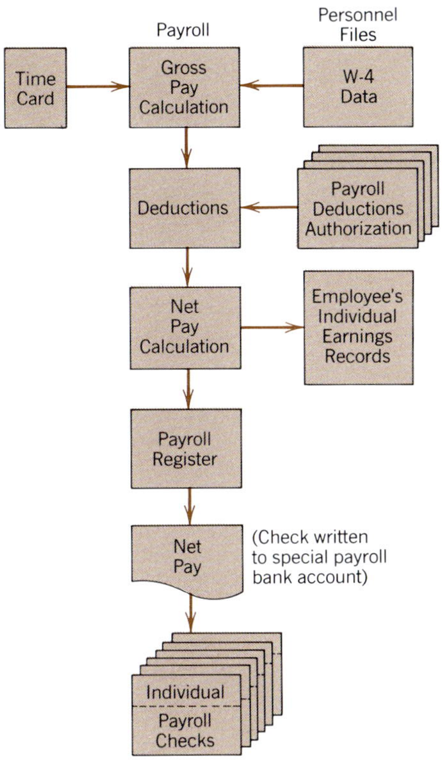

chapter highlights

Having studied this chapter, you should now be able to:

- Prepare checks or cash to pay the payroll.
- Journalize employee payments in the cash disbursements journal.
- Fill out the proper forms.
- Mail the forms with the correct amount to the proper agency.
- Journalize payments to the various agencies.

check figures to review exercises

1. \$20—39; \$10—2; \$5—3; \$1—8; 50 cents—2; 25 cents—3; 10 cents—6; 5 cents—1; 1 cent—8.
2. Nancy is incorrect. The special bank account requires one additional check to transfer funds from one bank account to another.
3.

FICA Taxes Payable	556.48	
Employees' Income Taxes Payable	440.50	
Cash		996.98

4. Assuming that November 4 is on Friday and that the bank is open on the following Monday, the deposit is due on November 10.

FICA Taxes Payable	5,320	
Employees' Federal Income Taxes Payable	3,988	
Cash		9,308

5. (a) $3,402; (b) $777.60; (c) $388.80.
6. (a) $777.60; (b) $1,701.

key terms

The following important terms are discussed in Chapter 9 and are defined in the Glossary at the end of the book:

eighth-month
experience rating
employer identification number
net pay
payroll bank account

questions

1. Why do some employers pay their employees with cash?
2. What is the purpose of the employer identification number?
3. If the regular checking account is used for the payroll, how are employees informed about deductions?
4. Why is it preferable to use a special checking account for the payroll?
5. Name the four payroll taxes that the employer must remit to the Federal government.
6. What Federal taxes are reported on the *Employer's Quarterly Federal Tax Return?*
7. What is meant by the term "eighth-month"?
8. Must payments to the Federal government be made directly to the Internal Revenue Service? If not, what alternatives are available?
9. Fabricated Products has accumulated $3,116.88 in Federal taxes by Friday, April 24. Assuming payday is each Friday and that the depository bank is open on the following Monday, what is the last day on which the employer may make a deposit?
10. What is the purpose of an experience rating? List some factors that affect a firm's state unemployment rate.
11. Discuss the situation in which the employer would lose a state unemployment tax exemption and be required to pay the 3.5% rate to the Federal government.
12. List ways that an employer can keep the unemployment rate at the lowest possible rate.

exercises

1. Fred's Auto Sales employs three salespersons who are paid in cash. Net pay for the three employees is shown below:

John Franks	$280.37
Jean Simmons	300.95
Bennett Wood	122.88

Determine the currency needed to pay these employees assuming the firm uses the fewest units. The largest currency used is a $20 bill.

2. Make an entry in general journal form to record the payment in Exercise 1.

3. Weiss Electronic paid the following gross amounts to its employees during 19X1:

Helen Baroni	$32,640
Roxanne Clark	16,200
Marvin Dalton	18,870
Sammy Feldman	5,604
Barbara Hampston	3,400
Shirley Seal	34,630
Michael Thrasher	29,340

Calculate the total (a) employees' FICA tax, (b) employer's FICA tax, (c) state unemployment tax, and (d) Federal unemployment tax charged during 19X1. Assume that the firm earned a state experience rate of 2.4%.

4. Sinclair Candy Store's records show the following Federal taxes for July:

	Employees' FICA Tax	Employer's FICA Tax	Employees' Federal Income Tax
July 6	$138.46	$138.46	$224.80
13	152.30	152.30	249.20
20	145.34	145.34	236.20
27	157.64	157.64	240.60

When must these taxes be paid? Make the necessary entry in general journal form.

5. Harris Insurance employs a small staff. An examination of the firm's records reveals that the following Federal taxes are due:

	Employees' FICA Tax	Employer's FICA Tax	Employees' Federal Income Tax
Nov. 5	$22.19	$22.19	$40.50
12	24.00	24.00	45.20
19	21.75	21.75	38.80
26	18.44	18.44	35.90

When must payment be made for these taxes? Make the necessary entry in general journal form.

6. Dot Discount Department Store's records show a *cumulative* total for employees' and employer's FICA taxes plus employees' Federal income taxes as follows:

Jan. 4	$2,360.42
11	4,277.30
18	6,511.18
25	8,604.84

Assume that payday is each Friday. When must the firm make its payments to the Federal bank? Assume that the store was closed during December because of a strike.

7. Wholesale Supply has earned a state experience rating of 2.2%. During the year, three employees exceeded $7,000 in wages and one earned $5,620. Calculate the firm's annual state and Federal unemployment tax.

8. Henderson Clothing paid wages and salaries of $23,640.50 that are subject to unemployment taxes. The firm has an experience rating of 1.8%. Through an oversight, the firm failed to pay the state tax on time. How much is due the Federal government for the firm's unemployment tax?

problems

1. COMPETENCY TESTED The ability to record the payment of wages.

On February 26, Read-A-Lot Book Store paid its five employees wages for work performed during the past week. The net pay for each employee and the number of the check issued is shown below:

	Net Pay	Check No.
Drozdowski, Edgar	$249.30	4761
Epps, Bryan	207.89	4762
Maxwell, Harlan	186.55	4763
Ray, Mary	215.88	4764
Weinrach, Eleanor	203.06	4765

Instructions Record paying the employees, assuming that the firm (a) does not keep a separate checking account for payroll, and (b) keeps a separate checking account for payroll.

2. COMPETENCY TESTED The skill to prepare payroll checks and payroll deduction statements.

Voluntary and involuntary deductions for the three employees of Chocolate Chip Shoppe, along with each employee's net pay, are shown below. The employees are being paid for five days ending on Friday, May 7, 19X1.

Employee	FICA Taxes	State Income Taxes	Federal Income Taxes	Kidney Foundation	Hosp. Ins.	Net Pay
Peggy Horn SS#142-00-7600	$14.70	$4.20	$18.80	$5.00	$12.10	$155.20
Bill Isbell SS#141-28-0000	15.40	4.60	27.40		8.60	164.00
Debbi Lafever SS#006-29-4500	12.95	3.70	23.20	5.00	8.60	131.55

Instructions Using the forms in your workbook, prepare payroll deduction statements. Chocolate Chip Shoppe does not use a special bank account for the payroll.

3. COMPETENCY TESTED The ability to determine payment date and amount to be sent to the Federal government for payroll taxes.

Felder's Fashion Store has the following Federal payroll items during the month of September:

	Employees' FICA Taxes	Employer's FICA Taxes	Employees' Federal Income Tax	Cumulative Total
Sept. 3	$81.15	$81.15	$173.20	$ 335.50
10	86.48	86.48	196.00	704.46
17	84.22	84.22	189.50	1,062.40
24	79.20	79.20	163.70	1,384.50

Instructions (a) Determine the payment date to the First Federal Bank, assuming that the bank is not open on weekends and that payday is always on a Friday. (b) Make the required journal entry in the cash disbursements journal to record using check 393.

4. COMPETENCY TESTED The skill to complete Form 941.

L. G. Laycox, owner of Hi-Flight Charter Service, provides you with the following information concerning Federal payroll taxes:

	Combined Employer and Employees' FICA Taxes	Employees' Income Taxes Withheld
July 3	$415.16	$ 934.10
10	440.54	1,011.30
17	390.78	902.40
24	400.12	915.70
31	380.16	885.20
Aug. 7	360.65	834.80
14	348.34	811.90
21	300.58	788.30
28	324.98	808.20

Sept. 4	$288.60	$740.10
11	290.76	754.70
18	250.34	710.50
25	277.34	729.40

Instructions Using the partial Form 941 found in your workbook, complete this form using the data from above. Assume that payday is each Saturday and that the Federal depository bank is closed on weekends, July 4, and September 6 during this quarter.

5. COMPETENCY TESTED The ability to calculate FICA taxes, state unemployment taxes, and Federal unemployment taxes.

CASE 1: The employees of Korner Drug have earned a total of $46,250. All of this amount is subject to FICA; $28,830 is subject to unemployment taxes. The state unemployment rate is 4.1%.

CASE 2: Technical Institute employs two workers. The first employee earned $36,400, while the second employee earned $28,960. The state unemployment rate is 2.3%.

CASE 3: Leaseco Equipment Company employs no more than four employees at any one time. Individual earning records show the following information:

Employee	Cumulative Pay	Other Data
Don Foister	$18,560	Employed all year
David Francis	5,280	Fired, March 3
Kim Key	6,460	Began September 8
Linda Moore	12,970	Began March 5
Merle Watts	2,400	Moved, February 15
Clark Wood	31,450	Employed all year

The state unemployment rate is 2.7%.

Instructions Calculate in each of these cases the annual amount paid by (a) the employee for FICA taxes and (b) the employer for FICA taxes, state unemployment taxes, and the Federal unemployment taxes.

6. COMPETENCY TESTED The skill to fill out an employer's quarterly contribution report.

By the end of the first quarter, Phil's Corner Grocery, located on Highway 97 in Klamath Falls, Oregon (97601), had paid total wages of $14,620. The store employs four workers on a salary basis and has a state unemployment rate of 1.8%.

Instructions Using the form provided in your workbook, complete the *Employer's Quarterly Contribution Report* for the first quarter ending on March 31, 19X1.

comprehensive problem Using the transactions prepared in Chapter 6 for purchases and sales of the Reed Supply Company, record the transactions in the cash receipts and cash disbursements journals for the cash transactions of the firm. Payroll transactions are recorded for this section of the comprehensive problem. Cash transactions for the month of January are as follows:

19X2

Jan. 1 Paid rent to Geraldine Fox for 3 months in advance for $900. Check No. 321.

1 John Reed, the owner, invested an additional $5,000 cash in the business.

3 Received a check from Ellis and Foster for the sale of December 26, less 2 percent discount.

4 Paid Plain View Electric for monthly utility expenses, $325. Check No. 322.

5 Paid Rush and Sons for the purchase of December 31, less discount of 2 percent. Check No. 323.

6 John Reed withdrew $400 for personal use. Check No. 324.

7 Cash sales were $865.

10 Received a check from Stevens Products Company for the amount due on the sale of January 2, less 2 percent discount.

12 Paid Swan Company for the amount due on the purchase of January 3, less discount. Check No. 325.

13 Paid Dodson Supply Company $170 on the purchase of office supplies on January 4, less discount. Check No. 326.

14 Paid employees as follows:

	Gross Pay	FICA Taxes Payable	Federal Income Taxes Payable	Net Pay	Check Number
Burt Williams	$400	$28	$52	$320	327
Martha Ziegler	500	35	75	390	328

FICA Taxes were withheld at 7.0%.
The employer payroll taxes were as follows:

FICA taxes	7.0 percent
State unemployment taxes	2.7 percent
FUTA taxes	.8 percent

Hint: Record the entry in the general journal with a credit to *Salaries Payable;* then record the net amount of each check in the cash disbursements journal.

16 Paid National Express for freight charges of $150. Check No. 329.

16 Received a $4,100 check from Ellis and Foster for the sales of January 2 and 5.

17 Paid Rush and Son the amount owed on the purchase of January 8, less returns and less discount at 2 percent. Check No. 330.

21 Nolan Supply Company returned merchandise (Invoice No. 599) valued at $80. Issued a credit memorandum.

21 Received a check from Bolt and Sons for the amount due on the sale of January 9.

21 Paid Walters Company the amount due on the purchase of January 11, less 2 percent discount. Check No. 331.

22 Paid Swan Company the amount due on January 13 purchase, less 2 percent discount. Check No. 332.

24 Received a check from Nolan Supply Company for the amount due from sale of January 15, less return and less 2 percent discount.

25 Cash sales were $1,232.

28 Paid employees as follows:

	Gross Pay	FICA Taxes Payable	Federal Income Taxes Payable	Net Pay	Check Number
Burt Williams	$400	$28	$52	$320	333
Martha Ziegler	500	35	75	390	334

FICA taxes were withheld at 7.0 percent.
The employer payroll transactions were as follows:

FICA taxes	7.0 percent
State unemployment taxes	2.7 percent
FUTA taxes	.8 percent

29 Received a check from Bolt and Sons for the amount due, less 2 percent discount on the sale of January 23.

31 Returned $100 of merchandise to Walters Company from January 25 purchase.

31 Paid KMXX for advertising expense for $80. Check No. 335.

31 Paid National Express for freight charges of $200. Check No. 336.

Instructions (continued from Chapter 6)

2. Record the above transactions in the journals provided in Chapter 6 of your workbook.

3. Total and rule the journals and post to the subsidiary ledger accounts and to the general ledger. Because you are posting from all five journals at once, you may have some difficulty in keeping transactions in chronological order. This will cause no problem in the statements, but you may have some abnormal balances during your posting. We encourage you to post the Sundry columns of the special journals first, then the items in the general journal; finally, the totals of the special journals. Note: This comprehensive problem will continue in Chapter 10.

chapter 10
WORK SHEET AND OTHER END-OF-PERIOD ADJUSTMENTS

overall competency THE ABILITY TO PREPARE A WORK SHEET AND ADJUSTING ENTRIES FOR A MERCHANDISING BUSINESS

career objectives In Chapter 3 we introduced you to the concept of preparing a work sheet for a service-type business. As you face the business world, you will find that the majority of firms have a product to sell. So that you will have the understanding to sell your skills to these merchandising firms, we began in Chapter 5 to expose you to the buying and selling of merchandise. New accounts connected with merchandise, such as *Purchases, Sales,* and *Freight-In,* will be combined with those from the work sheet presented in Chapter 3 to construct a merchandising firm's work sheet.

When you complete this chapter, you should be able to accomplish these tasks:

- PREPARE A TRIAL BALANCE FROM THE GENERAL LEDGER OF A MERCHANDISING FIRM.
- GIVEN THE ADJUSTING DATA, COMPLETE THE WORK SHEET.
- PREPARE ADJUSTING ENTRIES FROM THE WORK SHEET AND POST TO THE GENERAL LEDGER ACCOUNTS.
- USE ALTERNATIVE APPROACHES TO HANDLING DEFERRALS.

A merchandising concern must bring its accounts up to date in much the same way that a service-type business does. Since merchandise is debited to *Purchases* when bought and credited to *Sales* when sold, no entry is made to show that merchandise is actually owned by the company. We will look at how to deal with this problem and also how to show these new accounts on the work sheet. If you felt comfortable with Chapters 3 and 4, this chapter should be easy for you because it continues the same thought.

• task PREPARE A TRIAL BALANCE FROM THE GENERAL LEDGER OF A MERCHANDISING CONCERN

Preparing the trial balance

Just as you did for a service business, you must prepare a trial balance as the first step in making a work sheet for a merchandising business. At the end of each fiscal period, the ledger should be tested for equality of debits and credits. This testing, of course, is done by making a trial balance. We could call it the unadjusted trial balance because period-ending adjusting entries have not been made at this point. As indicated earlier, the trial balance merely indicates that total debits equal total credits and nothing more.

Making a trial balance in good form requires that you list the accounts as they appear in the ledger. As a refresher, recall that assets are always first, followed by liabilities, then by the owner's equity section, then revenues, then cost (actually, cost of goods sold), and finally, expenses. As you list these accounts, make a mental note as to whether the placement of the balance is logical. Keep in mind that ACE accounts (asset, cost, and expense) have debit balances unless a contra account or an account with an abnormal balance is involved (an overdrawn *Cash* account, for example).

For a better understanding of a trial balance prepared for a firm selling merchandise, refer to Illustration 10-1. Accounts that would not be found on a trial balance for a service business are shown in color.

Most of the accounts are the same as those used for the service firm. There could be many other accounts, such as *Delivery Supplies, Machinery, Interest Payable,* or *Entertainment Expense,* but these are just more of the type of accounts that even a service business could use. Your attention should be focused squarely on those accounts in color. *Sales Discounts* is missing from this list of new accounts because a grocery store deals primarily in cash sales.

illustration 10-1
trial balance.

Tush's Grocery
Trial Balance
December 31, 19X1

Account	Debit	Credit
Cash	4100 –	
Accounts Receivable	3250 –	
Notes Receivable	1000 –	
Merchandise Inventory	28018 –	
Office Supplies	80 –	
Store Supplies	125 –	
Prepaid Insurance	210 –	
Office Equipment	6200 –	
Accumulated Depreciation, Office Equipment		2050 –
Store Equipment	1160 –	
Accumulated Depreciation, Store Equipment		416 –
Building	140000 –	
Accumulated Depreciation, Building		34000 –
Accounts Payable		2980 –
Notes Payable		500 –
Mortgage Payable		78000 –
Walter Tush, Capital		61756 –
Walter Tush, Drawing	18000 –	
Sales		186540 –
Sales Returns and Allowances	4215 –	
Purchases	129760 –	
Purchases Returns and Allowances		1980 –
Purchases Discounts		8400 –
Freight-In	6235 –	
Advertising Expense	4550 –	
Delivery Expense	740 –	
License Expense	600 –	
Salaries Expense	24000 –	
Telephone Expense	1400 –	
Utilities Expense	2103 –	
Miscellaneous Expense	876 –	
	376622 –	376622 –

Locating errors

This section is only a reminder about the procedure to follow when totals do not match. All the rules of finding errors discussed in Chapter 3 apply here. Let's run through them again just to reinforce your skill. First, read the columns. If you add manually, you more than likely added from the top down. This time try adding from the bottom up. If you use an adding machine, compare the tape with the trial balance. If this procedure fails to locate the error, then find the difference between the two columns. If the difference is exactly divisible by 9, remember that the error could be either a *slide* or a *transposition*. If the difference is not divisible by 9, perhaps you omitted that number or included it twice. Next, divide the difference by 2 and look for that number (many times the account balance has been placed in the wrong column).

If you have tried all the quick tricks for locating the error, then you are faced with the tedious task of retracing your steps. Basically, the best approach is to do everything in reverse—beginning with transferring numbers from the ledger to the trial balance, then checking the addition in each ledger account, then the posting, and then the journalizing. If this does not turn up the error, you just have to start over again because *you missed it.* In the words of some forgotten bookkeeper, "It is easier to make a mistake than it is to find one."

To provide you with a continuous picture of how to handle the end-of-period procedures, we are using Brooks' Readywear, a sole proprietorship, throughout Chapters 10 and 11. The December 31, 19X1 trial balance appears in Illustration 10-2.

illustration 10-2
Brooks' Readywear trial balance.

Brooks' Readywear
Trial Balance
December 31, 19X1

Cash	2119 —	
Accounts Receivable	759 —	
Merchandise Inventory	17900 —	
Store Supplies	216 —	
Prepaid Insurance	640 —	
Store Equipment	9460 —	
Accumulated Depreciation, Store Equipment		3348 —
Office Equipment	4000 —	
Accumulated Depreciation, Office Equipment		1000 —
Building	116000 —	
Accumulated Depreciation, Building		67000 —
Accounts Payable		1721 —
Notes Payable		500 —
Mortgage Payable		28610 —
Mary Brooks, Capital		58710 —
Mary Brooks, Drawing	12650 —	
Sales		45018 —
Sales Returns and Allowances	1229 —	
Sales Discounts	220 —	
Purchases	24507 —	
Purchases Returns and Allowances		865 —
Purchases Discounts		314 —
Advertising Expense	812 —	
Delivery Expense	641 —	
License Expense	40 —	
Payroll Taxes-General	242 —	
Payroll Taxes—Selling	968 —	
Office Salary Expense	2500 —	
Sales Salary Expense	10000 —	
Subscription Expense	60 —	
Telephone Expense	632 —	
Utilities Expense	1491 —	
	207086 —	207086 —

sample problem You are a part-time employee for Harvey Ledbetter, owner of Harvey's Auto Parts, and one of your tasks is to keep the accounting records. He would rather you sell parts than do accounting, so he has taken the account balances from the ledger to save some of your valuable time. Unfortunately, he has no understanding of debits and credits, so he did not designate which were which.

Instruction Assuming that Harvey was very careful in copying the balances and made no errors and that no abnormal balances exist, use the following list to prepare a trial balance in good form for Harvey as of December 31, 19X1:

Cash	$14,158
Accounts Receivable	2,783
Notes Receivable	200
Merchandise Inventory	18,691
Supplies	435
Prepaid Insurance	838
Equipment	8,450
Accum. Depreciation—Equipment	2,964
Accounts Payable	3,467
Notes Payable	1,000
Harvey Ledbetter, Capital	42,855
Harvey Ledbetter, Drawing	14,200
Sales	89,784
Sales Discounts	2,121
Sales Returns and Allowances	1,356
Purchases	51,221
Purchases Discounts	982
Purchases Returns and Allowances	1,288
Freight-In	650
Advertising Expense	2,105
Postage Expense	491
Rent Expense	3,600
Repairs Expense	823
Salaries Expense	16,400
Telephone Expense	1,440
Utilities Expense	2,378

sample problem solution

Harvey's Auto Parts
Trial Balance
December 31, 19X1

Cash	$ 14,158	
Accounts Receivable	2,783	
Notes Receivable	200	
Merchandise Inventory	18,691	
Supplies	435	
Prepaid Insurance	838	

Equipment	$ 8,450	
Accumulation Depreciation, Equipment		$ 2,964
Accounts Payable		3,467
Notes Payable		1,000
Harvey Ledbetter, Capital		42,855
Harvey Ledbetter, Drawing	14,200	
Sales		89,784
Sales Discounts	2,121	
Sales Returns and Allowances	1,356	
Purchases	51,221	
Purchases Discounts		982
Purchases Returns and Allowances		1,288
Freight-In	650	
Advertising Expense	2,105	
Postage Expense	491	
Rent Expense	3,600	
Repairs Expense	823	
Salaries Expense	16,400	
Telephone Expense	1,440	
Utilities Expense	2,378	
	$142,340	$142,340

review exercises

1. Indicate the normal balance for each of the following accounts: (a) *Prepaid Insurance;* (b) *Supplies Expense;* (c) *Sales Discounts;* (d) *Purchases Returns and Allowances;* (e) *Accumulated Depreciation, Machinery;* and (f) *Julie Wright, Capital.*
2. The debit column of the trial balance totals $562,416, and the credit column totals $553,416. What would you do first, and what type or types of error(s) would you be looking for?
3. Boster's Sporting Goods Store's trial balance shows a matching debit and credit total of $182,041.16. What does this prove?

• task GIVEN THE ADJUSTING ENTRIES, COMPLETE THE WORK SHEET

Adjustments to the trial balance

We seem to be talking about Chapter 3 quite a bit, but we feel that it would be repetitious to spend your time going over the adjusting entries we have already discussed. If you do have questions about adjusting entries for accounts that include supplies, rent, insurance, wages, and the like, we encourage you to go back to Chapter 3 to refresh your memory. To be sure, these entries are just as important as those we are getting ready to introduce, so if you have any doubts, we want you to know that the need to review previous material is perfectly normal.

In Chapters 5 and 6, we discussed buying and selling merchandise. Recall that when merchandise was bought, you were told to debit *Purchases;* when it was sold, you were instructed to credit *Sales.* Yet, merchandise is something of value that the firm owns, and you were never told to show it as an asset. Since the balance sheet is designed to show everything a company owns, this ownership must be presented on the balance sheet.

Since most firms count their merchandise once each year, the asset account, *Merchandise Inventory,* is changed only once a year (unless a mistake is made). To illustrate adjustments for merchandise, assume that Brooks' Readywear was opened at the beginning of 19X0. During the fiscal year, no entry was made to *Merchandise Inventory* because all buying of merchandise was debited to *Purchases.* At the end of December, a physical (periodic) count was made. Merchandise that cost $17,900 was found to be on hand. The following adjusting journal entry will bring the account up to date:

GENERAL JOURNAL — Page 7

Date		Description	P.R.	Dr.	Cr.
19X0 Dec.	31	Merchandise Inventory		17900 —	
		Income Summary			17900 —

Note that *Income Summary,* the same account that is used to assist in closing entries, is used as the offsetting credit.

Continuing with the Brooks' Readywear illustration, assume that Brooks takes another inventory at the end of 19X1. This time the count of merchandise on hand amounts to $18,452. At this time, the *Merchandise Inventory* account has a balance of $17,900 that it has carried for an entire year. This amount must be removed by an adjusting entry.

Date		Description	P.R.	Dr.	Cr.
	31	Income Summary		17900 —	
		Merchandise Inventory			17900 —

A second entry is then needed to insert the latest inventory count:

31	Merchandise Inventory		18452 —	
	Income Summary			18452 —

Examine Illustration 10-3 carefully to make certain that you understand what is being done. The first entry removed the 19X1 inventory, and the second entry placed the 19X2 count on the books.

illustration 10-3 merchandise inventory account.

Merchandise Inventory — Account No. 114

Date		Item	P.R.	Dr.	Cr.	Balance Dr.	Balance Cr.
19X0 Dec.	31	Adjusting Entry	G7	17900 —		17900 —	
19X1 Dec.	31	Adjusting Entry	G13		17900 —	-0-	
	31	Adjusting Entry	G13	18452 —		18452 —	

In 19X0, the balance sheet should show a current asset of $17,900. In 19X1, the amount listed with *Merchandise Inventory* should be $18,452. As for *Income Summary*, it is closed into the capital account just as you did in Chapter 4. We will be looking at closing entries in more detail in Chapter 11.

Since the formal trial balance discussed in the first section of this chapter appears as the first two columns of the work sheet and the only new adjustments involve merchandise, let's continue with the Brooks' Readywear illustration by looking at the first four columns of the work sheet. The accounting clerk for the firm would first take either the unadjusted account balances from the ledger or use the formal trial balance (Illustration 10-2) and prepare the trial balance columns. These ledger balances are now in a prime position to be analyzed for adjustments. Therefore we proceed from an unadjusted trial balance to an adjusted trial balance. An examination of Illustration 10-4 will show that the first two columns contain the same information as the trial balance you prepared earlier. To be on the safe side, the columns should be added to be certain that no item was omitted or placed in the wrong column.

Brooks' Readywear
Work Sheet
For Year Ended December 31, 19X1

Account Titles	Trial Balance		Adjustments		Income Statement		Balance Sheet	
	Dr.	Cr.	Dr.	Cr.	Dr.	Cr.	Dr.	Cr.
Cash	2119 –						2119 –	
Accounts Receivable	759 –						759 –	
Merchandise Inventory	17900 –		(d) 18452 –	(c) 17900 –			18452 –	
Store Supplies	216 –			(a) 143 –			73 –	
Prepaid Insurance	640 –			(b) 290 –			350 –	
Store Equipment	9460 –						9460 –	
Accum. Deprec., Store Equipment		3348 –		(e) 450 –				3798 –
Office Equipment	4000 –						4000 –	
Accum. Deprec., Office Equipment		1000 –		(f) 100 –				1100 –
Building	116000 –						116000 –	
Accum. Deprec., Building		67000 –		(g) 1100 –				68100 –
Accounts Payable		1721 –						1721 –
Notes Payable		500 –						500 –
Mortgage Payable		28610 –						28610 –
Mary Brooks, Capital		58710 –						58710 –
Mary Brooks, Drawing	12650 –						12650 –	
Sales		45018 –				45018 –		
Sales Returns and Allowances	1229 –				1229 –			
Sales Discounts	220 –				220 –			
Purchases	24507 –				24507 –			
Purchases Returns & Allowances		865 –				865 –		
Purchases Discounts		314 –				314 –		
Advertising Expense	812 –				812 –			
Delivery Expense	641 –				641 –			
License Expense	40 –				40 –			
Payroll Taxes – General	242 –				242 –			
Payroll Taxes – Selling	968 –				968 –			
Office Salary Expense	2500 –				2500 –			
Sales Salary Expense	10000 –		(h) 320 –		10320 –			
Subscription Expense	60 –				60 –			
Telephone Expense	632 –				632 –			
Utilities Expense	1491 –				1491 –			
	207086 –	207086 –						
Store Supplies Expense			(a) 143 –		143 –			
Insurance Expense			(b) 290 –		290 –			
Income Summary			(c) 17900 –	(d) 18452 –	17900 –	18452 –		
Deprec. Expense, Store Equip.			(e) 450 –		450 –			
Deprec. Expense, Office Equip.			(f) 100 –		100 –			
Deprec. Expense, Building			(g) 1100 –		1100 –			
Salaries Payable				(h) 320 –				320 –
			38755 –	38755 –	63645 –	64649 –	163863 –	162859 –
Net Income					1004 –			1004 –
					64649 –	64649 –	163863 –	163863 –

illustration 10-4 completed work sheet.

Now let's examine the adjustments. Here are the data used to plan these adjusting entries:

(a) Store supplies on hand, $73
(b) Insurance expired, $290
(c & d) Merchandise on hand at December 31, 19X1, $18,452
(e) Depreciation on the equipment, $450
(f) Depreciation on office equipment, $100
(g) Depreciation on the building, $1,100
(h) Salaries accrued but not paid, $320

Since entries (c) and (d) are the only new entries on the work sheet, any questions you have about the other entries can probably be answered by referring to Chapter 3. As for entries (c) and (d), note that the first step is to credit *Merchandise Inventory* (remember that you add and subtract horizontally on a work sheet) to remove last year's inventory cost. The second step, entry (d), inserts the new inventory.

Completing the work sheet

Once you have checked the equality of totals for the adjustments columns, you will be ready to divide the adjusted account balances between the income statement and the balance sheet. To assist you in comparing a completed work sheet for a service-type business with one for a merchandising business, the new accounts involved are shown in Illustration 10-4 in color.

Note first that the December 31, 19X1, inventory cost is shown on the balance sheet. This cost was found by adding $17,900 to $18,452 (horizontally), then subtracting $17,900 to leave $18,452. Next, since revenue and cost accounts appear on the income statement, the accounts that fit into these categories should be shown in the Income Statement columns. Finally, both numbers found in the adjustments columns for *Income Summary* are carried forward to the Income Statement columns. The reasoning for this procedure will be explained in Chapter 11.

sample problem The Horseman Shop keeps its books on an annual fiscal year ending on December 31, 19X1. Using data from the following unadjusted trial balance, prepare a completed work sheet:

Cash	$2,417	
Accounts Receivable	3,692	
Merchandise Inventory	7,469	
Supplies	509	
Prepaid Insurance	240	
Equipment	4,523	
Accumulated Depreciation, Equipment		$ 2,156
Accounts Payable		1,611
Phil Hargrove, Capital		21,172
Phil Hargrove, Drawing	6,200	
Sales		16,915
Sales Discounts	1,015	
Purchases	8,749	
Purchases Returns and Allowances		488
Salary Expense	5,400	
Telephone Expense	429	

Utilities Expense	600	
Rent Expense	1,000	
Interest Expense	99	
	$42,342	$42,342

Other information:

(a) Supplies used, $164
(b) Insurance which is unexpired, $200
(c) Unexpired rent, $150
(d) Ending merchandise inventory, $9,229
(e) Depreciation on equipment, $462
(f) Accrued salaries, $315
(g) Accrued interest, $100

sample problem solution

The Horseman Shop
Work Sheet
For Year Ended December 31, 19X1

Account Titles	Trial Balance Dr.	Trial Balance Cr.	Adjustments Dr.	Adjustments Cr.	Income Statement Dr.	Income Statement Cr.	Balance Sheet Dr.	Balance Sheet Cr.
Cash	2417 –						2417 –	
Accounts Receivable	3692 –						3692 –	
Merchandise Inventory	7469 –		(d) 9229 –	(d) 7469 –			9229 –	
Supplies	509 –			(a) 164 –			345 –	
Prepaid Insurance	240 –			(b) 40 –			200 –	
Equipment	4523 –						4523 –	
Accum. Deprec., Equipment		2156 –		(e) 462 –				2618 –
Accounts Payable		1611 –						1611 –
Phil Hargrove, Capital		21172 –						21172 –
Phil Hargrove, Drawing	6200 –						6200 –	
Sales		16915 –				16915 –		
Sales Discounts	1015 –				1015 –			
Purchases	8749 –				8749 –			
Purchases Returns & Allowances		488 –				488 –		
Salary Expense	5400 –		(f) 315 –		5715 –			
Telephone Expense	429 –				429 –			
Utilities Expense	600 –				600 –			
Rent Expense	1000 –			(c) 150 –	850 –			
Interest Expense	99 –		(g) 100 –		199 –			
	42342 –	42342 –						
Supplies Expense			(a) 164 –		164 –			
Insurance Expense			(b) 40 –		40 –			
Prepaid Rent			(c) 150 –				150 –	
Income Summary			(d) 7469 –	(d) 9229 –	7469 –	9229 –		
Deprec. Expense, Equipment			(e) 462 –		462 –			
Salaries Payable				(f) 315 –				315 –
Interest Payable				(g) 100 –				100 –
			17929 –	17929 –	25692 –	26632 –	26756 –	25816 –
Net Income					940 –			940 –
					26632 –	26632 –	26756 –	26756 –

review exercises

4. The *Income Summary* account in the adjustments columns shows a debit of $39,432.76. What does this number represent?
5. Use an × to indicate where each of the following items would be shown in the last four columns of a work sheet.

	Income Statement Dr.	Income Statement Cr.	Balance Sheet Dr.	Balance Sheet Cr.
(a) Supplies				
(b) Prepaid Insurance				
(c) Income Summary				
(d) Purchases Returns and Allowances				
(e) Sales Discounts				
(f) Accounts Payable				
(g) Depreciation Expense, Truck				
(h) Interest Payable				
(i) Merchandise Inventory				
(j) Purchases				
(k) Bill Harper, Drawing				

• task PREPARE ADJUSTING ENTRIES FROM THE WORK SHEET AND POST TO THE GENERAL LEDGER ACCOUNTS

Journalizing the adjusting entries

Once you have completed the work sheet, you still must get the accounts to match the information in the last four columns. At this point, all you have done is to plan what you are going to do. Referring back to Illustration 10-4 and then to the ledger (Illustration 10-5), you will see that every account still has the balance as shown in the trial balance. For example, if *Supplies* has a debit balance in the trial balance, it should have a debit balance in the adjusted trial balance.

illustration 10-5 unadjusted ledger.

Cash Account No. 111

Date		Item	P.R.	Dr.	Cr.	Balance Dr.	Balance Cr.
19X1 Dec.	31	Balance	✓			2 1 1 9	

Accounts Receivable Account No. 112

Date		Item	P.R.	Dr.	Cr.	Balance Dr.	Balance Cr.
19X1 Dec.	31	Balance	✓			759 –	

Merchandise Inventory Account No. 113

Date		Item	P.R.	Dr.	Cr.	Balance Dr.	Balance Cr.
19X0 Dec.	31	Balance	✓			17900 –	

Store Supplies Account No. 114

Date		Item	P.R.	Dr.	Cr.	Balance Dr.	Balance Cr.
19X1 Dec.	31	Balance	✓			216 –	

Prepaid Insurance Account No. 115

Date		Item	P.R.	Dr.	Cr.	Balance Dr.	Balance Cr.
19X1 Dec.	31	Balance	✓			640 –	

Store Equipment Account No. 116

Date		Item	P.R.	Dr.	Cr.	Balance Dr.	Balance Cr.
19X1 Dec.	31	Balance	✓			9460 –	

Accumulated Depreciation, Store Equipment Account No. 117

Date		Item	P.R.	Dr.	Cr.	Balance Dr.	Balance Cr.
19X1 Dec.	31	Balance	✓				3348 –

Office Equipment Account No. 118

Date		Item	P.R.	Dr.	Cr.	Balance Dr.	Balance Cr.
19X1 Dec.	31	Balance	✓			4000 –	

illustration 10-5 (continued)

Accumulated Depreciation, Office Equipment — Account No. 119

Date		Item	P.R.	Dr.	Cr.	Balance Dr.	Balance Cr.
19x1 Dec.	31	Balance	✓				1000 –

Building — Account No. 120

Date		Item	P.R.	Dr.	Cr.	Balance Dr.	Balance Cr.
19x1 Dec.	31	Balance	✓			116000 –	

Accumulated Depreciation, Building — Account No. 121

Date		Item	P.R.	Dr.	Cr.	Balance Dr.	Balance Cr.
19x1 Dec.	31	Balance	✓				67000 –

Accounts Payable — Account No. 211

Date		Item	P.R.	Dr.	Cr.	Balance Dr.	Balance Cr.
19x1 Dec.	31	Balance	✓				1721 –

Salaries Payable — Account No. 212

Date		Item	P.R.	Dr.	Cr.	Balance Dr.	Balance Cr.

Notes Payable — Account No. 213

Date		Item	P.R.	Dr.	Cr.	Balance Dr.	Balance Cr.
19x1 Dec.	31	Balance	✓				500 –

Mortgage Payable — Account No. 214

Date		Item	P.R.	Dr.	Cr.	Balance Dr.	Balance Cr.
19x1 Dec.	31	Balance	✓				28610 –

Mary Brooks, Capital — Account No. 311

Date		Item	P.R.	Dr.	Cr.	Balance Dr.	Balance Cr.
19X1 Dec.	31	Balance	✓				58710 –

Mary Brooks, Drawing — Account No. 312

Date		Item	P.R.	Dr.	Cr.	Balance Dr.	Balance Cr.
19X1 Dec.	31	Balance	✓			12650 –	

Income Summary — Account No. 313

Date		Item	P.R.	Dr.	Cr.	Balance Dr.	Balance Cr.

Sales — Account No. 411

Date		Item	P.R.	Dr.	Cr.	Balance Dr.	Balance Cr.
19X1 Dec.	31	Balance	✓				45018 –

Sales Returns and Allowances — Account No. 412

Date		Item	P.R.	Dr.	Cr.	Balance Dr.	Balance Cr.
19X1 Dec.	31	Balance	✓			1229 –	

Sales Discounts — Account No. 413

Date		Item	P.R.	Dr.	Cr.	Balance Dr.	Balance Cr.
19X1 Dec.	31	Balance	✓			220 –	

Purchases — Account No. 511

Date		Item	P.R.	Dr.	Cr.	Balance Dr.	Balance Cr.
19X1 Dec.	31	Balance	✓			24507 –	

illustration 10-5 (continued)

Purchases Returns and Allowances Account No. 512

Date		Item	P.R.	Dr.	Cr.	Balance Dr.	Balance Cr.
19x1 Dec.	31	Balance	✓				865 –

Purchases Discounts Account No. 513

Date		Item	P.R.	Dr.	Cr.	Balance Dr.	Balance Cr.
19x1 Dec.	31	Balance	✓				314 –

Advertising Expense Account No. 611

Date		Item	P.R.	Dr.	Cr.	Balance Dr.	Balance Cr.
19x1 Dec.	31	Balance	✓			812 –	

Delivery Expense Account No. 612

Date		Item	P.R.	Dr.	Cr.	Balance Dr.	Balance Cr.
19x1 Dec.	31	Balance	✓			641 –	

License Expense Account No. 613

Date		Item	P.R.	Dr.	Cr.	Balance Dr.	Balance Cr.
19x1 Dec.	31	Balance	✓			40 –	

Payroll Taxes Expense – General Account No. 614

Date		Item	P.R.	Dr.	Cr.	Balance Dr.	Balance Cr.
19x1 Dec.	31	Balance	✓			242 –	

Payroll Taxes Expense – Selling Account No. 615

Date		Item	P.R.	Dr.	Cr.	Balance Dr.	Balance Cr.
19x1 Dec.	31	Balance	✓			968 –	

Office Salary Expense Account No. 616

Date		Item	P.R.	Dr.	Cr.	Balance Dr.	Balance Cr.
19X1 Dec.	31	Balance	✓			2500 –	

Sales Salary Expense Account No. 617

Date		Item	P.R.	Dr.	Cr.	Balance Dr.	Balance Cr.
19X1 Dec.	31	Balance	✓			10000 –	

Subscription Expense Account No. 618

Date		Item	P.R.	Dr.	Cr.	Balance Dr.	Balance Cr.
19X1 Dec.	31	Balance	✓			60 –	

Telephone Expense Account No. 619

Date		Item	P.R.	Dr.	Cr.	Balance Dr.	Balance Cr.
19X1 Dec.	31	Balance	✓			632 –	

Utilities Expense Account No. 620

Date		Item	P.R.	Dr.	Cr.	Balance Dr.	Balance Cr.
19X1 Dec.	31	Balance	✓			1491 –	

Store Supplies Expense Account No. 621

Date		Item	P.R.	Dr.	Cr.	Balance Dr.	Balance Cr.

Insurance Expense Account No. 622

Date		Item	P.R.	Dr.	Cr.	Balance Dr.	Balance Cr.

illustration 10-5
(continued)

Depreciation Expense, Store Equipment Account No. 623

Date	Item	P.R.	Dr.	Cr.	Balance Dr.	Balance Cr.

Depreciation Expense, Office Equipment Account No. 624

Date	Item	P.R.	Dr.	Cr.	Balance Dr.	Balance Cr.

Depreciation Expense, Building Account No. 625

Date	Item	P.R.	Dr.	Cr.	Balance Dr.	Balance Cr.

The next step is to journalize the adjusting entries from the adjustments columns just as you did in Chapter 4. First, find the last entry in the general journal, skip a line, then write "Adjusting Entries" in the center of the explanation column. This procedure does away with having to make an explanation each time. Then you date each entry *December 31,* the date of the work sheet. The rest is elementary. Just find (a) debits and (a) credits in the adjustments columns of the work sheet and journalize them exactly that way. Next, find item (b) and repeat the process. In so doing, you will find that the only new items will be *Merchandise Inventory* and *Income Summary.* You can see transactions from the work sheet in Illustration 10-4 journalized in Illustration 10-6. Use this as an example when you work the exercises and problems.

Posting the adjusting entries

If you have performed all the steps properly, once journal entries are posted to the ledger, the balance in each account should match the amount shown in the last four columns of the work sheet.

Now let's continue the illustration. Note that in Illustration 10-7 the accounts match the information found in the last four columns of Illustration 10-4. This means that we have used proper procedures in bringing the accounts up to date. Look especially at *Merchandise Inventory.* Recall our earlier discussion of this account, and you can see this same effect here. Last year's inventory balance has been removed, and this year's inventory balance has replaced it on the work sheet. This is exactly the way it should be because Brooks' Readywear has merchandise valued at $18,452—the amount shown in the account.

illustration 10-6
adjusting entries.

GENERAL JOURNAL — Page 23

Date		Description	P.R.	Dr.	Cr.
		Adjusting Entries			
19X1 Dec.	31	Store Supplies Expense		143 –	
		Store Supplies			143 –
	31	Insurance Expense		290 –	
		Prepaid Insurance			290 –
	31	Income Summary		17900 –	
		Merchandise Inventory			17900 –
	31	Merchandise Inventory		18452 –	
		Income Summary			18452 –
	31	Depreciation Expense, Store Equipment		450 –	
		Accumulated Depreciation, Store Equip.			450 –
	31	Depreciation Expense, Office Equipment		100 –	
		Accumulated Depreciation, Office Equip.			100 –
	31	Depreciation Expense, Building		1100 –	
		Accumulated Depreciation, Building			1100 –
	31	Sales Salaries Expenses		320 –	
		Salaries Payable			320 –

illustration 10-7
adjusted ledger accounts.

Merchandise Inventory — Account No. 113

Date		Item	P.R.	Dr.	Cr.	Balance Dr.	Balance Cr.
19X1 Dec.	31	Balance	✓			17900 –	
19X1 Dec.	31	Adjusting	G23		17900 –	–0–	
	31	Adjusting	G23	18452 –		18452 –	

Store Supplies — Account No. 114

Date		Item	P.R.	Dr.	Cr.	Balance Dr.	Balance Cr.
19X1 Dec.	31	Balance	✓			216 –	
	31	Adjusting	G23		143 –	73 –	

illustration 10-7 (continued)

Prepaid Insurance — Account No. 115

Date		Item	P.R.	Dr.	Cr.	Balance Dr.	Balance Cr.
19x1 Dec.	31	Balance	✓			640 –	
	31	Adjusting	G23		290 –	350 –	

Accumulated Depreciation, Office Equipment — Account No. 119

Date		Item	P.R.	Dr.	Cr.	Balance Dr.	Balance Cr.
19x1 Dec.	31	Balance	✓				1000 –
	31	Adjusting	G23		100 –		1100 –

Accumulated Depreciation, Store Equipment — Account No. 117

Date		Item	P.R.	Dr.	Cr.	Balance Dr.	Balance Cr.
19x1 Dec.	31	Balance	✓				3348 –
		Adjusting	G23		450 –		3798 –

Accumulated Depreciation, Building — Account No. 121

Date		Item	P.R.	Dr.	Cr.	Balance Dr.	Balance Cr.
19x1 Dec.	31	Balance	✓				67000 –
	31	Adjusting	G23		1100 –		68100 –

Salaries Payable — Account No. 212

Date		Item	P.R.	Dr.	Cr.	Balance Dr.	Balance Cr.
19x1 Dec.	31	Adjusting	G23		320 –		320 –

Income Summary — Account No. 313

Date		Item	P.R.	Dr.	Cr.	Balance Dr.	Balance Cr.
19x1 Dec.	31	Adjusting	G23	17900 –		17900 –	
	31	Adjusting	G23		18452 –		552 –

Sales Salary Expense — Account No. 617

Date		Item	P.R.	Dr.	Cr.	Balance Dr.	Balance Cr.
19x1 Dec.	31	Balance	✓			10000 —	
	31	Adjusting	G23	320 —		10320 —	

Store Supplies Expense — Account No. 621

Date		Item	P.R.	Dr.	Cr.	Balance Dr.	Balance Cr.
19x1 Dec.	31	Adjusting	G23	143 —		143 —	

Insurance Expense — Account No. 622

Date		Item	P.R.	Dr.	Cr.	Balance Dr.	Balance Cr.
19x1 Dec.	31	Adjusting	G23	290 —		290 —	

Depreciation Expense, Store Equipment — Account No. 623

Date		Item	P.R.	Dr.	Cr.	Balance Dr.	Balance Cr.
19x1 Dec.	31	Adjusting	G23	450 —		450 —	

Depreciation Expense, Office Equipment — Account No. 624

Date		Item	P.R.	Dr.	Cr.	Balance Dr.	Balance Cr.
19x1 Dec.	31	Adjusting	G23	100 —		100 —	

Depreciation Expense, Building — Account No. 625

Date		Item	P.R.	Dr.	Cr.	Balance Dr.	Balance Cr.
19x1 Dec.	31	Adjusting	G23	1100 —		1100 —	

sample problem From the partial December 31, 19X1 work sheet shown below, prepare the necessary adjusting entries in general journal form.

Account	Trial Balance Dr.	Trial Balance Cr.	Adjustments Dr.	Adjustments Cr.
Cash	$ 1,938			
Supplies	162			(a) $ 39
Merchandise Inventory	2,764		(c) $2,286	(b) 2,764
Equipment	5,280			
Accumulated Depreciation, Equipment		$1,773		(d) 244
Accounts Payable		511		
Notes Payable		200		
K. Rogers, Capital		12,261		
K. Rogers, Drawing	1,400			
Sales		12,000		
Sales Discounts	844			
Purchases	5,960			
Purchases Returns	340			
Advertising Expense	379			
Salaries Expense	6,200		(e) 175	
Rent Expense	1,400			
Telephone Expense	581			
Utilities Expense	955			
	$26,745	$26,745		
Supplies Expense			(a) 39	
Income Summary			(b) 2,764	(c) 2,286
Depreciation Expense, Equipment			(d) 244	
Salaries Payable				(e) 175
Interest Expense			(f) 15	
Interest Payable				(f) 15
			$5,523	$5,523

sample problem solution

Adjusting Entries

Date	Account	Dr.	Cr.
19X1			
Dec. 31	Supplies Expense	39	
	Supplies		39
31	Income Summary	2,764	
	Merchandise Inventory		2,764
31	Merchandise Inventory	2,286	
	Income Summary		2,286

31	Depreciation Expense, Equipment	244	
	Accumulated Depreciation, Equipment		244
31	Salaries Expense	175	
	Salaries Payable		175
31	Interest Expense	15	
	Interest Payable		15

review exercises

6. Bozeman Company had an inventory in 19X1 of $86,452.19. On December 31, 19X2, the count showed merchandise on hand costing $72,862.81. Make the adjusting entry as of December 31, 19X2, to update *Merchandise Inventory*.
7. If a firm took the inventory carelessly and overcounted the ending inventory by $1,000, would this error have any effect on the net income (since inventory is an asset and not a revenue, cost, or expense)?

• task USE ALTERNATE APPROACHES TO HANDLING DEFERRALS

Deferrals reviewed

Up to this point, whenever supplies were bought, *Supplies* was usually debited. The same is true for rent and insurance. Actually, the accountant has the option of debiting either an asset or an expense. In other words, when supplies are purchased, a debit to *Supplies Expense* is equally proper. Whenever payments are made or obligations are assumed in advance, a *deferral* is probably involved. To illustrate a situation in which a deferral is recorded initially as an asset, assume that on November 17, Tom Lamberson of Lamberson's Boat Dock contracts for advertising with the *Daily News*. Five ads are to be published in the local newspaper over the next two months at a cost of $100 per ad. If the firm pays for this advertisement in advance and the accountant desires to record deferrals in *real* (balance sheet) accounts, then *Prepaid Advertising* would be debited. As of December 31, 19X1, assume that two of the ads have appeared. The entry below is needed to adjust the accounts.

Dec.	31	Advertising Expense		200 –	
		Prepaid Advertising			200 –

Instead of recording the advertisement payment as an asset, assume that Lamberson chose to record all payments for advertising as an expense. Assume also that between January and November 17, $4,200 has been spent for advertising. All of the $4,200 has been used and shown as an expense since the expense account was debited in recording the transactions. After the payment on November 17, *Advertising Expense* would have a $4,700 balance:

Advertising Expense

Date	Item	P.R.	Debit	Credit	Balance Debit	Balance Credit
Jan.–Oct.			4,200		4,200	
Nov. 17			500		4,700	

On November 17, *Prepaid Advertising* would have a zero balance. The necessary adjusting entry on Lamberson's Boat Dock books would be:

Date		Account	P.R.	Debit	Credit
Dec.	31	Prepaid Advertising		300 –	
		Advertising Expense			300 –

It is important to note at this point that the amount shown in the adjusting entry is not always the amount "used up." In fact, as can be seen in the case of recording a prepayment (deferral) as an expense, the amount of the adjusting entry is the unused portion. After posting the adjusting entry, the accounts appear as follows:

Prepaid Advertising

Date	Item	P.R.	Debit	Credit	Balance Debit	Balance Credit
Dec. 31	Adjusting		300		300	

Advertising Expense

Date	Item	P.R.	Debit	Credit	Balance Debit	Balance Credit
Jan.–Oct.			4,200		4,200	
Nov. 17			500		4,700	
Dec. 31	Adjusting			300	4,400	

The balances of these two accounts after the adjusting entry are exactly the same as they would have been if *Prepaid Advertising* had been debited when the payment was made. Accuracy of the treatment depends on making the proper adjusting entry.

You can get a better understanding of the two approaches by examining Illustration 10-8. Data shown here are from the Lamberson's Boat Dock example.

Event	Recorded Initially as an Asset			Recorded Initially as an Expense		
Payments made for ads during Jan. 1–Oct. 31	Prepaid Advertising	4,200		Advertising Expense	4,200	
	Cash		4,200	Cash		4,200
Payments for five ads on Nov. 17	Prepaid Advertising	500		Advertising Expense	500	
	Cash		500	Cash		500
Adjusting entries, Dec. 31	Advertising Expense	4,400		Prepaid Advertising	300	
	Prepaid Advertising		4,400	Advertising Expense		300

Advertising Expense = $4,400
Prepaid Advertising = $300

illustration 10-8 comparison of adjusting approaches for prepaid expenses.

Unearned revenues

Just as payments for assets are deferred, money may also be *received* in advance. This transaction is also considered a deferral. Since money is being received, *Cash* must be debited. The big question is, "What do I credit?" Earlier, we chose to credit a revenue account. For example, when a tenant paid rent in advance, we simply debited *Cash* and credited *Rent Revenue*. Such a treatment is fine, but it requires more work if an unearned portion remains at the end of the fiscal period. Other cases might involve receiving a subscription payment, tuition, or interest in advance.

The other possibility available is to credit a liability account. You may think of liabilities as always ending in "payable," but the term "unearned" also indicates a liability. For example, *Unearned Rent Revenue* tells the reader that the rental revenue has not been earned—thus, a liability. To illustrate the liability approach, assume that Music Limited contracts for concerts in advance. Each concert is priced at $1,000, and during the course of the year, the firm signs contracts for 80 performances. Upon receipt of cash on May 12 for a June 3 performance, *Cash* would be debited and *Unearned Concerts Revenue* credited. The account *Unearned Concerts Revenue* is a current liability and indicates that Music Limited must either provide the concerts or refund the ticket receipts—which definitely sounds like a liability.

To continue with this example, assume that 73 concerts had been performed by December 31, 19X1. Music Limited has kept its end of the bargain for $73,000 in services and still owes $7,000 for future performances. Before the adjusting entry is made, the revenue account *Concerts Revenue* has a zero balance, while *Unearned Concerts Revenue* shows an $80,000 balance. To bring the accounts up to December 31, the following adjusting entry must be made:

Dec.	31	Unearned Concerts Revenue		73000 —	
		Concerts Revenue			73000 —

Once posted, the account *Unearned Concerts Revenue* will show that Music Limited still "owes" $7,000 in concerts, and the account *Concerts Revenue* reveals that the firm has earned $73,000 for performing 73 concerts during the year. After the adjusting entry has been posted, the accounts will appear as follows:

Unearned Concerts Revenue

Jan.–Dec.				80,000		80,000
Dec. 31	Adj.		73,000			7,000

Concerts Revenue

Dec. 31	Adj.			73,000		73,000

Unearned Concerts Revenue appears in the current liability section of the balance sheet with a $7,000 balance, while *Concerts Revenue* is shown on the income statement as a revenue item of $73,000.

Now let's look at the approach using a revenue account for the credit when *Cash* is debited. Assume the same facts as in the preceding section, except that a revenue account is credited. This means that *Concerts Revenue* would have a balance of $80,000 by December 31. Since $7,000 has not been earned, the following adjusting entry would be needed:

GENERAL JOURNAL — Page 19

Date		Description	P.R.	Dr.	Cr.
19X1 Dec.	31	Concerts Revenue		7000 —	
		Unearned Concerts Revenue			7000 —

After the foregoing entry has been posted, the two accounts would appear as follows:

Unearned Concerts Revenue

Dec. 31	Adj.			7,000		7,000

Concerts Revenue

Jan.–Dec.				80,000		80,000
Dec. 31	Adj.		7,000			73,000

The two approaches are compared in Illustration 10-9.

Event	Recorded Initially as a Liability	Recorded Initially as Revenue
Typical entry for cash received for a concert	Cash 1,000 Unearned Concerts Revenue 1,000	Cash 1,000 Concerts Revenue 1,000
Adjusting entry on Dec. 31	Unearned Concerts Revenue 73,000 Concerts Revenue 73,000	Concerts Revenue 7,000 Unearned Concerts Revenue 7,000

Unearned Concerts Revenue = $ 7,000
Concerts Revenue = $73,000

illustration 10-9 comparison of adjusting approaches for unearned revenue.

Note that the two accounts, *Unearned Concerts Revenue* and *Concerts Revenue,* have the same balance, regardless of the approach used. Other situations involving an unearned revenue occur when cash is received before the service is performed for such items as rent, tuition fees, magazine and newspaper subscriptions, and interest.

Reversing entries

Recall from Chapter 4 that once adjusting entries are made and financial statements prepared, all of the nominal accounts are closed into the *Income Summary* account. In the case of deferrals recorded initially in nominal accounts, this treatment could create a problem. For example, assume that McCracken Fruit Market pays its rent one month in advance on the tenth of each month. The accountant chooses to record this transaction as a debit to *Rent Expense.* As a result, after adjusting and closing entries, the prepaid portion will be on the books in *Prepaid Rent*—not in *Rent Expense* as the accountant prefers.

To solve this problem, a *reversing entry* (also known as a readjusting entry) can be made. The procedure is simple but very important. To illustrate, assume that in 19X1 Lamberson's Boat Dock recorded payment of $500 for five ads by initially debiting *Advertising Expense* and crediting *Cash.* After the adjusting entry, the accounts would appear as follows:

Prepaid Advertising

Dec. 31	Adj.		300		300	

Advertising Expense

Nov. 17			500		500	
Dec. 31	Adj.			300	200	

After closing entries are journalized, the *Advertising Expense* account would have a zero balance.

Prepaid Advertising

Dec. 31	Adj.		300		300	

Advertising Expense

Nov. 17			500		500	
Dec. 31	Adj.			300	200	
31	Clos.			200	0	

The balance began in a nominal account, *Advertising Expense,* and ended in a real account, *Prepaid Advertising.* If 19X2 payments for advertising are recorded in *Advertising Expense,* then a balance will appear in both the real and the nominal accounts during 19X2 (which is not desirable).

This difficulty can be avoided easily by using reversing entries, which are made as of the first working day of the new fiscal year. In 19X1, if the firm had reversed the adjusting entry affecting advertising, then the use of *Advertising Expense* would be consistent whenever advertising was purchased.

GENERAL JOURNAL — Page 23

Date		Description	P.R.	Dr.	Cr.
		Adjusting Entries			
19X1 Dec.	31	Prepaid Advertising		300 –	
		Advertising Expense			300 –

GENERAL JOURNAL — Page 24

Date		Description	P.R.	Dr.	Cr.
		Reversing Entries			
19X2 Jan.	2	Advertising Expense		300 –	
		Prepaid Advertising			300 –

In the entries above, note that the reversing entry is simply the adjusting entry of December 31, 19X1, "reversed." Posting of this reversing entry will balance out *Prepaid Advertising*, and *Advertising Expense* will again show the amount of unused advertising. Thus, only *Advertising Expense* will be open during the year—*Prepaid Advertising* is used only with the adjusting entry and the resulting balance sheet.

Prepaid Advertising

Dec. 31	Adj.		300		300	
Jan. 2	Rev.			300	0	

Advertising Expense

Nov. 17			500		500	
Dec. 31	Adj.			300	200	
31	Clos.			200	0	
Jan. 2	Rev.		300		300	

A number of "rules of thumb" are available to assist you in dealing with deferrals. One rule states that if the balance after the closing entry is in a different account from that used for initial recording, a reversing entry is needed. Another rule is that any adjusting entry that *created* an asset or liability is reversed. Fully understanding the purpose of reversing entries is fairly complex. Here we have just touched upon a few ideas to make you aware of available alternatives.

sample problem On December 31, 19X1, Toy Time's unadjusted trial balance has the following accounts that should be adjusted:

	Dr.	Cr.
Office Supplies	$ 450	
Merchandise Inventory	8,650	
Rent Expense	3,600	
Accumulated Depreciation, Equipment		$6,900
Interest Expense	85	
Prepaid Insurance	378	

Additional data:

(1) Office supplies used, $237

(2) Ending merchandise inventory, $10,364

(3) Unexpired Rent, $240

(4) Expired Insurance, $114

(5) Depreciation on equipment, $650

Instructions

(a) Make the necessary adjusting entries.

(b) Make the reversing entry or entries as of January 1, 19X2.

sample problem solution

(a) Adjusting Entries

Date	Account	Dr.	Cr.
19X1			
Dec. 31	Office Supplies Expense	237	
	Office Supplies		237
31	Income Summary	8,650	
	Merchandise Inventory		8,650
31	Merchandise Inventory	10,364	
	Income Summary		10,364
31	Prepaid Rent	240	
	Rent Expense		240
31	Insurance Expense	114	
	Prepaid Insurance		114
31	Depreciation Expense, Equipment	650	
	Accumulated Depreciation, Equipment		650

(b) Reversing Entry

Date	Account	Dr.	Cr.
19X2			
Jan. 1	Rent Expense	240	
	Prepaid Rent		240

review exercises

8. During the year, supplies costing $964.15 were bought. The *Supplies Expense* account had a debit balance of $121.89 at the beginning of the year. An inventory on December 31 showed $267.43 in supplies on hand. Make the necessary adjusting entry. Should this entry be reversed at the beginning of the next year?
9. Joe Parks had a policy of recording premium payments for insurance in the *Prepaid Insurance* account. At year end, this account had a balance of $642. A check of the different policies revealed that $490 had expired. Make the required adjusting entry. Would you reverse this entry?
10. If a firm pays rent of $320 on the first day of each month, would it be better to debit *Rent Expense* or *Prepaid Rent?* (Think in terms of the approach that will require the fewest entries.)

chapter highlights

Having studied this chapter, you should now be able to:

- Prepare a trial balance for a merchandising business.
- Prepare a work sheet for a merchandising business.
- Journalize and post adjusting entries.
- Use alternative approaches to handle deferrals.

check figures for review exercises

1. (a) debit, (b) debit, (c) debit, (d) credit, (e) credit, (f) credit
2. First, add the columns again. Since the difference is exactly divisible by 9, it could be a transposition or a slide. It is also possible that a $4,500 credit has been recorded incorrectly as a debit ($9,000/2).
3. That debits equal credits. It does not prove that the books are correct.
4. It is the offsetting amount to remove the previous year's merchandise inventory.
5.

	Income Statement		Balance Sheet	
	Dr.	Cr.	Dr.	Cr.
(a)			X	
(b)			X	
(c)	X	X		
(d)		X		
(e)	X			
(f)				X
(g)	X			
(h)				X
(i)			X	
(j)	X			
(k)			X	

6.			
	Income Summary	86,452.19	
	Merchandise Inventory		86,452.19
	Merchandise Inventory	72,862.81	
	Income Summary		72,862.81

7. Yes, the net income would be exactly $1,000 higher than it should be.

8.			
	Supplies	267.43	
	Supplies Expense		267.43

Reverse this entry.

9.			
	Insurance Expense	490.00	
	Prepaid Insurance		490.00

Don't reverse.

10. *Rent Expense.* Since all payments would be an expense by December 31, you have no reason to make an adjusting entry. If no adjusting entry, then there can be no reversing entry.

demonstration problem A trial balance and other data are shown below for Demo Limited.

Demo Limited
Trial Balance
December 31, 19X1

Cash	$ 2,215	
Accounts Receivable	4,810	
Merchandise Inventory	9,720	
Supplies	240	
Prepaid Insurance	630	
Equipment	7,800	
Accumulated Depreciation, Equipment		$ 2,940
Accounts Payable		5,110
Notes Payable		1,000
Mary Mason, Capital		19,945
Mary Mason, Drawing	4,800	
Sales		24,345
Sales Discounts	980	
Purchases	13,425	
Purchases Discounts		390
Advertising Expense	450	
Delivery Expense	375	
Rent Expense	1,200	
Salaries Expense	6,400	
Utilities Expense	685	
	$53,730	$53,730

Data for adjustments:

(a) Depreciation expense on equipment for year, $300.
(b) Prepaid insurance at December 31, 19X1, $310.
(c) Ending merchandise inventory, $8,310.
(d) Rent expense for the year, $700.
(e) Accrued salaries at end of the year, $280.
(f) Supplies on hand at the year end, $240.

Instructions From the information given above, perform the following:

(a) Prove the equality of total debits in the trial balance.
(b) Prepare an eight-column work sheet.
(c) Journalize the adjusting entries.
(d) List the letters of adjusting entries that could be reversed.
(e) Compute the net increase or decrease to *Mary Mason, Capital* for the year.

demonstration problem solution

(a) Total debits and total credits in the trial balance each equal $53,730.
(b) Work sheet

Demo Limited
Work Sheet
For The Year Ended December 31, 19X1

	Trial Balance		Adjustments		Income Statement		Balance Sheet	
	Dr.	Cr.	Dr.	Cr.	Dr.	Cr.	Dr.	Cr.
Cash	2215						2215	
Accounts Receivable	4810						4810	
Merchandise Inventory	9720		(d) 8310	(c) 9720			8310	
Supplies	240						240	
Prepaid Insurance	630			(b) 320			310	
Equipment	7800						7800	
Accum. Depr., Equipment		2940		(a) 300				3240
Accounts Payable		5110						5110
Notes Payable		1000						1000
Mary Mason, Capital		19945						19945
Mary Mason, Drawing	4800						4800	

	Trial Balance		Adjustments				Income Statement		Balance Sheet	
	Dr.	Cr.		Dr.		Cr.	Dr.	Cr.	Dr.	Cr.
Sales		24345						24345		
Sales Discounts	980						980			
Purchases	13425						13425			
Purchases Discounts		390						390		
Advertising Expense	450						450			
Delivery Expense	375						375			
Rent Expense	1200				(e)	500	700			
Salaries Expense	6400		(f)	280			6680			
Utilities Expense	685						685			
	53730	53730								
Depr. Exp., Equipment			(a)	300			300			
Insurance Expense			(b)	320			320			
Income Summary			(c)	9720	(d)	8310	9720	8310		
Prepaid Rent			(e)	500					500	
Salaries Payable					(f)	280				280
				19430		19430	33635	33045	28985	29575
Net Loss								590	590	
							33635	33635	29575	29575

(c)

General Journal
Adjusting Entries

19X1			
Dec. 31	Depreciation Expense, Equipment	300	
	Accumulated Depreciation, Equipment		300
31	Insurance Expense	320	
	Prepaid Insurance		320
31	Income Summary	9,720	
	Merchandise Inventory		9,720
31	Merchandise Inventory	8,310	
	Income Summary		8,310
31	Prepaid Rent	500	
	Rent Expense		500
31	Salaries Expense	280	
	Salaries Expense		280

(d) Adjusting entries labeled e (rent) and f (salaries) could be reversed.

(e) Mary Mason, Capital would have a net decrease of $5,390. (Drawing of $4,800 plus a net loss of 590).

questions

1. How does the trial balance differ from the balance sheet? What is the main reason for preparing a trial balance?
2. Why are adjusting entries necessary? Can we avoid making adjusting entries?
3. List the accounts appearing on a merchandising firm's trial balance but not normally shown on a trial balance for a service-type firm.
4. What accounts must be adjusted on a merchandising work sheet that would not be adjusted on a service company's work sheet?
5. Once the work sheet is complete, why is it necessary to make journal entries?
6. What journal is used to make adjusting entries? How would you avoid writing an explanation after each adjusting entry?
7. What is a deferral? Give an example.
8. If a firm begins the fiscal year with a $624 balance in *Supplies,* would it be wrong to debit *Supplies Expense* for the next purchase?
9. Assume a firm paid rent of $3,600 in advance on March 1 (fiscal year, January to December). Would it make any difference in the net income if the bookkeeper debits *Rent Expense* rather than *Prepaid Rent* if proper adjusting entries are made?
10. Why are reversing entries necessary?

exercises

1. Indicate the normal balances for the following accounts:
   (a) Rent Expense
   (b) Prepaid Advertising
   (c) Purchases
   (d) J. B. Marshall, Capital
   (e) Income Summary
   (f) Purchases Discounts
   (g) Freight-In
   (h) Accounts Receivable
   (i) Merchandise Inventory
2. Jonston Company had an inventory on the books before adjusting entries of $13,675.09. A count of merchandise on hand as of December 31, 19X1, showed $18,442.52. Make the required general journal entries.
3. Supplies on hand at the beginning of 19X1 amounted to $125. During the year, $834 in supplies were purchased and debited to the *Supplies* account. At the end of the year, $398 in supplies were still on hand. Make the needed adjusting entry.

4. Harris Medals shows a balance on January 1, 19X1, of $700 in the *Rent Expense* account. This amount covered January and February. On March 1, $4,800 was paid in advance for the next twelve months. This amount was also debited to *Rent Expense.* Make the adjusting entry needed on December 31, 19X1.
5. Dalton Publishing Company started a new magazine and sold subscriptions totaling $88,600 during the first year. Dalton's bookkeeper chose to credit *Unearned Subscriptions Revenue.* Make the needed adjusting entry, assuming $21,400 is still unearned at the end of the year.
6. On January 1, 19X1, the *Advertising Expense* account has a balance of $95. During 19X1, $1,076 was spent for advertising and debited to *Advertising Expense.* On December 31, 19X1, advertising still prepaid amounted to $215. Make the necessary adjusting and reversing entries.

problems

1. COMPETENCY TESTED The ability to prepare a trial balance for a merchandising concern.

   The following unadjusted trial balance accounts have been listed in alphabetical order. Without changing the order, prepare a trial balance for Bulford's Place dated November 30, 19X1.

Accounts Payable	$ 6,870
Accounts Receivable	5,466
Accumulated Depreciation, Equipment	5,932
Advertising Expense	4,210
Barney Buford, Capital	66,738
Barney Buford, Drawing	28,200
Cash	27,168
Equipment	16,900
Freight-In	1,250
Merchandise Inventory	36,482
Notes Payable	2,000
Prepaid Insurance	1,662
Postage Expense	982
Purchases	101,442
Purchases Discounts	1,854
Purchases Returns and Allowances	2,596
Rent Expense	7,200
Repairs Expense	1,602
Salaries Expense	32,800
Sales	194,113
Sales Discounts	4,242

Sales Returns and Allowances	$ 2,596
Supplies	887
Telephone Expense	2,440
Utilities Expense	4,574

2. COMPETENCY TESTED The skill to locate an error in the trial balance.

Harper Equipment Company's trial balance will not balance because of some errors that the bookkeeper cannot locate. You have been asked to look over the accounts to see whether you can spot the errors.

Harper Equipment Company
Trial Balance
December 31, 19X1

Cash	$ 2,400	
Accounts Receivable	3,300	
Merchandise Inventory	8,021	
Store Supplies	590	
Office Supplies	185	
Store Equipment	9,016	
Accumulated Depreciation, Store Equipment		$ 3,200
Office Equipment	1,500	
Accumulated Depreciation, Office Equipment		300
Accounts Payable	1,700	
Notes Payable		500
Harriet Harper, Capital		19,253
Harriet Harper, Drawing	4,650	
Sales		76,200
Sales Returns and Allowances		650
Sales Discounts		812
Purchases	52,500	
Purchases Returns and Allowances		380
Purchases Discounts		500
Freight-In		1,200
Salaries Expense	14,250	
Advertising Expense	900	
Insurance Expense	642	
Delivery Expense	1,869	
Miscellaneous Expense	524	
	$102,047	$102,995

Other information showed that the amount for merchandise was the inventory taken on December 31, 19X1. Last year's inventory was $7,036. Also, in tracing the ledger accounts, it was found that *Sales Discounts* should have been $821.

3. COMPETENCY TESTED Skill in preparing a complete work sheet for a merchandising firm.

A trial balance prepared for Thrasher Tomato Company for the year ending on December 31, 19X1, is shown below:

Thrasher Tomato Company
Trial Balance
December 31, 19X1

Cash	$ 1,828	
Accounts Receivable	374	
Merchandise Inventory	8,752	
Supplies	108	
Prepaid Insurance	320	
Equipment	4,820	
Accumulated Depreciation, Equipment		$ 1,237
Building	60,000	
Accumulated Depreciation, Building		39,462
Accounts Payable		2,898
Notes Payable		200
Mortgage Payable		15,333
Martin Thrasher, Capital		21,151
Martin Thrasher, Drawing	4,200	
Sales		22,965
Sales Returns and Allowances	773	
Purchases	12,056	
Purchases Discounts		162
Advertising Expense	402	
Delivery Expense	361	
License Expense	50	
Salaries Expense	8,200	
Subscription Expense	35	
Telephone Expense	355	
Utilities Expense	774	
	$103,408	$103,408

Adjustments:

(a) Supplies on hand, December 31, 19X1, $61

(b) Insurance expired, $294

(c) Depreciation on equipment, $225

(d) Depreciation on building, $600

(e) Ending merchandise inventory, $10,155

(f) Accrued salaries, $125

Instructions From the data given above, prepare a complete 8-column work sheet.

4. COMPETENCY TESTED The ability to prepare a work sheet.

The following trial balance was taken from the ledger of Feldman's Bakery at the end of its annual accounting period:

Feldman's Bakery
Trial Balance
December 31, 19X1

Cash	$ 2,620	
Accounts Receivable	880	
Merchandise Inventory	35,950	
Store Supplies	1,650	
Equipment	13,880	
Accumulated Depreciation, Equipment		$ 5,960
Accounts Payable		11,255
Milton Feldman, Capital		45,392
Milton Feldman, Drawing	8,500	
Sales		68,224
Sales Returns and Allowances	1,826	
Purchases	38,992	
Purchases Returns and Allowances		821
Purchases Discounts		299
Freight-In	1,224	
Salaries Expense	15,689	
Rent Expense	7,200	
Advertising Expense	2,413	
Utilities Expense	1,127	
	$131,951	$131,951

Instructions Prepare a work sheet for Feldman's Bakery using the following data to make adjustments:

(a) Merchandise on hand, December 31, 19X1, $29,334

(b) Store supplies used, $1,114

(c) Depreciation on equipment, $600
(d) Rent unexpired, $150
(e) Advertising unexpired, $1,460
(f) Accrued salaries, $620

5. COMPETENCY TESTED The ability to plan, journalize, and post adjusting entries.

An examination of the unadjusted trial balance revealed that the following accounts needed adjusting:

Unadjusted Balance		Data on 12/31/19X1
Supplies	$ 500	Supplies on hand, $115
Merchandise Inventory	76,434	Ending inventory, $58,119
Rent Revenue	2,400	Unearned rent, $1,800
Prepaid Insurance	862	Expired insurance, $161
Salaries Expense	14,100	Accrued, $620
Accumulated Depreciation, Equipment	6,665	Annual depreciation, $885
Unearned Subscription Revenue	18,934	Earned during year, $9,400

Instructions After planning the necessary adjusting entries, (a) journalize these entries on page 23 of a general journal; then (b) post these entries.

6. COMPETENCY TESTED The ability to prepare a work sheet and journalize the related adjusting entries.

The following account balances (all normal) were found on the books of Todd Candy Company.

Cash	$ 1,880
Merchandise Inventory	22,169
Store Supplies	440
Office Supplies	1,822
Store Equipment	8,650
Accumulated Depreciation, Store Equipment	4,490
Office Equipment	2,768
Accumulated Depreciation, Office Equipment	947
Accounts Payable	2,115
Kirk Todd, Capital	23,613
Kirk Todd, Drawing	6,840

Sales	$82,114
Sales Discounts	654
Sales Returns and Allowances	1,414
Purchases	40,335
Purchases Discounts	542
Purchases Returns and Allowances	809
Freight-In	1,102
Salaries Expense	12,887
Rent Expense	8,800
Insurance Expense	1,255
Delivery Expense	743
Telephone Expense	1,411
Utilities Expense	3,860
Rent Revenue	2,400

Instructions

(a) Prepare a complete work sheet as of December 31, 19X1, using the following data:
  (1) Merchandise inventory, December 31, 19X1, $26,889
  (2) Store supplies used, $314
  (3) Office supplies inventory, $513
  (4) Insurance unexpired, $235
  (5) Accrued salaries, $440
  (6) Unexpired rent, $800
  (7) Unearned rent income, $120
  (8) Depreciation on store equipment, $612
  (9) Depreciation on office equipment, $286

(b) Journalize the adjusting entries.

(c) Indicate the adjusting entries that should be reversed by placing an "R" to the right of the entry.

7. COMPETENCY TESTED The ability to use different approaches to recording deferrals.

Philpot Business School operates from September to June, but keeps its books on a calendar fiscal year.

Item 1: On September 3, 19X1, $8,650 in tuitions was collected for services to be provided during the school year. By the end of 19X1, $2,880 had been earned. Make the necessary entries for September 3 and December 31 assuming (a) the initial receipt was recorded as revenue and (b) the initial receipt was recorded as liability.

Item 2: Rent is paid on June 1 of each year for use of the building. Annual rent amounts to $2,400. Make the necessary entries for June 1 and December 31 assuming (a) the initial payment was recorded as an asset and (b) the initial payment was recorded as an expense.

Item 3: Office supplies of $300 were on hand at the beginning of the year. Through a reversing entry from the previous year, this amount appears in the *Office Supplies Expense* account. Office supplies of $1,416 were purchased during the year, and these purchases were debited to *Office Supplies Expense.* At the end of 19X1, an inventory of office supplies showed $652 on hand. Make the adjusting entry needed on December 31.

8. COMPETENCY TESTED The skill to deal with reversing entries.

Polar Bear Ice Company's accountant has chosen to record deferrals as follows:

(a) The firm sells contracts to maintain ice machines in the area. The vendors paid Polar Bear Ice Company $2,815 in advance for this service, and the accountant recorded this as a credit to *Contract Revenue.* By December 31, Polar Bear had provided $2,200 in services.

(b) Rent of $500 is paid in advance to Jackson Realty on the first day of each month for that month's use of the building. This payment is debited to *Rent Expense.*

(c) Insurance premium payments of $586.10 were debited to *Insurance Expense.* On December 31, $387.50 was unexpired.

(d) On November 5, the firm agreed to provide ice for three ice festivals to be held in December, January, and February. The charge of $3,000 ($1,000 per month) was collected on that date and credited to *Unearned Festival Revenue.*

Instructions Make the necessary adjusting entries. Then indicate which should be reversed by placing an "R" to the right of those entries identified.

comprehensive problem

Instructions Using your transactions and postings in the comprehensive problem at the end of Chapter 6 and at the end of Chapter 9, prepare the following:

4. Trial balance on the work sheet.

5. A complete work sheet, reflecting the adjustments listed below:

(a) Expired rent, $300.

(b) Ending merchandise inventory, $3,000.

(c) Depreciation of $100 per month on the delivery equipment.

(d) Office supplies used, $130.

(e) Store supplies used, $70.

(f) Accrued salaries, $235.

chapter 11
FINANCIAL STATEMENT PREPARATION AND CLOSING THE ACCOUNTS

overall competency THE ABILITY TO PREPARE FINANCIAL STATEMENTS AND CLOSING ENTRIES FOR A MERCHANDISING CONCERN

career objectives Once the work sheet has been completed, you must present the information from the work sheet in such a way that the owner or manager can see how the business is doing. Financial statements prepared from the work sheet are used for this purpose. Once this step is complete, you may use a closing procedure similar to that you used in earlier chapters for a service-type business. In some firms, an outside accountant prepares the financial statements, and the accounting clerk assumes the responsibility of journalizing and posting the closing entries in this end-of-the-year process.

Upon completing this chapter, you should be able to perform these tasks:

- PREPARE AN INCOME STATEMENT FOR A FIRM THAT SELLS MERCHANDISE.
- PREPARE A CAPITAL STATEMENT AND A CLASSIFIED BALANCE SHEET FOR A MERCHANDISING CONCERN.
- PREPARE CLOSING ENTRIES FOR A MERCHANDISING FIRM USING THE INCOME STATEMENT COLUMNS OF THE WORK SHEET.
- PREPARE A POST-CLOSING TRIAL BALANCE AND MAKE THE REVERSING ENTRIES.

We previously discussed the accounting cycle for a service-type business. This chapter continues the thought begun in Chapter 10 and shows you how to complete the end-of-the-period procedures. In Chapter 10, you were shown how to prepare a work sheet and adjusting entries. In this chapter, we will take this same work sheet and prepare the *financial statements* and *closing entries.* A post-closing trial balance will show whether debits and credits have been journalized and posted equally.

• task USING THE INCOME STATEMENT SECTION OF THE WORK SHEET, PREPARE AN INCOME STATEMENT FOR A FIRM THAT SELLS MERCHANDISE

Revenue section of the income statement

The revenue section will take on a new look only in that *Sales, Sales Returns and Allowances,* and *Sales Discounts* will replace accounts like *Commissions Revenue, Service Revenue,* and *Professional Fees.* The revenue category appears first on the income statement, just as it would for a service business. A typical situation can be seen in Illustration 11-1 for Hudson Motors. As is the case with all income statements, the heading must tell the reader how long it took the firm to earn the revenue and experience the costs and expenses.

illustration 11-1 partial income statement.

Hudson Motors
Income Statement
For The Year Ended December 31, 19X1

Revenue:			
Sales		246500 —	
Less: Sales Discounts	3100 —		
Sales Returns and Allowances	7800 —	10900 —	
Net Sales			235600 —

It is important to separate revenues from "normal" operations from revenues from transactions that are not part of the firm's basic purpose. To illustrate, assume that Frank's Shoe Mart leases part of the building it owns to an insurance firm for $2,400 a year. Since selling shoes and related items is the major activity of Frank's Shoe Mart, the rental revenue should be placed somewhere else on the income statement. It is still a plus to net income, but the statement reader can tell that this revenue was not caused by selling socks and shoes. Such revenue is reported in a category known as **other income** that is placed near the bottom of the statement. More will be said later about the location of this category. Examples of other items that would not be considered normal revenue are interest earned, gains from selling equipment or other assets, and collections from insurance of more than book value of items stolen or destroyed.

Cost of goods sold section

With the addition of cost items, the arrangement of the income statement becomes more complex than the one you used with a service-type firm. Now we must subtract both costs and expenses from revenues to find the net income. The *cost of goods sold* section does exactly what the title says—it tells the reader of the statement just how much it cost to buy the merchandise sold during the period. To help you see this part of the income statement, we will use a very simple example. Assume that Horace's Fruits started the period with 100 pineapples that cost $1 each and ended with 80 pineapples. During the period, Horace bought 350 pineapples at $1 each. How can we find out how many $1 pineapples Horace sold? The following arrangement would be one possible approach:

Pineapples on hand Jan. 1 100 @ $1	100 –	
+ Pineapples bought, 350 @ $1	350 –	
Cost of Pineapples available to sell	450 –	
– Pineapples on hand Dec. 31 80 @ $1	80 –	
Cost of Pineapples sold during year		370 –

Since pineapples are merchandise and those bought during the period would be debited to *Purchases,* the example above can be stated in accounting terms:

Merchandise Inventory, Jan. 1	100 –	
Add: Purchases	350 –	
Cost of Merchandise Available for Sale	450 –	
Less: Merchandise Inventory Dec. 31	80 –	
Cost of Goods Sold		370 –

The terms *goods* and *merchandise* are interchangeable, so the *cost of goods sold* section may be called the *cost of merchandise sold.* This cost figure can also be affected by such items as merchandise returned, freight charges, and discounts given for paying promptly. These three items would be identified in accounting terms as *Purchases Returns and Allowances, Freight-In,* and *Purchases Discounts,* respectively.

Now let's look at a more realistic example using returns, discounts, and freight charges. Assume that Felder's Jewelry began the year with $110,000 in merchandise and ended the year with $95,000 on hand. During the year, the firm purchased $450,000 in jewelry for resale. By paying within the discount period, cost savings of $7,100 were permitted. Because of damage to goods and errors in filling the orders, $2,400 in merchandise was returned to suppliers. Finally, freight charges on the merchandise bought totaled $950. Using an arrangement similar to the one just discussed, the cost of goods sold section for Felder's Jewelry would appear as follows:

illustration 11-2 Cost of goods sold section.

Cost of Goods Sold:			
Merchandise Inventory, Jan. 1		110000 –	
Purchases	450000 –		
Less: Purchases Returns & All. 2400			
Purchases Discounts 7100	9500 –		
	440500 –		
Add: Freight-In	950 –		
Net Purchases		441450 –	
Cost of Goods Available for Sale		551450 –	
Less: Merchandise Inventory Dec. 31		95000 –	
Cost of Goods Sold			456450 –

Cost of goods sold of $456,450 would then be subtracted from net sales to show the gross profit.

Expense section of the income statement

Actually, there are two types of expenses—**operating** and **other.** Just like the revenue category, items not connected with the principal operation of the business should be placed into a separate category called *other expenses.* Usually, items such as interest on notes and bonds payable or loss on selling an asset fall into this category. However, most expenses are considered operating if they are the expenses of carrying on the daily operation of the business. Operating expenses follow the cost of goods sold section on the income statement.

To give management the best possible information, operating expenses are divided into two subcategories—general and selling. *General expenses* are those connected with the office and administrative operation of the business. Examples are the depreciation expense connected with office equipment, office salaries, and supplies that have been used in the office. Some accountants like to refer to these as *general and administrative expenses. Selling expenses* are those related to the actual selling of the product. Usually, any expense preceded by the word "store" is in this subcategory. Examples would be the depreciation on store equipment, sales salaries, store supplies used, and gas for the delivery truck.

Some expenses are both selling and general and must be divided between the two subcategories. The fancy word used by accountants is to *allocate*, so from now on, we won't divide, we will allocate. For example, assume that rent for 19X1 of $4,800 was allocated between the office and the sales area on the basis of floor space. The office used 10%; selling used the rest. This would mean that an expense for rent would be shown twice on the income statement—totaling $4,800. Under selling expenses, *Rent Expense* would be shown as $4,320 (90%), while under general expenses, *Rent Expense* would be shown as $480. The same approach can be used for heat, supervisor's salary, telephone, or any other expense for which the benefit is shared by both selling and administration. How you allocate items like utilities, rent, supervisors' salaries, and janitorial services may be left to the accounting clerk or it might be a management decision. Whoever has this responsibility should attempt to find the most logical basis for dividing these expenses. Each item may have its own basis. For example, rent may be divided on square footage or quality of floor space, utilities on number or types of electrical units, and janitorial services on the number of employees in each area or time spent in different areas of the building.

It is important that you understand the difference between a *cost* and an *expense*. Since we have gone to all the trouble of explaining the cost of goods sold section, there must be a reason we do not just lump *Purchases* and other "cost" accounts with the expenses. What is the difference? Cost accounts are connected with buying the merchandise that the firm is selling. An expense, in contrast, is a past or future payment to carry on the operation of the business.

Preparing the income statement

Once the work sheet is complete, preparing the income statement is a matter of properly transferring the information. To walk you through this process, we need to continue with the Brooks' Readywear illustration we started in Chapter 10. Illustration 11-3 is a reproduction of Illustration 10-4. Every number that appears in the income statement columns of the work sheet must be shown on the income statement, including the beginning and ending inventories. Your first reaction to this last statement is that *merchandise inventory* is an asset, and these numbers must be taken from the balance sheet. However, a close look at the work sheet will show you that the debit to *Income Summary* in the Income Statement column is the beginning inventory and the credit to *Income Summary* is the ending inventory. So, we repeat, every number that appears on the income statement can be found in these two columns. Note that the items highlighted

Brooks' Readywear
Work Sheet
For Year Ended December 31, 19X1

Account Titles	Trial Balance Dr.	Trial Balance Cr.	Adjustments Dr.	Adjustments Cr.	Income Statement Dr.	Income Statement Cr.	Balance Sheet Dr.	Balance Sheet Cr.
Cash	2119 –						2119 –	
Accounts Receivable	759 –						759 –	
Merchandise Inventory	17900 –		(d) 18452 –	(c) 17900 –			18452 –	
Store Supplies	216 –			(a) 143 –			73 –	
Prepaid Insurance	640 –			(b) 290 –			350 –	
Store Equipment	9460 –						9460 –	
Accum. Deprec., Store Equipment		3348 –		(e) 450 –				3798 –
Office Equipment	4000 –						4000 –	
Accum. Deprec., Office Equipment		1000 –		(f) 100 –				1100 –
Building	116000 –						116000 –	
Accum. Deprec., Building		67000 –		(g) 1100 –				68100 –
Accounts Payable		1721 –						1721 –
Notes Payable		500 –						500 –
Mortgage Payable		28610 –						28610 –
Mary Brooks, Capital		58710 –						58710 –
Mary Brooks, Drawing	12650 –						12650 –	
Sales		45018 –				45018 –		
Sales Returns and Allowances	1229 –				1229 –			
Sales Discounts	220 –				220 –			
Purchases	24507 –				24507 –			
Purchases Returns & Allowances		865 –				865 –		
Purchases Discounts		314 –				314 –		
Advertising Expense	812 –				812 –			
Delivery Expense	641 –				641 –			
License Expense	40 –				40 –			
Payroll Taxes-General	242 –				242 –			
Payroll Taxes-Selling	968 –				968 –			
Office Salary Expense	2500 –				2500 –			
Sales Salary Expense	10000 –		(h) 320 –		10320 –			
Subscription Expense	60 –				60 –			
Telephone Expense	632 –				632 –			
Utilities Expense	1491 –				1491 –			
	207086 –	207086 –						
Store Supplies Expense			(a) 143 –		143 –			
Insurance Expense			(b) 290 –		290 –			
Income Summary			(c) 17900 –	(d) 18452 –	17900 –	18452 –		
Deprec. Expense, Store Equip.			(e) 450 –		450 –			
Deprec. Expense, Office Equip.			(f) 100 –		100 –			
Deprec. Expense, Building			(g) 1100 –		1100 –			
Salaries Payable				(h) 320 –				320 –
			38755 –	38755 –	63645 –	64649 –	163863 –	162859 –
Net Income					1004 –			1004 –
					64649 –	64649 –	163863 –	163863 –

illustration 11-3 completed work sheet.

in Illustration 11-4 have been allocated, supposedly on some realistic basis. For example, we might have used floor space occupied to allocate insurance.

The net income you calculated on the financial statement must match the net income shown on the work sheet. You need to stop here and carefully compare the income statement in Illustration 11-4 with the work sheet in Illustration 11-3 to make certain that you understand this transfer of numbers.

Before leaving the income statement, let's take a look at "other income"

illustration 11-4
income statement.

Brooks' Readywear
Income Statement
For Year Ended December 31, 19X1

Revenue:			
Sales			45018 –
Less: Sales Returns & Allowances		1229 –	
Sales Discounts		220 –	1449 –
Net Sales			43569 –
Cost of Goods Sold:			
Merchandise Inventory Jan. 1, 19X1		17900 –	
Purchases	24507 –		
Less: Purchases Returns & All. 865			
Purchases Discounts 314	1179 –	23328 –	
Cost of Goods Available for Sale		41228 –	
Less: Merchandise Inv. Dec. 31, 19X1		18452 –	
Cost of Goods Sold			22776 –
Gross Profit			20793 –
Operating Expenses:			
Selling Expenses			
Advertising Expense	812 –		
Delivery Expense	641 –		
Payroll Taxes Expense	968 –		
Sales Salaries Expense	10320 –		
Utilities Expense	1299 –		
Store Supplies Expense	143 –		
Insurance Expense	210 –		
Depreciation Expense, Store Equip.	450 –		
Depreciation Expense, Building	1000 –		
Total Selling Expenses		15843 –	
General Expenses:			
License Expense	40 –		
Payroll Taxes Expense	242 –		
Office Salaries Expense	2500 –		
Subscription Expense	60 –		
Telephone Expense	632 –		
Utilities Expense	192 –		
Insurance Expense	80 –		
Depreciation Expense, Office Equip.	100 –		
Depreciation Expense Building	100 –		
Total General Expenses		3946 –	
Total Operating Expenses			19789 –
Net Income			1004 –

and "other expenses." Assume Brooks' Readywear also had income from dividends on stocks owned of $100 and rental revenue on some equipment of $50. Assume further that the firm paid $75 in interest during the year. So that the reader of the statement will know that these are not revenue and expense items from the firm's main line of operations, a net income, known as **income from primary operations,** is shown before these other items. In reference to Illustration 11-4, we changed "Net Income" to "Income from Primary Operations" and added the other items shown in Illustration 11-5.

illustration 11-5
lower portion of income statement showing a net income.

Income from Primary Operations			1004 –
Other Income:			
Dividend Revenue	100 –		
Rental Revenue	50 –	150 –	
Other Expenses:			
Interest Expense		75 –	75 –
Net Income			1079 –

Should the firm have a **loss from primary operations,** just remember that you are dealing with a negative amount when handling other income and other expenses. This treatment can be seen in Illustration 11-6.

illustration 11-6
lower portion of income statement showing a net loss.

Loss from Primay Operations			793 –
Other Income:			
Dividend Revenue	100 –		
Rental Revenue	50 –	150 –	
Other Expenses:			
Interest Expense		75 –	75 –
Net Loss			718 –

sample problem The Music Shop closes its books on December 31 each year; and at the end of 19X1, the Income Statement columns of the work sheet showed the following amounts:

	Dr.	Cr.
Sales		$ 94,684
Sales Returns and Allowances	$ 711	
Sales Discounts	164	
Purchases	45,500	
Purchases Returns and Allowances		551
Purchases Discounts		256
Freight-In	129	
Advertising Expense	2,003	
Store Salary Expense	24,915	
Office Salary Expense	3,650	
Rent Expense	6,000	
Telephone Expense	1,838	
Utilities Expense	1,455	

Office Supplies Expense	$ 79	
Store Supplies Expense	128	
Depreciation Expense, Store Equipment	612	
Depreciation Expense, Office Equipment	248	
Dividend Revenue		$ 50
Interest Expense	20	
Income Summary	14,773	16,217
	$102,225	$111,758
Net Income	9,533	
	$111,758	$111,758

Allocation of different expenses is as follows:

	Store	Office
Rent	90%	10%
Telephone	50%	50%
Utilities	80%	20%

The beginning merchandise inventory was $14,773, while the ending is $16,217.

Instructions Prepare an income statement for the Music Shop for the year ending December 31, 19X1. Every number that appears in the Income Statement columns must be used on the statement (either allocated or as a whole).

sample problem solution

The Music Shop
Income Statement
For Year Ended December 31, 19X1

Revenue				
Sales			$94,684	
Less: Sales Returns and Allowances		$711		
Sales Discounts		164	875	
Net Sales				$93,809
Cost of Goods Sold:				
Merchandise Inventory, Jan. 1			$14,773	
Purchases		$45,500		
Less: Purchases Returns and Allowances	$551			
Purchases Discounts	256	807		
		$44,693		
Add: Freight-In		129	44,822	
Cost of goods available for sale			$59,595	
Less: Merchandise Inventory, Dec. 31			16,217	
Cost of Goods Sold				43,378
Gross Profit				$50,431

Operating Expenses:			
Selling Expenses:			
Advertising Expense	$ 2,003		
Store Salary Expense	24,915		
Rent Expense	5,400		
Telephone Expense	919		
Utilities Expense	1,164		
Store Supplies Expense	128		
Depreciation Expense, Store Equipment	612		
Total Selling Expenses		$35,141	
General Expense:			
Office Salary Expense	$3,650		
Rent Expense	600		
Telephone Expense	919		
Utilities Expense	291		
Office Supplies Expense	79		
Depreciation Expense, Office Equipment	248		
Total General Expenses		5,787	
Total Operating Expenses			40,928
Income from Primary Operations			$ 9,503
Other Income:			
Dividend Revenue		$ 50	
Other Expenses:			
Interest Expense		20	30
Net Income			$9,533

review exercises

1. From the following information, prepare the cost of goods sold section of an income statement: *Freight-In,* $1,446; *Delivery Expense,* $2,108; *Purchases,* $96,335; *Purchases Discounts,* $1,512; *Purchases Returns and Allowances,* $880; beginning inventory, $28,004; ending inventory, $19,556. Be careful; some of these accounts may not be part of the cost of goods sold section.
2. Here is a list of accounts for a firm selling groceries. Indicate whether the item is a (S) selling expense; (G) general expense; (O) other expense; or (NA) needs allocating. Assume a normal situation in all cases.
   (a) Depreciation Expense, Delivery Equipment
   (b) Office Supplies Expense
   (c) Rent Expense
   (d) Utilities Expense
   (e) Interest Expense
   (f) Depreciation Expense, Building
   (g) Advertising Expense
   (h) Miscellaneous General Expense
   (i) Delivery Expense
   (j) Sales Salaries Expense

3. Diana's Book Shop had a net loss from primary operations of $1,944. During the year she received $400 in dividends from investments she had made for the firm and $4,200 from renting the space next door. During the year she paid interest of $50 on a note. What is her final net income or net loss?

• task PREPARE A CAPITAL STATEMENT AND A BALANCE SHEET FOR A MERCHANDISING CONCERN

Review of the balance sheet

Unlike the income statement, the capital statement and balance sheet for a merchandising business are very similar to those of a service firm. The major difference in the balance sheet will be the account *Merchandise Inventory*. There probably will be more accounts since merchandising firms tend to be larger than service firms, but a large service firm could easily have as many or more accounts than a firm that sells a product.

As you construct a balance sheet, keep in mind what you are trying to tell the reader. Just as we mentioned earlier, it is simply a matter of saying "Stop! This is how much we own today, this is how much we owe, and this is how much we are worth." To prepare such a statement, you must first construct a capital statement.

Preparation of a capital statement

The purpose of the capital statement is to tell the reader why capital changed during the fiscal period. For a proprietorship, explanations are limited to these four possible items—net income, net loss, investments, and withdrawals. Since the capital statement is actually part of the balance sheet, all the information you need to prepare this statement can be found in the Balance Sheet columns of the work sheet.

We will use Illustration 11-3 as the basis for preparing the capital statement. To save you from turning back and forth, we have shown the important information below:

Mary Brooks, Capital	$58,710
Mary Brooks, Drawing	12,650
Net Income	1,004

If Mary invested $1,000 during the year, the capital account balance at the beginning of 19X1 would be $57,710. Brooks' Readywear capital statement for 19X1 is shown in Illustration 11-7.

illustration 11-7
capital statement.

Brooks' Readywear
Capital Statement
For Year Ended December 31, 19X1

Mary Brooks, Capital, Jan. 1, 19X1		57710 –	
Add: Net Income	1004 –		
Investment	1000 –	2004 –	
		59714 –	
Less: Withdrawals		12650 –	
Mary Brooks, Capital, Dec. 31, 19X1			47064 –

If the business had a net loss for 19X1, then the loss and the withdrawals would have been subtracted from $58,710 (beginning capital plus $1,000). In other words, losses are treated just like withdrawals. Before we leave the capital statement, remember that it can also be called a statement of owner's equity.

Preparing the balance sheet

Once you have finished the capital statement, you will be ready to use the Balance Sheet columns of the work sheet to prepare the balance sheet. However, you will not use all the numbers in the columns. Why? By preparing the capital statement, you have found the final capital balance for the year. Since the balance sheet shows net worth on a specific date (the last day of the fiscal period), the amount from the capital statement is more current than the one found in the balance sheet column of the work sheet. Likewise, since drawing was used in arriving at this updated capital balance, it is not shown on the balance sheet.

Illustration 11-8 shows a balance sheet constructed from the amounts in the Balance Sheet columns in Illustration 11-3. As you did with the income statement, take a few moments to trace the numbers, making certain that you understand what has been done. One caution in preparing the balance sheet: It is easy to overlook the amounts at the bottom of the work sheet that were created by adjusting entries (like *Salaries Payable*) since such accounts are separate from the other real accounts. Of course, omitting an account will be obvious when the assets do not equal the liabilities plus capital.

Balance sheet format classifications

To provide the statement reader with the best possible information, it is necessary to divide the balance sheet into subcategories. For example, assets fall mainly into five subcategories (there are more, but beyond the scope of this book), and liabilities are usually divided into two subcategories. In a proprietorship, owner's equity is not subdivided.

Current assets If a firm owns items of value with future use, they are considered **current assets** if they are to be converted into cash or used up, usually within one year. In some situations, the period can be longer, but

illustration 11-8
balance sheet.

Brooks' Readywear
Balance Sheet
For Year Ended December 31, 19X1

Assets			
Current Assets:			
Cash		2119 -	
Accounts Receivable		759 -	
Merchandise Inventory		18452 -	
Store Supplies		73 -	
Prepaid Insurance		350 -	
Total Current Assets			21753 -
Plant and Equipment:			
Store Equipment	9460 -		
Less: Accumulated Depreciation	3798 -	5662 -	
Office Equipment	4000 -		
Less: Accumulated Depreciation	1100 -	2900 -	
Building	116000 -		
Less: Accumulated Depreciation	68100 -	47900 -	
Total Plant and Equipment			56462 -
Total Assets			78215 -
Liabilities and Owner's Equity			
Current Liabilities:			
Accounts Payable		1721 -	
Notes Payable		500 -	
Salaries Payable		320 -	
Total Current Liabilities			2541 -
Long Term Liabilities:			
Mortgage Payable			28610 -
Mary Brooks, Capital			47064 -
Total Liabilities & Owner's Equity			78215 -

these are rare in a small proprietorship. Examples of current assets would be such items as *Cash, Accounts Receivable, Notes Receivable, Merchandise Inventory, Supplies,* and *Prepaid Insurance.*

Investments When a firm has some idle cash to be "put to work" for a long time, it can be placed in a fund that draws interest or dividends. When a bond is due in the future and management wants to be certain that funds are there to meet this debt, installment payments are made to such a fund. These commitments are usually long-term, so they are listed under the **investments** heading. Occasionally, a firm will buy a piece of land and use only part of it to construct a building. If the rest is held for resale in the distant future (one year or longer), then the land is also an investment. If the firm plans to use this property for later expansion, then carrying it in an "other asset" category would be best. Real estate, capital stock, bonds, and money market funds are specific examples of investments.

Plant and equipment assets This category is also known by such titles as fixed assets, plant assets, and property, plant, and equipment. These items of future value are not used up or converted to cash within a year.

Most **plant and equipment assets** are used to produce revenue, including land, a building in which to operate, and machinery and equipment used to carry on day-to-day operations. An asset such as a piece of equipment no longer used in the business but held for resale should be listed as an investment. The plant and equipment category should be reserved for productive long-term assets.

Intangible assets The term **intangible assets** indicates something that cannot affect the human senses, such as hearing or smelling. Yet, if it is an asset, it must be something of value to the firm. A firm can own certain privileges which it has paid for the right to exercise. For example, this textbook is protected by a copyright that states that nobody can duplicate the book without violating our rights. You cannot see this right; yet there was an expense in obtaining it, so its future value to the authors and the publisher makes it an asset. The same is true for copyrights for movies and songs. In like manner, a patent gives a degree of protection to the inventor. If a firm purchases this right from the inventor, its cost should be recorded as an asset. Other intangible assets are *Leasehold Improvements, Franchises,* and *Goodwill.*

Other assets There is some debate as to where some assets should appear on the balance sheet, such as a building under construction or a piece of equipment that is idle at present and may or may not be put back into production. Sometimes accountants simply have to use their best judgment as to which subcategory is appropriate. If it does not fit comfortably into one of the first four categories, then this "catch all" group is probably where it should be shown. The major requirements are that it must be (1) long-term, (2) owned by the business, and (3) valuable to the firm.

Current liabilities To fit into this subcategory, the item must definitely be a debt of the firm for current or past activities. When a firm buys merchandise and promises to pay in 30 days, it creates a **current liability.** To be current, management must intend to pay the debt by using either current assets (usually cash or merchandise) or creating another current liability (giving a note payable for an account payable). Examples of current liabilities would be accounts like *Accounts Payable, Notes Payable, Interest Payable,* and *Wages Payable.*

Long-term liabilities A debt of the company that management plans to pay in the distant future (one year beyond the balance sheet date), or with long-term assets (such as a special fund set aside to pay off bonds when they become due) is a **long-term liability.** Traditionally, most accounting clerks will use one year as a convenient dividing point between most current and long-term liabilities. This classification works fairly well most of the time, but there can be exceptions, so just use this suggestion as a general guideline. Examples of long-term liabilities are *Bonds Payable, Long-Term Notes Payable,* and *Mortgages Payable.*

Owner's equity section In a proprietorship, the owner's equity section is quite simple, involving only capital and drawing accounts. To the beginning capital balance, we either add the net income or subtract the net loss. Likewise, investments increase owner's equity; and withdrawals decrease it. As we have illustrated in this chapter, a separate capital statement can be prepared so that only one figure for owner's equity is displayed on the balance sheet.

sample problem Frosty Ice Cream Company's work sheet for 19X1 had the following items in the balance sheet columns:

	Dr.	Cr.
Cash	$ 8,940	
Merchandise Inventory	19,112	
Accounts Receivable	6,885	
Store Supplies	260	
Equipment	8,603	
Accumulated Depreciation, Equipment		$ 2,923
Accounts Payable		1,776
Notes Payable		2,000
Martin Mott, Capital		38,620
Martin Mott, Drawing	8,700	
Salaries Payable		550
	$52,500	$45,869
Net Income		6,631
	$52,500	$52,500

Instructions Martin started the year with a balance of $36,620 in his capital account and invested $2,000 during the year. Using this information and the work sheet data, prepare (a) a capital statement and (b) a balance sheet as of December 31, 19X1.

sample problem solution (a)

FROSTY ICE CREAM COMPANY
Capital Statement
For Year Ended December 31, 19X1

Martin Mott, Capital, Jan. 1		$36,620
Add: Investment	$2,000	
Net Income	6,631	8,631
		$45,251
Less: Withdrawals		8,700
Martin Moss, Capital, Dec. 31		$36,551

(b)

FROSTY ICE CREAM COMPANY
Balance Sheet
December 31, 19X1

Assets

Current Assets:		
Cash	$ 8,940	
Merchandise Inventory	19,112	
Accounts Receivable	6,885	
Store Supplies	260	
Total Current Assets		$35,197
Plant and Equipment:		
Equipment	$ 8,603	
Less: Accumulated Depreciation	2,923	
Total Plant and Equipment		5,680
Total Assets		$40,877

Liabilities and Owner's Equity

Current Liabilities:		
Accounts Payable	$ 1,776	
Notes Payable	2,000	
Salaries Payable	550	
Total Current Liabilities		$ 4,326
Martin Mott, Capital		36,551
Total Liabilities and Owner's Equity		$40,877

review exercises

4. Using the following symbols, indicate on which part of the December 31, 19X1 balance sheet each of the accounts would appear:

CA	= current asset	LL	= long-term liability
PE	= plant and equipment	OE	= owner's equity
IA	= intangible asset	CS	= item appears only on the capital statement
CL	= current liability		

(a) Building
(b) Heinz Schultz, Capital (Jan. 1, 19X1)
(c) Salaries Payable
(d) Heinz Schultz, Drawing
(e) Accumulated Depreciation, Equipment
(f) Merchandise Inventory
(g) Accounts Payable
(h) Investment by the owner
(i) Cash
(j) Copyright
(k) Interest Receivable

5. From the following information, prepare a capital statement for Hendrix Sporting Goods for the month ending March 31, 19X1: net loss, \$691.16; beginning balance of *Fred Hendrix, Capital,* \$18,634.12; withdrawals by the owner during March, \$1,200.

6. Prepare a balance sheet for Builder's Equipment Company assuming that the following information is taken from the work sheet and capital statements dated December 31, 19X1: *Cash,* \$8,215; *Accounts Receivable,* \$18,912; *Merchandise Inventory,* \$45,239; *Equipment,* \$9,340; *Accumulated Depreciation, Equipment,* \$1,875; *Truck,* \$12,140; *Accumulated Depreciation, Truck,* \$8,534; *Patent,* \$1,600; *Land* (being held for future expansion), \$10,000; *Accounts Payable,* \$12,160; *Notes Payable,* \$500; *Mortgage Payable* (due in 5 years), \$25,000; *Sarah Felder, Capital* from the capital statement's ending balance, \$57,377.

• task PREPARE THE REQUIRED CLOSING ENTRIES FOR A MERCHANDISING CONCERN USING THE INCOME STATEMENT COLUMNS OF THE WORK SHEET

Purpose of closing entries

The reasoning behind making closing entries is the same as that used earlier for a service-type business. All of the temporary (nominal) accounts must be brought back to zero to prepare for the next fiscal period. The closing entries transfer balances from expense, cost, and revenue accounts to *Income Summary.* The only differences here, as compared with procedures used for the service business, are that cost accounts are now involved and revenue accounts are more numerous.

Once closing entries have been completed, the capital account should show the same balance as that shown by the capital statement. To accomplish this, the *Income Summary* account and the drawing account must be closed into capital. The closing entries can be made by using information from either the ledger or the work sheet. The ledger approach is much more cumbersome since you have to look at the balance of every nominal account and decide whether to debit or credit to close out that particular account. This procedure would then be repeated until all the nominal accounts have been considered.

An easier method, in our opinion, is to use the work sheet approach. Since every account that appears in the Income Statement columns of the work sheet must be closed, just remember that every account in the Income Statement debit column can be closed by a credit and every account in the credit column can be closed by a debit.

Journalizing the closing entries

Recall that the closing process is a four-step procedure:

1. Close all accounts with debit balances in the Income Statement column of the work sheet into *Income Summary.*
2. Close all accounts with credit balances in the Income Statement column of the work sheet into *Income Summary.*
3. Close the *Income Summary* account to the capital account.
4. Close the drawing account to the capital account.

The order of these steps is not hard and fast. By that we mean that Steps 1 and 2 could be reversed without any change in results.

illustration 11-9 accounts on the work sheet to be closed.

Account Titles	Income Statement Dr.	Income Statement Cr.	Balance Sheet Dr.	Balance Sheet Cr.
Mary Brooks, Drawing			12650 –	
Sales		45018 –		
Sales Returns and Allowances	1229 –			
Sales Discounts	220 –			
Purchases	24507 –			
Purchases Returns and All.		865 –		
Purchases Discounts		314 –		
Advertising Expense	812 –			
Delivery Expense	641 –			
License Expense	40 –			
Payroll Taxes, General	242 –			
Payroll Taxes, Selling	968 –			
Office Salary Expense	2500 –			
Sales Salary Expense	10320 –			
Subscription Expense	60 –			
Telephone Expense	632 –			
Utilities Expense	1491 –			
Store Supplies Expense	143			
Insurance Expense	290 –			
Income Summary	17900 –	18452 –		
Deprec. Expense, Store Equip.	450 –			
Deprec. Expense, Office Equip.	100 –			
Deprec. Expense, Building	1100 –			
	63645 –	64649 –		
Net Income	1004 –			
	64649 –	64649 –		

Illustration 11-9, which is a portion of the same illustration we have been using throughout, illustrates the work sheet approach. Let us remind you again that as you go through the four steps, you should compare this procedure with that for a service-type business. The only difference is that cost accounts are involved. This means that when expenses are closed out with credits, accounts like *Purchases, Freight-In,* and *Sales Returns and Allowances* are also included. A comparison of the accounts in Illustration 11-9 with the journal entries in Illustration 11-10 will emphasize the four steps you must take:

illustration 11-10
closing entries.

GENERAL JOURNAL — Page 24

Date		Description	P.R.	Dr.	Cr.
		Closing Entries			
19X1 Dec.	31	Income Summary		45745 –	
		Sales Returns and Allowances			1229 –
		Sales Discounts			220 –
		Purchases			24507 –
		Advertising Expense			812 –
		Delivery Expense			641 –
		License Expense			40 –
		Payroll Taxes, General			242 –
		Payroll Taxes, Selling			968 –
		Office Salary Expense			2500 –
		Sales Salary Expense			10320 –
		Subscription Expense			60 –
		Telephone Expense			632 –
		Utilities Expense			1491 –
		Store Supplies Expense			143 –
		Insurance Expense			290 –
		Depreciation Expense, Store Equipment			450 –
		Depreciation Expense, Office Equipment			100 –
		Depreciation Expense, Building			1100 –
	31	Sales		45018 –	
		Purchases Returns and Allowances		865 –	
		Purchases Discounts		314 –	
		Income Summary			46197 –
	31	Income Summary		1004 –	
		Mary Brooks, Capital			1004 –
	31	Mary Brooks, Capital		12650 –	
		Mary Brooks, Drawing			12650 –

After making these adjusting entries, *Income Summary* and *Mary Brooks, Capital* would appear as follows:

Income Summary — Account No. 313

Date		Item	P.R.	Dr.	Cr.	Balance Dr.	Balance Cr.
19X1 Dec.	31	Adjusting	G23	17900 –		17900 –	
	31	Adjusting	G23		18452 –		552 –
	31	Closing	G24	45745 –		45193 –	
	31	Closing	G24		46197 –		1004 –
	31	Closing	G24	1004 –		–0–	

Mary Brooks, Capital — Account No. 311

Date		Item	P.R.	Dr.	Cr.	Balance Dr.	Balance Cr.
19X1 Dec.	31	Balance	✓				58710 –
	31	Closing	G24		1004 –		59714 –
	31	Closing	G24	12650 –			47064 –

One proof that you have possibly followed the correct procedure is that *Income Summary* closes out, and a second is that the ending balance of the capital account matches the final amount on the capital statement (see Illustration 11-7). Once the closing entries are posted, all revenue, cost, and expense accounts should have a zero balance.

sample problem A portion of Foster Eyewear's work sheet is shown below for the year ending December 31, 19X1. From the information shown, prepare the necessary closing entries.

Foster Eyewear
Work Sheet
For Year Ended December 31, 19X1

Account Name	Income Statement Dr.	Income Statement Cr.	Balance Sheet Dr.	Balance Sheet Cr.
Jerry Foster, Capital				37,480.66
Jerry Foster, Drawing			6,500.00	
Sales		41,763.13		
Sales Returns and Allowances	3,741.94			
Sales Discounts	2,887.12			
Purchases	20,419.83			
Purchases Returns and Allowances		1,513.18		
Purchases Discounts		3,966.40		
Advertising Expense	1,516.12			
Delivery Expense	744.93			
License Expense	156.00			
Payroll Taxes Expense	1,048.88			
Salaries Expense	14,984.00			
Telephone Expense	944.15			
Utilities Expense	1,955.43			
Income Summary	28,400.12	27,708.48		
Supplies Expense	189.40			
Insurance Expense	662.50			

Foster Eyewear
Work Sheet
For Year Ended December 31, 19X1

Account Name	Income Statement Dr.	Income Statement Cr.	Balance Sheet Dr.	Balance Sheet Cr.
Depreciation Expense, Equipment	746.20			
Depreciation Expense, Building	1,069.00			
Salaries Payable				512.00
	79,465.62	74,951.19	98,032.26	102,546.69
Net Loss		4,514.43	4,514.43	
	79,465.62	79,465.62	102,546.69	102,546.69

sample problem solution

Closing Entries

Date	Account	Dr.	Cr.
Dec. 31	Income Summary	51,065.50	
	Sales Returns and Allowances		3,741.94
	Sales Discounts		2,887.12
	Purchases		20,419.83
	Advertising Expense		1,516.12
	Delivery Expense		744.93
	License Expense		156.00
	Payroll Taxes Expense		1,048.88
	Salaries Expense		14,984.00
	Telephone Expense		944.15
	Utilities Expense		1,955.43
	Supplies Expense		189.40
	Insurance Expense		662.50
	Depreciation Expense, Equipment		746.20
	Depreciation Expense, Building		1,069.00
31	Sales	41,763.13	
	Purchases Returns and Allowances	1,513.18	
	Purchases Discounts,	3,966.40	
	Income Summary		47,242.71
31	Jerry Foster, Capital	4,514.43	
	Income Summary		4,514.43*
31	Jerry Foster, Capital	6,500.00	
	Jerry Foster, Drawing		6,500.00

*Includes $691.64, which is the difference between beginning and ending merchandise inventory.

review exercises

7. Indicate which of the following accounts should be closed: (a) *Prepaid Rent;* (b) *Howard Martin, Drawing;* (c) *Sales Returns and Allowances;* (d) *Notes Payable;* (e) *Salaries Payable;* (f) *Depreciation Expense, Store Equipment;* (g) *Telephone Expense;* (h) *Walter Davidson, Capital;* (i) *Cash.*

8. Totals of the work sheet for the income statement and the balance sheet were as follows:

$14,816.14	$16,119.50	$86,765.00	$85,461.64
1,303.36			1,303.36
$16,119.50	$16,119.50	$86,765.00	$86,765.00

What journal entry would be required to close the net income or net loss to the *Krista Sames, Capital* account?

• task PREPARE A POST-CLOSING TRIAL BALANCE AND MAKE THE REVERSING ENTRIES

Post-closing trial balance

Once the adjusting and closing entries have been posted, you must check for equality of debits and credits. This is the same procedure you followed earlier in this text after completing the adjusting and closing process for a service firm. Since all of the nominal accounts have been closed, the only accounts left are the real accounts, as shown in Illustration 11-11. This illustration lists all of the accounts as they appear in the ledger just before the post-closing trial balance is prepared.

illustration 11-11 ledger after closing entries.

Cash — Account No. 111

Date		Item	P.R.	Dr.	Cr.	Balance Dr.	Balance Cr.
19X1 Dec.	31	Balance	✓			2119 –	

Accounts Receivable — Account No. 112

Date		Item	P.R.	Dr.	Cr.	Balance Dr.	Balance Cr.
19X1 Dec.	31	Balance	✓			759 –	

Merchandise Inventory — Account No. 113

Date		Item	P.R.	Dr.	Cr.	Balance Dr.	Balance Cr.
19X0 Dec.	31	Balance	✓			17900 –	
19X1 Dec.	31	Adjusting	G23		17900 –	–0–	
	31	Adjusting	G23	18452 –		18452 –	

Store Supplies — Account No. 114

Date		Item	P.R.	Dr.	Cr.	Balance Dr.	Balance Cr.
19X1 Dec.	31	Balance	✓			216 –	
	31	Adjusting	G23		143 –	73 –	

Prepaid Insurance — Account No. 115

Date		Item	P.R.	Dr.	Cr.	Balance Dr.	Balance Cr.
19X1 Dec.	31	Balance	✓			640 –	
	31	Adjusting	G23		290 –	350 –	

Store Equipment — Account No. 116

Date		Item	P.R.	Dr.	Cr.	Balance Dr.	Balance Cr.
19X1 Dec.	31	Balance	✓			9460 –	

Accumulated Depreciation, Store Equipment — Account No. 117

Date		Item	P.R.	Dr.	Cr.	Balance Dr.	Balance Cr.
19X1 Dec.	31	Balance	✓				3348 –
	31	Adjusting	G23		450 –		3798 –

Office Equipment — Account No. 118

Date		Item	P.R.	Dr.	Cr.	Balance Dr.	Balance Cr.
19X1 Dec.	31	Balance	✓			4000 –	

Accumulated Depreciation, Office Equipment — Account No. 119

Date		Item	P.R.	Dr.	Cr.	Balance Dr.	Balance Cr.
19X1 Dec.	31	Balance	✓				1000 –
	31	Adjusting	G23		100 –		1100 –

Illustration 11-11 (continued)

Building — Account No. 120

Date		Item	P.R.	Dr.	Cr.	Balance Dr.	Balance Cr.
19X1 Dec.	31	Balance	✓			116000 –	

Accumulated Depreciation, Building — Account No. 121

Date		Item	P.R.	Dr.	Cr.	Balance Dr.	Balance Cr.
19X1 Dec.	31	Balance	✓				67000 –
	31	Adjusting	G23		1100 –		68100 –

Accounts Payable — Account No. 211

Date		Item	P.R.	Dr.	Cr.	Balance Dr.	Balance Cr.
19X1 Dec.	31	Balance	✓				1721 –

Salaries Payable — Account No. 212

Date		Item	P.R.	Dr.	Cr.	Balance Dr.	Balance Cr.
19X1 Dec.	31	Adjusting	G23		320 –		320 –

Notes Payable — Account No. 213

Date		Item	P.R.	Dr.	Cr.	Balance Dr.	Balance Cr.
19X1 Dec.	31	Balance	✓				500 –

Mortgage Payable — Account No. 214

Date		Item	P.R.	Dr.	Cr.	Balance Dr.	Balance Cr.
19X1 Dec.	31	Balance	✓				28610 –

Mary Brooks, Capital — Account No. 311

Date		Item	P.R.	Dr.	Cr.	Balance Dr.	Balance Cr.
19X1 Dec.	31	Balance	✓				58710 –
	31	Closing	G24		1004		59714 –
	31	Closing	G24	12650 –			47064 –

Mary Brooks, Drawing Account No. 312

Date		Item	P.R.	Dr.	Cr.	Balance Dr.	Balance Cr.
19X1 Dec.	31	Balance	✓			12650 -	
	31	Closing	G24		12650 -	-0-	

Income Summary Account No. 313

Date		Item	P.R.	Dr.	Cr.	Balance Dr.	Balance Cr.
19X1 Dec.	31	Adjusting	G23	17900 -		17900 -	
	31	Adjusting	G23		18452 -		552 -
	31	Closing	G24	45745 -		45193 -	
	31	Closing	G24		46197		1004 -
	31	Closing	G24	1004 -			-0-

Sales Account No. 411

Date		Item	P.R.	Dr.	Cr.	Balance Dr.	Balance Cr.
19X1 Dec.	31	Balance	✓				45018 -
	31	Closing	G24	45018 -			-0-

Sales Returns and Allowances Account No. 412

Date		Item	P.R.	Dr.	Cr.	Balance Dr.	Balance Cr.
19X1 Dec.	31	Balance	✓			1229 -	
	31	Closing	G24		1229 -	-0-	

Sales Discounts Account No. 413

Date		Item	P.R.	Dr.	Cr.	Balance Dr.	Balance Cr.
19X1 Dec.	31	Balance	✓			220 -	
	31	Closing	G24		220 -	-0-	

Purchases Account No. 511

Date		Item	P.R.	Dr.	Cr.	Balance Dr.	Balance Cr.
19X1 Dec.	31	Balance	✓			24507 -	
	31	Closing	G24		24507 -	-0-	

illustration 11-11 (continued)

Purchases Returns and Allowances — Account No. 512

Date		Item	P.R.	Dr.	Cr.	Balance Dr.	Balance Cr.
19X1 Dec.	31	Balance	✓				865 –
	31	Closing	G24	865 –			–0–

Purchases Discounts — Account No. 513

Date		Item	P.R.	Dr.	Cr.	Balance Dr.	Balance Cr.
19X1 Dec.	31	Balance	✓				314 –
	31	Closing	G24	314 –			–0–

Advertising Expense — Account No. 611

Date		Item	P.R.	Dr.	Cr.	Balance Dr.	Balance Cr.
19X1 Dec.	31	Balance	✓			812 –	
	31	Closing	G24		812 –	–0–	

Delivery Expense — Account No. 612

Date		Item	P.R.	Dr.	Cr.	Balance Dr.	Balance Cr.
19X1 Dec.	31	Balance	✓			641 –	
	31	Closing	G24		641 –	–0–	

License Expense — Account No. 613

Date		Item	P.R.	Dr.	Cr.	Balance Dr.	Balance Cr.
19X1 Dec.	31	Balance	✓			40 –	
	31	Closing	G24		40 –	–0–	

Payroll Taxes Expense - General — Account No. 614

Date		Item	P.R.	Dr.	Cr.	Balance Dr.	Balance Cr.
19X1 Dec.	31	Balance	✓			242 –	
	31	Closing	G24		242 –	–0–	

Payroll Taxes Expense—Selling — Account No. 615

Date		Item	P.R.	Dr.	Cr.	Balance Dr.	Balance Cr.
19X1 Dec.	31	Balance	✓			968 —	
	31	Closing	G24		968 —	—0—	

Office Salary Expense — Account No. 616

Date		Item	P.R.	Dr.	Cr.	Balance Dr.	Balance Cr.
19X1 Dec.	31	Balance	✓			2500 —	
	31	Closing	G24		2500 —	—0—	

Sales Salary Expense — Account No. 617

Date		Item	P.R.	Dr.	Cr.	Balance Dr.	Balance Cr.
19X1 Dec.	31	Balance	✓			10000 —	
	31	Adjusting	G23	320 —		10320 —	
	31	Closing	G24		10320 —	—0—	

Subscription Expense — Account No. 618

Date		Item	P.R.	Dr.	Cr.	Balance Dr.	Balance Cr.
19X1 Dec.	31	Balance	✓			60 —	
	31	Closing	G24		60 —	—0—	

Telephone Expense — Account No. 619

Date		Item	P.R.	Dr.	Cr.	Balance Dr.	Balance Cr.
19X1 Dec.	31	Balance	✓			632 —	
	31	Closing	G24		632 —	—0—	

Utilities Expense — Account No. 620

Date		Item	P.R.	Dr.	Cr.	Balance Dr.	Balance Cr.
19X1 Dec.	31	Balance	✓			1491 —	
	31	Closing	G24		1491 —	—0—	

illustration 11-11 (continued)

Store Supplies Expense — Account No. 621

Date		Item	P.R.	Dr.	Cr.	Balance Dr.	Balance Cr.
19x1 Dec.	31	Adjusting	G23	143 -		143 -	
	31	Closing	G24		143 -	-0-	

Insurance Expense — Account No. 622

Date		Item	P.R.	Dr.	Cr.	Balance Dr.	Balance Cr.
19x1 Dec.	31	Adjusting	G23	290 -		290 -	
	31	Closing	G24		290 -	-0-	

Depreciation Expense, Store Equipment — Account No. 623

Date		Item	P.R.	Dr.	Cr.	Balance Dr.	Balance Cr.
19x1 Dec.	31	Adjusting	G23	450 -		450 -	
	31	Closing	G24		450 -	-0-	

Depreciation Expense, Office Equipment — Account No. 624

Date		Item	P.R.	Dr.	Cr.	Balance Dr.	Balance Cr.
19x1 Dec.	31	Adjusting	G23	100 -		100 -	
	31	Closing	G24		100 -	-0-	

Depreciation Expense, Building — Account No. 625

Date		Item	P.R.	Dr.	Cr.	Balance Dr.	Balance Cr.
19x1 Dec.	31	Adjusting	G23	1100 -		1100 -	
	31	Closing	G24		1100 -	-0-	

Now you are ready to prepare the post-closing trial balance. The amount can be taken either from the balance sheet columns of the work sheet (except for capital and drawing) or directly from the ledger. Since the ledger is shown in Illustration 11-11, let's use it for this purpose. By transferring the balances to the statement, we arrive at Illustration 11-12.

illustration 11-12
post-closing trial balance.

Brooks' Readywear
Post-Closing Trial Balance
December 31, 19X1

Account	Debit	Credit
Cash	2119 -	
Accounts Receivable	759 -	
Merchandise Inventory	18452 -	
Store Supplies	73 -	
Prepaid Insurance	350 -	
Store Equipment	9460 -	
Accumulated Depreciation, Store Equipment		3798 -
Office Equipment	4000 -	
Accumulated Depreciation, Office Equipment		1100 -
Building	116000 -	
Accumulated Depreciation, Building		68100 -
Accounts Payable		1721 -
Salaries Payable		320 -
Notes Payable		500 -
Mortgage Payable		28610 -
Mary Brooks, Capital		47064 -
	151213 -	151213 -

If you would rather use the work sheet to make the post-closing trial balance, simply list all the accounts as they appear on the work sheet in the Balance Sheet columns. Remember to pick up those accounts at the bottom of the column that were created by adjusting entries (such as *Salaries Payable* for Brooks' Readywear). Also keep in mind that the capital amount must be found by calculating the change. To illustrate by using the Brooks' Readywear work sheet, note that the ending balance is shown as \$58,710. To find the amount for the post-closing trial balance, you must subtract the amount withdrawn (\$12,650) and add the net income (\$1,004). This means that the calculated balance on December 31, 19X1 is \$47,064.

Balance as shown on work sheet	\$58,710
Less: Withdrawals	(12,650)
	\$46,060
Add: Net Income	1,004
Balance as shown on post-closing trial balance	\$47,064

If a loss had been experienced, then the loss would have been subtracted from the \$46,064 in the example above.

If the two numbers on the post-closing trial balance do not agree, use the same approach to find the error that you use for a trial balance:

1. See whether the difference can be divided equally by 9. If so, look for a transposition or a slide.

2. Divide the difference by 2 and look for that amount. Often a number is carried from the work sheet, or the ledger is listed in the wrong column. This makes the mistake twice the amount incorrectly listed.
3. Read the column. If you use a manual approach, read each column in the opposite direction from that used the first time. If you use an adding machine, compare the tape with the statement amounts.

Students today very often add with a calculator. Unless your calculator has a tape (and most don't), find yourself a ten-key adding machine with a tape. If that is impossible, go back to a system that accountants used for years—add the columns in your head. If these steps do not uncover the mistake, then you will have to check every step in reverse until the mistake is discovered, and that can be a long process.

Reversing entries

The idea that we talked about in Chapter 4 should be expanded here. In Chapter 4 we talked about handling reversing accruals for a service-type operation. The procedure for a merchandising concern is the same, so you should not have any difficulty with this section if you understood the earlier presentation.

In Chapter 10, we discussed reversing entries as they relate to deferrals. Now we need to review accruals so that you will feel comfortable in dealing with both deferrals and accruals. When debt is built up (either by a customer who owes the firm money or by the firm as it owes money to a creditor) and the debt remains unpaid at the end of the fiscal period, the question of whether an accrual is involved must be considered. An accrual is a building-up process, much like a conveyor belt continually feeding a pile of sand. Occasionally, a front-end loader will scoop up a load and take it away from this pile. This is the effect that a payment has upon an accrual. Recall the illustration in Chapter 4 in which the firm paid the employees every two weeks at the end of the second week. If August began on Sunday, then we would make the first payment (assuming the firm was closed on Saturdays and Sundays) on August 13. The second payment would be made on August 27, leaving Monday and Tuesday, August 30 and 31, built up but not paid at the end of the fiscal period (assuming it ends on August 31). This building-up process is an accrual.

Other items that fall into this category are taxes, interest, and rent. You might wonder if *Accounts Payable* and *Accounts Receivable* are accruals. The answer is "No," since there is not the continual building up of debt or receivable that is needed to be an accrual. To illustrate why this isn't an accrual, let's make a graphic comparison. Assume that $150 of merchandise is sold to Art Wilson on June 3 and he pays us $50 on July 1. He buys $200 more merchandise on account on August 19; finally, he pays $300. Now, examine Illustration 11-13 and note how *Rent Receivable* grows steadily until the amount due is received.

illustration 11-13 accrual versus nonaccrual comparison.

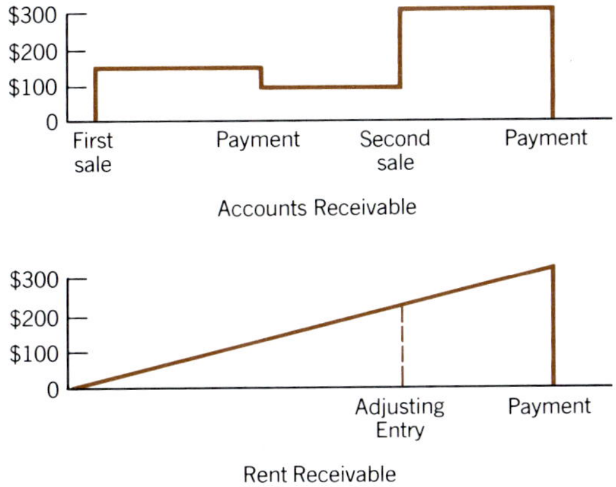

The purpose of a reversing entry to deal with accruals is simply to present the same financial picture as that shown before the adjusting and closing entries were made (and after the financial statements have been prepared). If we do so we won't have to look back to see what was done in the past. You can make the same entry that you would have made if the fiscal period had not ended and the books had not been closed. To illustrate, in the Brooks' Readywear example, the only accrual that appears is *Salaries Payable* for $320. If a reversing entry had not been made, then the following entry would have been necessary when salaries were paid on January 3, 19X2.

GENERAL JOURNAL — Page 25

Date		Description	P.R.	Dr.	Cr.
19X2					
Jan.	3	Salaries Payable		320 –	
		Office Salary Expense		20 –	
		Sales Salary Expense		60 –	
		Cash			400 –

If you make a reversing entry (which, you should recall, is nothing more than the adjusting entry reversed), you will have no need to look back to check the adjusting entry. All you have to know is that on January 3 a salary payment of $400 is being made. Continuing with the Brooks' Readywear illustration, note the reversing entry:

GENERAL JOURNAL — Page 25

Date		Description	P.R.	Dr.	Cr.
		Reversing Entry			
19X2 Jan.	1	Salaries Payable		320 –	
		Sales Salary Expense			320 –

And the payment:

GENERAL JOURNAL — Page 25

Date		Description	P.R.	Dr.	Cr.
19X2 Jan.	3	Sales Salary Expense		380 –	
		Office Salary Expense		20 –	
		Cash			400 –

By setting up accounts, the reversing process can be shown as it applies to *Office Salary Expense* and *Sales Salary Expense*.

Office Salary Expense — Account No. 616

Date		Item	P.R.	Dr.	Cr.	Balance Dr.	Balance Cr.
19X1 Dec.	31	Balance	✓			2500 –	
	31	Closing	G24		2500 –	–0–	

Sales Salary Expense — Account No. 617

Date		Item	P.R.	Dr.	Cr.	Balance Dr.	Balance Cr.
19X1 Dec.	31	Balance	✓			10000 –	
	31	Adjusting	G23	320 –		10320 –	
	31	Closing	G24		10320 –	–0–	
19X2 Jan.	1	Reversing	G25		320 –		320 –
	3		G25	380 –		60 –	

Salaries Payable — Account No. 212

Date		Item	P.R.	Dr.	Cr.	Balance Dr.	Balance Cr.
19X1 Dec.	31	Adjusting	G23		320 –		320 –
19X2 Jan.	3	Reversing	G24	320 –			–0–

If a receivable were involved, the same procedure would be followed for accrual. To illustrate, assume that the firm sold merchandise by accepting a note from a customer. On December 31, $15 of interest has accrued, but it is not receivable until January 20. The adjusting entry on December 31, 19X1, would be:

GENERAL JOURNAL — Page 19

Date		Description	P.R.	Dr.	Cr.
19X1 Dec.	31	Interest Receivable		15 –	
		Interest Revenue			15 –

The asset, *Interest Receivable,* is shown on the balance sheet, while the revenue account, *Interest Revenue,* is shown as other income on the income statement. When the closing entry is made, the nominal account is closed out. Next, on January 1, 19X2, the following reversing entry is made:

GENERAL JOURNAL — Page 20

Date		Description	P.R.	Dr.	Cr.
19X2 Jan.	1	Interest Revenue		15 –	
		Interest Receivable			15 –

When the interest is received, the following entry will be recorded:

GENERAL JOURNAL — Page 18

Date		Description	P.R.	Dr.	Cr.
19X2 Jan.	20	Cash		60 –	
		Interest Revenue			60 –

By examining the following accounts, you can see that the entries above do show the proper information in the books.

Interest Receivable — Account No. 114

Date		Item	P.R.	Dr.	Cr.	Balance Dr.	Balance Cr.
19X1 Dec.	31	Adjusting	G 19	15 –		15 –	
19X2 Jan.	1	Reversing	G 20		15 –	–0–	

Interest Revenue — Account No. 711

Date		Item	P.R.	Dr.	Cr.	Balance Dr.	Balance Cr.
19X1 Dec.	31	Adjusting	G 19		15 –		15 –
	31	Closing	G 19	15 –			–0–
19X2 Jan.	2	Reversing	G 20	15 –		15 –	
	20		CR 31		60 –		45 –

The result is that interest revenue of $45 is shown for 19X2. Since $45 of the $60 was earned in 19X2, this amount should be the balance of *Interest Revenue.* The other $15 was earned in 19X1 and was shown as revenue in that year. Look at the *Interest Revenue* account again, and you will see that making the reversing entry brought the accounts into agreement with the facts.

review exercises

9. The post-closing trial balance of Bohannon Furs for December 31, 19X1, has a debit total of $14,690 and credit total of $14,150. If you were helping the bookkeeper to find the error in a hurry, what suggestions would you make?

10. On November 30, 19X1, the last day of the fiscal year, Harley's Appliances owes its workers $350 in wages (*Note:* not salaries). On that date, the expense account has a debit balance of $14,160. Make the required (a) adjusting entry, (b) closing entry, and, if necessary, the (c) reversing entry on December 1.

chapter highlights

After studying this chapter, you should be able to:

- Prepare an income statement for a merchandising business.
- Use the work sheet to prepare a capital statement.
- Prepare a classified balance sheet.
- Prepare closing entries.
- Construct a post-closing trial balance.
- Prepare appropriate reversing entries.

check figures for review exercises

1. Cost of goods sold, $103,837 (do not include *Delivery Expense*).

2. Selling expenses—a, g, i, j; General expenses—b, h; Other expenses—e; Needs allocating—c, d, f

3. Net income, $2,606

4. a—PE; b—CS; c—CL; d—CS; e—PE; f—CA; g—CL; h—CS; i—CA; j—IA; k—CA

5. Ending capital balance, $16,742.96

6. Total assets, $95,037. *Land* should be shown as other assets.

7. b, c, f, and g

8. Dr. *Income Summary,* $1,303.36 and Cr. *Krista Sames, Capital,* $1,303.36

9. Since the difference is exactly divisible by 9, look for a transposition or a slide. Also check out any account that has a balance of $270 ($540

÷ 2), because the amount could be listed in the wrong column. Finally, look for $540 since it could have been listed twice or omitted.

10. (a) Dr. *Wages Expense* and Cr. *Wages Payable,* $350
(b) Dr. *Income Summary* and Cr. *Wages Expense* for $14,510
(c) Reverse entry (a)

key terms

The following key terms are discussed in Chapter 11 and defined in the Glossary at the end of the book.

current assets
current liabilities
income from primary operations
intangible assets
investments
long-term liabilities
loss from primary operations
operating expense
other expense
other income
plant and equipment assets

demonstration problem

Examination of the income statement and balance sheet columns of the work sheet of the Conway Company revealed the following accounts and amounts. Unless otherwise indicated, all accounts have normal balances.

Cash	$ 4,000
Accounts Receivable	9,000
Merchandise Inventory	12,000
Office Equipment	15,000
Accumulated Depreciation, Office Equipment	4,000
Accounts Payable	7,000
Luther Conway, Drawing	12,000
Luther Conway, Capital	16,800
Sales	81,000
Sales Discounts	1,500
Purchases	29,000
Purchases Discounts	1,200
Advertising Expense	900
Salaries Expense	16,000
Rent Expense	6,000
Utilities Expense	1,300
Supplies Expense	800
Depreciation Expense, Office Equipment	600
Dividend Revenue	500
Interest Expense	400
Income Summary (from inventory adjustment)	2,000 (Dr)

Additional data: Beginning *Merchandise Inventory*, $14,000.

Instructions From the information above prepare:

(a) closing entries in general journal form.

(b) an income statement.

(c) a balance sheet.

(d) a capital statement.

demonstration problem solution

(a)

GENERAL JOURNAL

		Closing Entries		
19X1				
Dec.	31	Sales	81,000	
		Purchases Discounts	1,200	
		Dividend Revenue	500	
		Income Summary		82,700
	31	Income Summary	56,500	
		Sales Discounts		1,500
		Purchases		29,000
		Advertising Expense		900
		Salaries Expense		16,000
		Rent Expense		6,000
		Utilities Expense		1,300
		Supplies Expense		800
		Depreciation Expense, Office Equipment		600
		Interest Expense		400
	31	Income Summary	24,200	
		Luther Conway, Capital		24,200
		(Note that the $24,200 includes the $2,000 difference between beginning and ending inventory as shown in the *Income Summary* account.)		
	31	Luther Conway, Capital	12,000	
		Luther Conway, Drawing		12,000

Income Summary 313

				Balances	
		Dr.	Cr.	Dr.	Cr.
Dec. 31	Adjusting	14,000		14,000	
31	Adjusting		12,000	2,000	
31	Closing		82,700		80,700
31	Closing	56,500			24,200
31	Closing	24,200			0

(b)

Conway Company
Income Statement
For Period Ending December 31, 19X1

Revenue:			
Sales			$81,000
Less: Sales Discounts			1,500
Net Sales			$79,500
Cost of Goods Sold:			
Merchandise Inventory, Jan. 1		$14,000	
Purchases	$29,000		
Less: Purchases Discounts	1,200		
Net Purchases		27,800	
Goods Available for Sale		$41,800	
Less: Merchandise Inventory, Dec. 31		12,000	
Cost of Goods Sold			29,800
Gross Profit			$49,700
Operating Expenses:			
Advertising Expense		$ 900	
Salaries Expense		16,000	
Rent Expense		6,000	
Utilities Expense		1,300	
Supplies Expense		800	
Depreciation Expense, Office Equipment		600	
Total Operating Expenses			25,600
Net Operating Income			$24,100
Other Income and Expense:			
Dividend Revenue		$ 500	
Interest Expense		400	
Net Other Income and Expense			100
Net Income			$24,200

(c)

Conway Company
Balance Sheet
December 31, 19X1

Assets

Current Assets:		
Cash	$ 4,000	
Accounts Receivable	9,000	
Merchandise Inventory	12,000	
Total Current Assets		$25,000
Plant and Equipment:		
Office Equipment	$15,000	
Less: Accumulated Depreciation, Office Equipment	4,000	
Total Plant and Equipment		11,000
Total Assets		$36,000

Liabilities and Owner's Equity

Current Liabilities:	
Accounts Payable	$ 7,000
Luther Conway, Capital	29,000
Total Liabilities and Owner's Equity	$36,000

(d)

Conway Company
Capital Statement
For Period Ending December 31, 19X1

Luther Conway, Capital, Jan. 1, 19X1		$16,800
Add: Net Income	$24,200	
Less: Withdrawals	12,000	
Net Increase to Capital		12,200
Luther Conway, Capital, Dec. 31, 19X1		$29,000

questions

1. What is the difference between a cost account and an expense account?
2. Why is it necessary to separate "other expenses" from "operating expenses"?
3. If the warehouse is kept at 50 degrees in the winter, while the office area and showroom are kept at 68 degrees, would square footage be a good basis for allocating the heat bill? Why?
4. What is the purpose of the capital statement?
5. Name one account that fits into each of the following categories: current assets, plant and equipment assets, intangible assets, investments, other assets, current liabilities, and long-term liabilities.
6. What is the effect of the following items on the owner's final capital balance? (a) net loss; (b) an investment by the owner of equipment in the business; (c) an investment by the owner of cash in the business; (d) a net income; (e) a withdrawal from the business.
7. What is the purpose of closing entries? How do closing entries for a merchandising firm differ from those for a service-type firm?
8. What is another name for temporary accounts that must be closed?
9. Are there any nominal accounts on the capital statement and balance sheet? If so, list them.
10. What is another name for balance sheet accounts that are not closed out? Are any of these accounts on the income statement? If so, list them.
11. If the balance sheet debit column is smaller than the balance sheet credit column in the work sheet, does the firm have a net income or a net loss?
12. What is the purpose of a post-closing trial balance? What classification of accounts are found on this statement?

13. How would you describe an accrual to someone who has no understanding of accounting?
14. In dealing with accruals, are reversing entries necessary, or are they just a convenient tool for accountants?
15. If *Salaries Payable* is an accrual, why isn't *Accounts Payable* one also?
16. If *Interest Expense* ended with a debit balance of $10 after the adjusting entry, where would the balance in this account be after the reversing entry?

exercises

1. From the accounts listed below, prepare the revenue and cost of goods sold section of an income statement for Willis Supply:

Sales	$114,550
Sales Returns and Allowances	2,970
Sales Discounts	1,888
Merchandise Inventory, Jan. 1	26,502
Merchandise Inventory, Dec. 31	29,663
Purchases	60,389
Purchases Discounts	1,012
Freight-In	950
Delivery Expense	2,600

2. Prepare the operating expense section of an income statement from the expenses listed below:

Rent (25% office; 75% showroom)	$6,600
Office Supplies Expense	490
Depreciation Expense, Store Equipment	1,458
Depreciation Expense, Office Equipment	640
Interest Revenue	60
Utilities (20% office; 80% showroom)	1,800
Dividend Revenue	140
Store Supplies Expense	290
Delivery Truck Expense	600
Advertising Expense	540
Interest Expense	75

3. Last year's balance sheet for Etter's Computer Sales showed an ending capital balance of $29,654. During the current year, the firm made a net income of $16,955 and Etter withdrew $18,000 from the business. What would her ending capital balance be for the current year?
4. James Daisy had a beginning capital balance of $49,110. During 19X1 he invested $6,000 in the business and made no withdrawals. The proprietorship had a net loss of $13,228. Prepare a capital statement for Daisy Farms for the year ending December 31.

5. Prepare the assets portion of a balance sheet by properly classifying the following accounts:

Cash	$ 8,960.41
Accounts Receivable	6,422.80
Merchandise Inventory	25,669.20
Interest Receivable	215.00
Accumulated Depreciation, Equipment	5,600.00
Store Supplies	120.15
Prepaid Rent	600.00
Copyright	2,200.00
Patent	1,600.00
Equipment	24,650.00

6. Indicate which of the following accounts must be closed and whether a debit or credit would be necessary to close that account:

(a) *Rent Expense*

(b) *Accounts Receivable*

(c) *Accumulated Depreciation, Building*

(d) *Notes Payable*

(e) *Rent Revenue*

(f) *Income Summary (assume a net loss)*

(g) *Hal Watts, Drawing*

(h) *Purchases*

(i) *Freight-In*

(j) *Sales Returns and Allowances*

(k) *Purchases Discounts*

(l) *Prepaid Insurance*

(m) *Salaries Payable*

(n) *Sales*

7. After adjusting *Merchandise Inventory* to remove the beginning inventory and inserting the ending inventory, *Income Summary* has a credit balance of $1,874. If the firm has a net income for the year of $7,094 and the owner has withdrawn $8,600, what entry is necessary to close *Income Summary* to *Ann Franklin, Capital?*

8. Each week Coffin Dress Shop pays its employees a total salary of $600. For the year, the firm had paid out salaries of $30,600 going into the final week. During the final week, a liability of $200 for salaries was accrued by December 31. On January 3 the employees are paid. Make the adjusting, closing, reversing, and payment entries in general journal form.

problems

1. COMPETENCY TESTED The ability to prepare an income statement and make closing entries.

These are some of the accounts from the adjusted trial balance of Double Discount Company as of December 31, 19X1:

Cash	$ 3,000
Accounts Receivable	8,000
Merchandise Inventory	13,000
Accounts Payable	6,000
John Doaks, Drawing	13,000
John Doaks, Capital	14,000
Sales	72,000
Sales Discounts	1,000
Purchases	27,000
Purchases Returns and Allowances	1,500
Freight-In	500
Advertising Expense	800
Store Salaries Expense	10,000
Office Salaries Expense	8,000
Rent Expense (50% is Selling Expense)	6,000
Utilities Expense (33 ⅓% is related to selling)	1,200
Office Supplies Expense	700
Store Supplies Expense	600
Depreciation Expense, Store Equipment	400
Depreciation Expense, Office Equipment	500
Dividend Revenue	400
Interest Expense	200

Additional data:
Beginning merchandise inventory, $10,000.

Instructions From the list of accounts shown above, (a) prepare an income statement for the year and (b) make the closing entries. All accounts have normal balances. Since some of the balance sheet accounts are shown, you will need to select the nominal accounts in preparing the income statement.

2. COMPETENCY TESTED Skill in preparing an income statement and closing entries.

A partial list of ledger accounts, including all income statement accounts and some balance sheet accounts, is shown below for the Scott Company for 19X1. All accounts have normal balances and have been adjusted to the correct balances.

Cash	$ 3,250
Accounts Receivable	7,725
Merchandise Inventory	11,168
Accounts Payable	8,112
James Scott, Drawing	6,200
James Scott, Capital	17,120
Sales	91,000
Sales Returns and Allowances	1,100
Sales Discounts	1,300
Purchases	42,500
Purchases Discounts	1,600
Advertising Expense	1,200
Store Salaries Expense	11,000
Office Salaries Expense	9,500
Rent Expense (40% Selling Expense)	8,000
Utilities Expense (30% Selling Expense)	1,300
Depreciation Expense (20% Selling Expense)	2,000
Interest Expense	800

Additional data: Beginning merchandise inventory, $12,888.

Instructions (a) Select the appropriate accounts and prepare an income statement for the year ending on December 31, 19X1; then (b) prepare the required closing entries.

3. COMPETENCY TESTED Skill in preparing adjusting and reversing entries.

The Hanshake Company had the following transaction entries during the year 19X1.

Date	Account	Debit	Credit
May 1	Prepaid Insurance	2,400	
	Cash		2,400
	Paid insurance for 12 months' coverage.		
June 1	Rent Expense	3,600	
	Cash		3,600
	Paid rent for 12 months in advance.		
July 1	Cash	5,000	
	Rental Revenue—Computer Time		5,000
	Rent received in advance to be allocated evenly over the next 10 months.		

Instructions

(a) Prepare the appropriate adjusting entries at December 31, the end of the accounting period.

(b) Journalize any required reversing entries.

(c) What type of accounts are *Prepaid Rent* and *Unearned Rental Revenue—Computer Time?*

4. COMPETENCY TESTED The ability to prepare a capital statement.

The Jack Lewis Company has the following partial financial information available for the year 19X1.

Net sales	$99,000
Cost of goods sold	55,000
Total operating expenses	18,000
Withdrawals of cash by owner	11,000
Beginning capital balance	27,000

Instructions

(a) Compute net income or loss for 19X1 and prepare a capital statement as of December 31, 19X1.

(b) Using the same data as in (a) except an additional investment by the owner of $12,000 and an operating loss of $7,000 rather than net income, prepare a capital statement for 19X1.

5. COMPETENCY TESTED The ability to prepare a capital statement.

The John Ellis Company has the following partial data available for the year 19X1.

Net sales	$103,000
Cost of goods sold	78,000
Total operating expenses	31,000
Withdrawals of cash by owner	8,000
Beginning capital balance	19,500

Instructions

(a) Compute net income or net loss for 19X1 and prepare a capital statement.

(b) Using the same data as in (a) except an additional cash investment of $9,000 by the owner and a net income of $12,500 rather than a net loss, prepare a capital statement for 19X1.

6. COMPETENCY TESTED The ability to prepare a balance sheet and capital statement.

A complete list of balance sheet accounts for the Hector Company for 19X1 after all adjustments have been made appears below:

	Dr.	Cr.
Cash	$11,240	
Accounts Receivable	13,560	
Merchandise Inventory	19,300	
Store Supplies	3,400	
Equipment	26,000	
Accumulated Depreciation, Equipment		$18,800
Accounts Payable		11,250
Salaries Payable		1,200
Notes Payable		9,000
Hector Manning, Capital		33,250

Nominal accounts have been closed through *Income Summary* to capital with a net income of $22,000. The drawing account balance of $9,000 was closed directly to capital.

Instructions Prepare (a) a balance sheet and (b) a capital statement assuming the owner invested $5,000 in cash during the year.

7. **COMPETENCY TESTED** The ability to prepare a balance sheet and capital statement.

A complete list of balance sheet accounts for the Bobby Perkins Company for 19X1, after all adjustments have been made, appears below:

	Dr.	Cr.
Cash	$13,500	
Accounts Receivable	16,200	
Merchandise Inventory	19,400	
Store Supplies	4,800	
Prepaid Insurance	3,600	
Equipment	30,000	
Accumulated Depreciation, Equipment		$17,700
Accounts Payable		18,500
Salaries Payable		1,600
Notes Payable (short-term)		23,000
Bobby Perkins, Capital		26,700
	$87,500	$87,500

Nominal accounts have been closed through *Income Summary* to capital with a net income of $19,000. The drawing account balance of $11,000 was closed directly to capital.

Instructions

(a) Prepare a balance sheet.

(b) Prepare a capital statement assuming the owner invested $7,000 in cash during the year.

8. COMPETENCY TESTED The ability to prepare a balance sheet, income statement, capital statement, and closing entries.

The Income Statement and Balance Sheet columns of a work sheet for the Stanley Hendrix Company on December 31, 19X1, are given below.

Account Titles	Income Statement Dr.	Income Statement Cr.	Balance Sheet Dr.	Balance Sheet Cr.
Cash			6,100	
Accounts Receivable			13,300	
Merchandise Inventory			16,400	
Store Supplies			2,800	
Store Equipment			10,500	
Accumulated Depreciation, Store Equipment				6,300
Accounts Payable				5,000
Notes Payable (short-term)				4,000
Stanley Hendrix, Drawing			10,000	
Stanley Hendrix, Capital				16,300
Sales		87,900		
Sales Discounts	2,100			
Purchases	39,000			
Purchases Returns and Allowances		1,100		
Freight-In	1,500			
Advertising Expense	4,000			
License Expense	1,800			
Salaries Expense	12,000			
Telephone Expense	600			
Utilities Expense	1,300			
Income Summary	15,600	16,400		
	77,900	105,400	59,100	31,600
Net Income	27,500			27,500
	105,400	105,400	59,100	59,100

Additional data:
Beginning inventory, $15,600.

Instructions

(a) Prepare an income statement (do not divide operating expense into selling and general).

(b) Prepare a capital statement.

(c) Prepare a balance sheet.

(d) Journalize the closing entries.

9. COMPETENCY TESTED The ability to prepare an income statement, balance sheet, capital statement, and closing entries.

The Income Statement and Balance Sheet columns of a work sheet for the Hank Spencer Company, at December 31, 19X1, are shown below:

Account Titles	Income Statement Dr.	Income Statement Cr.	Balance Sheet Dr.	Balance Sheet Cr.
Cash			4,900	
Accounts Receivable			12,200	
Merchandise Inventory			15,700	
Store Supplies			2,800	
Prepaid Rent			1,800	
Office Equipment			15,300	
Accumulated Depreciation, Office Equipment				10,100
Accounts Payable				6,000
Notes Payable (short-term)				7,000
Hank Spencer, Drawing			9,000	
Hank Spencer, Capital				20,400
Sales		76,800		
Sales Discounts	1,500			
Purchases	37,400			
Purchases Discounts		900		
Advertising Expense	3,000			
Rent Expense	4,000			
Salaries Expense	11,000			
Utilities Expense	2,200			
Income Summary	16,100	15,700		
	75,200	93,400	61,700	43,500
Net Income	18,200			18,200
	93,400	93,400	61,700	61,700

Additional data:
Beginning inventory, $16,100.

Instructions

(a) Prepare an income statement without separating operating expense into selling and general expense.

(b) Prepare a capital statement.

(c) Prepare a balance sheet.

(d) Journalize the closing entries.

comprehensive problem From the completed work sheet for Reed Supply Company prepared for Chapter 10, complete the accounting cycle by performing the following tasks at the end of January:

6. Prepare the income statement, capital statement, and balance sheet. Note: To simplify the problem, do not divide operating expenses between selling and general.
7. Prepare the adjusting journal entries and post to the general ledger accounts.
8. Prepare the closing journal entries and post to the general ledger accounts.
9. Prepare a schedule of accounts receivable and a schedule of accounts payable.
10. Prepare a post-closing trial balance.

part three

ACCOUNTING FOR ASSETS AND LIABILITIES

chapter 12
BANKING ACTIVITIES

overall competency THE ABILITY TO PREPARE BANK DEPOSITS, RECONCILE THE BANK STATEMENT, AND RECORD CASH SHORTAGES AND OVERAGES

career objectives No single item catches the attention of business people more frequently than cash. It is the "lifeblood" that keeps the firm healthy. An adequate amount must be kept flowing through the firm to pay both employees and creditors and to cover other cash needs. The accountant must be able to help the company keep track of the firm's funds in an easy yet accurate manner. Since money bears no identification as to the owner, it is tempting to thieves. If properly followed, the procedures introduced in this chapter will help your employer know the firm's cash position.

Upon completing this chapter you should be able to:

- PREPARE THE DAILY BANK DEPOSIT SLIP BASED ON THE INTAKE OF CURRENCY, COINS, AND CHECKS.
- PREPARE A BANK RECONCILIATION.
- JOURNALIZE AND POST ENTRIES CONNECTED WITH THE BANK RECONCILIATION.
- SET UP A PETTY CASH FUND AND RECORD ENTRIES CONNECTED WITH REPLENISHING THE FUND.
- ACCOUNT FOR CASH SHORTAGES AND OVERAGES.

Because cash is such an important item to the firm, a good grasp of day-to-day cash control is critical. The more comfortable you become with procedures such as writing checks or making deposits, the more valuable you will become to the firm. One task that you will face every month is preparing the bank reconciliation and using your findings to make the necessary journal entries. You should find this chapter somewhat challenging but quite enjoyable, since it deals with an item you already understand something about—cash.

• task PREPARE THE DAILY BANK DEPOSIT SLIP BASED ON THE BASIS OF THE INTAKE OF CURRENCY, COINS, AND CHECKS

Initial preparation

On the surface, preparing a deposit slip seems to be a rather simple task, and it can be. There are some steps, however, that will help you if it becomes necessary to review a deposit. These steps will also make you popular with the bank clerks. Doing this task well is really a combination of organization and consideration.

Let's assume that we are dealing with a company that follows the cash controls we discussed in Chapter 7. You might want to refresh your memory by looking at Illustration 12-1. This diagram repeats Illustration 7-2 from the cash receipts discussion. In this diagram, three clerks are involved. The size of a firm has a lot to do with how many steps of protection the owner can build into the operation. If the owner makes the deposit, good control involves fewer people. In the illustration, note that the third clerk compares a copy of the deposit slip with the cash receipts report. This procedure reduces the temptation for someone to "borrow" from the cash receipts. Using the same person to count the cash receipts and also to make the bank deposit is unwise, for research has shown that even the stout-

illustration 12-1 control of cash.

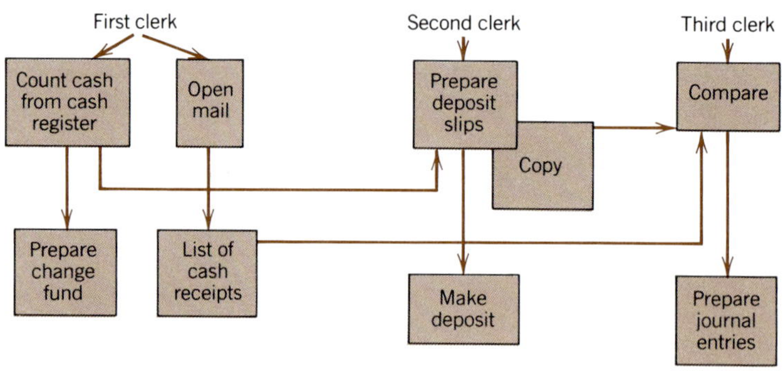

hearted can be tempted. Using good internal accounting controls, on the other hand, helps to detect unintentional as well as intentional errors and irregularities.

As we mentioned in Chapter 7, a designated member of the firm should make a *daily* deposit to reduce the potential loss from robbery. By doing so, the accounting clerk will find that locating an error is considerably easier since the daily cash receipts should match the deposit slip amount.

To illustrate a typical small firm's approach, assume that a business has one cash register. Each day $100 is taken out of the safe and placed in this cash register as a change fund. At the end of each day, $100 is returned to the safe as a change fund for the following business day. After the change fund has been removed, the change, currency, and checks are counted to see whether the amount matches cash sales for that particular day (as shown on the cash register's totals). Before going any further, we should define currency. In the general sense, **currency** includes paper money, government and bank notes, and coins. Banks, however, tend to think of currency as paper money only. This money is combined with payments received on account and other miscellaneous cash receipts to prepare a cash receipts report, which was discussed in Chapter 7.

Endorsements

When arranging the currency, if you want to make a friend at the bank in a hurry, arrange the money in denominations of descending order. Put all the twenties together (all turned the same way), then the tens, and so on. Next, stamp (or write) *for deposit only* on the back of each check. This is known as a **restrictive endorsement.** It allows the firm to which the check is made payable to deposit it in its account; probably more important, it means that the check cannot be cashed, which is a protection in case of robbery. You can see a restrictive endorsement in Illustration 12-2.

illustration 12-2 restrictive endorsement.

For Deposit Only
JAY SMITH WORLD TRAVEL
0135976

An exception to this rule occurs when a check written to someone else is used to pay a third party. To illustrate, assume that Joe Baker received a $10 check from Hattie Strong. Joe uses the check to buy a tool from Vinson's Hardware. Mr. Vinson accepts the check after Joe signs his name on the back. This procedure is known as a **blank endorsement** since it imposes no restrictions. Mr. Vinson can either cash the check or deposit it in his account. He then endorses it *For deposit only, VINSON'S HARDWARE,* and includes it with his daily deposit. This endorsement procedure is shown in Illustration 12-3. A **qualified endorsement,** a third type of endorsement shown in Illustration 12-4, usually includes the phrase "without recourse." Such an endorsement frees the endorser of future liability in case the maker of the check does not have sufficient funds to cover it. Obviously, the maker of the check would have to have a good credit rating for any business to accept such an endorsement.

illustration 12-3
blank endorsement changed to a restrictive endorsement.

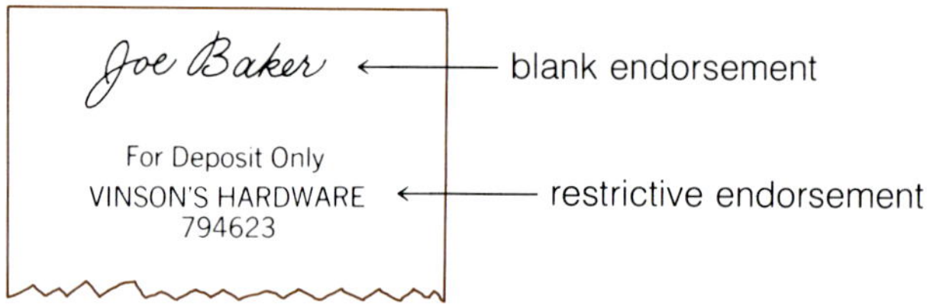

illustration 12-4
qualified endorsement.

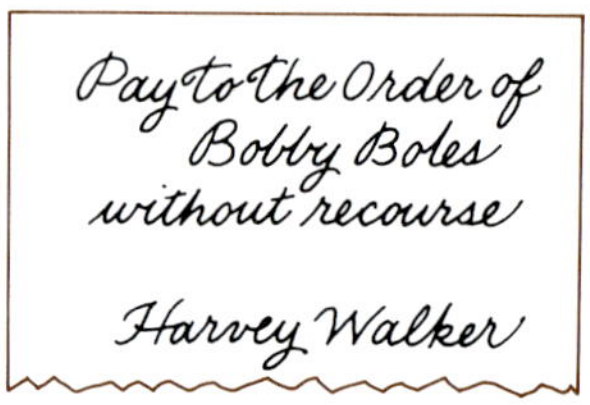

Other currency items

Hotels, travel agencies, campgrounds, and other businesses that deal with the traveling public may receive traveler's checks and foreign currency. *Traveler's checks* are usually purchased from a bank in denominations of \$10, \$20, \$50, and \$100 for an amount equal to the face of the checks plus a service fee. The buyer of the checks signs each check in the presence of an employee of the firm, usually the cashier. The check serial numbers are listed on a separate sheet so that in case of loss or theft, a claim can be made for checks that have not been spent. Upon using the check, the person buying merchandise or services should again sign the document in the designated place in the presence of the seller. The recipient should then place a restrictive endorsement on the back of the check and place it in the cash register.

On the deposit slip, traveler's checks are treated just like regular checks. *Foreign currency* can create some problems that are beyond the scope of this book; however, for the infrequent foreign check, simply take it to a bank and request that it be converted. The bank (after about a week) will send you a new check for the converted amount less the bank charge. To make a deposit, you then treat this check like any other.

In recent years, *food coupons* (or **food stamps**) have been provided by the Federal government to help needy people buy food. The program may be administered by the state or handled directly by the Federal agency. Food coupons come in \$1, \$5, or \$10 denominations. They can be used only for edible items, which can range from garden seed to rib-eye steaks. A specimen food coupon is shown in Illustration 12-5.

illustration 12-5
food coupon. (reprinted with permission of U.S. Department of Agriculture)

When food stamps are deposited, they must be accompanied by a **Food Stamp Redemption Certificate.** This form provided by the U.S. Department of Agriculture is shown in Illustration 12-6. A supply preprinted with the store's name and address is received about every three months. No other store can use this certificate. The accounting clerk completes the form in pencil, which allows for easy correction of errors. The food coupon takes on the same status as currency and checks in that it is valued at the face amount.

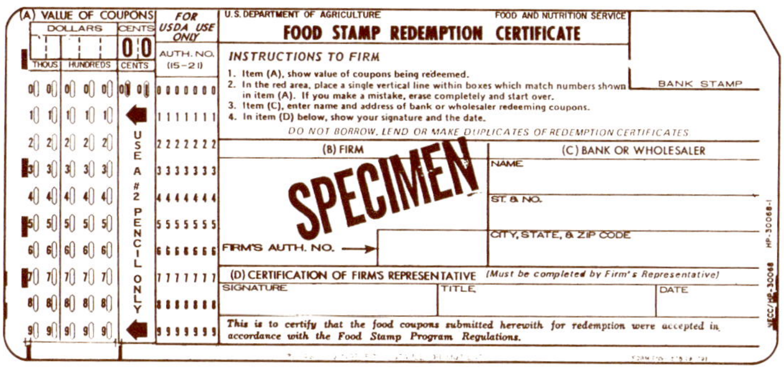
(A) VALUE OF COUPONS — DOLLARS — CENTS — THOUS — HUNDREDS — CENTS
FOR USDA USE ONLY — AUTH. NO. (15-21)
USE A #2 PENCIL ONLY
U.S. DEPARTMENT OF AGRICULTURE — FOOD AND NUTRITION SERVICE
FOOD STAMP REDEMPTION CERTIFICATE
INSTRUCTIONS TO FIRM
1. Item (A), show value of coupons being redeemed.
2. In the red area, place a single vertical line within boxes which match numbers shown in item (A). If you make a mistake, erase completely and start over.
3. Item (C), enter name and address of bank or wholesaler redeeming coupons.
4. In item (D) below, show your signature and the date.
BANK STAMP
DO NOT BORROW, LEND OR MAKE DUPLICATES OF REDEMPTION CERTIFICATES
(B) FIRM — (C) BANK OR WHOLESALER
NAME
ST. & NO.
CITY, STATE, & ZIP CODE
SPECIMEN
FIRM'S AUTH. NO.
(D) CERTIFICATION OF FIRM'S REPRESENTATIVE (Must be completed by Firm's Representative)
SIGNATURE — TITLE — DATE
This is to certify that the food coupons submitted herewith for redemption were accepted in accordance with the Food Stamp Program Regulations.

illustration 12-6
food stamp redemption certificate. (reprinted with permission of U.S. Department of Agriculture)

Preparing the deposit slip

Once all the currency, coins, and checks have been arranged and, when appropriate, endorsed, you will fill out the **deposit slip.** Most deposit slip books come with carbon paper that allows you to make at least two copies of each deposit—one for the bank and one for the firm. Currency and coins are usually listed first. Make certain that you are not including items that do not qualify as currency, such as money orders, traveler's checks, credit card receipt forms, or the boss's daughter's IOU (you may find some strange things in the cash register). You can see in Illustration 12-7 how the accounting clerk for Silky Trip Travel Agency would list currency of $475 and coins of $3.93.

If you have any traveler's checks and money orders to deposit, list them next. Silky received five $20 traveler's checks and one $75.63 money order.

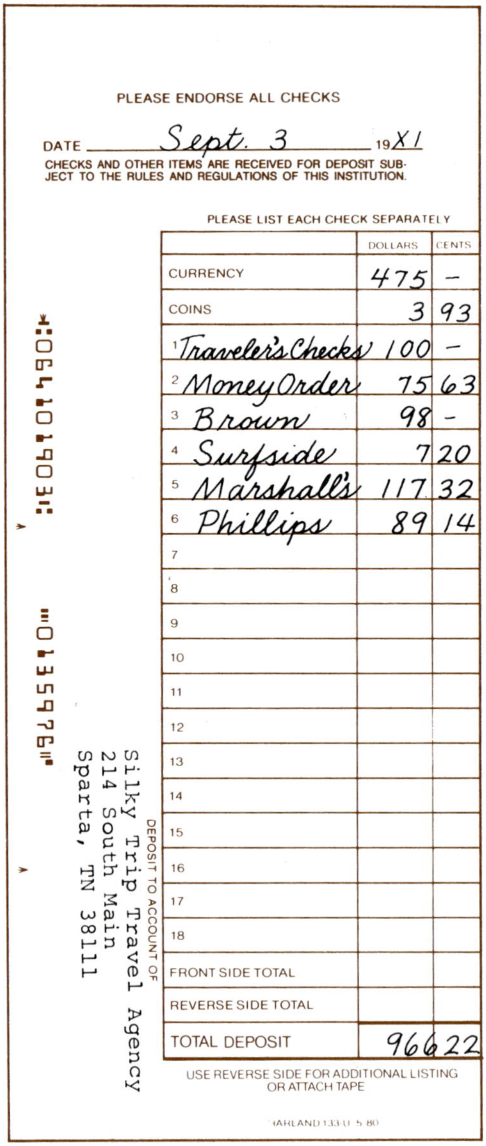

PLEASE ENDORSE ALL CHECKS

DATE Sept. 3 19X1

CHECKS AND OTHER ITEMS ARE RECEIVED FOR DEPOSIT SUBJECT TO THE RULES AND REGULATIONS OF THIS INSTITUTION.

PLEASE LIST EACH CHECK SEPARATELY

	DOLLARS	CENTS
CURRENCY	475	–
COINS	3	93
1 Traveler's Checks	100	–
2 Money Order	75	63
3 Brown	98	–
4 Surfside	7	20
5 Marshall's	117	32
6 Phillips	89	14
7		
8		
9		
10		
11		
12		
13		
14		
15		
16		
17		
18		
FRONT SIDE TOTAL		
REVERSE SIDE TOTAL		
TOTAL DEPOSIT	966	22

USE REVERSE SIDE FOR ADDITIONAL LISTING OR ATTACH TAPE

DEPOSIT TO ACCOUNT OF
Silky Trip Travel Agency
214 South Main
Sparta, TN 38111

⑆064101903⑆ ⑈0135976⑈

HARLAND 133-U 5 80

illustration 12-7 completed deposit slip. (courtesy of John H. Harland Company)

Notice in Illustration 12-7 that only one line was used for the traveler's checks. If you wish to note who gave you each traveler's check, you may do so, but the extra work is usually unnecessary.

Next, note that Silky Trip Travel's accounting clerk listed the checks received. To assist the bank cashier, checks should be listed in the order in which you have stacked them. Some easy label that fits into a small space should be used to identify each check. In Silky's case, an abbreviation of the client's name is used. For example, a commission check from Surfside Hotel for $7.20 is listed as *Surfside,* and Marshall's Institutional Wholesale

Corporation's check for $117.32 is simply *Marshall's* on the deposit slip. Keep in mind that this deposit slip is for your firm as much as it is for the bank, so if you want to show categories, such as on account, tours, or whatever, go ahead and do it unless the bank has a definite deposit slip format that it insists you follow. Some banks do insist that you list checks by the **American Bankers Association (ABA) number.** The location of this number and a deposit slip prepared using ABA numbers are shown in Illustration 12-8.

illustration 12-8
A. B. A. numbers. (courtesy of John H. Harland Company)

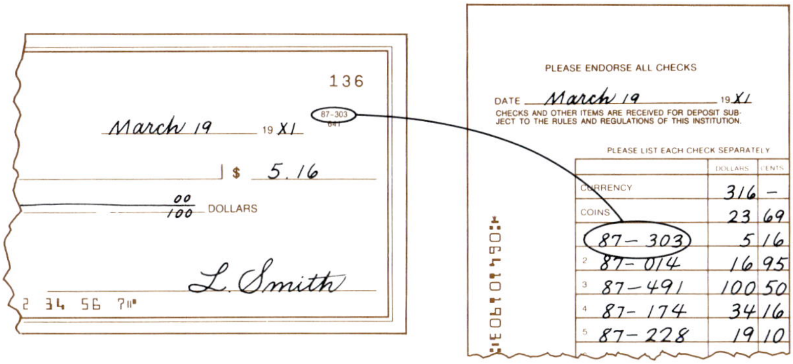

The total you derive should be the same amount as that counted by the person who emptied the cash register. Take both copies, the money, and your adding machine tape (not required) to the bank. If a night deposit is made, the bank will return by mail a copy of the deposit that shows a bank stamp acknowledging receipt of the deposit and verifying the currency and coins. If you deal with the cashier directly, you might ask that the bank stamp not be placed across your writing. Smile politely, of course, when you make this request.

Credit card sales

In Chapter 7 we discussed the procedure to follow when a credit card sale is made. VISA and MasterCard sales drafts are treated like cash. Since *Cash* is debited for the sales drafts, the funds must be placed in the bank. To do this, a special deposit is prepared. First, all of the sales drafts for each type of bank card are grouped together. To illustrate the purchase, assume that on March 13 the accounting clerk for Jayson's finds 20 credit card sales drafts and two credit slips in the receipts. Twelve of the drafts, totaling $487.50 are on a VISA card and eight drafts totaling $658.42 are on a MasterCard credit card. The two credit slips totaling $16 are both on a VISA card. This information is entered on a **Merchant Deposit Summary** similar to the one shown in Illustration 12-9. The two credit slips are subtracted from the total VISA card sales drafts to arrive at a net amount. The two bank groups are then added together to arrive at the total deposit of $1,129.92. This summary form is run through the imprinting machine to show the vendor's identification plate information and the date.

illustration 12-9 merchant deposit summary.

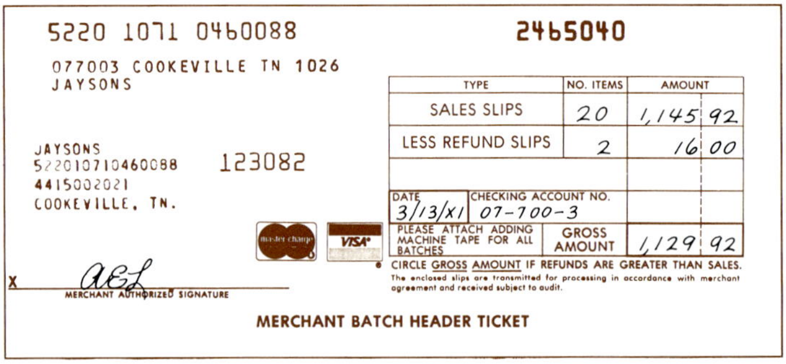

5220 1071 0460088 2465040

077003 COOKEVILLE TN 1026
JAYSONS

JAYSONS
5220107104600088 123082
4415002021
COOKEVILLE, TN.

TYPE	NO. ITEMS	AMOUNT
SALES SLIPS	20	1,145 92
LESS REFUND SLIPS	2	16 00
DATE 3/13/X1	CHECKING ACCOUNT NO. 07-700-3	
PLEASE ATTACH ADDING MACHINE TAPE FOR ALL BATCHES	GROSS AMOUNT	1,129 92

• CIRCLE GROSS AMOUNT IF REFUNDS ARE GREATER THAN SALES.
The enclosed slips are transmitted for processing in accordance with merchant agreement and received subject to audit.

X AEL
MERCHANT AUTHORIZED SIGNATURE

MERCHANT BATCH HEADER TICKET

After the merchant completes the *Merchant Deposit Summary,* a deposit slip only for credit card sales must be prepared. This deposit slip probably will look like the one you use for coins, currency, and checks, but we thought you might like to see a different style. The March 13 credit card deposit slip for Jayson's is shown in Illustration 12-10. The total combined net VISA card and MasterCard credit card sales must match the net deposit.

illustration 12-10 credit card deposit.

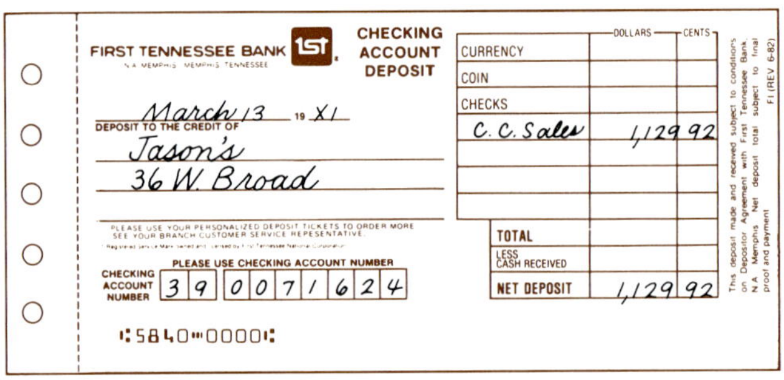

FIRST TENNESSEE BANK 1st
N.A. MEMPHIS MEMPHIS, TENNESSEE

CHECKING ACCOUNT DEPOSIT

March 13 19 X1
DEPOSIT TO THE CREDIT OF
Jason's
36 W. Broad

	DOLLARS	CENTS
CURRENCY		
COIN		
CHECKS		
C. C. Sales	1,129	92
TOTAL		
LESS CASH RECEIVED		
NET DEPOSIT	1,129	92

PLEASE USE CHECKING ACCOUNT NUMBER
CHECKING ACCOUNT NUMBER 3 9 0 0 7 1 6 2 4

⑆5840⑈0000⑆

This deposit made and received subject to conditions on Depositor Agreement with First Tennessee Bank N.A. Memphis. Net deposit total subject to final proof and payment. F1 (REV 6-82)

sample problem Jimmy Walker, an employee of Fiddler Office Supply, is assigned the task of making the daily deposit. On April 23, 19X1, he is handed the following:

Dollars	$643.00
Coins	49.83
Money orders	15.62
Traveler's check	50.00
IOU from customer	25.16
Postage stamps	.90
Checks from	
Amos Smihor	88.19
Beatrice Studios	17.10
Amalgamated Tool and Die Company	6.42
Tommy Dorman	32.55

Prepare the deposit, assuming that you are getting it ready for the night depository.

sample problem solution

PLEASE ENDORSE ALL CHECKS

DATE April 23 19 X1

CHECKS AND OTHER ITEMS ARE RECEIVED FOR DEPOSIT SUBJECT TO THE RULES AND REGULATIONS OF THIS INSTITUTION.

PLEASE LIST EACH CHECK SEPARATELY

	DOLLARS	CENTS
CURRENCY	643	—
COINS	49	83
1 Money Order	15	62
2 Traveler's Checks	50	–
3 Smihor	88	19
4 Beatrice	17	10
5 Amalgamated	6	42
6 Dorman	32	55
7		
8		
9		
10		
11		
12		
13		
14		
15		
16		
17		
18		
FRONT SIDE TOTAL		
REVERSE SIDE TOTAL		
TOTAL DEPOSIT	902	71

DEPOSIT TO ACCOUNT OF

Fiddler Office Supplies

⑆064101903⑆ ⑈0135976⑈

USE REVERSE SIDE FOR ADDITIONAL LISTING OR ATTACH TAPE

HARLAND 133-U 5 80

review exercises

1. Which of the following would be included in a daily deposit slip? (a) Check from Paris (France) Hotel, (b) stamps, (c) savings bond, (d) money order, (e) post-dated checks, (f) note from boss's son, (g) newspaper coupons accepted from a customer in partial payment for merchandise, (h) food stamps, (i) credit card sales draft.
2. Harvey Walker, a new bank employee, examines a number of check

American BANK and TRUST
COOKEVILLE, TENNESSEE 38501

MEMBER FDIC

JAMES SPENCER'S LUGGAGE SHOPPE
400 NORTH MAIN
COOKEVILLE, TN 38501

ACCOUNT NUMBER	
210 124 9	
DATE OF STATEMENT	PAGE
JULY 29, 19X1	1
BRANCH	
4	

****************** CHECKING *****************

ADDITIONS

DEPOSITS AND OTHER CREDITS

DATE	AMOUNT	DESCRIPTION
7/3	500.50	DEPOSIT
7/15	387.00	DEPOSIT
7/29	798.00	DEPOSIT
7/29	110.00	NOTE COLLECTION

SUBTRACTION

CHECKS PAID (*INDICATES A SKIP IN CHECK NUMBERS)

CHECK NO.	AMOUNT	DATE	CHECK NO.	AMOUNT	DATE
862	71.14	7/1	886	6.93	7/16
869*	516.14	7/1	887	315.94	7/17
883*	30.36	7/1	888	308.99	7/21
884*	344.00	7/7	890*	10.00	7/23
885	108.20	7/9	891	29.07	7/29
			SC	13.30	7/29

SUMMARY OF ACTIVITY ON THIS STATEMENT

AVERAGE BALANCE 442.62

	LAST STATEMENT WAS 6/30/X1 BALANCE	421.90
+	4 DEPOSITS AND OTHER CREDITS	1,795.50
-	11 CHECKS AND OTHER DEBITS	1,754.07
=	YOUR CURRENT BALANCE ON 7/29/X1	463.33

*********** SEE US ABOUT OPENING YOUR IRA ACCOUNT **********

Please notify us of any change in your address.
For direct inquiry contact:
AMERICAN BANK & TRUST, P. O. BOX 100, COOKEVILLE, TN. 38501 PH. (615) 528-7561

FOR YOUR CONVENIENCE SEE BACK FOR RECONCILEMENT FORM. 1

illustration 12-11 bank statement. (courtesy of American Bank & Trust)

endorsements. He asks you to help him determine the types of endorsement and restrictions (if any) involved.

(a) Check stamped "For Deposit Only; Martin Department Store, 786543."

(b) Check signed "Betty Swallows."

• task PREPARE A BANK RECONCILIATION

Purpose of a reconciliation

The term **reconciliation** may strike you as being rather awesome, but its meaning is actually simple. If two people take different positions on an issue, such as where to locate a store, the difference can be resolved only if one or both parties compromise. By discussing the issue or seeking outside advice, they may arrive at a compromise position acceptable to both; then a reconciliation has taken place. A bank reconciliation also involves two parties—the bank and the firm. The bank indicates the amount it shows the company to have in its trust by providing a **bank statement.** This document, furnished monthly by the bank, shows the beginning balance, all checks that have been processed by the bank, all deposits made, the daily balance, any other charges or credits, and the ending balance. Such a statement for James Spencer's Luggage Shoppe can be seen in Illustration 12-11.

The bank indicates that James has $463.33 on hand, while the firm's check stub shows that James has cash of $314.75. The firm's cash balance on July 31, 19X1, can be seen on Check Stub 893 in Illustration 12-12.

illustration 12-12 check stub. (courtesy of John H. Harland Company)

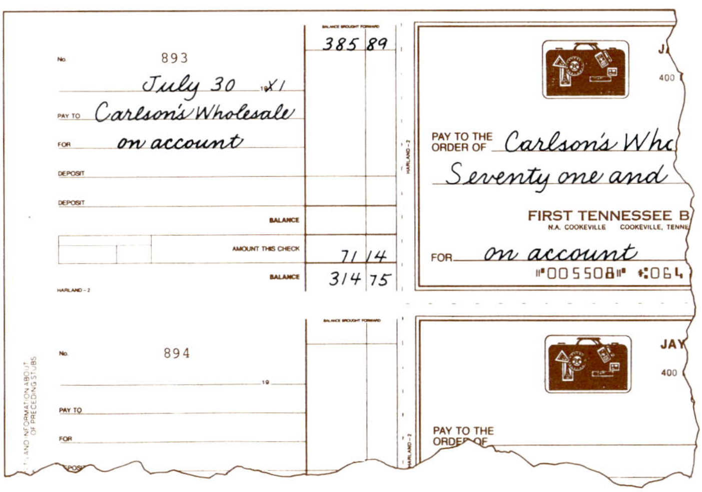

How do two businesses (the bank and the firm) using all the information available to them in determining the ending cash balance arrive at different amounts? Any one of the following items would cause the bank to show a different ending balance:

1. Outstanding checks.
2. Late deposits.
3. Accommodation collection.
4. Error by the bank.
5. Error by the company.
6. Checks with nonsufficient funds (NSF).
7. Bank service charge.

Preparing the reconciliation

The accounting clerk should approach a reconciliation through a logical, step-by-step procedure. Here is a suggested approach:

1. Examine the previous month's bank reconciliation to see whether there were any outstanding deposits. If so, check the current bank statement to see whether the deposits are shown. Since all of the deposits should have been processed, call the bookkeeping department of the bank and trace the missing deposit. If a deposit has been made that was not shown, add it to the balance on the bank statement.
2. Compare the other deposits listed on the current bank statement to see whether they agree with the deposits shown on the check stubs. Check off each one as you verify it. Any unrecorded deposits must be added to the balance on the bank statement.
3. Compare the previous month's bank reconciliation with the current bank statement to see whether all listed outstanding checks have cleared. Since most checks should have cleared, examine the check stub to see to whom the check was written and see whether further investigation is needed.
4. Compare listed check numbers and amounts with the check stubs to determine which checks are outstanding for the current period. Total the outstanding checks and subtract this amount from the balance in the checkbook.
5. Examine all other charges and credits made by the bank, such as service charges, printing charges, and NSF checks to determine what action to take on the reconciliation.
6. Complete the reconciliation by correcting the balances for any errors.
7. Make the necessary journal entries.

Outstanding checks The key to doing a reconciliation is to ask yourself in each case (except when an error was made), "Which party did not know about this?" Let's begin with the first item listed—**outstanding checks.** These are the checks that have not been processed by the bank by the bank statement date. Those that have cleared and have been honored (and cancelled) are boldly marked so that reuse is very unlikely. These **cancelled checks** are returned to the firm along with the bank statement. To keep the illustration simple, assume that Checks 867, 892, and 893, adding up to $216.42, are outstanding on the reconciliation date. This means that the company subtracted this amount from the check stub balance, but the bank is unaware of these checks. We ask "Who did not know about the outstanding checks?" and come to the conclusion that the bank did not. So we go to the bank side of the equation. Next, we ask ourselves, "What happens to the bank balance when these checks clear?" The conclusion must be that cash will decrease as these checks clear. Here is the result:

Bank	$463.33	Check stub	$314.75
− Outstanding checks	216.42		
	$246.91	⟵ does not equal ⟶	$314.75

Late deposit By comparing our bank deposit slips with the bank statement, we find that a deposit of $146.54 made on July 31 did not appear on the bank statement. This is commonly referred to as a **deposit in transit.** Again, the bank did not know about this deposit, so we go to the bank side of the reconciliation. Since cash will increase by $146.54, we must add this amount to the bank side, bringing the equation to this position:

Bank	$463.33	Check stub	$314.75
+ Late deposit	146.54		
	$609.87		
− Outstanding checks	216.42		
	$393.45	⟵ does not equal ⟶	$314.75

Accommodation collection During July, the bank collected a $100 note plus $12 interest from Joe Williams, a customer of the firm. The customer was instructed to make payment directly to the bank since James Spencer gave the note to the bank for collection. He had turned this note over to the bank for collection because the customer, Joe Williams, had an account in the same bank. Hence, all the bank had to do was transfer funds from one account to another on the maturity date or whenever Joe gives the bank permission to reduce his account. The bank informs James of the collection by adding this amount plus interest to his deposit column and deducting any service charge. In this case, assume that the bank charged a $2 fee for this service. To simplify the illustration, we will net all of this together. Since the company did not know that it had been collected, we go to the check stub side and increase this balance by $110.

Bank	$463.33	Check stub	$314.75
+ Late deposit	146.54	+ Note plus interest (less collection fee)	110.00
	$609.87		
− Outstanding checks	216.42		
	$393.45 ⟵	does not equal ⟶	$424.75

Errors Unfortunately, errors do occur in dealing with daily check writing. Sometimes a check is incorrectly recorded in the journal, either by entering the wrong information on the check stub or by transferring correct stub information incorrectly to the journal. Although errors are less frequently committed by banks, they do occur—errors such as subtracting $35.50 for $355, for example, or deducting an amount from another company's account. To continue with Spencer's Luggage Shoppe, assume that Check 871, correctly written to a creditor, Jasper Supply, for $97, was incorrectly journalized and posted as $79. This means that *Cash* was credited for $18 less than it should have been. Incidentally, this *transposition* is identifiable since it is exactly divisible by 9. When an error is made, we change our approach to the analysis. In the case of a mistake, we ask, "Who made the mistake?" In this instance the error was committed by the company, so we move to the checkbook side of the reconciliation. Then, in asking what effect correcting the mistake will have on cash, we should conclude that since *Cash was credited for $18 less than it should have been, we must credit Cash* for this amount. To do so would decrease *Cash*, giving us the following analysis:

Bank	$463.33	Check stub	$314.75
+ Late deposit	146.54	+ Note plus interest (less collection fee)	110.00
	$609.87		$424.75
− Outstanding checks	216.42	− error correction	18.00
	$393.45 ⟵	does not equal ⟶	$406.75

Checks with nonsufficient funds Occasionally, a check will be returned from the bank because of **nonsufficient funds (NSF).** Some banks return them with the bank statement, while others return NSF checks upon learning that funds in the account will not cover a particular check. Upon receiving notification, the merchant usually notifies the customer and then runs the check through the bank again. Although there are a number of practical shortcuts, the proper approach is to make an entry when an NSF check is received. Otherwise, the firm might overdraw its own bank account. To illustrate, assume that John Biggers gave the firm a check for $50 on July 7. Five days later, a document is received from the bank stating that the check could not be honored because of nonsufficient funds. A typical form sent out by a bank is shown in Illustration 12-13. The NSF check is also returned with this form to allow the company to take further action.

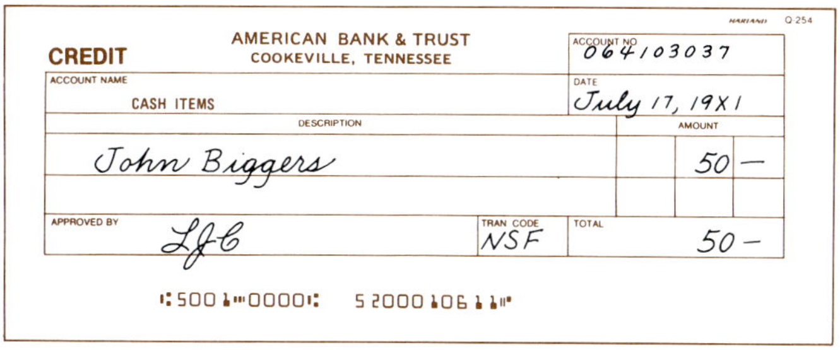

CREDIT

AMERICAN BANK & TRUST
COOKEVILLE, TENNESSEE

ACCOUNT NO. 064103037

ACCOUNT NAME: CASH ITEMS

DATE: July 17, 19X1

DESCRIPTION	AMOUNT
John Biggers	50 —

APPROVED BY: LJC — TRAN CODE: NSF — TOTAL: 50 —

⑆500⑈0000⑆ 52000106⑈⑈

illustration 12-13 bank memorandum. (courtesy of American Bank & Trust)

At this time the firm would do two things: (1) make a journal entry and (2) deduct $50 from the latest check stub balance. Since John Biggers owes us $50, we would make the following entry:

GENERAL JOURNAL — Page 16

Date		Description	P.R.	Dr.	Cr.
19X1					
July	12	Accounts Receivable/John Biggers		50 –	
		Cash			50 –
		Received bad check			
		from customer.			

This entry could be made either in the cash disbursements journal or the general journal. If it is placed in the cash disbursements journal, we will indicate that no check was written by placing a dash in the check number column. Since there is no designated place on the check stub to make such a deduction, we suggest using one of the unused deposit lines around July 12. Make certain that you indicate that this $50 amount is a deduction by placing a minus before the $50, or better yet, brackets around the $50. Also, be sure that you clearly label the purpose of this deduction.

If Mr. Biggers does not deposit enough funds to allow the check to be honored before the end of the fiscal period, no further action will be required, since an entry has been made and the check stub balance has been properly reduced. In many cases, however, handling the check is simply a matter of calling the bank to see whether the balance is now large enough to cover the check. If the funds are still not sufficient, then call the customer; the customer will usually apologize and ask you to run the check through again in a day or two. Whether your firm adds a service charge for this trouble depends on company policy.

Let's back up and assume that on July 12, after receiving the notice from the bank, Mr. Biggers tells us that he has just made a deposit so we should run the check through again. A wise approach is to prepare a separate deposit slip for the one check. In this way, tracing what has been done is easier. Assume also that Mr. Biggers paid us a $5 service charge, which we also deposited with the check. At this point you would make the following entry:

GENERAL JOURNAL Page 17

Date		Description	P.R.	Dr.	Cr.
19X1					
July	13	Cash		55 –	
		Accounts Receivable/John Biggers			50 –
		Miscellaneous Income			5 –
		Collected for bad check			
		plus service charge			

The deposit of $55 would also be entered on the check stub, which means that the bank statement and the check stub would agree (as far as this one item is concerned).

Some accounting clerks may prefer to wait until the end of the period and treat NSF checks as a bank reconciliation adjustment. This procedure is fine, except that failure to deduct NSF checks could result in overdrawing the firm's bank account. However, if the firm keeps a substantial working fund and the overdraft is protected by the bank, then it would be safe to wait until the statement is reconciled before taking any action.

Bank service charge This **bank service charge** category might include a fee for collecting a note, a printing charge on new checks, or a charge for handling the firm's account. A few banks have a policy of "no service charge" for handling the firm's account, but most have adopted a minimum balance approach. Such a system can be seen in Illustration 12-14, which shows a service charge that varies from $1 to $3 a month. In the case of James Spencer's Luggage Shoppe, a service charge of $13.30 was levied by the bank for handling the account and for some printing. Since the printing charge was relatively small, the accounting clerk decides to debit the entire service charge to an expense account.

illustration 12-14 minimum balance policy. (courtesy of First Tennessee Bank)

It has always been our aim to give our customers the best possible service. In the past it has been possible to offer all our customers a checking account with no charge. Because of increased costs, it has become necessary to apply a service charge to some accounts.

As of October 1, 1980, we will apply a monthly service charge to checking accounts that fall below a minimum balance of $300. These charges will be as follows:

Minimum Balance from $ 0.00 to $ 99.00........................$3.00 Per Month Service Charge
Minimum Balance from $100.00 to $199.00........................$2.00 Per Month Service Charge
Minimum Balance from $200.00 to $299.00........................$1.00 Per Month Service Charge

You can continue free checking if your balance does not fall below $300.00.

You can also continue free checking if you are a member or become a member of BanClub.

We value your relationship and appreciate having your checking account at First Tennessee Bank. Please call or come by and see us if we can be of assistance to you in any of your financial needs.

FIRST TENNESSEE BANK

When the question is asked as to who did not know about this item, the response has to be "the company." Since the bank deducted $13.30 from James's account, the decrease in *Cash* results in the following equation:

Bank	$463.33	Check stub		$314.75
+ Late deposit	146.54	+ Note and interest		110.00
	$609.87	(less collection fee)		$424.75
− Outstanding checks	216.42	− Error correction	$18.00	
		Service charge	13.30	31.30
	$393.45 ←	equals		→ $393.45

Bank reconciliation adjustments

Now the bank figure agrees with the check stub, and the statement is said to be *reconciled.* The amount of cash the firm actually has on July 31 is $393.45, which is also the adjusted cash balance. Showing this balance on the check stub is important. To do so, as well as to get the information in the ledger, we must make journal entries to reflect changes on the check stub side of the reconciliation. First, the plus item is $110, meaning that *Cash* must be debited for $110. Since a note, along with its related interest less the collection fee, was collected, the following entry (in general journal form) would be made:

GENERAL JOURNAL — Page 22

Date		Description	P.R.	Dr.	Cr.
19x1 July	31	Cash		110 —	
		Miscellaneous General Expense		2 —	
		Notes Receivable			100 —
		Interest Revenue			12 —
		To bring cash into			
		agreement with bank			
		reconciled amount			

The minus portion on the check stub side indicates that *Cash* must be decreased by $31.30, requiring a credit to the *Cash* account for this amount. The offsetting debits must indicate what caused this decrease. The first minus item is an error correction connected with payment made to a creditor. Recall that *Accounts Payable/Jasper Supply* was debited for only $79 when the check was actually written correctly for $97. To correct this error, an additional $18 must be debited to the liability account and Jasper Supply. As for the service charge, it is similar to simply writing a check to the bank—except the bank does it for us. *Service Charge Expense* could be debited for this charge; but since it is a minor item, *Miscellaneous General Expense* is often used. The resulting entry (in general journal form) would be:

GENERAL JOURNAL — Page 22

Date		Description	P.R.	Dr.	Cr.
19X1 July	31	Accounts Payable/Jasper Supply		18 –	
		Miscellaneous General Expense		13 30	
		Cash			31 30
		To bring cash into agreement with bank reconciled amount			

Keep in mind that the first entry should actually be journalized in the cash receipts journal and the second one in the cash disbursements journal. After posting these two entries, the *Cash* account would show the proper adjusted cash balance of $393.45.

Cash — Account No. 111

Date	Item	P.R.	Dr.	Cr.	Balance Dr.	Balance Cr.
31		G22	110 –		424 75	
31		G22		31 30	393 45	

James's check stub (see Illustration 12-12) still shows a balance of $314.75, rather than the adjusted amount of $393.45. Illustration 12-15 shows one easy approach to handling this situation. Numerous other approaches, such as listing all the items adjusted individually, would work as well.

illustration 12-15 check stub with adjustment. (courtesy John A. Harland Company)

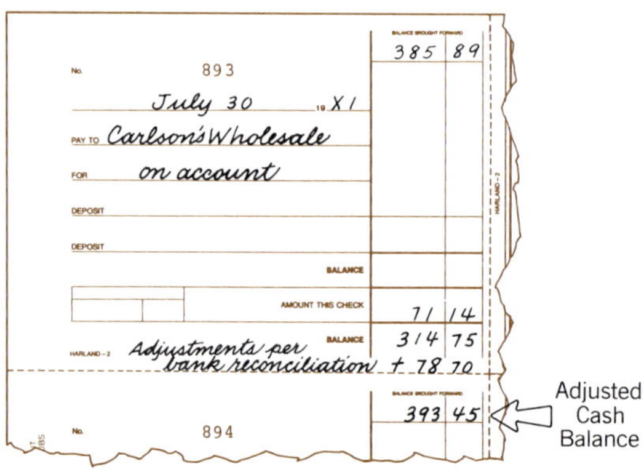

The problem here is that space is too limited to make many adjustments. In Illustration 12-15, all of the adjustments are summarized into one number ($112 in plus items less $31.30 in minus items). Remember that we are not concerned with the bank's side of the reconciliation since those adjustments will be made on the bank's books as the deposits and checks clear.

To help firms prepare their bank reconciliations, most banks supply a printed form on the back of the bank statement. There is no set design, but Illustration 12-16 is a sample of such a form with the information from James Spencer's Luggage Shoppe.

illustration 12-16 back of bank statement.

American BANK and TRUST
COOKEVILLE, TENNESSEE 38501

MEMBER FDIC

OUTSTANDING ITEMS

TO WHOM	DATE	CHECK NUMBER	AMOUNT
Fred's Supply	7/13	867	$ 102.93
John Rodgers	7/29	892	42.35
Carlson's Wholsale	7/30	893	71.14
		Total Amount Outstanding →	216.42

YOUR RECORDS			BANK STATEMENT	
ENTER YOUR CHECKBOOK BALANCE	314.75		$ 463.33	ENTER THE ENDING BALANCE SHOWN ON BANK STATEMENT
*(1) SUBTRACT ANY SERVICE CHARGE	13.30		146.54	+ ADD ANY DEPOSITS NOT SHOWN ON BANK STATEMENT
SUB TOTAL	301.45		609.87	SUB TOTAL
*(2) + ADD ANY INTEREST PAID			216.42	− SUBTRACT TOTAL AMOUNT OUTSTANDING
SUB TOTAL				SUB TOTAL
ADJUSTMENTS (IF ANY)	+110.— −18.—			ADJUSTMENTS (IF ANY)
YOUR ADJUSTED CHECKBOOK BALANCE	393.45	SHOULD ←→ EQUAL	393.45	YOUR ADJUSTED STATEMENT BALANCE

*(1) Be sure you deduct from your checkbook

*(2) Be sure you add to your checkbook.

IF STATEMENT DOES NOT BALANCE

1. Recheck addition & subtraction in checkbook and above.
2. Compare check amount to checkbook.
3. Compare check amount to amount on statement.

AFTER BALANCING, "YOUR ADJUSTED CHECKBOOK BALANCE," SHOULD BE EQUAL TO THE BALANCE IN YOUR CHECKBOOK.

Some firms prepare formal statements similar to the one shown in Illustration 12-17.

illustration 12-17
bank reconciliation.

James Spencer's Luggage Shoppe
Bank Reconciliation
July 31, 19X1

Balance per bank statement		463 33
Add: Deposit not credited by bank		146 54
		609 87
Deduct: Outstanding checks		216 42
Adjusted cash balance		393 45
Balance per check stub		314 75
Add: Note collected	100 –	
Interest on note	12 –	112 –
		426 75
Deduct: Error on Jasper check	18 –	
Service charge	13 30	
Collection fee	2 –	33 30
Adjusted checkbook balance		393 45

sample problem Nellie's Florist received its monthly bank statement dated August 31, 19X1, showing a balance of $1,149.62. On that date, the checkbook showed a balance of $965.11. Analysis of the bank statement and related data showed the following:

1. Outstanding checks, $297.71
2. Late deposit, $64.90
3. Check 443 was correctly written for $6.90, but recorded as $9.60
4. Bank service charge, $10
5. A check written for $141 was incorrectly entered on the check stub as $100

On notebook paper, prepare a simple bank reconciliation for Nellie's Florist.

sample problem solution

Bank statement balance		$1,149.62
+ Late deposit		64.90
		$1,214.52
− Outstanding checks		297.71
Adjusted bank balance		$916.81
Check stub balance		$965.11
+ Error in recording check		2.70
		$967.81
− Bank service charge	$10	
Error on check stub	41	51.00
Adjusted bank balance		$916.81

review exercises

3. Indicate on which side of the bank reconciliation each item would appear and whether it would have a positive or negative effect on cash.
   (a) Outstanding checks, $416.93.
   (b) Bank service charge, $5.
   (c) Check received from bank marked NSF, $50.
   (d) Error made by company on deposit slip total. It should have been $1,462 rather than $1,642.
   (e) Bank collected note of $500, plus interest of $25 (no collection fee).
4. Make the necessary journal entries, in general journal form, for the following bank reconciliation:

Balance per bank		$4,914	Balance per checkbook	$3,614
+ Late deposit	$412		+ Note $200 and interest	220
Error	2	414		$3,834
		$5,328	− Service charge	6
− Outstanding checks		1,500		
		$3,828		$3,828

5. Joe Carr, owner of a proprietorship, correctly wrote a check to Jensen Realty for $250 to pay the rent. In filling out the check stub, he incorrectly entered $205. This amount was then journalized and posted at $205. What steps must be taken in preparing the reconciliation and making journal entries to correct this error?

• task SET UP A PETTY CASH FUND AND RECORD ENTRIES CONNECTED WITH REPLENISHING THE FUND

Petty cash fund

For internal control, all payments should be made by prenumbered checks. Yet making small payments by checks is both expensive and inefficient. Also, small payments are often unexpected. For example, taxi fare may be needed to send an office employee to pick up certain supplies. These small expenditures are best paid by cash instead of by check. By establishing a *petty cash fund*, a company can still follow its policies of cash control. A **petty cash fund** is a fixed amount of money provided for the convenience of the company.

To establish the petty cash fund, the owner of the business must decide on the amount of cash to be provided—an amount large enough to take care of the needs of the business for several weeks to avoid having to replenish it frequently. A petty cash fund for $200, for example, might be large enough to provide for the company's needs for several weeks. The petty cash entry in the partial cash disbursements journal is as follows:

CASH DISBURSEMENTS JOURNAL

Page 2

Date		Ch. No.	Payee	Account Debited	P.R.	Sundry Accounts Dr.	Accounts Payable Dr.	Purchases Discounts Cr.	Cash Cr.
19X1 Mar.	20	455	Petty Cash	Petty Cash	12	200 –			200 –

Once the check has been cashed, the money is placed in a safe or petty cash drawer. A single person is responsible for making all payments from the petty cash fund. A second person, usually the owner of a small firm, is responsible for approving additional checks to replenish the fund. The *Petty Cash* account will remain at a fixed amount as indicated in the following asset account:

Petty Cash

Account No. 12

Date		Item	P.R.	Dr.	Cr.	Balance Dr.	Balance Cr.
19X1 Mar.	20		CD2	200 –		200 –	

The only time that the $200 amount in the account above is changed is upon instruction from the owner or another person in authority to lower or raise the amount of the fund. For example, the owner may decide that $150 is sufficient. The following entry in general journal form explains the lowering of the fund and the return of $50 to the *Cash* account.

GENERAL JOURNAL

Page 1

Date		Description	P.R.	Dr.	Cr.
19X1 May	1	Cash		50 –	
		Petty Cash			50 –
		To reduce the petty cash			
		fund			

Payments from petty cash

When cash is paid from the fund, a voucher should be completed to show the account to be debited and the proper approval. An excellent control form is a prenumbered **petty cash voucher.** The person receiving the money should also sign the voucher to verify that approved small cash payments have been made to the right person or company.

To illustrate, assume that a petty cash voucher in the amount of $10 is approved for delivery expenses. The completed voucher would include all

illustration 12-18
petty cash voucher.

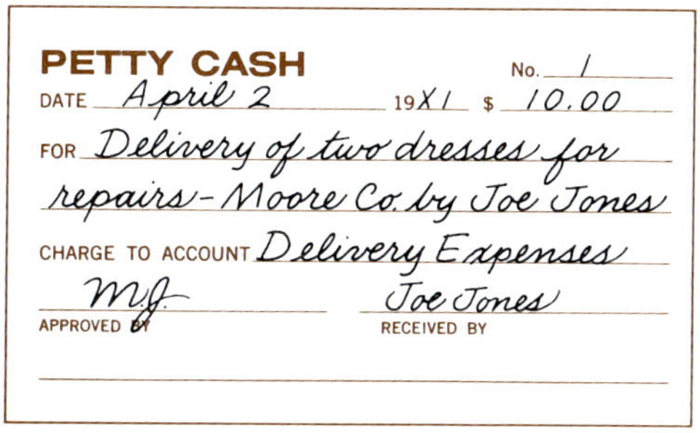

PETTY CASH No. 1

DATE April 2 19X1 $ 10.00

FOR Delivery of two dresses for repairs - Moore Co. by Joe Jones

CHARGE TO ACCOUNT Delivery Expenses

M.J. — APPROVED BY

Joe Jones — RECEIVED BY

required data as shown in Illustration 12-18. The voucher indicates the purpose of the expenditure, the account charged, and the person receiving the cash. All paid petty cash vouchers should be kept with the remaining petty cash funds. At any time, the total of the paid petty cash vouchers plus the remaining cash should equal the original petty cash fund. Assume that you have petty cash vouchers for the following approved payments.

Delivery Expenses	$30.00
Supplies	26.30
Postage Expense	35.20
Freight-In	57.50
Miscellaneous Expense	18.25
	$167.25

These petty cash expenditures would leave a balance of \$32.75 (\$200.00 − \$167.25) in the petty cash box. A lesser balance would require a debit to a petty cash shortage account, and a greater balance would require a credit to this same account. This account will be discussed later in the chapter.

Replenishing of petty cash

Petty cash funds must be **replenished** when there isn't enough money left in the fund to provide the services of the fund. The fund also will be replenished when the company needs to prepare financial statements. The information concerning the expenses on the petty cash vouchers must be recorded in the accounting system. Therefore, petty cash funds are replenished mainly for two reasons:

1. When funds are low.
2. When financial statements are prepared.

Replenishing petty cash requires that a check be written for the total of the petty cash vouchers that have been paid. The transaction for the $167.25

in a cash disbursements journal for the paid vouchers on March 31 would be:

CASH DISBURSEMENTS JOURNAL Page 17

Date	Ch. No.	Payee	Account Debited	P.R.	Sundry Accounts Dr.	Accounts Payable Dr.	Purchases Discounts Cr.	Cash Cr.
19X1 Mar. 31	461	Petty Cash	Delivery Expense		30 00			
			Supplies		26 30			
			Postage		35 20			
			Freight-In		57 50			
			Miscellaneous Expense		18 25			167 25

Note that the *Petty Cash* account is not involved in the transaction. The check is made payable to cash or petty cash, and the money is placed in the petty cash drawer. The expense accounts are debited for expenditures that represent payments from the fund prior to March 31, 19X1. Individual expense accounts are posted from the Sundry Accounts Dr. column and now they are included on the income statement.

Petty cash record

A company may prefer to maintain a petty cash record to account for petty cash receipts and disbursements. The petty cash record is not considered to be a journal from which postings are made to general ledger accounts. This record book merely provides information concerning petty cash activities. A petty cash record with the previous payments and reimbursement information is presented in Illustration 12-19.

Petty Cash Record

Date	Explanation	Receipt No.	Receipts	Payments	Postage	Freight-In	Misc. Gen. Expense	Miscellaneous Payments Account	Miscellaneous Payments Amount
19X1 Mar. 20	Establish Petty Cash fund		200 00						
21	Purchase of Office Supplies	459		26 30				Office Supplies	26 30
21	Stamps for Special Mailing	460		10 00	10 00				
22	Special Order Deliveries	461		30 00				Delivery Expense	30 00
22	Paper Cups for Coffee—Office	462		18 25			18.25		
26	F.O.B. Shipping Point Deliveries	463		57 50		57 50			
29	Special Mailing	464		25 20	25 20				
31	Reimbursement of Petty Cash		167 25						

illustration 12-19 petty cash record.

sample problem Prepare entries in general journal form for the following petty cash activities:

(a) The Morgan Company decided that $150 would be adequate for a petty cash fund established on July 1, 19X1.

(b) A review of petty cash vouchers revealed the following expenditures for July:

Postage Expense	$21.80
Miscellaneous General Expense	12.60
Freight-In	40.30
Office Supplies	62.40

Prepare the July 31 reimbursement entry in general journal form.

sample problem solution

(a)	19X1			
	July 1	Petty Cash	150.00	
		Cash		150.00
		To establish petty cash fund.		
(b)	July 31	Postage Expense	21.80	
		Freight-In	40.30	
		Office Supplies	62.40	
		Miscellaneous General Expense	12.60	
		Cash		137.10
		To reimburse petty cash fund.		

review exercises

6. James Company decided to establish a petty cash fund of $100 for convenience in making small payments. Paid petty cash vouchers amounted to $87.32. How much cash should be in the petty cash box?

7. Donaldson Company had a petty cash fund of $250, an amount too large for the company's needs. Mr. Donaldson decided to reduce the fund by $50 on August 1, 19X1. Paid petty cash vouchers for August are grouped in the following categories:

Freight-In	$52.30
Office Expense	25.70
Miscellaneous Expense	20.10

Prepare the journal entries to reduce the petty cash fund on August 1 and to reimburse the fund on August 31, 19X1. Do you think the fund is still too large?

• task ACCOUNT FOR SHORTAGES AND OVERAGES OF CASH

Shortages and overages from daily sales

Cash shortages and overages were discussed briefly in Chapter 7. Now we would like to spend more time on this topic so that you will feel comfortable dealing with it. To illustrate, assume that Boatman's Donut Shoppe has only one cash register. A change fund of $150 is kept to handle daily transactions. This amount is kept in a bag in the safe overnight and placed in the cash register drawer each morning. At the end of the day on August 19, the cash register is totaled. The tape showed cash sales of $416 plus $24.96 for sales taxes for a total of $440.96. This means that the cash register drawer should have $590.96 in checks, currency, and coins. If the change fund were removed, $440.96 should be left for deposit. A count showed only $439.43 on hand. Since $1.53 is missing because of error or theft, a cash shortage exists. As we discussed in Chapter 7, you would make the following entry:

GENERAL JOURNAL — Page 21

Date		Description	P.R.	Dr.	Cr.
19X1					
Aug.	19	Cash		439 43	
		Cash Short and Over		1 53	
		Sales			416 –
		Sales Taxes Payable			24 96

If, on the other hand, $442.96 had been found in the drawer, then *Cash Short and Over* would have been credited.

GENERAL JOURNAL — Page 21

Date		Description	P.R.	Dr.	Cr.
19X1					
Aug.	19	Cash		442 96	
		Sales			416 –
		Sales Taxes Payable			24 96
		Cash Short and Over			2 –

At the end of the fiscal year, if *Cash Short and Over* ends with a debit balance, it should be shown on the income statement as an operating expense. If the amount is relatively small, it can be combined with *Miscellaneous General Expenses.* In contrast, if a credit balance results, then this account should be shown as *Other Income.*

Since customers are more likely to complain when they are short-changed than when they are given too much change, the account will more than likely have a debit balance. Finally, keep in mind that the amount debited to *Cash* must be the same as the deposit slip total.

Shortages and overages in petty cash

In earlier discussions, the amount in the drawer plus the vouchers exactly matched the balance of *Petty Cash.* Here let's assume that the vouchers plus cash do not agree with *Petty Cash,* that the vouchers total $79.23 and the cash in the drawer is $20, a shortage of 77 cents if *Petty Cash* shows a $100 balance. To bring the balance back to $100, $80 is needed. When the check to replenish the petty cash fund is written, the check stub must explain how the entire $80 is used so that proper accounting can be provided. To continue this illustration, assume that vouchers for the following items are found in the drawer and grouped together:

Supplies	$23.19
Postage	15.00
J. L. Jones, Drawing	20.00
Miscellaneous Expense	21.04
	$79.23

To account for the entire $80, a cash shortage of 77 cents must be listed. The accountant then has information to make the following entry (in general journal form):

GENERAL JOURNAL — Page 45

Date		Description	P.R.	Dr.	Cr.
19X1 July	31	Supplies		23 19	
		Postal Expense		15 —	
		J.L. Jones, Drawing		20 —	
		Miscellaneous Expense		21 04	
		Cash Short and Over		77	
		Cash			80 —

Note that for both the shortage and overage, enough cash is needed to bring the drawer back to the balance of the *Petty Cash* account (which was $100 in this illustration).

sample problem Bryson's Discount Store has six cash registers. Each register has a $200 change fund that is taken from the safe and placed in the register each working day. Total sales and sales tax for each machine are as follows:

	Sales	Sales Tax
Register 1:	$420	$21.00
Register 2:	$608	$30.40
Register 3:	$516	$25.80
Register 4:	$243	$14.58
Register 5:	$765	$38.25
Register 6:	$447	$22.35

Machines 1, 2, 3, and 6 are correct, but Register 4 has $259.30 after removing the change fund, and Register 5 has $802.16 after the change fund is removed. Make one entry to record sales and tax liability for all six registers along with the overages or shortages.

sample problem solution

Cash	3,152.01	
Sales		2,999.00
Sales Taxes Payable		152.38
Cash Short and Over		.63

Machine 4: $243 + $14.58 − $259.30 = $1.72 Over

Machine 5: $765 + $38.25 − $802.16 = $1.09 Short

$ .63 Over

review exercises

8. Ginny's Furniture uses one cash register. At the end of the day after the change fund was taken out, $1,643.18 in currency, coins, and checks was removed from the cash register. The totals tape shows sales of $1,570 and sales taxes of $73.50. Make the required entry in general journal form.

9. Fowler Chicken and Dumpling Diner had total sales of $363.25 for August 27. Fowler's business is located in a state with no sales tax. After the change fund was removed, $353.25 remained in the drawer. Fowler found a note from one of his regular customers, Harry Holmes, who had bought four meals for himself and his family, only to discover he had not brought his wallet. The cashier allowed him to sign the note that promises to pay the $10 on August 28. Make the necessary journal entry in general journal form.

10. Marge Williams, the petty cashier, decides that it is time to replenish the petty cash fund. Petty cash vouchers give the following information:

Supplies	$14.73
Postage on packages mailed	4.19
Withdrawals by the owner, Fred Rocker	8.00
Miscellaneous general items	3.00

The *Petty Cash* account shows a balance of $40, and the petty cash drawer contains $9.08 in currency and coins. Make the necessary journal entry in general journal form to replenish the petty cash fund.

chapter highlights

After studying this chapter, you should be able to:

- Prepare a daily bank deposit.
- Prepare a bank reconciliation.

- Journalize and post entries related to a bank reconciliation.
- Maintain records for a petty cash fund.
- Replenish the petty cash fund and provide information in the cash disbursements record.
- Account for cash shortages and overages.

check figures for review exercises

1. (c), (d), (h); credit card sales (i) are listed on a separate deposit form.

2. (a) Restrictive endorsement. The holder of the check could deposit it only to the account of Martin Department Store.

(b) Blank endorsement. Because this endorsement imposes no restrictions, Betty could have cashed it or deposited it to any account she chose.

3. (a) Bank (−)
(b) Check stub (−)
(c) Check stub (−)
(d) Check stub (−)
(e) Check stub (+)

4.

Cash	220	
Notes Receivable		200
Interest Earned		20
Miscellaneous General Expense	6	
Cash		6

5. Since the error was made by Carr, the mistake should be shown on the checkbook side. When the accounting clerk wrote $205 instead of $250 on the check stub, *Cash* was incorrectly reduced $45 less than it should have been. Therefore, the checkbook side should be reduced. To correct the account, debit *Rent Expense* for $45 and credit *Cash,* $45.

6. Petty cash fund balance, $12.68.

7. Aug. 1 Credit *Petty Cash,* $50; Aug. 31 credit *Cash,* $98.10.

8.

Cash	1,643.18	
Cash Short and Over	.32	
Sales		1,570.00
Sales Taxes Payable		73.50

9.

Cash	353.25	
Accounts Receivable/Harry Holmes	10.00	
Sales		363.25

10.	Supplies (or Supplies Expense)	14.73	
	Postage Expense	4.19	
	Rocker, Drawing	8.00	
	Miscellaneous General Expense	3.00	
	Cash Short and Over	1.00	
	Cash		30.92

key terms

The following important terms are discussed in Chapter 12 and defined in the Glossary at the end of the book.

American Bankers Association (ABA) number
bank service charge
bank statement
blank endorsement
cancelled checks
currency
deposit in transit
deposit slip
food stamp
food stamp redemption certificate
merchant deposit summary
nonsufficient funds (NSF)
outstanding checks
petty cash fund
petty cash voucher
qualified endorsement
reconciliation
replenished
restrictive endorsement

questions

1. Why is it important to deposit money daily?
2. What is meant by *currency?*
3. What items are listed in the check category on the deposit slip?
4. How does writing *for deposit only* and the bank number on the back of a customer's check protect the depositor? What type of endorsement is this?
5. If the firm accepts a check made out to the customer, and the customer endorses the check with only a name, what type of endorsement is involved?
6. What is the primary purpose of a bank reconciliation?
7. Name at least five items that would cause disagreement between the company's check stub balance and the bank statement.
8. How does a bank indicate that a check has cleared and is no longer outstanding?
9. What is meant by the notation *NSF,* and what effect does it have on the cash balance?
10. Why is it necessary to make journal entries in connection with the bank reconciliation?

11. Why aren't entries made for the bank side of the reconciliation?
12. Is it possible to tell whether proper journal entries were made in connection with the bank reconciliation (i.e., is there a check figure)?
13. Briefly discuss the steps followed in handling the cash register count. How can you determine if a shortage has taken place in daily sales?
14. On what two occasions are petty cash funds replenished?
15. If petty cash vouchers total $83.21, the petty cash drawer contains $17.79, and the firm maintains a balance of $100 in the *Petty Cash* account, is there a cash shortage or a cash overage? Would you debit or credit *Cash Short and Over* to record this amount?

exercises

1. Determine the total amount of the daily deposit for these cash register items:

Coins	$ 24.63
Dollars	519.00
Money order	50.00
IOU from customers	10.00
Stamps	5.00

Reserve a change fund of $80 in dollars and $20 in coins.

2. Determine which of the following items should be considered as currency, which should be listed along with the checks, and which should not be included with the daily deposit:

Traveler's check

Check from Banco de Espana in pesos

Check from customer

Money order

Check issued to customer as a refund that was endorsed by the customer and returned to company toward another purchase

Italian currency received from customer

3. Marquis Tax Consulting Company received its February bank statement showing an ending balance of $1,413.61. At the same time, the check stub balance showed $1,077.89. Analysis of the data shows that (a) a late deposit of $149.66 was not included by the bank; (b) an error had been made by the bank when it treated a $100 deposit by another client as a Marquis deposit; (c) there was a $5 bank service charge; and (d) several checks were outstanding. Assuming no other items, what is the total of checks outstanding?
4. Using the general journal form, make the required journal entry or entries for Exercise 3.

5. Indicate the effect that each of the following would have on a bank reconciliation by using (+b) increase bank side, (−b) decrease bank side, (+c) increase check stub side, (−c) decrease check stub side, or (n) no effect.
   (a) NSF check received from customer. Upon redeposit, it cleared the bank within the same banking period
   (b) Outstanding checks
   (c) Check correctly written for $56.13 was incorrectly recorded on the stub as $65.13 and journalized as such
   (d) Service charge
   (e) Bank collected note for firm, plus interest
   (f) Late deposit
6. Lomas Company maintains a petty cash system of $200 for small convenience payments. The expenditures from the fund for which vouchers are maintained are:

Delivery Expense	$125.00
Miscellaneous General Expense	25.00
Postage Expense	12.30

   (a) What should be the petty cash fund balance?
   (b) What will you do if the balance in the petty cash fund differs from the proper amount?
7. Upon replenishing the petty cash fund to $50, the petty cashier assembled the vouchers in the following groups:

Office Supplies	$8.43
Store Supplies	7.98
Postage Expense	3.19
Miscellaneous General Expense	11.14
Miscellaneous Selling Expense	5.50
J. Wilson, Drawing	10.00

In addition to the vouchers, the drawer contained $4.74 in currency and coins. Make the necessary adjusting entry in general journal form.

problems

1. COMPETENCY TESTED The ability to prepare a deposit slip.

On November 28, 19X1, Arnold, an employee of the firm, empties out all three of the store's cash registers and finds the following after removing the change fund.

Register 1:	Currency	$214.00
	Postage stamps	15.00
	Coins	17.63
	Note from employee stating that money had been borrowed	5.00

Register 2:	Currency	$394.00
	Coins	13.42
	Check from Mo Walker	64.94
	Check from Joy Meaders	15.74
Register 3:	Currency	$263.00
	Traveler's checks (six $20 and one $50)	170.00
	Money order	50.00
	Check from Martin Wilson	17.21

Instructions Prepare a deposit slip for the appropriate items listed above.

2. COMPETENCY TESTED The ability to prepare deposit slips when credit card sales are involved.

Melanie, an employee of Diana's TV Sales and Service, has the task of making the daily deposit. On October 7, 19X1, Melanie finds the following items in the cash register:

Currency	$656.00
Coins	39.49
Traveler's checks	40.00
Checks from:	
Bernard Keys	430.00
Martin Ferris	18.00
Walter Prescott	22.57
Beatrice Floore	295.95
Five VISA card sales drafts	812.62
One MasterCard credit slip	95.70
Postage stamps	8.00

The firm began the day with $100 in currency and $20 in coins.

Instructions Prepare the necessary forms to make the deposit.

3. COMPETENCY TESTED The ability to prepare a simple bank statement.

Strong's Deli received a bank statement dated March 31 from Citizen's State Bank showing a balance of $567.90. On this date, the check stub showed a balance of $644.56. By comparing the bank statement and the books, the following differences were noted:

(a) The bank had collected a $100 note from Bobby Spurlock plus $5 interest.

(b) A deposit of $445.94 made on March 31 did not appear on the bank statement.

(c) A service charge of $6 was charged by the bank.

(d) Checks 134 for $100 and 144 for $152.28 had not cleared the bank.

(e) Check 129 for $141.16 was incorrectly shown on the check stub (and later journalized) as $159.16. This check was written to pay the telephone bill.

Instructions

(a) Prepare a bank reconciliation for Strong's Deli.

(b) Make the necessary journal entries on Strong's books.

4. COMPETENCY TESTED The ability to prepare a bank reconciliation.

You have been given the task of reconciling the following bank statement dated September 30, 19X1, for Foster Company:

AMERICAN NATIONAL BANK
Livingston, AZ

01-231-92

Foster Company
204 West Main St.
Livingston, AZ 85261

9/30/X1
Ending balance $1,199.91

	Checks and Other Debits			Deposits
381	$ 2.00	396	$433.00	$558.00
382	25.00	397	75.00	180.00
383	152.79	398	607.86	165.00
386	12.50	399	59.71	664.22
387	216.50	402	18.00	428.00
388	20.00	SC	4.00	850.52
389	200.00	NSF	75.00	766.00
390	393.25			600.00
391	10.00			275.65
392	64.33			743.70
393	97.33			167.38
394	59.71			290.00
395	10.00			288.00

The check stub balance on September 30 was $313.05. Outstanding checks totaled $1,193.25:

No. 400	$393.25
No. 401	100.00
No. 402	500.00
No. 403	200.00

On September 11, Foster Company received a check from Walter Brett for $75 in payment on account. The bank returned the check because of insufficient funds in Brett's account with the bank statement; the first notification that the check was not honored. A $216.14 deposit made by Foster Company on September 30 does not appear on the statement. During September, service charges amounted to $4. A review of the facts also indicated that a check written by the firm for $12.50 (No. 386) was recorded on the check stub as $1.25. This check was in payment for a newspaper ad.

Instructions

(a) Prepare a bank reconciliation.

(b) Journalize the necessary transactions to bring the books in line with the reconciliation.

5. COMPETENCY TESTED The ability to prepare a complex bank reconciliation along with the related journal entries.

The following bank statement showing transactions ending June 30, 19X1, was received from the Hudson Bay Bank:

HUDSON BAY BANK
2916 Berry Ave.
Mesa City, New York 10173

Ending Balance: $4,765.79 Date: 6/30/X1

Check and Other Debits				Deposits
153	$ 304.00	163	$ 41.50	$ 197.08
154	256.30	164	65.00	615.00
155	105.09	165	863.00	209.00
156	75.00	166	760.00	963.00
157	3,131.28	167	238.00	1,407.00
158	200.00	169	459.00	284.00
159	14.25	SC	8.00	968.00
160	57.39	NSF	23.00	375.00
161	18.15			1,957.00
162	256.30			577.50

Other important facts:

(a) At the beginning of the month, Checks 153, 154, and 155 were outstanding.

(b) At the end of the month, Checks 168 ($214.16), 170 ($18.53), and 171 ($265) are still outstanding.

(c) On the May statement, a deposit made on May 31 for $197.08 did not appear.

(d) At the end of June, deposits made on June 29 and 30 of $404 and $586, respectively, were not listed on the statement.

(e) The bank charges an $8 service charge.

(f) A check for $23 was returned by the bank because of insufficient funds. B. G. Honeybroom had given the firm this check as payment on account early in June.

(g) Close examination showed that Check 165 for $863 was actually written for $836 and properly entered as this amount on the firm's check stub.

(h) Received notice that the bank collected a $450 note for us, along with $9 interest.

(i) The check stub balance on June 30 was $4,857.10.

Instructions

(a) Using the form provided in your workbook (which is similar to that found on the back of most bank statements), prepare a bank reconciliation for Alden's Hardware Store as of June 30, 19X1.

(b) Prepare the necessary journal entries in general journal form to record all entries related to (a) on Alden's books.

6. COMPETENCY TESTED The ability to prepare journal entries based on cash register tapes.

Zetmer's Discount Store has four checkout registers. The cash count (after removing the change fund from each cash register) and the register tapes provide you with the following information:

Register	A	B	C	D
Cash intake	$229.21	$509.84	$339.00	$294.85
Sales per tape	216.40	480.22	319.40	280.00
Sales tax per tape	12.98	28.81	19.60	16.80

Instructions Analyze the information above and make a single entry to record the intake of all four cash registers. Use general journal form.

7. COMPETENCY TESTED The ability to analyze cash register tapes and make journal entries.

Crossville Grocery Store has two cash registers. Myrtle examined the first tape on August 19, 19X1, and found the following:

Cash	$635.90
Sales	560.00
Sales tax	28.00

One of the items, a $2 sale, was circled and initialed by the cashier as being a mistake. The sale did not take place and should be removed. Cash in the register was correct. A change fund of $35 is used for each cash register.

The second cash register tape indicated the following:

Cash	$653.18
Sales	602.10
Sales tax	30.10

Instructions Make the necessary journal entry to record sales for August 19, 19X1.

8. COMPETENCY TESTED The ability to establish and reimburse a petty cash fund for 19X1.

Stover Company decided to establish a petty cash fund for the convenience of making small disbursements. Prepare the general journal entries (a) to establish the fund, (b) to make reimbursements at the appropriate time, and (c) to reduce the petty cash fund.

Aug. 1 Established the petty cash fund for $250. Petty cash vouchers indicated the following expenditures for the month of August.

Gas for delivery truck	$85.50
Postage	24.25
Miscellaneous general items	32.40
Repairs on office machines	22.60

Aug. 31 Replenished the petty cash fund.

Sept. 30 Reduced the petty cash fund by $50.

chapter 13
RECEIVABLES AND NOTES PAYABLE

overall competency THE ABILITY TO MAKE COMPUTATIONS, RECORD TRANSACTIONS, AND PRESENT FINANCIAL STATEMENT DATA FOR ACCOUNTS RECEIVABLE, NOTES RECEIVABLE, BAD DEBTS, AND NOTES PAYABLE

career objectives When you complete this chapter, you should be able to:

- COMPUTE INTEREST ON A NOTE USING THE FORMULA APPROACH AND THE 6 PERCENT METHOD.
- RECORD RECEIPT OF NOTES RECEIVABLE, CASH RECEIVED FOR INTEREST, ACCRUED INTEREST, AND MATURITY OF THE NOTE.
- RECORD ISSUANCE OF NOTES PAYABLE, INTEREST PAID, ACCRUED INTEREST, AND MATURITY OF THE NOTE.
- ASSIST IN ESTIMATING BAD DEBTS AND RECORDING ADJUSTMENTS, WRITE-OFFS, AND RECOVERIES.
- PRESENT THE PROPER BALANCE SHEET AND INCOME STATEMENT DATA FOR NOTES AND ACCOUNTS RECEIVABLE.

At one time or another, most businesses borrow money to use for day-to-day operations or for specific nonrecurring needs. Most often they do so with short-term or long-term notes payable. Most businesses, other than financial institutions such as banks, however, do not lend money. They do sometimes accept a note receivable from a customer for a sales transaction or in exchange for accounts receivable. Because notes payable and receivable are interest bearing, the business will have an interest expense or interest earned related to the notes.

Accounts receivable and notes receivable cannot always be collected on time. Under the accrual basis of accounting, estimates of uncollectible accounts and notes should be made and appropriate recognition given in the accounts and financial statements at the end of each accounting period.

• task USING THE FORMULA APPROACH AND THE 6 PERCENT METHOD, COMPUTE INTEREST ON A NOTE

Notes and stated interest rates

A **note,** often called a *promissory note,* is a promise in writing to pay a specified sum of money at a fixed and stated date. Most notes are interest bearing, a term that means that an amount in addition to the principal will be paid and received. An example of a note appears in Illustration 13-1.

In Illustration 13-1, James B. Barksdale is the *maker* of the note, Harold Hawkins is the *payee,* and the *principal* of the note is $400. To Barksdale the note is a *Notes Payable,* and *Interest Expense* will be recognized by him. To Hawkins, the note is a *Notes Receivable,* and *Interest Revenue* will be recognized by him.

The time value of money, usually called *interest,* is measured by the **interest rate** stated on the note. Interest, calculated by applying the interest rate of 12 percent times the principal of $400, will be interest expense for the maker and interest revenue for the payee. The principal plus interest will be paid by Barksdale and received by Hawkins.

The interest rate of 12 percent is stated on an annual basis. Since the note is for 90 days, an adjustment must be made for the time factor. This adjustment will be shown later as a part of the interest calculation.

Interest calculation

The rate of interest on a note is stated as an annual rate. The principal amount of the note is multiplied by the rate to determine the amount of interest related to the note. If the note is for other than one year, an

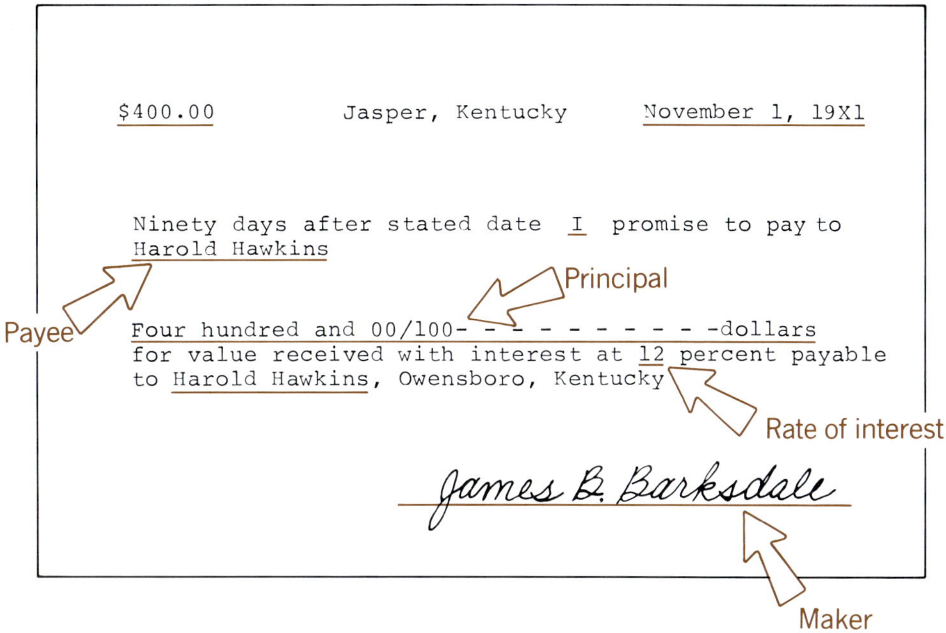

$400.00 Jasper, Kentucky November 1, 19X1

Ninety days after stated date I promise to pay to Harold Hawkins

Four hundred and 00/100- - - - - - - - - - -dollars for value received with interest at 12 percent payable to Harold Hawkins, Owensboro, Kentucky

James B. Barksdale

illustration 13-1 promissory note.

adjustment must be made for the time factor. The formula for calculating interest follows:

Principal Amount	×	Interest Rate	×	Time Factor Adjustment	=	Interest Amount

For example, interest on a $3,000 note for 90 days at 12 percent would be computed:

$$\$3{,}000 \times .12 \times 90/360 = \$90$$

If the note is for one year, the time factor adjustment could be stated as 360/360, the whole number 1, so it can be omitted from the calculation. The number of days used as the denominator in the time factor adjustment fraction was 360 days rather than 365 days. This is a common business practice, one that is usually acceptable by the maker and payee.

To find the exact **maturity date** of a note, a precise calculation is necessary, since the number of days in a month varies. For a 90-day note at 12 percent dated June 9, the maturity date would be September 7, determined as follows:

Days in June	30
Less the date of the note	9

Number of days in June	21	
Add days in July	31	
Add days in August	31	
Days through August 31	83	
Add days in September to bring total to 90	7	(maturity date)
Total days of note	90	

Before we go on, let's stop and deal with a troublesome problem. Although we deal with the months of the year every day, an amazing number of people do not know the number of days in each month. So that you will not be among this group, we have included some easy ways to remember these numbers.

The first approach is the "knuckle" method. If you will make a fist and hold up your hand with your fingers away from you, humps and valleys should appear on the top of your fist. The hump (or knuckle) is 31 and the valley between the knuckes is 28, 29, or 30. Starting from either end, the hump is January (or 31 days), the valley is February (28 or 29 days), the hump is March (31 days), etc., until the last hump is July (31 days). Then start over again with August at a hump (31 days) and complete the year.

The second approach may be easier for some of you. It is a widely known poem:

Thirty days has September
April, June, and November
All the rest have thirty-one
Except the second month alone
Which has twenty-eight, except
In a leap year it has twenty-nine.
Source: *Mother Goose*

A convenient way to determine interest, especially if a calculator is not available, is the *60-day, 6 percent method* or a variation called the 6-day, 6 percent method. Each method is based on the fractional part of a year for the number of days used; 60 days and 6 days, respectively. Sixty days is 1/6 of a year. If the interest rate on a note is 6 percent, then 1/6 of 6 percent is equal to 1 percent. The 1 percent applied to the principal amount would give the same amount of interest as using the formula. An easy way to apply the 60-day, 6 percent method is merely to point off two places to the left in the principal amount. For a \$2,000 note at 6 percent for 60 days, the interest would be \$20, determined by pointing off two places in the \$2,000. Observe that the formula gives the same amount: $\$2,000 \times .06 \times 60/360 = \$20$.

The 6-day, 6 percent method uses the same basic idea as does the 60-

day method. Six days are 1/60 of a year or 1/10 of 1 percent (6 days are 1/10 of 60 days), which may be expressed by the decimal .001. Therefore, to get the interest for 6 days at 6 percent, three places to the left should be pointed off in the principal amount. Assume that we have a $7,000, 6 percent note for 6 days. The interest would be $7. Determining interest with a hand calculator is quite simple. To illustrate, assume a note for $6,200 at 13 percent for 90 days. The interest of $201.50 is found by multiplying $6,200 times 13 times 90, then dividing the results by 36,000. The 60-day, 6 percent rule can still be used as a test of reasonableness. Interest on $6,200 for 60 days at 6 percent is $62, so an answer of $20.15 or $2,015 (rather than $201.50 on the $6,200 for 90 days at 13 percent) would be unrealistic.

Stated and true interest rate

Stated and true effective interest rates may be the same, or they may be different. If the rates are different, the true rate is usually higher than the stated rate. The stated rate is always used to compute the amount of interest and is printed on the note. The **true interest** rate is the **stated interest** amount for a year divided by the proceeds of the note. If $10,000 is borrowed by a business from a bank at a stated rate of 12 percent for one year, the true rate will also be 12 percent if the business has use of the entire $10,000 for the year. Interest of $1,200 would be paid to the bank at the end of the year, along with the principal of $10,000. We will refer to this type of note as a **regular note payable.** If, on the other hand, the bank deducts the interest of $1,200 at the beginning of the year, the effective rate would be higher than 12 percent. In this situation the business has use of only $8,800 for the year and pays back $10,000, which includes the interest. The latter case is called a **discounted note payable.** The effective rate for the discounted rate would be 13.636 percent, determined as follows:

$$\$10{,}000 \times .12 \times 360/360 = \$1{,}200$$
$$\$1{,}200/\$8{,}800\ (\$10{,}000 \text{ less } \$1{,}200) = 13.636 \text{ percent}$$

The concept of comparing a true interest rate with a stated interest rate is very important in business transactions, as well as in personal transactions for individuals.

sample problem The Brock Company has an option to borrow from either of two local banks as follows:

1. First National—A $6,000 regular note payable at 12 percent for one year.
2. American State—A $6,000 discounted note payable at 12 percent for one year.

Instructions

(a) Calculate the amount of interest for each bank's note using the 60-day, 6 percent method.

(b) Calculate the true rate of interest for each potential loan.

(c) From which bank should the business borrow the $6,000?

sample problem solution

(a) 1. First National Bank:
$6,000 at 6 percent for 60 days = $60
12 percent for 60 days = $120
12 percent for 360 days (60 days × 6) = $720

2. American State Bank:
Interest calculation the same = $720

(b) 1. First National Bank:
$720/$6,000 = 12 percent effective rate

2. American State Bank:
$720/$5,280 ($6,000 less $720) = 13.636 percent effective rate

(c) The Brock Company should borrow from the First National Bank since the true rate is 12 percent, the same as the stated rate. In addition, Brock would have use of the entire $6,000 rather than only $5,280 for the one-year period.

review exercises

1. The Alexander Company borrows $7,000 from the First National Bank at 15 percent for 120 days. The note is dated March 20, 19X8. The Alexander Company has use of the entire $7,000 for the 120 days.

Instructions

(a) Which party is the maker of the note? The payee?
(b) Calculate the maturity date of the note.
(c) Calculate the amount of interest using the 60-day, 6 percent method and verify this amount by using the formula method.

2. Calculate the interest for these notes:
(a) $2,800 at 6 percent for 24 days.
(b) $4,500 at 8 percent for 60 days.
(c) $5,000 at 12 percent for 78 days.

3. Calculate the true interest rate for these notes:
(a) $4,000 discounted note payable at 8 percent for one year.
(b) $6,000 discounted note payable at 12 percent for 180 days.
(c) $8,000 regular note payable at 10 percent for 120 days.

• task RECORD RECEIPT OF NOTE RECEIVABLE, CASH RECEIVED FOR INTEREST, ACCRUED INTEREST, AND MATURITY OF THE NOTE

Notes receivable

Most businesses do not have very many notes receivable; many do not issue notes receivable for a year or longer. The reason is rather apparent if you remember the purpose of a service, merchandising, or manufacturing company. The purpose is not to lend money but to provide a service, sell a product, or make and sell a product.

Financial institutions such as banks, however, have numerous notes receivable since these notes relate directly to the business purpose of lending money.

Note receivable transactions

A note receivable may be accepted in a credit sale or in exchange for an account receivable. Assume that a sale in the amount of $5,000 is handled on credit by accepting a 60-day, 12 percent note. Usually notes would not be received for small credit sales, such as those for $18 or $30.

GENERAL JOURNAL — Page 25

Date		Description	P.R.	Dr.	Cr.
19X1					
Dec.	16	Notes Receivable		5000 –	
		Sales			5000 –
		Sold merchandise on credit			
		with terms of 60-day, 12			
		percent note			

Also, assume that this same business that accepts the note made a credit sale for $3,000 on November 1 with terms of n/30. On December 1 an agreement is made between the buyer, Alex Jones, and seller, Henry Smith, to exchange the account receivable for a note receivable at 9 percent for 90 days. This arrangement permits Jones, who is having cash flow problems, additional time to pay the amount owed. Two basic differences distinguish an open account receivable from a note receivable. A note requires a formal signed document and usually produces revenue in the form of interest.

Date		Account	Debit	Credit
Nov.	1	Accounts Receivable/Alex Jones	3000 –	
		Sales		3000 –
		Sold merchandise with		
		terms of n/30		

Date		Account	Debit	Credit
Dec.	1	Notes Receivable	3000 –	
		Accounts Receivable/Alex Jones		3000 –
		Exchanged on accounts		
		receivable for a 90-day,		
		9 percent notes receivable		

Both of these notes receivable would be outstanding at the end of the accounting period on December 31. Therefore, accrued interest revenue would be calculated and recorded on December 31.

Date		Account	Debit	Credit
Dec.	31	Interest Receivable	47 50	
		Interest Revenue		47 50
		To record interest earned on		
		notes receivable in current		
		year but not received in cash.*		

*Determined as follows:

\$5000 X .12 X 15/360 = \$25.00 (12/15 note)

\$3000 X .09 X 30/360 = \$22.50 (12/1 note)

Total Accrued Interest \$47.50

For the balance sheet dated December 31, *Notes Receivable* of \$8,000 and *Interest Receivable* of \$47.50 would be shown as current assets. *Interest Revenue* of \$47.50 would be presented on the income statement as other revenue and would be closed to the *Income Summary* account, along with all other nominal accounts as of December 31. Financial statement presentation will be discussed later in this chapter.

On February 14, the \$5,000 note will mature. If the maker of the note pays on the maturity date, the following entry would be prepared, assuming no reversing entry was made.

The entry below shows collecting $25 interest earned in 19X1 and $75 interest earned in 19X2.

				Debit	Credit
Feb.	14	Cash		5100 –	
		Notes Receivable			5000 –
		Interest Revenue			75 – *
		Interest Receivable			25 –
		To record receipt of principal amount plus interest earned.			

* If reversing entries are used for the two notes, then Interest Revenue would be $100 on Feb. 14 and $67.50 on March 1.

				Debit	Credit
Mar.	1	Cash		3067 50	
		Notes Receivable			3000 –
		Interest Revenue			45 – *
		Interest Receivable			22 50
		To record receipt of the principal and interest earned.			

The $3,000 note matures on March 1, and an entry is made to record the receipt of cash if the maker pays on the maturity date.

The entry above records receipt of $3,000, which is the principal of the note, plus interest of $67.50. *Interest Receivable* represents the amount earned in the prior fiscal period and *Interest Revenue* indicates the amount earned in the current fiscal period.

Dishonored notes receivable

Sometimes a note is not paid by the maker at the maturity date. If the note was received in exchange for an account receivable, postponing payment of the account by giving a note may indicate that the customer is having financial difficulties. This fact suggests that the payee should be aware of the possibility of nonpayment. Assume that The Oakley Company is holding a note receivable dated March 1 for $3,000 for 60 days at 12 percent interest. On May 2 Peggy Freeman, maker of the note, tells Oakley she cannot pay the note at this time but expects to pay at least part of the amount in three months. Oakley transfers the principal and interest due to *Accounts Receivable* by this entry:

May	2	Accounts Receivable/Peggy Freeman	3060 —	
		Notes Receivable		3000 —
		Interest Revenue		60 —
		To record dishonored note and interest as accounts receivable.		

This account would be of special interest in establishing the estimate of bad debts if not paid by the end of the period. Estimating bad debts is discussed later in this chapter.

Notes receivable discounted

A business may need cash for operations before a note receivable becomes due. Rather than issue a note payable, the business can take the other party's note to a bank and receive cash before the maturity date. This procedure is referred to as **discounting a note receivable.** The bank will, of course, charge interest for this service. The business is usually contingently liable to pay the bank if the maker does not pay at maturity date. A **contingent liability** is an event that may happen in the future, but is related to some event that has already occurred. It should be contrasted with an actual liability. The Haygood Company holds a $9,000, 120 day, 9 percent note receivable dated June 1 from Terri Sharp. Haygood discounts the note (sells it to the bank) on July 25 at a 12 percent interest rate. Steps in the process of determining and recording the terms of this transaction follow:

1. Maturity date of the note receivable:
   The **maturity date** of a note is the date that the note becomes due. The period of time between the issuance date and the maturity date can be expressed in either days or months.

Term of the Note		120 days	
June	30		
less	1		
		29	
		91	
July	31		
August	31		
		62	
September		29	(maturity date)

2. Maturity value of note:
   The amount that the holder of the note will receive from the maker on the maturity date is known as the **maturity value.**

$$\$9{,}000 \times .09 \times 120/360 = \$270 + \$9{,}000 = \$9{,}270$$

3. Days of discount (or bank holding period):

June 1		90 days July 25		September 29
	54 days		66 days	
Date of Note		Date of Discount		Maturity Date

The days of discount are counted from the date of discount to the maturity date.

July	31
less	25
	6
August	31
September	29
	66 (days of discount)

4. Amount of discount:
The amount of **discount** is calculated by multiplying the maturity value times the discount rate times the time factor adjustment, using the days of discount. The discount is the amount the financial institution charges for interest.

$$\$9{,}270 \times .12 \times 66/360 = \$203.94$$

5. Proceeds:
The **proceeds,** the net amount received from the financial institution, are calculated by subtracting the amount of discount from the maturity value.

$$\$9{,}270 \text{ less } \$203.94 = \$9{,}066.06$$

6. Record the proceeds:

Date		Account	Debit	Credit
July	25	Cash	9066 06	
		Interest Expense	203 94	
		Notes Receivable		9000 —
		Interest Revenue		270 —
		To record proceeds of discounted note.		

Note that *Interest Revenue* of $270 and *Interest Expense* of $203.94 are both recorded in the transaction. Also, the business is contingently liable to pay the bank if Terri Sharp does not pay as agreed. The proceeds may be recorded to show this liability in a ledger account and to net revenue and expense.

			Debit	Credit
July	25	Cash	9066 06	
		Interest Revenue		66 06
		Notes Receivable		9000 —
		To record proceeds of discounted note.		

Rather than report both *Interest Revenue* and *Interest Expense* in the income statement, only the net amount of $66.06 would be presented. If the maker pays the bank on the maturity date, no entry is necessary on the discounter's books. If the maker does not pay the bank on the maturity date, an entry is required on the discounter's books. To illustrate, assume that the bank notifies Haygood on October 2 that Terri Sharp (the maker) has not paid and the bank asks for the maturity value plus a $5 protest fee.

			Debit	Credit
Oct.	3	Accounts Receivable/Terri Sharp	9275 —	
		Cash		9275 —
		To record payment including the $5-protest fee for dishonored discount note.		

sample problem A $7,000 note receivable is received from Holton Company in exchange for an account receivable. The note is for 120 days at 12 percent interest and is dated November 1.

Instructions Assuming the company's accounting period ends on December 31, prepare journal entries supported by calculations to: (1) record receipt of the note, (2) accrue interest on December 31, (3) reverse the December 31 adjusting entry, and (4) record receipt of principal and interest on the maturity date.

sample problem solution

			Debit	Credit
(1)	Nov. 1	Notes Receivable	7,000	
		Accounts Receivable/Holton Co.		7,000
(2)	Dec. 31	Interest Receivable	140	
		Interest Revenue		140
		($7,000 × .12 × 60/360 = $140)		
(3)	Jan. 2	Interest Revenue	140	
		Interest Receivable		140
(4)	Mar. 1	Cash	7,280	
		Notes Receivable		7,000
		Interest Revenue		280
		($7,000 × .12 × 120/360 = $280)		

Maturity date:			
November		30	days
November		1	date of note
		29	
Add:	December	31	
	January	31	
	February	28	
		119	
	March	1	(maturity date)
		120	days

review exercises

4. The Hang Company receives a $8,000, 90-day, 10 percent note receivable for a credit sale of a machine to Ron Bruce. The note is dated August 1 and the accounting period ends December 31. Calculate or provide answers for the following:
   (a) Maturity date.
   (b) Interest revenue.
   (c) Maturity value (principal plus interest revenue).
   (d) List all the journal entries needed for the note.
   (e) Would a reversing entry be appropriate in this situation? Explain.
5. Assume that the note in Exercise 4 was dated November 21. On the maturity date, the note was dishonored by Ron Bruce. Prepare entries related to this note, assuming that a reversing entry is used.
6. The Crosby Company holds a $11,000 note receivable from Bob Dye dated August 1 for 90 days at 10 percent interest. Crosby discounts the note at the bank on August 31 at 12 percent. Calculate the proceeds and make the journal entry to record them.

• task RECORD ISSUANCE OF NOTE PAYABLE, INTEREST PAID, ACCRUED INTEREST, AND MATURITY OF THE NOTE

Notes payable

Most businesses need to borrow to finance their operations. The borrowing may be either long-term or short-term. If it is long-term, the company may choose to issue bonds, mortgages, or notes. Bonds and mortgages may be issued for 10 or 20 years or longer. Although notes may be long-term, many notes are for relatively short periods, such as one year or less. Some notes are for 30, 60, or 90 days. These short-term notes may be renewed in some cases, or a new note may be issued.

The cash flow of a business is important to its overall operation. This cash flow is a separate stream from net income and often is very different from it. Although a business may be expanding and showing substantial net income, it often may be short of cash. For example, additional cash is needed during expansion to increase inventories and accounts receivable, pay additional rent, construct new buildings, or purchase equipment. A note payable is an easy way to handle some of the additional cash needs. A note might be issued by a business to take advantage of cash discounts or to pay taxes or salaries. The cost of borrowing, called *interest expense,* is an additional cost of doing business.

Interest-bearing notes payable

A regular note payable is issued to the bank for $9,000 for 90 days at 15 percent interest. The note is dated November 11.

Nov.	11	Cash	9000 –	
		Notes Payable		9000 –
		Issued a 90-day 15		
		percent note to the bank.		

If the company's accounting period ends on December 31, an adjusting entry is necessary to recognize accrued interest expense.

Dec.	31	Interest Expense	187 50	
		Interest Payable		187 50
		To accrue interest for 50		
		days at 15 percent.		
		($9000 X .15 X 50/360 = $187.50)		

The entry at the maturity date follows:

Feb.	9	Notes Payable	9000 –	
		Interest Expense	150 –	
		Interest Payable	187 50	
		Cash		9337 50
		To record note and interest		
		paid at maturity date.		
		Interest recognized in		
		current year for 40 days.		
		($9000 X .15 X 40/360 = $150–)		

Notice that no reversing entry was used in January. Had such an entry been used, *Interest Expense* would have been debited for $337.50. Using a reversing entry with accrued interest will be illustrated in the sample problem.

The December 31 balance sheet would show both the $9,000 note and *Interest Payable* as current liabilities at December 31. The income statement would present *Interest Expense* of $187.50 as part of other expenses for the year ended December 31. Financial statement presentation will be shown in more detail later in this chapter.

Discounted notes payable

In contrast with regular notes payable, which were discussed above, a note may be discounted by the bank at the time it is issued. Discounting means that the bank deducts the interest at the issue date, and the payee has only the net amount to use during the time the note is outstanding. Using the same note as that shown for the regular notes payable, we will make the entries for a discounted note. Reversing entries are not appropriate in this situation.

				Debit	Credit
Nov.	11	Cash		8662 50	
		Discount on Notes Payable		337 50	
		Notes Payable			9000 –
		To record discounted note			
		for 90 days at 15 percent.			

				Debit	Credit
Dec.	31	Interest Expense		187 50	
		Discount on Notes Payable			187 50
		To recognize interest expense			
		for 50 days of the 90 day			
		note.			
		(50/90 X $337.50 = $187.50)			

				Debit	Credit
Feb.	9	Notes Payable		9000 –	
		Interest Expense		150 –	
		Cash			9000 –
		Discount on Notes Payable			150 –
		To record payment of 90-day			
		note at maturity date and			
		remaining interest			
		recognized.			

The discounted note requires a payment of only $9,000, rather than $9,337.50, since the $9,000 includes the interest, and the borrower receives only $8,662.50. The stated rate of interest is 15 percent, but the true rate of interest is slightly higher. The true rate may be calculated as follows:

$$\$8{,}662.50 \times 90/360 = \$2{,}165.63$$
$$\$337.50/\$2{,}165.63 = .1558 \text{ or } 15.58 \text{ percent}$$

The net amount borrowed is first converted to a 90-day period since the stated 15 percent rate is an annual rate. In the regular note situation previously discussed, the true rate is the same as the 15 percent stated rate.

$$\$337.50/\$2{,}250\ (\$9{,}000 \times 90/360) = .15 \text{ or } 15 \text{ percent}$$

The write-off of the discount on the note to *Interest Expense* is similar to other adjusting entries, such as the adjustment for *Prepaid Insurance* to *Insurance Expense.*

The regular note is always better for the borrower than the discounted note because of the lower true effective interest rate. Of course, the discounted note is advantageous to the lender.

sample problem

The Manchester Company borrows $12,000 from the First National Bank at 12 percent interest for 120 days, receiving the entire $12,000 at the issuance date. The note is dated December 1, and the accounting period for Manchester ends on December 31. Prepare all the necessary journal entries for the 120-day period, using a reversing entry on January 2.

sample problem solution

Date	Account	Debit	Credit
Dec. 1	Cash	12,000	
	Notes Payable		12,000
31	Interest Expense	120	
	Interest Payable		120
Jan. 2	Interest Payable	120	
	Interest Expense		120
Mar. 31	Notes Payable	12,000	
	Interest Expense	480	
	Cash		12,480

review exercises

7. The Jennings Company borrows $6,000 from the bank for 90 days at 12 percent, receiving the entire $6,000 to use during the 90 days. The note is dated November 21, and the accounting period for Jennings ends December 31. Prepare all the entries for the 90-day period without using a reversing entry.

8. Using the same note as that described in Exercise 7, prepare the reversing entry on January 2 and the entry to be made at maturity if a reversing entry has been used.
9. Using the note in Exercise 7, except that the bank discounts the note, prepare all necessary journal entries for the 90-day period. A reversing entry is not appropriate for a discounted note.

• task ASSIST IN ESTIMATING BAD DEBTS AND RECORDING ADJUSTMENTS, WRITE-OFFS, AND RECOVERIES

Accounting for uncollectible accounts

An account receivable or a note receivable usually arises as a part of the revenue making process. It follows that any losses from uncollectible accounts or notes should be recognized in the same accounting period in which the revenue is recognized. Since there is some lag time in determining whether a note or account is collectible, the only way to match bad debt losses with revenues properly is to estimate the amount and make an adjusting entry at the end of the year. This method, called the **allowance method,** is more important for accounts or notes arising near the end of the accounting period. Another method sometimes used is called the **direct write-off method,** which means that the loss is recognized when the specific account or note is identified as uncollectible. The direct write-off method is not acceptable unless the results are not materially different from those obtained using the allowance method. Under the direct write-off method, *Bad Debt Expense* is not matched with revenue in the year of the revenue recognition.

Percentage of credit sales method

Since most businesses do not have many notes receivable, no overall procedure of estimating uncollectibles is appropriate. Most businesses have many accounts receivable, however, and an overall procedure tends to give satisfactory results. A frequently used approach of estimating bad debts is the **percentage of credit sales method** (also called the *income statement approach*). Users of this method have the option of using credit sales or net credit sales. In our example, we will be using net credit sales.

In Illustration 13-2 we show data for a firm that began in 19X1. This company adjusts its percentage each year based on a five-year average. Because 19X1 did not have previous data for analysis, 2 percent was arbitrarily chosen. Beginning in 19X2, the 19X1 net credit sales amount ($82,000) was divided into bad debt losses experienced in 19X1 ($1,260). The resulting percentage (1.54%) served as the basis for estimating bad debt losses in 19X2. In 19X3 the percentage was found by dividing the sum of the bad debt losses for 19X1 and 19X2 ($1,260 + $1,190) by the sum of the net credit sales for these two years ($82,000 + $85,500). The resulting percentage (1.46%) was used to estimate bad debt losses for 19X3. This procedure is followed each year to calculate the expected losses from bad debts. After the firm has been in operation for five years, the oldest year's data can be dropped as current data are added.

illustration 13-2 percentage of net credit sales method.

	19X1	19X2	19X3	19X4	Totals
Credit Sales	$82,000	$85,500	$84,000	$87,600	$339,100
Bad Debt Losses	1,260	1,190	1,400	1,310	5,160
Percentage of Sales	2.00	1.54	1.46	1.53	1.52*

*The 1.52 percent is to be applied to the total credit sales of $89,300, for 19X5, and the $1,357 ($89,300 × .0152) used as the bad debt loss estimate for 19X5, the current year. The 1.52 percent is used because it is the average for the four-year period.

Aging method

Another method of estimating losses is to analyze the make-up of *Accounts Receivable.* We discussed this *aging method* briefly in Chapter 6. The accounts may be separated into different age groups. The idea is that the oldest accounts are less likely to be collectible. This method is often called the *balance sheet approach.* A brief example is shown in Illustration 13-3.

illustration 13-3 aging method of estimation.

Total Accounts Receivable	0-30 Days	31-60 Days	61-90 Days	Over 90 Days	Estimated Bad Debts
$128,000	$98,000	$20,000	$7,000	$3,000	(total of all
5 year average	× .01	× .015	× .03	× .20	age groups)
Estimation	$980	$300	$210	$600	$2,090

For individual accounts, additional information may be obtained from the credit department about correspondence with the debtor and past collection experience, especially for accounts more than 60 days past due. This data could be used to adjust the amount calculated from the percentages representing past experience.

Notes receivable are usually analyzed on an individual basis for collectibility. Since notes receivable are infrequent, percentages of uncollectible notes from prior years would not usually be a good measure of current notes. If certain notes are considered to be either partially or wholly uncollectible, the allowance method would be appropriate to match the losses with revenue of the same year.

Recording the adjustment

Under the allowance method, an adjusting entry should be made at the end of the accounting period for the estimated uncollectible accounts. For the amount estimated for 19X5 in Illustration 13-2, using the percentage of credit sales method, the adjustment for accounts receivable would be:

19X1				
Dec.	31	Bad Debts Expense	1357 —	
		Allowance for Uncollectible Accounts		1357 —
		To record estimated bad debts.		

Bad Debts Expense of $1,357 is shown as an operating expense in the income statement. *Allowance for Uncollectible Accounts* of $1,357 is deducted from the *Accounts Receivable* balance in the balance sheet. The allowance account is a contra asset account and has a normal credit balance. When using the percentage of credit sales method, the calculated amount is the basis for the adjusting entry *regardless of the balance in the allowance account.*

For the aging method shown in Illustration 13-3, assuming a debit balance in the allowance account of $200, the entry would be:

Dec.	31	Bad Debts Expense	2290 —	
		Allowance for Uncollectible Accounts		2290 —
		To record estimated bad debts		

Note that the accounts in the above journal entry are exactly the same as those used for the percentage of credit sales method. The amount calculated by using the aging process is the ending balance desired in *Allowance for Uncollectible Accounts* after the adjusting entry is made. Based on the information in 13-3, a balance of $2,090 is desired. In the above journal entry, the entry amount needed to bring the allowance account's balance from a negative $200 to a positive $2,090 balance (contra asset accounts have credit balances) was $2,290. Had the balance in the allowance account been a $100 credit, the amount of the adjusting entry would have been $1,990 ($2,090 − $100).

The ledger account for *Allowance for Uncollectible Accounts* would appear as shown below for the two different situations.

(1) Debit balance:

Allowance for Uncollectible Accounts — Account No. 114

Date		Item	P.R.	Dr.	Cr.	Balance Dr.	Balance Cr.
19X1 Dec.	31	Balance	✓	200 —		200 —	
	31	Adjusting	G23		2290 —		2090 —

(2) Credit balance:

Allowance for Uncollectible Accounts Account No. 114

Date		Item	P.R.	Dr.	Cr.	Balance Dr.	Balance Cr.
19X1 Dec.	31	Balance	✓		100 –		100 –
	31	Adjusting	G23		1990 –		2090 –

In either case the balance after posting the adjusting entry is the amount estimated in the calculation, $2,090.

Note that the adjustment can be made without identifying specific uncollectible accounts. The expense is matched with revenue in the correct year, even though specific accounts are not written off until later. The adjustment also permits the current asset, *Accounts Receivable,* to be stated at its **net realizable value,** the amount expected to be collected. Thus, the allowance method is proper from both an income statement and balance sheet effect.

Writing off a bad debt

Uncollectible accounts will be identified during the months after the adjustment has been made, the old year closed, and the new accounting period begun. As specific accounts are identified as uncollectible, a write-off will be made against the allowance previously established. Assume that John Gentry, with a $625 balance in *Accounts Receivable,* is determined on February 10, 19X1, to be unable to pay the account. The entry would be as follows:

Date		Account	P.R.	Dr.	Cr.
Feb.	10	Allowance for Uncollectible Accounts		625 –	
		Accounts Receivable/John Gentry			625 –
		To write-off uncollectible			
		account of John Gentry.			

After all uncollectible accounts have been written off during the year, *Allowance for Uncollectible Accounts* will usually have a small debit or credit balance. A *debit* balance would be caused by writing off a total amount larger than the amount carried in the account. A *credit* balance would follow if total write-offs were less in dollar amount than the amount carried in the account. This situation is to be expected since the adjustment to this account was based on an estimate. Unless this balance, either debit or credit, in the allowance continues to grow from year to year, the amount may be carried forward without undue concern. If the balance continues to build up through a few years, the percentages used might be adjusted slightly to compensate for the situation.

If notes receivable are analyzed separately, as suggested earlier in this chapter, they would be written off directly since the specific note has been identified and can be credited rather than the allowance. If a business does have a number of notes and a percentage is used, an allowance would be used as illustrated for an account receivable.

Bad debt recoveries

Sometimes a previously written off account receivable may be collected in part or in full. Since the write-off decision is a judgment call, this occurrence is to be expected. Assume that John Gentry, after six months have passed, pays $400 on his account, which was written off by debiting the allowance account. The entry would be as follows:

19X1				
Aug.	11	Accounts Receivable/John Gentry	625 –	
		Allowances for Uncollectible Accounts		625 –
		To set up the amount		
		previously written off based		
		on John Gentry's Payment of $400.–		
	11	Cash	400 –	
		Accounts Receivable/John Gentry		400 –
		To credit John Gentry for		
		partial payment of		
		written-off account.		

Observe that the entire amount of $625 is reestablished in the account. There are two basic reasons for this procedure. Since Gentry has made a partial payment, he may possibly pay all or a portion of the remaining amount. This action will alert the credit department to attempt to collect the remainder. In addition, the customer, John Gentry, should be given credit for his payment, and it should be fully reflected in the records for future credit ratings. The same final results would be obtained, of course, by debiting *cash* and crediting the allowance for any amounts collected, but the approach shown is much preferred.

sample problem The Assurance Company has a debit balance of $200 in *Allowance for Uncollectible Accounts* at December 31, 19X1. Credit sales for the year amounted to $128,000, and past experience indicates that 2 percent of credit sales is a satisfactory way to establish estimated bad debts.

Instructions

(a) Calculate the amount to be used in the adjusting entry for bad debts at December 31, 19X1.

(b) Make the adjusting entry on December 31, 19X1.

sample problem solution

(a) $128,000 × .02 = $2,560, the $200 debit balance would not be used to adjust the computed amount.

(b)

19X1			
Dec. 31	Bad Debt Expense	2,560	
	Allowance for Uncollectible Accounts		2,560

review exercises

10. If the amounts in the sample problem above are used, *Allowance for Uncollectible Accounts* would have a credit balance of $2,360. Assume that on March 14, 19X2, a decision is made that Hershall Pennyworth cannot pay a $900 balance in his account. Prepare the journal entry on March 14.

11. Hershall Pennyworth, from Exercise 9, pays $580 on his account, which was written off on March 14. Prepare journal entries on April 12.

• task PRESENT THE PROPER BALANCE SHEET AND INCOME STATEMENT DATA FOR NOTES AND ACCOUNTS RECEIVABLE

The balance sheet

Financial statements are the final product of the accounting process. Therefore, financial statement presentation and disclosure are very important to the entire process. Users of these statements expect information adequate to make business decisions.

On the balance sheet, the basic separation in the asset and liability sections is between *current* and *long-term* items. As discussed in Chapter 11 of this textbook, the usual criterion used to make this separation is one year. If a note receivable or note payable is due eight months from the balance sheet reporting date, it would be a current item. Notes due fifteen months from the statement date would be reported as long term, but the next year, with only three months until maturity, they would become current items. The abbreviated relevant sections of the balance sheet in Illustration 13-4 show classifications discussed in this chapter for *Accounts Receivable, Notes Receivable,* and *Note Payable.*

illustration 13-4
balance sheet.

The Weekly Journal
Balance Sheet
December 31, 19X1

Assets			
Current Assets:			
Cash			8200 –
Accounts Receivable		10100 –	
Less: Allowance for Uncollectible Accounts		1200 –	8900 –
Notes Receivable (Due in less than 1 yr)			10000 –
Interest Receivable on Notes			350 –
Long-Term Assets			
Notes Receivable (Due in more than 1 yr)			8000 –
Liabilities and Owner's Equity			
Current Liabilities:			
Accounts Payable			7300 –
Notes Payable (Due in less than 1 yr)			9000 –
Interest Payable on Notes			560 –
Long-Term Liabilities:			
Notes Payable (Due in more than 1 yr)			11000 –

The income statement

Presentation and disclosure are just as important for the income statement as for the balance sheet. A condensed income statement is shown in Illustration 13-5, which includes classifications discussed in this chapter.

illustration 13-5
income statement.

The Weekly Journal
Income Statement
For Year Ended December 31, 19X1

Sales		79000 –
Cost of Goods Sold		43000 –
Gross Profit		36000 –
Operating Expenses:		
Bad Debt Expense	1300 –	
Salaries Expense	8000 –	
Rent Expense	1800 –	
Total Operating Expenses		11100 –
Net Operating Income		24900 –
Other Revenues:		
Interest Revenue	400 –	
Other Expenses:		
Interest Expense	900 –	
Net decrease to income		500 –
Net Income		24400 –

sample problem Listed below are classifications that would be shown on financial statements. For each item listed, state whether the item is current or long term for assets and liabilities and whether it would be shown on the balance sheet or income statement.

a. Accounts Receivable
b. Notes Receivable (due in 6 months)
c. Notes Payable (due in 14 months)
d. Allowance for Uncollectible Accounts
e. Interest Receivable
f. Interest Payable
g. Bad Debt Expense
h. Interest Revenue
i. Interest Expense
j. Notes Payable (due in 4 months)

sample problem solution

a. Balance sheet; current item.
b. Balance sheet; current item.
c. Balance sheet; long term item.
d. Balance sheet; current item.
e. Balance sheet; current item.
f. Balance sheet; current item.
g. Income statement.
h. Income statement.
i. Income statement.
j. Balance sheet; current item.

review exercises

12. From the classifications shown below, select the balance sheet items and state the heading under which they would be presented.

1. Accounts Receivable
2. Allowance for Uncollectible Accounts
3. Interest Payable
4. Interest Expense
5. Interest Receivable
6. Interest Revenue
7. Bad Debt Expense
8. Notes Payable (due in 3 months)
9. Notes Receivable (due in 9 months)
10. Notes Payable (due in 14 months)

chapter highlights

After studying this chapter, you should be able to:

- Calculate the interest on a note.
- Prepare all general journal entries involving receivables and notes payable.
- Estimate the amount of bad debts, write off bad debts, and record subsequent collections.
- Present receivables and notes payable properly on the financial statements.

check figures for review exercises

1. (a) Maker is the Alexander Company; payee is the First National Bank.
(b) Maturity date is July 18.
(c) Interest amount is $350.

2. (a) $11.20
(b) $60
(c) $130

3. (a) 8.6957 percent or 8.70 percent ($320 ÷ $3,680)
(b) 12.7659 percent or 12.77 percent ($360 ÷ $5,640) × 2
(c) 10 percent

4. (a) October 30
(b) $200
(c) $8,200
(d) Entries for receipt of note and for the receipt of the interest revenue and the principal amount at the maturity date.
(e) No; since there is no adjusting entry, no consideration would be made for a reversing entry.

5.

Nov. 21	Notes Receivable	8,000	
	Machinery		8,000
Dec. 31	Interest Receivable	88.89	
	Interest Revenue		88.89
Jan. 2	Interest Revenue	88.89	
	Interest Receivable		88.89
Feb. 19	Accounts Receivable/Ron Bruce	8,200	
	Notes Receivable		8,000
	Interest Revenue		200

6. Proceeds are $11,049.50.

7. The entry for the payment at the maturity date would be:

Feb. 19	Notes Payable	6,000	
	Interest Expense	100	
	Interest Payable	80	
	Cash		6,180

8. The entry for the payment at the maturity date would be:

Feb. 19	Notes Payable	6,000	
	Interest Expense	180	
	Cash		6,180

9. The entry for the payment at the maturity date would be:

Feb. 19	Notes Payable	6,000	
	Cash		6,000

10.

Mar. 14	Allowance for Uncollectible Accounts	900	
	Accounts Receivable/Hershall Pennyworth		900

11.

Apr. 12	Accounts Receivable/Hershall Pennyworth	900	
	Allowance for Uncollectible Accounts		900
12	Cash	580	
	Accounts Receivable/Hershall Pennyworth		580

12. (1) Balance sheet; current assets.
(2) Balance sheet; current assets.
(3) Balance sheet; current liability.
(4) Income statement.
(5) Balance sheet; current asset.
(6) Income statement.
(7) Income statement.
(8) Balance sheet; current liability.
(9) Balance sheet; current asset.
(10) Balance sheet; long-term liability.

key terms

The following key terms are discussed in Chapter 13 and defined in the Glossary at the end of the book.

allowance method
contingent liability
direct write-off method
discount
discounting a note receivable
discounted note payable
interest rate
maturity date
maturity value
net realizable value
note
percentage of credit sales method
proceeds
regular note payable
stated interest
true interest

questions

1. How would you determine the maturity date of a note?

2. What is meant by maturity value of a note?

3. What are the differences between an account receivable and a note receivable?
4. Distinguish between the maker and the payee of a note.
5. What is the difference between a regular note payable and a discounted note payable?
6. Would a regular note or a discounted note be better for a borrower? A lender?
7. Should one use the formula method or the 60-day, 6 percent method in calculating interest? Explain.
8. There seems to be general agreement that a business should borrow at say 12 percent, if cash is not available, to take advantage of a 2/10, n/30 cash discount. Explain why this statement is either true or false.
9. Why is the allowance method of handling bad debts preferable to the direct write-off method? Is the direct write-off method ever acceptable? Explain.
10. The percentage of credit sales method for estimating bad debts is a balance sheet approach to the problem. Is this statement true or false and why?
11. What is a dishonored note receivable? What journal entry would you make for this event?
12. What type of account is *Allowance for Uncollectible Accounts* and what is its normal balance?
13. For each item listed below, state whether it is a balance sheet or income statement item and under what heading it should be shown.
    (a) *Allowance for Uncollectible Accounts.*
    (b) *Notes Payable* (due in 8 months).
    (c) *Interest Payable.*
    (d) *Interest Receivable.*
    (e) *Bad Debt Expense.*
14. Describe discounted notes receivable and how to compute the proceeds.

exercises

1. Compute the interest on the following notes:
    (a) \$3,280 at 9 percent for 60 days.
    (b) \$5,000 at 10 percent for 24 days.
    (c) \$6,000 at 12 percent for 90 days.
    (d) \$8,000 at 13 percent for 120 days.
    (e) \$9,000 at 6 percent for 72 days.
2. Compute the maturity date on these notes:
    (a) 60-day note dated January 16.
    (b) 90-day note dated March 10.
    (c) 120-day note dated October 21.

3. Jimmy Carlson has an option to borrow $9,000 for 60 days at 12 percent on a regular note payable from the People's Bank or $9,000 from Citizens' Bank discounted at 12 percent for 60 days. Calculate the amount of interest on each note. From which bank should Carlson borrow? Explain your answer.
4. John T. Lee, Ltd. purchased $2,800 of merchandise from the Hamrock Supply Company on January 30, terms 2/10, n/30. On February 28, an agreement is reached between the two parties to exchange the open account for a 60-day, 12 percent note. Record all transactions for the sale and note on the books of both companies, assuming that the note and interest are paid on the maturity date.
5. The Center Hill Company, with an accounting period ending December 31, borrows $6,000 from the bank on a 9 percent, 90-day note dated December 1. Prepare all journal entries for the note, using a reversing entry on January 2.
6. The Heritage Company sells merchandise to Everrett Roberts on December 1 for $7,000 accepting a 60-day, 12 percent note. The accounting period for Heritage ends December 31. Prepare all journal entries for the note without using a reversing entry if the note is dishonored at the maturity date.
7. Overnight Delivery made credit sales for 19X1 of $110,000 in 19X1 and has a five-year average of 1.5 percent bad debts rate based on the percentage of credit sales method. Prepare the adjusting entry on December 31, 19X1, using the allowance method of handling bad debts.
8. Referring to Exercise 7, on February 22, 19X2, Hank Custer, a customer of Overnight Delivery, is determined to be unable to pay the account of $750. Prepare the entry to write off the account on Overnight's books.
9. Referring to Exercise 7 and 8, Hank Custer inherits a substantial amount of money and pays $600 on his past-due account on October 1. Prepare the journal entries needed on the books of Overnight for this transaction.
10. The Bowser Company holds Joey West's note receivable for $7,000 for 90 days at 10 percent dated July 1. Bowser discounts the note at the bank on July 31 at a 12 percent discount rate. Compute the proceeds and record the proceeds.

problems

1. COMPETENCY TESTED The ability to compute interest for notes.

   For the accounting year 19X1, the Fleetwood Company has the following notes.

   (1) A $3,000, one-year note receivable at 10 percent dated July 1.

   (2) A $5,000, 120-day note receivable at 12 percent dated November 1.

(3) A $7,000, six-months note payable at 9 percent dated September 1.

(4) An $8,000, 90-day, noninterest-bearing note payable discounted at 12 percent dated November 16.

Instructions

(a) Calculate the interest and the maturity value of each note.

(b) Calculate accrued interest payable, accrued interest receivable, and the amount of the discount on notes payable to be expensed at December 31.

2. COMPETENCY TESTED The ability to calculate interest for notes.

For the accounting year 19X1, the Hamdorff Company has the following notes.

(1) A $4,000, one-year note receivable at 9 percent dated September 1.

(2) A $6,000, 120-day note receivable at 10 percent dated December 1.

(3) An $11,000, six-month note payable at 12 percent dated October 1.

(4) An $8,000, 90-day, noninterest-bearing notes receivable discounted at 12 percent dated November 21.

Instructions

(a) Calculate the interest amount and the maturity value of each note.

(b) Calculate accrued interest payable and accrued interest receivable at December 31 and the interest expense that should be recognized from the discount on the notes payable.

3. COMPETENCY TESTED The ability to journalize transactions and adjustments.

The Caprice Company had the following transactions for 19X1:

Jan. 20	Sold merchandise to Henry Lane, $925, terms 2/10, n/30.
Feb. 23	Accepted cash of $125 and an $800, 90-day, 12 percent note dated February 20 in settlement of Lane's past-due account.
Apr. 10	Sold merchandise to Helen Gray, $3,000, accepting a 12 percent, six-month note dated April 10 for payment.
May 21	Received notice that the $800 note dated February 20 will not be paid.
30	Discounted a $8,000, one-year, 10 percent note payable dated May 30 at the bank.
Sept. 30	Issued a $10,000, six-month, 12 percent regular note payable dated September 30 at the bank.
Oct. 11	Received principal and interest on the $3,000 note dated April 10.
Nov. 16	Sold merchandise to Dean Goodman for $5,000, accepting a 120-day, 10 percent note receivable dated November 16 for the goods.

Instructions

(a) Prepare journal entries for all transactions.

(b) Calculate accrued interest receivable, accrued interest payable at December 31, and the amount on notes payable that should be expensed.

(c) Prepare adjusting entries for the accrued interest and expense from discount.

4. COMPETENCY TESTED The ability to journalize transactions and adjustments.

The Lolly Company had the following transactions for 19X1:

Jan.	14	Sold merchandise to Susan Stark, $1,100, terms 2/10, n/30.
Feb.	15	Accepted cash of $200 and a $900, 60-day, 12 percent note dated February 15 in settlement of her account.
Apr.	18	Received notice that the $900 note dated February 15 will not be paid at this time.
	30	Sold merchandise to Robert King, $4,000, accepting a 9 percent, six-month note dated April 30 for payment.
June	1	Discounted a $9,000, one-year, 10 percent note payable dated June 1 at the bank.
Sept.	15	Issued a $7,000, six-month, 12 percent regular note payable dated September 15 at the bank.
Oct.	30	Received payment of principal and interest on note dated April 30.
Dec.	1	Sold merchandise for $6,000, accepting a 90-day, 9 percent note receivable dated December 1 for the goods.

Instructions

(a) Prepare journal entries for all transactions.

(b) Calculate accrued interest receivable and accrued interest payable at December 31 and the expense to be recognized from the discount on notes payable.

(c) Prepare adjusting entries for the accrued interest.

5. COMPETENCY TESTED Skill in preparing journal entries for notes payable.

The Beckler Company issues two notes payable during 19X1:

(1) A regular one-year note payable for $12,000 at 12 percent dated August 1.

(2) A discounted six-month note payable for $9,000 at 12 percent dated September 1.

Instructions

(a) Prepare journal entries for both notes to record issuance of the notes, adjustments on December 31, reversing entries on January

2, 19X2, if appropriate, and receipt of principal and interest on maturity dates.

(b) Calculate the true interest rate for each note.

(c) Which is the better deal for the Beckler Company?

6. COMPETENCY TESTED Skill in preparing journal entries for notes payable.

The Sandlin Company issues two notes payable during 19X1.

(1) A regular one-year note payable for $9,000 at 10 percent dated June 1.

(2) A discounted six-month note payable for $7,000 at 10 percent dated October 1.

Instructions

(a) Prepare journal entries for both notes to record issuance, adjustments on December 31, reversing entries on January 2, 19X2, if needed, and receipt of principal and interest on maturity dates.

(b) Calculate the true interest rate for each note.

(c) Which is the better deal for the Sandlin Company?

7. COMPETENCY TESTED The ability to estimate bad debts using the allowance method.

The Freeman Company has the following data available for *Accounts Receivable:*

(1) Credit sales and bad debt losses:

	19X1	19X2	19X3	19X4	19X5
Credit sales	$46,000	$49,000	$51,000	$55,000	$52,000
Bad Debts	800	900	1,000	1,200	1,300

(2) Freeman used the percentage of credit sales method to estimate bad debts and the allowance method to handle bad debts.

(3) In 19X7 the following accounts were identified as uncollectible:

Feb. 20	Ed Watson	$300
Mar. 18	Charles Click	$450
Apr. 29	Don Crump	$250

(4) On June 27, Charles Click paid $300 on his past-due, written-off account.

(5) *Allowance for Uncollectible Accounts* has a $75 credit balance on December 31, 19X6.

Instructions

(a) Assuming Freeman had credit sales of $60,000 for 19X6, estimate bad debts for 19X6 and make the adjusting entry.

(b) Prepare entries to write off the uncollectible accounts in 19X7.

(c) Prepare entries for collecting $300 from Charles Click on August 2, 19X7. This was for the written-off account of $450.

8. COMPETENCY TESTED The ability to estimate bad debts using the allowance method.

The Edmonds Company has the following data available for accounts receivable:

(1) Five-year experience shows a bad debt loss percentage of 1.8 based on credit sales.

(2) Credit sales for 19X1 amounted to $112,000 of total sales of $178,000.

(3) For bad debts, Edmonds is using the allowance method based on a percentage of credit sales.

(4) In 19X2 the following accounts for 19X1 sales were identified as uncollectible:

Feb. 24	Patty Deason	$600
March 17	Thomas Duke	525
April 26	Homer Gardner	900

Instructions

(a) Estimate bad debts for 19X1 and make the reversing entry.

(b) Prepare entries to write off the uncollectible account in 19X2.

(c) Prepare journal entries for collecting $400 from Patty Deason on July 21, 19X2. This was for the written-off account of $600.

9. COMPETENCY TESTED The ability to present financial statements data.

The Lester Company has the following information about financial statement classifications for 19X1:

Sales	$140,000
Cost of Goods Sold	65,000
Operating Expenses, except Bad Debts Expense and Interest Expense	33,000
Bad Debts Expense	1,500
Interest Expense	1,200
Interest Revenue	900
Cash	4,000
Accounts Receivable	29,000
Allowance for Uncollectible Accounts	3,100
Notes Receivable (Due in 5 months)	7,000
Equipment	18,000

Accumulated Depreciation, Equipment	7,000
Accounts Payable	12,000
Notes Payable ($8,000 due in 4 months and $6,000 due in 14 months)	14,000
Mona Lester, Capital	(?)
Interest Receivable	300
Interest Payable	400

Fill in the amount needed to balance, which will include net income you calculated for 19X1.

Instructions Prepare (a) an income statement and (b) a balance sheet for 19X1.

10. COMPETENCY TESTED The ability to discount a note receivable.

The Meyer Company had the following transactions for notes receivable:

March	1	Received a $5,000, 60-day note at 9 percent interest for a sale of merchandise dated March 1. Maker of the note is Pam Barnett.
	31	Discounted the note dated March 1 at the bank at a 12 percent interest rate.
April	1	Received a $4,000, 90-day note at 10 percent in exchange for an accounts receivable dated April 1. Maker of the note is Gary Martin.
May	3	Received a notice from the bank that the Pam Barnett note was dishonored. The bank requested payment of maturity value and a $6 protest fee.
	11	Discounted the note dated April 1 at the bank at a discount rate of 12 percent.
July	2	Received notice from bank that Gary Martin paid the note at maturity.

Instructions

(a) Record all necessary journal entries.

(b) List the steps you went through to calculate the proceeds of the notes.

11. COMPETENCY TESTED The ability to present financial statements data.

The Blankenship Company has among its classifications for financial statements the following items for 19X1:

1.	Bad Debts Expense	$ 1,700
2.	Interest Expense	1,400
3.	Interest Revenue	800
4	Accounts Receivable	31,000

5.	Allowance for Uncollectible Accounts	2,900
6.	Notes Receivable (Due in 6 months)	8,000
7.	Notes Payable (Due in 8 months)	16,000
8.	Notes Payable (Due in 14 months)	6,000
9.	Interest Receivable	700
10.	Interest Payable	1,000

Instructions

(a) State whether each of the items listed above is a balance sheet or income statement classification.

(b) For each item, provide the proper heading for financial statement presentation.

chapter 14
INVENTORY PROCEDURES

overall competency THE ABILITY TO TAKE THE INVENTORY COUNT AND, AFTER PRICING THE INVENTORY, CALCULATE BOTH THE ENDING INVENTORY AND THE COST OF GOODS SOLD

career objectives The inventory clerk must be competent in several areas if inventory procedures are to be completed correctly. You must understand how the inventory is taken and what should be done with the data listed on the inventory sheets. You also must be able to select the appropriate price for the inventory units on hand and to calculate both the inventory balance and the cost of goods sold.

In this chapter we will examine both the periodic system and the perpetual system. We will also examine the different tasks necessary to handle inventory. Remember to test your understanding of the material by working the review exercises.

Upon completing this chapter, you should be able to:

- COUNT AND PRICE THE INDIVIDUAL ITEMS AND CALCULATE THE INVENTORY TOTAL.
- CALCULATE THE COST OF GOODS SOLD.
- USE A PERIODIC OR A PERPETUAL SYSTEM TO RECORD AND ACCOUNT FOR INVENTORY BALANCES.

Inventory procedures represent a very important function of a merchandising business. Buying items for resale is essential to any business whose primary purpose is selling products. Accurate inventory data are important in preparing both the balance sheet and the income statement. While *Merchandise Inventory* is shown as a current asset on the balance sheet, this account also appears on the income statement so that the difference between the beginning and ending inventories can be measured. These increases or decreases affect the cost of goods sold, which in turn affects net income.

Inventory procedures range from a very basic periodic system to the most detailed perpetual system. Basically, periodic systems depend entirely on a physical count at the end of the accounting period, while the perpetual systems give a running balance throughout the accounting period. This chapter will explore the tasks necessary to produce an accurate inventory.

• task COUNT AND PRICE THE INDIVIDUAL ITEMS AND CALCULATE INVENTORY TOTAL

Tagging the inventory

Written instructions are provided for the employees who are responsible for counting the inventory. The workers usually are told to work in teams of two as each person makes an independent count. After the two separate counts, totals are compared. If they disagree, the items are recounted until both counts show the same quantity. Some system for tagging or marking the stacks, bins, boxes, or space sections must be used. The tag or marker, which is attached to the groups of items, will show the type of items, size and color, and the number of items as shown in Illustration 14-1. The data on the **inventory tags** are listed on **inventory sheets,** usually after all items have been counted and tagged.

illustration 14-1
inventory tag.

Tag No.

Warehouse Location: *Section B-3*

Description of Items (Color, Size, etc.):
4 X 12 X ½" sheetrock

No. of Items: *250*

Counted by: *JM*

The inventory-taking procedure is made easier if there is no business activity when the counts are being made. Preferred days for this task are holidays, weekends, or other nonbusiness dates. If items are being added to the inventory or shipped to customers from the inventory, counting, tagging, and listing on the inventory sheets are more difficult.

Items that are not selling (usually as a result of changes in consumers' tastes) and damaged inventory units should be segregated in the warehouse and listed separately with notations about the special conditions. Also, items in the warehouse that are not owned by the business should be segregated or given special handling to make sure they are not included as a part of the inventory.

illustration 14-2
inventory sheet.

Size	Color	Identification Number	Number of Items	Unit Price	Total Price
42″	White	X-10	30		
42″	Red	X-11	45		
42″	Green	X-12	51		
42″	Gray	X-13	28		
42″	Brown	X-14	39		

The inventory sheet for five products might look like the data shown in Illustration 14-2. Note in this illustration that the unit price and total price columns are not filled in by the inventory-taking team. The employees taking the inventory only count, tag, and list the number of items, not the price. To assist you in understanding the inventory procedure, one of the items, Commodity X-10, will be used in the next task statement for pricing the inventory by the inventory clerk.

Pricing the inventory

Specific invoice prices may be used to place a value on the inventory items. However, if these prices are difficult or impossible to trace, other procedures may be followed. The **specific identification** method would require a serial or stock number on both the inventory item and the invoice as a means of identification.

In some businesses, tracing items in the inventory to specific purchase invoices is impractical; too much time would be required to make the effort worthwhile. In other businesses, this task would be impossible. If specific identification of wholesale prices is not used, one of three acceptable cost flow methods is generally employed. These acceptable alternatives are: (1) **first-in, first-out (FIFO);** (2) **last-in, first-out (LIFO);** and (3) **weighted average.** To illustrate the four methods, assume that a business enterprise uses a periodic inventory system and has selected the calendar year as its accounting period. The illustration will include computing cost of goods sold, as well as ending inventory. A separate discussion of cost of goods sold will follow later in the chapter. Only one product, Commodity X-10, will be illustrated, but a similar analysis would apply to each product listed on the inventory sheet. The following data will be used to illustrate the four methods:

Jan. 1	Beginning inventory	20 units at $10.00	=	$ 200.00
Apr. 5	Purchased	22 units at $12.00	=	264.00
Aug. 30	Purchased	30 units at $13.00	=	390.00
Nov. 27	Purchased	20 units at $12.50	=	250.00
	Total units available for sale	92		$1,104.00

Specific identification We noted in Illustration 14-2 that the final count of Commodity X-10 was 30 units. Since 92 units were available for sale and 30 units were left, 62 units must have been sold. If 12 of the 30 items were purchased on April 5 (as part of the 22) and 18 on November 27 (as part of the 20), the costs can be assigned to inventory and costs of goods sold as shown in Illustration 14-3.

illustration 14-3 specific identification method.

Inventory cost				
12 units @ $12	=	$144		
18 units @ $12.50	=	225		
30 units in the ending inventory			=	$ 369
Cost of goods sold:				
20 units @ $10	=	$200		
10 units @ $12	=	120		
30 units @ $13	=	390		
2 units @ $12.50	=	25		
62 units assigned to cost of goods sold			=	735
Total cost of 92 units available for sale			=	$1,104

Beginning inventory and each purchase may be considered as layers and partial layers. The display in Illustration 14-4 shows the flow to ending inventory and cost of goods sold.

First-in, first-out If it is not possible or practical to identify specific products in the inventory, an acceptable "cost flow assumption" must be used. Cost flow should be emphasized since this flow does not necessarily mean that the physical products move in this order. For example, inventory items such as canned goods on a shelf in a grocery store might remain

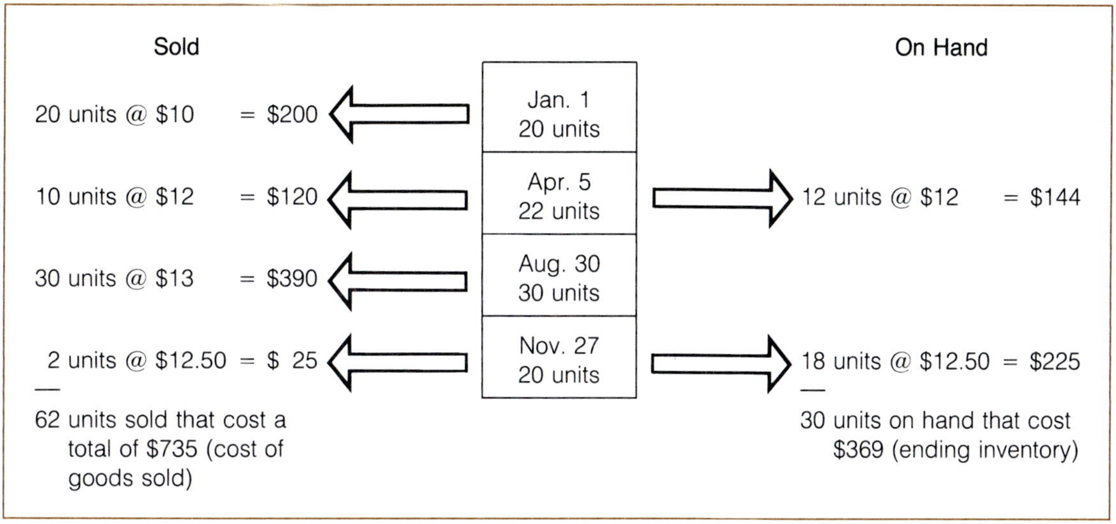

illustration 14-4 specific identification inventory layers.

for years toward the back of the shelf if stocking were not supervised properly. However, with perishable items like fresh vegetables, older items would be arranged to sell first. One of the acceptable cost flow assumptions is **first-in, first-out (FIFO).** The 30 units in inventory and cost of goods sold would be assigned as indicated in Illustration 14-5.

illustration 14-5 first-in, first-out method.

Inventory cost:				
10 units @ $13	=	$130		
20 units @ $12.50	=	250		
30 units in the ending inventory			=	$ 380
Cost of goods sold:				
20 units @ $10	=	$200		
22 units @ $12	=	264		
20 units @ $13	=	260		
62 units assigned to cost of goods sold			=	724
Total cost of 92 units available for sale			=	$1,104

Beginning inventory and each purchase may be considered as layers and partial layers. For example, in assigning costs to ending inventory, the entire layer of the November 27 purchase plus 10 units of the August 30 purchase are included to account for the 30 units in inventory. Illustration 14-6 gives you a visual display of this concept.

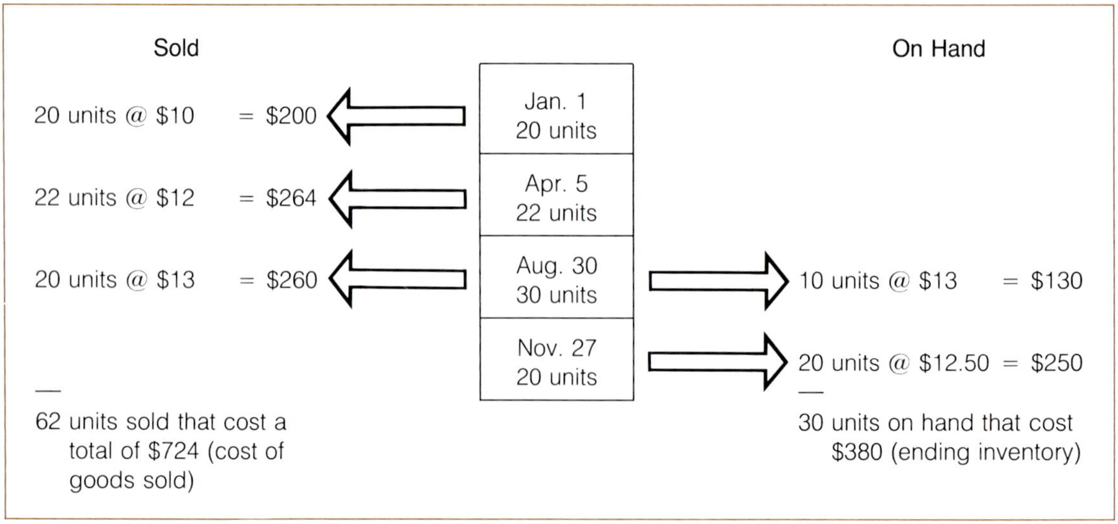

illustration 14-6 FIFO inventory layers.

Note that the term *first-in, first-out* applies directly to cost of goods sold rather than to the ending inventory to which the term is applied. That is, the cost of the first or earliest purchases flows into cost of goods sold, and the last or latest purchases are assigned to ending inventory to be carried forward on the balance sheet to the next accounting period as the beginning inventory.

Last-in, first-out Another widely used flow assumption is the **last-in, first-out (LIFO)** method. Under this method, the latest or most current costs are matched against revenue in arriving at gross profit and net income. The example of the last-in, first-out procedure that follows uses the same costs as those in the previous examples.

illustration 14-7 last-in, first-out method.

Inventory cost:				
20 units @ $10	=	$200		
10 units @ $12	=	120		
30 units in the ending inventory			=	$ 320
Cost of goods sold:				
20 units @ $12.50	=	$250		
30 units @ $13	=	390		
12 units @ $12	=	144		
62 units assigned to cost of goods sold			=	784
Total cost of 92 units available for sale			=	$1,104

Compare this assignment of cost between the two categories in Illustration 14-7 with the FIFO flow costs. Note that in Illustration 14-8 the last (most current) costs flow into cost of goods sold and that the first (oldest) costs are assigned to the ending inventory to be carried forward on the balance sheet as a current asset.

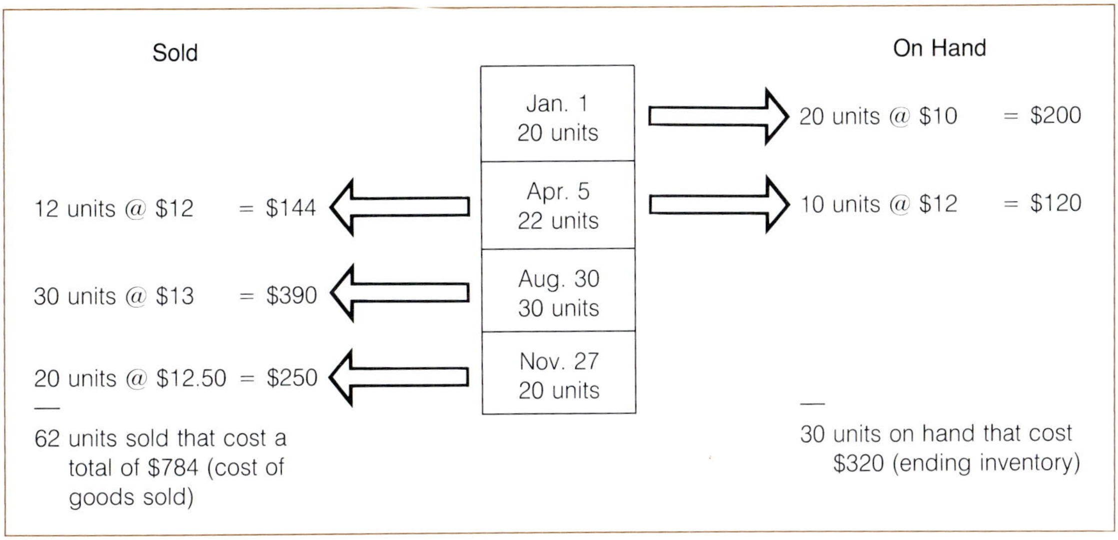

illustration 14-8 LIFO inventory layers.

Weighted average Under the **weighted-average method,** the same unit cost is assigned to both the ending inventory and the cost of goods sold. Using the same data as before, you can obtain a weighted average cost of $12 per unit by dividing the total costs of $1,104 by the total number of units, 92. The assigned costs would be as listed in Illustration 14-9.

illustration 14-9 weighted-average calculation.

Cost of ending inventory, 30 units @ $12*	=	$ 360
Cost of goods sold, 62 units @ $12	=	744
Total cost of 92 units available for sale	=	$1,104

* $1,104/92 = $12

The weighted-average method can be thought of as a process of mixing all the purchase prices together and arriving at an average price per unit. This process can be seen in Illustration 14-10.

illustration 14-10 weighted-average method.

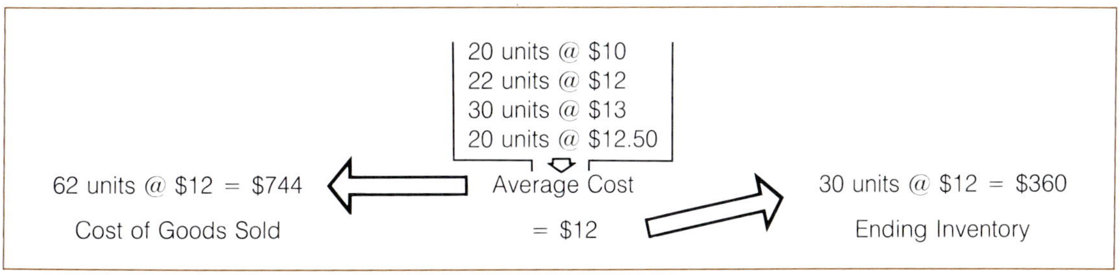

Note that under each of the four methods, a different amount is obtained for ending inventory and cost of goods sold, as shown in the comparison in Illustration 14-11. You can see in this illustration that cost of goods sold is highest under the LIFO method.

illustration 14-11
comparison of cost flow methods.

	Specific Identification	FIFO	LIFO	Weighted Average
Cost of Goods Sold	$735	$724	$784	$744
Merchandise Inventory	$369	$380	$320	$360

Gross profit and net income would differ under each method as summarized in the condensed income statements displayed in Illustration 14-12.

illustration 14-12
comparison of condensed income statements.

	Specific Identification	FIFO	LIFO	Weighted Average
Sales	$1,500	$1,500	$1,500	$1,500
Cost of Goods Sold	735	724	784	744
Gross Profit	$ 765	$ 776	$ 716	$ 756
Operations Expense	300	300	300	300
Net Income	$ 465	$ 476	$ 416	$ 456

Under each of the cost flow methods, the balance in the capital account would differ by the same amount as the merchandise inventory and net income. This fact is evident if you recall that net income is closed into the capital account.

sample problem The information below is for Commodity X-11; the ending inventory showed 45 units (Illustration 14-2).

Jan. 1	Beginning inventory	25 units at $40	=	$1,000
Mar. 22	Purchase	30 units at 41	=	1,230
Aug. 20	Purchase	32 units at 42	=	1,344
Dec. 18	Purchase	40 units at 44	=	1,760
	Total goods available for sale =	127		$5,334

Instructions Calculate the amounts for ending inventory and cost of goods sold for (1) specific identification—the 45 units in ending inventory can be identified as 20 units from the December 18 purchase, 15 from the August 20 purchase, and 10 from the March 22 purchase; (2) first-in, first-out; (3) last-in, first-out; and (4) weighted average.

sample problem solution In each case, you should calculate ending inventory and cost of goods sold. Add these amounts to determine whether the total agrees with the total goods available of $5,334.

1. Specific Identification:

Ending inventory	=	$1,920
Cost of goods sold	=	3,414
Goods available for sale	=	$5,334

2. First-In, First-Out:

Ending inventory	=	$1,970
Cost of goods sold	=	3,364
Goods available for sale	=	$5,334

3. Last-In, First-Out:

Ending inventory	=	$1,820
Cost of goods sold	=	3,514
Goods available for sale	=	$5,334

4. Weighted Average:

Unit weighted average price	=	$ 42
Ending inventory	=	1,890
Cost of goods sold	=	3,444
Goods available for sale	=	$5,334

review exercises

1. Set up a format for an inventory count sheet and fill in the columns for your products as you, the accounting clerk, would expect to receive the sheet from the inventory clerk.
2. A company has 12 units at $5.03 per unit in beginning inventory. Two purchases are made during the accounting period: 1st purchase, 15 units at $6, and 2nd purchase, 18 units at $7. Twenty-five units were sold during the accounting period. Calculate the ending inventory and cost of goods sold, assuming that half of the units on hand are identified with the first purchase and half with the second purchase.
3. The following data are available for a business that sells a product: Beginning inventory, 100 units at $80 = $8,000. 1st purchase, 150 units at $85 = 12,750; 2nd purchase, 200 units at $90 = $18,000; 3rd purchase, 130 units at $88 = $11,440. The inventory count sheet shows 160 units in the ending inventory. Other records show that 420 units were sold at $115 per unit. Compute the ending inventory using (a) FIFO, (b) LIFO, (c) weighted average.

• task CALCULATE THE COST OF GOODS SOLD

Calculating cost of goods sold

The income statement for a business that sells a product or many products has the primary classifications presented in Illustration 14-13:

illustration 14-13 income statement.

Sales	$122,000
Cost of Goods Sold	60,000
Gross Profit on Sales	$ 62,000
Operating Expenses	35,000
Net Income	$ 27,000

If the $122,000 revenue in Illustration 14-13 was made by selling 10,271 units of various products, we need to find the cost of those 10,271 units. In other words, we must determine the cost of goods sold.

Information for the cost of goods sold calculation is taken from various business documents (invoices, purchase orders, inventory reports, inventory counts, etc.) for the following categories—beginning inventory, purchases, and ending inventory. The calculation for the income statement will show totals for these categories. You have already seen the calculation for a separate product in Illustrations 14-3 through 14-13. The calculation for totals in each category follows in Illustration 14-14.

illustration 14-14 cost of goods sold section.

Cost of Goods Sold:	
Merchandise Inventory, beginning of period	$ 8,000
Purchases during the period	43,000
Cost of Goods Available for Sale	$51,000
Merchandise Inventory, end of period	9,000
Cost of Goods Sold	$42,000

sample problem From the list of accounts shown below, select the data you need to calculate the costs of goods sold using the format shown in Illustration 14-13.

Depreciation Expense	$ 7,000
Sales	90,000
Purchases	52,000
Salaries Expense	12,000

Jack Smith, Capital	$ 9,000
Ending Inventory	11,000
Accounts Receivable	15,000
Beginning Inventory	13,000

sample problem solution

Beginning Inventory	$13,000
Purchases	52,000
Cost of Goods Available for Sale	$65,000
Ending Inventory	11,000
Cost of Goods Sold	$54,000

Note that some of the accounts listed are not a part of the cost of goods sold section. Some are balance sheet accounts, and some would be shown in other sections of the income statement.

review exercises

4. Beginning inventory is $22,000; purchases amount to $60,000; and cost of goods sold is $62,000. Compute the ending inventory.
5. Sales amount to $105,000; net income is $16,000; and operating expenses total $34,000. Calculate the cost of goods sold. *Hint:* Refer to Illustration 14-14.
6. Given the same facts stated in Exercise 5 above, what is the gross profit on sales? *Hint:* Refer to Illustration 14-13.

• task USE A PERIODIC OR A PERPETUAL SYSTEM TO RECORD AND ACCOUNT FOR INVENTORY BALANCES

Periodic inventory method

Under the **periodic inventory system,** when merchandise is bought, *Purchases* is debited. Because of this procedure, *Merchandise Inventory* remains at the beginning balance, unchanged during the year. At the end of the period, a physical count of the inventory items is made and the items are priced. Another name for the periodic inventory system is the *physical inventory system*. The cost of goods sold is then calculated for the accounting period as shown in Illustration 14-14.

If a business had purchases, sales, and inventory balances as shown below, the data would be posted eventually to the ledger as shown in Illustration 14-15.

Beginning Merchandise Inventory balance		$16,000		
Purchases:				
Feb. 10	$19,000			
May 17	22,000			
Aug. 21	17,000			
Nov. 27	18,000	76,000		
Cost of Goods Available for Sale		$92,000		
Sales:				
	Cost		Sales Price	
Feb. 20	$18,000		$27,000	
Apr. 25	19,000		28,000	
Aug. 2	20,000		30,000	
Dec. 6	21,000	$78,000	31,000	$116,000
Ending Merchandise Inventory (from physical count)		$13,000		

Journal entries for buying, selling, and adjusting merchandise inventory can be seen below:

Date	Account	Debit	Credit
10	Purchases	19000 –	
	Accounts Payable/Creditor		19000 –
	To record purchases on account.		
20	Accounts Receivable/Customer	27000 –	
	Sales		27000 –

(Each of the other purchases and sales would be recorded in a similar manner.)

Date	Account	Debit	Credit
31	Income Summary	16000 –	
	Merchandise Inventory		16000 –
31	Merchandise Inventory	13000 –	
	Income Summary		13000 –

Note that even though the ending inventory should have been $14,000 ($16,000 + $76,000 − $78,000), the $13,000 amount determined by a physical count is used to record the ending inventory. The $1,000 difference is included in cost of goods sold even though the shortage may be from lost or stolen goods. The ending inventory amount would be determined, as discussed earlier, by using specific identification, FIFO, LIFO, or weighted-average methods. The relevant ledger accounts follow:

illustration 14-15 posted ledger accounts.

Merchandise Inventory — Account No. 114

Date		Item	P.R.	Dr.	Cr.	Balance Dr.	Balance Cr.
19X1 Jan.	1	Balance	✓			16000 –	
Dec.	31	Adjusting	G14		16000 –	–0–	
	31	Adjusting	G14	13000 –		13000 –	

Purchases — Account No. 411

Date		Item	P.R.	Dr.	Cr.	Balance Dr.	Balance Cr.
19X1 Feb.	10		G7	19000 –		19000 –	
May	17		G9	22000 –		41000 –	
Aug.	21		G12	17000 –		58000 –	
Nov.	27		G13	18000 –		76000 –	

Perpetual inventory method

Under the perpetual method, *Merchandise Inventory, Cost of Goods Sold,* and the individual item records have balances that are kept current. A physical count should be taken periodically and the perpetual records adjusted to show the balances indicated by the physical count. Differences between the perpetual records and the physical count may be caused by theft, spoilage, shrinkage, or errors. If a shortage occurs, *Cost of Goods Sold* is debited and *Merchandise Inventory* is credited. In the event of an overage, *Merchandise Inventory* is debited and *Cost of Goods Sold* is credited. An exception is made when the shortage or overage is very large. In case of a large shortage, *Inventory Loss* is debited and in the case of a large overage, *Gain on Inventory Overage* is credited.

To illustrate the perpetual inventory, assume that Miller Supply Company keeps its inventory by using the first-in, first-out method of pricing the inventory, along with a perpetual inventory system. During the month of January, the following purchases and sales took place:

Beginning Merchandise, Jan. 1		$1,200
Purchases:		
Jan. 9	300 units @ $4.20	
Jan. 14	400 units @ $4.50	
Jan. 24	250 units @ $5.00	
Sales (at sales price):		
Jan. 11	500 units @ $6.00	
Jan. 17	300 units @ $6.80	
Jan. 30	100 units @ $7.00	
Ending Inventory count, 300 units.		

Entries that would be made (in general journal form) for January 9, 11, and 30 are shown on the next page:

GENERAL JOURNAL Page 15

Date		Description	P.R.	Dr.	Cr.
19x1 Jan.	9	Merchandise Inventory		1260 –	
		Accounts Payable/Creditor			1260 –
		To record purchases on Account.			
		(Each of the other two purchases would be recorded exactly the same way.)			
	11	Accounts Receivable/Customer		3000 –	
		Cost of Goods Sold		2040 –	
		Sales			3000 –
		Merchandise Inventory			2040 –
		To record sale on account and reduction of inventory.			
		(Each of the other sales would be recorded in the same way. See Illustration 14–16 for details of the cost of the 500 units.)			
	30	Cost of Goods Sold		225 –	
		Merchandise Inventory			225 –
		To adjust the perpetual records showing 350 units on hand to the physical count of 300 units.			
		(The cost is computed using the $4.50 per unit that follows the FIFO costing method used for the flow of all units.)			

Assuming this business has only one product, 100-2A, the perpetual record and *Merchandise Inventory* are shown in Illustrations 14-16 and 14-17.

The journal entries and illustrations shown under this task followed the first-in, first-out method of pricing. Perpetual inventory records may be maintained for the other inventory methods similar to the way the first-in, first-out method is handled in Illustration 14-16. These other methods for the perpetual system will not be discussed in detail in this text.

sample problem The Sunrise Company's records show the following information about the inventory transactions and balances.

Beginning inventory	$14,000
Total purchases during the year	68,000
Ending inventory per physical count	10,000
Merchandise inventory, perpetual inventory balance	12,000
Sales during year (retail price $108,000), wholesale price	72,000
Operating expenses	19,000

Instructions

(a) Use the periodic system to record the buying and selling of merchandise, as well as operating expenses.

(b) Use the periodic system to prepare an income statement.

(c) Use the perpetual system to record the buying and selling of merchandise.

(d) Prepare an income statement using the perpetual system.

[Sample Problem Solution follows Illustrations 14-16 and 14-17.]

Perpetual Inventory Record
Product 100-2A

	Received			Sold			Balance		
Date	Units	Unit Cost	Total Cost	Units	Unit Cost	Total Cost	Units	Unit Cost	Total Cost
Jan. 1							300	$4.00	$1,200
9	300	$4.20	$1,260				300	$4.00	$1,200
							300	4.20	1,260
11				300	$4.00	$1,200			
				200	4.20	840	100	$4.20	$ 420
14	400	$4.50	$1,800				100	$4.20	$ 420
							400	4.50	1,800
17				100	$4.20	$ 420			
				200	4.50	900	200	$4.50	$ 900
24	250	$5.00	$1,250				200	$4.50	$ 900
							250	5.00	1,250
30				100	$4.50	$ 450	100	$4.50	$ 450
							250	5.00	1,250
30				50*	$4.50	$ 225	50	$4.50	$ 225
							250	5.00	1,250

*Adjustment from perpetual inventory of 350 units to 300 units as determined by physical count.

illustration 14-16 perpetual inventory.

illustration 14-17 merchandise inventory account using a perpetual system.

Merchandise Inventory Account No. 114

Date	Item	P.R.	Dr.	Cr.	Balance Dr.	Balance Cr.
19X1 Jan. 1	Balance	✓			1200 –	
9		G 19	1260 –		2460 –	
11		G 20		2040 –	420 –	
14		G 20	1800 –		2220 –	
17		G 21		1320 –	900 –	
24		G 23	1250 –		2150 –	
30		G 24		450 –	1700 –	
31	Adjusting	G 24		225 –	1475 –	

sample problem solution

(a)

Purchases	68,000	
Accounts Payable/Creditor		68,000
To record credit purchases, in a summary entry. (Numerous entries would be made for purchases during the year to these same accounts rather than this one summary entry.)		
Accounts Receivable/Customer	108,000	
Sales		108,000
To record credit sales for the year, in a summary entry. (Numerous entries would be made for sales rather than this one entry.)		
Operating Expenses	19,000	
Accounts Payable (or Cash)		19,000
To record expenses incurred during the year. (This is also a summary entry.)		

(b) Income Statement:

Sales		$108,000
Cost of Goods Sold		
Beginning Merchandise Inventory	$ 14,000	
Purchases	68,000	
Cost of Goods Available for Sale	$ 82,000	
Less: Ending Merchandise Inventory	10,000	
Cost of Goods Sold		72,000
Gross Profit		$ 36,000
Operating Expenses		19,000
Net Income		$ 17,000

(c)

Merchandise Inventory	68,000	
Accounts Payable/Creditor		68,000
To record, in a summary entry, the purchases on a credit basis.		
Accounts Receivable/Customer	108,000	
Sales		108,000
To record credit purchases, in a summary entry.		

Cost of Goods Sold	72,000	
Merchandise Inventory		72,000
To record, in a summary entry, the wholesale price of the sales as a reduction of the inventory account and a charge to the cost of goods sold. (Note that this entry was not made under the periodic system.)		

(d) These two presentations would be identical to those shown in Solution (2) for the periodic system, since the perpetual records would be adjusted by $2,000 to reduce the inventory records to the $10,000 from the physical count amount. The entry would be:

Cost of Goods Sold	2,000	
Merchandise Inventory		2,000

Closing entries at the end of the accounting period were discussed and illustrated in Chapter 11.

review exercises

7. Prepare an adjusting entry for *Merchandise Inventory* when the physical count shows $17,000 and the perpetual records have a balance of $18,600.
8. Record the purchase on account of inventory items for $1,500 under (a) the periodic system, and (b) the perpetual system.
9. Record the sale on account of items from the inventory that have a sales price of $2,500 and a wholesale price of $1,500 using (a) the periodic system, and (b) the perpetual system.
10. If beginning inventory is $21,000, purchases are $63,000, and ending inventory is $18,000, calculate the cost of goods sold.
11. Using the answer you calculated for Exercise 10, assume that a firm had sales of $99,000 and operating expenses of $13,000. What would be the gross profit and net income?

chapter highlights

After studying this chapter, you should be able to:

- Count and price the individual inventory items and calculate the total inventory.
- Calculate the inventory under the various cost flow assumptions.
- Calculate the cost of goods sold.
- Use a periodic or perpetual system to record and account for inventory balances.

Flowcharting

The flow of merchandise through a business is shown in Illustrations 14-18 and 14-19 for a periodic system and for a perpetual system.

illustration 14-18
periodic inventory system.

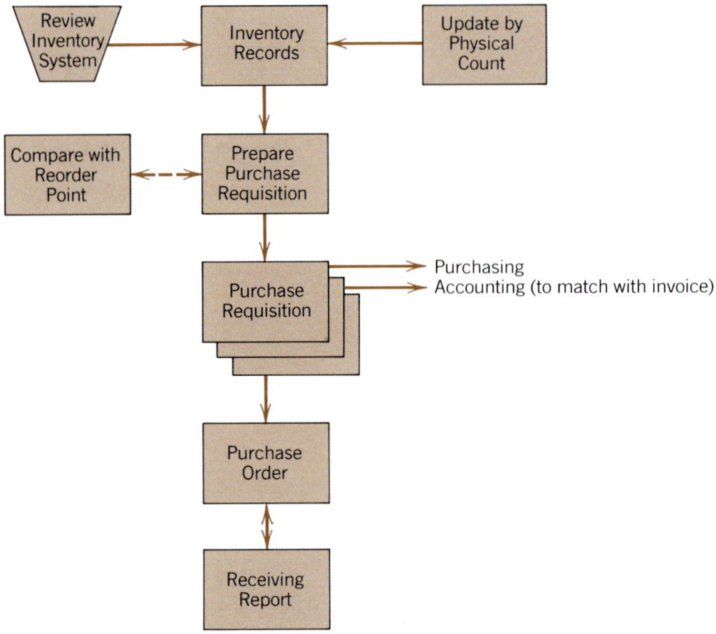

illustration 14-19
perpetual inventory system.

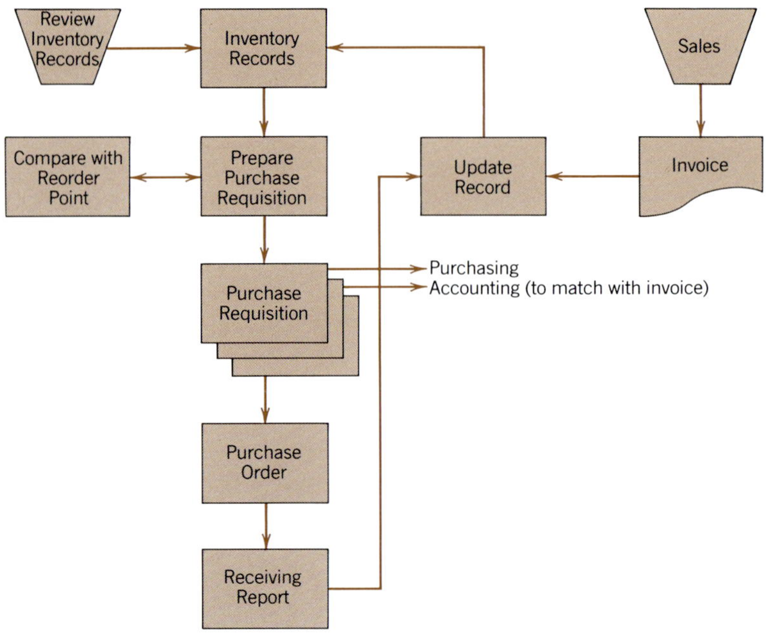

check figures for review exercises

1. The inventory count sheet would have data such as size, color, identification number, and number of items.
2. Ending inventory of 20 units with 10 at $6 and 10 at $7 for a total of $130. Cost of Goods Sold would be $146.36.
3. (a) $14,140.
   (b) $13,100.
   (c) $13,845 (rounded).
4. $20,000.
5. $55,000.
6. $50,000.
7. Debit *Cost of Goods Sold* and credit *Merchandise Inventory* for $1,600.
8. (a) Debit *Purchases* for $1,500.
   (b) Debit *Merchandise Inventory* for $1,500.
9. (a) Record the sale as usual and no other entry.
   (b) Record the sale as usual and another entry with a debit to *Cost of Goods Sold* and a credit to *Merchandise Inventory* for $1,500.
10. Cost of goods sold is $66,000.
11. Gross profit is $33,000 and net income is $20,000.

key terms

The following important terms are discussed in Chapter 14 and are defined in the Glossary at the end of the book:

first-in, first-out (FIFO)
inventory sheet
inventory tag
last-in, first-out (LIFO)
periodic inventory system
perpetual inventory system
specific identification
weighted average

questions

1. Briefly describe the steps in taking inventory.
2. What part does the inventory bookkeeper play in counting the inventory?
3. What is meant by the term *pricing the inventory?*
4. What is meant by the *specific identification* method of pricing inventory?
5. List the different cost flow methods for pricing the inventory.
6. What is the difference between a simple average and a weighted average?
7. How do the FIFO and LIFO methods differ?

8. What category is added to the income statement for a business that sells a product that does not appear on the income statement for a service-type business?
9. For a firm that sells a product, explain how to calculate: (a) cost of goods sold, (b) gross profit, and (c) net income.
10. State the basic differences between the periodic system and the perpetual system for inventory accounting.
11. What should be done if balances for the physical inventory count and the perpetual records differ?

exercises

1. List the types of information a bookkeeper would expect to receive from the inventory custodian in the inventory count sheet. What information would be needed to complete the inventory count sheet?
2. The merchandise inventory of a business enterprise contains the following data:

Beginning inventory,	40 units @ $42
First purchase,	50 units @ $43
Second purchase,	54 units @ $44
Third purchase,	60 units @ $43.50
Sales during year,	130 units @ $69

Calculate the ending inventory assuming (a) first-in, first-out; (b) last-in, first-out; (c) weighted average; (d) specific identification if one-half of the inventory is from the third purchase and one-half is from the second purchase.

3. Calculate the cost of goods sold using the same data as in Exercise 2 above for (a), (b), (c), and (d).
4. Prepare a formal cost of goods sold section as it would appear in an income statement from the data in Exercise 2 above, assuming (a) FIFO, (b) LIFO.
5. If operating expense amounts to $2,300, prepare an income statement showing sales, cost of goods sold, gross profit, operating expenses, and net income. Use the data in Exercise 2 for the weighted-average method.
6. Records for a merchandising business show the following totals for the accounting period:

Beginning inventory	$ 80,000
Purchases for the year	200,000
Ending inventory, physical count	75,000
Ending inventory, perpetual records	79,000
Sales during year, wholesale price	201,000
Sales during year, retail price	308,000
Operating expenses	48,000

(a) Prepare in summary form general journal entries necessary to record the information shown above, assuming a periodic system is used.
(b) Prepare an income statement, assuming a periodic inventory system is used.

7. Using the information in Exercise 6, prepare general journal entries in summary form to record the activities during the year if a perpetual system is used. What are the gross profit and net income under a perpetual system?

problems

1. COMPETENCY TESTED The ability to take a physical inventory.

Describe the procedures that should be followed in taking a physical inventory (counting the items) for a business that sells 23 different products with various sizes and colors for each product.

2. COMPETENCY TESTED Skill in pricing the inventory.

The Zero Company uses the specific identification pricing method. At the end of the period, the inventory count sheets show 20 units of X-1 and 38 units of X-2. The 20 units can be traced to an invoice dated March 30, 19X1, that shows a unit cost of $10.30. The 38 units are traced to two different invoices—25 units to an invoice dated July 10, 19X1, at $11.70 per unit, and 13 units to an invoice dated Oct. 21, 19X1, at $12.10 per unit.

Instructions (a) Describe the procedure of pricing the inventory using the specific identification method. (b) Calculate the ending inventory value using the specific identification method. (c) Why wouldn't this method be used for all pricing situations?

3. COMPETENCY TESTED The ability to price the inventory using cost flow methods.

The Enchon Company shows the following merchandise inventory data for year 19X1:

Beginning inventory	3,000 units @ $3.00
January 31 purchase	4,000 units @ $3.40
February 18 sale	3,500 units @ $6.00
April 22 purchase	4,400 units @ $3.80
May 30 sale	3,400 units @ $6.10
October 11 purchase	3,600 units @ $3.50
November 27 sale	4,100 units @ $6.20

Instructions

(a) Calculate the ending merchandise inventory amount using (1) first-in, first-out, (2) last-in, first-out, and (3) weighted average.

(b) Assuming that operation expenses amounted to $8,800, calculate the net income under FIFO and LIFO.

4. COMPETENCY TESTED The ability to calculate the ending inventory, cost of goods sold, gross profit, and net income.

The Hall Company has the following data relating to Product XZ-10:

Beginning inventory	6,200 units @ $12.00
1st purchase	5,000 units @ $13.00
2nd purchase	6,000 units @ $14.00
3rd purchase	5,400 units @ $13.50

An inventory count of product XZ-10 shows 6,800 units on hand at the end of the accounting period.

Instructions

(a) Calculate the ending inventory assuming (1) FIFO pricing, (2) LIFO pricing, and (3) weighted-average pricing.

(b) If all the units sold during the year were sold at $25 per unit, calculate the cost of goods sold and gross profit on sales using (1) FIFO, (2) LIFO, and (3) weighted average.

(c) If the selling price were still $25 per unit and operating expenses were $105,000, what would be the net income or net loss assuming (1) FIFO, (2) LIFO, and (3) weighted average?

5. COMPETENCY TESTED Skill in computing cost of goods sold.

From the data shown below, select the proper accounts and prepare the cost of goods sold section as it would appear in an income statement. The periodic system is used for inventory.

Cash	$ 6,000
Accounts Receivable	9,000
Merchandise Inventory	13,000
Building and Equipment	21,000
Accounts Payable	7,000
Purchases	41,000
Merchandise Inventory (physical count)	11,000

Instructions Present the cost of goods sold section.

6. COMPETENCY TESTED The ability to prepare an income statement.

A trial balance is shown for the General Company at the end of 19X1.

	Dr.	Cr.
Cash	$ 11,000	
Accounts Receivable	15,000	
Merchandise Inventory	21,000	
Machinery	18,000	
Accounts Payable		$ 30,000
J. C. Nanney, Capital		10,000
Purchases	51,000	
Sales		85,000
Operating Expenses	9,000	
Totals	$125,000	$125,000

The physical count shows an ending merchandise inventory (periodic system) of $22,000.

Instructions Select the appropriate accounts and prepare an income statement for the year.

7. COMPETENCY TESTED The ability to record the buying and selling of inventory items.

The High-Low Company has the following transactions for the first week of year 19X1.

Jan.	7	Purchased merchandise inventory items on account, $1,700.
	10	Sold goods on account, sales price $2,000. Cost of the items is $1,200.

Instructions

(a) Prepare general journal entries to record the transactions when a periodic inventory system is used.

(b) Prepare general journal entries to record the transactions when a perpetual system is used.

8. COMPETENCY TESTED Skill in recording the buying and selling of merchandise inventory items.

The Helton Company had the following transactions for the month of July:

July	4	Purchased merchandise inventory items on account, $3,400.
	19	Sold goods on account, sales price $5,000. Cost of the items is $3,100.

Instructions

(a) Prepare general journal entries to record the July transactions, assuming a periodic inventory system is used.

(b) Prepare entries to record the July transactions, assuming a perpetual system is used.

(c) If the physical count of inventory amount at the end of the accounting period is $15,000 and the perpetual records show a balance of $18,000, make the appropriate entry to adjust the *Merchandise Inventory* account.

9. COMPETENCY TESTED The ability to record entries for inventory transactions.

The Kerr Company had the following events and data available during the accounting year 19X1:

Beginning inventory	$ 18,000
Purchases	88,000
Sales, at retail prices	123,000
Sales, at cost prices	83,000
Physical count of ending merchandise inventory	21,000
Merchandise Inventory (Perpetual)	23,000

Instructions

(a) Prepare journal entries to record transactions and adjust the inventory amounts, assuming that the company uses a periodic method.

(b) How would these entries differ if the company uses the perpetual method?

10. COMPETENCY TESTED The ability to record details under a perpetual inventory system.

Assuming that the inventory shows only one item, use the information below to fill in the (a) detailed perpetual record for Product X-2A and the (b) general ledger control account. Assume that the first-in, first-out method is used.

Inventory Received:	
March 2	200 units @ $7.00
March 10	300 units @ $7.20
March 19	250 units @ $7.50
March 30	150 units @ $7.30
Inventory Sold:	
March 4	300 units
March 15	250 units
March 21	100 units
March 22	100 units
March 31	300 units
March 1 balance 400 units at $7.	

Ignore posting references and assume that the entries have been journalized.

chapter 15
PROPERTY, PLANT, AND EQUIPMENT

overall competency THE ABILITY TO RECORD THE PURCHASE OF PLANT AND EQUIPMENT ASSETS, TO CALCULATE DEPRECIATION BY SEVERAL METHODS, AND TO RECORD BOTH DEPRECIATION AND ASSET DISPOSALS

career objectives Land, buildings, equipment, and machinery make up a considerable part of most firms' assets. To handle these large investments properly, the accounting clerk must develop the skill needed to record the buying, selling, trading, and discarding of these items in the firm's accounting records. Two critical decisions have to be made: (1) whether the expenditure is an asset or an expense, and (2) if it is an asset, which asset account should be debited. The accounting clerk must also be able to calculate depreciation in various ways and to make the necessary journal entries based on these calculations. Whenever property, plant, and equipment are sold, traded, or junked, the accounting clerk must know how to show depreciation to that point and recognize any gain or loss.

Upon completing this chapter, you should be able to:

- DETERMINE THE COSTS AND JOURNALIZE TRANSACTIONS INVOLVING BUILDING, EQUIPMENT, OR LAND ITEMS.
- GIVEN THE METHODS OF DEPRECIATION, COMPUTE THE AMOUNT OF DEPRECIATION AND JOURNALIZE THE RESULTS.
- MAINTAIN SUBSIDIARY RECORDS AND RECONCILE THEM WITH CONTROL ACCOUNTS.
- JOURNALIZE THE REMOVAL OF PLANT AND EQUIPMENT ITEMS FROM THE ACCOUNTING RECORDS.

The classification *Property, Plant, and Equipment* includes such items as land, building, structures, machinery, equipment, furniture, and fixtures. These property items are sometimes called **fixed assets** because of their long-term nature. Assets with these characteristics have utility or "stored-up" benefits for future accounting periods. Property, plant, and equipment items are relatively permanent since they are not held for resale in the normal operation of the business.

Long-term fixed assets can be classified into three broad categories:

1. **Tangible assets:** Fixed assets that have physical characteristics subject to wear or that lose their technical ability to perform the tasks for which they were acquired are known as **tangible assets.** Trucks, machinery and equipment are examples of tangible assets. With the exception of land, these assets usually depreciate over time.
2. **Intangible assets:** Long-term assets that do not have physical characteristics, but give the business certain operational rights or benefits that are of value are known as *intangible assets.* Patents, copyrights, and goodwill are examples of intangible assets.
3. **Natural resources:** Assets such as minerals, ores, and trees that the firm plans to take from the land are known as **natural resources.** These assets deplete when the valuable resources are separated from the earth.

This chapter is concerned only with the accounting for tangible assets. Since tangible assets are used by a business for a number of years, depreciation accounting methods are used to allocate the cost of the fixed asset to present and future accounting periods. When the plant or equipment asset loses its usefulness to a company, it is sold, traded, or junked. Gains or losses may be involved when the business disposes of items of its plant and equipment. Finally, the fixed assets must be removed from the general ledger accounts and subsidiary ledgers when the company no longer owns them.

• task DETERMINE THE COST AND JOURNALIZE TRANSACTIONS INVOLVING PROPERTY, PLANT, AND EQUIPMENT ITEMS

Acquisition cost

Cost is the accounting principle that determines the amount shown in the ledger accounts. When two reasonable parties get together to negotiate the exchange price of a piece of property, the resulting cost is probably the best indication of the value that should be given to this property. To illustrate this concept, assume that a drill press was purchased for a cash outlay of $5,000. The required journal entry (with the expenditure listed in the items column for your benefit) would be:

June	1	Machinery		5000 –	
		Cash			5000 –
		To purchase drill press			

Note that the amount spent is recorded as a debit to the asset account, *Machinery*, instead of an expense account, such as *Machinery Expense*. When the outlay is expected to benefit more than one accounting period, an asset account should be debited. The drill press was purchased with the obvious hope of using it for a number of years. By comparison, payments connected with plant and equipment that are expected to benefit only the current period are expensed. For example, if you spent $10 for new spark plugs for the delivery truck, an expense account would be debited.

Generally, the purchase price and the market value of plant or equipment assets are the same on the purchase date, but as time passes, cost and market value for the asset may differ by significant amounts. Thus, the company books do not attempt to show the current market value of its property, plant, or equipment. After the purchase date, the term *historical cost* is often used to refer to the original cost.

In addition to the exchange price, other costs are debited to the asset. An important point to remember is that any reasonable and necessary expense to prepare the asset for use is debited to the asset account, while routine repairs and services are charged to an expense account. To illustrate, assume that after the press was purchased, the following additional costs were incurred:

June	1	Transportation cost	$100
	7	Concrete foundation for machine	300
	15	Materials used in adjusting machine	200
		Total	$600

Instead of showing only the original cost, *Machinery* shows the total cost of $5,600 ($5,000 invoice cost + $600 preparation), since these expenditures are necessary to prepare the machine to service the company's products. The total debits of $5,600 should be depreciated, not just the invoice price of $5,000. Depreciation starts as soon as the drilling press is operating and providing a service to the firm. Even though the drill press was purchased on June 1, depreciation does not begin until the press is in place and is being used.

Land and building accounts

Expenditures for land and building purchases should be kept in separate accounts because of the depreciable characteristic of buildings and the nondepreciable characteristic of land. To illustrate, assume that on August 7, 19X1, Whitney Discount Center purchases a piece of land for $10,000 on which the firm plans to erect a building. On the same date the firm pays $250 in legal and title fees and $700 for the broker's commission. To get the property ready for construction, $100 is paid for surveying and $2,050 for land grading. Since these two costs are necessary to get the land ready for use, both payments are debited to *Land.* After all related entries have been posted, the *Land* account shows that the land actually cost a total of $13,100—not just the base cost of $10,000. The *Land* account, after all postings have been made, is shown in Illustration 15-1.

illustration 15-1
land account showing costs connected with the purchase of property.

Land — Account No. 116

Date		Item	P.R.	Dr.	Cr.	Balance Dr.	Balance Cr.
19X1 Aug	7	Purchased Property	CD1	10000 –		10000 –	
	7	Legal Fees	CD1	250 –		10250 –	
	7	Brokerage Commission	CD1	700 –		10950 –	
	22	Surveying & Grading	CD2	2150 –		13100 –	

If the property had an old building on it that should be torn down, an additional cost of preparing the land is involved. However, the bricks, doors, windows, and other parts may have some salvage value that can reduce the cost of removing the old building. To illustrate, assume in the example above that $10,000 was paid for both the land and the old building. Since the old building is to be torn down immediately, no value is assigned to it. Cost to tear down the old structure amounts to $1,000, but a local salvage company allows Whitney Discount Center $450 for usable parts, thereby reducing the removal cost to $550. Under this assumption, the land would have a total cost of $13,650 ($10,000 + $250 + $700 + $2,150 + $1,000 − $450).

Care must be taken to make a distinction between land and land improvements. **Land improvements** can be identified as added expenditures having definite lives that increase the usefulness of the land. Examples are lighting fixtures, fences, and pavement on parking lots. Since these items have limited lives, the improvement costs should be depreciated in the same manner as equipment or buildings.

The make-up of the cost of a building depends upon the decision by Whitney Discount Center as to whether the firm purchased the building or had the building constructed. No gain is recognized if the company builds at a savings. An example of common costs for the two possibilities is shown below in Illustration 15-2.

illustration 15-2
buy or construct comparison.

Purchase Cost		Construction Cost	
Purchase price	$100,000	Labor, materials, and overhead	$90,000
Brokers' commission	7,000	Excavations	8,000
Legal fees	1,000	Architects' fees	9,000
Title and escrow fees	500	Building permits	100
Reconditioning and alterations	9,000	Fire and workman insurance	1,000
		Temporary buildings	2,000
	$117,500		$110,100

Purchases discount

In addition to certain acquisition costs that are obvious in buying plant and property, other purchasing procedures should be identified to calculate the cost of the asset. Manufacturers of fixed assets often encourage prompt payment by offering cash discounts. This concept is the same as the one you studied in Chapter 5 when merchandise was being purchased. A preferred method of handling discounts is to show the *net* amount of the cash payment agreed upon. The net amount represents the dollars that the seller willingly accepts for equipment as part of the sales contract. Because the difference between the gross and net amounts should be considered a penalty for not making a prompt payment, this penalty should not increase the value of the asset. Cash discount agreements for property, plant, and equipment are similar in accounting to inventory purchasing procedures. To illustrate, assume that Whitney Discount Center purchases equipment for $2,000 with terms of 2/10, n/30. The following entry would be journalized:

Date		Account	Debit	Credit
19X1				
Mar.	1	Equipment	1960 –	
		Accounts Payable/Bell Co.		1960 –
		Purchased display cases		
		from Bell Co. 2/10, n/30.		
		Recorded at net figure.		

If payment is made within the discount period, the following entry should be made:

Date		Account	Debit	Credit
19X1				
Mar.	10	Accounts Payable/Bell Co.	1960 –	
		Cash		1960 –
		Paid for display cases		
		within discount period.		

If payment were made after the discount period, the journal entry should show that the discount was lost.

Date		Account	Debit	Credit
19X1				
Mar.	31	Accounts Payable/Bell Co.	1960 –	
		Discounts Lost - Equipment	40 –	
		Cash		2000 –
		Paid for display cases after discount period expired.		

The cost to be depreciated should not exceed $1,960, the net purchase agreement. *Discounts Lost—Equipment* should be classified on the income statement as an administrative expense. This account would bring to management's attention the fact that cash was not used effectively to take advantage of discounts available.

sample problem The Green Corporation purchased land with a usable building on it from the Zee Company. Representative costs were detailed for March 15 as follows:

Title fees to land	$ 200
Land grading	500
Land purchase price	8,000
	$ 8,700
Building purchase price	$40,000
Broker's commission	2,000
	$42,000

Machinery purchase price $5,000, 2/15, n/30

Assuming a cash purchase, prepare a general journal entry.

sample problem solution

Mar. 15	Land	8,700	
	Building	42,000	
	Machinery (5,000 − [.02 × 5,000 = 100])	4,900	
	Cash		55,600

review exercises

1. The Nome Company made a cash purchase for land and building from the Fremont Company that included the following costs:

Legal fees for title to land	$ 200
Purchase price for land	2,900
Building purchase price	40,000

Prepare a general journal entry.

2. Machinery was purchased on account, $8,000. Terms of the purchase price were 2/10, n/30. These additional costs were required to place the machine in operation:

Concrete platform for machine	$300
Freight costs	250

Prepare a general journal entry.

• task GIVEN THE METHODS OF DEPRECIATION, COMPUTE THE AMOUNT OF DEPRECIATION AND JOURNALIZE THE RESULTS

What is depreciation?

Depreciation is a systematic and reasonable procedure for spreading the cost of a plant or equipment over the accounting periods benefited. Depreciation is not a procedure used to determine the market value of a fixed asset. The market price of an asset most likely will differ from the book values of the plant and equipment items in the accounts. To refresh your memory, **book value** for plant and equipment accounts is calculated by subtracting the accumulated depreciation from the initial cost.

Acquisition cost (including freight, installation, and testing)	$8,000
Less accumulated depreciation	2,000
Book value	$6,000

There are a number of depreciation methods available, and care should be taken to select the one that best indicates the actual use of the equipment in the business.

To illustrate the need for depreciation, assume that in January of 19X1, Whitney Discount Center purchased a machine with an expected production life of 5 years for $25,000. The firm could look at this expenditure as an expense in the year of purchase, 19X1. Obviously, this treatment would distort the financial statements since the firm would benefit from this machine for four more years without cost. This approach is shown as Possibility A in Illustration 15-3.

illustration 15-3 comparison of possibilities of spreading depreciation costs.

	19X1	19X2	19X3	19X4	19X5
Possibility A: Depreciation Expense	$25,000	0	0	0	0
Possibility B: Depreciation Expense	0	0	0	0	$25,000
Possibility C: Depreciation Expense	$5,000	$5,000	$5,000	$5,000	$5,000

An alternative would be to carry the cost as an asset of $25,000 until it is sold, traded, or scrapped, and then recognize the $25,000 as an expense at that point. Possibility B in Illustration 15-3 shows the entire cost being expensed when the asset is scrapped in the fifth year. Neither Possibility A nor Possibility B is a satisfactory procedure. What is needed is a system of spreading the cost over the expected life (and benefited period). Possibility C, shown in Illustration 15-3, is the only acceptable one since the first two violate the **matching principle** by not distributing the cost of the machine over the years the firm benefited from having the asset. By using Possibility C, the cost of the machine is matched properly with the revenues.

Estimating the useful life and salvage value

In each of the methods discussed, the life of the asset, either in terms of years or output, must be estimated. This figure is rather subjective since few of us have crystal balls that work. However, two factors can be considered to arrive at a realistic number—*obsolescence* and *deterioration*. **Obsolescence** has to do with the capacity of a plant or equipment item to perform up to expectations. An asset may have the physical capacity to perform its service function, but it becomes obsolete (out-of-date) when a more efficient asset is developed. In business, we often use automated machinery to replace man-operated machinery. In highly technical industries, the obsolescence factor becomes more important than physical wear in determining the estimated life. Machinery and buildings become inadequate to carry out their expected tasks when business volume increases. The *going-concern concept* assumes that a plant asset has the ability to perform successfully. If not, it is traded, sold, or junked.

Deterioration (physical wear and tear) occurs as the equipment is subjected to use. Because of excessive wear, the machine may lose its capacity to perform the task it was designed to do. This loss becomes quite obvious to the owner of a business when the delivery truck breaks down and is no longer available for service. Managers should be aware of the opportunities to extend the life of the equipment by overhauling, preventive maintenance, and major part replacements. All of these factors must be considered when the expected life of newly acquired equipment is determined.

The second estimation used to calculate the annual depreciation is **salvage value.** The term "salvage" may be misleading since an expensive bulldozer that is being traded in on a larger model may be far from salvage. Some accountants prefer the term **residual value.** On the other hand, salvage value may be so small in some instances that it can be ignored when calculating the depreciation charges. When the equipment is fully depreciated, the book value should equal the salvage value.

The four most popular depreciation procedures are straight-line, units of output, sum-of-the-years'-digits, and double-declining balance. The amount of depreciation to be charged off each accounting period differs under each of these methods.

Straight-line depreciation

Straight-line depreciation procedures produce an equal amount of depreciation expense to be matched against revenues for each accounting period. The fact that straight-line depreciation is easy to apply is a major reason for its popularity. Depreciation expense computed by the straight-line method is based on the passage of time; it is not tied to the number of items produced or the hours used. Therefore, the straight-line method would be appropriate when the asset is used evenly over its life.

Salvage value must be taken into consideration in calculating the total amount to be depreciated. To illustrate, assume a machine is purchased by Whitney Discount Center at a cost of $5,000. The estimated salvage value is $500, with an estimated life of 5 years. The annual depreciation is $900 as shown below:

Initial cost	$5,000
Less salvage value	500
Amount to be depreciated	$4,500

$4,500 ÷ 5 Years = $900 Annual Depreciation

The calculation may be expressed by the following formula:

$$\frac{\text{Cost} - \text{Salvage Value}}{\text{Estimated Life}} = \text{Annual Depreciation}$$

Adjustments for depreciation can be given as an annual depreciation rate based upon initial cost as follows:

$$\frac{\text{Annual Depreciation}}{\text{Cost}} = \text{Depreciation Rate} \qquad \frac{\$900}{\$5{,}000} = 18 \text{ percent}$$

Depreciation expense can be calculated easily now by taking this percentage and multiplying it by the cost ($5,000 × .18 = $900) to determine the amount of depreciation each year.

Units-of-output methods

When a direct relationship exists between the use of equipment or machinery and the fixed asset's decline in utility, one of the **units-of-output methods** is appropriate. Two widely used techniques in this depreciation approach are the *estimated units of production* method and the *estimated service-hours* method. The more the fixed asset is used, the greater the amount of depreciation to be recorded for that particular asset. When the straight-line method is used, the amount of depreciation remains the same, regardless of the change in units produced or service hours used. Since the units of production and the service hours methods are very similar, only the service hours method will be discussed. A useful formula for the service/output method of depreciation follows:

$$\text{Yearly Output Depreciation} = \frac{\text{Cost} - \text{Salvage Value}}{\text{Estimated Total Output (in Hours or Units)}}$$

$$= \text{(Depr. per Hr. or Unit)} \times \text{Yearly Output (Hours or Units)}$$

To illustrate the service-hours method, assume that machinery costing $5,000 (estimated salvage value, $500) has an estimated service-hours life of 10,000 hours. The depreciation rate per hour is 45 cents ($5,000 − $500/10,000). If 2,400 service hours were consumed in one year's operation, the depreciation adjustment would be $1,080 (2,400 hours × 45 cents per hour). Now, putting this together, we have:

$$\frac{\$5{,}000 - \$500}{10{,}000} = .45 \text{ per hour} \times 2{,}400 = \$1{,}080$$

If the machine was used 1,500 hours during the second year, depreciation expense for this period would be $675 (1,500 hours × 45 cents).

19X1					
Dec.	31	Depreciation Expense, Machinery		1080 —	
		Accumulated Deprec., Machinery			1080 —
		To record depreciation for			
		one year.			

Sum-of-the-years'-digits method

The **sum-of-the-years'-digits method** is a popular method of accelerated depreciation. Accelerated depreciation methods provide more depreciation expenses in the earlier years than straight-line when the asset is new. As the asset ages, increased repair expenses and more frequent overhauls are required to maintain the equipment's efficiency and productivity. Depreciation expenses will be lower than straight-line in the latter years of the equipment's estimated useful life and, along with expected higher repair expenses, will have a tendency to even out the cost of using the equipment over its total life. In addition, rapid technological advancements increase the probability that equipment must be replaced earlier than expected. The sum-of-the-years'-digits method may be expressed in the following formula:

Sum-of-the-years'-digits depreciation:

$$(\text{Cost} - \text{Salvage Value}) \times \frac{\text{Yearly Digit}}{{}^{*}n\left(\frac{n+1}{2}\right)}$$

$^{*}n$ = useful life

$$\text{Therefore,}\quad \text{SYD} = (\text{C} - \text{SV}) \times \frac{\text{Yearly Digit}}{n\left(\frac{n+1}{2}\right)}$$

Both the denominator and numerator in straight-line depreciation calculations are constant, while the sum-of-the-years' digits method uses a constant denominator and a decreasing numerator. (For those who have forgotten their math terminology, the part of the fraction on the bottom is the denominator, and the top part is the numerator.) The denominator is the sum of the years (1 + 2 + 3 + 4 + 5 = 15), and the numerator is the years in reverse order (5, 4, 3, 2, 1). Using the previous data ($5,000 cost; 5 years; $500 scrap value), let's complete the formula.

$$\text{Annual depreciation} = (\$5{,}000 - \$500) \times \frac{5}{5\left(\frac{5+1}{2}\right)}$$

$$= \$4{,}500 \times \frac{5}{15}$$

$$= \$1{,}500 \text{ for the first year}$$

illustration 15-4
sum-of-the-years'-digits method.

Year	Fraction		Asset Cost − Scrap Value		Depr. Expense
1	5/15	×	$4,500	=	$1,500
2	4/15	×	4,500	=	1,200
3	3/15	×	4,500	=	900
4	2/15	×	4,500	=	600
5	1/15	×	4,500	=	300
15	15/15				$4,500

A complete display for all five years can be seen in Illustration 15-4. Note that this approach gives a smaller amount of depreciation expense each year. The total amount to be depreciated is \$4,500, the initial cost less scrap value. When the estimated life of a plant asset is long, the denominator can be calculated by the formula efficiently. For example, assume a 20-year estimated life for a building. The denominator would be: $20 \times [(20 + 1)/2] = 210$; the first year fraction for depreciation would be 20/210.

Declining balance at a fixed percentage

Fixed percentages are applied to a declining balance to determine the periodic depreciation charges for the **declining-balance method** of depreciation. As the asset ages, efficiency decreases and repair and maintenance costs increase. The repair costs are low in the early years for routine operations. Another reason for using this method is that benefits received from certain classes of special equipment are less definite in future years.

The declining-balance at a fixed-percentage method is popular with business firms that want an accelerated depreciation method, since it usually allows more depreciation expense in the early years of the asset. This approach is based on a fixed rate that is applied to a declining balance. One popular approach is to take the straight-line rate (ignoring salvage value) and double it. To illustrate how this is done, we first find annual depreciation (using the same amounts from our previous illustration) by the straight-line method.

$$\text{Annual Depreciation} = \frac{\text{Cost}}{n} = \frac{\$5{,}000}{5}$$

$$= \$1{,}000$$

Next, we calculate the straight-line rate.

$$\text{S/L rate} = \frac{\text{Annual Depreciation}}{\text{Cost}} = \frac{\$1{,}000}{\$5{,}000} = 20 \text{ percent}$$

The 20 percent rate is then doubled to give a 40 percent rate. A shortcut is simply to divide the denominator "n" into 1. Thus, 5 divided into 1 is 20 percent. A 4-year life would be 25 percent ($1 \div 4 = .25$), a 20-year life would be 5 percent ($1 \div 20 = .05$), and a 50-year life would be 2 percent ($1 \div 50 = .02$).

To express the discussion above in a formula, the declining-balance method at twice the straight-line rate would be:

$$\text{Twice the S/L Rate} \times \text{Book Value} = \text{Annual Depreciation}$$

If this approach for the five-year period is used, depreciation is calculated as follows:

illustration 15-5
declining balance at twice the S/L rate.

Year	Depreciation Rate (%)	Declining Book Value Balance	Depreciation Expense	Accumulated Depreciation	Book Value
					$5,000
1	40%	$5,000	$2,000	$2,000	3,000
2	40%	3,000	1,200	3,200	1,800
3	40%	1,800	720	3,920	1,080
4	40%	1,080	432	4,352	648
5	40%	648	148	4,500	500

The fixed rate is applied to the declining balance of the equipment item in all years except the fifth year. An amount of depreciation necessary to reduce the book value to estimated scrap value is used. The computed amount of depreciation for the last year will not usually give the required salvage value. In Illustration 15-5, $148 is a "plug" figure to lower the declining balance from $648 to $500. While scrap value is not used in determining the fixed rate, it is important for you to recognize that the estimated scrap value provides a lower limit or base for the final year's depreciation.

For all four basic depreciation methods illustrated, allocating cost over the useful life of an asset does not imply that the resulting book value closely approximates market value. Nor does the selected depreciation method measure the exact amount of physical wear.

Illustration 15-6 compares the depreciation expense and book values for the four depreciation methods presented. The same data were used to illustrate the four methods ($5,000 cost; $500 estimated scrap value; and 5 years estimated life).

illustration 15-6
comparison of depreciation methods.

	Straight-line			Units of Output		
Year	Rate (%)	Depr.	Book Value	Hours	Depr.	Book Value
1	18	$900	$4,100	2,400	$1,080	$3,920
2	18	900	3,200	1,500	675	3,245
3	18	900	2,300	2,000	900	2,345
4	18	900	1,400	3,000	1,350	995
5	18	900	500	1,100	495	500

Sum-of-the-Years'-Digits			Double-Declining Balance		
Rate	Depr.	Book Value	Rate (%)	Depr.	Book Value
5/15	$1,500	$3,500	40	$2,000	$3,000
4/15	1,200	2,300	40	1,200	1,800
3/15	900	1,400	40	720	1,080
2/15	600	800	40	432	648
1/15	300	500	40	148	500

Each depreciation method allocated the initial acquisition cost by varying amounts over the five-year period, yet reduced the book value to the estimated $500 scrap value.

Accelerated cost recovery system

A new depreciation method has recently become a part of the tax code. This new method of straight-line depreciation may be used for tax purposes. Since some businesses, especially the small ones, may use this new method for financial reporting as well as for their tax returns, we will briefly describe the method. The **accelerated cost recovery system** is a tax method created by the *Economic Recovery Tax Act of 1981*. The assets to which this new method apply are called **recovery property.** Examples of recovery property are components of real property and improvements made on leased property. Assets are separated into 3-, 5-, 10-, and 15-year property. Percentages to be used in computing depreciation expense for each year are specified for each group. Percentages for each of these groups are shown in Illustration 15-7.

3-Year Property	
1st Year	25%
2nd Year	38
3rd Year	37
	100%

5-Year Property	
1st Year	15%
2nd Year	22
3rd Year	21
4th Year	21
5th Year	21
	100%

10-Year Property	
1st Year	8%
2nd Year	14
3rd Year	12
4th–6th Year	10
7th–10th Year	9
	100%

15-Year Property	
1st Year	5%
2nd Year	10
3rd Year	9
4th Year	8
5th and 6th Year	7
7th–15th Year	6
	100%

15-Year Real Property Other Than Low-Income Housing

Year	Use the Column for the Month Placed in Service											
	1	2	3	4	5	6	7	8	9	10	11	12
1st	12%	11%	10%	9%	8%	7%	6%	5%	4%	3%	2%	1%
2d	10%	10%	11%	11%	11%	11%	11%	11%	11%	11%	11%	12%
3d	9%	9%	9%	9%	10%	10%	10%	10%	10%	10%	10%	10%
4th	8%	8%	8%	8%	8%	8%	9%	9%	9%	9%	9%	9%

illustration 15-7 accelerated cost recovery tables.

When using the accelerated cost recovery system, use the same percentage regardless of the month of acquisition, unless 15-year real property other than low-income housing is involved. For all property except the 15-year real property, no depreciation expense is allowed in the year of disposal.

To illustrate the accelerated cost recovery system, assume that space in a shopping center is remodeled at a cost of $4,000. The lease covers an 8-year period, so it qualifies as "3-year property" since the tax rule states that the midpoint for this category is four years or less. Referring to the first-year line in Illustration 15-7, we find that 25 percent of the cost is allowed to be depreciated. By applying this rate to the cost, we arrive at depreciation for the year of $1,000. We need to note another important difference between accounting and tax depreciation—the accelerated cost recovery system does not allow for a salvage value.

Because the accelerated cost recovery system is based on tax philosophy and not on sound accounting theory, it should not be used for financial reporting except in limited situations. Generally, this new tax approach should be used only when the amounts of depreciation expense are not materially different from those calculated by a method that is acceptable for reporting on financial statements.

Partial year

It is highly unlikely that management will be so nice to the accounting clerk that it will buy fixed assets only at the first of the fiscal period. In actual practice, equipment and other fixed assets are purchased on dates like March 23, November 6, and December 19. Since depreciation is an estimation process anyway, you can round the purchase (for depreciation purposes only) to the nearest full month. So, March 23 would be treated as if the asset were purchased on April 1; a November 6 purchase as November 1; and a December 19 acquisition as January 1. It is acceptable to "round" to the nearest year.

Straight-line Assume that Whitney Discount Center purchased a $5,000 piece of machinery on April 18, 19X1. At the end of the year, depreciation should be calculated on eight months (May through December). Two ways can be used to arrive at the correct amount. First, multiply the $900 just as it was derived earlier by 8/12, or $600. The second approach is to divide the number of months the machine was used this year by its total life to get a fraction; then multiply this figure by $4,500. This procedure would give the following formula:

$$8/60 \times \$4{,}500 = \$600$$

In 19X2, the depreciation is for a full year—so $900 would be used.

Units of output Neither the service-hours nor the units-of-production method requires special treatment for partial years. Since the denominator is based on usage or production, the date of purchase is not a direct factor. In the earlier illustration, if 2,400 units had been used, it would not have made any difference if the machine had been bought on January 1 or February 12.

Sum-of-the-years'-digits and declining balance at a fixed percentage To demonstrate partial-year depreciation using sum-of-the-years'-digits method, assume that the machine was purchased on May 4, 19X1. This purchase date means that depreciation for this year should be for only 8/12 of the year (8 months from May 1 through December 31). Now by repeating the formula for 5 years, we come up with this table:

Calculation	Amount	Total	Year
5/15 × \$4,500 × 8/12 =	\$1,000	= \$1,000	19X1
5/15 × \$4,500 × 4/12 =	500		
4/15 × \$4,500 × 8/12 =	800	= 1,300	19X2
4/15 × \$4,500 × 4/12 =	400		
3/15 × \$4,500 × 8/12 =	600	= 1,000	19X3
3/15 × \$4,500 × 4/12 =	300		
2/15 × \$4,500 × 8/12 =	400	= 700	19X4
2/15 × \$4,500 × 4/12 =	200		
1/15 × \$4,500 × 8/12 =	200	= 400	19X5
1/15 × \$4,500 × 4/12 =	100	= 100	19X6

If the declining-balance at a fixed-percentage method is used, calculating partial-year depreciation is simply a matter of using the same approach. To illustrate, in the first year the calculation would be:

$$.40 \times \$5,000 \times 8/12 = \$1,333.33$$

the second year would be:

Calculation	Amount	Total
.40 × \$5,000 × 4/12 =	666.67	
.40 × \$3,000 × 8/12 =	800.00	= \$1,466.67
12/12		

The recording process

An understanding of depreciation concepts and the application of these concepts can be improved by following depreciation-related data through the steps of the accounting cycle.

1. A two-ton delivery truck, with an estimated life of 5 years and an estimated salvage value of \$500, is purchased by Whitney Discount Center

on January 1, 19X1, for $6,500. The company selects sum-of-the-years'-digits as its depreciation method.

Date		Description	P.R.	Dr.	Cr.
19X1 Jan.	1	Equipment		6500 –	
		Cash			6500 –
		To record purchase of delivery truck.			

2. Adjustment for annual depreciation.

Fraction × (Cost − Salvage Value)
Calculations: 5/15 × ($6,500 − $500) = $2,000

Date		Description	P.R.	Dr.	Cr.
19X1 Dec.	31	Depreciation Expense, Equipment		2000 –	
		Accumulated Deprec., Equipment			2000 –
		To record annual depreciation.			

3. Closing entry (condensed to show only *Depreciation Expense Equipment*).

Date		Description	P.R.	Dr.	Cr.
19X1 Dec.	31	Income Summary		2000 –	
		Depreciation Expense, Equipment			2000 –
		To close expense account.			

4. The ledger postings of the transactions above and the accounts involved can be illustrated as follows:

Equipment — Account No. 114

Date		Item	P.R.	Dr.	Cr.	Balance Dr.	Balance Cr.
19X1 Jan.	1		G12	6500 –		6500 –	

Accumulated Depreciation, Equipment — Account No. 118

Date		Item	P.R.	Dr.	Cr.	Balance Dr.	Balance Cr.
19X1 Dec.	31	Adjusting Entry	G20		2000 –		2000 –

Income Summary Account No. *313*

Date		Item	P.R.	Dr.	Cr.	Balance Dr.	Balance Cr.
19X1 Dec.	31	Closing Entry	G20	2000 –		2000 –	

Depreciation Expense Equipment Account No. *619*

Date		Item	P.R.	Dr.	Cr.	Balance Dr.	Balance Cr.
19X1 Dec.	31	Adjusting Entry	G20	2000 –		2000 –	
	31	Closing Entry	G20		2000	–0–	

After all income statement accounts have been closed to the *Income Summary,* the balance of the *Income Summary* account (which now includes the *Depreciation Expense* balance) is closed to the capital account.

sample problem Moore Company acquires equipment with an estimated life of five years and with $100 estimated scrap value at a cost of $2,200 from Jones Company. It is estimated that the machine will operate efficiently for 21,000 service hours. The Moore Company would like to know the amount of depreciation under each of the four methods for the first and second years. The company estimated the machine's use at 3,000 hours in Year 1 and 5000 hours in Year 2.

1. Fill in the schedule below.

	Straight-line	Sum-of-the-Years'-Digits	Double-Declining	Units of Output
Year 1				
Year 2				

2. Determine the book value after the second year by the different depreciation methods.
3. Prepare the journal entries for the sum-of-the-years'-digits method for both years' depreciation.
4. Prepare the closing entry for Year 2 assuming that the double-declining method was used.

sample problem solution 1.

	Straight-line	Sum-of-the Years'-Digits	Double-Declining	Units of Output
Year 1	$420	$700	$880	$300
Year 2	420	560	528	500

	Straight-line	Sum-of-the Years'-Digits	Double-Declining	Units of Output
2. Book value End-of-Year 2	$1,360	$940	$792	$1,400

3. Depreciation entries for sum-of-the-year's digits.

Year 1 Dec. 31	Depreciation Expense	700	
	Accumulated Depreciation, Equipment		700
Year 2 Dec. 31	Depreciation Expense	560	
	Accumulated Depreciation, Equipment		560

4. Closing entry for Year 2—double-declining balance.

Year 2 Dec. 31	Income Summary	528	
	Depreciation Expense		528

review exercises

3. Jones Company purchased equipment from the Green Company, $4,000. Estimated scrap value of the equipment is $400 with an estimated life of five years. Determine the amount of depreciation at the end of the years 1 and 2 by (a) the straight-line method, and (b) the double-declining balance method.

4. Prepare an adjusting journal entry for the Jones Company for the first year by the straight-line method and at the end of the second year by the double-declining balance method.

5. Foster Company uses the accelerated cost recovery system for both its tax report and its accounting records. How much depreciation would be reported for the second year for an asset that qualifies as 5-year property if the asset cost $10,000 and has a $1,000 salvage value? Use Illustration 15-7 for the depreciation rate.

• task MAINTAIN SUBSIDIARY RECORDS AND RECONCILE THEM WITH CONTROL ACCOUNTS

Plant and equipment information

In addition to detailed subsidiary records for plant and equipment, several reports, statements and work sheets give you information about depreciable assets. An individual subsidiary record contains information concerning acquisition cost, depreciation, major overhauls, routine maintenance, and disposition of the asset. A typical subsidiary ledger sheet for *Delivery Equipment* is shown in Illustration 15-8.

illustration 15-8
subsidiary ledger sheet.

Equipment item *Two-ton delivery truck* — Identification No. *1236C*
Purchased from *Motor Express, Inc.* — Address *Detroit, Michigan*
Cost *$6,500* — Scrap Value *$500* — Depreciation Method *SYD*

Date of Purchase *Jan. 1, 19X1*

Date	Cost	Depreciation For Year	Depreciation Balance	Book Value	Routine Main. Date	Disposition of Asset Date	Amount Received	Gain or Loss
19X1 Jan. 1	6,500			6,500	19X1 July 1	19X4 Apr. 6	1,000	(500)
19X1 Dec. 31		2,000	2,000	4,500	19X1 Dec. 15			
19X2 Dec. 31		1,600	3,600	2,900	19X2 July 10			
19X3 Dec. 31		1,200	4,800	1,700	19X3 Dec. 2			
19X4 Apr. 6		200	5,000	1,500				

The concept of controlling accounts was introduced in the earlier discussions of *Accounts Receivable* and *Accounts Payable*. You should recall that a *controlling account* is a general ledger account that summarizes a secondary set of records known as a *subsidiary ledger*. *Delivery Equipment* is the controlling account for all delivery trucks used in the business, including the two-ton delivery truck with a company identification number of 1236C. Detailed information included in the subsidiary record includes cost, routine maintenance check, book value, and information concerning the final disposition of the item. Such detailed information aids management in planning for future purchases of delivery equipment and setting up depreciation schedules.

Depreciation adjustments are first recorded as part of the work sheet preparation at the end of the accounting period. Two partial work sheets are given to illustrate the procedures of the initial work sheet depreciation adjustment and the work sheet adjustment for the second year. Assume that the two-ton truck is the only item of delivery equipment owned by the Whitney Discount Center in Illustration 15-9 and 15-10.

The initial cost of the delivery truck is recorded in a separate account. The credit balance in *Accumulated Depreciation, Delivery Equipment* increases each accounting period. The amount is $2,000 for the first year and an additional $1,600 for the second year. The balance in *Accumulated Depreciation, Delivery Equipment* will be $3,600 at the end of the second year of use.

Information about depreciable assets is presented on the balance sheet section of the work sheet and is formally presented in the *Property, Plant, and Equipment* section of the balance sheet. Partial balance sheets for the years 19X1 and 19X2 are presented in Illustration 15-11.

Whitney Discount Center
Work Sheet
For Year Ended December 31, 19X1

Account Titles	Trial Balance		Adjustments		Adjusted Trial Balance		Income Statement		Balance Sheet	
	Dr.	Cr.	Dr.	Cr.	Dr.	Cr.	Dr.	Cr.	Dr.	Cr.
Cash	4000 –								4000 –	
Delivery Equipment	6500 –								6500 –	
Land	8000 –								8000 –	
Totals	50000 –	50000 –								
Depreciation Expense			2000 –				2000 –			
Accumulated Depreciation Delivery Equipment				2000 –						2000 –

illustration 15-9 partial 19X1 work sheet.

Whitney Discount Center
Work Sheet
For Year Ended December 31, 19X2

Account Titles	Trial Balance		Adjustments		Adjusted Trial Balance		Income Statement		Balance Sheet	
	Dr.	Cr.	Dr.	Cr.	Dr.	Cr.	Dr.	Cr.	Dr.	Cr.
Cash	6200 –								6200 –	
Delivery Equipment	6500 –								6500 –	
Accumulated Depreciation Delivery Equipment		2000 –		1600 –						3600 –
Land	8000 –								8000 –	
Totals	70000 –	70000 –								
Depreciation Expense			1600 –				1600 –			

illustration 15-10 partial 19X2 work sheet.

WHITNEY DISCOUNT CENTER
Balance Sheet
December 31, 19X1

Current Assets:		
Cash		$4,000
Property, Plant, and Equipment:		
Delivery Equipment	$6,500	
Less: Accumulated Depreciation	2,000	4,500
Land		8,000

WHITNEY DISCOUNT CENTER
Balance Sheet
December 31, 19X2

Current Assets:		
Cash		$6,200
Property, Plant, and Equipment:		
Delivery Equipment	$6,500	
Less: Accumulated Depreciation	3,600	2,900
Land		8,000

illustration 15-11 partial balance sheets.

Formal presentations of partial income statements for the two years based upon information contained in the income statement section of the work sheet are given in Illustration 15-12.

WHITNEY DISCOUNT CENTER Income Statement For the Year Ended December 31, 19X1			WHITNEY DISCOUNT CENTER Income Statement For the Year Ended December 31, 19X2		
Revenues:			Revenues:		
Sales		$10,000	Sales		$12,000
Operating Expenses:			Operating Expenses:		
Depreciation Expense	$2,000		Depreciation Expense	$1,600	

illustration 15-12 partial income statements.

All nominal account balances, including *Depreciation Expense* presented on the income statement, are closed to *Income Summary*, which is then closed to capital. All real account balances, including *Delivery Equipment* and *Accumulated Depreciation, Delivery Equipment* presented on the balance sheet, are carried forward in the accounts. At the end of the accounting cycle, *Delivery Equipment* and the contra account, *Accumulated Depreciation, Delivery Equipment,* are the only accounts related to the depreciation procedure that are a part of the post-closing trial balance.

sample problem The Pont Company purchased a delivery truck on January 1, 19X1 for $8,000 (Identification No. 8673D). The estimated life is 4 years with a $2,000 estimated scrap value. Routine maintenance is scheduled every six months and is to be charged to an expense account. The truck is sold for $3,500 on July 1, 19X3. Pont Company uses straight-line depreciation procedures.

1. List the information you would expect to find on a typical subsidiary ledger card for this truck.
2. What is the book value of the truck as of July 1, 19X3?
3. How is the adjusting entry made on the work sheet as of December 31, 19X2?
4. How do you report depreciation expense and accumulated depreciation on the financial statements?
5. Do you remove both the original cost of the truck and its accumulated depreciation account from the accounting records when the truck is sold?

sample problem solution

1. Items on the subsidiary card
   (a) Date of purchase and price.
   (b) Method of depreciation and book value.
   (c) Maintenance record and major repairs.
   (d) Disposal date of asset with gain or loss.
2. Book value

Delivery Equipment	$8,000
Accumulated Depreciation	3,750
Book Value	$4,250

3.

Account Titles	Trial Balance Dr.	Trial Balance Cr.	Adjustments Dr.	Adjustments Cr.
Delivery Equipment	8,000.00			
Accumulated Depreciation		1,500.00		1,500.00
Depreciation Expense			1,500.00	

4.

Income Statement

Operating Expenses:		
Depreciation Expense	$1,500	

Balance Sheet

Plant and Equipment:		
Delivery Equipment	$8,000	
Accumulated Depreciation, Delivery Equipment	3,000	5,000

5. Yes.

review exercises

6. Monroe Company purchased an item of equipment with an estimated scrap value of $2,000 for $10,000 on July 1, 19X1. Monroe Company follows the straight-line method of depreciation and estimates a service life of four years. The company prepares adjusting entries yearly on December 31.

Instructions

(a) Prepare the adjusting entries as they would appear on the work sheet as of December 31, 19X1.

(b) Present financial information to show *Equipment, Accumulated Depreciation, Equipment,* and *Depreciation Expense* on the balance sheet and income statement as of December 31, 19X1.

7. Using the data in Review Exercise 6, (a) present the required adjusting entries and then (b) show how *Equipment, Accumulated Depreciation,*

Equipment and *Depreciation Expense* would appear on the financial statements for Year 19X3.

8. Jones Company purchased a delivery truck for $11,000 on January 1, 19X1. Estimated life of the truck is four years with an estimated scrap value of $2,000. The firm uses the straight-line method for depreciation.

Instructions

(a) Present the adjusting entry on December 31, 19X3.

(b) Present information as it would be shown on the balance sheet to show *Delivery Equipment* and the related accumulated depreciation account. Then show the amount of *Depreciation Expense* that would be presented on the income statement.

• task JOURNALIZE THE REMOVAL OF PLANT AND EQUIPMENT ITEMS FROM THE ACCOUNTING RECORDS

Sale of equipment

Property, plant, and equipment costs are kept in the general ledger until the assets are sold, junked, or traded. Fully depreciated plant and equipment still being used in productive services and processes of the firm are kept in the accounting records. However, once the total purchase cost has been allocated, no additional depreciation expenses can be taken.

If a depreciable asset is removed from the accounts during an accounting period, you must first bring the depreciation accounts up to date. An updating of depreciation will also give the correct book value, which you will need to determine the gain or loss on the disposal of the equipment.

Assume that the two-ton truck from Illustration 15-8 is sold on April 6, 19X4, for $1,000. According to Illustration 15-8, the book value on December 31, 19X3, is $1,700 ($6,500 − $4,800). Using the following formula, depreciation from January 1 through April 6 can be determined:

$$\text{Cost} - \text{salvage value} \times \text{SYD formula for 4th year} \times \text{fraction of year}$$
$$\$6{,}500 - \$500 \times 2/15 \times 3/12 = \$200$$

Note that April 6 is treated as if it were April 1; thus, we have exactly 3/12, or one-fourth of a year. An entry must be made first to bring depreciation up to date; then a second entry should be made to show the sale. Both these transactions are given below.

Date		Description	P.R.	Debit	Credit
19X1					
Apr.	6	Depreciation Expense, Delivery Equipment		200 –	
		Accumulated Deprec., Delivery Equipment			200 –
		To adjust one-fourth of			
		years depreciation.			
	6	Cash		1000 –	
		Accumulated Deprec., Delivery Equipment		5000 –	
		Loss on Disposal of Equipment		500 –	
		Delivery Equipment			6500
		To record sale of equipment.			

Delivery Equipment and *Accumulated Depreciation, Delivery Equipment* will have zero balances after the transactions above have been posted to the general ledger accounts. A loss on equipment disposal is recorded to show the difference between the book value of $1,500 and the $1,000 received in cash. Losses or gains on the sale of equipment are classified as "Other Revenues and Expenses" on the income statement. *Depreciation Expense* and *Loss on Disposal of Equipment* are closed to *Income Summary* at the end of the accounting cycle and will be reported on the income statement as of December 31, 19X4. All ledger accounts affected are shown in Illustration 15-13.

Accumulated Depreciation, Delivery Equipment — Account No. 119

Date		Item	P.R.	Dr.	Cr.	Balance Dr.	Balance Cr.
19X1 Dec.	31	Adjusting Entry	G 24		2000 –		2000 –
19X2 Dec.	31	Adjusting Entry	G 28		1600 –		3600 –
19X3 Dec.	31	Adjusting Entry	G 31		1200 –		4800 –
19X4 Apr.	6	Adjusting Entry	G 34		200 –		5000 –
	6		G 34	5000 –			–0–

Delivery Equipment — Account No. 118

Date		Item	P.R.	Dr.	Cr.	Balance Dr.	Balance Cr.
19X1 Jan.	1		G 21	6500 –		6500 –	
19X4 Apr.	6		G 34		6500 –	–0–	

illustration 15-13 general ledger accounts related to delivery equipment.

Depreciation Expense, Delivery Equipment — Account No. 637

Date		Item	P.R.	Dr.	Cr.	Balance Dr.	Balance Cr.
19X1 Dec.	31	Adjusting Entry	G 24	2000 -		2000 -	
	31	Closing Entry	G 24		2000 -	-0-	
19X2 Dec.	31	Adjusting Entry	G 28	1600 -		1600 -	
	31	Closing Entry	G 28		1600 -	-0-	
19X3 Dec.	31	Adjusting Entry	G 31	1200 -		1200 -	
	31	Closing Entry	G 31		1200 -	-0-	
19X4 Apr.	6		G 34	200 -		200 -	

Loss on Disposal of Equipment — Account No. 680

Date		Item	P.R.	Dr.	Cr.	Balance Dr.	Balance Cr.
19X1 Apr.	6		G 34	500 -		500 -	

Discarding equipment

If a $9,400 item was discarded (junked) on July 1, 19X4, when the book value was $1,300, an under depreciation exists in the original estimate of the life of the asset and its salvage value. The book value of $1,300 would have to be written off to the account, *Loss on Disposal of Equipment.* Since depreciation policies are subjective estimating procedures, care should be exercised in examining past depreciation records along with future expectations to establish realistic depreciation estimates. Losses or gains on disposals of property and plant assets represent final settlement accounts in the life cycle of individual equipment. After the depreciation has been brought up to date, the following journal entry would be required to record the disposal:

Date		Account		Dr.	Cr.
19X4 July	1	Accumulated Depreciation, Equipment		8100 -	
		Loss on Disposal of Equipment		1300 -	
		Delivery Equipment			9400 -
		Discarded equipment item 1416 J as worthless.			

Exchanging equipment—financial accounting approach

Plant and equipment assets are often traded for new and similar assets needed in the operations of the firm. Accounting theory requires that the life cycle of the traded equipment be ended and that the new asset be recorded in the accounts. Accounting rules permit the recording of a loss on an exchange of similar equipment but generally prohibit the recording of a gain. Trade-in values are set by the seller for the asset given in exchange. A high trade-in value is one method of reducing the price of a new fixed asset.

To illustrate trading fixed assets, assume that a trade-in allowance of $1,500 is allowed on July 1 for the two-ton delivery truck on a purchase of a new two-and-one-half ton truck with a current price of $7,600. You can see a gain of $200 ($1,500 − $1,300), but the gain is not recorded in the accounts. The amount of cash to be paid is $6,100 ($7,600 − $1,500). Journal entries to record the exchange of the two-ton truck and $6,100 cash for the new truck on July 1, 19X4 are as follows:

19X4				
July	1	Depreciation Expense, Delivery Equipment	400 –	
		Accumulated Deprec., Delivery Equipment		400 –
		To bring depreciation up to		
		date of exchange.		
	1	Delivery Equipment	7400 –	
		Accumulated Deprec., Delivery Equipment	5200 –	
		Delivery Equipment		6500 –
		Cash		6100 –
		To record exchange of		
		assets.		

Since acceptable accounting principles prohibit recognizing a gain on the equipment traded in, the new equipment will have to be valued at $7,400, not at $7,600. The new equipment will be valued at the book value of the old equipment plus the cash paid.

Cost	$6,500
Accumulated Depreciation	5,200
Book Value	$1,300
Add: Cash paid	6,100
	$7,400

If the trade-in allowance is only $1,000, the following general journal entry would indicate a loss of $300 (book value of $1,300 less trade-in allowance, $1,000). The amount of cash to be paid is $6,600 (current price of $7,600 less trade-in allowance of $1,000), as compared with $6,100 in the prior transaction. As we explained earlier, accounting rules permit the recognition of a loss on the exchange of similar fixed assets. After the depreciation is brought up to July 1, the following exchange transaction would be recorded:

19X4			
July 1	Delivery Equipment	7600 –	
	Accumulated Deprec., Delivery Equipment	5200 –	
	Loss on Exchange of Delivery Equipment	300 –	
	Delivery Equipment		6500 –
	Cash		6600 –
	To record trade of two ton trucks with $1000 trade-in allowance.		

Exchanging equipment—income tax approach

Income tax regulations do not allow gains or losses on exchanges of similar fixed assets on the tax return. The established value of the new equipment would be the amount of cash paid plus the book value of the asset given in exchange. In practice, many companies follow income tax procedures in the accounts so that financial statements will agree with income tax returns. Unless cash is *received* in the trade, acceptable accounting procedures and income tax regulations provide the same treatment of gains on exchanges.

When a loss is experienced on an exchange, it is not recorded. Instead, the cost of the asset is adjusted to "absorb" this loss. To illustrate, assume that the delivery truck exchange required a cash payment of $6,600, rather than the $6,100 amount used earlier. The cost would be calculated as follows:

Cost	$6,500
Accumulated Depreciation	5,200
Book Value	$1,300
Cash paid	6,600
Adjusted Cost	$7,900

Equipment is recorded in the accounts at $7,900, the book value of the old truck. The loss on the equipment of $300 is added to the $7,600 list price to be depreciated over the estimated life of the new equipment.

19X4			
July 1	Delivery Equipment	7900 –	
	Accumulated Deprec., Delivery Equipment	5200 –	
	Delivery Equipment		6500 –
	Cash		6600 –
	To record trade of two ton trucks with $1000 trade-in allowance.		

A summary of the exchange of similar plant and equipment items under the financial accounting method and the Federal income tax method follow:

Financial Accounting		Federal Income Tax
Loss recognized		No loss recognized
No gain recognized	← (unless cash is received) →	No gain recognized

sample problem Use the information in the previous sample problem to provide journal entries on July 1, 19X3, for each of the following unrelated assumptions (Pont Company uses straight-line depreciation):

(1) The truck is scrapped.

(2) The truck is sold for $3,500.

(3) The truck is exchanged for a similar truck with a list price of $10,000. The old truck has a trade-in value of $5,000 (use the accounting method).

(4) Assume the same facts in (3) above, but use the tax method.

sample problem solution

1.

Date		Account	Debit	Credit
19X3				
July	1	Depreciation Expense, Delivery Equipment	750	
		Accumulated Depreciation, Delivery Equipment		750
	1	Accumulated Depreciation, Delivery Equipment	3,750	
		Loss on Disposal of Equipment	4,250	
		Delivery Equipment		8,000

2.

Date		Account	Debit	Credit
19X3				
July	1	Depreciation Expense, Delivery Equipment	750	
		Accumulated Depreciation, Delivery Equipment		750
	1	Cash	3,500	
		Accumulated Depreciation, Delivery Equipment	3,750	
		Loss on Disposal of Equipment	750	
		Delivery Equipment		8,000

3.

Date		Account	Debit	Credit
19X3				
July	1	Depreciation Expense, Delivery Equipment	750	
		Accumulated Depreciation, Delivery Equipment		750

1	Delivery Equipment	9,250	
	Accumulated Depreciation, Delivery Equipment	3,750	
	Delivery Equipment		8,000
	Cash		5,000
	Trade-in Value	$5,000	
	Book Value	4,250	
	Exchange gain	$ 750	
	New Truck Value:		
	Book Value	$4,250	
	Cash paid	5,000	
	Cost (adjusted)	$9,250	

4. Same entry as in 3—no gain recognized on exchange.

review exercises

9. Mont Company had $10,000 recorded in the *Equipment* account and $6,000 recorded in the *Accumulated Depreciation, Equipment* account. What is the book value? Journalize the scrapping of the equipment, assuming that no cash was received for the junked equipment.
10. Using the information in Exercise 9 above, record the sale of the equipment for $4,500.
11. Using the information in Exercise 9 above, record the exchange of the equipment for a similar item of equipment with a cash equivalent price of $12,000. A trade-in allowance of $5,000 is permitted.

chapter highlights

After studying this chapter, you should be able to:

- Determine the total cost for *Land, Equipment,* and *Building* accounts.
- Journalize and post to control and subsidiary accounts.
- Compute depreciation expense using the different methods.
- Understand the effects of the different depreciation methods.
- Journalize disposal of fixed assets.

check figures for review exercises

1. Debit *Land,* $3,100
2. Debit *Machinery,* $8,390
3. (a) Straight-line—Year 1, $720
   (b) Double-declining balance—Year 2, $960

4. For double-declining balance

Dr. Depreciation Expense	$960	
Cr. Accumulated Depreciation, Equipment		$960

5. $2,200

6. Balance sheet presentation

Equipment	$10,000	
less accumulated depreciation	1,000	$9,000

7. Balance sheet presentation

Equipment	$10,000	
less accumulated depreciation	5,000	$5,000

8. Income statement presentation

Operating Expenses:		
Depreciation Expense	$ 2,250	

9. Book Value $4,000

Accumulated Depreciation, Equipment	$ 6,000	
Loss on Disposal of Equipment	4,000	
Equipment		$10,000

10. Cr. Gain on Sale of Equipment $500

11.

Equipment (new)	$11,000	
Accumulated Depreciation, Equipment	6,000	
Equipment (old)		$10,000
Cash		7,000

key terms

The following important terms are discussed in Chapter 15 and are defined in the Glossary at the end of the book.

accelerated cost recovery system

book value

declining-balance method

deterioration

fixed assets

land improvements

natural resources

obsolescence

recovery property

residual value

salvage value

straight-line depreciation

sum-of-the-years' digit method

tangible assets

units of output method

questions

1. Define depreciation and name the financial statement on which it appears.
2. Distinguish between a tangible and an intangible asset.
3. What is the nature of the *Accumulated Depreciation, Building* account? Name the financial statement on which it appears.
4. Name two accelerated methods of computing depreciation.
5. What is the purpose of using a subsidiary ledger for plant and equipment assets?
6. How do you determine the book value of a plant or equipment asset?
7. Why is it necessary to record the amount of depreciation when an equipment item is sold or traded during an accounting period?
8. What is meant by "the exchange of similar fixed assets"?
9. What factors are considered in determining the length of time an asset might be useful to a business?
10. If the financial accounting approach is used, are gains recognized on the exchange of similar fixed assets? What about losses on the exchange?
11. How do income tax laws treat the exchange of similar fixed assets?

exercises

1. The Blue Company acquired an item of machinery with an invoice cost of $3,000. Terms of the purchase were 2/10, n/30. Freight charges of $200 were paid and installation costs of $100 were incurred. In adjusting the machinery, materials of $50 were used. What is the amount that should be debited to the *Machinery* account?
2. From the following list determine the cost of the building and the land.

Purchase price of land	$10,000
Title search fees (land)	200
Purchase price building	40,000
Commissions—Broker (building)	2,000
Survey costs	300
Installation of air conditioning	5,000

3. Determine the depreciation expenses for the first and third years using the straight-line method and the double-declining balance method. Equipment had a cost of $10,000 with a 10-year expected life and $2,000 estimated trade-in.
4. The original cost of a plant asset and its associated accumulated depreciation account are related to determine the book value. Information concerning an equipment item is given in the T accounts listed on the next page.

Equipment		Accum. Depr. Equipment	
1/1/X1 5,000			12/31/X1 800
			12/31/X2 800
			12/31/X3 800

(a) As of 12/31/X3, what is the book value of the equipment?
(b) What is the estimated life of the equipment if the estimated scrap value is $1,000?
(c) If the equipment were sold for $2,000 on 12/31/X2, what would be the amount of the gain or loss?

5. The Bono Company prepares financial statements every six months. The annual rate of depreciation on a building owned by Bono that cost $100,000 is 4 percent. Using the straight-line method, prepare the adjusting and closing entries for the six-month period ending July 31, 19X2.

6. A delivery truck was purchased for $6,000 on January 2, 19X1. It had an expected life of six years and an expected salvage value of $600. On July 1, 19X3, the company disposed of the truck. The company prepares financial statements on a calendar-year basis. Prepare journal entries on July 1, 19X3, for each of the following situations, assuming that the company uses straight-line depreciation.
(a) The delivery truck is junked with no salvage value.
(b) The delivery truck is sold for $3,500.
(c) The delivery truck is sold for $4,600.

problems

1. COMPETENCY TESTED Skill in recording the total cost of tangible fixed assets.
Classify each of the following expenditures as a land cost, a building cost, or a machinery cost.

Land survey fees	$ 400
Construction of sidewalks to the building	1,200
Sales taxes on new machinery	100
Renovations of building	8,000
Installation cost of machinery	500
Payment of delinquent taxes on land at time of purchase	600
Installation of air conditioning system	5,000

Instructions

(a) Prepare a schedule with headings for land, building, and machinery.

(b) Why is it important to separate land costs from building costs?

2. COMPETENCY TESTED The ability to compute depreciation expense and book value.

On January 1, 19X1, Boone Company purchased machinery for $7,000 with an estimated $1,000 scrap value. The machine is estimated to have a useful life of 5 years, operating for a total of 10,000 hours. The machine is expected to operate the following number of hours each year:

19X1	1,500	19X4	2,000
19X2	2,500	19X5	1,000
19X3	3,000		

Instructions

(a) Prepare a five-year schedule comparing the sum-of-the-years' digits method and the units of output method with headings for rate, *Depreciation Expense,* and *Accumulated Depreciation, Machinery* for each year.

(b) What is the book value of the machine after three years of expected use by each of the two methods?

3. COMPETENCY TESTED The ability to compute total cost of fixed assets and depreciation.

Lavi Company purchased a machine for $10.000. While the machine was being placed upon a concrete foundation that cost $200 to prepare, the employees dropped the machine. Costs of $300 were incurred to repair the damage. In addition, sales taxes of $500 and freight charges of $300 were paid in connection with buying the machine. The company plans to use the double-declining balance method. An estimated life of 10 years and an estimated scrap value of $2,000 is established for the machine.

Instructions

(a) Calculate the total amount to be debited to *Machinery*.

(b) Calculate the depreciation for the first year and for the third year assuming the double-declining method is used.

(c) For comparison, calculate the first and third years' depreciation by the straight-line method. Which method gave more depreciation in the first year? In the third year?

4. COMPETENCY TESTED Expertise in recording transactions for fixed assets.

Jones Hauling Company purchased three delivery trucks during its first year of operations. Prepare all journal entries related to the truck purchases, depreciation, operations, and disposals over two years of use.

19X1	
Jan. 4	Purchased Truck A and Truck B for $8,000 each. Estimated life is 5 years with a $1,000 estimated scrap value.
May 2	Paid routine repair expenses on the trucks, $200.
July 1	Purchased Truck C for $10,000. Estimated life is 8 years with an estimated scrap value of $2,000.
Jan.–Dec.	Oil and gas expenses for the year were $9,000.
Dec. 31	Trucks A and B are depreciated by the straight-line method and Truck C by the double-declining balance method.
31	Prepare all closing entries pertaining to truck use for the year.
19X2	
Apr. 1	Truck A is traded for Truck D. Truck D has a list price of $12,000, and a trade-in allowance of $5,000 is allowed on Truck A. The company follows the income tax method in the trade of similar fixed assets. Truck D has an estimated life of 4 years and a $2,000 estimated scrap value. Use straight-line depreciation.
July 1	New tires at a cost of $400 were placed on Truck B and are to be depreciated over the remaining life of Truck B.
Jan.-Dec.	Oil and gas expenses were $12,000 for the year.
Dec. 31	Prepare the depreciation entry for the trucks being used.
31	Prepare closing entries for the Year 19X2.

Instructions Prepare the journal entries with explanations.

5. COMPETENCY TESTED The ability to prepare a work sheet and financial statements.

Jackson Company had the following trial balance as of December 31, 19X1.

Jackson Company
Trial Balance
December 31, 19X1

Cash	$9,800	
Accounts Receivable	4,000	
Merchandise Inventory	7,000	
Prepaid Insurance	500	
Equipment	12,000	
Accumulated Depr., Equipment		$ 2,400
Accounts Payable		3,000
Larry Jackson, Capital		12,000
Larry Jackson, Drawing	5,000	
Sales		50,000
Purchases	10,000	
Rent Expense	2,400	
Salary Expense	16,700	
	$67,400	$67,400

Adjustment Data

(a) Inventory count, Dec. 31, 19X1, $4,000.

(b) Depreciation is 10 percent per year.

(c) Prepaid insurance of $200 has expired.

(d) Accrued salary expense, $400.

Instructions

(a) On the work sheet provided, prepare the adjusting entries and complete the work sheet.

(b) Prepare the financial statements.

6. COMPETENCY TESTED Expertise in recording transactions for fixed assets.

Kay Company provides delivery services for its customers. Two service trucks were purchased at first and additional trucks will be added as needed. The company wants to maintain accounting records to determine the cost of providing the delivery service. Transactions concerning the trucks and related expenses to keep them operating are given for two years of operations.

19X1

Jan. 8	Purchased Delivery Truck A for $12,000 and Delivery Truck B for $15,000. The company uses straight-line depreciation methods. Truck A has an estimated life of 5 years and an estimated trade-in value of $2,000. Truck B has an estimated life of 10 years and an estimated trade-in value of $3,000.
July 1	Routine repairs of $100 were charged to *Repairs Expense.*
Jan.-Dec.	Salaries for drivers were $18,000 for the year.
Dec. 31	Journalize the depreciation adjustment for the year.
31	Close all expense accounts to *Income Summary.*

19X2

April 1	Delivery Truck C is purchased for $14,000. Estimated life is 5 years with an estimated salvage value of $2,000. The company plans to use the sum-of-the-years'-digits method.
Jan.-Dec.	Salaries for drivers were $25,000 for the year.
Dec. 31	Journalize the depreciation expense adjustment for the year.
31	Close all expense accounts to *Income Summary.*

Instructions Prepare general journal entries for the transactions above.

7. COMPETENCY TESTED The ability to record the exchange of similar assets.

Wilson Company purchased an item of machinery for $11,000, with an estimated scrap value of $1,000 after 10 years of use. The firm acquired the machine on January 5, 19X1. On July 1, 19X6, the company exchanged the machine for a similar model with a list price of $15,000. Trade-in allowance on the new machine was $4,000. The company prepares financial statements on December 31 and uses straight-line depreciation.

Instructions

(a) Prepare the journal entry for both the financial accounting method and the tax method.

(b) Assume the trade-in allowance was $6,000. Prepare the journal entries for both the financial accounting method and the tax method.

8. COMPETENCY TESTED The ability to record plant and equipment transactions and to post to the general ledger accounts.

The Dove Company owns a drill machine that cost $2,400 and has accumulated depreciation of $1,100 on May 1, 19X1. Additional transactions for the month of May follow:

May	1	Purchased cutting equipment at a cost of $3,800. Freight costs were $200 and installation costs were $100. Estimated scrap value is $500 at the end of the estimated life of 3 years. The company uses straight-line depreciation.
	5	Routine repair expenses on the drill machine were $120.
	15	Sold the drill press for $800. The drill press is being depreciated at $50 per month.
	31	Journalize the depreciation entry for the month.

Instructions Prepare all transactions and post to the general ledger accounts.

GLOSSARY

This Glossary contains accounting terms and their definitions. A chapter number follows each definition so that the student can locate a more complete discussion.

accelerated cost recovery system A tax depreciation method created by the Economic Recovery Tax Act of 1981. Assets are divided into 3-, 5-, 10-, and 15- year property. (Ch. 15)

account An accounting form used to record and summarize financial information related to assets, liabilities, owner's equity, revenues, costs, and expenses. (Ch. 1)

accounting cycle The step-by-step procedures for handling the financial records of a business for a fiscal period to determine how well the business is progressing. (Ch. 4)

accounting pegboard A device that serves as a holder and writing surface which allows for the recording of information on more than one accounting record with a single writing. (Ch. 25)

accounts receivable turnover A measure of the number of times that sales on account are collected during the year. (Ch. 20)

accrual A process that adds continually to account totals. Basically, it is an expense that has been incurred but not recorded or a revenue that has been earned but not recorded. (Ch. 3)

accrual accounting An accounting system that requires revenues and expenses to be recorded as they are earned or incurred, although cash has not been received or paid. (Ch. 25)

acid-test ratio A quick ratio that is similar in purpose and computation to the current ratio but omits the inventory account and prepaid expenses in its computation. (Ch. 20)

adjusted trial balance A test of the equality of debits and credits after adjusting entries are planned. The adjusted trial balance is found on the work sheet. (Ch. 3)

adjusting entries A series of entries made at the end of each accounting period to bring certain accounts up to date. This type of entry is used to separate the deferred (or mixed) accounts as well as to record the accruals. (Ch. 3)

administrative expenses Those expenses related to the general operation and management of a business firm. These administrative expenses are sometimes referred to as general expenses. (Ch. 3)

aggregate cost The total cost of all marketable securities. (Ch. 18)

aging of accounts receivable A procedure used to determine the length of time that each customer's account is past due. From this analysis, an estimation of bad debt losses can be made. (Ch. 6)

allocate To divide into parts, such as dividing a partnership's net income among the partners or dividing factory overhead among the various jobs. (Ch. 16)

allowance method A method of recognizing bad debt losses during the period of revenue recognition. This method requires the estimation of a bad debt before specific accounts receivable have been identified as being uncollectible. (Ch. 13)

allowances A reduction in price to the purchaser due to the item of merchandise being defective or not meeting specifications. (Ch. 5)

American Bankers Association (ABA) number A set of numbers located in the upper-right-hand corner of each check. These numbers identify the bank holding the company's funds and the Federal Reserve district in which the bank is located. (Ch. 12)

amortization A process of spreading the difference between the selling price of a bond and its face value over the remaining life of the bond. (Ch. 18)

appropriate To set aside or segregate a portion of *Retained Earnings*. (Ch. 17)

arithmetic/logic The part of the central processing unit that is capable of performing calculations. (Ch. 24)

articles of copartnership A written contract that covers all of the important aspects of operating a partnership. Also known as a *partnership agreement*. (Ch. 16)

asset An item of value owned by a business that can be used to benefit the firm in the future. (Ch. 1)

balance sheet A financial statement prepared as of a given date, showing the assets, liabilities, and owner's equity of a firm. This statement also is known as a "statement of financial position." (Ch. 1)

bank service charge A charge imposed by a bank for such items as collecting a note, printing charges, or handling a firm's account. (Ch. 12)

bank statement A monthly document received from a bank listing all transactions between a firm and the bank. Items such as deposits, checks, and service charges are displayed on the bank statement. (Ch. 12)

basic accounting equation The fundamental accounting equation which states that assets equal liabilities plus owner's equity. (Ch. 1)

batch processing The processing of a group of business transactions that have accumulated for a period of time, such as a day, a week, or a month. (Ch. 24)

bill of sale A billing form that provides information on the type and number of items sold and the total amount of the sale made on credit terms to an individual customer. (Ch. 6)

blank endorsement An endorsement that includes only the signature of the check holder. (Ch. 12)

block of stock At least 100 shares of a corporation's stock. (Ch. 18)

bond discount Bonds sell at a discount if they sell at less than par value. (Ch. 18)

bond premium Bonds sell at a premium if they sell at more than par value. (Ch. 18)

book of original entry Another name for the journal, given because it is the first place an entry is recorded. (Ch. 2)

book value When this term is applied to plant assets, it refers to historical cost less accumulated depreciation. (Ch. 15)

cancelled check A check issued by a company that has cleared. It is marked by the bank in such a way that its reissuance would be highly unlikely. (Ch. 12)

capitalize When used in connection with *Retained Earnings*, the term means to transfer a portion of *Retained Earnings* to the paid-in capital category, usually because of a stock dividend. (Ch. 17)

capital statement A financial statement showing the changes in the proprietor's capital for an accounting period. The financial statement also is referred to as the statement of owner's equity. (Ch. 1)

cash change fund An amount of cash placed in each cash register that is used to make change on cash sales transactions. (Ch. 7)

cash disbursements journal A special journal used to record all cash payments. (Ch. 7)

cash discount A discount allowed by the seller if payment is made by the buyer within a specified time period, such as 2/10, n/30. A discount is given if payment is made within 10 days from the date of the invoice. (Ch. 5)

cash dividend A payment from a corporation to its stockholders. The payment is considered a return of the stockholders' investment and is often described as a distribution of earnings. (Ch. 17)

cash flow statement Another name for the statement of changes in financial position when it is prepared on a cash basis. This statement reports the sources and uses of cash for an accounting period. (Ch. 19)

cash receipts and fees charged journal A form designed primarily for attorneys to record charges and receipts using the one-write system. (Ch. 26)

cash receipts journal A special journal used to record the collections of all cash received by a business. (Ch. 7)

cash register tape A source document generated by a cash register providing information about cash sales. (Ch. 6)

cash short and over The amount by which a physical count of cash differs from amounts on the cash register tapes. (Ch. 7)

cathode-ray tube (CRT) A visual display device used for the retrieval of information. (Ch. 24)

center-write check A check used with the one-write system that allows for the check and journal entry to be recorded with one writing. Center write refers to the check design that requires the payee's name and the amount to be written on a line located at the center of the check. (Ch. 25)

central processing unit (CPU) The component unit of a computer, consisting of a memory or storage, an arithmetic/logic section, and a central section. (Ch. 24)

chart of accounts A list of accounts located at the beginning of a ledger and used to help locate accounts in the ledger. (Ch. 2)

charter A document issued by a state that serves as a contract between the state and a firm; sets forth certain requirements and rights of the corporation. (Ch. 17)

check register A special type of cash disbursements journal that is used in connection with the voucher register. A cross reference is established in the voucher register and the check register through the use of check numbers and voucher numbers. (Ch. 7)

check request form A document authorizing the issuance of a check. A responsible person must sign this form. (Ch. 7)

classified balance sheet A balance sheet with assets subdivided into current, plant and equipment, and other assets, while liabilities are subdivided into current and long-term. (Ch. 3)

client's ledger sheet An unbound sheet used with the one-write accounting system in which all transactions involving each client are maintained. (Ch. 26)

closing entries Entries prepared at the end of the fiscal period to facilitate the orderly closing of all temporary accounts along with the owner's drawing account. (Ch. 4)

common stock One type of stock that is issued by a corporation. This class of stock carries voting and other privileges (along with certain risks) not available to holders of preferred stock. (Ch. 17)

compound entry An entry containing more than one debit and/or more than one credit. (Ch. 2)

contingent liability A possible debt that may or may not come due; usually related to another event taking place. (Ch. 13)

contract interest rate The stated rate that is used to compute cash and accrued interest. (Ch. 18)

control A computer component section that selects, interprets, and executes stored programs that have been fed into the computer. (Ch. 24)

controlling account A single account contained in the general ledger that summarizes all of the accounts found in a subsidiary ledger. (Ch. 5)

conversion cost The combined cost of direct labor and factory overhead. (Ch. 23)

cost concept This concept states that the proper basis for recording a transaction is the agreed price between a buyer and a seller determined in an objective manner. (Ch. 1)

cost of production report A report prepared for each process or department that summarizes the quantities, costs, and unit costs for a given time period. (Ch. 23)

credit The right side of the ledger account. When used in connection with a specific account, this term indicates whether that account increases or decreases. (Ch. 2)

credit card A form of "plastic money" used by customers for the purpose of making credit purchases. (Ch. 7)

credit memorandum A document prepared by a seller that indicates the buyer's outstanding debt has been reduced by the amount of the memorandum. (Ch. 5)

credit terms Required payment dates to qualify for certain percentage reductions in the selling price for early payments by the buyer. See **cash discount**. (Ch. 5)

currency The paper monetary units used as a medium of exchange, in contrast to coins, money orders, cashier's checks, and traveler's checks. In the United States a five-dollar bill is considered currency, while a quarter is a noncurrency item (a coin). (Ch. 12)

current assets Items of value that are expected to be converted into cash, sold, or used within one year or during the normal operating cycle, whichever is longer. (Ch. 11)

current liabilities The financial obligations that are expected to be paid with current assets or by creating another current liability. Current liabilities usually are due within one year of the balance sheet date. (Ch. 11)

current ratio A ratio that develops the relationship between the current assets of a firm and the current liabilities of a firm. It indicates by ratio comparison the excess of current assets available to pay for currently maturing obligations. (Ch. 20)

customer receipt form A form designed to provide a record of information: customer's name, accounts to be debited or credited, date received, explanation, and initials of the person receiving the cash. (Ch. 7)

daily cash receipts report A report to reconcile the cash collected against the cash receipts record, such as a cash register tape. (Ch. 7)

data processing A series of planned actions that convert raw data into useful information. (Ch. 24)

date of record A date specified by the board of directors of a corporation that determines the individuals who will receive cash dividends. (Ch. 17)

day sheet An accounting record that is used primarily by physicians and dentists to keep a record of daily charges and receipts. Often this accounting record is referred to as a record of charges and receipts. (Ch. 25)

debit The left side of a ledger account. When used in connection with a specific account, this term indicates whether that account increases or decreases. Often the term "charge" is used interchangeably with debit. (Ch. 2)

debit memorandum A document prepared by a buyer that indicates a creditor's account balance has been debited by the amount of the memorandum. (Ch. 5)

declaration date The date a board of directors declares a cash dividend. If all legal requirements are met, the item becomes a liability to the corporation on this date. (Ch. 17)

declining-balance method A depreciation method that assigns a greater expense for depreciation in the earlier years of an operational asset. It is a fixed percentage applied to a declining balance. (Ch. 15)

deferral A delay in recognizing a revenue or an expense until a future accounting period. (Ch. 3)

deficit Refers to a debit balance in a partner's capital account. This condition indicates a negative equity; that is, the partnership has a claim on a partner for cash or other assets. (Ch. 16)

dependent The number of exemptions allowed by the taxing authority based on a number of factors, such as age and amount of support provided. Each dependent allowance reduces the amount of taxes that must be paid. (Ch. 8)

deposit in transit A deposit made by the firm that does not appear on the bank statement, usually because the deposit has not had enough time to be processed by the bank. (Ch. 12)

deposit slip A convenient bank form that provides space for listing currency, coins, and checks a firm or individual wishes to deposit. (Ch. 12)

depreciation The arbitrary method of spreading the capitalized cost of fixed assets over present and future accounting periods. (Ch. 15)

deterioration An indication that a fixed asset is losing productivity or requiring an increased amount of maintenance due to wear and aging. (Ch. 15)

direct labor Labor that can be traced or charged directly to a product or operation, thus identifying this labor with the goods manufactured. (Ch. 21)

direct materials Material costs that are applied directly to products based upon the fact that the material becomes a significant part of the product. (Ch. 21)

direct write-off method A method of writing off bad debts to the expense account when the specific account or note is identified as uncollectible. (Ch. 13)

discount The amount a financial institution charges for interest. A discount is interest collected in advance. (Ch. 13)

discounting a note payable The process of deducting the interest on a note payable at the time of issuance rather than at the maturity date. (Ch. 13)

discounting a note receivable Exchanging a note received from another party to a bank earlier than the maturity date for cash or in settlement of a debt. (Ch. 13)

division of earnings One step in the process of dividing the partnership's net income or net loss among the partners. No payment of cash to partners is indicated by this process. (Ch. 16)

effective interest rate The true interest rate on bonds, which may be more than the contract rate if bonds sell at a discount or less than the contract rate if bonds sell at a premium. (Ch. 18)

eighth-month Dividing the month into eight equal parts for the purposes of preparing payroll Form 941. (Ch. 9)

electronic spread sheet A work sheet displayed on a computer screen that allows simulations of different alternatives by changing key amounts in the format. (Ch. 24)

employee pay statement A form used with the one-write system that shows the deductions taken from the employee's paycheck. (Ch. 25)

employee's earnings ledger card A form designed for each individual employee showing current payroll information together with deductions withheld. This form is used with the one-write accounting system. (Ch. 26)

employee's earnings record A record designed for each individual employee showing current payroll information together with cumulative total earnings and deductions for the year. (Ch. 8)

employer identification number A number that is similar to an employee's Social Security number. This number is assigned by the Internal Revenue Service and must appear on all reports submitted to the Federal government. (Ch. 9)

Employer's Tax Guide A publication of the Federal government showing how much to deduct from paychecks based on gross pay, number of exemptions, marital status, and frequency of payment. This publication also contains a table to calculate FICA taxes. (Ch. 8)

entity concept The idea that each business unit is, for accounting purposes, separate from every other business unit and also from the owner or owners of the business. (Ch. 1)

equivalent units The number of fractional units of materials, labor, or factory overhead required to equal one whole unit of production during a period of time. (Ch. 23)

exemption A deduction from adjusted gross income for each exemption claimed by the employee. (Ch. 8)

expense An expenditure that is necessary to carry on the operations of the business. (Ch. 1)

experience rating A system that rewards the employer for not laying off workers by reducing the firm's unemployment tax rate. Another term widely used in the same context is merit rating. (Ch. 8)

face value The par or maturity value of bonds. This amount is due at the maturity date regardless of the selling price. (Ch. 18)

factory overhead All manufacturing costs except direct labor and direct materials. Factory overhead costs are not directly traceable to products or operations. (Ch. 21)

finished goods The cost of the products that have been manufactured completely and are ready for sale. (Ch. 21)

first-in, first-out (FIFO) A cost flow method that uses the cost of the earlier purchases for cost of goods sold and leaves the most recent cost for purchases in the ending inventory. It is based on the assumption that the first items bought are the first items sold. (Ch. 14)

fiscal period The length of the accounting or reporting period, typically 12 consecutive months. (Ch. 1)

fixed assets A term to describe long-term assets that are used in the operation of a business, such as buildings, equipment, and machinery. See **plant and equipment assets**. (Ch. 15)

fixed costs Manufacturing costs that remain the same in total as the volume increases or decreases over a relevant range of production. (Ch. 22)

flexible budgets A series of budgets that give the variable costs, fixed costs, and total costs at various levels of volume activity. (Ch. 22)

floppy disks A term often applied to small (5 1/4-inch) flexible disks used to input information into a computer. (Ch. 24)

FOB destination Shipping term that determines when title to merchandise passes to a buyer. Under this designation, title is assumed to pass to the buyer when the merchandise arrives at the buyer's place of business. (Ch. 5)

FOB shipping point A term of shipment that determines when title to merchandise passes to a buyer. According to this concept, title passes to the buyer when the merchandise is delivered to the point of shipment. (Ch. 5)

food stamp A coupon provided by the Federal government to assist the needy in acquiring adequate meals. Food coupons are provided in denominations of $1, $5, and $10. (Ch. 12)

food stamp redemption certificate A form provided by the U.S. Department of Agriculture to accompany the food stamps when they are deposited at the bank. (Ch. 12)

general account disbursements journal A cash disbursements journal used with the one-write system to record payments out of the general cash fund. (Ch. 26)

general ledger A book or file containing all ledger accounts pertaining to a business. (Ch. 5)

going concern An assumption that a firm will continue in operation for a relatively long period of time. (Ch. 1)

gross pay The employee's total pay before deductions. (Ch. 8)

hardware A computer and its related equipment. (Ch. 24)

horizontal analysis A technique for comparing the same account or items for two years or for a series of years on a percentage basis. (Ch. 20)

income from primary operations The net income from normal operations before considering other items. In other words, this is the net income after a firm's costs and operating expenses are subtracted from its revenues. (Ch. 11)

income statement A financial statement comparing revenues and expenses for an accounting period to determine whether a firm has a net income or a net loss. (Ch. 1)

indirect labor Labor not directly associated with the products being manufactured, such as supervisors, plant guards, and custodians. (Ch. 21)

indirect materials Materials that are necessary to support the manufacturing process, but are not directly identified with the finished product. Examples are cleaning supplies, glue, nails, and lubricating oils. (Ch. 21)

input The device used to enter information into a computer. This may consist of punched cards, magnetic tapes, punched paper tapes, magnetic disks, or documents with magnetic ink or optical characters. (Ch. 24)

intangible assets Items, owned by a company, with future value but with no physical characteristics. (Ch. 11)

integrated data processing (IDP) The computer processing operation designed to minimize the rehandling and resorting of data by human involvement. (Ch. 24)

interest allowance One step in the process of division of earnings. This is not a payment or receipt of cash or other assets. (Ch. 16)

interest rate The time value of money expressed as a percentage. The rate is stated as an annual rate unless otherwise specified. (Ch. 13)

inventory sheet A sheet used to list all items of merchandise owned by a firm for the purpose of determining the amount to record as *Merchandise Inventory*. (Ch. 14)

inventory tag Markers used for tagging the stacks, bins, boxes, or space sections for inventory purposes. (Ch. 14)

investments Long-term investments in items such as stocks and bonds of other firms. Usually, these items are held for a period exceeding one year. (Ch. 11)

involuntary deductions Deductions from employees' gross pay for which the employees have no choice. (Ch. 8)

job order cost sheet A sheet to accumulate direct labor, direct materials, and factory overhead by specific job orders. The unit cost of production is determined from information accumulated on the job order cost sheet. (Ch. 22)

journal A bound book with pages designed to record transactions. It is also known as the "book of original entry" because transactions are first recorded completely in the journal. (Ch. 2)

land improvements Expenditures related to land that have limited lives, such as paving on parking lots, light posts, and fences. (Ch. 15)

last-in, first-out (LIFO) A cost flow method that uses the cost of the most recent purchases for the cost of goods sold and leaves the earliest costs in the ending inventory. (Ch. 14)

ledger A loose-leaf book or file containing the accounts of a business. (Ch. 2)

legal capital The amount of paid-in capital determined by the par value or stated value of stock. Cash dividends are not to be paid from assets represented by the legal capital. (Ch. 17)

liability The debts and obligations incurred by a business. (Ch. 1)

limited liability Stockholders of corporation stock cannot be held responsible to a firm's creditors beyond the extent of their investment in shares of the corporation's stocks. (Ch. 17)

liquidation The process of closing out a firm for business purposes. In this process, all assets are sold, creditors are paid, and the remaining cash is distributed to the proprietor, partners, or stockholders. (Ch. 16)

long-term liabilities Debts of a firm that are expected to be paid beyond one year from the balance sheet date or paid with noncurrent assets. (Ch. 11)

loss from primary operations A loss that is determined by deducting normal operating expenses and the cost of goods sold from a firm's revenue. This loss is listed on the income statement before other income and other expenses. (Ch. 11)

market value The value of stock established in the marketplace based upon past performance and expectations. (Ch. 17)

marketable securities Short-term investments in stocks and bonds. (Ch. 18)

matching concept This concept requires that expenses be recorded in the same accounting period as the revenue generated by these expenses. (Ch. 3)

materials requisition form A form used to formally request specific materials to be charged to specific jobs and to specific departments. Such requisitions are approved by designated persons. (Ch. 22)

maturity date The date a note is due to be paid by the maker. (Ch. 13)

maturity value The total principal of a note plus the amount for interest. (Ch. 13)

memory A computer component in which data are stored mechanically or electronically. (Ch. 24)

merchandise Items that a firm normally handles for the purpose of resale. An inventory of merchandise is a count that is made usually once a year to determine how much is owned by a company. (Ch. 5)

merchandise inventory turnover An indication of the number of times that an average inventory is sold during the year. The calculation is made by dividing the cost of merchandise sold by the average inventory. (Ch. 20)

merchant deposit summary A form provided by banks for making deposits of credit card sales drafts. (Ch. 12)

microcomputer A small special computer with limited primary memory. It is often restrictive in terms of how much additional hardware can be attached for expanded procedures. (Ch. 24)

minicomputer A small-scale computer that is capable of performing many of the operations of a large computer, only on a more limited scale. (Ch. 24)

mixed account An account in the ledger that is part asset and part expense or part revenue and part liability. (Ch. 3)

modified cash basis An accounting system that allows revenues to be recorded when cash is received and expenses to be recorded when cash is paid. This system also allows depreciation to be recorded. (Ch. 25)

mutual agency Under normal circumstances, each partner is an agent of a business and can bind the partnership to a contract within the scope of its business operations. (Ch. 16)

natural resources Assets such as minerals, ores, and trees that a firm plans to take from the land. (Ch. 15)

NCR paper No carbon required. All information appears on two or more copies in a single writing. (Ch. 25)

net assets Total assets less total liabilities. (Ch. 17)

net income The excess of all of a firm's revenues over its expenses for a single accounting period. (Ch. 1)

net loss The excess of all of a firm's expenses over its revenues for a single accounting period. (Ch. 1)

net pay The amount of take-home pay an employee receives after all voluntary and involuntary deductions are deducted. (Ch. 8)

net realizable value This is the amount that is expected from credit customers. It can be found by deducting *Allowance for Doubtful Accounts* from *Accounts Receivable*. (Ch. 13)

no-par value stock Stock authorized by a corporation's charter that does not have a par value assigned to it. (Ch. 17)

nominal account Primarily income statement accounts with expense and revenue characteristics that are closed at the end of the accounting period because of their temporary nature. (Ch. 4)

nonsufficient funds (NSF) A customer's check returned by the bank because of insufficient funds. (Ch. 12)

normal balance The expected debit or credit balance of a ledger account. Assets and expenses are expected to have debit balances, and liabilities, revenues, and owner's equity are expected to have credit balances. (Ch. 2)

note A promise in writing to pay a certain sum of money at a fixed date to a named party to the transaction. (Ch. 13)

obsolescence This term is used in connection with a fixed asset that is less productive than a newer model. (Ch. 15)

odd lot Less than 100 shares of capital stock. (Ch. 18)

one-write accounting system An accounting system that allows for the recording of information on more than one accounting record with a single writing. (Ch. 25)

operating expenses Expenses necessary to carry on the normal operations of a firm. Operating expenses are divided into selling and general expenses on a classified income statement. (Ch. 11)

other expense An expense not connected with a firm's primary line of operations. *Interest Expense* is usually included in this category. (Ch. 11)

other income Revenue that is not caused by a firm's primary line of business must be separated into this category. Other income is listed on the income statement after Income (or loss) from Primary Operations. *Interest Revenue* and *Dividends Revenue* fall into this category. (Ch. 11)

output The end result ot a data process system. Usually, it consists of reports used for making business decisions. (Ch. 24)

outstanding check A check that has been issued by a firm which has not yet been received by the bank for payment by the date of the bank statement. (Ch. 12)

owner's equity The owner's net worth in the business. Expressed in a formula, this would be assets minus the liabilities of a firm. (Ch. 1)

paid-in capital The total amount of assets invested in a corporation by its stockholders. (Ch. 17)

partnership An association of two or more persons who have established ownership interests for the purpose of carrying on a business for profit. (Ch. 16)

partnership agreement See **articles of copartnership**. (Ch. 16)

par value An arbitrary value of capital stock set by a charter. This value is also called legal capital for the overall purpose of the protection of the creditors of a corporation. (Ch. 17)

patient's charge slip A prenumbered slip attached to an accounting pegboard so that a patient's bill (amount due for services rendered) can be calculated by a receptionist. (Ch. 25)

patient's statement A bill prepared from a patient's charge slips and sent to the patient to indicate the balance due. (Ch. 25)

payment date The date on which a dividend is paid. (Ch. 17)

payroll bank account A special checking account used to pay a company's employees. The use of this special account allows payroll checks to be designed with spaces for payroll information. (Ch. 9)

percentage of credit-sales method A method of estimating bad debts based upon past experience of bad debts compared with the total credit sales for the same year. (Ch. 13)

periodic inventory system Under this system, the balance in an inventory account remains at the beginning balance during the accounting period. Purchases and sales of merchandise are recorded by using nonasset accounts. This approach requires that the ending inventory be determined by a physical count. (Ch. 14)

permanent account An account that is not closed out at the end of an accounting period. Also known as a real account. (Ch. 4)

perpetual inventory system An inventory system that allows for a continuous recording of merchandise on hand and the cost of goods sold. (Ch. 14)

petty cash fund A special fund set aside for payment of minor items, such as a small amount of supplies or postage. This fund is usually under the control of a person known as the petty cashier. (Ch. 12)

petty cash vouchers Business forms used with the petty cash fund. A typical voucher contains a voucher number, the name of the person receiving the money, the amount of the voucher, the reason for payment, the general ledger account to be debited, and the signature or initials of the person granting the approval. (Ch. 12)

plant and equipment assets Assets that are used in the normal operation of a business that are expected to last for a relatively long period of time. (Ch. 11). See **fixed assets**.

post-closing trial balance A listing of real accounts after nominal accounts have been closed. It is a trial balance used to prove the equality of debits and credits after posting the adjusting and closing entries. (Ch. 4)

posting The procedure of transferring data from the journal to the ledger. (Ch. 2)

preferred stock Stock issued in addition to common stock that grants its shareholders a certain preferential treatment over common stockholders, such as in the receipt of dividends. (Ch. 17)

present value The current value of a future benefit. Money held today is worth more than the same amount of money received in the future because of the time value of money. (Ch. 18)

proceeds The amount received by a party discounting a note receivable computed by deducting the discount amount from the maturity value. (Ch. 13)

process cost system A manufacturing operation that brings raw materials to a stage of completion with the application of direct labor and factory overhead. All costs are accumulated for a certain time period in a department or cost center prior to transfer to the next department for additional processing. (Ch. 23)

profitability An analysis that dictates whether investors are making a fair return on their investments. Profitability margins may vary in different industries. (Ch. 20)

program The instructions on software that direct the computer to perform various tasks and generate outputs. (Ch. 24)

proprietorship A single-owner business. (Ch. 1)

purchase order A document issued for the purpose of ordering approved merchandise and other items. (Ch. 5)

purchase requisition An internal document sent from a department of a business to the purchasing department for the purpose of requesting items to be ordered by the purchasing department. (Ch. 5)

purchases journal A special journal designed to record a firm's purchases of merchandise on credit. When the journal is expanded to a multicolumn design, it can be used to record the purchase of other needed items on credit. (Ch. 5)

qualified endorsement A check endorsement that usually includes the phrase "without recourse." This type of endorsement frees the endorser of future liability in case the maker of the check does not have sufficient funds to cover the check. (Ch. 12)

quantity schedule A schedule that accounts for all whole units committed to a production department in terms of those which have been transferred to the next department during the period plus those units remaining in the ending inventory. (Ch. 23)

random access A method of locating information stored on a computer input device (such as a diskette) by skipping unneeded information. (Ch. 24)

rate of return on common stockholders' equity A rate measurement that indicates the return on the stockholders' investment. The calculation is made by dividing net income by the average stockholder's equity. (Ch. 20)

ratio The division of the remainder of the net income or net loss after subtracting all of the requirements of the partnership contract. This remainder is usually divided in a predetermined relationship between the partners, such as equally. (Ch. 16)

ratio analysis An evaluation of the relationship between two amounts. (Ch. 20)

ratio of property, plant, and equipment to long-term debt A ratio that indicates the margin of safety provided for the payment of long-term obligations represented by property, plant, and equipment. (Ch. 20)

ratio of sales to total assets A ratio that indicates how efficiently the firm is using its assets to generate sales. (Ch. 20)

real account See **permanent account**. (Ch. 4)

real-time processing A form of processing that updates individual accounts as transactions occur. (Ch. 24)

receiving report A report prepared by the receiving department listing the type and quantity of goods received. (Ch. 7)

reconciliation The procedure of reconciling an amount shown on a bank statement with the amount shown on a check stub. (Ch. 12)

record of charges and receipts See **day sheet**. (Ch. 25)

recovery property Real property, such as a building, and improvements made on leased property. (Ch. 15)

regular note payable A note for which the interest is paid at the time the note matures. (Ch. 13)

replenished The procedure followed when a check is written to replace the funds spent from a petty cash fund. (Ch. 12)

residual value The trade-in or scrap value of a depreciable asset. (Ch. 15)

restrictive endorsement An endorsement that states a check can be deposited only to the account of the party whose name or account number follows the words "For Deposit Only." (Ch. 12)

returns From the seller's viewpoint, it refers to merchandise previously sold that is being returned. From the purchaser's viewpoint, it refers to merchandise previously purchased that is being sent back. (Ch. 5)

revenue The inflow of assets into a firm from providing a service or selling a product. (Ch. 1)

reversing entry An entry to reverse adjusting entries involving accruals and certain deferrals. Reversing entries are dated the first business day of the new fiscal period. (Ch. 4)

salary A set amount of pay, such as an annual contract, whereby the number of hours worked or units produced does not cause the amount of gross pay to change. (Ch. 8)

salary allowance A basis for dividing partnership net income and net loss by allowing varying salaries for services performed or talent rendered. (Ch. 16)

sales discount A cash discount issued on a sale used to urge buyers to pay their bills earlier. (Ch. 6)

sales draft A form designed to be used with credit card sales. Space is provided to imprint the customer's credit card information and to write in information about the sale. (Ch. 7)

sales invoice See **bill of sale**. (Ch. 6)

sales journal A special journal used to record all sales of merchandise on account. (Ch. 6)

salvage value See **residual value**. (Ch. 15)

schedule of accounts payable A listing of individual creditors together with balances due. (Ch. 5)

schedule of accounts receivable A listing of individual credit customers together with balances due. (Ch. 6)

schedule of changes in working capital A schedule showing changes in all the current items between two balance sheet dates. (Ch. 19)

selling expenses Expenses related to the selling or marketing/promotion function of a business firm. (Ch. 3)

sequential access Memory stored on an input device to a computer, such as a tape, that can only be found by examining each section until the desired material is located. (Ch. 24)

shares of stock Evidence of ownership in a corporation. (Ch. 17)

slide An incorrect amount caused by moving the decimal point to the right or to the left. (Ch. 2)

software Programs and instructions contained on input devices that are used to control the behavior of a computer. (Ch. 24)

solvency The ability of a business entity to pay its debts as they currently mature. On a going concern basis a firm is solvent if it is able to pay its debts on time. (Ch. 20)

special journals Journals developed to record similar and repetitious business transactions. For example, all cash receipts are recorded in the cash receipts journal. (Ch. 5)

specific identification An inventory costing method in which merchandise, both sold and unsold, can be identified in terms of the specific cost of each item. (Ch. 14)

stated interest The interest rate that is shown on the face of a note. (Ch. 13)

stated value A value assigned to a share of no-par stock by a board of directors. (Ch. 17)

statement of account A business form prepared and forwarded to a customer showing all charges, amounts credited, and current balances of the account. (Ch. 6)

statement of changes in financial position A financial statement summarizing all of the financing and investing activities of a business between two balance sheet dates. (Ch. 19)

statement of cost of goods manufactured A financial statement prepared for a manufacturing firm that provides a detailed accounting of manufacturing costs. This cost is shown on the income statement as part of the cost of goods sold. (Ch. 21)

statement of owner's equity See **capital statement**. (Ch. 1)

stock dividend A distribution of the company's own stock to the stockholder. Usually this dividend is based on the number of shares the stockholders presently hold. (Ch. 17)

stockholders The owners of a corporation through the purchase and retention of shares of stock. (Ch. 17)

stockholders' equity to liabilities ratio A ratio of stockholders' equity to liabilities compares the margin of the investment of the stockholders to the investment of the creditors. (Ch. 20)

stock split An action taken by a corporation to issue additional shares of stock, such as two-for-one, to reduce the par or stated value. (Ch. 17)

straight-line depreciation A method of depreciation based on an equal amount of depreciation charged each accounting period. (Ch. 15)

subsidiary job order ledger A ledger containing the individual job order sheets showing the detailed cost of labor, materials, and factory overhead. (Ch. 22)

subsidiary ledger A group of accounts contained in a separate ledger that is summarized in one account in the general ledger. (Ch. 5)

sum-of-the-years'-digits method An accelerated method of depreciation based on a fraction of the total of all the years. The numerator declines by one each year while the denominator remains constant. (Ch. 15)

tangible assets Long-term assets that have characteristics subject to wear, tear, obsolescence, and deterioration. (Ch. 15)

target number The increase or decrease in working capital. (Ch. 19)

temporary account Income statement accounts that are closed, along with the owner's drawing account for a proprietorship, at the end of an accounting period. (Ch. 4)

time card A card used to record the number of hours an employee works each day during a work period. This card is used to calculate the employee's gross pay when the employee is working on a wage basis. (Ch. 8)

time sharing A method of obtaining access to a computer by sharing its cost and related expenses with other users. (Ch. 24)

top-write check A check that is part of the one-write system that comes in "shingled sets." This design calls for the date, payee, and amount to be written in boxes at the top edge of the check. (Ch. 25)

transaction An economic event during which something of value is exchanged for another item of value. (Ch. 1)

transposition An exchange of two or more digits within the same amount. (Ch. 2)

treasury stock Shares of stock that have previously been outstanding but have been reacquired by a corporation. Treasury shares have no voting or dividend rights. (Ch. 17)

trend analysis A percentage analysis that aids in the study and understanding of the positive or negative directions a company has taken for a number of years. A base year is selected and percentage changes are calculated to indicate the trend and magnitude of change. (Ch. 20)

trial balance A listing of all account balances found in a ledger to test the equality of total debits and credits. (Ch. 2)

true interest The actual interest rate that a borrower is paying on a note when the interest is deducted at the beginning. (Ch. 13)

true no-par value stock A corporation's stock that has no par or stated value. (Ch. 17)

trust account disbursements journal A cash disbursements journal used as part of the one-write system to record payments made from the *Trust Account*. (Ch. 26)

unadjusted trial balance The first two columns found on a work sheet. The accounts on this trial balance have not been adjusted. (Ch. 3)

unamortized The amount of bond discount or bond premium that has not been written off as an adjustment to the cash interest. (Ch. 18)

unappropriated A term applied to *Retained Earnings* that indicates the amount available for dividends. (Ch. 17)

unit costs The accumulated costs of a product stated on a unit basis as developed in a process cost system. (Ch. 23)

units-of-output method A method of depreciation based on an activity, such as the number of units produced. (Ch. 15)

unlimited liability A characteristic of both proprietorships and partnerships whereby each partner is responsible for all of the debts of a firm. Personal assets can be required to pay creditors' claims. (Ch. 16)

variable cost A cost that will vary in direct proportion to an increase or a decrease in volume change. (Ch. 22)

vertical analysis A percentage analysis that compares an individual account balance with a total within the same statement. For example, all components of the income statement are compared with net sales. (Ch. 20)

voluntary deductions Deductions chosen by an employee to be withheld from their paycheck. Some examples of voluntary deductions are union dues, medical insurance premiums, and savings bond plans. (Ch. 8)

voucher register A journal of special design in which all approved payments are recorded. It is used by firms that need a good internal control system. (Ch. 7)

voucher system A system designed for internal cash control in which all cash disbursements are made from approval vouchers. (Ch. 7)

wage A method of determining an employee's gross pay based on some set unit rate, such as hours worked or merchandise handled. (Ch. 8)

weighted average A method of valuing the inventory by which an average cost per unit is calculated. This amount is applied to both those items sold and those items still on hand. (Ch. 14)

word processor A program designed for use with a computer that allows for creating and editing text. (Ch. 24)

work sheet A multicolumned accounting form used to plan the adjusting and closing entries. This form also is used in preparing financial statements. Since the work sheet is a planning device, it is usually prepared in pencil. (Ch. 3)

working capital Current assets minus current liabilities. (Ch. 19)

INDEX

NOTES

NOTES

NOTES

NOTES

NOTES

NOTES

NOTES

NOTES

NOTES

NOTES

NOTES

NOTES

NOTES

NOTES